"Hillerbrand's years of expertise in sixteen: work. With fresh insights and the voice of a story well told, he does an exquisite job of weaving together the social, economic, political, and religious strands of a very complex history. Hillerbrand deftly paints a picture of how the 'great conflagration' of one man can explode beyond his control and alter the course of history."

—G. Sujin Pak, Assistant Professor of Church History,
Garrett-Evangelical Theological Seminary

"As one of America's leading historians of the sixteenth century, Hans Hillerbrand has poured a lifetime of scholarship and learning into this history of the Reformation. His strength and experience as a teacher are apparent in every chapter. Hillerbrand ably combines scholarly engagement and thoughtful narrative. What one ends up with, then, is a book that is both very readable and deeply informative."

—David M. Whitford, Associate Professor of the History of Christianity,
United Theological Seminary, Trotwood, Ohio; Associate Editor,
Sixteenth Century Journal; and author of *Tyranny and Resistance:
The Magdeburg Confession and the Lutheran Tradition*

"In this revised version of his earlier work published in 1971, Hillerbrand continues to probe multifarious factors that made Luther's Reform movement in Germany a pivotal point in history, leading to a clear division in Western Christendom. In this historical narrative, Hillerbrand skillfully weaves the results of expansive research in the field of Reformation studies over the last three decades. . . . [This is] an excellent textbook for current theological students as well as for any pastor's continuing education."

—Haruko Nawata Ward, Assistant Professor
of Church History, Columbia Theological Seminary

The Division of Christendom

The Division of Christendom

Christianity in the Sixteenth Century

Hans J. Hillerbrand

Westminster John Knox Press
LOUISVILLE • LONDON

© 2007 Hans J. Hillerbrand

Book design by Sharon Adams
Cover design by Mark Abrams
Cover art: Martin Luther (1483–1546) Publicly Burning the Pope's Bull in 1521 (engraving), English School (19th century) / Private Collection, Ken Welsh / The Bridgeman Art Library

First edition
Published by Westminster John Knox Press
Louisville, Kentucky

This book is printed on acid-free paper that meets the American National Standards Institute Z39.48 standard. ∞

PRINTED IN THE UNITED STATES OF AMERICA

07 08 09 10 11 12 13 14 15 16 — 10 9 8 7 6 5 4 3 2 1

Library of Congress Cataloging-in-Publication Data

Hillerbrand, Hans Joachim.
    The division of Christendom : Christianity in the sixteenth century / Hans J. Hillerbrand.
        p. cm.
    Includes bibliographical references and index.
    ISBN 978-0-664-22402-8 (alk. paper)
    1. Church history—16th century.   2. Reformation.   3. Counter-Reformation.   I. Title.
BR305.3.H55   2007
270.6—dc22

                                                                                2007009017

Contents

Chapter 4
*In which the divisions in the movement of reform triggered by Huldrych
Zwingli in Zurich and Switzerland are explained*

Chapter 5
*In which attention is called to further divisions on the Reformation
movement brought by those called Anabaptists, Hutterites, Spiritualists,
and Antitrinitarians*

Chapter 6
*In which further developments in Germany are recounted; how reform
began to be consolidated; how peasants and townspeople took to arms
in 1524*

Chapter 7
*In which the continuing story of reform after 1525 is presented; the decisions
of several imperial diets concerning the religious controversy are summarized;
the creation of the alliance of the League of Schmalkald is explained, together
with the crisis that occurred in Switzerland, and finally the war of the emperor
against the League of Schmalkald, and the eventual outcome of the conflagration
in Germany*

Chapter 8

In which is related the story of the Reformation in England, pointing to King Henry VIII's role; the king's great matter is explained, as is also how the Reformation was enforced; the Edwardian revolution; the Marian reaction; the Elizabethan Settlement is thoroughly discussed as is the Puritan dissent; the close of the reign; as well as the establishment of Anglicanism

Chapter 9

In which is recounted the story of Roman Catholicism in the sixteenth century, beginning with the Catholic reaction to the Reformation movement; the Council of Trent, the manifestations of spiritual renewal in Catholicism; the implementation of the Tridentine reform as well as descriptions of new forms of spirituality and religious life

Chapter 10

In which are presented John Calvin and the Reformed tradition, together with details of the life of John Calvin; his theology, and his leadership in the Genevan church

Chapter 11

In which the reader is informed of the Reformation changes occurring in Europe, notably in such countries as France, Scandinavia, Scotland, Poland, Hungary, and the Low Countries

Chapter 12
*In which are summarized the Protestant theologies, the common Protestant vision,
the affirmations and disagreements over the Lord's Supper and baptism; how
a new church emerged, and what that meant; church life and popular religion*

Chapter 13
*In which the author presents his reflections of the subject matter; rehearses
the consequences of the conflagration, and offers comments on the Reformation
and women; the Reformation and society; the Reformation and political life
and the wider world*

Epilogue

Preface

This book presents my understanding of the Reformation of the sixteenth century in the context of the broader story of Christianity at that time. It is, I must confess, not the first such effort on my part. Earlier in my career as a student of the Reformation I was invited to write a history of the Protestant Reformation that received the title of *Christendom Divided*. The book was well received, even though—due to the vicissitudes of publishing—it was remaindered two months after its publication. Since then, a large number of scholars—I am thinking of Carter Lindberg, Euan Cameron, Patrick Collinson, Diarmaid MacCullouch, James Tracy, Glenn Sunshine, Ulinka Rublack—have published histories of the Reformation, each with a particular focus. This plethora of narratives is all the more surprising in light of the diminished importance the Reformation seems to have in the broader context of European history. The German historian Heinz Schilling remarked that the Reformation seems to have "evaporated."

The invitation of Westminster John Knox Press to write a history of the Reformation has proved to be a welcome opportunity to revisit *Christendom Divided* both in light of new scholarship and my own maturing understanding of the Reformation. Not only have I changed my mind on a number of issues, important and not so important, I have also been forced to change my mind—not something that I was particularly eager to do—through the work of Bob Scribner, Heiko Oberman, Peter Blickle, Bernd Moeller, Martin Brecht, Scott Hendrix, Mark Edwards, Susan Karant-Nunn, Lyndal Roper, and others.

This book will tell how the Augustinian monk and professor of theology Martin Luther stumbled into a conflagration, how this conflagration coalesced into a movement, and how this movement marked a moment of historical importance. The book will thus tread familiar ground, and even though it will resist the temptation (I hope) to stake out excessive claims for the significance of this Reformation, it will tell the story as an important story.

As the epilogue points out, histories of the Reformation have had a way of being confessionally biased, Catholic scholars painting a quite different picture than did

Protestant scholars. Moreover, the foci of scholarly interest have had a way of shifting. A century ago, the interest of Reformation historians related to the historical course of events. Then, about half a century ago, the interest turned theological, prompting the German Reformation historian Bernd Moeller to warn of the danger of a "theologized" Reformation. A great deal of the excitement of recent scholarship has come from an interest in social issues and the suggestion to see religious issues from a social perspective.

My own understanding is simply stated: The Reformation was a striking interplay of religious and political forces. While religion, however, played the leitmotif, a great deal of serendipity also characterized the course of events. I hope to demonstrate—for example, with a detailed narrative of events and ideas in England—that the story of sixteenth-century Christianity was more than variations on themes of Martin Luther and Germany, more than a trip up and down the Rhine. It formed a rich matrix of diversity but also of common themes and motifs. Its cohesiveness derived from the common determination to restore what was perceived to be biblical religion, and do so in a striking relationship to the civil authorities.

There is presently a widespread preference for the use of the plural "Reformations" when talking about sixteenth-century reform phenomena. If I understand this use of the plural, it is used to characterize the variety of reform efforts occurring over an extended period of time, roughly from the fourteenth to the seventeenth century, denoting that time as a period of "reforms" or of "Reformations." A second perspective suggests that what has been traditionally called "Reformation" was so diverse and so lacking in homogeneity that it is best denoted by the use of the plural "Reformations."

The first point is well taken. Since it argues a conceptualization much broader than the chronological scope of this volume, however, it does not lend itself for utilization here. As regards the second point, I have retained the traditional use of the singular not only because I see an essential cohesiveness in the heterogeneous pursuits of religious reform in the sixteenth century, but also because I endeavored through judicious use of the terms "reform," "movement of reform," and "Reformation" to acknowledge the diversity that existed in the early years of the conflagration.

The alert reader will, in this connection, have noticed that title and subtitle of this book blatantly omit any reference to the Reformation. That is altogether intentional and expresses my conviction that the most important feature of the story of sixteenth-century Christianity was that a fundamental and fateful division occurred. Of course, there had been another division in 1014 that divided the East and the West, a happening that led Western Christians on a path of ignorance and indifference about the East. In this book, my concern was to depict the inner dynamic of reform-related events in sixteenth-century Europe, and that precluded a consideration of the story of Orthodoxy at the time.

It remains for me to thank those whose criticism and reactions have contributed, however inadvertently, to this book. A long list of colleagues has made my preoccupation with the sixteenth century a challenging and, at times, a delightful venture: Tom Brady, Eric Middelfort, Steven Ozment, Peter Kaufman, Scott Hendrix, Tom Robisheaux, as well as two good friends no longer with us, Heiko Oberman and Lewis Spitz. I also gratefully acknowledge the help of John M. Headley, Martin Brecht, Barbara

Norton, and Dorothea Wendebourg, who read parts of various drafts of the manuscript and proffered their opinions. A special recognition is due J. Samuel Hammond, of Duke University, who combines a wonderful mastery of the Duke Chapel carillon with an equally impressive understanding of the sixteenth century. He labored through the entire manuscript and compiled a most helpful and thoughtful index. Don McKim of Westminster John Knox Press first suggested that I undertake this project, and he has been a good friend and counselor. The book is better because of the suggestions and criticism of these colleagues. In a way, it is *their* book. And I am grateful.

Finally, I thank my family—Eric, Michael, Stephan, their spouses and children—for understanding what it means to have a father whose mind always seems to be in the sixteenth century. The years during which I wrote this book (as well as the others that preceded it) have been a challenge for my wife Bonnie, who many years ago commented that it was not easy to live with a husband who was really married to the sixteenth century. Many years ago I with deep appreciation dedicated my first book, my doctoral dissertation, to her with the acknowledgment that I could not have done it without her. Now, many years later, I dedicate this book to her, and I do so with the same heartfelt gratitude—as well as with the emotions that Edward Gibbon recorded upon the completion of his *Decline and Fall of the Roman Empire*: "I will not dissemble the first emotions of joy on recovery of my freedom, and perhaps the establishment of my fame. But my pride was soon humbled, and a sober melancholy spread over my mind, by the idea that I had taken an everlasting leave of an old and agreeable companion. . . ."

Hans J. Hillerbrand
Duke University
February 18, 2007

Chapter 1

THE SETTING

Anno Domini, the Year of the Lord, 1517, was a year much like any other. That year no bloody wars rampaged the German countryside, nor did the chroniclers' pens record unusual calamities, natural disasters, or mysterious signs in the skies. Sun and moon came at their appointed times, and the harvest that year was rich and full, even though the Augsburg chronicler Wilhelm Rem felt bound to record that because of inclement weather the wine was going to be poor—perhaps a timeless complaint of those whose livelihood depends on the forces of nature.[1]

Forests covered much of the land, and the earth that was tilled with crude tools afforded sufficient food only if the harvest was plentiful. Otherwise, when there was too much rain or too bitter a winter, hunger and starvation became constant companions. There were a few towns, Cologne, Nuremberg, or Augsburg, for example, whose economic importance, just like that of centers such as Venice, Florence, or Antwerp, had been steadily increasing over the years. But most people lived in hamlets and villages, and they were illiterate and little aware of what was going on in the wider world.

Anno Domini, the Year of the Lord, 1517, in faraway Spain, a seventeen-year-old, Carlos or Charles by name, had succeeded to the Spanish throne, altogether unexpectedly. He and others in seats of power throughout Europe were concerned about the military intentions of the Ottoman Empire in the eastern Mediterranean and about the failing health of the aged emperor of the Holy Roman Empire, Maximilian I. Others that year discussed a striking book, written by the English humanist and lawyer Thomas More, about a perfect society he called Utopia, where harmony, justice, tranquility, and communalism prevailed, while others marveled at that paradigm of Christian matrimony, the marriage of the dashing English king Henry VIII and his somber (and quite a bit older) wife, Catherine of Aragon.

The theologians and intellectuals of the day did, so the chronicler must report, what theologians and intellectuals have always done—they wrote, argued, and published. The invention of the printing press, that is, of movable type, a little over half a century earlier had made it immensely easier than ever before to put ideas, good and bad, into print. Some intellectuals were in the public eye: the German humanist Johannes Reuchlin, for example, who was engaged in a fierce controversy with a Dominican monk, Johann Pfefferkorn, over the question of whether in Christian society books by

---

1. Wilhelm Rem, "Chronica," in *Chroniken der schwäbischen Städte: Augsburg* (Göttingen: 1965), 69, 72, 77.

Jewish authors should be allowed to be published. Desiderius Erasmus, called Rotero-damus because he hailed from Rotterdam, had attained European renown as an inde-fatigable editor of ancient texts, including the New Testament in Greek, and a challenging proponent of Christianity as the "philosophy of Christ," which saw the Christian religion more as a moral rule of life than as theology.

Anno Domini 1517, few had ever heard of one Martin Luther, Augustinian friar and professor of biblical studies at the University of Wittenberg in central Germany. Wit-tenberg was a small and undistinguished town of some three thousand; Luther himself later observed that it was situated "on the edge of civilization. One more step, and I would have landed in the midst of the Barbarians."[2] He might as well have spoken of academic Siberia. Compared to the prestigious universities of the day, such as those at Cologne, Leipzig, or Erfurt, Wittenberg had few students and even less reputation.[3] It was barely two decades old in 1517 and hardly a distinguished place of higher learning.

By the time the year 1517 turned, however, this unknown professor had begun to blaze into public consciousness, and before long he overshadowed everything and everybody else. An innocuous event stood at the beginning of the greatest conflagra-tion Western Christendom ever experienced. Toward the end of October 1517, Luther prepared a set of theological theses or propositions, ninety-five in number, for an aca-demic disputation at Wittenberg. Such was customary at universities in those days, when intellectual brilliance was to be displayed or unresolved theological topics were to be resolved. Luther's Ninety-five Theses dealt with the relatively unimportant topic of indulgences, a complicated matter in which popular perception and church teach-ing were not altogether in harmony and where the church had not rendered a final doctrinal verdict. For good measure Luther added in his theses a few asides against the role of the papacy in this matter (not really saying anything that had not been said before, merely echoing the widespread German sentiment that Rome was exacting too much money from Germany). He also sent copies of his theses to several friends and colleagues at other places—and there the problem began. As matters turned out, much to their author's surprise and consternation, the Ninety-five Theses became the cata-lyst for an increasingly vehement theological controversy, not the least because Luther had seen to it that an intra-university affair became known elsewhere.

Within three years this controversy had embroiled central Europe. Indeed, a move-ment was beginning to coalesce, vague and inchoate, to be sure, but a movement nonetheless. It began its sweep across Germany and before long took in the rest of Europe, precipitating one of the most serious crises Christendom and even European society had experienced for some time. The "squabble among monks," as Pope Leo X had called the initial discussion of Luther's Ninety-five Theses, turned into a confla-gration, and before too long into a movement.[4] It soon was called the Reformation.

Until recently, historians, at least those of a Protestant disposition, have tended to be of one mind as to how to explain this story. They noted how church and society in the early sixteenth century were characterized by weaknesses that, in various ways,

2. Martin Luther, *Werke: Kritische Gesamtausgabe: Tischreden* (Weimar: 1883ff.), 3:1432 (hereafter WA TR).
3. On universities in the early sixteenth century, see Paul Grendler, "The Universities of the Renais-sance and Reformation," *Renaissance Quarterly* 57 (2004): 1–41.
4. WA TR 2635b.

greatly facilitated the progression of a single individual's protest to a movement. Indeed, some historians have talked about a systemic crisis of society in the early sixteenth century, while others pointed to a variety of stark abuses and perversions in the church. Historians seem to have agreed that the clue to what happened after 1517 must be sought in the years before.

The reason is obvious: if church or society revealed signs of fateful weaknesses or tensions, if there were telltale symptoms of a deepening crisis in either church or society, or even both—if the handwriting was on the wall, so to speak—the task of explaining the phenomenon of the Reformation becomes one of relating the structural crisis of church or society to the upheaval. Of course, this smacks of some form of historical determinism; and, indeed, traditionally historians of the Reformation, especially Protestant historians, have so paid homage, seeing the Reformation as a reaction against a decadent church that had fallen into grave theological error. German nationalism, social class, and the general intellectual climate were the catalysts for reform.

According to this perspective, an analysis of early-sixteenth-century church and society will identify a variety of forces that constituted an irresistible, inevitable thrust toward upheaval. There would have been a Reformation, in other words, even if Luther had died in the cradle. In essence, such a view entails the argument that one can posit a line of causality between pre-Reformation church and society and the ensuing Reformation. This would mean, for example, that the widespread immorality of the clergy or the new vision of humanism created a profoundly destabilizing situation, that intellectuals had become alienated from church and society, that people were consciously hostile and dissatisfied, and that the critical voices evident in theology, in literature, in society, were deeply symptomatic of these troubles.

Another perspective shows the causes of the Reformation to lie not so much in overt aspects as in fundamental characteristics of society in the early sixteenth century. The "crisis" of the early sixteenth century is seen to have been structural, even though the surface may have been peaceful and tranquil—and the worldly cleric an exception, and ecclesiastical greed rare, and loyalty to the church universal. External considerations notwithstanding, the harmony of forces that formed a cohesive mantle over late medieval society was disappearing. Changing political, economic, and social conditions challenged the traditional place of the church in society. These developments took place, as often as not, underneath the surface and had few dramatic manifestations. For example, the accelerating migration from country into towns meant that these new urbanites lived "uprooted," in new social settings and often without full legal rights. Unaffiliated with the traditional guilds, they may well have been prone to be open to new ideas, including those that challenged the status quo, making them disposed to embrace the challenge of the Reformation to order things anew.

What, then, is to be said about the state of affairs on the eve of the Reformation? Politically, two realities on the periphery of Europe were of critical importance in the early years of the sixteenth century. In the southeast, not too far from Vienna, there was the Ottoman Empire, powerful and menacing. It had attained significance under the rule of Mohammed II, "the Conqueror" (1451–1481), and had steadily expanded its realm, first by conquering the shores of the eastern Mediterranean, then, in 1453, by the conquest of Constantinople, the capital of the fading Byzantine Empire. Mohammed II also conquered the Balkan Peninsula, with forays in 1477 and 1480 into the Adriatic. Like a mighty river, the Ottoman Empire had separated the western and eastern Mediterranean.

By the end of the second decade of the sixteenth century, this expansionist empire, driven in part by the cry of a holy war against the non-Muslim world, was massed to the southeast of Vienna, threatening to overrun central Europe. To be sure, Ottoman expansion during the previous half century had been anything but steady. Times of aggression were followed by extended periods of calm, when the Ottoman Empire was forced to deal with domestic problems or turned its aggressiveness to the south to play the two sacred sites of Mecca and Medina into its hands. Indeed, calm prevailed in central Europe between the death of Mohammed II in 1481 and the reign of Suleiman II, "the Magnificent" (1520–1566), giving Western Christendom a welcome respite that may well have saved it from annihilation: chances are that Europe could not have withstood an Ottoman onslaught.[5]

Europe was thus deeply apprehensive, but no consensus prevailed as to how to deal with this threat. Since the Ottoman Turks were Muslim, some in Christendom understood military action against the Turks as the defense of the Christian faith against unbelievers. They were ready to take up arms and undertake once more a crusade against the enemy of Christendom, who now was no longer a thousand miles away but stood massed outside the gates. Others, paying homage to realpolitik, sought to reach a political accommodation with the Ottoman Empire.

When the German diet met in Augsburg in 1518, the foremost issue before the estates was how to counter a possible Ottoman military onslaught. There was no agreement as to the seriousness of the Ottoman threat; after all, there had been that extended period of peace. The raising of an army required financial resources, and then as now new taxes were problematic. That a German monk by the name of Martin Luther was interrogated about a theological squabble by the papal legate Cajetan during that same diet was of minor importance.

The Ottoman domination of the eastern Mediterranean had another dramatic consequence, symbolized by the Turkish conquest of the island of Rhodes in 1522. The traditional commercial trade route between the Far East and central Europe had utilized the eastern Mediterranean sea route, which ended in Venice. From there spices, silk, and other goods were then moved northward across the Alps. Turkish dominance of the eastern Mediterranean made this traditional trade route increasingly dangerous, or made trade and commercial contact dependent on Ottoman goodwill. The pursuit of new trade routes along the western coast of Africa, not to mention the European determination to find a western sea route to India, was the fateful consequence. Hovering over the course of the sixteenth century was the increasing reality that the Mediterranean was beginning to lose its pivotal role in European affairs and that the axis was shifting westward, toward the Atlantic Ocean. The proud cities and city-states of Italy began their decline.

---

5. Stephen Fischer-Galati, *Ottoman Imperialism and German Protestantism, 1521–1555* (New York: 1959).

The developments on the western periphery of Europe proved to be of even greater revolutionary impact. They were intimately connected to the Ottoman domination of the East and meant the beginning of what has been called the Age of Discovery, Europe's westward expansion across the Atlantic. Christopher Columbus had succeeded in 1492 in traversing the ocean that had been seen as the end of the world. Now European merchant vessels began to plow the Atlantic Ocean both westward and southward, bringing fur, tea, sugar, gold, and silver from other continents back to Europe. A new commercial and economic era was dawning, characterized by the transfer of the intra-European conflict between Spain and Portugal to the new lands. In 1494 the pope was called upon to negotiate the Treaty of Tordesillas between Portugal and Spain, which stipulated how the South American continent should be divided into Spanish and Portuguese spheres of influence.

A political reality of equal importance was the struggle between France and Spain over the possession of northern Italy. In a way, this struggle, which lasted for the better part of half a century, had to do with the traditional importance of Italy as trading center with the East. Because there had been no further Ottoman aggression for a generation, the European powers focused their attention on the struggle between Spain and France and were themselves drawn into the conflict. Intra-European belligerence was made possible, perhaps even encouraged, by the calm that prevailed in the southeast of Europe.

Between east and west hovered the Holy Roman Empire of the German Nation, so named in Emperor Charles V's election agreement of 1519. Named to evoke continuity with the greatest of all empires—that of Rome—and named "holy" to denote that the emperor received his authority from God, its boundaries stretched from the Baltic southward through much of present-day Poland and the Slovak Republic to the Adriatic, encompassing northern Italy, Switzerland, and eastern France as well as present-day Belgium and the Netherlands. The "of the German Nation" aspect of the empire's name explains why historians have often used the appellation "Germany" for the empire. Although they justified the shorthand by reasoning that by the early sixteenth century, what might be called "Germany" or "the German lands" constituted the functioning part of the empire, it embraced in fact far more than that.[6]

These territories and cities in the area roughly identical with that of present-day Germany formed a unity, tenuous though it was, primarily because of their German language, even though this language comprised a number of quite distinct dialects. The non-German territories and principalities of the Holy Roman Empire, Burgundy and Bohemia, had become virtually autonomous by the end of the fifteenth century and were only casually involved in affairs of the empire. The king of Bohemia, for example, formally one of the seven electors, attended the meetings of the imperial diet only to participate in the election of a new emperor.

This Holy Roman Empire was the most formidable political entity in Europe. Unlike other European countries, such as France or England, however, it had not

---

6. *Grimm's Deutsches Wörterbuch* shows that the word "Germany" was in usage in the early sixteenth century, even though no political entity corresponded to that term. It referred to the lands in which the various German dialects were spoken, roughly identifiable, of course, with Germany.

succeeded in resolving the long-standing ambivalences in the power relationships between the central authority, the emperor, and the nobility. At the Diet of Worms in 1495, important reform measures were agreed upon that, though not altogether successful, provided the crucial context for the course of the religious controversy that was to ensue in 1517. Indeed, what happened after 1517 was to provide the ultimate test of the viability of the reforms agreed upon in 1495. This *Handhabung Friedens und Recht* (How Law and Order Are to Be Maintained) provided that the emperor was bound by the decisions of the *Reichstag* (diet), which was to convene annually. The *Reichstag* was composed of three "colleges" that deliberated separately: the college of electors; the college of ecclesiastical and secular territorial rulers; and the free cities, called "free" because they were constitutionally subject only to the emperor as overlord (there were some eighty-six of such "free cities" in 1521, most of them located in the south), though in the end the three colleges sought to agree on common action and policy. A *Reichsregiment* was instituted as a kind of executive authority for the emperor, especially in his absence from the empire. The emperor was elected by seven electors (*Kurfürsten*). By the early sixteenth century, the election of the emperor hinged on the candidates' willingness to make various commitments, embodied in the so-called *Wahlkapitulation*, or election agreement, which essentially reinforced the autonomy of the territorial rulers, both secular and ecclesiastical. In short, the distribution of power in the empire made for a peculiar situation, for it meant that as long as no strong central authority existed that might have enforced decisions, the territorial rulers, either in consort with the diet or acting unilaterally, were the major players.

THE INTELLECTUAL ATMOSPHERE

The slogan *ad fontes* (to the sources) had exerted a revolutionary impact on European intellectuality ever since the fourteenth century. The "sources" that were to be studied and taken seriously were not the ones of which the medieval scholastics had been so fond, but those of Roman and Greek antiquity. These sources needed to be discovered, uncovered so to speak, from under the scholastic overlay, as the deep roots of European thought. First in Italy, then elsewhere in Europe, small groups of like-minded individuals committed themselves to an exciting and exhilarating pursuit of the intellectual sources of classical antiquity.

The challenge was thus the recovery of the literature, art, and philosophy of classical antiquity, including the sources of the earliest Christianity. Those who were so engaged saw themselves as reformers, and much later, in the eighteenth century, they were described as humanists.[7] The term derived from what was central: the *studia humaniora,* humanistic studies.

Humanistic studies meant the intensive study of Plato and Aristotle, without the Christianizing mantle that had accompanied the preoccupation with these thinkers in the Middle Ages. It also meant attention to classic Ciceronian Latin philosophy, rhetoric, and history. A different ideal of erudition stood behind this: learning was to

---

7. Leif Grane, *Martinus Noster. Luther in the German Reform Movement* (Mainz: 1994), 29ff.

be acquired from classical antiquity and not from medieval scholasticism. Humanists had noted that the noble qualities in human nature might be enhanced by the study of good authors, the cultivation of eloquence, and the pursuit of a pleasant setting for learning, and they were persuaded that they found these elements in classical antiquity. A new age was dawning, when the stultifying limitations of the old one would be removed. "Oh century, Oh sciences! It is a pleasure to be alive!" Ulrich von Hutten's ecstatic declaration of 1518 was indicative of the widespread mood of exuberance among humanists at the time.

Those enthralled with these notions banded together in circles, first in Italy, and then, by the second half of the fifteenth century, in all parts of Europe. These circles were part mutual-admiration societies, part eighteenth-century salon, part continuing-education effort. Their members published feverishly. In Germany it was Rudolf Agricola who had imbibed these new notions during a lengthy stay in Italy (where he wrote a biography of Petrarch). Agricola, who eventually occupied a professorship at the University of Heidelberg, inspired not so much with his pen—he wrote very little—as with his charismatic personality. His pupil Konrad Celtis, poet, professor at Ingolstadt, and, since 1498, professor in Vienna, was a traveling evangelist who inveighed against scholastic learning. Celtis established communalities of humanists (*sodalitates*) that exerted considerable influence in such places as Strassburg, Nuremberg, and Augsburg. The very fact that these flourishing urban centers immediately became humanist strongholds suggests the connection between the humanists' intellectual agenda and the increasing economic and political vitality of the cities in early-sixteenth-century Germany.

Alongside this high-spirited affection for classical antiquity and everything that went with it, the German humanists also expressed a pointed national consciousness. Celtis's inaugural lecture at Ingolstadt challenged the "German men" to embrace again that "ancient spirit which was so many times a terror and spectacle to the Romans."[8] Interestingly, cultural nationalism became a major theme for the German humanists.

ERASMUS AND REFORM

In 1504 Erasmus, thirty-five years old and increasingly renowned in Europe, published the *Adnotationes* of Lorenzo Valla on the New Testament. It was to be a revolutionary venture, since Valla sought to recover the original text, a point of which Erasmus himself seemed quite aware. He wrote: "I consider Valla deserving of the highest praise." As the next years passed, Erasmus increasingly became the pivotal figure in the theological scene before Martin Luther published his Ninety-five Theses in 1517. Some humanists (they themselves did not use the term) focused their attention on the Christian religion and concluded that it was in dire need of renewal. Those who so argued came to be known as "Christian" humanists, and Erasmus of Rotterdam was their most eloquent and influential spokesman.

Erasmus was born in Rotterdam, probably in 1469, the illegitimate son of a Dutch priest and an unknown mother (to the end of his life Erasmus never quite got over his

8. Lewis Spitz, *Conrad Celtis: The German Arch Humanist* (Cambridge: 1957), 50.

ignominious origins). He seems to have received thorough schooling in his childhood
and youth, though most of what we know about that time comes from his own pen,
written when he sought a papal dispensation to release him from his monastic vows.
In later years Erasmus complained a lot about the shortcomings of his education, especially the instruction he received in dreadful medieval Latin.

At age sixteen Erasmus entered the monastery at Steyn, not too far from the Dutch
town of Gouda. Soon thereafter, however, the opportunity to become the Latin secretary to the bishop of Cambrai ended his monastic sojourn. He had hoped for tranquility and intellectual friendship in the monastery, and had instead encountered
stifling regulations and uncouth companions. His treatise *Antibarbarorum Liber*,
composed around 1495 but not published until 1520, indicted the "barbarians" for
their lack of interest (and even laziness) in ancient studies. At the same time, he also
repudiated the traditional Christian contempt of the "world"—that is, wealth, pleasure, and reputation—which constituted, in fact, the underpinnings of the monastic
life.[9] In a striking phrase, one of the participants of the fictitious colloquy that forms
the structure of Erasmus's treatise observes that the trouble with the religious is that
they "continually hide like tortoises in their shells, and worry more morosely about
the smallest details of physical comfort," a sentiment that was to be echoed with
Luther's argument that the religious commitment to live in the monastery was a cow-
ardly way to avoid the challenges of the "world."

After Erasmus's monastic life ended, he matriculated at the University of Paris in
1495. He found the College of Montaigu, its discipline and rote learning, stultifying,
though he did have the opportunity to deliver sermons on the saints. He stayed hardly
a year. He pursued influential (and wealthy) patrons and was reasonably successful in
this regard, but he never quite lost his worries about money, managing always to live
just slightly above his means, and also constantly fretting about his health—and about
what others thought of him.

When Erasmus found his way to England, he introduced himself to John Colet as
"a man of little or no fortune, foreign to ambition, much given to love, burning with
desire for letters, though without experience, with respect to religion admiring the
propriety of others, without having any of his own, easily yielding to others in learning, though not in loyalty, who is simple, open, free, ignorant of both pretense and
deceit; in disposition without ambition and corruption."[10]

It was in England that Erasmus decided to study Greek in order to become a "primitive theologian." What he meant by that was a theologian who would seek to recover
the tenets of the earliest, primitive Christianity. The literary fruits promptly followed,
starting with his *Enchiridion militis Christiani* (The Dagger of the Christian Soldier)
in 1503, after Colet had unsuccessfully insisted that he take up a professorship in Old
Testament at Oxford. The winsomeness of the *Enchiridion* derived mainly from Erasmus's successful juxtaposition, echoing the sentiment of the church father Origen, of
the notions of antiquity and Christianity.

9. James Tracy, *Erasmus: The Growth of a Mind* (Geneva: 1972), 52.
10. *Opus epistolarum Des. Erasmi* (Oxford, 1906f.), Letter 107, p. 244. Tracy, *Erasmus*, 61. My translation differs from Tracy's.

The *Enchiridion* was a somewhat strange title: the word meant "dagger." Erasmus used it allegorically to describe the "spiritual" dagger as the indispensable tool for the Christian. By the time Erasmus died, the little book had been reprinted over thirty times and had been translated into the major European languages. It was arguably the most important introduction to Christianity published in the early sixteenth century before the Reformation controversy ensued. Its content was as simple as its title was strange. Erasmus espoused an inner piety of the heart, and in so doing inveighed against the religion of external observances, of ceremonies and ritual, of the veneration of saints and relics. In a way Erasmus's book was elitist, because it showed small patience for the various crutches the common people used to express and live their religion. To be sure, the *Enchiridion* was ambivalent—for example, it is not at all clear whether it argued the essential equality of laity and clergy—but Erasmus's conviction of the essential harmony between the ideals of classical antiquity and Christianity comes through on page after page.

It was in the second decade of the century that Erasmus turned from his preoccupation with the style of classical letters and rhetoric, manifest in his seemingly endless editions of classical authors, to a more gargantuan task, that of the restoration (*restitutio*) of Christianity to its original biblical intentions. It was a Christianity marked, above all, by its fidelity to the "sources"—and that did not mean the scholastic sources but those of antiquity, foremost among them, of course, the Bible itself. At issue was the program that other Christian humanists, such as Colet, Guillaume Briçonnet, or Jacques Lefèvre d'Étaples, had enunciated—that scholastic theology had brought about a fundamental misunderstanding of the true Christian message—but Erasmus refined this program to insist that a false theology had led to a neglect of the moral behavior of Christians, and rectifying that was the most urgent need and challenge.

When Erasmus reached Basel in 1514, secure in his European-wide reputation, his writings focusing on Christian themes became more forthright and audacious. Although Erasmus's main occupation was to edit ancient texts, he also published a number of works that, before long, made him a household name among the literate throughout Europe. Later, after Erasmus had published his satirical *Encomium moriae* (The Praise of Folly), in which he subjected all human endeavors, including the church, to churning criticism as "folly," he found himself attacked by a twenty-nine-year-old upstart from Louvain, Martin Dorp.[11] Dorp chided Erasmus for his indiscriminate attack in his *Encomium* on the guild of theologians, who were, after all, the mainstay of the church. More important, Dorp's biting criticism argued that there was a gulf between Erasmus's "philosophy of Christ," with its elements of simplicity, love, meekness, and self-discipline, and profound notions of sin and divine omnipotence that the theologians of the church were seeking to work out.

In 1516 Erasmus's greatest legacy appeared: his edition of the Greek New Testament. In a way, it was much like the numerous other editions that he published. He hoped that by making the wisdom of classical antiquity available, religion and morality would improve. Scholars could have recourse to the Gospels and the Epistles of

11. Ibid., Letter 347, 27 August 1515.

New Testament, and that would lead to a revival of true biblical religion: the moralizing stories of Jesus and the epistolary exhortations of the apostles would become available in the powerful language in which they were written—Greek. Erasmus's edition offered both the Greek and the Latin Vulgate texts in a parallel translation. He ventured a few emendations of the Vulgate text, but his changes were modest, even though he offered, at the end of his edition, notes on various chapters and verses.

There were other writings as well: *Julius Exclusus, Enarratio in Ps. 1*, a new edition of the *Encomium moriae*. These not only enhanced his reputation but also made his dismay over the state of the church increasingly obvious, expressing his sentiment that "reform" was necessary. He charged that there were too many monasteries, that nuns were allowed to marry as late as the fourth century, that married priests were better than priests living in concubinage. The sporadic anticlerical denunciations of the late medieval period found eloquent restatement in Erasmus's writings.

The key theme of Erasmus's writings was that of Christian freedom. Erasmus argued that the common folk were burdened with rules that obscured and hid the true meaning of the Christian faith. He denounced the "tyranny of ceremonies," by which he meant the unending obligations imposed by the church on the common people. Instead, he believed, Christians should be free from obligatory rules and fulfill the law of Christ in freedom. Clearly, these themes were echoed by Luther and other advocates of reform once the controversy over the Ninety-five Theses had erupted. No wonder, then, that Erasmus was quickly seen by many as the true source of Luther's protest, an inference he at first gladly enjoyed and then, once Luther's theological issues had come to the fore, emphatically rejected. There can be no doubt that Erasmus and those who shared his program of a *restitutio Christianismi* prepared the ground for Luther's decisive repudiation of the religious and ecclesiastical status quo. Unlike Luther, however, Erasmus never relinquished his fundamental belief in the values of classical antiquity and the essentially moral character of the Christian profession.

Erasmus had comrades-in-arms, and although their emphases, concerns, and complaints were diverse, most of them concurred in a pointed dislike for the traditional scholastic method of theology. The anonymous *Epistolae virorum obscurorum* (*Letters of Obscure Men*) of 1515 is a case in point: the book was a biting, satirical attack upon the obscurantist scholastic theologians who pondered the number of angels that could dance on the head of a pin or who wondered about the moral implications of eating an egg on a meatless day if they happened to discover, in the process of gulping—alas, too late!—that the chick had already hatched.[12] Not only did the humanists' animosity toward scholasticism derive from an aversion to their stilted and structured method of doing theology, which in the humanists' judgment obscured the true Christian religion, it also postulated the knowledge of Greek (and Hebrew) as indispensable for proper theologizing. Indeed, precisely because the scholastics were doing bad theology, they were largely responsible for the church's lamentable condition.

In addition to reacting against hairsplitting theological sophistry, as found in scholasticism, the humanists emphasized the pivotal importance of the moral precepts of the Bible, particularly those of Jesus, and embraced a different scholarly method.

12. Hajo Holborn, ed., *On the Eve of the Reformation: Letters of Obscure Men* (New York: 1964).

It was based on the reading of ancient texts of the church fathers in order to get as close to the sources of Christian theology as possible. This concern for the original texts had been the catalyst for the publication of the *Letters of Obscure Men* by Ulrich von Hutten in order to assist Johannes Reuchlin, whose support for Hebraic studies and the publishing of Hebrew texts had triggered intense opposition from the traditionalist scholastic theologians at Cologne. The humanists scorned the stultified Latin of the scholastic theologians and argued that the ancient language should be "modernized" so that the snowball fights of schoolboys could be described in exciting Latin.

Rather than the scholastic method of tediously outlined questions and answers, the humanists preferred a free-flowing exposition, with form and structure governed by content rather than by preconceived categories. Moreover, they stressed the need to go "back to the sources," to the writers of Christian antiquity, rather than dwell on the pronouncements of the medieval scholastics. Erasmus edited the writings of Jerome and Cyprian, while his French comrade-in-arms, Jacques Lefèvre d'Étaples, occupied himself with the writings of St. Paul.

Much of this humanist emphasis was latent and implicit. With few exceptions, there was no outright clash; the prestigious academic positions, after all, were occupied by scholastically oriented theologians. The humanists were the younger generation and tended to be associated with faculties of the (liberal) arts, while those steeped in scholasticism were theologians. After the turn of the century, humanist emphases were embraced by an increasing number of intellectuals and theologians. The Christian humanists added a novel element of heterogeneity.

CHURCH AND RELIGION

The church hovered over everything. From Brabant to Tuscany, from the Baltic Sea to Santiago de Compostela, travelers approaching a village or a town would see the church steeples rise up from the horizon, and those steeples, unmatched in height by any other edifice, symbolized the place of the church in society. Rarely has any society since then been so completely and so comprehensively permeated by the church as that of the late Middle Ages. Indeed, the label used to describe this all-embracing political, social, and religious phenomenon was "Christendom" (*Christianitas*), and it expressed the notion that from Ireland to Poland, from Finland to Sicily, there existed a community of a single faith and a single set of values. To be sure, this winsome unity and harmony had all sorts of exceptions and deviations. There were intra-Christian squabbles with heretical movements and theological deviation. There was the sporadic presence of Jewish communities. Although increasingly segregated in ghettos, they nonetheless made their Christian neighbors aware of religious diversity, often tinged with strange fear and suspicion. There also was awareness of Islam, at home along the northern shores of the Mediterranean, increasingly in the Balkan Peninsula, and only tardily retreating from Spain.[13] Nonetheless, these were all minor exceptions, irritants at times, that only confirmed the larger rule.

13. Michael Borgolte, *Christen, Juden, Muselmanen: Die Erben der Antike und der Aufstieg des Abendlandes 300 bis 1400 n. Chr.* (Berlin: 2006), argues the case for extensive religious diversity in the Middle Ages.

The ancient saying, "Outside the church there is no salvation," expressed the universality of the church's claim. The church was more than the bearer of the revelatory truth that determined the eternal fate of all, even though only the priests were said to provide the sole access to God. The laws and principles of the church reached into the daily lives of the faithful by ordering all of life from marriage to inheritance, from schooling to the arts. The church had a monopoly on education, from the learned universities that prepared men for prestigious careers in church and state to local schools that focused on reading and writing. The church cared for the sick and the poor, for orphans and widows. Monasteries and convents provided shelter and learning and spiritual solace. Even as the liturgical calendar ordered the religious life of the faithful through the course of the year, so did it reach into the daily life with its rich celebration of saints' days and feast days, punctuated by seasons of fasting and penance. Birth, marriage, and death were made meaningful by the ritual celebrations of the church; there was very little in the lives of the faithful that did not entail its sacralization by a ubiquitous church.

This church was well aware of its authority and its place in society. Some of its spokesmen advanced far-reaching and extravagant claims to authority and power. According to ancient documents the emperor Constantine was said to have at his deathbed "donated" all his worldly power to the church, thereby making the popes the superiors of emperors and kings. But increasingly, the civil powers refused to accede to Constantine's wishes, and the Middle Ages turned into an unending story of a fierce clash between the secular and the ecclesiastical powers. Pope Boniface VIII, whose bull *Unam Sanctam*, of 1302, constituted the high-water mark of the claims of papal supremacy over civil government, had cut his teeth in his fierce clash with Philip IV of France. Even though there never was a time when churchly claims to supremacy remained uncontested, these claims continued to be persistently advanced.

By the late fifteenth century, the new self-confidence of the civil powers and a papacy weakened by internal strife had given way to increased secular power over the church. This was particularly noticeable in France, where, by the time Francis I succeeded to the throne in 1515, the church was largely under royal control. The following year Francis concluded a concordat with Pope Leo X that gave the French king the power to nominate episcopal appointees and the right to tax the clergy in return for the continued payment of the annates (the tax of one year's revenue, paid by each new holder of a church office, to Rome). Elsewhere in Europe the scales had not tilted quite so dramatically in the direction of the secular power—though it was said that the Duke of Cleves "est papa in suo regno" (is pope in his realm)—but no doubt developments in France were copiously watched.

Observers of religious life in Germany were uniformly impressed by the religiosity of the people.[14] Johann Cochlaeus's *Brevis Germaniae descriptio* (Brief Description of Germany), of 1512, painted a picture of vibrant church life, and an Italian cardinal traveling in Germany at the time remarked upon the piety of the common people and found the city of Ulm "molto religiosi."[15]

---

14. M. Miller, "Das römische Tagebuch des Ulmer Stadtammanns Konrad Locher," *Historisches Jahrbuch* 60 (1940): 293.

15. G. Giacalone, *Il Viaggio in Alamagna di F. Vettori ei miti del Rinascimento* (Arezzo: 1982), 73, 107.

Much has been written about the theological currents of the fifteenth century. Scholars have talked about a distressing lack of familiarity with authentic Catholic teaching, about a "long fifteenth century" that anticipated much of what was argued theologically in the Reformation.[16] There is no doubt that fifteenth-century theologizing threw a long shadow over the beginnings of the Reformation.

By the late fifteenth century, the lively medieval debate between the proponents of the "old way," the *via antiqua*, and the proponents of the "new way," the *via moderna*, had coalesced into distinct and fixed camps. At issue had been the question as to whether "universals" were real, as the old way maintained, or simple constructs of the human mind, as claimed by the new way. Underneath this philosophical debate, heavily influenced by Aristotle, was one over human reason. Here the proponents of the old way wrote splendidly about the ability of reason to penetrate even the most complex metaphysical questions, while the new way thought in terms of paradox—some metaphysical issues would not be elucidated by human reason.

By the end of the fifteenth century the rich complexity of medieval theological discourse had given way to a rather one-sided emphasis on nominalist assertions. This scholastic system, traceable to William of Occam, the English Franciscan friar who was involved in the major intellectual and political controversies of the fourteenth century, stressed the utter omnipotence of God, whose commands derived from his will and not from his being (for example, if God were so to will, murder would be a good). By the same token, and in unmitigated paradox, theologians just before the Reformation stressed human freedom as the crucial category in theological reflection. Human beings were not puppets, without freedom to choose; they were able to act morally, and so salvation was made contingent, to some extent, on their efforts. To be sure, divine grace constituted the primary factor, without which human effort was useless; but that effort was seen as more important than it had been in previous theological discussion.

A generation before the outbreak of the indulgences controversy, the theological firmament was dominated by Gabriel Biel (c. 1410–1495), professor at Tübingen and author of a widely used commentary on the *Sentences* of Peter Lombard, entitled *Collectorium circa quatuor libros Sententiarum*, which despite much keen independence seemed to be an homage to William of Occam.[17] Occam's insistence on the paradoxical nature of talking about faith and the failure of philosophy to be a perfect guide proved to be enormously significant in the subsequent theological reflection of the Reformation. Luther, in a set of theological theses of September 1517 that antedated his more famous Ninety-five Theses of the following October, inveighed against the entire scholastic tradition—Duns Scotus no less than Biel, as well as Aristotle. Even more important, however, was the much broader current of late-medieval theologizing that focused on the relationship between the freedom of the human will and the freedom of God's will. This topic had reverberated in the West ever since Augustine battled with Pelagius, and through the centuries all sorts of mediating positions had

16. Joseph Lortz, *History of the Reformation in Germany* (New York: 1968); Heiko Oberman, *The Two Reformations* (New Haven: 2003).

17. *Collectorium circa quatuor libros Sententiarum*, ed. Wilfried Werbeck, 4 vols. (Tübingen: 1973–1977).

been advanced. In the late fifteenth century Biel ventured forth with a remarkable notion that related human effort to divine grace: if humans "facere quod in se est" (do what is within them), not more though also not less, then God will not refuse his grace.[18] Thomas Bradwardine recalled from his student days, "In the philosophical faculty I seldom heard a reference to grace. . . . What I heard day in and day out was that we are masters of our own free acts, that ours is the choice to act well or badly."[19]

Theologically, the scene was thus both restive and serene. Inasmuch as freedom entails responsibility, this theological emphasis is understandable, though it upset the balance between God and humanity characteristic of most medieval theological reflection, as exemplified by Thomas Aquinas. When the balance was disrupted, theologians moved further from Augustine's view of God as pivotal and central.

A second aspect of the late medieval theological scene had to do with the question of the ultimate authority in the church. In the course of the fifteenth century its major focus was the tension between conciliar and papalist disposition. Conciliarism, the notion that a general council, composed of the bishops of the church, possessed final authority, experienced both a spectacular victory and a devastating defeat. The former happened at the Council of Constance (1414–1418), which healed the schism in the church created by competing popes, and the latter in 1460, when Pope Pius II condemned the notion of the primacy of a council over the pope. That condemnation by no means ended the discussion, however, nor was conciliar sentiment dead; and by the early sixteenth century the question of the legitimate range of power and authority attributed to the papal office was by no means clear.

A related issue pertained to the source of religious authority. Needless to say, Scripture was viewed as revealed truth, and its authority was fundamental to all theologizing. But over the centuries another source of authority had emerged, at first by way of explanation and commentary of biblical truth: church tradition. The issue of how the two were to be related was increasingly viewed in the fifteenth century as a pressing one. Tradition was seen either as the explanation of scriptural truth or as autonomous revelation in itself. Theologians could not agree upon an answer, nor could they completely silence the nagging suspicion that Scripture and tradition themselves might possibly be in disagreement.

Despite these focal points of theological dispute, there is no evidence of a state of theological tension or unresolved paradox in the decades preceding the Reformation. On the issue of human freedom, the pendulum had swung to one side and sooner or later was bound to swing back; in theology positions tend to move dialectically. Such a turn was hardly urgent, however.

Practical piety in the early sixteenth century was marked by several characteristics, primarily perhaps by the flourishing of the so-called private masses (celebrated alongside the regular, canonical masses). In distinction to regular masses, these private masses tended to be generally celebrated, not at the high altar but at side altars or chapels, by ordained members of a monastic community, monks who were priests.

18. See here Leif Grane, *Contra Gabrielem: Luthers Auseinandersetzung mit Gabriel Biel* (Copenhagen: 1962).

19. Heiko A. Oberman, ed., *Forerunners of the Reformation*, 135.

Such masses were called private because generally no worshipers were present. This was not just a practical outcome of the services' multiplicity; the key reason was that their role and place were not canonically prescribed. They generally resulted from endowment gifts of private donors, who wished to speed up the transition of the (wealthy) donors from purgatory to eternal bliss. Estimates are that in Cologne no less than one thousand such private masses were celebrated each day.[20]

The intense religiosity of the late medieval period also found expression in the increased popularity of the cult of the saints, an understandable development in view of the fact that God and Jesus were seen as distant, one as ruler of the universe, the other as its judge, whose wrath was perceived with fear and trembling. The saints thus rose to greater prominence as welcome (and human) intermediaries.

At the same time, saints were understood as companions in the pilgrimage of life. Because infants tended to be given at baptism the name of the saint on whose commemorative day the baby was born, baptism was understood as inaugurating a lifelong bond between saint and individual. Above all, saints offered assistance in need. They became patron saints, and the richness of the medieval panoply of saints meant that just about every situation in life had a patron saint—shoemakers, pregnant women, soldiers, hunters. Men and women prayed to St. Appoline in case of a toothache, St. Sebastian for deliverance from the plague, or St. Loy for protection of horses. An important happening occurred both in 1445 and 1446, when a shepherd by the name of Hermann Leicht from Upper Franconia had a vision of fourteen individuals who identified themselves as "holy helpers" and asked him that a chapel in their honor be built at the site. Among these fourteen were Christopher (who helped with an unprepared death), Dionysius (who helped against headaches), Erasmus (who helped against stomach problems), and Margaret (who helped women in childbirth).

Mary became queen of heaven, and her veneration brought her an increasing centrality that found expression in numerous statues, altars, paintings, and the devotional "Hail Mary," a combination of two verses from the Gospel of Luke.

In support of the contention of a religiously dynamic age, scholars have called attention to the various manifestations of lay religiosity, such as the Brethren and Sisters of the Common Life in Holland and northwest Germany, the "confraternities of the Rosary," or the "oratories of the divine love," as cases in point. Indeed, the existence of these groups allows us to reconcile otherwise incompatible characteristics: the simultaneous presence of deep piety and ecclesiastical alienation. The argument is that people were spiritually inclined but found their spirituality no longer being met by the church and therefore sought (and formed) new structures. Such an argument would be persuasive if continuity could be shown between these pre-Reformation lay groups and the Reformation—if the former became proponents of the latter. Unfortunately, the facts indicate otherwise.

The increasing veneration of the saints explains the importance of the relics, the remains (bones, hair, teeth, pieces of clothing, etc.) of saints as well as items related to Jesus, such as pieces of the cross, the crown of thorns, his robe, earth from the site of his crucifixion. These relics were displayed in magnificent reliquaries, often exquisite

---

20. Arnold Angenendt, *Geschichte der Religiösität im Mittelalter* (Darmstadt: 1997), 48ff.

exemplars of the jeweler's and goldsmith's art. To view these relics generally required going on a pilgrimage, but the vicissitudes of such an undertaking were amply made up by the indulgences that were earned: viewing and praying in the presence of relics provided indulgences that, according to a somewhat vague church teaching, short-ened one's time in purgatory.

What about the men and women in the pews? In the past historians have seized upon criticisms and allegations of perversions in the church to paint a picture of large-scale depravity and yearning for reform. The reality would seem to have been quite differ-ent. To be sure, there were grievances and aberrations, complaints and tension. But most people at the time appear to have been as religious and loyal to their church as those in the generations preceding (and following) them. This is a risky judgment, for it raises a tricky matter, the definition of "religious," not to mention the distinction between what was understood as the true and the false Christian religion. Is religiosity measured by indices of formal religious observance, such as attendance at mass, reception of the sacraments, acceptance of dogmatic propositions, or explicit individual testimonials? A massive study of half a century ago undertook to measure the religiosity of the people in pre-Reformation Flanders by ascertaining the frequency of Communion.[21] This was done by using wine receipts for parishes, since it was the custom to give unconsecrated wine to communicants so that they might cleanse their palates upon having received the wine. This kind of social science methodology offers a clue, a hint, a suggestion, but hardly more than that. That some people were lukewarm toward receiving the sacra-ments might well mean that they placed greater emphasis on inward spirituality and thus were religious in their own particular way. In addition, the profession of formal theological notions says little about the intensity of inner conviction. Faith, conscience, and the like are realities far easier claimed than possessed and analyzed, more sweep-ingly conjectured than actually ascertained. They pertain to people's innermost being; people seldom wear their convictions on their sleeves, unless they want to score a point.

There can be little doubt that in the early sixteenth century the subtle mysteries of the official dogma of the church were beyond most of the faithful. Indeed, one is inclined to suggest that theology was as far removed from them as is Einstein's rela-tivity theory for most people in the twenty-first century. Ignorant of most doctrines, the common people undoubtedly tended to reduce the Catholic faith to its lowest common denominator: a simple religion of rewards and punishments, mingled with vague ideas of God, Jesus, Mary, and the saints. Given the illiteracy of the time, the sophisticated theology of the church, as the scholastic theologians had delineated it, was beyond the faithful. Whatever the intensity of the religious conviction of the peo-ple, it could not but be thwarted by a lack of familiarity with basic theological asser-tions. The church was aware of this reality, and it formed the notion of "fides implicita," implied faith, meaning that the common people were called upon to believe implicitly what the church taught—even if they themselves were not cognizant of what that might be.

A technological feat—Johann Gutenberg's invention of movable type halfway through the fifteenth century—proved to have consequences for popular religion,

---

21. Jacques Toussaert, *Le sentiment religieux en Flandre à la fin du moyen-âge* (Paris: 1963).

indeed, for religion in general. The simplified manner of printing brought a dramatic proliferation of book production, and by far the most popular genre dealt with theology or religion. Of the approximately thirteen hundred volumes published in German between 1510 and 1520, almost half were on religious topics.[22] One needs to keep in mind, of course, that the requirement of literacy and affluence for book purchasers meant that only a small, albeit growing, part of the population were book buyers. For example, a Nuremberg patrician owned, in 1464, a library of some 29 books, of which no less than 18 were on religious topics.[23] The library of a monastery in north Germany had 187 books, including the Bible, Augustine, Ambrose, and Chrysostom.[24] And—Martin Luther's disparaging comment about never having seen a Bible in his youth notwithstanding—Bibles were available, including in vernacular translations, in Germany more than twenty complete editions.[25] In his famous satire *Narrenschiff* (Ship of Fools), Sebastian Brandt noted the dissemination of the Bible and the writings of the "holy fathers."[26]

To the best of our reconstruction, the religion of the common people on the eve of the Reformation entailed a combination of crude and noble spirituality, of new impulses and old complaints. Theirs was a religion of doing. Theologically, this meant an emphasis on doing good works, which God, after all, demanded be done—from which followed those merits that assured eternal salvation. This intense religiosity found expression in an impressively rich spectrum of piety, often driven by an impressive activism of a religious sort.

The details of ecclesiastical politics and maneuvering were undoubtedly beyond the knowledge, interest, and competence of most people—such as the demeanor of the papacy in Rome in the latter part of the fifteenth century or the details of the arrangements for the sale of the special indulgence involving Albert of Brandenburg that precipitated the Reformation. The common people knew little, if anything, of what was going on in high places, and a blatant instance of local clerical immorality or misbehavior assuredly weighed more heavily than the sum total of the financial and political involvement of the papacy. Historians are always tempted to assume that the abundance of sources available to them was also common knowledge in the past.

Rome, the "eternal city," the center of the church, was far away from the regions north of the Alps, which proved both blessing and curse. While such distance avoided the likelihood of intimate knowledge, the center of power and final authority appeared distant and removed, and was thus easily blamed for everything from the misdemeanor of the local cleric to the threat of Turkish invasion. Rumors and allegations

---

22. R. Crofts, *Ecclesiastical Reform Prospects in Germany 1510–1520*. Ph.D. dissertation (Duke University, 1969), 43.

23. L. Sporhan-Krempel, "Der Bücherbestand eines Nürnberger Patriziers im 15. Jahrhundert," *Archiv für die Geschichte des Buchwesens* 3 (1961): 1651.

24. L. Michaelsen, *Die Geschichte des Benediktinerklosters St. Pauli bei Bremen* (Göttingen: 1953), 72; V. Hasak, *Der christliche Glaube des deutschen Volkes beim Schluss des Mittelalters* (Regensburg: 1868), lists the religious books published before the Reformation.

25. B. Moeller, "Frömmigkeit in Deutschland um 1500," *Archiv für Reformationsgeschichte* 56 (1965), 20. English translation: Imperial Cities and the Reformation (Philadelphia, 1972).

26. As quoted in H. Dannenbauer, *Luther als religiöser Volksschriftsteller* (Tübingen: 1930), 7, "Bibel, der heiligen väter ler, und auch ander dergleichen bücher mer in mass." ("The Bible, the teachings of the ancient fathers, and similar books in great quantities.")

came easily; facts were few. The disposition to charge local irritants or the imperfections of the universe to a distant "them" seems to be universal in history; in the early sixteenth century "they" were "Rome." This hostile sentiment found salient expression in Germany with a formal list of "grievances" (*gravamina*) that were part and parcel of every diet from the 1490s onward.[27] These grievances, however, pointedly focused on financial and legal rather than theological issues. The theology of the church, in other words, remained unchallenged.

There is no evidence to suggest that ecclesiastical conditions on the whole were either better or worse than at earlier times. The characteristic of the higher clergy seems to have been involvement in sundry secular pursuits. Since positions of ecclesiastical eminence entailed prestige, money, and frequently even power, the incumbents were often more concerned about such matters than about their spiritual functions. The secular preoccupation of the so-called Renaissance papacy is a matter of record, as are the various financial and political involvements of the episcopacy. In a speech in 1517, the Augsburg bishop Christoph von Stadion bewailed the preoccupation with luxury, attire, and food on the part of his episcopal colleagues: "I weep over these men who live for the flesh, who flee solitude, piety, and humility, and who cherish conversations with women, business affairs, lawsuits, and money."[28] Other late-fifteenth-century chroniclers report similar weaknesses of the high dignitaries of the church, for example, their preoccupation with hunting, the arts, politics, or high finance. Perhaps this was the outgrowth of their uncommonly high income. Many of the church leaders, especially in Germany, were also political rulers—the bishops of Würzburg, for example, were also dukes of Franconia, the archbishop of Mainz also was the sovereign of the city of Erfurt—and the disposition to adapt to the lifestyle of their worldly colleagues is understandable.

To be sure, there was noisy criticism of the clergy, and one could, indeed, make much of prevailing currents of anticlericalism as a major catalyst of the Reformation.[29] No doubt, one need not read far in the *gravamina* or other sources to find a persistent and noisy criticism of the universal lack of moral standards on the part of the clergy, both higher and lower, who held concubines, had long abandoned their vows of poverty, and lacked monastic discipline and the disciplined life. The charges against the higher clergy were that they neglected their spiritual responsibilities and were mainly concerned about prestige and advancement in power. The criticism was harsh and pointed, but one must be careful not to be carried away by the flamboyant and emotional indictments that frequently pitted the simplicity and poverty of Jesus against the greed and worldliness of the prelates, such charges made in different ways by burghers in the cities, by peasants, and by the nobility. This anticlericalism undoubtedly helped parlay an atmosphere of discontent and unhappiness with the status quo, which in turn helped fuel the fires of Reformation change. But, impor-

27. Heinz Scheible, "Die Gravamina und der Wormser Reichstag 1521," *Blätter für pfälzische Kirchengeschichte und religiöse Volkskunde* 39 (1972): 167–83.
28. As quoted by W. Andreas, *Deutschland vor der Reformation* (Stuttgart: 1949), 119.
29. This is done by Hans-Jürgen Goertz, especially in his *Antiklerikalismus und Reformation* (Göttingen: 1995).

tantly, none of this critical anticlericalism turned to a fundamental repudiation of the ecclesiastical or theological status quo. Not, that is, until after 1517.

The parish priests and the monks and nuns in the monasteries were a different story. Financially, the priests were in a lamentable state, their incomes hardly sufficient for even a modest livelihood. Not surprisingly, some took to moonlighting—some priests actually operated taverns! Their educational background was unpretentious. A good many of them had never darkened the door of a university, though we must add that the scope of their responsibilities was rather restricted: their principal duties were to celebrate Mass, which required merely a rudimentary knowledge of Latin, and to hear confession. For Württemberg the estimate is that some 10 percent of the monks had been to a university and about 50 percent of the priests.[30] For those responsibilities their background was probably sufficient. The literacy of the general populace, especially in rural areas, was also low, so the ill-trained priest fit harmoniously into the society that he was to serve.

The traditional characterization of the lower clergy on the eve of the Reformation shows them as not only ignorant but immoral as well. Volumes were written in earlier generations, generally by historians, about drunkenness, violations of celibacy, and other assorted moral shortcomings of the clergy. The boisterous criticism of a few contemporaries depicted each parish house as a den of iniquity, each monastery as a house of ill fame. Such was, for example, the sentiment of the royal visitors to the English monasteries in 1535, who claimed this condition to be a heartbreaking story up and down the land. Naturally, specific instances of clerical misdemeanors were easily cited.

Whatever statistical evidence is available suggests a quite different situation. The systematic interrogations of the clergy in the diocese of Lincoln at mid-century, for example, revealed an insignificant digression from the standard rules of behavior, though also an embarrassingly low level of theological literacy among the clergy. Of some 1,006 visitations of parishes between 1514 and 1521, there were only 12 incidents of insobriety and only 25 men of the cloth were "definitely suspect" of "having a woman."[31] In a visitation in Jülich in 1533, 45 of the 105 clerics examined about their understanding of the sacraments were declared to be "unlearned"—hardly an encomium to ministerial learning.[32]

The harsh rhetoric of humanists, reformers, and rulers drowned out the sober realities. While the evidence must be taken with the proverbial grain of salt, it is all that is available, other than a few scattered, melodramatic causes célèbres. In England, there was John Colet's Convocation Sermon of 1510 with its acid indictment of the "unlearned and wicked priests," and later, in 1528 or 1529, Simon Fish's vitriolic *Supplication for the Beggars*. Fish, an attorney and "gentleman at Gray's Inn," was anything but a "hot gospeller," as the adherents of the Continental Reformation were labeled,

30. M. Brecht, "Herkunft und Ausbildung der protestantischen Geistlichen des Herzogtums Württemberg im 16. Jahrhundert," *Zeitschrift für Kirchengeschichte* 80 (1969): 167.

31. M. Bowker, *The Secular Clergy in the Diocese of Lincoln, 1495–1520* (Cambridge: 1968), 107, 116.

32. F. W. Oediger, *Über die Bildung der Geistlichen am Ausgang des Mittelalters* (Cologne: 1909), 2, 17. One might need to keep in mind that in all likelihood the deficient clergy had received their ministerial training well before the Reformation emphasis on improved ministerial education.

though he was emotionally anticlerical. He denounced the clergy as "idle thieves" and the nuns as "idle whores" of whom there were, so he insisted, "an hundred thousand" in the realm.[33] Fish invoked specious statistics to score a religious point and to bolster his argument, for with unflappable confidence he announced that the church owned one-third of the property in England and that the mendicant monks annually extracted no less than £43,000 from the English people. Fish adroitly understood the power of careless statistics as a tool of propaganda. Somewhat more dispassionate historians, however, have noted that the English clergy were more educated and competent from the turn of the sixteenth century onward.[34]

Another incident is customarily cited as descriptive of pre-Reformation popular sentiment about the church and the clergy. The notorious case of the London merchant tailor Richard Hunne brought existing anticlerical sentiment to the fore.[35] Hunne, a man of both good reputation and prosperity, had at the death of his infant son in 1511 refused to pay the mortuary, the customary fee paid to the priest. Since the priest had (merely) demanded the "bearing sheet," in which the infant had been wrapped for his baptism, Hunne's refusal had to do more with symbolism than with money. Not surprisingly, a church court found in the church's favor, but Hunne took the matter to a fundamental level when, early in 1513, he filed a suit under the Statute of Praemunire. This statute, promulgated in 1353 as a cudgel against the French popes residing in Avignon, was to prevent ecclesiastical courts from usurping jurisdiction of secular courts and at the same time prohibit appeals to the pope in matters that should be decided in England. The statute gave the king enormous power, but, since king and church wanted to live harmoniously, it was seldom applied; and by the early sixteenth century nobody seemed to know exactly what it meant.

The ecclesiastical establishment countered by charging Hunne with Lollard heresy and having him arrested. In December 1514 (the matter had dragged on and on) Hunne's lifeless body was found hanging by the neck in his prison cell. The official version was that he had hanged himself, but promptly the accusation made the rounds that he had been murdered by charges of the London bishop. Parliament had expressed its own unhappiness with the traditional exemption of clerics by passing a bill in 1512 that curtailed this exemption of clerics from secular jurisdiction, but it was a mild and temporary bill, though when time came to renew it the Hunne affair had gotten everybody into a frenzy.

In the end, however, a compromise ruled the day: the king had neither reason nor interest to trigger a confrontation with the church. That was the striking difference between what took place in 1515 and what was to take place in 1531, even though in 1515 the fundamental considerations that were to influence Henry VIII's Reformation Parliament, namely to bring the English church under the jurisdiction of the king and civic law, were already in place. Indeed, when the Convocation met in 1515, an ambitious and passionate cleric, Henry Standish, argued the case that clerics

33. Simon Fish, *A Supplication for the Beggars*, in *English Historical Documents 1483–1553* (ed. C. H. Williams; London: 1967), 672, 676; note, for example, p. 674, "Have they not gotten into their hands more lands than any duke?"
34. P. Heath, *The English Parish Clergy on the Eve of the Reformation* (London: 1969), 188ff.
35. A. Ogle, *The Tragedy of the Lollards' Tower* (Oxford: 1949).

accused of crimes must be tried by secular courts, which argument earned him the reputation of a turncoat and made him suspect of heresy. He appealed to the king, and the common-law judges ruled for him and against convocation, recalling the prae-munire statutes. When Parliament met in the presence of the king, Wolsey got down on his knees—that ancient gesture of humility—and apologized for the clergy and begged that the case be transmitted to Rome for adjudication. But the king refused, insisting that only God had a right to overrule his decision. How God was to exercise this right remained unexplained.

Then there were the monasteries, at this time as at all times integral parts of the church, for centuries splendid places for dedicated men and women to live commit-ted Christian lives. Over time, however, some convents and monastic houses had fallen from their high ideals, and by the early sixteenth century the number of reli-gious, both male and female, was on a decline. Some religious orders had relaxed their stringent rules, as in Leicester.[36] All the same, the educational and social activities of the religious houses persisted—monasteries and convents fed the poor, tended the sick, taught the young, and lodged the weary—even as they continued to follow the ancient monastic rule to spend the days "orare et labore," praying and working. None other than Martin Luther vowed to become a monk and joined the Augustinian eremites in Erfurt to attain the salvation of his soul.

In short, the criticism of contemporaries grossly exaggerated reality and facts. Moreover, as Erasmus illustrates, criticism frequently came from men with an ax to grind. In all probability, most of the lower clergy, while not well educated and per-haps not even particularly spiritual, performed their tasks with reasonable conscien-tiousness. Sensitive souls were grieved by deviation from the ideals professed by the church, but outright abuse and deviation among the lower clergy, although they undoubtedly existed, were anything but widespread, and thus hardly a burning issue. Priests falling short of the professed ideal evidently did not seriously alarm or outrage the people in a parish.

Professional competence may well be a matter of definition. The local clergy min-istered to congregations made up of illiterate men and women, even though everywhere in Europe a new class of laypeople was emerging—the increasingly self-conscious and literate urban burghers. The main requirement for priests was that they knew enough Latin to get through the Mass, which of course stood at the center of worship and reli-gion. One visitation record from the diocese of Constance phrased a disarmingly neat assessment of priests: "bene legere, canere, textum planum bene exponere, bene prac-ticare" (to read and sing well, expound the plain text well and officiate well).[37]

Moreover, priests tended to be poor and numerous. In the early sixteenth century, some 137 priests were attached to the Strassburg cathedral, and in a typical town, such as Mainz or Worms, clergy easily made up 10 percent of the population. The main responsibility was to celebrate mass, generally private masses, and the income from the foundations and legacies established by pious donors provided their financial

36. David Knowles, *The Religious Orders in England* (Cambridge, 1957–1960), 3:67.
37. A. Braun, *Der Klerus des Bistums Konstanz im Ausgang des Mittelalters* (Münster: 1938), 100, "to read, sing well, to expound the plain text well, to practice well."

support. The ubiquitous monasteries and convents added further to ecclesiastical presence in towns and villages; the church was an ever-present reality.

But the priests' livelihood was inadequate and their spiritual responsibilities hardly extensive enough to occupy their waking hours. If some priests ventured into financial involvements and others behaved inappropriately, the reason was surely that they had too much time on their hands. Some priests improved economic livelihood by creative moonlighting in a variety of ways, in Flanders, for example, as barbers, gardeners, or tailors. In fact, the church had developed principles in this regard; some trades, such as the ones mentioned, were officially permitted, while those of innkeepers or lawyers were prohibited.[38] One suspects that the large-scale desertion of Catholic priests in the early years of the Reformation movement may well have been prompted not only by the persuasiveness of the new theology but also by the pursuit of a better material well-being. While the law of supply and demand may well have dictated the low incomes of the lower clergy, the practice of pluralism, that is, of holding several ecclesiastical positions at the same time, although officially strictly prohibited, seemed to be a practical solution to allow incumbents an augmented style of living. It is difficult to judge the extent of the practice, though it is clear that formidable problems stood in the way of eliminating it: during the administration of Matthew Parker, who was archbishop from 1559 to 1575, pluralism continued to be fairly extensive in the diocese of Canterbury.[39]

In short, no matter how ardently Protestant historiography has employed the few shrill partisan voices of complaint, there is not much evidence of a widespread alienation from the church in the decades before the Reformation. To be sure, there is the difficulty of attempting to measure such evasive categories as "spirituality" or "allegiance"; yet the evidence seems to suggest that no marked turnabout occurred in the decades before the Reformation. People were as observant in their Catholic faith as they had always been. Flanders, for example, showed little change in the frequency of the reception of Communion in the course of the fifteenth century, while in England and Germany bequests for religious causes continued at even a slightly increasing rate until the outbreak of the Reformation.[40] Even the much-publicized denunciation of the so-called Renaissance papacy, the popes in the second half of the fifteenth century, whose lives were said to be hardly a paragon of Christian virtues, must be seen in its own distinctive setting. A great deal of what we know about these pontiffs comes from contemporary sources demonstrably hostile to them. The demeanor of Pope Alexander VI during his pontificate was, in that context, more a matter of a breakdown of personal morality than a general breakdown of sexual morality in either late-fifteenth-century Rome or the church.

Of course, some people were overwhelmed by such noisy criticism or dismayed by even the slightest departure from the standards the church claimed for itself and its clergy. Thus the call for reform was voiced by a wide variety of individuals; the En-

38. Toussaert, *Le Sentiment religieux en Flandre à la fin du moyen-âge,* 565.

39. J. I. Daeley, "Pluralism in the Diocese of Canterbury during the Administration of Matthew Parker," *Journal of Ecclesiastical History* 18 (1967): 41ff.

40. There are statistics in W. K. Jordan, *Philanthropy of England* (London: 1959), 374, table VI.

glish historian Owen Chadwick stated a generation ago that "at the beginning of the sixteenth century everyone that mattered in the Western Church was crying out for reformation."[41] Pope Julius II had convened a council, the Fifth Lateran Council, which met from 1512 to 1517 and addressed three objectives: achieving peace among Christian rulers, church reform, and the defense of the faith and the rooting out of heresy. Concerning reform the pope noted, "When we notice, out of solicitude for our said pastoral office, that church discipline and the pattern of a sound and upright life are worsening, disappearing and going further astray from the right path throughout almost all the ranks of Christ's faithful, with a disregard for law and with exemption from punishment, as a result of the troubles of the times and the malice of human beings, it must be feared that, unless checked by a well-guided improvement, there will be a daily falling into a variety of faults under the security of sin and soon, with the appearance of public scandals, a complete breakdown." Those words may well have been mere window dressing of a pope known for his "wordly" activities and pursuits but show the complexity of the times.

The crucial issue is whether there were underlying structural tensions in the Catholic Church on the eve of the Reformation, and whether the church had lost its hold upon the people. In a way this view seems to be the consensus of scholarship, Catholic historians arguing that the overall theological emphasis before the outbreak of the Reformation was so one-sided (and thus altogether "uncatholic") that a reaction was inevitable. Other scholars have called attention to contemporary evidence of disaffection and anticlericalism in the early sixteenth century. In Germany secular authorities compiled extensive lists of grievances against the church. At the Diet of Worms in 1521 the *gravamina* listed (with a persistent repetitiveness) no less than 102 specific points, all the way from complaints about the reservation of certain lawsuits to Rome to the exemption of clerics from ordinary jurisdiction.

Even if the alleged charges of clerical abuse and corruption are dismissed as sensation-mongering, the fact remains that there were various tensions between church and society. The church had accumulated, over the centuries, a variety of legal and financial prerogatives. Its clerics were exempt from general judicial procedure, as already noted, and it was entitled to exact various legal fees. In the beginning most of these prerogatives had a persuasive rationale, but circumstances had changed. The prerogatives were increasingly felt as a burden, indeed, an unnecessary one. It was not easy to perceive, for example, the connection between the exemption of the clergy from taxation (in view of its enormous wealth) and the eternal destiny of the believers' souls. The tensions between church and society led to constant attempts by secular authorities to curtail and restrict the place of the church. The new breed of economic activists and political rulers could only be frustrated by the restrictions that the formidable presence of the church imposed. Of course, modifications were made as decades passed, and by the early sixteenth century much that entrepreneurs and rulers had wanted was achieved. Thus interest up to 5 percent was accepted in theory (and a much higher rate in practice), while in town and country a great deal of

---

41. O. Chadwick, *The Reformation* (Baltimore: 1964), 11.

control was exercised by political authorities over the external affairs of the church, a concomitant to the widespread process of governmental administrative consolidation.

Before speaking too easily of a "crisis," a disjointed society, or a time gone awry, one needs to remember that the notion of a golden age in the past, with which the present no longer conforms, is probably found in all ages. Sensitive individuals have a way of agonizing over their own time and in so doing are tempted to invoke the image of a splendid past. This disposition is particularly true in religion, where the real has a way of perpetually falling short of the ideal. The fifteenth and sixteenth centuries were no exception. The question is whether a particularly striking sense of urgency existed in the early sixteenth century with respect to the problems, real or alleged, in the church—and the concomitant necessity of reform. Arguably, antagonism and opposition to the church existed; it is impossible to say whether in the early sixteenth century such sentiment was more intense then than it had been fifty or a hundred years earlier.

In sum, then, the picture of the church on the eve of the Reformation presents an intriguing mixture of tensions and tranquility. There were weaknesses, even abuses, in the church; but even as the demand for reform was raised, many people were as loyal to the church and as pious as they had always been. After all, even the immoral cleric is hardly an argument against the teaching of the church concerning the eternal salvation of one's soul.

With the proverbial insight of hindsight, the historian can easily detect "causes" or "factors" that subsequently gained significance in the Reformation. But such detection stems from knowing the outcome of the story. Quite the contrary, in the early sixteenth century society was in a state of equilibrium. This observation does not deny the existence of uneasiness, grievances, or even alienation—contemporaries, after all, did not completely manufacture their accusations—but merely places them in perspective.

When the century turned in 1500, life for most men, women, and children was what it had always been, generation upon generation. It was hard and demanding and difficult; few could enjoy the luxury of reflecting on matters beyond their unending struggle for daily food, so severely dependent were they on the vicissitudes of the weather and the annual harvest. To be sure, in some places in Europe—in cities such as Florence, Venice, Nuremberg, Basel, London—a new world was emerging that offered a different life and thus posed different questions.

But all—men and women—looked to the church to provide ultimate as well as practical meaning for their lives. The church was the solid foundation for their lives and their daily struggles. The church offered meaning with principles that served people in ritual and celebration from the hour of birth to the hour of death. The church also painted a splendid picture of a life beyond. To be sure, a heavy price was often exacted for all this, for the church had skillfully succeeded in merging the exhortation and solace of its message with the demand of sundry fiscal obligations, legal curtailments, and political impositions. To say, however, that the church had outlived its usefulness or no longer fulfilled its function of supplying the spiritual needs of the people or that it was in a state of crisis, simplifies a complex reality beyond recognition. Church and society were stable. However, this judgment is not to suggest that some individuals—or even groups of individuals, such as the humanists—did not perceive there to be a crisis.[42] Some undoubtedly did, even as some secular authorities were undoubtedly troubled by what they perceived as the excessive authority of the church in secular matters. Clearly, there were tensions. However many points of tension are identified in pre-Reformation church and society, one cannot speak of a crisis. To say, as I myself did many years ago, that the time before the Reformation was a powderkeg with a lit fuse, invokes a neat metaphor but not an accurate appraisal of the time.

CONCLUSION

Somehow, this scene began to be profoundly disturbed in the fall of 1517, and scholars have long sought to find the explanation for this turn in the features of the time I have sought to summarize here in all too brief a fashion. Of course, to do full justice to all the aspects of the time, a lengthier and more detailed exposition would be necessary. The time possessed its own integrity and must be understood as having been more than a mere prelude to a new era. This book, however, is about the sixteenth century, and its most significant aspect, the Reformation.

Even though the main features of the time before the Reformation should be clear, a basic question still begs to be asked: Was there a cogent reason for the subject of indulgences to become the tinderbox that caused the conflagration? In a strange way the answer is affirmative. However inadvertently, the indulgences sale of John Tetzel brought together a number of annoying issues.

In retrospect it should be obvious that the indulgences sales were an almost perfect catalyst. Over the centuries, the practice had become both theologically complicated and practically corrupt. One indulgence seemed to follow another. Each new indulgence sale seemed to offer greater spiritual benefits than the one that had preceded it: the one that got Tetzel into trouble seemed to offer—in a model of theologically imprecise language—the full remission of all sins, surely an exquisitely generous proposition for all the faithful. Nonetheless, there is plenty of evidence that things did not go well either for this particular jubilee indulgence or for other indulgences at the time. People coveted the spiritual benefits indulgences offered, but they were irritated, dismayed, even disgusted with all that went with it.

In the end, then, one might almost forget about the sundry features and characteristic described here, and concentrate on a single issue, a simple action, and a single individual.

42. R. Wohlfeil, "Reformation in sozialgeschichtlicher Betrachtungsweise," in *Reform, Reformation, Revolution* (ed. S. Hoyer; Leipzig: 1980), 96–97. Hans J. Hillerbrand, *The Reformation* (New York: 1965).

Chapter 2

THE LUTHER AFFAIR

The Augustinian monk and professor of theology Martin Luther, whose Ninety-five Theses triggered the controversy in the fall of 1517, was assuredly not one of the theological luminaries and celebrated intellectuals of the day. He was, for those days, an inappropriately youthful professor, barely thirty-four years of age, and his school was a newcomer to the university scene in Germany. Founded in 1502 by the Saxon Elector Frederick at the behest of his personal physician, Martin Polichius, who was promptly appointed its first rector, the Universitas Leucoreum was in only its second decade by 1517. Its faculty was not overly renowned and enrollment was modest. The university had opened with 416 students, a number that quickly declined, however, in the subsequent semesters.

If the university was not particularly distinguished, Wittenberg was not either. Situated on the banks of the Elbe River, the town of Wittenberg and its buildings rose from the river plain and luscious meadows. The traveler approaching the town from the river would see the steeple of the parish and the castle church and the fortress-like castle of the elector on the northern side of the town. Three gates provided entrance into the city, and two streets (the *Kollegiumstrasse* and the *Mittelgasse*) traversed the town from one end to the other. Alongside the two churches, there were two monasteries, that of the Augustinian friars near the Elster Gate, and that of the Franciscans near the northern end of town. Most noticeable in this town of some two thousand people and some 350 houses was the *Schlosskirche*, the castle church, dedicated to All Saints' and built by Elector Frederick as impressively as possible: two balconies and no less than sixteen altars but above all the elector's magnificent collection of relics, which was open to the public on the Monday after Miseriocordia Domini, the second Sunday after Easter, and on All Saints' Day in November.

Contemporaries found few good things to say about Wittenberg. The townsfolk derived their livelihood from agriculture and fishing, though there also were vineyards in the immediate vicinity.[1] The town boasted of two distinctions: the university and the (intermittent) residence of the Saxon elector. The former meant a crowd of (at times quite unruly) students, while the latter meant an electoral residence at the other end of town from the university and a castle church to go with it. Neither, however, altered the negative image of the town. In fact, there had been discussions at the time of the establishment of the university as to whether the poverty of the Wittenbergers and their decrepit houses did not call for another site for the new Saxon institution

---

1. Karlheinz Blaschke, *Wittenberg als Lutherstadt* (Berlin: 1977), 3ff.

of higher learning.[2] "A poor, unseemly town with old, ugly, low, wooden houses," wrote one contemporary, and another added, "The poor, miserable, dirty little town of Wittenberg is not worthy to be called a town in German lands. It would be nothing if it were not for the castle, the castle church, and the university."[3] Here Martin Luther lived and taught, first as a student in 1509, then from 1512 as a professor until his death in 1546.

The story of the great conflagration begins with this man. While at one time rather self-evident, this place of priority for Luther for the beginning of what eventually became the Reformation of the sixteenth century requires explanation, since his centrality has been challenged.[4] Nowadays, Luther's role in the emerging movement of reform tends to be rather minimized. To begin the story with him is to run the risk of making the German Reformation a synonym for Luther, or to turn the story of the Reformation into a story of great men, with some elite theology and elite politics thrown in for good measure. Events were more complicated, and to begin with Luther is simply to acknowledge the obvious: at the outset, that is, in the years between 1518 and 1522, perhaps a bit longer, Luther was the central figure and dominated the public agenda—whatever the larger and more complex forces driving events may have been and however different forces and different individuals later came to dominate the scene, pushing Luther into the background.

Luther's centrality is explained not only by his impressive qualities of intellect and uncommon charisma. He was also catapulted onto the public stage at a propitious time. He encountered forces and benefited from trends that were intriguingly tailor-made for letting events run an unexpected course. Of course, there were other forces of formidable historical importance along the way: for example, Charles V and his peripatetic dynastic concerns; Elector Frederick the Wise of Saxony, and his protective hand over Luther; the quarrel between Spain and France; the complicated distribution of political power in Germany; the threat of a military attack by the Ottoman Empire; the inadequate attention of the papacy to German affairs; Pope Leo X's and Nuncio Aleander's inability to understand the dynamics of the emerging movement; the lack of dogmatic clarity on some major theological points. These are a few factors that heavily influenced the course of events. Luther happened to mesh with these factors in the most striking way. It is a moot question if a different personality encountering the same factors (or the same personality encountering different factors) would have produced a different course of events. No matter, the historian of the Reformation must allow Luther, for a brief time, center stage.

Indeed, but for these forces and factors, Luther would have died an early and ignominious death once the church had concluded that he was a heretic. His words and his message, no matter how profound, would have been written as on water. It was the combination of person and circumstances that elevated him to a pivotal place in the annals of the sixteenth century. Thus the story of the early Reformation in Germany will have to focus on him. That this early story turned into a formidable soci-

2. *Großes vollständiges Universal-Lexikon aller Wissenschaften und Künste* (Leipzig, 1732ff.), 1726.
3. Otto Scheel, *Martin Luther* (Tübingen: 1916), 2:267ff.
4. So, for example, by Heiko Oberman, *The Two Reformations* (New Haven: 2003).

etal conflagration and eventually brought the emergence of a new Christian tradition called Protestantism is another matter.

The irony is that Luther became a public figure altogether unintentionally and against his will. His entrance onto the public stage with his Ninety-five Theses in October 1517 was mainly meant as an internal university matter (though he sent copies of the theses to a few friends, astutely, since this assured that the theses would become known outside Wittenberg). He himself thought little of his person and his role in the course of events, always speaking with painful acrimony about himself. "I am but a stinking bag of worms," he said on one occasion, and on another, "the teaching is not mine. I was crucified for no one."[5] He may well have gotten his cue from the Old Testament prophets, who also minimized their role; but that paradigm, flattering though it must have been for him, was profoundly serious, and in the year before his death he wrote the unthinkable for any author—that he wished to see all of his books committed to oblivion.[6] Understandably, his followers demurred, and in the years and decades after his death they waxed ever more ecstatically about him, likening him to the biblical prophet Elijah and finding his theology to have been the only authentic iteration of New Testament Christianity since John wrote the book of Revelation on the Isle of Patmos.[7] Needless to say, his enemies always saw things quite differently.[8]

Luther was born at Eisleben on the eastern slope of the Harz Mountains in central Germany on November 10, 1483. His father, Hans Luther (or Luder), was a mining entrepreneur who had achieved a measure of financial success and was determined to give his son the benefits of this newly acquired prosperity. For Martin this meant sound schooling and eventually a university degree as the prerequisites for a career in public service both distinguished and prosperous. In Luther's later recollections of his childhood and youth in his Table Talks, dinner conversations of the 1530s recorded by eager student-boarders, little is said about his mother, while his father appears repeatedly as a stern and opinionated character. The picture of an intense father-son conflict prompted the psychoanalyst Erik Erikson to suggest that Luther's theological liberation derived from the resolution of an identity crisis that brought liberation from his oppressive father. But the record of the relationship between father and son hardly intimates future significance.[9]

Luther's childhood and youth were routine enough for a time when life was as Brueghel's canvases depict it: earthy, severe, austere, each day a new struggle of modest joys and many sorrows. Luther's recollections from his childhood convey not only the timeless romantic nostalgia of adults for the innocence of a childhood lost but also take us into a strange world of medieval credulity. Luther reports, for example, that a woman at Eisenach gave birth to a mouse, that he never heard the Lord's Prayer or the Ten Commandments, or that he had to sing for his food in Mansfeld, where he

5. WA 8:685.

6. WA 50:657.

7. Robert Kolb, *Martin Luther as Prophet, Teacher, Hero: Images of the Reformer, 1520–1620* (Grand Rapids: 1999).

8. See here the thorough biography of Luther's first Catholic biographer, Cochlaeus, by Martin Spahn, *Johannes Cochlaeus* (Nieuwkoop: 1964).

9. Erik Erikson, *Young Man Luther* (New York: 1958). Erikson's book was published at a time of great excitement over the new "psychohistory."

had been sent to boarding school.[10] The historian is hard-pressed to know what to make of these pronouncements or to see lasting significance in them. That young Martin was promptly recognized as intellectually talented, however, is beyond doubt.

In 1501 "Martinus Ludher ex mansfelt" matriculated at the University of Erfurt, a sign that his intellectual gifts were recognized and his ambitious father was seeing his hopes for his son being realized. Martin was declared "in habendo" in the university matriculation records, meaning that his father's financial circumstances made him ineligible for financial aid. Hans Luther had become prosperous. Martin pursued the customary course of study in the liberal arts, and received, probably in 1503, the baccalaureate and, in 1505, the master's degree (of seventeen students taking the examination, Luther ranked second), both prerequisites for his planned study of law. That same summer, in line with his father's wishes, he entered law school at Erfurt, clutching his copy of the *Corpus juris civilis*, the standard legal text of the late Middle Ages (and the revival of Roman law), which his proud father had bought for him. Less than three months later, however, Martin had abandoned his legal studies and had entered the monastery of the Observant Augustinian Order in Erfurt. His law career was over before it had really begun.

The explanations for this remarkable decision vary. It may well have been that the span of a few weeks proved sufficient to convince Martin that he was pursuing an erroneous vocation. Luther's is not the only recorded instance of a sudden ending of a vocational pursuit proposed by a parent. However, he himself noted other factors related to his abrupt decision: the sudden death of a close friend, a cut to an artery of his leg that might well have been fatal. But he singled out on several occasions many years later one decisive incident: the experience of a fierce thunderstorm near the village of Stotternheim, some three miles north of Erfurt, on July 2, 1505. On his way home from a visit to his parents in Mansfeld, a thunderstorm so terrified him that he vowed to become a monk if his life were spared.

His life was spared, Luther later explained, and so he was obligated to fulfill his vow. But the matter was not so simple since, according to the teachings of the church, vows made under such duress did not have to be kept. In other words, any spiritual counselor would have assured Luther that he could be relieved of the obligation. That he nonetheless fulfilled his vow suggests that there were other reasons. In later years Luther gave his decision a spiritual meaning. He had entered the monastery, so he stated, in order to obtain "my salvation," and one may well see this as the fundamental cause.[11] Spiritual concerns triggered Luther's decision, and they converged with—perhaps overshadowed—the mistaken pursuit of the study of law. In his later years, Luther clearly saw his decision as fundamentally flawed; in the monastery, so he observed, "I should have killed myself with vigils and prayers."[12]

On July 17, two weeks after the thunderstorm experience, Luther entered the Augustinian monastery, having disposed of his law books and having celebrated a farewell meal with friends and "chaste maidens and ladies."[13] The choice of the Augus-

10. WA 58:2–3; TR 2:1429, 2370; 3:2982b.
11. A. Zumkeller, "Martin Luther und sein Orden," *Analecta Augustiniana* 25 (1962): 254–90.
12. WA 38:143.
13. Hartmann Grisar, *Luther* (Berlin: 1911), 1:1.

tinian monastery was undoubtedly due to its scholarly as well as spiritual reputation. Since there were no less than eleven monasteries in Erfurt, including the prestigious (and wealthy) Benedictine monastery, the choices were many. One year later, in 1506, Luther made his monastic profession, and in April 1507 he was ordained, quite routinely, to the priesthood. At that point, his monastic superior, Johann Staupitz, instructed him—not at all routinely—to pursue formal theological studies. Luther demurred, reminding Staupitz that the long and arduous course of studies would see him dead before its completion. This prompted Staupitz's retort that God in heaven always was in need of learned advisors.[14] Luther complied and pursued his studies, first at Erfurt, then briefly in 1508 at Wittenberg, and then again in Erfurt as well as Wittenberg. In the fall of 1512, after an amazingly short period of study, which prompted raised eyebrows on the part of the Erfurt faculty, he received the doctorate in theology at Wittenberg. Since the Augustinian Order supplied four professorships in theology at the University of Wittenberg, Luther was at once appointed to assume the *lectura in Biblia*, the professorship in biblical studies. This proved to be his life's vocation.

From all accounts, Luther was a splendid addition to the faculty. He was "a man of middle stature," reported one student, "with a voice that combined sharpness in the enunciation of syllables and words and softness in tone. He spoke neither too quickly nor too slowly, but at an even pace, without hesitation and very clearly, and in such fitting order that every part flowed naturally out of what went before."[15] Since professorial instruction in those days was a virtual dictation session (in light of the absence of accessible textbooks), courses covered little ground (a professor at Vienna succeeded in covering only the first few chapters of the book of Genesis in the span of ten years!). The need to speak distinctly and with a loud voice may well have overshadowed the need for theological expertise or rhetorical brilliance.

During the next years Luther offered courses on various biblical books, twice on the book of Psalms, as well as on Romans, Galatians, and Hebrews. Though some of his course lectures are extant only in the form of student notes (which must be used with caution), they do provide important evidence of theological maturing. Gradually, Luther abandoned the traditional fourfold exegetical scheme of the medieval expositors (which distinguished between the historical, theological, moral, and eschatological meaning of a text) and focused on the literal meaning. Also, references to Augustine appeared ever more prominently in Luther's exposition. This Augustinian emphasis put him in conflict with his senior colleague on the faculty, Andreas Bodenstein Carlstadt, who promptly purchased a copy of Augustine's *De Spiritu et Littera* in order to disprove his younger colleague. It speaks for Luther's influence on his faculty colleagues that by 1517 they had begun to share his aversion to scholastic theologizing. A set of theses, ninety-seven in number, "against scholastic theology," of September 1517, were an indication of his search for a new theological perspective.

That fall an innocuous event catapulted the youthful professor into the public limelight. Perturbed by claims made in the sale of indulgences by the Dominican John Tetzel, Luther drafted a set of ninety-five theses dealing with the topic of indulgences.

---

14. Of course, we are dependent on Luther's own recollection in the matter, see WA TR 2:2255A.
15. E. Gordon Rupp, *Luther's Progress to the Diet of Worms* (Chicago: 1951).

His underlying premise was that the church had not yet doctrinally defined the practice and that the attempt to achieve theological clarification in a university disputation was altogether in order. Luther may have intended to hold a disputation on the topic, perhaps in conjunction with the regular weekly disputations held on Fridays.[16] On October 31 he sent a copy of the theses, together with a covering letter, to Archbishop Albert of Mainz, to whom Tetzel was responsible in this matter. The letter enumerated the preposterous claims made by Tetzel about the benefits of indulgences. Some of these claims—for example, that an indulgence would free even someone who had violated the Virgin Mary or that indulgences could also be purchased to cover the sins of the deceased—grew out of the imprecise language found in the *Summary Instructions* issued by Albert for the indulgences preachers. In his letter Luther asked the archbishop to put an end to Tetzel's preaching.[17] Luther's letter (a similar letter went to his bishop, Hieronymus Schulze of Brandenburg, but none to his ruler, Elector Frederick) was a paradigm of servility and political astuteness: his point was that the indulgences preachers parlay personal views of indulgences as dogma and that it was Albert's responsibility to call a halt to this unsavory practice.

If we can trust the contemporary accounts, Tetzel had been carried away in his own rhetoric, as sometimes befalls preachers in pulpits. One might also observe—to do justice to this tragic catalyst of the conflagration—that since indulgences, while a long tradition in the church, had not as yet been doctrinally defined, Tetzel's notions had as much merit as Luther's explosive reaction. Moreover, the formal teaching of the church (and, for that matter, the theological consensus) was one side of the matter, and the perception of the common people, who had flocked to hear (and pay) Tetzel, quite another.

The practice of indulgences was related to the premise that the penitent sinner, upon having been absolved through confession of the "guilt" of a sin, was obligated to do certain good works demonstrating penance. These good works might be going on a pilgrimage or praying the Lord's Prayer, which would, as remission of the "punishment" for the sin committed, shorten the time to be spent in purgatory. In the late Middle Ages indulgences were increasingly based on the notion of substituting a monetary payment for a good work in lieu of doing the good work oneself. The prerequisite was penance; only for the penitent sinner did the purchase of a letter of indulgence offer spiritual relief. But that not so subtle distinction evidently got lost in the shuffle.

Tetzel appears to have simplified this somewhat complicated matter. One would like to think that he did so because he himself did not fully understand its theological complexities, nor appreciated the ease with which the common people were likely to misunderstand it. Earlier generations depicted a Luther with hammer in hand nailing his theses to the door of the Wittenberg Castle Church, which served as a kind of bulletin board for the university. Often these accounts noted that on All Saints' Day, November 1, Elector Frederick's magnificent collection of relics was opened to the people, who could earn no less than 1.9 million days of indulgences from pious reflection on the relics in the collection.

16. This is questioned, however, by Martin Brecht, *Martin Luther* (Stuttgart, 1981).

17. Luther's letter is found in WA *Briefwechsel*, 1:111 (hereafter Br); a section of the *Summary Instructions* is in Hans J. Hillerbrand, *The Reformation* (New York: 1965), 37ff. The entire set of relevant documents is found in Walther Koehler, *Dokumente zum Ablasstreit von 1517* (Tübingen: 1934).

The story of a determined, even furious, Luther in front of the Castle Church, surrounded by puzzled townspeople and intrigued students, began to make its rounds many years later, after Luther's death; in recent decades scholars have cast doubts on this gripping story and relegated it to the realm of pious fiction.[18] In any case, Luther meant his theses to be an effort at theological clarification, and while it bears noting that he supplied not only Archbishop Albert with a copy of his theses but also several friends, he surely wanted the topic discussed in Wittenberg. The program for a routine academic disputation proposed for the university at Wittenberg became known at other places. If the transmittal of the theses to Albert triggered the commencement of official heresy proceedings against Luther in Rome, sending the theses to friends apprised a wider circle of colleagues of the matter. The proposed disputation in Wittenberg never took place, and it is not clear why, since it was weeks before Luther's theses became an official item of business for the church, rendering an academic disputation moot as well as unwise. One suspects that Luther's real intent was not so much an internal university disputation at Wittenberg. The extant copies of the theses give no indication of time or place of the proposed disputation, making it rather impossible for outsiders (assuming they wished to participate) to know when and where to present themselves in Wittenberg. By all odds, an actual disputation at Wittenberg was a secondary concern; Luther's letter to Albert and his sending copies of the theses to friends clearly suggests that he wanted to fire a shot across the bow about a practice that in his judgment endangered the souls of simple believers.

"When our Lord and Master Jesus Christ said 'Repent,' he meant the entire life of his faithful to be one of repentance." This first thesis set the tone with a subtle questioning of traditional piety, which focused on particular acts or times of penance. Succeeding theses sought to define several key terms pertaining to the theology and practice of indulgences and then discussed the effectiveness of indulgences for the dead (theses 8–29) and for the living (theses 30–80). A summary of various popular arguments against the sale of indulgences, which included several thinly veiled barbs against papal practices, together with a few repetitions, brought the total number to ninety-five.

Written in Latin and intricate in their theological pronouncements, Luther's theses were anything but a clarion call for an ecclesiastical revolution. They were a quintessential academic document. Even where Luther dissented from the theological consensus, as in his insistence that indulgences can free one only from canonically imposed punishment, he did so in the form of probing rather than categorical assertions. "This I presented for debate and did by no means put the theses into emphatic affirmations," he wrote a few months later, correctly, though perhaps with a bit of self-serving defensiveness.[19] Surely, participants in the proposed debate, had it actually taken place, or mere readers of the theses, would concur that something needed to be done. By the same token, the Ninety-five Theses declared topics that in the subsequent controversy aroused enormous discussion—indulgences, purgatory, and papal

18. The issue was raised by E. Iserloh, *Luthers Thesenanschlag, Tatsache oder Legende?* (Wiesbaden: 1962). While few Reformation scholars have outrightly agreed with Iserloh, most have acknowledged the lack of explicit sources for posting. But since the Castle Church door was the bulletin board of the University and Luther's theses were meant to be discussed, the conclusion of a posting is altogether reasonable.
19. WA 1:567.

power—to have their proper place in the church. In short, Luther's theses were seemingly moderate in tone and content (certainly in comparison with Luther's ninety-seven theses of September), and essentially called for a clarification of an article of faith and ecclesiastical practice that had not been doctrinally defined by the church.

By the same token, while theologically moderate, several theses sounded shrill tones about church and hierarchy, including the pope. Luther asked, for example, if the pope presided over the treasury of merit, that treasure of superabundant good works performed by some of the departed faithful, why did he not dispense this treasure freely, without charge? Or: "To say that the crucifix erected with the papal coat of arms can do as much as the cross of Christ is blasphemy." Or: "They preach human opinions who assert that, as soon as the coin in the coffer rings, the soul from purgatory springs."[20] Luther propounded heady arguments!

Luther was unaware that he had reached into a hornet's nest with his theses and his letter to Archbishop Albert. Tetzel's indulgences preaching was not merely an ecclesiastical undertaking; it was an integral part of an elaborate financial and political scheme that involved the curia, Archbishop Albert, the banking house of the Fuggers, and German politics. Luther could not possibly have chosen a more inopportune political and financial occasion to express a theological concern.

It all had begun in 1505 when Pope Julius II announced a jubilee indulgence to support two "good works," the one to finance a military campaign against the Ottoman Empire, which threatened to overrun central Europe, the other to build a new St. Peter's basilica in Rome. Both the military defense against the Turks and the building of a new basilica were worthwhile purposes, as such purposes go. The "infidel" Turks were a military threat to Christendom, and the construction of magnificent houses of worship, often more magnificent than practical needs required, seemed to be burdens quite willingly assumed by the faithful, as any present-day visitor to Europe, with its lavish Romanesque, Gothic, and baroque churches, will readily confirm. The construction of a new basilica in honor of St. Peter became a pet project of Pope Julius II, but—since he possessed a grandiose vision of a magnificent new house of God—adequate financial funding was lacking. Julius's successor, Leo X, was no less interested, embracing the project with enviable enthusiasm. The jubilee indulgence continued.

As matters turned out, however, the sale of the indulgence proved anything but a success. Virtually all territories in north Germany prohibited its proclamation, for it was seen as an indirect taxation of the German people to undertake a pet project of the curia in a foreign land (when there were many worthwhile ecclesiastical projects in Germany). One suspects that the jubilee indulgence would have fallen into the obscurity of history had there not been an unexpected turn of events.

That happened in 1514. Albert, Margrave of Brandenburg and brother of the Brandenburg elector, barely twenty-four years of age, was elected archbishop of Mainz that year, after having attained the previous year two important ecclesiastical positions, the archbishopric of Magdeburg in 1513 and the administration of Halberstadt. Such accumulation of ecclesiastical offices, especially by someone not yet of the canon-

---

20. WA 1:234.

ical age for the episcopal office, violated canon law. A papal dispensation was necessary to legitimize the new appointment.

Today, we marvel at the ease with which canon law was slighted as such arrangements were made (and the concomitant dispensations granted). In the sixteenth century, however, they were viewed in the church as purely administrative arrangements; those involved, from the curia on down, would have reacted with genuine dismay if chided that such arrangements would effect the cure of souls. The curia's benevolent view of Albert's astounding progression of ecclesiastical dignities (of course, with an eye on Albert's future role as German elector), found new expression in 1518 with Albert's elevation to a cardinal's purple. For Albert there was the prospect of substantial income from his new archbishopric and the splendor of his powerful political stature. The archbishop of Mainz also served as imperial chancellor, who presided over the meetings of the electors, cast the last vote in an imperial election, and crowned the emperor. Intoxicating stuff for the youthful Albert.

After lengthy negotiations, Albert received the desired dispensation in return for a special fee to be paid in addition to the customary tax for receiving the *pallium* (paid by new appointees to the curia in the amount of the annual revenue of the new position). In this instance fee and *pallium* tax, ordinarily paid by the new archbishop's dioceses, were covered by the Augsburg banking house of the Fuggers (at an exorbitant interest rate) and by Albert's brother, Elector Joachim I of Brandenburg, whose political importance as German elector explains at once why Albert won out over the other candidates for the Mainz position. Moreover, since the archbishop of Mainz was one of the seven German electors, the papacy could rest assured that it had two of the electors on its side when a new emperor was to be elected.

To make this agreement attractive to Albert and his brother, the curia proposed that the languishing proclamation of the jubilee indulgence for the construction of St. Peter's should be extended to north Germany, specifically to Brandenburg and Saxony. While the proceeds from the proclamation were stated to be for the construction of St. Peter's in Rome, a secret agreement stipulated that half of the revenue was to accrue to Albert. The assumption underlying this arrangement was that Albert's brother would prompt the north German territorial rulers, as a concession to him, to allow the indulgence being proclaimed in their territories.

Albert had thus become involved in a major financial transaction in return for a prestigious ecclesiastical and political position, and the youthful archbishop may well have had sleepless nights about his enormous financial burden. Of course, the presumption was that a host of indulgence buyers would assume the major share of Albert's fiscal obligation. In short, for Albert and the curia the arrangement was a win-win situation, for everyone was to profit: Albert for the reasons cited, the curia for the anticipated revenue for the construction of a new St. Peter's basilica, and the enhanced political influence in Germany through Albert's electorship, and—last but not least—the Augsburg banking house of the Fuggers, which handled the finances at high interest and a hefty profit. Indeed, a holy business!

Luther, professor at a university in the provinces, knew nothing of this. Had he known, one hopes he undoubtedly would have written a different letter to Albert. He was only aware of the practical side of the whole matter—the way Tetzel, the chief commissioner of the indulgence in north Germany, was reported to be parlaying its benefits. When Luther obtained a copy of the *Instructio Summaria*, the instruction issued by Albert for the indulgences preachers, he was shocked by its theological ambiguities, its mercenary spirit, and its blatant disregard of what Luther took to be the teaching of the church.[21] Importantly, both Luther's Ninety-five Theses and his cover letter to Albert placed the responsibility for the matter squarely on Tetzel, making clear that Albert and the church were doubtless ignorant of Tetzel's preaching. With winsome naiveté Luther seemed to assume that on receipt of his letter, Albert would posthaste instruct Tetzel to halt his provocative preaching. Luther's theses sought to blackmail Albert, plain and simple, with the threat to go public with such an instance of theological perversion.

Friedrich Myconius, later a staunch partisan of Luther, wrote that the Ninety-five Theses spread throughout Germany within weeks "as if angels from heaven themselves had been their messengers." One must be skeptical about the accuracy of this statement, both with regard to its metaphysical assertion and its breathless chronology. Luther's fame (or notoriety) took some time in coming, and the speed with which he became a public figure must not be overestimated. When the year turned, Luther was still an unknown, and awareness of his theses was restricted to a small circle of officials and scholars. Public awareness of the theses and the ensuing controversy grew slowly; the theses (and their author) began to be known more widely during the early months of 1518.

Luther's theses began to be the catalyst for a theological controversy in the spring of 1518. Tetzel, upon learning of the theses, launched a vehement if somewhat superficial counterattack, characterized by the kind of overkill that is often the hallmark of controversy. Understandably, he admitted to no wrongdoing. His sermons were fully in accord with the teachings of the church, he asserted. Indeed, not yielding an inch, he wrote, for example, that souls were freed more quickly from purgatory than the time it took for a coin to fall into the coffer (as payment for an indulgence); after all, the coin needed time to fall to the bottom. Promptly, Luther's theses and Tetzel's countertheses became the first indications of an emerging controversy. Elsewhere, some of Luther's friends, to whom he had sent copies, began to discuss the theses. These friends, humanists many of them, were to become the prime agents in circulating the theses; thereby they helped turn a local matter into a wider affair. Not only did these friends discuss and disseminate, they also cheered what they took to be a challenge to the theological establishment. But no one during those early months of 1518 was prepared to assume that the church itself was being challenged, except perhaps Erasmus, that astute observer, who sending Thomas More in England a copy of Luther's theses remarked, "I am sending you theses concerning the vices of the papacy"—a characterization hardly calculated to see the theses as yet another routine academic venture.[22]

Indeed, on closer purview it was obvious that Luther had hurled a fundamental challenge to the church to mend its ways. Unlike his humanist confreres, he did not

---

21. The entire document is in B. J. Kidd, ed., *Documents Illustrative of the Continental Reformation* (Oxford: 1911), document 6.
22. *Erasmi Epistolae*, Letter 785, 3:239.

focus on clerical shortcomings or practical abuses. While clad in the evasive format of propositions for an academic debate, the truth of which was yet to be ascertained, Luther's theses argued that the eternal salvation of the faithful was in jeopardy because the church had come to misrepresent the authentic teaching of the gospel. That was the "vice of the papacy" of which Erasmus spoke, and that made the stakes very high. Only a blatant misunderstanding of the church's teaching on indulgences on Luther's part, or Luther or the church promptly throwing in the towel, could forestall a major confrontation. One may only talk about a "moderate" or "conservative" tone of the theses (as was suggested above), if one notes that there is no outright challenge of the entire theological system of the church in Luther's theses.

Not surprisingly, then, by the spring of 1518 an increasingly intense theological controversy was in the making. Luther published an explanation, in German, of his Ninety-five Theses, his immensely popular *Ein Sermon von dem Ablass und Gnade* (*A Sermon on Indulgence and Grace*), in which he elaborated his understanding of the relationship between divine grace and indulgences. At a meeting of the German congregations of the Augustinian Order in Heidelberg in April, Luther presented a set of theses that became a salient expression of his theological thinking, even though the theses seemed to stay far from the topics prominent in his Ninety-five Theses of the previous fall.

These "Heidelberg Theses" turned into a succinct statement of his new theological thinking. The key notion was Luther's distinction between what he called a theology of "glory" and a theology of the "cross." Drawing on the medieval mystical tradition and on the book of Isaiah as sources, Luther offered a theological perspective that showed how he differed from scholastic theology (or at least set different accents): "The theology of glory calls evil good and good evil: the theology of the cross calls things by their name."[23] The difference was between human seeking and divine response, between self-glory and self-humiliation, between speculation that fails to perceive God and the true knowledge of God in the "cross." Luther passionately attacked an erroneous understanding of God: "He is not a true theologian who beholds God's invisible being in created things, but who beholds and knows God as he has visibly manifested himself through suffering and the cross." God is found, Luther argued, "only in his suffering and the cross, not through works, effort, striving, but through *humilitas, infirmitas, stultitia* (humility, weakness, folly)." In other words, God is other than what humans think, and Christ's death on the cross (outwardly the execution of a criminal, actually the divine reconciliation with humankind) provided a powerful illustration for how God always acts (and manifests) "in hiding."

The Heidelberg Theses conveyed that Luther was beginning to formulate a radically new theology. There has been much discussion in scholarship as to exactly when Luther broke with the medieval theological consensus. The question has bearing on the nature of the controversy triggered by Luther's Ninety-five Theses. Were these theses the cause or consequence of a new theology? If the cause, then Luther must have begun to challenge the theological consensus before the fall of 1517 and his Ninety-five Theses were vivid consequences. If the consequence, then the controversy surrounding the

---

23. WA 1:364ff.

theses was the catalyst prompting Luther to rethink his theology. From all accounts, it was the latter. In either case, Luther's new theological vision was related to a personal religious experience.

When Luther made his monastic profession in the fall of 1506 and began his two-decade sojourn as an Augustinian monk, he committed himself to a scrupulous observation of the spiritual life as his monastic order and the church had defined it. Luther was an unusually conscientious monk if his own recollections of his life in the monastery, offered many years later, serve as a trustworthy guide. With great determination he sought to live a spiritual life. "If ever a monk came to heaven through monkery, it should have been I," he observed on one occasion, and added on another, "In the monastery I lost both the salvation of my soul and the health of my body."[24] Luther was overwhelmed by his fundamental inability to rise to the standards God (according to the church) had set for him. He brooded over whether he had done enough penance, had prayed and fasted enough to be acceptable to God—and always concluded that he had not. The sacraments of the altar and of penance, which provided meaningful spiritual consolation for so many, failed to offer comfort.

One is tempted to assume, of course, that Luther's dilemma lay in the fact that there were serious sins in his life, perhaps of a sexual sort; but if so, the evidence is lacking. If anything, the nature of his inner conflict points in the opposite direction. Luther's troublesome spiritual problem was that precisely despite proper demeanor, despite his efforts to be moral and spiritual, he always concluded that he was unacceptable to God. Since the church taught him that he had to do his share, marshaling his moral resources in order to be worthy of divine grace, he knew himself to be in a terrifying bind. As he acknowledged many years later, he came to hate the God who appeared to be playing a game, insisting that he contribute his share to his salvation, yet knowing full well that he was incapable of doing that. Luther's liberating insight was that sinners are justified *coram Dei*, before God, not by contributing their moral effort, to which divine grace is added. Rather, humans must acknowledge that their self-centered sinfulness pervades their entire being (hardly a modern notion!) rendering all human moral effort futile. With this acknowledgment, the sinner "justifies" God, who in the Bible declared all humans to be sinners. By so identifying themselves as sinners, humans can claim the forgiveness that God has offered to sinners. Justification takes place by faith since the sinner appropriates by faith, and by faith alone, the divine promise of forgiveness as found in the gospel. Such forgiveness is contrary to the experience of sinfulness: humans continue to experience themselves as sinners, but God has accepted them. And faith itself is a gift of God.

"I felt as though I had been born again and entered the gates of paradise," Luther reported later in life on his experience. The key scriptural passage that offered him spiritual deliverance was Romans 1:17, "For in it [the gospel] the righteousness of God is revealed through faith for faith; as it is written, 'He who through faith is righteous shall live.'" Luther concluded that God's righteousness, as revealed in the Bible, does not give humans what they deserve, but offers them the gift of forgiveness. As far as Luther was concerned, his discovery was new, dramatically new, indeed, "contrary to

24. WA TR 1:502; 4:3944. Luther offered a number of similar comments.

the opinion of all the doctors." Unfortunately, there was more exuberance than accuracy in Luther's reflection. Was it really so dramatically "contrary to the opinion of all the doctors"? Had Luther not read widely enough in medieval theology? Had he misunderstood the "doctors," or had his Catholic protagonists misunderstood them? These are the perplexing scholarly questions hovering over Luther's spiritual maturing and thereby over the early Reformation.[25] In any case, Luther himself saw his insight as dramatically new.

Luther's "evangelical insight" occurred in all probability in 1518, well after the indulgences controversy had erupted, though at one time it was the nearly unanimous consensus of scholarship to argue for an early date. A late date would not only agree with Luther's own comment that in 1517 he was "scribendo et docendi" (that is, in a process of writing and teaching) but also confirm that in the fall of 1517, when he drafted the Ninety-five Theses, he still was—as he had been—a loyal son of the church.

No matter how important the timing of Luther's new theological insight, something else was even more significant: Luther's new theology was forged in the context of a personal religious experience. In other words, for Luther the ensuing controversy was about more than theological issues. His new theological understanding was, as he himself put it, as if "the gates of paradise had opened up before him."[26] One can well understand his rigidity, dismay, and anger when as the controversy progressed he discovered that his theological affirmations, wrought in existential agony, were treated blithely.

In the unfolding controversy Luther's prime antagonist was Johann Eck, a distinguished and well-published theologian at the University of Ingolstadt in south Germany.[27] Ingolstadt was arguably the most distinguished German university, and Eck one of its bright stars, whose eminence did not keep him from serious engagement in local matters, as for example, when the students threatened to leave the university because Ingolstadt beer was so horrible—in their judgment! Three years younger than Luther, Eck was a brilliant theologian with encyclopedic knowledge and a razor-sharp mind, though also with a combative temperament that made it difficult to let his antagonists have the last word. Perhaps Eck and Luther debated so fiercely because they were so much alike. This observation should not reduce Eck's role in the controversy to his personality (unless one would make the same comment about Luther's temperament). Once Eck had concluded that Luther's notions were heretical, he was determined to set forth correct church teaching and proper theology and prompt the church to render the appropriate judgment.

Upon receiving a copy of the Ninety-five Theses Eck had jotted down a few *obelisci* (comments), negative as they were, and had circulated them among friends. Luther, not surprisingly, got hold of a copy and composed an aggressive reply, entitled *asterisci* (asterisks), in which homely comparisons of the protagonist and the animal kingdom

---

25. A long line of scholars has challenged Luther's accuracy on this point, for example, H. Denifle, *Die abendländischen Schriftausleger bis Luther über Justitia Dei und Justificatio* (Mainz: 1905); see also H. A. Oberman, *The Harvest of Medieval Theology: Gabriel Biel and Late Medieval Nominalism* (Grand Rapids: 2000).

26. This in Luther's autobiographical notes, WA 54:183–84.

27. See Walter L. Moore, "Eck, Johann," *Oxford Encyclopedia of the Reformation* (ed. H. J. Hillerbrand; 4 vols.; New York: 1996), 2:17–19.

made their entrance into the polemics. Eck had used heavy artillery as well, calling Luther a "Bohemian," a follower of Jan Hus, the heretic who had been burned at the stake in Constance in 1416. That was bound to send shivers up and down the spines of contemporaries for Hus's heresy—and the bloody conflict the Hussite movement had generated, even after Hus's death—had deeply upset Christendom. Eck's charge was the ultimate denunciation and drew a clear line in the sand. Luther, in response, insisted on his orthodoxy, and for the time being this settled the matter.

But there was Andreas Bodenstein Carlstadt, Luther's senior colleague at Wittenberg. Temperamentally much akin to Eck, Carlstadt's exuberance propelled the controversy forward. While Luther was at Heidelberg for the meeting of the Augustinian friars, Carlstadt compiled 379 theses, subsequently enlarged to 405, which offered an exhaustive statement of the new Wittenberg theology. Eck promptly responded with a set of theses of his own, and since Carlstadt was unwilling to let his opponent have the last word, he retorted with yet another set of theses against Eck in late summer. With each round the tone became more bitter and vehement.

In August 1518 Luther published the *Resolutiones*, or "Explanations Concerning the Theses on the Power of Indulgences," meant as a clarifying statement on various topics programmatically stated in his Ninety-five Theses. The *Resolutiones* were thus a detailed exposition of the Ninety-five Theses, and they offered Luther the opportunity to put forward his own views and positions.[28] They were Luther's own response to the invitation in the preface of the Ninety-five Theses, where he had asked for a scholarly discussion of his propositions. After all, Luther had steadfastly argued that his Ninety-five Theses merely offered propositions for debate. Now, he wanted his voice to be heard. Theologically, the *Resolutiones* showed Luther in a state of transition. Luther affirmed the centrality of Scripture but allowed a place for tradition. He acknowledged papal primacy but advocated certain restrictions of papal power. Nonetheless, it is clear that Luther propounded a new understanding of sin, repentance, and forgiveness.

Alongside the increasingly intense theological controversy, another development was taking shape, tentative at first, but of crucial, if tragic, significance in the end: the official ecclesiastical proceedings against Luther. The reality was that from the very beginning Luther was embroiled in more than a theological controversy. While he and Carlstadt exchanged theological barbs with Eck, the curia in Rome was contemplating action against him. This was an ominous turn, even though initially few knew how Luther's affair was treated in Rome. Luther, at any rate, had to be portentously aware that every word spoken in the theological feud was likely to be placed on a golden scale in Rome to ascertain orthodoxy.

The first step in the ecclesiastical proceedings against Luther had come with surprising speed. On December 1, 1517, within a couple of weeks of having received a copy of Luther's Ninety-five Theses, Archbishop Albert asked the University of Mainz to render a theological assessment of Luther's document. Two weeks later, without having heard (not surprisingly) from the academicians, he reported Luther's theses to Rome, asking that the *processus inhibitorius*, the first step in formal heresy proceedings, be initiated against Luther.

28. WA 1:530–628.

The formal proceedings against Luther promptly commenced in the spring of 1518. At issue was the suspicion of heresy, the challenge of ecclesiastical authority, and lack of obedience to the papal office. The Thomist theologian Sylvester Mazzolini, known as Prierias, who held the title Master of the Sacred Palace, or chief theologian of the curia, was assigned the task of examining Luther's theses.[29] Prierias quickly composed a response, completed in June, noting with disappointment that this official assignment to respond to Luther had kept him from the more serious task of completing a commentary on Thomas Aquinas. Entitled *Dialogus in praesumptuosas M. Lutheri conclusiones de potestate Papae* (Against the Presumptuous Theses of Martin Luther Concerning the Power of the Pope), Prierias's reply astutely observed—despite a certain superficiality of approach and an unwillingness to engage Luther seriously—that the main problem with Luther's theses was that they had implicitly challenged papal authority. Prierias argued, in effect, that any ecclesiastical practice was vindicated by being a practice of the church. To challenge any practice of the church that pertained to faith and morals was tantamount to being a heretic. Since Prierias's argument drew no distinction between matters already defined as normative dogma, where the authority of the church had to be accepted, and theologically undefined matters, where freedom of discussion was possible, it was not likely to be the final word. Nonetheless, Prierias's reply served notice, right at the beginning of the tumult, that at issue was the question of authority.

Prierias displayed a great deal of learning in his book, especially with respect to his conversance with Thomas Aquinas—not at all surprising, since he was a foremost Aquinas expert. In addition, he exhibited theological flair, as, for example, when he remarked that Luther's theses suggested that he was about to emigrate to Bohemia, of course, no matter what the wit, also a fateful suggestion about Luther's theological proximity to Jan Hus.

Luther was little impressed by Prierias's response. The reason may have had to do as much with a personal aspect—Luther's "evangelical" experience added a deeply personal existential note to his theological views—as with the schoolmasterly tone of Prierias's work, surely offensive to Luther, who after all was a professor of biblical studies himself.

Prierias's assessment of Luther's theses resulted in Luther being served early in August 1518 the *admonitio caritativa*, or "loving admonition," to appear within sixty days in Rome as a reputed heretic, to be questioned about his views. Promptly, toward the end of that month, the head of the Saxon province of the Augustinian Order and Thomas Cardinal Cajetan, papal legate in Germany, were instructed to have Luther apprehended as a notorious heretic. Pope Leo X wrote Elector Frederick of Saxony to be mindful of the faith of his fathers and to turn the "son of iniquity" over to the authorities.

The wheels of the official ecclesiastical machinery had moved swiftly and with determination. Hardly a year after the Ninety-five Theses, the case of Martin Luther,

---

29. Details of the proceedings against Luther in Rome still remain unclear or controversial. The best guide is W. Borth, *Die Luthersache (1517–1524)* (Hamburg: 1970); P. Kalkoff, *Forschungen zu Luthers römischem Prozess* (Rome: 1905ff.), includes important documents.

Augustinian monk and professor of theology, writer of bold theological theses—and possibly a heretic—was about to be closed.

At this juncture (late summer 1518) political considerations impinged upon the ecclesiastical course of events. A German diet had convened in session in Augsburg. The ailing Emperor Maximilian I was preoccupied with the question of his succession, but the most important matter before the German estates was the financing of a military campaign against the Turks. Their persistent presence not too far to the southeast of Vienna seemed to herald imminent disaster. The papacy supported strong military measures against the Turks, and its concern was underscored by the presence of Cardinal Cajetan as papal legate. The estates were reluctant, however, to agree to the proposed tax. They agreed that resisting the infidels was both an honorable matter and a Christian responsibility, but insisted that the mood among the common people did not allow for levying a new tax. Some argued that the curia should shoulder a heavier burden.

On August 27, 1518, the Estates formally declared a new tax out of the question. In so doing, they called attention to the widespread complaint about moneys already contributed to various worthy causes and, for good measure, added a long list of grievances—culled from the traditional *gravamina*—against the Roman see, such as the appointment of foreigners to ecclesiastical positions in Germany and the increasing financial burdens imposed by the church on the common people. Further negotiations followed, and in the end the Estates' bark was worse than their bite. The official recess of the diet provided that for three years communicants should pay a tax to be used for financing a military campaign against the Turks. To convey dramatically that this was no done deal, the Estates declared that they first had to consult with their subjects concerning this matter.

The next phase of Luther's case took place in this setting. Apprehensive about being questioned in Rome, Luther had appealed to his ruler Elector Frederick to secure a hearing in Germany, and Frederick's active interest in his Wittenberg professor caused Luther's case to take a different turn. Frederick had strongly opposed the notion of a "Turkish" tax, which he saw as an ill-disguised scheme to funnel moneys to Rome, and he had also not taken kindly to Emperor Maximilian's active lobbying for his nephew Charles as his imperial successor. There was, in short, an independent streak in Frederick, who was not likely to hand Luther over to the Roman judiciary. Matters were made worse by a papal missive of late August that sharpened the situation by declaring Luther guilty of heresy: Cajetan was to apprehend Luther and give him the opportunity to recant. Elector Frederick's unwillingness to go along with Roman routine complicated matters, but Cajetan's new instructions meant that Luther's recantation could occur at Augsburg.

The Saxon Elector's intervention on Luther's behalf to have him examined in Germany, not in Rome, deserves reflection. Without Frederick's involvement in the summer of 1518, Luther arguably would not have survived. Why did the elector protect Luther? Was he a partisan—whatever that may have meant in the summer of 1518? Luther's attack on indulgences had been implicitly directed also against Frederick's collection of relics in the Castle Church at Wittenberg, and so there was every reason for the elector to be cool toward his outspoken professor. Frederick did not know

Luther personally, the two men never met, though there was extensive indirect contact through George Spalatin, Frederick's influential chaplain and secretary. What is more, there is no evidence that Frederick, who continued to attend mass in his private chapel until 1525, shared Luther's religious views. Nonetheless, when Albrecht Dürer did an etching of Frederick in 1523, he noted in his inscription: "Deo Verbo magna pietate favebat" (he favored the word of God with great piety).

Religious considerations thus hardly suffice as a full explanation; considerations of diplomacy and politics surely must be added. Frederick's support of Luther was an anti-Roman gesture to the gallery that could be sure of widespread applause. By the late summer of 1518 the controversy triggered by the Ninety-five Theses had reached wider circles. Even if nothing more than a forceful reminder to the Curia that it could not proceed unilaterally and that the cooperation of the secular arm was necessary, Frederick's intervention may well have been an act of political prudence. Spalatin, who early on had become a staunch supporter of Luther, exerted enormous influence not only by portraying Luther to the elector as a deeply spiritual person, but also by noting the political advantages to the elector of assuring that Luther received due process.

From all accounts, Elector Frederick was a man of simple principles and virtues. He believed in due process, a principle that he wished to apply to Luther, of whose religiosity he was persuaded even if he himself did not share it. Frederick's awareness of Roman processes may have raised doubts in his mind as to whether Luther would be treated fairly in Rome. Fairness was his concern, and he was willing to go to considerable lengths to achieve it. Whatever the motivation, Frederick's stand in the summer of 1518 saved Luther and thereby made possible that Luther's ideas gained an ever-wider audience.

Thomas Cardinal de Vio, known as Cajetan, represented the papacy at the Augsburg diet. One of his early biographers recorded his mother's dream that Thomas Aquinas himself taught her son and had carried him to heaven. Such pious anticipation may have guided her son's childhood and youth, who would soon have a brilliant career. His theological eminence was celebrated and his ecclesiastical achievements were distinguished. Cajetan was the head of the Dominican Order and one of the most learned men of the curia. Indeed, his nine-volume commentary on Thomas's *Summa theologiae* continues to be an impressive exposition of the magnum opus of the Angelic Doctor.[30] He was also known to be arrogant and temperamental, though he could be fair and judicious.

Cajetan's legatine assignment to Germany was to influence the German Estates to remain committed to a vigorous suppression of the Hussites and to finance an army against the Ottoman Turks. At the same time, he was to keep a watchful eye on the paramount political issue in Germany—the succession to the ailing Emperor Maximilian. It was precisely on this point that Elector Frederick's request to have Luther examined in Augsburg was bound to fall on fertile soil. As one of the seven German electors, Frederick was to play a crucial role in the selection of the new emperor. The curia, vitally interested in influencing the outcome of the election, was hardly in a

---

30. On Cajetan, see B. A. R. Felmberg, *Die Ablasstheologie Kardinal Cajetan (1469–1534)* (Boston: 1998), as well as the older book by Gerhard Henning, *Luther und Cajetan* (Stuttgart: 1966).

position to slight him. Thus Fredrick's request to have Luther examined at Augsburg was honored.

Luther's examiner could not have been a more erudite and learned churchman. He met Luther three times, on October 12, 13, and 14. Cajetan had done his homework. Prior to his arrival at Augsburg he had written a treatise on indulgences and had attempted to familiarize himself with Luther's writings. It is obvious that he took Luther seriously and that he did not intend to deal offhandedly or cavalierly with him. Luther, in turn, could not have asked for a better examiner. Nonetheless, the encounter between the two men ended in failure. The urbane cardinal, deeply steeped in scholastic thought, and the uncouth monk, full of religious fervor, disagreed about theology and lacked proper chemistry.

Their three meetings ranged through the whole diapason of politeness, theological discussion, and explosive anger. Neither was much impressed by the other. Cajetan thought Luther an obstinate monk, with "ominous eyes and wondrous fantasies in his head, who did not recant because of fear of personal shame rather than because of his conviction." Luther, on the other hand, opined that Cajetan "perhaps might be a famous Thomist, but he is an evasive, obscure, and unintelligible theologian and Christian."[31]

This mutual condemnation attests that the cardinal and the professor did not speak the same theological language. Cajetan, prepared to engage in theological discussion with Luther, confronted Luther with two errors: he had denied the treasury of merit as the basis of indulgences, contrary to the bull *Unigenitus Dei filius* of 1343, and he had argued that faith was indispensable for justification. Luther, in arguing his case, cited Scripture; Cajetan, in turn, cited scholastic theology and canon law. Agreement was difficult, for the fateful distinction between "Scripture" and "tradition," between the "Word of God" and "human traditions," came to the fore when the two argued. Luther asserted bluntly that Cajetan's authorities—the scholastics and canon law—were irrelevant since they did not measure up to the authority of Scripture.

Luther insisted that church traditions and teachings had to be measured against Scripture. At the heart of Cajetan's argument, however, was a view of the church as a mystical body that was more than its empirical expression in the hierarchical structure. It was an entity nurtured by continued sacramental union with Christ, and the traditions embedded in the bosom of the church could not be anything other than authentic reflections of Scripture.

At the end of their third meeting Cajetan dismissed Luther with the exasperated comment that he need not return unless he was ready to recant. Luther, realizing his acute danger, quickly drafted an appeal to "a not-well-informed pope so that he be better informed," in which he explained that ill health, poverty, and the threat of sword and poison had made his journey to Rome impossible. He volunteered not to write anything against Scripture, the Fathers, and canon law, and then fled from Augsburg, after Johann Staupitz, his monastic superior, had formally released him from his monastic vow of obedience. This vow of obedience might have forced Luther to silence, in response to orders from his monastic superiors, or put him him into out-

31. WA Br 1:216.

right defiance. Whatever limitations his vow had placed on Luther during the preceding months, Staupitz freed him of it. He was now free to speak—a fact that may well explain his increasingly adamant posture as the controversy continued.

Luther had good reason to be apprehensive. The papal instructions of the end of August had empowered Cajetan—even though the sixty days given Luther in the "charitable admonition" had not expired—to have Luther arrested as a heretic and sent to Rome.

Back in Wittenberg, Luther published a winsomely subjective account of his encounter with Cajetan, entitled *Acta Augustana*, and drew up an appeal to a general council. Then he settled back into his academic routine to await the future. His meager belongings packed, he was ready to leave Wittenberg on a moment's notice. His appeal to a general council was in line with the notion that a council was superior in authority to the pope. Though such appeals had been condemned in the fifteenth century, Luther's move had recent precedents, for example, an appeal of the faculty of the University of Paris in the spring of 1517. Indeed, at points Luther followed the Parisian document almost word for word. Luther's appeal to a general council had been printed to be available when needed, but had not been intended for distribution. However, Luther's printer, all business, sensed the sensational character of the document and promptly began to print it. Luther reacted with a public declaration of his distress over this indiscretion, though this may well have been an intentional leak since publicity undoubtedly aided Luther's cause.

On November 9 the papal bull *Cum Postquam* defined the doctrine of indulgences and affirmed the authority of church and pope to absolve penitent sinners from the (temporal) punishment of sin. The driving force behind the bull was Cajetan, who thus put his coda to his Augsburg encounter with Luther. Luther's views were declared to be incompatible with those of the church. Everything now depended on Luther's response.

At this point a bizarre interlude began to dominate the scene. Karl von Miltitz, a young Saxon nobleman and papal chamberlain, had been entrusted with the delivery of the Golden Rose, a prestigious papal decoration, to Elector Frederick along with the grant of special papal indulgences for the Wittenberg Castle Church. This papal move—hardly astute, given that indulgences had triggered the controversy in the first place—was calculated to make Frederick receptive to papal interests in the forthcoming election of a new emperor. Frederick, for his part, could have cared less about the presumed honor.

Miltitz had no official mandate to become involved in the controversy, but being young, ambitious, hardly a major player, and Saxon, he ventured forth to use his routine assignment to resolve it. His effort failed, and within the increasingly complex interweaving of ecclesiastical and political scheming, his one-person diplomatic tour de force had only peripheral significance. Yet Miltitz was the one individual who possessed a realistic notion as to how to resolve the controversy, namely to use a period of silence to calm tempers and to reduce the matter to an academic squabble.

Miltitz met with Luther at Altenburg early in January 1519, and his persuasiveness apparently succeeded in winning Luther over. Luther wrote the pope, explaining his religious concerns, his awareness of the problems and anxieties he had caused, and his desire to find an acceptable solution to the controversy. Luther declared himself willing to be silent, if his opponents remained silent, and to write a treatise exhorting everyone to honor the church. Clearly, the letter conveyed that Luther was not a trouble maker, and at Altenburg he gave evidence that he would respond to conciliatory gestures. Still, the agreement came to naught, and in the annals of Reformation history Miltitz is only a fleeting interlude in the swiftly moving course of events though for some to this day an indication that Luther wanted to remain a faithful Catholic.[32] The agreement brokered by Miltitz failed not because it was the wrong solution (on the contrary, it seems to have been the right one), but because some people fail to respond to irenic gestures: Miltitz should be chided not for his effort but for his failure to understand the temper of the protagonists.

One might interject that the deeply rooted theological divergence between Luther and the Catholic Church made a parting of the ways inevitable. But as late as the fall of 1518 Luther's theological opinions might yet have been relegated by the church to the periphery. His radical theological pronouncements, such as the treatise *De captivitate Babylonica ecclesiae praeludium* (*The Babylonian Captivity of the Church*) of 1520, lay still in the future. In fact, historical precedents come to mind, suggesting that the church has had a way of not appropriating certain theological opinions without excommunicating those holding them. In early Christianity Augustine's anti-Pelagian writings were not accepted by the church, and in the sixteenth century Erasmus, despite denunciation and partial condemnation, died in peace with the church. Why could not Luther's story have become that of Erasmus? Arguably, he was the more orthodox of the two.

The reason is twofold. Luther chose what proved to be a most inopportune occasion to propound his theological message. He became embroiled in both theological controversy and ecclesiastical protocol, and there were pointed political overtones to both. Erasmus, on the other hand, always skillfully managed the former so as to avoid the latter. Moreover, the chronicler of events must guard against viewing the early phase of the controversy from the perspective of its eventual outcome—the dividing of Western Christendom. In 1519 the likelihood that the Luther affair might lead to a major conflagration, indeed, to a major schism in Western Christendom, was not very great. There had been heretics before, and the church had always successfully dealt with them. Even Jan Hus's dissent of the previous century, no matter how much of a nagging problem for the church, had remained geographically restricted to Bohemia, a small speck on the map of Europe. Was the Luther affair different? Was there reason to be overly concerned, reason to make accommodations? Only with the insight of hindsight. Of course, the policy and action of the church should have been guided by prudence. Of course, a course of curial action was possible in 1518 different from prompt and outright confrontation.

The Altenburg agreement was broken not by Luther, who kept his pledge, but by two protagonists with brilliant minds unconcerned about larger considerations: Eck

32. Gordon Rupp, the insightful English Reformation historian, called Miltitz "a kind of ecclesiastical Von Ribbentrop," the Nazi foreign minister, whose hallmark was a combination of diplomatic ineptitude and arrogant self-conceit: see his *Luther's Progress to the Diet of Worms* (Chicago: 1951). Since Ribbentrop has largely faded into historical oblivion, the comparison has lost its punch.

and Carlstadt. Their feud came to dominate the controversy and eventually brought Luther back into the arena. Eck and Carlstadt had agreed to settle their theological differences with a disputation, for which Eck had published twelve theses. Luther found that these theses were directed against him rather than Carlstadt, and promptly responded with a set of twelve theses of his own. The Altenburg agreement was thus thrown overboard, though Luther was able to declare that it had been Eck who had broken the informal truce. Eck and Carlstadt continued their feud, touching on an ever growing range of topics, but the focus was on the question of papal authority. One of Eck's theses had been, "We deny that the Roman Church was not superior to other churches in the time of Pope Sylvester," an assertion that had prompted Luther to undertake extensive historical studies in order to understand the past of the church.

The disputation arranged between Eck and Carlstadt, now to include Luther, took place in Leipzig in June 1519. In line with academic custom, a High Mass and an academic convocation opened the proceedings on June 27. A member of the Leipzig faculty delivered an oration for the occasion—a two-hour exercise that gave him the opportunity to display his rhetorical and scholarly expertise. The oration covered the range of history as well as of religion, spoke of the great debates of the past, and of the need for truth and modesty. Duke George of Saxony, present for this oratorical feat, expressed surprise that theologians were so godless as to need such exhortations.

The disputation itself began inauspiciously. Carlstadt, who had insisted on speaking first, cut a poor figure beside the more eloquent and flamboyant Eck, who cited his authorities, several at one time, from memory (whether accurately or inaccurately proved to be contested). Carlstadt, in turn, had to look up his citations, causing tedious delays in the debate. The topics discussed were free will and grace. Both Eck and Carlstadt succeeded in obtaining minor concessions from one another, but on the whole their exchange, no matter how profound, was listless. Nonetheless, Carlstadt articulated several crucial characteristics of subsequent Reformation thought.[33] When Luther took Carlstadt's place, the debate shifted to the question of papal supremacy, and Eck at once reiterated his charge that Luther echoed Hussite heresy. This elicited deep anxiety among those who heard it, for the University of Leipzig had an intimate connection with the Hussite movement: it had been founded, roughly a century before, by German emigrants who had left the University of Prague in opposition to Hussitism. Luther's remark that not all of Hus's views had been heretical, and that some had indeed been Christian, such as his assertion that there is one holy Christian church, created high drama.

At this point the atmosphere of the disputation changed dramatically. Eck again and again accused Luther of being a Hussite, with Luther retorting each time that Eck tell him what was heretical with the statement that there was one holy Christian church, for which Hus had been condemned. In exasperation, Luther finally insisted that the condemnation of this statement of Hus at Constance showed that councils, too, can be in error. Upon hearing Luther's words, Duke George burst out, "I'll be damned!" (in German, "das walt die Sucht") and left the room, an indication that

---

33. Ulrich Bubenheimer, ed., *Querdenker der Reformation: Andreas Bodenstein von Karlstadt und seine frühe Wirkung* (Würzburg: 2001).

Luther's words had profound implications. Eck announced that Luther was a "heathen and publican," hardly a compliment, of course, but actually a much milder statement than his earlier denunciation that Luther was "heretical, erroneous, blasphemous, presumptuous, seditious, and offensive to pious ears."

Carlstadt and Eck continued to debate for another several days about such topics as purgatory, indulgences, penance, and the forgiveness of sins. But the climax of the debate had passed, and the minds of the two men must have wandered back more than once to the incisive exchange about conciliar authority. To everybody's relief, one suspects, the debate concluded on July 15. Promptly, and not surprisingly, both sides claimed victory in letters to friends and in public pronouncements that spread the news of the disputation far and wide. Officially, the universities at Erfurt and Paris had been asked to render a decision about who had won—the debate had been an academic affair, a scholarly exchange—though the two universities took so long to come to a judgment (favoring Eck) that their verdicts were hopelessly outdated by the time they were issued.

Word about the disputation spread quickly, both in Latin and in vernacular publications; instead of remaining an esoteric theological affair, the disputation became a widely known event that symbolized Luther's defiant rejection of ecclesiastical authority. In fact, of course, Luther had used rather careful language when he challenged the authority of councils. Astutely, he had tempered his rejection of councils with the qualification that councils have erred in "matters not *de fide*," not concerning faith and doctrine. Luther had meant to argue that councils should not be understood as having been infallible in absolutely everything they had promulgated. But his important qualification got lost in the shuffle.

Before too long, the controversy was once more overshadowed by political developments. Emperor Maximilian had died, not unexpectedly, in January 1519, and the powerful in Europe began to involve themselves in the election of his successor. Formally the election lay in the hands of the seven German electors, but it was a cause célèbre of European politics during the first six months of 1519. Four candidates were in the running at one time or another: Henry VIII of England, Frederick of Saxony, Francis I of France, and Charles I of Spain, but only the latter two were serious contenders. The most obvious candidate was Charles, then eighteen years of age.

Charles had succeeded to the Castillian throne when his father Philip, the "Fair," died rather unexpectedly—the official version was of fever, the result of playing too engaged an outdoor game. Those seemingly in the know, however, such as Emperor Maximilian, alleged that he had been poisoned. The pope had counseled Philip not to touch any food that had not been prepared by his own cooks.

Through his father, Charles inherited the Burgundian lands, roughly comparable to present-day Netherlands, Belgium, and Luxemburg; and through his mother, Donna Juana, the lands of Castile and Aragon, that is, Spain. It was a powerful configuration of realms and power, even though for geopolitical reasons it almost automatically created tensions with France. Charles himself had never been in Germany nor was he able to speak German. As Maximilian's grandson he possessed a nominal claim to the imperial office, and his grandfather had almost succeeded in formalizing his succession. Charles ruled Castile and Aragon as well as the Habsburg territories—

the Dutch provinces, Burgundy, and Austria. The imperial crown suggested itself as a means to consolidate these geographically heterogeneous possessions.

The other serious candidate, Francis I of France, was bound to enter the race if for no other reason than to keep the prize from Charles who, as Holy Roman emperor, would control lands virtually all along the entire French border. The papacy, too, saw serious dangers in Charles's candidacy, and a glance at the map tells the reason. The Habsburgs already ruled Naples to the south of the Papal States, and the prospect of Charles's rule in northern Italy as emperor meant potential encroachment from north and south. French domination in northern Italy also was problematic, but, compared with Charles, Francis seemed the lesser of two evils.

Pope Leo X proceeded to marshal his influence in support of Francis, promising cardinal's hats to the electors of Cologne and Trier and a permanent papal legateship for the archbishop of Mainz. But the intensity of papal support for Francis alienated the German electors. German nationalism, antipathy toward things French, and good memories of Emperor Maximilian became important elements as the election approached. In the end, the election turned into a combination of political strategizing—which candidate for the imperial crown was most likely to enhance the electors' political power—and of fiscal maneuvering with the prize going to the higher bidder. The bribes expended by both Charles and Francis stagger the imagination, but Charles's political importance and financial strength were more impressive—and persuasive.

Charles's election was unanimous. A *Wahlkapitulation*, an "election agreement," spelled out the relationship between the emperor and the territorial rulers, and indicated the significant concessions Charles had to make to win the imperial crown. Imperial offices were to be occupied only by Germans; the German language was to be used in official matters; all diets were to be held in Germany; no foreign soldiers were to be brought to Germany; no one should be condemned as an outlaw without a hearing; a *Reichsregiment* (imperial governing body) was to be established for the purpose of administering affairs during the emperor's absence from Germany, though the exact nature of this institution was left to subsequent clarification.

The reaction to Charles's election was boundless enthusiasm. Poems, sermons, and odes sang his virtues. A new day seemed to be dawning, and the German people eagerly looked forward to Charles's rule. Luther remarked in his *Open Letter to the Christian Nobility* that "God has given us a young, noble blood to be our head and thereby awakened many hearts to great and good hopes."[34] In part, of course, Luther's encomium was meant to make sure that the new emperor would be sympathetic to his cause. No matter. Soon Luther's "great and good hopes"—if in fact he had entertained them—vanished.

THE WILD BOAR IN THE VINEYARD

The curial proceedings against Luther, which had come to a halt after Luther's encounter with Cardinal Cajetan because of the curia's involvement in the imperial

---

34. WA 6:405.

election, were resumed in the fall of 1519. Elector Frederick's intervention to have Luther examined at Augsburg rather than (as should have been routine) in Rome, had shown that the case had political dimensions, though the implications of this reality were not altogether clear. It was obvious that the "Luther affair" was beginning to be complicated, and Pope Leo X was groping for a constructive resolution. Given the other issues—imperial politics, the confrontation between France and Spain, the threat posed by the Ottoman Empire—the case of the German Augustinian monk seemed of minor importance, and there is evidence that it was seen that way by many in the curia.

The fateful hardliner was Johann Eck. He had sent detailed reports of the Leipzig disputation to Rome, combining remarkable self-confidence and self-congratulation in his account of how he had exposed Luther's fatal theological errors with pessimistic prognoses about the spread of Luther's notions in Germany. His gloomy picture incited action.

In January 1520 a consistory in Rome was apprised that Luther's orthodoxy should be examined and, if necessary, his teachings condemned. Within a month a papal commission had hastily condemned several of Luther's errors, but at that point members of the curia counseled that further deliberations were appropriate. Consequently a second commission, composed of the heads of the major monastic orders, was appointed to examine Luther's teachings. This commission took its responsibilities seriously, and in its report rendered the verdict that some of Luther's notions were erroneous and a few seemed heretical. Mainly, however, Luther's ideas were "scandalous and offensive to pious ears." This was a surprisingly mild conclusion, and if matters had been left there, the outcome of the whole affair would have been nothing more than a reprimand, a word of counsel.

At this juncture, Eck decided to travel to Rome to make sure that Luther's errors were fully understood. His presence in Rome poured fuel on the fire. "It was appropriate that I came to Rome at this time," Eck wrote a friend, "for no one else was sufficiently familiar with Luther's errors." And he made sure that such ignorance was promptly dispelled. A new commission, greatly influenced by Eck, examined Luther's writings one more time and resulted in the promulgation of the papal bull *Exsurge Domine*. The bull, issued on June 15, 1520, threatened Luther with excommunication unless he recanted.

Exsurge Domine is assuredly one of the best-known documents of the entire Reformation. Its title, "Arise, O Lord," was a prayerful invocation of God, Jesus Christ, Peter, Paul, the apostles, the saints, indeed the entire church, to arise and defend their cause against the onslaught of Luther, who—like a wild boar (a vague biblical allusion to Psalm 68)—had invaded the Lord's vineyard. The drafters of the bull surely were deliberate in their use of a biblical allusion, but the comparison of Luther with a wild boar was hardly calculated to evoke sympathy for the manner of Luther's censure. The bull described Luther's history and declared forty-one sentences, or parts of sentences, culled from his writings to be "heretical, offensive, erroneous, objectionable to pious ears, misleading to simple minds, and contrary to Catholic teaching." The bull expressed regret about Luther's stubborn refusal to recant. Like all heretics, Luther was stubborn, scoffed at the scriptural interpretation of the church, and substituted his own views for those of the church. He was given sixty days during which to recant and another sixty days to report his recantation to Rome. Otherwise he and his supporters were to be declared heretics.

The church had spoken.

By all counts, *Exsurge Domine* was a strange summary of Luther's theological views. Most (but by no means all) of the forty-one condemned sentences can be found in Luther's writings, but a curious quality characterized the quotations. For example, the bull compressed into a single sentence what Luther wrote at different places on a page.[35] In one instance Luther merely cited the opinion of others, for which he was censured, and in another he was faulted for expressing his hope as to what a general council might do. Some of the sentences dealt with peripheral points of theology (concerning which the Catholic Church has long come to different positions), such as "the spiritual and temporal rulers would be well advised to do away with begging" or "the burning of heretics is against the Holy Spirit." The bull also was not free from ambiguities. At one place it indicated that all of Luther's writings were to be burned, while at another it condemned to the fire only those containing any of the forty-one condemned errors. If knowledge of Luther's views were extant only in the form provided by the bull, we would be sorely misled—this quite apart from the reality that by late 1519 Luther had not written much, certainly not explicitly, about those major theological themes that subsequently defined the Reformation and the Lutheran tradition. The topic of justification, for example, is not mentioned at all in the bull, except that the bull rejected Luther's denial of free will. More than half of the forty-one censured sentences came from the Ninety-five Theses and the *Resolutiones*; most of the others were taken from the proceedings of the Leipzig disputation.

In short, while the bull was clear in its fundamental conclusions, it also suggests that speed had been more important than accuracy. Those familiar with Luther's writings (above all, of course, Luther himself) were bound to conclude that his notions about the Christian faith had been neither seriously considered nor fully understood. Far from clarifying the controversy, the bull was bound to intensify the uncertainty among the theologians and the common people. Once all of this had become obvious, people were forced to conclude that the sloppiness of the bull was evidence of Luther's unfair treatment by the church. Ever more loudly the demand was made that Luther should receive a real hearing. If one argues that the bull did not take Luther seriously, and that his early views were compatible with the broad spectrum of permissible Catholic positions, to be labeled "offensive" but not at all "heretical," an important caveat must be added. Had the framers of the bull been able to include Luther's later writings, for example his 1520 treatise on the Babylonian Captivity, their judgment would have been reinforced, for Luther's attack on the sacramental system of the Catholic Church did constitute a radical break with the church. *Exsurge Domine* was thus both faulty and profound.

Luther himself was aware, in the early summer months of 1520, that closure of the official proceedings was imminent. In this atmosphere of uncertainty, he feverishly

35. Hans J. Hillerbrand, "Martin Luther and the Bull Exsurge Domine," *Theological Studies* 30 (1969): 109.

devoted himself to garner support. Three of his most famous writings came off the press that summer: *An den christlichen Adel deutscher Nation von des christlichen Standes Besserung* (*An Open Letter to the Christian Nobility of the German Nation*); *De captivitate Babylonica ecclesiae praeludium* (*The Babylonian Captivity of the Church*); and *Von der Freiheit eines Christenmenschen* (*The Freedom of the Christian*). These writings contained an intriguing mixture of his understanding of the Christian faith and his notions of necessary reform in church and society, coupled with a clear appeal for support. Not at all surprisingly, Luther dedicated the treatise on the Christian nobility to the newly elected German emperor, Charles V.

The *Open Letter to the Christian Nobility* was an appeal to the German nobility to understand the proper relationship of secular and ecclesiastical authority (a thorn in the flesh of the secular powers for some time). It also identified the various areas in church and society in need of reform. Luther's appropriation of the traditional German grievances—surely a pointed nationalist stance—was put into the context of important theological reflections. At the beginning of the treatise Luther repudiated the "three walls of the Romanists": that ecclesiastical power was superior to temporal power, that no one can authoritatively interpret Scripture except the pope, and that no one can convene a general council except the pope. Luther's repudiation of these assertions derived from his new theological insights, particularly the postulate of the priesthood of all believers. Faith and baptism make all Christians "priests," Luther wrote; they are the spiritual estate and need no intermediary to God. This assertion was truly revolutionary in that it rejected the traditional Catholic hierarchical understanding of the church. Luther also argued that theological reform was necessary, and he challenged the Christian nobility to take the lead in the reform of society and church. If the pope failed to convene a church council, any Christian assembly under the leadership of its secular authority had the right and the duty to do so.

The second and far longer part of the treatise contained no less than twenty-six reform proposals for church and society. There was not much that was new here; virtually all of these proposals had been made before. Some echoed the traditional German *gravamina* against the fiscal practices of the church; others dealt with more general societal concerns, such as the restriction of the importation of costly spices, the reform of university curricula, or the need for laws against extravagance and excess in dress. The *Open Letter* conveyed that Luther had appropriated the traditional German grievances, some of which bore no relationship to church and theology. Nonetheless, the sentiment was clear and unmistakable. The hour of reform had struck.

The *Babylonian Captivity of the Church*, written in Latin (though promptly published also in a German version), was an appeal to fellow theologians. Luther called it a *praeludium*, a "prelude," to convey that more was yet to come. "I know another little song about Rome and about them," Luther had written at the end of his *Open Letter to the Christian Nobility*, "and if their ears itch for it I will sing them that song too, and pitch the notes to the top of the scale."[36] And so he did. His topic was the sacramental teaching of the church, and he delineated a defining criterion for assessing that teaching—fidelity to the Scriptures. Luther concluded that the church had perverted

---

36. WA 6:469.

the authentic biblical teaching and therefore found itself in a "Babylonian Captivity." Scripture, so Luther argued, teaches that a sacrament is a divine promise to which an external sign is attached. He concluded that there were only two sacraments—baptism and Communion—and not seven as the Catholic Church taught. Moreover, the Mass was falsely understood as a sacrifice. And Communion was incorrectly observed, since the cup was withheld from the laity and the philosophical notion of transubstantiation was used to explain Christ's presence in bread and wine. "The Holy Spirit is greater than Aristotle," Luther wrote, and added that "in order that the real body and the real blood of Christ may be present in the sacrament, it is not necessary that bread and wine be transubstantiated and Christ be contained under their accidents." The faithful must turn their "eyes and hearts simply to the institution of Christ and to this alone, and set naught before us but the very word of Christ by which he instituted this sacrament."[37] The word of Christ is a word of promise—the remission of sins— and the proper approach to the sacrament must be that of faith. For a sacrament to be effective, nothing is required but the word of divine promise, which is appropriated in faith.[38] Luther's emphasis on both the Word and on faith as the constituting elements in the beneficial reception of the sacraments fits harmoniously into his broader understanding of the gospel as a word of forgiveness to be appropriated by faith.

The treatise on the *Freedom of a Christian* was prefaced by an important document, urged on Luther by two friends: a conciliatory letter to Pope Leo X. Luther seems to outdo himself with gracious words about the pope—he mentions the pope's good reputation and blameless life and makes the point that he had only spoken "good and honorable words" about the pope. "So I come, most blessed Father, and, prostrate before you, pray that if possible you intervene." Luther's point was that the good king was surrounded by evil advisors: the Roman Church, "once the holiest of all, has become the most licentious den of thieves." Luther carefully distinguished between Pope Leo as a person and the state of the church over which he presided. It was an appeal of support, reinforced by Luther's declaration that the accompanying treatise, the tract of Christian freedom, was indicative of his foremost concern.

The *Freedom of a Christian* is about the principles of Christian faith and morality. The Christian life, Luther asserted, is a life of freedom, and thus the Christian is "a perfectly free lord over all things," bound, or restricted, only by love. In other words, the Christian faith is not defined by rules and mandates and laws, but by freedom. It is not an accumulation of "oughts" but an exercise of the liberated spirit. Today these notions sound simple enough and even a Christian commonplace. To Luther's contemporaries they were no less than revolutionary, for the medieval church had expressed the Christian ethos with innumerable rules. Luther countered with the principle of "freedom." The Christian, bound only by love, is a "free lord over all." "It will not hurt the soul," Luther wrote, "if the body is clothed in secular dress, dwells in unconsecrated places, eats and drinks as others do."[39] No detailed rules; no minute prescriptions, but freedom. "Christians," Luther observed, "are free from all things

---

37. WA 6:511.
38. WA 6:550, "ad sacramenti enim constutionem ante requiritur verbum divinae promissionis, quo fides exerceatur."
39. WA 7:21.

and over all things, so that they need no works to make them righteous and to save them, since faith alone confers all these things abundantly. But should they grow so foolish as to presume to become righteous, free, saved, and a Christian by means of some good work, they will at once lose faith and all its benefits." And again: "From faith flow forth love and joy in the Lord, and from love a cheerful, willing, and free disposition that serves the neighbor willingly, without considering gratitude or ingratitude, praise or blame, gain or less."[40]

In the second part of the treatise Luther wrote about those who, "misled by the word 'faith' and by all that has been said, now say, 'If faith does all things and is alone sufficient unto righteousness, why then are good works commanded?'" Freedom does not mean license. Christians, though free from rules, are called upon to be "Christ" unto their neighbors—to serve them in their needs, even as Christ served all people by his life. God calls humans to be both free and a servant: free because God has loved them and servant because they are called upon to love their neighbors.

More than anything else Luther had written up to that time, these three treatises expressed the full range of his new understanding of the Christian faith. All three, but particularly the *Babylonian Captivity*, showed the gap between their author and the church. Reportedly, one reader angrily threw the *Babylonian Captivity* to the ground upon finishing reading it and another said that it made him shiver from head to toe. Luther had acknowledged that, no matter how serious were issues of reform in church and society, his concern was not merely the correction of abuses or the alleviation of grievances, but a new understanding of the gospel.

Luther also propounded a new understanding of the church. As he wrote at the time, "Wherever you see baptism, bread, and the gospel, wherever it may be, by whomever administered, do not doubt that there is the church."[41] What was so strikingly new was that Luther outlined here dimensions of the true church that could be perceived only by faith, for it is only by faith that baptism and bread and wine are taken to be sacraments, even as it is only by faith that the gospel is accepted as the Word of God.

The printing history of the three treatises of 1520 suggests that their impact must have been enormous. Each treatise was reprinted and reprinted, the tract on Christian freedom no less than eighteen times and the *Open Letter to the Christian Nobility* fourteen times in the span of just a few years. While before too long his writings triggered Catholic responses, including the famous *Assertio* supposedly from the pen of the English king Henry VIII, Luther achieved what he had set out to do: he had put his case before a wider public.[42]

The defining event of the late summer of 1520 was the bull *Exsurge Domine*. When, after weeks of anxious uncertainty, Luther was officially notified of its content, which triggered the two sixty-days deadlines to recant and report his recantation to Rome, he knew that it was neither a phony document nor an unsubstantiated rumor. Pro-

40. WA 7:36ff.
41. WA 7:720.
42. By contrast, the tract on the Babylonian Captivity, written in Latin and meant for the much smaller circle of theologians, was only reprinted half a dozen times, though it did have five German-language reprints. This total of eleven reprints is impressive as well.

foundly convinced of the rightness of his biblical interpretation, Luther concluded that the bull was the work of the antichrist, a charge he proved to his satisfaction in a brief treatise entitled *Adversus execrabilem Antichristi bullam* (Against the Execrable Bull of the Antichrist). The treatise was published just about on the last day allowed by the bull for his recantation; it thus constituted Luther's response to the papal judgment and exhortation. At the same time he issued an appeal to a general council to hear his case. Defiantly, he stood his ground.

Then, on the morning of December 10, 1520, sixty days after his official notification, Luther, accompanied by a throng of students, whose classes were canceled for the day, went outside the Wittenberg city walls near the Elster gate. (Though one is tempted to translate "Elster" as "magpie," and see symbolism in the location, the gate took its name from the nearby Elster River.) A bonfire had been started on that cold December morning and as students and faculty were milling around it, a number of theological books were tossed into the fire. They were books by second-rate authors; none of the professors was willing to part with valuable books in their libraries. All the same, a copy of canon law found its way into the fire, a blatant gesture of rejection and defiance in that the book governed much of the lives of individuals and society (as Henry VIII was to learn less than a decade later, when he sought to free himself from the marital bond to Catherine of Aragon). A copy of the papal bull was also burned, almost so it seems as an afterthought: "Because you have grieved the saints of the Lord, may eternal fire grieve you," Luther said as he committed the bull to the flames. In the afternoon this literary auto-da-fe event was repeated, undoubtedly much to the delight of the students, for whom this was a great joke, and it must have been disturbing for Luther to see the occasion made ridiculous by collegiate pranks. The next day Luther, who had "trembled and prayed" at the occasion, told his students that "now things will turn serious."[43] A contemporary called the burning "a crime such as has not been seen for centuries, a lese majesty." It was not so much the burning of the bull that was so offensive, although papal authority had been dramatically defied with this act, but the burning of copies of the decretals and canon law, the very foundation of societal and religious law and order. Quite profoundly Luther noted to Spalatin "the dice has been cast." He had defied the church.

On January 3, 1521, the bull *Decet Romanum pontificem* duly declared that, since Luther had not recanted his erroneous views, he was excommunicated.[44] The church had spoken. The next step in the process was clear enough: the secular authorities— in this case Elector Frederick of Saxony—were to execute the ecclesiastical verdict. Strangely, that did not happen. Indeed, Luther's papal condemnation proved singularly ineffective; the widely stated sentiment was that Luther's case (and his concerns) required a different resolution than a papal condemnation. It was not that Luther's message had gained overpowering support; rather, his case seemed for many the opportune occasion to push particular agendas. Some called for a general council of the church to address not only Luther's case but also issues of reform; others proposed

43. J. Luther, "Noch einmal Luthers Worte bei der Verbrennung der Bannbulle," *Archiv für Reformationsgeschichte* 54 (1954): 260–65.

44. *Magnum bullarium Romanum: bullarum, privilegiorum ac diplomatum Romanorum Pontificum amplissima collectio* (Graz: 1964–1966), 5:761–64.

that Luther should receive a hearing at the forthcoming diet of the empire. Luther himself led the foray with his incessant charge that he had been condemned without a fair hearing.

With the proposal to give Luther a hearing at the forthcoming imperial diet, the case was tossed into the lap of the new emperor. But Charles had other worries. His attention was focused on his Spanish possessions, where domestic problems seemed to be endless. German affairs were foreign to him, and one may well question if Charles possessed a deep commitment (not to mention ability) to make German affairs his own. As far as he was concerned, Luther's case was open and shut: Luther had been condemned as a heretic by the church and had to be given the punishment prescribed by the church. No sooner had he assumed office after an elaborate ceremony in Aachen than the Luther affair became his responsibility. But there were other issues. Charles's election agreement had provided for the creation of a standing body to govern, together with an emperor, German affairs. Charles—or rather his advisors—began to have second thoughts about this provision, and so the early months of 1521 were occupied by inconclusive wrangling between emperor and estates. Even as the chorus of voices demanding a full and fair hearing for Luther continued to swell, Charles did not see much importance in the affairs of an Augustinian monk in Saxony, whom the church had declared a heretic. His own initial response to Luther had been to echo the verdict of the church, but he soon had to realize that the resolution of the matter depended on more than his own convictions. His election agreement had stipulated that no German should be outlawed without a proper hearing, and thus Luther's case triggered a conflict with the estates over the nature and implementation of the agreement that had put him, in fact, onto the imperial throne.

It became clear that Charles could not win this one. More and more voices argued that Luther had not received a proper hearing. Those who yearned for reform felt that Luther's notions, despite the intensity of their form and content, deserved more careful consideration than they had been afforded. German nationalists resented the curial condemnation of Luther as foreign intrusion, while some of the territorial rulers saw unilateral imperial action against Luther, undertaken at the very beginning of the new emperor's rule, as a fateful step in the direction of increased imperial power.

In short, for a variety of reasons Luther's condemnation by the church did not appear to be (as bizarre as that was) the end of the matter. The proposal that Luther should receive a hearing gained increasing support, even though the details—the form of such a hearing and who should conduct it—remained nebulous. Eventually, this sentiment turned into the practical suggestion that the hearing should take place in conjunction with the forthcoming German diet to be held at the city of Worms.

That, of course, was something the church neither wanted nor condoned. The papal nuncio Aleander bluntly reminded the emperor and the estates that the church had spoken, that a condemned heretic could not receive a further hearing, and that it was the responsibility of the secular authorities to issue a mandate against Luther and his followers without delay. The emperor shared Aleander's sentiment for prompt action, but his chancellor Gattinara urged him not to proceed against Luther without consultation with the estates. Gattinara realized that the emperor could hardly afford a confrontation with the estates at the very beginning of his rule since he needed their support in the future. In February the estates promptly refused to pass a bill suppressing Luther's writings and demanded, in view of the evident restlessness of the common people, that Luther should be cited to appear before the diet "to the benefit and advantage of the entire German nation, the Holy Roman Empire, our Christian faith, and all estates."[45] At this juncture Charles recognized that the sentiment among the estates made Luther's citation the only practicable option. He yielded.

Understandably, some rulers, especially those of ecclesiastical territories, had bitterly opposed this turn, but in the end all parties gained by it. The emperor conformed to the stipulation of his election agreement and could strengthen his claim to be the ultimate arbiter of Christendom; Elector Frederick of Saxony manifested his continued concern for a fair treatment of his professor; the territorial rulers asserted their importance in German politics; the humanists and others saw the issue as a possible breakthrough in the quest for reform of the church. In the end, even the papal nuncio Aleander realized that Luther's citation was in the best ecclesiastical interest: Luther's recantation might resolve the whole controversy, and if he did not recant, his condemnation by the diet would put the blame on the German rulers rather than on the Roman curia. All parties were united (for different reasons, of course) in their determination to resolve the issue according to their particular interests. At the same time, it also is obvious, especially in light of what was to happen in Worms, that emperor and nuncio concurred with Luther's citation to the diet merely to provide him with the opportunity to recant. That, of course, is not precisely what took place.

So it happened that Luther, the condemned heretic, received an invitation to appear before the dignitaries of the empire assembled in Worms. His citation addressed him as "honorable," "dear," "pious"—a fact that must have so impressed Luther that even many years later at the dinner table he produced the invitation and spelled out to his listeners exactly how he had been addressed.[46] The emperor's invitation assured him of formal and legal safe conduct, understandably an important concern for a condemned heretic, but since Jan Hus's safe conduct a century earlier had not been honored, hardly an ironclad certainty. The citation employed rather general language as to the reason for his invitation to Worms: "Information is requested from you concerning your teaching and your books," a phrase that could be easily understood (erroneously, as matters turned out) as an invitation to a thorough exploration of Luther's ideas and pronouncements.[47]

On Tuesday of Holy Week, March 26, the imperial herald Kaspar Sturm reached Wittenberg (his journey of some 260 miles from Worms had taken ten days) and delivered the citation to Luther. It was by no means a foregone conclusion that Luther would accept—the emperor and Nuncio Aleander hoped that the "monster" would not—but he did as he had intimated in a letter to Spalatin back in December: "There is no doubt but that the summons of the emperor means that I am summoned by God. But since the summons surely does not mean that I can properly instruct them, they will probably use force. I must then commit my case to the Lord."

---

45. *Deutsche Reichstagsakten, Jüngere Reihe* (Munich: 1823ff.), 2:515.
46. Ibid., 526.
47. Ibid.

Luther was in no hurry to be on his way to Worms: it was Holy Week, and his preaching responsibilities in Wittenberg had priority. He preached twice on Maundy Thursday, Good Friday, Easter Sunday, and Easter Monday, without referring in any of the sermons to his forthcoming journey. Finally, on Tuesday after Easter, April 2, the journey began. The Wittenberg city council provided its official carriage, with three horses, and even provided funds for expenses along the way. In addition to the emperor's herald with the imperial banner, who had been sent to assure Luther's safety, three companions—Nikolaus von Amsdorf, later the reformer of Pomerania; the young nobleman Peter Swaven; and the Augustinian friar Johann Pezensteiner— accompanied Luther. Wherever this little caravan was recognized on its progress to Worms, enthusiastic welcomes took place, with dinners, and toasts with wine, and exuberant assurances of support. When Luther reached Erfurt, the university welcomed his arrival with a delegation of some forty faculty and a host of students. The humanist Crotus Rubeanus delivered an academic oration in which he hailed Luther as having been sent by God and declared him to be the avenger of the lies of the time that robbed men and women of their faith—all very festive. Luther's response, which declared that he was not worthy of this honor but would accept it gratefully, was the epitome of modesty. (A few years later Rubeanus entered the service of Albert of Mainz and became a bitter enemy of the Reformation.)

Luther had clearly become a public figure and his case had begun to reverberate among the people. There was also the disquieting news that on March 10 the emperor had issued a mandate ordering the confiscation and destruction of Luther's writings and severe punishment for those who propagated them. While this mandate was issued only for his own territory, it was a grave foreboding of the emperor's position. No wonder that, as the little caravan approached Worms, well-meaning if anxious supporters warned Luther not to proceed, for he would be burned to ashes, as had been happened with Hus at Constance. Hus, like Luther, had been given official safe conduct, but then the council fathers at Constance had found that it was not necessary to keep faith with a convicted heretic, and Hus died at the stake. Even Kaspar Sturm, the imperial herald, queried Luther, when he found him playing the lute in the inn in Frankfurt, "Doctor, do you really want to continue?" "We will come to Worms," retorted Luther, "in spite of all the gates of hell," a phrase that he afterward changed into the more picturesque phrase, "even if there were as many devils ready to jump on me as there are tiles on the roofs."[48] The pace was slow as the carriage moved from village to village, from town to town.

Luther reached Worms, welcomed by hundreds, on April 16. The following day, shortly after six o'clock in the evening, after he had been kept waiting for two hours, Luther appeared before the dignitaries of the diet: emperor, electors, secular and ecclesiastical rulers, representatives of the cities, and the imperial knights. The site was the large hall of the episcopal residence, where the emperor was staying. Since the hall was far too small to accommodate all the dignitaries, some 150 of them, many had to stand crowded together. Rich woodcarvings in the Renaissance style covered the ceiling of the hall, and an enormous tile stove that reached almost to the ceiling stood in a cor-

48. WA Br 2:298.

ner. Benches were placed against three walls, while the emperor sat at the far end of the room on a platform three steps higher than the rest, a tapestry with the empire's coat of arms behind him.

Here was the epicenter of power in Europe, and those in the room were attired in splendor and confident of their authority and power. Here they faced one another— monk and emperor, dissenter and the rulers of the empire. Here were those who later were to turn into bitter enemies over the teachings of the individual who stood now before them: Landgrave Philip of Hesse, Duke George of Albertine Saxony, as well as Elector Frederick, Luther's territorial ruler, making it the only time Luther and Frederick were in the same room, even though Frederick, more than anyone else, ensured that Luther did not die a heretic's death.

Seeing Luther escorted into the hall, Charles remarked that this man would never turn him into a heretic. Luther was told by the imperial chancellor that he had been cited for two reasons: to acknowledge the books placed on the table as his own and to repudiate their content. Before Luther was able to respond, a Saxon counselor jumped to his feet and asked that the titles of the books on the table be read. This request must have struck many in the hall, perhaps even the emperor, as bizarre, for the issue was surely not so much what was literally on the table in front of Luther but the content of the treatises widely disseminated under his name. The counselor's intervention was meant to provide time to decide on the next step. When Luther answered, he acknowledged himself to be the author of the books, adding with that timeless confidence of authors, "I have written many more," but then continuing "in a very soft voice," he requested time to ponder his answer to the second question. This caused consternation, but after a brief consultation between the emperor and the electors, Luther was given twenty-four hours for his answer. The emperor's chancellor began a surprisingly extensive speech, dripping with impatience and reprimands. Brother Martin, so he noted, had enjoyed more than sufficient time to ponder the accusations of heresy against him and had known exactly why he had been cited to appear before emperor and the estates. Thus it surely was perplexing that he was unable to give an answer; nonetheless, the emperor, in his graciousness, was willing to give him until 4 o'clock of the next day to answer—but he had to speak freely and not present a written statement. And he should be mindful that he had written against his holiness the pope, against the chair of St. Peter, and had propagated heretical teachings. Much evil had resulted from his teachings and a mighty fire would break out if the necesary action were not taken. Then the flames would not be extinguished through Luther's recantation or the might of the emperor. "Therefore, I admonish you, Brother Martin, to change your mind."

On the following day Luther appeared once more before the dignitaries of the empire, again late in the afternoon. Luther had overcome his timidity of the previous day. "My gracious lords," he began, "I humbly ask for your understanding if I, a simple monk, fail to show proper etiquette in this illustrious setting." His writings fell into three groups, he stated. Some dealt with faith and morals, some with papal tyranny, some were written against literary opponents. At times he had been vehement in tone, more vehement than became a Christian; for this he apologized. As to their content, some of what he had written even his enemies approved; some expressed noncontroversial biblical truths. But to revoke all that he had written? If he were convinced by Scripture, he would do so and be the first to burn his own books. "Therefore, I pray by the grace of God that your Imperial Majesty and Lordships provide such testimony, convict me of error, and convince me with biblical writings. Should I thus be persuaded, I am truly ready and willing to revoke all errors and be myself the first to throw my books into the fire." Luther had astutely combined the categorical insistence on Scripture with a willingness to be instructed.

Eck of Trier, the imperial chancellor who conducted the questioning, told Luther that his answer had not been clear enough. Did he, or did he not, recant? Luther's simple response made history: "Since your majesty and your lords demand a simple answer, I shall give one without horns and teeth. Unless I am convinced by the testimony of Scripture and evident reasoning, I am convicted by the Sacred Scripture I have cited—for I believe neither solely the pope nor the councils, for it is evident that they have often erred and contradicted one another. My conscience is captured by the Word of God. I cannot and will not recant, since to act against one's conscience is neither safe nor honest." The answer ended as if Luther had uttered a prayer: "Amen."[49]

Eck retorted that Luther should forget about his conscience; he could never prove that councils had erred. Luther insisted that he could, but at that point the emperor, who had to have every word translated, interjected that enough had been said, and Luther was escorted from the hall. Aleander reported to Rome that Luther, when leaving, raised his arms "as is the custom of German soldiers when they rejoice over a good hit."[50]

The following day Charles convened the territorial rulers to ask for their judgment in the matter. When they expressed the need for further reflection, he told them that he for one did not need to ponder his position. Pulling notes from his pockets, he began to read a brief statement, the first one we have from his pen. His ancestors, so he said, had been faithful sons of the Catholic Church and had bequeathed their faith to him. Now, a single monk had set his own opinions above the consensus of the church for more than a thousand years. "I am therefore determined to use all my dominions, possessions, and friends, my body and blood, my life and soul to settle this matter."[51]

The emperor had spoken, and his pronouncement was to guide his religious policy from then on until the day of his abdication thirty-five years later. While unsuccessful, as matters turned out, his religious policy proved to be his destiny. Indeed, when speaking to the members of the Spanish *consejo real* and *consejo de estade* a few years later, Charles remarked that while future historians would record the outbreak of the Lutheran heresy during his reign, they would also acknowledge that it was "extinguished through my help and determination." Charles abhorred heresy, and at Worms he wanted to make clear that he would use everything in his power and authority to suppress it.

When Charles demanded the concurrence of the estates to proceed against Luther, he found them reluctant. They proposed further conversations with Luther since he

49. *Deutsche Reichstagsakten*, 2:555–56.
50. P. Kalkoff, ed., *Die Depeschen des Nuntius Aleander* (Halle: 1886), 143.
51. *Deutsche Reichstagsakten*, 2:595–96.

had not been told his specific errors. Luther had expressed his willingness to be shown his errors, and this should be done. The emperor diplomatically agreed. In the ensuing conversations Luther was told that he was dividing the Christian church; that pious men had read the Scriptures before him and had not broken with the church; that, by not recanting, the good that he had written would also be condemned. In turn, Luther insisted that his scriptural interpretation was correct and declared that he would accept decisions of a general council only if they agreed with the Word of God. Even a compromise put forward by Aleander (surely an indication that he had at long last understood the complexity of the situation), that Luther refrain from writing and in return be assured of a quiet and peaceful living, led nowhere. The situation was hopeless, especially since the vindictive comments made by ecclesiastical and secular rulers in Worms about Luther—that his heresy was ten times worse than that of Hus, that his preaching was an invitation to rebellion, murder, and thievery—sharply increased. When Luther was asked, in exasperation, how the matter was to be resolved, he elusively responded with a passage from Scripture: "If it is a work of men, it will perish; if it is from God, you will not quench it." The evident impossibility to secure Luther's recantation meant that his stay in Worms had to come to an end.

On May 8 the emperor ordered an edict against Luther, drawn up by Aleander several days earlier, to be put into proper legal form. Four days later he was ready to sign, with pen in hand, when he decided to consult once more with the estates to gain their concurrence. The diet had formally adjourned and many of the rulers had left town; yet this unfinished business remained. Finally, on May 25, Elector Joachim of Brandenburg having assured the emperor of the consent of the estates, Charles signed the draft of May 8. Luther and his supporters were declared political outlaws, and his books were to be burned.[52]

This edict promptly proved to be an ambiguous matter (much like the bull *Exsurge Domine* itself), for doubts about its legality were raised at once and may well have been an important factor in the practical insignificance of the edict in the subsequent course of events. The edict was issued after the adjournment of the diet, and so the phrase "with the unanimous counsel and will of the electors, rulers, and estates" was patently inaccurate. Many of the rulers, such as Elector Frederick and Philip of Hesse, had left Worms by the middle of May. Only the emperor's authority stood behind the document, which was not part of the official recess of the diet, and that fact made for a further complication. The emperor clearly meant the edict to be relevant for the entire empire, but since one could argue that all the estates had not explicitly agreed to it, it could be seen as relevant only for the emperor's possessions.

Charles, who used the wording "with the unanimous counsel and will" to attain this objective, argued with some justification that the estates had assured him, prior to Luther's appearance at Worms, that he could act if Luther did not recant—and this was what Charles now proposed to do. Charles conveniently overlooked, however, that during the negotiations in May, subsequent to Luther's appearance, several of the estates had reversed their position. It also was an open legal question if Charles had the authority to proceed unilaterally if the edict was understood to have been issued

52. Ibid., 654.

on the authority of the diet. The emperor wanted his imperial authority to stand behind the edict, but at the same time have the concurrence of the estates. Legally, things were murky, and some challenged the emperor's authority to issue such an edict applicable to the empire, and not just to his own possessions, including none other than Albert of Mainz, the imperial chancellor. Albert refused to countersign the edict, which meant the edict was of dubious imperial legality. If, on the other hand, the edict was considered a mandate, its applicability was restricted to those territories over which the emperor had immediate and direct control. A fateful legal uncertainty hovered over the edict. Intriguingly, Charles refrained from transmitting the edict to Elector Frederick, who was able to claim that no legal basis for proceeding against Luther existed.

In short, confusion hovered over the edict, though those who objected to its legality were also those who in one way or another felt sympathy for Luther. With the insight of hindsight it is easy to see how this confusion contributed to the subsequent course of events. Nonetheless, with the edict the curtain fell on what should have been the final act of Luther's drama. Most of the contemporaries were convinced that the edict was indeed the end of the Luther affair. It was not, and from the vantage point of subsequent events the reason is not difficult to discern.

An unknown professor of Bible had been catapulted into empirewide limelight, and his cause, whatever it was, had become an affair of state. Between the Ninety-five Theses of the fall of 1517 and the Edict of Worms in the sping of 1521 three developments had taken place. While frequently intertwining, they remained separate developments. First, there were the excommunication proceedings against Luther in Rome. Albert of Mainz had triggered them in December 1518, and they had continued, at times haphazardly, at times vigorously, until Luther's excommunication. The site of the action was faraway Rome, and while some knew about these proceedings, they were initially a distant matter. By the same token, given the complex nature of events, Rome was not always well informed of the nature of the theological discussion, Eck hardly being a reliable informant. Luther's alleged statements that had found their way into the bull *Exsurge Domine* were by no means an authentic summary of his theology even at that time.

Hand in hand went a second development: the theological controversy. Luther had initiated it with his Ninety-five Theses, and it was kept alive by the likes of Sylvester Prierias and Eck, on the one side, and Carlstadt on the other. Its focus shifted, from the peripheral and dogmatically undefined topic of indulgences to the question of authority in the church. The Leipzig debate of the summer of 1519 was the climax of this controversy.

Luther was the pivotal figure in a third development, which might be called the challenge to spirituality. In the short run, it overshadowed everything else. Luther's prolific publication frenzy between 1518 and 1521 shows that most of his titles were in the German vernacular, and that most of them dealt with devotional, not theological, topics. Their printing history indicates that these devotional writings enjoyed reprint after reprint, often in the dozens, and thus helped in making Luther a household name in Germany. His theological pronouncements in Latin, addressed to the learned theologians (and the church), were reprinted considerably fewer times.

It was the Luther of these devotional pamphlets whom ever more people came to know—the Luther who wrote about how to pray, who counseled how to die a Christian death, who instructed about good works and about marriage. For the common people, the ecclesiastical proceedings against Luther were far away and the theological controversy largely incomprehensible. What Luther wrote in their own language, however, could be easily grasped. To be sure, there were a few defenders of the church who also took to the pen and wrote in the vernacular, but they failed to write with Luther's eloquence, passion, and simplicity. People resonated with Luther's challenge to live a committed Christian life and took to heart his concern for reform. They found it all the more startling that this pious man who had challenged them to deeper faith and commitment was now a declared heretic of the church.

What about Luther himself? When the futility of further discussions with him in Worms and the emperor's threatening observation that his safe conduct was soon to expire, Luther hurriedly left the city. On May 1 he and his small cohort had reached Eisenach, where he was able to preach, though not until the local priest had been given the opportunity to voice a notarized protest. Two days later, Luther was told that his "abduction" was imminent and the small convoy should not use the major road, frequented by many travelers, but a side road. Luther formally discharged Kaspar Sturm, imperial herald and guarantor of the imperial safe conduct. The following day masked horsemen appeared dramatically out of the woods, frightening Luther's uninitiated companions beyond measure. The horsemen demanded in rough language that Luther identify himself, then grabbed him and had him run, like an animal, beside them until they were out of sight.

For those not in the know, the conclusion was that Luther's abduction had been carried out by Catholics. Luther was in their hands; the sentence against him would be carried out.

The Luther affair was over and a thing of the past.

Chapter 3

THE BEGINNINGS OF THE MOVEMENT OF REFORM

The traditional story of the Reformation had a winsome persuasiveness, for it pitted a depraved and corrupt pre-Reformation church against a Hercules who enthralled his contemporaries with his vision of the Christian gospel. The story is more complicated, however, if the premise of a corrupt church is not the point of departure of the story. If, on the eve of the Reformation, the church was in a secure and acceptable state—and the noisy criticism was but the fiery denunciations of a few disgruntled souls—the challenge is to explain the dramatic impact and increasingly widespread support garnered by Luther's message. How could it be that within the span of less than a decade, the church in Germany began to crumble and found itself in the most serious crisis it had ever experienced?

As we have seen, the beginnings of the conflagration were rather innocuous. The events between 1517 and 1521 pertained to one individual, Martin Luther. To be sure, events had many facets—political blackmail and maneuvering, ecclesiastical action, religious exhortation, theological discussion—and it distorts the happenings to see Luther in splendid isolation. There was Luther's colleague Carlstadt and an increasing throng of supporters. Nonetheless, at the center of it all stood Luther, and the story of those four years was his story, from the publication of his Ninety-five Theses in 1517 to his excommunication and political condemnation in 1521. While Luther was increasingly at pains to share his new theological insights, his most popular tracts and treatises dealt with devotional themes. His burden was to help men and women to be more serious about their Christian profession, not to "Christianize" or even "re-Christianize" them, as has been suggested, for they were all proper if ignorant members of the mystical body, the church, but to challenge them to devout lives. It is not too far from the mark to see Luther as a kind of modern revival preacher, consumed by zeal to preach the message, just as the prophets of the Old Testament cried out "woe is me. . . ."

To label these events the "Reformation" or "Reformation movement" is to employ a precarious kind of shorthand. During the first few years of the controversy, nobody thought of categorically rejecting the church, nobody thought of the whole range of possible theological implications to the arguments put forward. The theological significance of the controversy was by no means clear nor were its political ramifications fully obvious.

Supporters appeared on the scene in mounting numbers, and little by little the Luther affair began to coalesce into a movement. No longer was it about a single individual, for increasingly people who had read the pamphlets of Luther and those of his followers were touched and excited and enthralled by their message. Again, one wonders why this was so, and the answer not only points in the direction of Luther's winsome appeal to a simpler yet deeper understanding of the Christian faith but also his impressive rhetorical eloquence. An old word entered the vocabulary anew and was enthusiastically embraced by Luther and his supporters—the word "reform." Scanning Luther's writings of those years one sees how slowly that word made its appearance, gingerly in his Ninety-five Theses, then notably in his *Open Letter to the Christian Nobility*—it became like a torrent and overwhelmed everything else. Now it was no longer the esoteric issue of indulgences that was on the table; it was all of the church and all of society.

The "Martinians," as they were promptly dubbed, did not come from a single corner of Germany or from a particular section of the people. Soon they were found everywhere, north and south, learned and illiterate, young and old, male and female. The call for reform did not remain confined to a small circle of the intellectual elites, but increasingly touched all aspects of society, with religion a core concern. All the same, those who eagerly devoured Luther's pamphlets, incessantly talked about him, and proudly carried the label "Martinian," had no clear notion what the whole matter was about. Or, to say it differently, many understood (perhaps misunderstood) Luther to be the advocate of a reformed Catholic church, challenging Christians to be more spiritually committed, whatever that meant.

This steady increase of partisans of Luther's cause took place in the face of the ecclesiastical and political censures against Luther and his followers. From the spring of 1521 onward, taking up the cause of Luther was not a neutral option, the support of one theological position over another; rather, it was the support of someone labeled a heretic by the church. It was support that invoked the wrath of Christendom.

Nonetheless, the stage began to be crowded with followers, some idiosyncratic, like Andreas Carlstadt or Ulrich von Hutten; others more in accord with Luther's theology, like Philip Melanchthon, Urban Rhegius, Huldrych Zwingli, Ambrosius Blaurer, and Martin Bucer. Luther began to fade from the scene, even though he continued to issue striking (and provocative) theological pronouncements. In the cities and territories that resonated to this wave of proclamation, questions arose that tended to be answered locally. What did it mean, for example, to proclaim "the gospel" or what was a proper "evangelical" service? Soon it also became evident that the key figures in the story were the political authorities—town councils or territorial rulers. Indeed, political figures, such as George Spalatin, Frederick of Saxony, and Philip of Hesse, occupied center stage. After 1521 these political figures gained increasing importance, because the foremost issue had turned into a legal one: were the estates and cities authorized to undertake ecclesiastical changes in their territories and cities? The ruling elites determined they were, and they thereby influenced the course of events. The theological controversy turned into an affair of state.

Something dramatic had happened during the previous half decade. Luther's formulation of the Christian faith with its focus on the Word had come to be the ground that brought together the various notions of reform and gave them a startling dynamic. At the core stood an amazingly simple assertion, which proved to be electrifying to the core: all of Christian faith and life had to be subjected to the "Word." This Word was to be applied to all the aspects of church and society that appeared to be in need of reform. That Luther had been declared a heretic and an outlaw mattered little, because the principle underlying reform in church and society was clear. It was the Word. Trouble came with the implementation.

There are problems with this perspective, and in recent years historians have been rather persistent in pointing them out. They begin with the term "Reformation" itself, its usefulness as historical shorthand notwithstanding. The problems have to do with the complexity of what is described by the term "Reformation." The simple fact is that a great deal was going on at the same time. It is tempting to view all events from the perspective of the eventual outcome—that is, to see the beginnings in terms of the ending, drawing a line from the beginnings of the indulgences controversy in 1517 to the promulgation of official legal recognition of Lutheran churches at the Diet of Augsburg in 1555. Such a view runs the risk of ignoring the diversity of sentiment in the early years of the conflagration, of not appreciating the open-ended dynamic of the events along the way (especially the essential stability of the ecclesiastical and societal situation in Germany before the outbreak of the controversy), and of insisting that the character of events all along the way was such as to allow the label of "Reformation." Recently, historians have also emphasized that there were reform impulses well before the early sixteenth century, that in the early sixteenth century a variety of notions of reform were being bandied about, and they have suggested that we better speak of "reformations" of the sixteenth century so as to reject the notion of a discrete epoch or a unitary movement. Any inkling of Luther's overriding centrality in the story is thereby likely to be disavowed.

We will best understand the nature of events by distinguishing between various stages of the larger story, since events differed rather dramatically at different times. A precise definition of the phenomenon "Reformation" must entail a chronological schematization that recognizes that events between 1517 and 1521 had a different character from those ten, or even five, years later. At the beginning was the controversy surrounding a single individual, the Augustinian friar and professor of biblical studies, Martin Luther. This controversy had two identifiable aspects. First, it was a theological dispute, a "squabble among monks," as Pope Leo X called it with uncanny insight, a demonstration of the kind of theological hairsplitting of the sort that had made medieval theologians experts in determining the number of angels on the head of the pin. That this dispute quickly attained notoriety had to do neither with the importance of the debated theological issues nor with the state of church or society, but with what might be called the lifeblood of theologians, their disposition to engage in fierce polemics, with elements of personal jealousy and jurisdictional disputes thrown in for good measure. A second aspect of the controversy hung like a dark cloud over this theological dispute: the heresy proceedings against Luther. That was serious business, and by the time Luther met with Cardinal Cajetan in Augsburg in October 1518, he was aware of the seriousness of his situation. This was more than a theological dispute. In light of Luther's (and that of his supporters') censure as heretics and political outlaws, the theological controversy had become a matter of life and death.

Around the time of Luther's formal censure by church and state in early 1521, the character of the events began to change. What had been "the Luther affair," characterized by a theological dispute and formal proceedings in Rome, began to coalesce into a movement. This turn of events clearly grew out of Luther's skillful strategy not to limit his concerns and values to the small circle of professional theologians and churchmen but to communicate to a broader public. At the same time, the "Luther affair" became the catalyst bringing various long-held personal and societal grievances, concerns, and notions of reform to the attention of a larger circle of people. In fact, Luther had himself embraced, in his *Open Letter to the Christian Nobility of the German Nation Concerning the Reform of Christian Society* (1520), a wide range of ecclesiastical and societal reform proposals that had swirled around Germany for the better part of three decades. Thus the compass widened from a narrow set of theological topics to a broad societal agenda. The stage was set for an avalanche of pronouncements that criticized various aspects of societal life, including religion, and urged reform. The call for a "reformation" now became part of the societal discourse.

The flood of pamphlets that issued from the printing presses, large and small, made for a new agenda. As we have seen, while the church was secure in the loyalty of its members, and immoral clergy and corrupt hierarchy existed mainly in the minds of reform propagandists, there were critics and criticisms of church and society. But reform was not, despite the repeated, albeit abortive efforts of the imperial diet to agree on a list of *gravamina* against Rome, "on the front burner." Rather, the avalanche of pamphlets descending on society—not the least those by the most prolific publicist, Luther—undertook a grandiose consciousness-raising. These treatises did so by introducing (in the mind of the contemporaries for the first time a startlingly new category) the notion of the "Word of God"; or to say it differently, they insisted that anything and everything wrong in church and society could be ameliorated by recourse to the "Word." As the splendor of the pristine biblical message was juxtaposed to the grim realities of life, for example, in the woodcuts of Lucas Cranach's *Passional Christi und Antichristi*, the need for reform became all the more patent and evident.

It is not easy to find a proper definition for this "Word," since after all the medieval church had embraced the *Verbum Dei*, the Word of God, with reverence and awe. So what was different? The dynamic impulses of the early 1520s presupposed that this true Word had been perverted and that direct and simple recourse to it would provide the solution and panacea to all ecclesiastical and societal ills. What so strikingly characterizes the writings and pronouncements of those who jumped into the literary fray in the early 1520s was what might well be called a "rhetoric of excess."[1] A penchant for overstatement, for categorical judgments, for assertive pronouncements seemed to carry the day. No matter how different in scope, topic, perspective, the pamphlets all shared a quality of self-confident certainty. The Reformers' pronouncements were not judiciously probing explorations; they were overconfident, and arrogant, and proud. An emotional intensity marked their statements. The world lost its colorful brilliance; it turned into stark black and white—the forces of good versus the forces of evil. The Catholic Church was perverted; all the priests were incompetent; all the monks were immoral; all monasteries and convents were dens of iniquity; all the church was interested in was money, and more money. It was not that some in the

---

1. The term has been applied to insights from biblical and theological studies, e.g., S. H. Webb, "A Hyperbolic Imagination: Theology and the Rhetoric of Excess," *Theology Today* 50 (1993): 56–67.

church had sinned a little; all had sinned a lot. And what the church taught was equally perverted—its disregard of the Bible in favor of human traditions; its rejection of the way of Jesus in favor of the opinions of churchmen.

No wonder, then, that this rhetoric of excess escalated the discourse. Soon there was no more dialogue, no more listening to those who defended old church—most of whom were dumbfounded and stricken with silence. And when all had been said, this rhetoric of excess had been successful. Its emotional intensity had garnered followers and supporters.

The people responded in a surprisingly striking manner to both the criticisms advanced and the reforms proposed. The result of this consciousness-raising was a new mind-set that made the situation in the early 1520s dramatically different. One is tempted to call this public mind-set a "movement," but that would be incorrect. To be sure, before too long a movement did coalesce. But there was an intermediate stage, characterized simply by a new public consciousness, by the universal concern, where there had been no such concern, and by widespread frustration, where there had been no frustration.[2] This new mind-set was relatively vague, undefined, heterogeneous, unstructured, even as it revolved around the twin banners of reform and the Word. Perhaps a kind of "utopian" restlessness and exuberance prevailed in those months and years, the awareness that things ought to be different than they actually were and that the Word would provide the answer. This new mentality brought about a pervasive sense of crisis in church and society.

Social psychologists have told us that a crisis, perceived by individuals or by society, may be real or may be merely imagined.[3] In other words, a "crisis" is as much a psychological as an empirical phenomenon. This insight is relevant for understanding the early stage of the movement of reform, for in the early 1520s men and women became convinced of something they had not been convinced of before, or had not given much thought: there was a crisis in church and society and the "Word" was the God-given tool to set things straight. It matters little, therefore, that one can cull from the rich matrix of pre-sixteenth-century theology a voice here and there that bestowed a crucial primacy to the Word. What was missing was a sense of deliverance from a profound predicament, from a deep crisis. If we ask what made the early 1520s so dramatically different, the answer is clear enough: Luther and the other Reformers succeeded in persuading their contemporaries of the stark reality of crisis and the "Word" as panacea, solution, and lodestar.

The general sense of crisis overshadowed nagging details as to what, exactly, was in crisis in church or society. Some followed Luther's lead in the matter, others the free-wheeling pamphleteering of Ulrich von Hutten or Eberlin von Günzburg. Between 1522 and 1526 Eberlin published some three dozen pamphlets, all of which advocated reform and defined reform in the broadest way. The pamphlets were concerned

2. I am using the term "public consciousness" as a rendering of Jürgen Habermas's term *Öffentlichkeit*, delineated in his *Strukturwandel der Öffentlichkeit: Untersuchungen zu einer Kategorie der bürgerlichen Gesellschaft* (Frankfurt am Main: 1990), Engl. tr. *The Structural Transformation of the Public Sphere* (Cambridge: 1989).

3. This is the thesis of Kai T. Erikson's provocative monograph, *Wayward Puritans: A Study in the Sociology of Deviance* (New York: 1966).

about religious matters as well as economic and political issues, and expressed diverse religious views. While Luther was a forceful voice in this chorus, his role must be seen as that of a catalyst rather than of the towering leader. If we understand that the dominant issue was how to employ the Word of God as the solution to a profound crisis, it becomes clear how more and more people were able to reconcile their endorsement of Luther, even though he was a declared heretic and a political outlaw, with allegiance to the Catholic Church. At least at the outset—things were to change radically before too long—there was surprisingly little tension between the two.

So, a movement coalesced. There is a rich sociological literature on social-religious movements, though there is, alas, no full agreement as to their features.[4] Nonetheless, a few salient features stand out. A social-religious movement involves a group of people who are involved in a common purpose; it is a source of spiritual and political empowerment that involves attempts to alter the existing order; it is global in scope, effects, action, and practice; it articulates both defensive (reactive) and offensive (proactive) claims; it interprets and meliorates personal crisis of meaning and identity.[5] If one applies these criteria to the situation in Germany in the early 1520s, the foremost feature of the emerging Reformation movement was the evolution of a common consciousness of spiritual and political empowerment.

The coalescing movement was thus a movement with a general rather than a specific focus. While it did have a negative aspect—one pamphlet had the title *The Main Articles in Which Christendom Has Heretofore Been Misled* (Hauptartickel durch welch), while another offered *A Christian Warning to All Christians How the Gospel Is to Be Understood* (Ermanung des missbrachs)—the thrust was positive. Even as it lacked clear theological assertions, it possessed no cohesiveness. Pamphleteers propounded a general vision of how the crisis could be overcome by recourse to the "Word." In more and more communities ministers proclaimed new notions, Huldrych Zwingli in Zurich, Andreas Osiander in Nuremberg, or Urbanus Rhegius in Augsburg. Contemporaries began to call the adherents of the emerging movement "Martinians," yet another indication of Luther's perceived prominence.

The medium of propaganda was the sermon. To be sure, sermons were not at all new in the early 1520s, as Protestant historians used to argue, but had an important ancestry, in Geiler von Kaysersberg, for example, or even Savonarola, the one preaching to great renown in Strassburg, the other combining fiery eschatological frenzy with political activism in Florence. As Zwingli's appointment to the position of Leutpriester in Zurich suggests, increasing attention was paid to preaching in the pre-Reformation church. But the vital focus, unchallenged and majestically in the center whenever faithful Catholics gathered for worship, continued to be the Mass. What began to be characterstic in the emerging centers of reform activity in the 1520s was that the pulpit became the pivotal vehicle of a call for religious and societal reform. The Luther affair became a movement through the sermon.

Sermons were preached and sermons were also published. Another catalyst of the coalescing movement, strikingly related to the sermon, was the printed page. A tech-

4. See the summary appraisal in John A. Harrigan, "Social Movement Theory and the Sociology of Religion: Toward a New Synthesis," *Sociological Analysis* 52 (1991): 311–31.

5. Ibid., 329–30.

nological innovation—Gutenberg's invention of movable type—half a century earlier had created unheard-of possibilities for the dissemination of ideas. Readily available as printing had become by the early sixteenth century, it might have been a tool for both sides of the Reformation controversy; however, it was utilized mainly by the proponents of change, much to the detriment of those who defended the established church. The historian may offer any number of conjectures why that was so—that the defenders of the old faith focused their attention on the theological polemic; that they lacked the gift of popular discourse; that the old church was weak—with few exceptions, the agenda was set by those who advocated reform. Without the creative utilization of the printing press the Reformers would have been bereft of their single most effective means of communication and propaganda.

Even the contemporaries understood this significance, including none other than Luther himself, who praised printing as a divine gift for spreading the gospel.[6] Others echoed this sentiment; for example, John Foxe, the English martyrologist and chronicler of the English Reformation, introduced his narrative of the Reformation with a lengthy commentary on the invention of printing: "To restore the church again by doctrine and learning, it pleased God to open to man the art of printing."

What took place during those early years was the revolutionary shift from a luxury item, the book, to a "mass article," the pamphlet. It was the creative appropriation of a format of publication that had hardly been much in use—the pamphlet, the brief, eight- or sixteen-page publication, unbound—that exerted an enormous impact. Without pamphlets, the movement of reform would hardly have gained momentum. The pamphlets offered the means of transmitting ideas from one locale to another. People who had never set foot outside the walls of their community, for whom Saxony and Zurich, or Alstedt and Augsburg, were located at the edge of the universe, could with the help of the pamphlets read the very words their authors had preached to their congregations.

Two catalysts, then, the one dependent on a technological invention, the other on the oratorical feats of individuals, were crucial for creating a movement. The common denominator of both sermon and pamphlet was the appeal to the "common man," the common people, the artisans and burghers in the cities, and to some extent the peasants out in the country; in other words, those whose enthusiasm for the new "gospel" and the "Word" carried the story forward.

In addition, the passing of time brought the increasing sharpening of the theological focus on the part of the "Martinians." In fact, their homogeneity had been more ideal than real; they were muddled by differences of emphasis and perspective, and as time passed this divergence of theological positions became more evident. Disagreements arose over the theological propensity of the "Lutheran" movement, and these disagreements promptly began to dominate the scene.

The mounting recourse to the "Word" as the means to ameliorate the sense of crisis entailed an increasing awareness that reform meant practical change. If the care for the poor in a community was to be the responsibility of that community, and not of the church, resources and structures had to be found to make this possible. If monastic vows were unbiblical, something had to be done about the ubiquitous monasteries

6. WA TR 1:523; and 2:649, "per eam enim Deus toti terrarum orbi voluit negotium verae religionis."

and convents in town and country. If the sacrifice of the Mass was called into question, its celebration had to be discontinued. The awareness of a myriad of possible practical ramifications of proposed ameliorations of the crisis in church and society promptly triggered disagreement about strategy: should the changes be undertaken now or later?

Different partisans of the reform cause, in other words, had different ideas of the details of the new faith they were proclaiming. Their disagreements were intense, an indication of the depth of emotional and existential engagement. Indeed, the clash among the various "reforming" factions became as vehement as that between the reformers and Catholics. The Reformation became a house divided, and a loss of inner strength and resilience was the consequence. When, in the years after 1525, the great decisions affecting the future of the Reformation movement were made in the councils of state, Luther and Zwingli were preoccupied with their bitter feud over the interpretation of the Lord's Supper.

The outward manifestation of these disagreements was the emergence of several theological-ecclesiastical factions for which new labels became necessary. As a result, the term "Martinian" underwent change; it became specific, exclusive, detailed, no longer referring to adherents of the reform movement in general. New labels appeared, such as "Zwinglian," "Anabaptist," and "Calvinist." Opposition to Rome as expressed in the label "evangelical" no longer sufficed as the mark of distinction. The hallmark of each grouping became its uniqueness vis-à-vis the other Protestant groupings.

THE AFTERMATH OF WORMS

The news of Luther's dramatic disappearance spread quickly. Of course, only a few knew what had actually happened, and most were convinced of foul play—that in violation of his safe conduct Luther had been arrested, perhaps even killed. The artist Albrecht Dürer penned some moving lines in his diary upon learning of Luther's disappearance: "O God, if Luther is dead, who will henceforth proclaim to us the holy Gospel?"[7] Later, in 1526, when Dürer painted the four apostles as a gift for the Nuremberg city council, he had these words inserted at the bottom of the two gigantic panels: "all secular rulers in these dangerous times must exercise great care that they do not accept human enticements as God's word."[8] This was quite a change from the words in his *Gedenkbuch* (Memorial Book) at the death of his mother in 1514, when he wrote that she had "died in a Christian manner, supplied with all sacraments, freed by papal authority from punishment and guilt."[9] Elector Frederick had decided to hide Luther at a safe place, presumably until the storm had blown over. The place was the Wartburg, an eleventh-century castle on the outskirts of the town of Eisenach,

7. E. Heidrich, *Albrecht Dürer's schriftlicher Nachlass* (Berlin: 1908), 96.

8. "Alle weltliche Regenten in disen ferlichen zeitten Nemen billicht acht, das sie nit fur das gottlich wort menschliche verfuerung annemen."

9. Albrecht Dürer, *Gedenkbuch,* "verschiden crystlich mit allen sacramenten, aus pepstlicher gewalt von pein und schuld geabsolfyrt" (died in a Christian way with all sacraments, absolved by papal power from all punishment and guilt).

rich in history, later utilized by Richard Wagner for his medieval operatic themes. Luther's identity was not known to the various attendants in the castle, only to its captain. Luther had removed his monastic habit and began to sport a beard. He was "Junker Jörg," Knight George. His home during his stay from May 1521 to March 1522 was a small room, where in feverish activity of some ten weeks he translated the New Testament into German, a feat made possible because Luther had thoughtfully put a copy of the Greek New Testament in his satchel when the masked highwaymen kidnapped him.

We do not know if Emperor Charles had at the time considered apprehending Luther at Worms; he observed many years later that it had been a major mistake of his rule to have honored Luther's safe conduct. While there seems to be persuasive logic in this purported insight of hindsight—had Luther been promptly apprehended and punished as a heretic, the storm might have yet proved to be a tempest in a teapot—things were not quite that simple. The deliberations at Worms had surely demonstrated to Charles the extent of support for due process in Luther's case; the emperor's edict was unequivocal in spelling out how to deal with the declared heretic. Nothing expressed better Charles's self-confidence that he had dealt adequately with all of the German problems than his immediate departure for Spain upon the formal adjournment of the diet in May of 1521.

Charles conveniently overlooked what was, in fact, taking place: the dynamics of events had outrun Luther. To be sure, Luther had been the catalyst of both the indulgences controversy and the creation of a widespread awareness of a crisis in church and society. At the same time, he had also provided the liberating solution for this crisis, the "Word." But soon the crisis and solution of the coalescing movement were far more crucial—not to mention the stark reality that for all practical purposes it seemed indeed as though Luther were dead, certainly for that better part of the year between May 1521 and early March 1522, when he returned to Wittenberg. The issue was not, as Charles assumed, a single monk with heretical ideas, but a movement of increasingly widespread dimension. Thus neither the honoring of Luther's safe conduct nor Elector Frederick's melodramatic intervention should be seen as crucial.

And Luther? The drama and tension of the preceding weeks and months had left their mark on him. His dismay over having inadvertently become embroiled in a controversy, his conviction that he had discovered the authentic message of the gospel, his clarion call that church and society were in a deep crisis that only the "Word" would resolve, his nagging awareness that he had challenged a long and honorable tradition—all these caused intense spiritual turmoil. He knew, of course, that the emperor had declared him an outlaw, and that any day, any moment, the emperor's charges might disturb the idyllic peace of the Wartburg, break into his room, and haul him away in chains to the pyre. "My heart often trembled and pounded and reproached me," Luther wrote. "Are you alone wise? Is everyone else in error? Have so many centuries been in ignorance? What if you have been wrong and dragged many with you into error and eternal damnation?"[10]

---

10. WA 8:421, "wie, wenn du yrrest und sso viel leit yn yrthum verfurest, wilche all ewiglich verdamnet wurden?" (what if you are in error, lead many people into eternal temptation?).

Luther devoted himself to vigorous studying, which proved to be both a therapeutic help and a theological challenge. Several of his most influential works flowed from his pen during those months at the Wartburg, beginning with a volume of sermons in German, expressing the profound insight that the vehicle for the communication of the new gospel had to be the sermon, so as to engage the men and women in the pews. Luther used the prescribed Scripture passages from the Epistles and the Gospels to reflect on issues of Christian faith and life.[11] This *Kirchenpostille* (Church Postil) could be read privately, of course, but it was mainly intended for clergy, who could read the sermons from the pulpit. Indeed, Luther encouraged this use of his sermon book; he astutely surmised that many clergy did not know how to write and deliver a sermon, and felt they deserved help. Thus Luther's words echoed from a thousand pulpits and the mouths of clergy for decades, if not centuries, to come, in later years undoubtedly more for the sake of convenience than lack of training. In his book Luther offered an intriguing homiletical distinction between "teaching" and "exhortation," the former transmitting knowledge about the faith, the latter inspiring the faithful to live it.

Later that year Luther began to reflect on the issue that had become paramount in Wittenberg and elsewhere: were monastic vows valid? The problem was of extreme urgency. Monks and nuns had heard the message that the monastic life lacked biblical justification. But these nuns and monks had made the monastic vows (we today would speak of sacred oaths), and the agonizing problem for many, even as for Luther himself, was whether their vows, made to God, were more important than new insights about the monastic life. Luther's treatise on monastic vows, published under the title *De votis monasticis M. Lutheri iudicium* (M. Luther's Judgment Concerning Monastic Vows), in February 1522, was yet another salvo against the traditional understanding of the Christian faith. As far as Luther was concerned, the very heart of the gospel was at stake: the fundamental conviction that humans could not offer any "good work" to God. Luther bluntly declared the monastic institutions, heretofore understood as the very epitome of Christian commitment, to be a denial of true faith and true Christian freedom.

Luther could hardly have put forward a more revolutionary pronouncement, especially since he thereby opened the door for nuns and monks to renounce, in Christian freedom, the vows they had made. Luther maintained that the monastic vow of celibacy brought about a permanent inner conflict and that the vows of poverty and ecclesiastical obedience ran counter to Scripture. Luther noted subsequently that he himself would "remain [in the celibate state] where I am." He dedicated his treatise to his father (with lengthy reflections on his conflict with him at the time of his entrance into the monastery, when his father had pointed out that alongside his son's monastic vows there was also the commandment to honor father and mother). Luther's words show the depth of his own feelings even as they suggest that the conflict with his father was beginning to be resolved.[12]

---

11. WA 10, 1/1:1ff.

12. The treatise is in WA 8:564ff., Luther's comment in WA 10, 1/1:708. The psychoanalyst Erik Erikson's *Young Man Luther: A Study in Psychoanalysis and History* (New York: 1958), sought to understand Luther from the perspective of his conflict with his father. The book received few endorsements from historians, but enthusiastic responses from social scientists.

Luther wrote an important treatise immediately upon his arrival at the Wartburg. The Louvain theologian Jacobus Latomus had taken up Luther's charge that Catholic teaching did not conform to Scripture and had produced in his *Articulorum doctrinae fratros Martini per theologos Louaniensis damnatorum Ratio ex sacris literis et veteribus tractoribus* (Explanation, from Sacred Writings and the Writings of the Fathers of the Articles), a learned and thorough treatise that could be neither ignored nor labeled an exercise in "human traditions." Latomus's treatise was a reach for Luther's jugular since Latomus, endlessly citing Scripture, argued the case for Catholic doctrine on the basis of a consensus of Scripture, the ancient fathers, and scholastic theologians. Luther's response, *Rationis Latomianiae pro incendiaries Louaniensis scholae sophistis reddita, Lutheriana confutatio* (A Lutheran Rejection of the Explanation of Latomus), challenged Latomus's notions arguing the utter clarity of Scripture, which, because of its clarity, did not need an interpretive authority. Theologically, Luther's treatise also elaborated his understanding of sin, including the nature of the Christian life, which is forever deeply embedded in sin.

Luther's other literary efforts focused on the church requirement of confession and a bout with Archbishop Albert of Mainz. Albert had organized an ambitious exhibit of relics in a church in Halle, hoping to fill his coffers through the sale of indulgences connected with pilgrimages to the church. Albert was devastatingly short of cash. Luther learned about Albert's plan at the same time he also learned of how the ecclesiastical authorities in Mainz had begun to pursue priests who had married.

Luther apprised Elector Frederick's secretary, George Spalatin, of his intention to make a public pronouncement in the matter, who promptly alerted Albert of what was in the offing. Using diplomatic channels, Albert retorted that Luther should be silenced, a threat that hardly fazed Luther, who remained adamant. In a bold and aggressive letter, Luther told Albert that he would indeed go public, both about the indulgence connected with the Halle relics and also about Albert's stern measures against priests. The latter point was touchy, since it was well and widely known that Albert had a concubine. Albert's response was amazingly conciliatory. He promised Luther that in the future he would act as became a "pious, spiritual, and Christian prince."[13]

Amid his other concerns Luther's main effort during his Wartburg stay was directed to a project that over time constituted his most significant contribution to both religion and society—the German translation of the Bible. Luther's assertion that Scripture was the sole norm of faith raised the necessity of the availability of Scripture in the vernacular; how otherwise could the common people make it their norm?

Luther's translation was one of his pillar achievements. To this day, the *Luther Bibel* continues as the widely used German translation of the Bible, despite various revisions through the centuries. It has often been cited as the major influence that made Luther's Saxon dialect (which he used) the normative German language. Friedrich Nietzsche, master of German prose and no friend of Luther, found high words of commendation: "In comparison with Luther's Bible, almost everything is just literature, that is, it is a thing that has not grown in Germany and has not grown, and is not growing, into German hearts as the Bible has done."[14]

German translations of the New Testament existed before Luther; his translation was not at all novel. If it was a sensation, while earlier translations, scarcely tolerated by the church, had fallen into oblivion, the explanation lies in the change of the religious and even societal climate in Germany. The theological controversy had been taken to the people, and in so doing had involved an unheard-of use of the vernacular. Virtually all of the pamphlets flooding from the printing presses were in German, prompting Eberlin von Günzburg to write in 1521, "German books are becoming numerous, and one finds these days all of divine and human wisdom in the German language."[15]

Moreover, in the span of less than half a decade, Luther had succeeded in persuading his contemporaries of the pivotal importance of Scripture and its crucial role in defining the Christian faith. As important as the translation itself, then, was Luther's defining a new consciousness about Scripture. Theretofore people had been content to let the church expound the Scriptures and had accepted the church's notion that tradition was as important as Scripture. Luther's plea for men and women was to read and to study, for Scripture was clear and needed no formal interpreter. Thus it had to be available in the vernacular.

Luther's flair for language, so evident in all of his writings, made the words of the Bible come alive and breathe an exhilarating spirit. It showed Luther's remarkable eloquence. Luther himself observed in his *Sendbrief vom Dolmetschen* (Open Letter about Translating), which he wrote when his opponents charged him with gross mistranslations, that the translator must "look at the people's mouths," that is, use contemporary idiom to express historical language. In so doing he transformed biblical Galilee into Saxony and biblical Jerusalem into Wittenberg. The personages of the Gospels, their speech, their customs, their environment, became those of the sixteenth century. When Jesus spoke to his disciples, he spoke as a burgher in Wittenberg or Nuremberg would speak to his neighbors. Lucas Cranach's woodcuts, which accompanied the text, conveyed the same message by providing a sixteenth-century setting for the biblical events. In a way, the biblical iconography of fifteenth- and sixteenth-century religious paintings both anticipated and reinforced Luther's approach, for the men and women who populate Grunewald's or Brueghel's paintings of the crucifixion, for example, are those of the painters' own time.

It took Luther just about ten weeks to complete his translation of the New Testament. After his return to Wittenberg in March of 1522, he solicited the help of Philip Melanchthon's linguistic competence. The translation appeared in September 1522 and became known as the "September Bible." Two reprints within months followed, ·and there were some fifty reprintings within four years, attesting to the phenomenal popularity (and perhaps successful marketing) of Luther's translation. Understandably, Catholics were less impressed by Luther's feat, but neither the offer, of Duke

14. As quoted in H. Bornkamm, *Luther im Spiegel der deutschen Geistesgeschichte* (Heidelberg: 1955), 228.

15. Ludwig Enders, ed., *Johannes Eberlin von Günzburg, Sämtliche Schriften* (Halle a. S.: 1900), 69.

George of Saxony, to reimburse the purchase price to anyone turning in a copy of Luther's translation nor the speedy publication of a translation by Luther's arch foe Hieronymus Emser diminished the popularity of Luther's work. Catholics quickly charged that at some places Luther translated rather loosely. For example, he had rendered Romans 3:28 to read: "the just shall live by faith *alone*," even though the Greek text did not include the word "alone." Scripture à la Luther proclaimed Luther's gospel. Luther claimed that he did not intend to falsify the text and pointed out that none other than Thomas Aquinas had translated the verse the same way.[16] Luther made the change, as he wrote in his *Sendbrief vom Dolmetschen,* because his wording expressed the meaning of the passage and conformed to the structure of the Greek language.[17]

When Luther's translation of the New Testament was published, it included a preface on how Scripture was to be understood, and this preface equaled the translation in importance, for here Luther delineated his hermeneutic principles. While it might be seen as a strange turn of events for Luther, who argued that Scripture was clear and self-evident, to provide an introductory guide to how to understand Scripture (as did, by the way, virtually all sixteenth-century Protestant vernacular translations), the controversy with Latomus, who had extensively quoted Scripture to support the Catholic position, had forced Luther to recognize that *sola scriptura* was a problematic source of authority. Scripture was heterogeneous; a principle was necessary to transform this heterogeneity into a consistent whole. It was not enough to quote Scripture; it had to be quoted properly. Was the Catholic Church therefore correct when it insisted on the need for authoritative interpretation by the church? In the preface of his translation, Luther offered his answer. To be an authentic source of faith a biblical passage must "Christum treiben," "proclaim Christ."[18] Luther insisted that not all of Scripture did so: certainly not the Epistle of James (an "epistle of straw," Luther remarked, that is, not worth much), certainly not the book of Revelation. Luther was also ambivalent about the Synoptic Gospels but spoke most highly of the Gospel of John, of Romans, Galatians, Ephesians, and 1 Peter.

Luther's rather open attitude toward certain parts of Scripture (he did not acknowledge that all parts were created equal) was surely problematic. Luther eased his blunt differentiation in later years to make sure that no one understood him to advocate a revision of the biblical canon. The Epistle of James, after all, was in the canon, and Luther never questioned the decision of the early church in this regard. He meant to call attention to the fact that not all of the Christian canon equally expressed the divine salvation history culminating in Jesus Christ. A hermeneutic principle was necessary, and Luther found this principle in Paul, or, more precisely, in Romans 1:17. This passage was, for Luther, the theme and the key to the New Testament and indeed the entire Bible. Luther acknowledged that Paul's assertion of justification by faith alone and James's notion of justification by works needed to be harmonized—without invoking the authority of the church—and his conclusion was that such harmony

---

16. In contemporary discussion the argument that translations always entail bias has been variously advanced. See, for example, Edwin Gentzler, *Contemporary Translation Theories* (Clevedon, UK: 2001).

17. WA 30, 2:636ff.

18. WA Deutsche Bibel 7:385.

could be attained by looking at all of Scripture. If one took the entire Bible seriously, Luther concluded, one would be compelled to interpret all of it through the message of Paul: James and the Synoptic Gospels had to be interpreted through Paul, rather than vice versa.

Modern biblical scholars have not only questioned Luther's positing the centrality of Paul in the entire canon; they have also challenged Luther's (and the subsequent Lutheran tradition's) interpretation of Paul, specifically his understanding of the law.[19]

REFORM INSTITUTIONALIZED

In the summer of 1521 several Wittenberg theologians, notably Andreas Carlstadt and Philip Melanchthon (Luther, of course, was in hiding at the Wartburg), discussed with friars from the Augustinian monastery whether the new theological insights mandated changes in prevailing ecclesiastical practice. The prime issues were clerical celibacy and the validity of monastic vows, but promptly two other topics—the role of the secular authorities in religious reform and Communion under both kinds—came to the fore. There seemed to be agreement that practical "reforms" were necessary and that they should be carried out at once. This quest for practical reform beyond theological reflection constituted a dramatic step, for it meant taking the controversy unleashed by Luther into the realm of ecclesiastical practice.

Changes took place promptly. In September Melanchthon and some of his students received both bread and wine in a Communion service, and soon thereafter the Augustinian friar Gabriel Zwilling began to preach against the Mass, particularly the so-called private Masses as well as the notion of the sacrifice of the Mass. With such agitation, changes were bound to be imminent. Luther, who in his pastoral idyll at the Wartburg was regularly informed of what was going on in Wittenberg, made a clandestine visit to Wittenberg to show his support of practical reform.

Luther had left Wittenberg back in early April 1521 at a crucial moment. He had urged reform based on the Word of God, but who should determine the necessary reforms: the theologians, such as Luther, or the pastors, or the secular authorities? Should one wait for the church at large to order changes, for a general council of the church, perhaps? Were cities and territories free to proceed on their own?

Later, elsewhere in Europe, such as in England, the political authorities quickly took charge of the processes of ecclesiastical and societal reform. But they enjoyed the benefit of knowing how reforms had begun to be undertaken in Germany in the early 1520s. That benefit was the result of hindsight; at the time uncertainty prevailed as to how to proceed. Luther himself was of little help; his sojourn at the Wartburg kept him removed from the involvement in ecclesiastical practices that in Wittenberg increasingly led to disturbed consciences. For a while, in Wittenberg, as in other centers of reform, the new message of reform did not seem to lead to actual reform. Tra-

---

19. My distinguished colleague E. P. Sanders has been a major contributor to this debate, which involves the charge that Luther misunderstood the Jewish understanding of the law; see especially his *Paul* (New York: 2001).

ditional ecclesiastical and community practices continued as if nothing had happened: the Mass was celebrated as it had been for centuries, the Communion cup continued to be withheld from the laity, life in the monasteries was what it always had been. Was that proper in light of the new theological insights? If not, what was to be done?

It was one thing, however, to call for a conformity of ecclesiastical practice with biblical insight, but quite another to know exactly which practices were biblically legitimate. The simplest—and certainly the most consistent—answer was that Scripture contained explicit instructions on every topic; the difficult answer was that for some ecclesiastical practices no explicit biblical warrant existed.

The issue was one of principle as well as expediency. The first practice challenged in Wittenberg—and subsequently in just about every place the reform movement found partisans—was the Mass, especially the withholding of the cup from the laity, the "private masses," and the sacrifice of the Mass. In December things grew a bit tumultuous in Wittenberg. Early that month students harangued priests who were about to celebrate Mass in the town church and subsequently did the same with monks from the Franciscan monastery in town. The city council was dismayed and spoke of "disturbances" (*Aufruhr*), a term subsequently used by Elector Frederick and by historians ever since. In fact, they were nothing but student pranks. What took place in Wittenberg during those cold days of December, January, and February was a lot of verbal agitation, students and burghers taking sides one way or the other and arguing intensely, with isolated instances of student unruliness and iconoclasm. Subsequent Protestant hagiography (as well as Catholic dismay) turned this fairly benign event into the "Wittenberg disturbances," as if the city's rule of law and order had been completely overturned.

The elector demanded that the disturbers of the public peace be punished, with the city council blaming the students, over whom it had no authority, for the problem. Into this rather tense situation burst Carlstadt's announcement that he would celebrate an "evangelical mass" on New Year's Day. When the elector prohibited it, Carlstadt proceeded (with exquisite legalism) to celebrate such a "Mass" on Christmas Day. On that day, the centuries-long customs of a revered ecclesiastical rite were abandoned. The service began with a Communion homily, followed by a new liturgy that had been stripped of anything suggestive of a sacrificial meaning. The words of institution were spoken in German, and Carlstadt performed the ceremony in simple clothes—in his "shirtsleeves," as a hostile observer noted. There must have been many curious souls in the town church on that occasion, as well as partisans of the new gospel; an eyewitness reported that everyone of rank and station in Wittenberg had come to witness the radical break with liturgical and theological tradition. Clearly, it was an occasion both radical and awkward. When a consecrated host fell onto the ground, none of the worshipers dared pick it up. Carlstadt uttered repeated entreaties to bystanders but eventually had to pick up the wafer himself.

Soon therafter Carlstadt volunteered to read publicly a chapter from the Bible each day. He also instigated further changes in the liturgy: images were to be removed from churches, and the elaborate singing in the Mass was to be discontinued, Carlstadt comparing such singing to "shrieking geese." He also startled everyone with his announcement that rather than celebrate Mass, he would purchase a house in Wittenberg and earn his living as a beer brewer and innkeeper, undoubtedly (as far as he was concerned) the ultimate manifestation of the new notion of the priesthood of all believers.[20]

The agitation for change came from university faculty, such as Carlstadt, from students, from Augustinian friars. On the other hand, the Franciscan monastery in town and the chapter of the Castle Church were adamantly against change, while the Wittenberg city council, in sympathy with the proponents of reform, was primarily concerned that things not get out of hand. Elector Frederick, informed of the restless situation, demanded that the sacrament be treated in a "most orderly and Christian fashion," that images not be removed from churches, and that Carlstadt, who seemed to be the driving force behind the quest for reform, not be allowed to preach.

At this juncture, political considerations intruded. The rulers of Albertine Saxony, Brandenburg, and Braunschweig, all loyal Catholics, prohibited students from their territories to study at Wittenberg. The same rulers had also brought about a mandate of the *Reichsregiment* of January 20, 1522, which prohibited all changes in established Catholic worship and specifically admonished Elector Frederick to make sure that traditional worship continued in Wittenberg and elsewhere in Electoral Saxony. Luther, kept abreast of the Wittenberg happenings, wrote a treatise entitled *Vermahnung M. Luthers zu allen Christen, sich zu hüten vor Aufruhr und Empoerung* (M. Luther's Admonition to All Christians Not to Be Involved in Uproar and Rebellion).[21] The January mandate of the *Reichsregiment* and the evident concerns of Elector Frederick led Luther to conclude that the exuberance of those who pushed for reform in Wittenberg endangered the larger effort at reform. In early March Luther returned to Wittenberg without having secured Elector Frederick's approval; Luther merely informed him of his decision, adding that because Frederick was still weak in the faith, he could not protect or save him anyhow.

Much depended on Luther's stance at this point. Would he follow Carlstadt's example and preside over an evangelical Communion service in his shirtsleeves? Would he insist that biblical norms and practices be implemented at once? His answers came in a series of sermons known as the Invocavit Sermons (for the Sunday Invocavit of the church year on which he preached the first sermon). Those present in the overcrowded town church on that Sunday could discern Luther's answer before he ever opened his mouth for the first sentence of his first sermon on the first day. Luther stood in the pulpit, wearing the habit of an Augustinian monk and with a freshly shaved tonsure (gone were the beard and the knight's attire he had sported during his ten months at the Wartburg), as if nothing had happened ever since his Ninety-five Theses precipitated the controversy. That is how the Wittenbergers had seen him preach all these years, and that is how he stood in front of them—as if he had never preached against monasticism, never argued against monastic vows, and as if he himself had not been the foremost agent of calling for reform.

"We are all called upon to die," Luther began his sermon, "and then you will not be with me nor will I be with you. We may well shout into one another's ears, but we

20. Wolfgang Simon, "Karlstadt neben Luther. Ihre theologische Differenz im Kontext der 'Wittenberger Unruhen' 1521/22," in *Frömmigkeit—Theologie—Frömmigkeitstheologie. Festschrift für Berndt Hamm zum 60. Geburtstag* (ed. Gudrun Litz, Heidrun Munzert, and Roland Liebenberg; Leiden: 2005), 317–34.
21. WA Br 2:410.

must all die by ourselves, alone." What a strange way to begin a sermon on the expediency of liturgical change! Luther was seeking to focus on a fundamental point: in the hour of one's death, only the truly important issues of the Christian faith will matter. The peripheral and secondary issues will have no importance at all.

Luther then enunciated a vision of the faith where externals were secondary, where Communion under both kinds, pictures and statues in churches, monastic vows, and clerical marriage were, in the final analysis, insignificant and secondary issues. If true Christians are those who take the Communion wafer into their hands rather than have the priest place it on their tongues, said Luther referring to a point of controversy, then sows can also be Christian, since they too can take the wafer with their snouts. Hearts must first be changed, and this can only by done by the Word. Luther told the crowded gathering in the town church that he had preached the Word of God—and "while I was sleeping or drinking Wittenberg beer with my friends Philip [Melanchthon] and Amsdorf, the papacy was damaged more than any ruler or emperor had ever been able to do."[22]

Luther's return meant that the challenge was no longer to turn Wittenberg overnight into a "Christian city." At issue, more narrowly, was a strategy of slow yet deliberate reform, characterized by a concern for those weak in faith, who needed time to understand and accept change. Luther promptly published several tracts dealing with the controversial topics, including one on the "two forms of Communion": *Von beider gestalt des Sacraments zu nehmen*, whose title bore an uncanny resemblance to a tract his colleague Carlstadt had earlier published in November 1521 (*Von beiden Gestalten der heiligen Messe*). Initially Carlstadt had been a moderating influence on the course of events in Wittenberg, recognizing the need for patience and acknowledging the authority of the city council not to mention the elector to determine the scope and timing of reform. However, over time he had become caught up in the dynamics of the quest for change and emerged as one of the driving forces advocating immediate reform. Luther's strategy of making haste slowly, which the elector's counsellors had argued, strained the relationship between the two colleagues to the breaking point: Carlstadt saw in Luther a weak compromiser, while Luther found Carlstadt a danger to the success of reform.

THE NATURE OF THE CHANGE

In the spring of 1521 the papal nuncio Aleander reported from Worms that "daily there is a veritable downpour of Lutheran tracts in German and Latin . . . nothing is sold here except Luther's tracts."[23] Aleander may have exaggerated the German situation to convey its seriousness to Rome, but there can be no doubt that something was taking place, expressed by an avalanche of reform pamphlets. That turn of events, both novel and revolutionary, conveyed that at issue was no longer a single individual but a widespread concern and yearning.

---

22. WA 10, 3:5.
23. P. Kalkoff, *Die Depeschen des Nuntius Aleander* (Halle: 1886), 44.

In his pamphlet *Von den guten Werken* (Sermon on Good Works) Luther acknowl-edged that he had been accused of "writing only little tracts and German sermons" and retorted, "I am not ashamed that I preached and wrote in German for the unlearned laity—even though I can also do it the other way—for I do believe that if we had been more concerned about these matters in the past, Christendom would show more improvement than has been the case from the high and mighty books and the questions typical of the academicians of the universities."[24] To be sure, both the accusation and the response may have reflected narrow academic prejudice and pride, but Luther's comment did touch on an important aspect of the early Reformation controversy: he employed a rather unusual means of conveying his message. Of course, he too was one of those "academicians of the universities" who wrote massive tomes in Latin, on topics sometimes important, sometimes not. Some of these made a pro-found impact on their own time and beyond—one thinks of Thomas Aquinas's *Summa theologiae*—and the history of theology is hardly thinkable without them.

It would appear from Luther's statement that he was well aware of the limitations (and consequences) of such an approach ("Christendom would show more improve-ment") and that his preaching and writing "little tracts" in the German vernacular were a deliberate strategy on his part. At stake was the question of how to bring about change. Should the appeal be to the elites—the intellectual powerbrokers—or to the common people? In the course of human affairs both strategies have been used, and both have a measure of cogent persuasiveness. In the early sixteenth century Erasmus of Rotterdam, no less committed to reform than Luther, chose the former strategy. By publishing in Latin Erasmus intended to influence the course of events by rallying his fellow intellectuals. In this he undoubtedly was successful, for by the early 1520s "Erasmian" humanists were found throughout Europe. But what he marshaled was a circle of like-minded spirits, not a social movement.

Luther and the other reformers, on the other hand, chose the populist strategy. Although a few of Luther's writings—the *Babylonian Captivity of the Church,* for example, or the *Bondage of the Will*—were heavy-duty theology published in Latin and meant for fellow theologians, his overall strategy was to appeal to the common people in their language in order to make his case and to solicit support for his pro-gram of reform.[25] His first effort to do so came in the spring of 1518 with his expla-nation of the Ninety-five Theses in his German-language *Eyn Sermon von dem Ablass und Gnade* (Sermon on Indulgence and Grace), a kind of defensive gesture to set the record straight about what he believed rather than proposed for debate. The pamphlet was reprinted no less than twenty-three times within three years. Most of Luther's German tracts enjoyed the same popularity. Ten, fifteen, even twenty reprints of a particular pamphlet were not at all unusual. Although any attempt to quantify for sixteenth-century publications how many copies of a given pamphlet were in actual circulation is, given the absence of reliable data, an exercise in conjecture, something on the order of one million copies of Luther's pamphlets may have been in circula-

---

24. WA 6:203.
25. See here the excellent survey by Mark Edwards, *Printing, Propaganda, and Martin Luther* (Berke-ley: 1994), as well as the slightly older work by Elizabeth L. Eisenstein, *The Printing Press as an Agent of Change: Communications and Cultural Transformations in Early Modern Europe* (Cambridge: 1979).

tion by 1524, a stunning figure given that the German population at the time probably numbered only some six million. Luther was joined by a phalanx of other authors who wrote prolifically and stridently on a wide assortment of topics related to reform. The impact made by these publications on the mind-set of the German people would have been unthinkable had these authors written in Latin rather than the vernacular.

But it was not only the vernacular language that gave the pamphlets their particular character; the format of publication also changed. Previously, the quintessential publication had been the book, weighty and voluminous. The new format was the pamphlet (*Flugschrift*)—eight, sixteen, thirty-two pages in length, convenient in use, affordable in price, and accessible in language. While one may trace its antecedents to the fifteenth century—Savonarola in Florence, for example, published some of his sermons in the vernacular in the form of brief pamphlets, while the *Ars Moriendi* (The Art of Dying) was published in illustrated editions (evidently the macabre subject matter enticed artists to pictorial portrayals)—the controversy of the early 1520s altered the landscape. What had been isolated publications turned into a genre. The *Flugschriften* became the means by which the new notions of reform were propagated. They laid the groundwork both for a comprehensive consciousness raising and for the coalescing of a movement.[26]

The use of the vernacular to propound religious ideas had no real precedent. With rare exceptions the religious and theological literature before the Reformation was in Latin, as were the writings of the humanists, such as *Praise of Folly, Julius a coelo exclusus,* or the *Epistolae obscurorum virorum.* The medium of the humanists was Latin, the language of the learned. The humanists were concerned with more than the revival of an elegant and versatile language: their writings expressed a program of reformatory renewal. Their appeal for change was addressed to the educated elites to influence them and, through them, society at large.

Those advocating reform, on the other hand, chose to speak directly to the common people to persuade them. The Reformers' publishing effort was a large-scale attempt to confront the common people with the challenge to take their religion seriously, as Luther had argued in his *Letter to the Christian Nobility,* in which he had implored the laity to help in the reform of the church. The Reformers were concerned about the people—about the artisans and the burghers in the towns, and the peasants in the country. Erasmus had waxed lyrical about his desire to have the peasant recite the words of Sacred Writ behind his plow, but he always wrote in Latin. Theretofore considered incompetent to deal with religious issues, the people found themselves in a different role. They were wooed by these publications and exposed to fervent appeals to embrace the new teaching. Nothing is more symptomatic of this temper than the dramatically new position occupied by the lowliest of the lowly, the peasant. Pamphlets appealed to peasants, depicting them as wise and perceptive observers of the

---

26. U. Weiss, ed., *Flugschriften der Reformationszeit: Colloquium im Erfurter Augustinerkloster 1999* (Tübingen: 2001); Th. Hohenberger, *Lutherische Rechtfertigungslehre in den reformatorischen Flugschriften der Jahre 1521–22* (Tübingen: 1996); B. Moeller, *Städtische Predigt in der Frühzeit der Reformation: Eine Untersuchung deutscher Flugschriften der Jahre 1522 bis 1529* (Göttingen: 1996). The comprehensive bibliography is that of Hans J. Koehler, *Flugschriften als Massenmedium der Reformationszeit: Beiträge zum Tübinger Symposion 1980* (Stuttgart: 1981).

religious controversy, indeed, frequently making them arbiters of the controversy. The pamphlet *Karsthans*, published in 1521 and reprinted no fewer than nine times, made a simple peasant the judge of a theological disagreement between Luther and his Catholic opponent, Thomas Murner.

Luther's own *Eine einfältige Weise zu beten, für einen guten Freund* (A Simple Way to Pray, Written for a Good Friend) illustrated this concern for the propagation of the gospel among the common folk: the "good friend" was Luther's barber. Few theologians in Christian history have bothered to expound the Christian faith to their barber or grocer or neighbor; Luther did so, and with flair and rhetoric. "A competent and conscientious barber must keep his thoughts, mind, and eyes completely on his scissors and the customer's hair. Nor must he forget what he is about—if he talks too much, thinks of other matters, or looks at something else, he is likely to cut his customer's mouth or nose, perhaps even his throat. Anything, if it is to be done well, must be done with complete attention. . . . How much more does prayer call for a single-minded and sole attention, if it is to be good and proper?"[27] The language and style say something about the secret of the Reformation's appeal.

Luther's linguistic elegance, his gift for style, his ability to state a complicated argument simply and succinctly, combining substance with elegance, proved a crucial element in the force of his message. He could on occasion be boring; he could grind on endlessly; he could belabor the obvious. But in general his writings breathe an electrifying spirit. That he was a genius with language can be seen in this description of the burdens (and blessings) of marriage:

> The clever harlot, namely natural reason, comes along, looks at marriage, turns up her nose, and says: "Why should I rock the baby, wash his diapers, change his bed, smell his odor, heal his diaper rash, and do all sorts of such things? It is better to remain single and live a quiet and carefree life." But what does the Christian faith say? A father opens his eyes, looks at all these lowly, distasteful chores—and knows that they are adorned with divine approval as with precious gold and silver. God, and all his angels, will rejoice, not because diapers are changed, but because it is done in faith.[28]

The pamphlets sought to accomplish two purposes: to expound, in simple terms, the need for reform in the understanding of the gospel, and to respond to objections from Catholic antagonists. The latter explains the widespread use of the dialogue, a traditional genre, which made it possible to voice objections (in as vulnerable a form as possible) to the new teaching and then dismiss them with a skillful combination of logic, biblical references, and rhetoric. Today these dialogues appear stilted and not altogether convincing, especially since their eventual outcome is all too obvious from the outset, rather like a minister's sermon on sin. But people of the sixteenth century, unaccustomed to reading anything in their own language, found it all both exciting and persuasive.

The dialogue format offered not only literary dash, but also a subtle kind of argumentation that presented the Catholic demurrers and then eloquently dismissed them.

---

27. WA 38, 368.
28. *Vom ehelichen Leben*, WA 10, 2:295.

The dialogues took place between an endless variety of participants—father and son, student and teacher, Christian and Jew, the Apostle Peter and a peasant, professor and peasant, monk and layman. One pamphlet had no fewer than four participants in the conversation (a priest, peasant, artisan, and monk), while another included Erasmus, Johann Faber, a Catholic theologian—and Satan. Other pamphlets used rhyme to present the new message.

Naturally, these pamphlets moved all too obviously in the direction of the conversion of those who opposed the Lutheran cause. Such was the case, for example, in the *Dialogue between a Father and His Son* (1523), in which, rather in keeping with the youthful orientation of the Reformation as a whole, the son converts his father to the "true faith." In *Ein Gesprech Bruder Heinrichs von Kettenbach mit aim frommen Altmutterlein von Ulm von etlichen Zufeln und Anfechtung des Altmutterlein* (A Conversation of Brother Heinrich of Kettenbach with a Pious Old Widow from Ulm concerning Her Doubts and Temptations; 1523), the widow observed that because Luther had been condemned by the church, he should not be heeded, whereupon "Bruder Heinrich" retorts, "you only need to compare Luther's writings and those of the papists with Sacred Scripture to find that for every error in Luther there are three hundred in the papists."[29]

A variety of other literary forms was used as well—sermons, open letters, poems. There were also satires, such as *Absag oder Fehdschrift Lucifers an Luther* (Satan's Declaration of War against Luther; 1524), and parodies, such as an account of Luther's appearance at Worms clad in the form of the Gospel narratives of Jesus's passion. Another genre of pamphlets purported to speak in the voice of Jesus. Nikolaus Hermann's *Eyn Mandat Jhesu Christi an alle seyne getrewen Christen* (Mandate of Jesus Christ for All His Faithful Christians; 1524), for example, was an appeal from Jesus on behalf of the new interpretation of the gospel. It was reprinted twelve times in the 1520s (twenty-two times in all in the sixteenth century, as well as a few additional times in the early seventeenth century): "I painted and depicted your foe, who his helpers are, with whom he might fight, wolves in sheep's clothing—ecclesiastical, pious, and works-righteous men, Pharisees, scribes, prelates, cardinals, bishops, officials, canons, deans, abbots, monks, popes: all tempters."[30]

The visual arts also played an important role in the transmission of the ideas of reform, from the time the first simple woodcut of Luther made its appearance on the title page of a published sermon of 1519 to Lucas Cranach's drastic, if vulgar, cartoons accompanying Luther's portrayal of the "abomination" of the papacy in the 1540s.[31] Luther became a favorite subject of this propagandistic art. He was depicted as Hercules, with a saintly halo, in knight's armor, while his antagonists were transformed into replicas of the lower animal kingdom. The most popular instance of pictorial propaganda of the early 1520s, the *Passional Christi und Antichristi* (Passion of Christ and Antichrist), depicted in parallel woodcuts the contrast between the simplicity of Christ

29. O. Clemen, ed., *Flugschriften aus den ersten Jahren der Reformation* (repr. Nieuwkoop: 1967), 2:75.
30. Arnold Erich Berger, *Die Sturmtruppen der Reformation* (Leipzig, 1931), 61–62.
31. Martin Luther, *Wider das Papsttum zu Rom vom Teufel gestiftet* (Wittenberg: 1545, in WA 54, 218ff.).

and the splendor of the papacy: Christ washing his disciples' feet, the pope having his feet kissed; Christ wearing a crown of thorns, the pope wearing the papal tiara.[32]

The immense number of these pamphlets makes generalizations about their content difficult. The argument has been made that they were staunchly Lutheran, but this can only mean that they reflected the major themes Luther had published until the mid-1520s rather than what emerged as Lutheran theology later: the centrality of the "Word," salvation by faith alone, or the need for reform. The overwhelming number of pamphlets propounded Luther's theological views in utterly simple form.

A number of key themes were sounded with the monotonous simplicity of Gregorian plainsong: the notion that Scripture, rather than ecclesiastical traditions, was the sole source of the Christian faith; the rejection of "human traditions," the pronouncements of the church and the opinions of theologians; salvation was not by works, but by faith; one did not earn it by striving, but received it by grace; the rejection of the complex medieval understanding of the Christian faith with its ubiquitous mandates in favor of a "simple" faith. Indeed, such simplicity, as found in Luther's tract on Christian freedom, may well be said to have been the key slogan.

This call to the gospel and to reform in church and society was simple. The restoration of the true gospel was to be accomplished by the removal of the welter of human traditions. Men and women were told that theirs was simply to trust that their sins were forgiven upon their confession of sin—and this happened freely without works or efforts on their part. Thus the pamphlet *Eine verständige trostliche Lehre* (An Understandable Comforting Teaching), by Jakob Strauss, argued that "the whole summary of our faith consists in our confession and faith that Christ died for us"—a declaration that surely would have caused no problem for Catholic theologians (it was the fine print that made all the difference) but shows the far-reaching assertions staked out by the Reformers.[33]

The simple gospel, then, concerns a Christian life of faith and trust, not of externals and ritual. Moreover, authentic Christianity allowed for no spiritual distinction between clergy and laity, nor did it claim superiority of the clerical profession over lay vocation. These easily understood assertions electrified the common people. Indeed, they were deeply meaningful to all those who wished for a deeper understanding of the Christian faith. A host of testimonials acknowledged that the new message had effected a kind of conversion. Albrecht Dürer, for example, acknowledged that Luther "had delivered one from terrible distress," while Thomas Müntzer called him "a lamp of the friends of God."[34]

The message was a call for deeper spirituality, for inward spirituality in contrast to a religion of external observances. To be sure, there were theological ramifications (or presuppositions) to what the Reformers were proclaiming and writing. However, the insistence of the advocates for reform on explicit theological particularities and the delineation of new theological systems came later. To be sure, during the first years of

---

32. Bob Scribner explored the various uses of Reformation propaganda with great insight in *For the Sake of Simple Folk: Popular Propaganda for the German Reformation* (New York: 1994).

33. Quoted in G. Blochwitz, "Die antirömischen deutschen Flugschriften der frühen Reformationszeit," *Archiv für Reformationsgeschichte* 27 (1930): 152.

34. G. Franz, ed., *Thomas Müntzer. Schriften und Briefe* (Gütersloh: 1968), 361.

the conflagration, the theologians—Luther, Eck, Carlstadt, and Prierias—were fiercely arguing theological issues, but even a casual glance at Eck's and Carlstadt's theses of 1518 surely conveys that the notions expressed in these documents would hardly have triggered an avalanche of widespread popular response.

Surely it is not accidental that the most popular of Luther's pamphlets included such titles as *Sermon von der Bereitung zum Sterben* (Concerning the Proper Preparation for Dying); *Auslegung Deutsch des Vaterunser für einfältige Laien* (The Lord's Prayer Expounded for Simple Laymen); *Ein Sermon von der Betrachtung des heiligen Leidens Christi* (A Meditation on Christ's Passion); *Tröstung für eine Person* (Comfort When Facing Grave Temptations); *Sermon von der würdigen Empfahun* (A Sermon on the Worthy Reception of the Sacrament). These pamphlets conveyed the central point of Luther's concern, the recovery of true spirituality. We can thus speak of the initial reform impulses as a "recultivation of the vineyard," when, despite the increasing awareness of underlying theological issues, the consuming emphasis was on the enhancement of spirituality.[35] However, it also became quickly obvious that false theology was the cause of the lack of spirituality in the church.

Reformation historians have argued that the quest for reform beginning in 1518 enjoyed immense popular support, and that without the support of the common people the reform initiative would have remained unsuccessful.[36] The strategies of communication employed by the Reformers focused not so much on the learned elites as on the people, particularly on the opinion makers. The propaganda effort was directed toward those whose societal standing made them intermediaries between the elites and the common people—the local priests, the schoolteachers, the merchants. They appropriated the pamphlets and communicated them to the populace at large.

THE RESPONSE

The amazing aspect of the first few years of the Reformation controversy was that the writings of Luther (and of those who rallied to his side) enjoyed a vast (and utterly unexpected) resonance. People responded appreciatively for a variety of reasons, just as those who supported the notion that Luther should receive a hearing at the diet at Worms had different rationales. One suspects that quite a few people imposed their own notions on the discourse that was beginning to gather steam, and there may have been little religious interest on the part of some who rallied to Luther's side. As in other periods of Christian history, politics and economics may have been more important.

That people rallied to the cause of reform, however, can hardly be contested. The Reformers succeeded, and their insistence on reform turned into a social movement, because their contemporaries responded to their message. The extent to which this was the case, however, says little, if anything, about the reasons for the historical success (or

35. See Scott Hendrix, *Recultivating the Vineyard: The Reformation Agendas of Christianization* (Louisville: 2004). The question is how long this "christianizing impulse" persisted and when the theological underpinnings of the "impulse" became explicit and turned the movement into a theological phenomenon.

36. W. Reinhardt, *Probleme deutscher Geschichte*, in *Gebhardts Handbuch der deutschen Geschichte* 10 (Stuttgart: 2001).

failure) of the movement that ensued. The number of partisans had nothing to do with the Reformation's success or failure.

Initially, Luther's influence grew out of a combination of curiosity about him and the devotional quality of his writings. People were drawn to him because his writings appeared to be theologically orthodox (at least they emphatically made that claim). They assumed that the church would come to realize his orthodoxy and spiritual concerns before long. Certainly until Luther's excommunication in 1521, support for Luther was not taken to entail defiance of the Roman Church. Luther—we do well to remember—outdid himself with expressions of loyalty to church and pope as late as 1520, for example, in his cover letter to Pope Leo in the treatise of Christian freedom.

For a while the controversy could be believed to pertain to doctrinally peripheral matters, so that acceptance of the new message of Scripture and grace and faith did not mean repudiation of the Catholic Church. Unless we keep this in mind, the course of events between 1521 and 1541 loses its inner rationale, because we fail to understand the repeated assertions of key figures—Luther's colleague Melanchthon among them—that the disagreements pertained to matters about which conciliation should prove to be possible. Of course, Luther and his followers had long been declared heretics, which complicated matters. At any rate, the situation in the early years of the Reformation was characterized by an intriguing paradox: the repudiation of traditional religious norms, which was both courageous and defiant, was coupled with the insistence that no fundamental theological issues were at stake. We must ponder whether this insistence was realistic or a self-delusion (or, worse, a subtle deceit).

Soon, however, support for those who joined the chorus of reform became no easy thing. In fact, it turned into a fundamental existential decision: Luther or the church. To opt for Luther meant the repudiation of the church and all that this church stood for—above all, its insistence that it alone assured eternal salvation. However, support coalesced not in a few isolated instances, but over and over again. Monks who had vowed obedience to the pope became his mortal enemies. Nuns who had pledged lives of celibacy got married. Priests who had taken the Mass to be the very heart of the Christian faith denounced it as the abomination of abominations. These decisions called not only for conviction, but for courage. The switch in loyalties was not made lightly.

The number of those who so decided must remain uncertain. In 1521 the papal nuncio Aleander remarked that nine-tenths of the German people had rallied around Luther, and two years later Ferdinand of Austria reported that "Luther's teaching is so firmly embedded in the empire that among a thousand persons not a single one is completely untouched; it could hardly be worse." While both comments (as well as many others that might be cited) make up in exuberance what they lack in hard facts, they express the mood of the time.

There are other means of gauging the impact of the emerging Reformation movement. As we will see, the free imperial cities in Germany provide evidence for the impact of the new message. In most of these cities the burghers had a voice in the conduct of civic affairs. Popular agitation for reform in the cities was thus bound to find easy expression, in contrast to the larger territories where the single ruler's disposition was able to make all the difference. In the Swiss cities, for example, the acceptance of the new faith encountered difficulties wherever there was little popular participation in municipal governance. Zurich, with a contingent of artisans on the city council, moved with speedy ease, whereas Bern and Basel, where patrician families dominated the council, took almost a decade to effect religious change. In a few instances, the city councils were the retarding forces with respect to religious change, with the agitation for change coming from the burghers and the guilds.

This ambivalent role of city councils suggests that the issue could not have been one of greater control of ecclesiastical affairs by the secular authorities. If this had been the case, city councils everywhere would have jumped on the bandwagon of change. They did not. On the contrary, they frequently showed themselves determined to thwart the propagation of the new faith. The cause of reform was advocated by those who seemed to derive no obvious political advantage.

But one must be careful. If some of those who had earlier battled with the church over legal ecclesiastical prerogatives in society did not stand in the forefront of seeking reform, those who did advocate change frequently had political objectives as well. They were concerned not only about true religion; they also wanted social and political change in their communities.

Why did the common people respond positively to the reform proclamation? Of course, there must have been nonreligious factors: greed for the church's wealth; resentment over its legal prerogatives in society; the desire of the ruling elites to control all affairs of the community, including those of the church. In some places the demand for discontinuation of payments of taxes to the church and for "evangelical" ministers was made in the same breath as that for greater popular participation in governmental affairs. On the other hand, assuredly religious concerns were present; people found the new faith a persuasive interpretation of biblical religion. All in all, the evidence is ambiguous, and the historian will never know what went on in the minds of men and women in the third decade of the sixteenth century. Clearly, there was no single factor that caused people to become "Martinians." Different circumstances prevailed at different times and in different places. In the 1530s, when Protestantism in Germany had attained political strength, political prudence may well have made the acceptance of the new faith a viable decision. In the early 1520s, however, the situation was precarious: both ecclesiastical and political authorities had condemned Luther and his followers, the emperor had left no doubt about his intention to suppress the Lutheran heresy. To support Luther meant to support heresy—and heresy had never prevailed. No matter how many hundreds of pamphlets hailed Luther's cause, he was still a heretic against whom the universal church had rendered its verdict of condemnation.

In the end, Luther and most of the other major reformers died peacefully in bed, and acceptance of the new faith, far from entailing loss of property or life, could be economically profitable as well as politically prudent. But all this could not have been foreseen in 1523 or 1524, when the prospects seemed rather grim for anyone siding with the new faith. If, in the face of such difficulties, many were willing to do so, genuine religious enthusiasm must have been present.

Importantly, during the first few years of the controversy, support of Luther did not at all mean the categorical rejection of the church or the determination to part company with it. It was support for, rather than opposition against—for deeper spirituality, for example, or for a more committed faith. Once the reformers had succeeded in consciousness raising that church and society were in trouble, support for Luther turned at once into a challenge of existing conditions in church and society.

The foremost demand of the proponents of reform was for "evangelical" preaching, a program that was as precise as it was innocuous. The goal was not to repudiate the church, nor to break away from it, but to undertake changes within it. The corollary was the challenge, once the church had shown itself closed to change, to discern whether theological differences with the church did indeed require separation.

The question of possible patterns of "conversion" or "loyalty" remains. It would be splendid if the matter of becoming (or not becoming) a supporter of Luther followed a discernible pattern, so that all people in the cities (or in the country), in the north (or in the south, or east), with education (or without), with wealth (or without), became "Martinians" and "evangelicals." If such a pattern existed, it has remained obscure. Initially, most of Luther's supporters had come from the ranks of the humanists. In fact, all of the Reformers had been humanists of one stripe or another so that there can be little doubt that the humanist circle provided the reservoir from which the reform movement drew its initial adherents. They had wanted a reformed religion and the correction of what they perceived as ecclesiastical abuses. They employed their pens to bring about such a reform, and they rendered their vigorous support of Luther. But soon they abhorred Luther's theological reformulation as radical and confused. None expressed this sentiment better than Erasmus when in 1527 he wrote, "The reformers should have not heedlessly wrecked anything without having something better ready to put in its place. As it is, those who have abandoned the Hours do not pray at all. Those who have put off pharisaical clothing are worse in other matters than they were before. Those who disdain the episcopal regulations do not obey the commandments of God." In the end, humanists could be found on both sides of the conflagration.

The youthfulness of the Reformers helps to explain the exuberance with which the message of reform was propagated. It was not only that the Reformers were young; they had matured in a different theological climate than had their elders. In particular, Erasmus's Christian humanism, with its opposition, implicit as well as overt, to scholasticism and its adherents had many followers among the younger generation, which had a different *Erlebnisschicksal* (experiential horizon), to use Karl Mannheim's term. The importance of the younger generation was recognized even at the time: Luther wrote that "through the increase of good books the young are far more accomplished than the old."

Most of those who became reformers were too young to have become deeply immersed in traditional scholastic thought. They were at the beginning of their careers. The downside of their youth was a lack of experience, but that deficiency was made up by their exuberance about a new vision of Christianity. They were convinced that their exuberance would be shared by their contemporaries and that their optimism about a perfect church and society would be vindicated. Later in the century, when England began to be beset by Reformation turbulence, it was observed that

Cambridge "ran much divided into two factions, whereof the younger sort, which are the majority, was much for innovation."[37]

Virtually all "Martinians" were young men when the controversy erupted. Luther was thirty-four years of age at the time he published his Ninety-five Theses in 1517, and Zwingli was only a few months younger. Melanchthon was twenty, prompting Duke George of Saxony to remark that he was "far too young to understand these matters."[38] Of some fifty Reformers in German lands, only seven were older than Luther. Considering the enormously long time required in those days for the pursuit of a theological course of study—a doctorate in theology easily required over a decade—this youthfulness of the proponents of reform is significant. To cite a few illustrations: Wolfgang Capito was born in 1478; Balthasar Hubmaier, in 1480; Johann Oecolampadius, in 1482; Wenzeslas Link, in 1483; Jakob Strauss, in 1485; Guillaume Farel and Urban Rhegius, in 1489; Thomas Müntzer, in 1489; Martin Bucer and Friedrich Myconius, in 1491; Johannes Bugenhagen, in 1485; Hans Denck, about 1495; Andreas Osiander, in 1498; Johann Brenz, in 1499. Elsewhere in Europe, the same youthful preponderance prevailed: Miles Coverdale was born in 1488; Thomas Cranmer, in 1489; William Tyndale, in 1494; Olaus Petri, in 1493; Hans Tausen, in 1494; Robert Barnes and Thomas Bilney, in 1495. Youthfulness helps to explain the vitality of the reform movement.

But youthfulness did not mean lack of recognition. Andreas Bodenstein Carlstadt, born in 1480 and thus a bit older than most reformers, distinguished himself by being the first member of the Wittenberg faculty to appear in print. Thomas Müntzer's theological erudition was praised well before 1517, and in 1518 Zwingli had been appointed, despite his obscure background, to a prestigious preaching post in Zurich. Nicolas Cop was, despite his youth, rector of the University of Paris. Other future Reformers, such as Capito, Bucer, and Matthäus Zell (born 1487, 1491, and 1477, respectively), also held preaching and university positions and before long undoubtedly would have attained greater eminence in the church had it not been for the conflagration. Several Reformers held doctorates in theology—Luther, of course, but also Urban Rhegius, the reformer of Augsburg; Balthasar Hubmaier, the future Anabaptist leader; and in England, Thomas Cranmer and Robert Barnes. The quip of a twentieth-century Catholic historian, that had Luther been better versed in scholastic theology he would have become a Catholic saint, misses the mark.[39] The Reformers were neither theological ignoramuses nor illiterates.

It has been argued that the Reformation began as a university movement, particularly with Luther's lectures—a rather surprising statement, given the conservative nature of the academic enterprise—but in fact it neither was a university movement nor received its impetus from there.[40] The established professors of theology at the

37. John Strype, ed., *The Life and Acts of John Whitgift, D.D., the Third and Last Lord Archbishop of Canterbury in the Reign of Queen Elizabeth* (Oxford: 1822), 1:50–51.

38. Felician Gess, ed., *Akten und Briefe zur Kirchenpolitik Herzog Georgs von Sachsen* (Leipzig: 1905), 1:234.

39. Jared Wicks, ed., *Catholic Scholars Dialogue with Luther* (Chicago: 1970).

40. Hermann Schöffler, *Die Wirkungen der Reformation* (Frankfurt: 1960), has extended reflections on the role of the universities, but he is too exuberant in his argument that the Reformation was a university movement, confusing "university trained" and "university faculty." On the negative attitude of the faculty at Rostock toward the Reformation, see A. Vorberg, *Die Einführung der Reformation in Rostock* (Halle: 1897), 29–30.

universities remained aloof from the reform movement. Indeed, most of the fiercest opponents of change came from the ranks of university professors. Wittenberg was an exception; at the other universities the reaction of the academicians was uniformly negative. At Leipzig a phalanx of theologians opposed Luther; at Erfurt, his own alma mater, he had a few supporters, but the eminent members of the faculty failed to make his cause their own. Cologne, Ingolstadt, Heidelberg, Freiberg, Tübingen, and Frankfurt likewise remained Catholic hotbeds; none embraced the Reformation. Several universities did so later, but more on account of governmental fiat rather than the theologians' conviction.

If the university community showed itself immune to the challenges of the Reformation, the clergy was a different picture. Although the higher clergy (for whom, perhaps, too much was at stake in a change) remained faithful to the church, the lower clergy joined the reform movement in significant numbers. Indeed, most of the men who carried the new gospel to success had been priests and monks. They became the foot soldiers of the Reformation, and without them success would not have been possible, since they took the new message into the pulpits, the market squares, and the village inns. The printed word alone would not have sufficed to effect a socialization of the new faith, no matter how formidable the flood of reform pamphlets. These erstwhile monks and priests were the "little Luthers" who shared with their congregations the new proclamation even as they subsequently facilitated the restructuring of ecclesiastical life in their communities.

Not all who supported Luther during the first few years of the controversy remained committed to the cause of reform. Quite a few had second thoughts, especially after the church officially censured Luther and it became obvious that support of Luther's notions of reform was the support of notions declared heretical by the church. The humanist jurist Ulrich Zasius was one of these. Another was Theobald Billican, an oscillating theologian who moved seamlessly between Luther, Zwingli, and the Anabaptists, only to return to Catholicism, marry a prosperous widow, and wind up teaching rhetoric at Marburg. The eventual return of men such as Zasius and Billican to the church underscores the atmosphere of ambiguity and uncertainty that prevailed during the first half-decade or so of the controversy.

Chapter 4

THE DIVISION

In late December 1521 three men arrived in Wittenberg from Zwickau, a town some fifty miles to the southeast, to see Luther. They must have not been well informed of Luther's whereabouts—only the initiated, of course, knew that he was hiding at the Wartburg. So he was not available, and his younger colleague Melanchthon took his place. None of the three men was a trained theologian. Two were weavers by occupation, the third a university dropout. Their lack of formal training notwithstanding, they had been caught up in the controversy and had come to talk theology, and Melanchthon heard some rather strange notions: doubts about the legitimacy of infant baptism; claims of direct communication with God, who gave them instructions in their dreams; and much more of the like. Since in their dreams they also had conclusions about the future, they later received the appellation "Zwickau prophets." Melanchthon confided his bafflement to several friends and colleagues, including Luther, whose nonchalant reply that he had always expected Satan to tempt the church in bizarre ways was hardly much comfort to the impressionable young colleague.

This Wittenberg encounter was the first indication that those who were committed to reform were not all of the same mind. Indeed, it foreshadowed what was to be a characteristic of the movement of reform—its lack of cohesiveness, which became evident at precisely the time when the Lutheran identity of the movement for reform was beginning to be sharpened. Luther dominated the discourse for several of those important initial years, and nothing illustrates his centrality better than ascription of the label "Martinian" or "Lutheran" to those who took up his cause or went on record in support of reform. The label did not imply theological coherence or cohesiveness; it simply meant that Luther was the dramatic personification of all those who were persuaded that they had discovered a better way to run society and the church.

By 1523, however, it became evident that a good deal of diversity existed among those who had taken up the banner of reform, even though their essentially Lutheran character is well documented.[1] Most of this diversity, being the opinions of theologians and laypeople, of individuals of influence and of the common people, uttered from pulpits and printed in pamphlets, discussed in taverns and at village wells, had little bearing on the larger course of events. When these opinions found formal literary expression, they undoubtedly prompted an occasional raised eyebrow (and in our

---

1. The important essay is by Bernd Moeller, "Was wurde in der Frühzeit der Reformation in deutschen Städten gepredigt?" *Archiv für Reformationsgeschichte* 75 (1984): 176–93.

own day excite the fancies of writers of dissertations). Of the many reformers few, if any, agreed completely with Luther; most had their own particular slants and views.

None of this should come as a surprise. A relatively cohesive movement did not emerge until the mid-1520s. The sweep of Christian history shows that at no time did all the theologians ever agree with one another on all the theological topics. In one respect, though, the theological characteristic of the early reform movement was different. In the sixteenth century, theological disagreements were likely to find expression in new ecclesiastical structures. Theological differences had a way of leading to sociological differentiation. Distinct Protestant churches emerged, and the depth of theological disagreement did not always prove to be the key to the matter, though lesser differences tended to get resolved (or ignored) while bigger ones led to division.

In some instances geographic factors played a role in the emergence of different ecclesiastical bodies as did the temperament of the protagonists and the timing of the controversy. There was an accidental quality to what we might call the "theological consolidation" of the Reformation.

HULDRYCH ZWINGLI AND REFORM IN ZURICH

The division of the movement of reform may have been as inevitable as it was obvious. Not only was there a broad spectrum of notions of reform among its advocates; there also was, at least initially, no defining authority among these advocates. The exuberant atmosphere of a reforming free-for-all prevailed.

This initial diversity did not last long (though some might object that it has lasted nearly five hundred years). While a variety of biblical and theological perspectives continued to characterize the Reformation, a process of consolidation took place where some Reformers—those with deep theological insights, perhaps, or with strength of commitment—became seminal figures in the emergence of new and permanent ecclesiastical traditions.

The Zurich reformer Huldrych Zwingli is a good case in point. Even though his theology shared commonplaces with that of other Reformers, it had its own distinctive character, which found superb expression in the nineteenth century, when, after much controversy, a Zwingli monument was erected in Zurich, the site of Zwingli's activity. Strangely, it was not placed at the Grossmünster, Zurich's most prominent church, where Zwingli had labored for the reform of city and church, but at the far more modest Wasserkirche. There the Zurich reformer is depicted on a high pedestal, a Bible under his right arm, and in his left hand a sword: a man of the Word and of the world.

More than the pious patriotism of Zurich burghers bespeaks this memorial: Zwingli was as much a Swiss patriot as he was a Christian theologian. For him, "reform" meant reform not only of theology and the church, but also of society. Indeed, he lost his life on a battlefield because of his vision of how religion might change the politics of the entire Swiss Confederation.

Zwingli was born in Wildhaus in 1484, his birthplace then as now a small village nestled in the rugged mountains in eastern Switzerland, close to the Austrian border. Lush meadows with gentle slopes on mountain flanks still are sprinkled with farmhouses, the soil too poor for farming so that cows are the main source of nourishment, providing not only cheese but also meat. Zwingli's first biographer suggested that the birthplace possessed theological significance: the nearness of heaven in the Alpine mountains, he wrote, made God a powerful reality for the young boy. The family home still stands today, half a millennium later, turned into a museum and piously guarded by Zwingli's compatriots. It is a typical alpine chalet, one of the oldest wooden houses in Switzerland, tiny windows to the front of the house, while heavy stones on the flat roof keep snow from accumulating in winter and secure the dwelling in case of an avalanche.

One need not pay homage to the geographic determinism of the first biographer to acknowledge that Zwingli's closeness to nature, his reserved temperament, and his rustic language betray the setting in which he grew to manhood, in the sight of the grandeur of the mountains, where humans and nature appear to exist in harmony even though life is harsh and the winters long. Huldrych's father was a peasant who had been mayor of Wildhaus, and deep loyalty to the church characterized not only him but also the whole family. Of the eleven children in the family, no fewer than five committed themselves to serve the church. Early recognized for his intellectual talents, young Huldrych was first sent to an uncle in Weesen to attend school, after which he went to Basel, then to Bern. Eventually he studied at the University of Vienna and, between 1502 and 1506, in Basel, where he received the baccalaureate degree in 1504 and the master's degree two years later.

In 1506, without having pursued formal theological studies, Zwingli was ordained to the priesthood in his native village. He assumed pastoral responsibilities in Glarus, then a small village, now an important commercial center, a short distance to the south, where he spent ten years. Though tucked away in a forlorn place, Zwingli applied himself to serious intellectual pursuits. Through a rigid schedule he attained a solid competence in classical studies and theology, with the Christian humanism of Erasmus forming a towering influence. The notebook he kept for studying the Greek language tellingly shows both the positives and negatives of what we would call today his "long-distance" learning. Zwingli made certain grammatical mistakes over and over again—there was no one to correct him—and yet the notebook shows his steady progress.

In 1516 Zwingli moved to Einsiedeln and two years later to Zurich, where he was appointed *Leutpriester*, people's priest, a prestigious preaching position that offered opportunities for scholarly pursuits and a welcome proximity to humanist friends. His appointment in Zurich was almost derailed by rumors of an affair with the barber's daughter in Einsiedeln, but his candor in facing up to the matter (not to mention his putting all the blame on the woman) resolved the complication.

Zurich was a town of some five thousand; its subjects in the surrounding canton numbered over fifty thousand. It was prosperous and politically influential among Swiss cities. In line with a constitutional agreement of 1498, government power was exercised by a Large Council, the "Two Hundred," and a Small Council, with fifty members. The Large Council, which dealt with foreign affairs, taxation, and chose the mayor, wielded greater power; the Small Council supervised domestic administrative matters. Membership on both councils was by election, with the twelve guilds exercising considerable influence in civic affairs. The canton of Zurich included a number of outlying villages for which the city provided protection, general support, and spiritual care. In turn, these villages had to pay a tithe, which in part supported the priests who supplied the spiritual needs of the villagers. Religiously, Zurich was in the diocese of Constance, and no fewer than some 250 priests resided in the town, of whom 50 were attached to the major church, the Großmünster.

On January 1, 1519, his thirty-fifth birthday, Zwingli began his ministerial responsibilities in Zurich. He promptly gained attention with striking homiletic innovation. Instead of taking as his preaching text the prescribed biblical pericopes for the day, he preached on the first chapter of the Gospel of Matthew. In subsequent sermons he proceeded to cover the entire Gospel. But before Zwingli had settled down in his new environment—indeed, well before his forceful preaching was making an impact on Zurich—the echoes of the indulgences controversy surrounding Luther's Ninety-five Theses began to be heard in Zurich. In December 1518 Luther's name appeared for the first time in Zwingli's correspondence. Zwingli was deeply curious and undertook to obtain Luther's writings. He promptly began to praise them and became active in disseminating them. A "new Elias" had been given to the world, he exclaimed exuberantly; Saul (Erasmus) had slain a thousand, but David (Luther), ten thousand.

Yet, when later asked about Luther's influence on him, Zwingli adamantly denied any influence. "I do not want to be called Lutheran," he wrote in 1522, "for I did not learn the teachings of Christ from Luther, but from the Word of God." What is one to make of Zwingli's strange and categorical denial? One suspects that political considerations were operative in this protestation of aloofness from Luther. By 1522 the church had declared Luther and his followers to be heretics, and the Edict of Worms had declared them political outlaws; for Zwingli to acknowledge himself as Luther's disciple would have meant a personal threat to his physical well-being as well as to his work in Zurich. His disavowal of Luther therefore was an act of understandable prudence. But more was involved. Zwingli was profoundly convinced that he had preached the "gospel" before he had ever heard of Luther. The accuracy of his disclaimer hinges on his meaning of "gospel." When he used the word to describe his theology before Luther appeared on the scene, he gave it a particular connotation that it did not later possess. His "gospel" in those early years was that of Erasmus, and it meant the rejection of Scholasticism and the primacy of the Bible. Missing was the Pauline notion of law and grace. Initially, Jesus was the exemplar, the giver of the Sermon on the Mount. Later Zwingli emphasized Christ as redeemer and liberator from the law. The Wittenberg reformer was a catalyst, confirming an insight here and suggesting a new understanding there, but he never was an overpowering influence. Zwingli quite appropriately summed it up by acknowledging that Luther "propelled me to eagerness."

Zwingli argued the independence of his new religious views all the more forcefully after an intensely personal experience wove his life and thought into a single inextricable pattern. In August 1519 the plague struck Zurich. Zwingli contracted the dreadful disease and for weeks wrestled with death until, after a slow recovery, he was restored to full health. From this illness came a personal religious document, the *Pestlied*, or Hymn of Pestilence:

Help, Lord God, help
in this anguish!
Death stands at the door.
Stand before me, O Christ,
For you have overcome death.
To you I cry!

But, if it were to be your will
That Death should take me
In the midst of my days,
So let it be!
Your will be done,
I am completely in your hands,
Indeed, your vessel.[2]

Zwingli, in facing the reality of death, became persuaded of the reality of God; personal experience merged with theological insight.

REFORM IN ZURICH

Two pork sausages eaten in 1522 during Lent by several eager partisans of the cause of reform marked the beginning of the ecclesiastical changes in Zurich. The dinner guests, even though they were in the privacy of the printer Christoph Froschauer's dining room, had violated the rule of the church, which prohibited the consumption of meat during Lent. Somehow this culinary feat became publicly known and turned into an *affaire d'état*, particularly when an extensive investigation on part of the city council revealed additional instances of violation of the fast. Zwingli's teaching and preaching had borne intriguing fruit. The explanation of the culprits was of a rather fundamental sort: "We must keep all our lives and our doings in accord with the Gospel," one of them wrote, "or else we are not Christians." Froschauer himself, however, took a more pragmatic tack when he noted somewhat aggressively that the demands of his print shop to publish devotional writings for Lent and Easter required him to have substantial nourishment. Since each dinner guest had eaten only a small piece of the sausage, this seems a somewhat lame excuse. Zwingli, who had been present at the dinner, had refrained from eating the forbidden "fruit" though he had also not interfered by upholding church teaching.

Shortly afterward Zwingli took the pen and published a sermon entitled *Von Erkiesen und Freiheit der Speisen* (Concerning the Choice and Freedom of Food), the first public statement of his new theology. Defending the sausage eaters, the sermon explored the relationship between faith and works, between inward piety and outward rules. Its theme echoed Luther's 1520 tract on the freedom of the Christian: the Christian is not under the mandates of the law, but above the law. The impetus for moral action does not come from external rules, but from inward commitment.

2. H. Bullinger, *Reformationsgeschichte*, 2 vols. (ed. J. J. Hottinger; Frauenfeld: 1838–1840), 1:29.

This notion of Christian freedom took Zwingli to another violation of a rule of the church, that of clerical celibacy. He and a widow, Anna Reinhart, had formally attended church together, a seemingly quite innocent act, which, however, in the culture of the time, made public a marital commitment on their part. Zwingli requested that Hugo von Hohenlandenberg, the bishop of Constance, authorize the marriage. This was, of course, a skillful political move on Zwingli's part, for a bishop could hardly rescind general church teaching. Not surprisingly, the bishop declined, prompting Zwingli's publication of a sharply antiepiscopal tract entitled *Apologeticus Archeteles* (First and Last Explanation). Zwingli's repudiation of the rule of clerical celibacy found cogent expression.

In the meantime, disagreements were emerging on the two city councils—Zwingli's strong support on the Large Council notwithstanding—as to what ecclesiastical policy should be pursued in light of the religious agitation. Zwingli's reform proclamation was causing commotion in the city. Eventually, the city council announced that a theological disputation in Zurich should resolve the contested religious issues, a momentous decision that begs for explanation. After all, by that time (1523) both church and state had rendered their verdict on the theological innovators: they were heretics and thus political outlaws. On the face of things, the Zurich council should have implemented official policy as promulgated by church and empire rather than act as if such policy did not exist. The explanation for the decision of the Zurich city council (not only in Zurich, but in other centers of reform as well) is found in the convergence of several factors: the desire of the council to rein in the traditional role of the church in the community; the impact of the new evangelical message; the judgment that order and calm in the community called for acommo-dating the advocates of reform; and the sentiment that the decisions of church and state concerning reform were not final and definitive.

The call for a disputation implied that the Zurich city council saw itself as arbiter in matters of religion. If the church at large did not convene a council to resolve the controversy, so the argument ran, then the Christian community in Zurich was at liberty to proceed on its own to ponder the issues and arrive at proper conclusions. Such a claim to ecclesiastical and theological autonomy—first advanced in April 1522 in a statement of the city council to a delegation from the bishop of Constance—was startling, indeed revolutionary. Although Zwingli's voice could be heard in the statement of the city council, a new self-understanding of Zurich's secular government as the custodian of religious affairs in the city found expression here.

In preparation for the disputation Zwingli compiled a set of propositions, sixty-seven in number, which outlined his understanding of the Christian faith. These Sixty-seven Articles (*Schlussreden*) covered the whole range of theology, ethics, and liturgy. Two basic assertions set the tone: the centrality and self-sufficiency of Scripture, and the centrality of Christ and the need for the proclamation of his gospel ("Those who assert that the gospel is nothing without the confirmation of the church are in error and blaspheme God"). Most of the Sixty-seven Articles dealt with the papal office, ecclesiastical practices, church property, clerical celibacy, and monasticism. Although Zwingli discussed each topic on its own terms, his general judgment was clear: major changes were necessary in the life and thought of the church in order to make them conform to biblical norms.

The disputation took place on January 29, 1523, and accordingly is known as the January Disputation. More than six hundred people crowded the city hall, though the defenders of the status quo and the church were few. Not surprisingly, the bishop of Constance had protested the disputation, noting that chaos would result if each community could claim jurisdiction over what constituted the authentic Christian faith. He sent observers rather than participants in the disputation.

Accordingly, the disputation turned out to be a lame affair, hardly worth its name. Essentially Zwingli gave an account of his preaching along the lines of the *Schlussreden*. One suspects that everybody knew that the collective mind of the city council was made up. Indeed, after a listless morning, the city council announced that "Master Huldrych Zwingli" had demonstrated that he was not a heretic and that he "should continue, as heretofore, to proclaim the Holy Gospel and the Sacred Scriptures." The same exhortation was given to the other Zurich clergy. On the face of things, of course, this exhortation to biblical preaching was hardly a cry for theological reform. But it was code language, unassailable by those siding with the Roman Church: because the Reformers had taken ownership of the "Holy Gospel and the Sacred Scriptures," the council pronouncement allowed Zwingli and his increasing throng of supporters to change the nature of the Christian faith in Zurich.

In the wake of the disputation, monks and nuns left the monasteries in town, and the endowments of the Großmünster church were earmarked for charitable purposes. In August 1523 the first baptism was performed in which the German language, not Latin, was used. By and large, however, ecclesiastical life in the city continued unchanged. The Mass was celebrated in its traditional form, as were most of the other rituals. Nor surprisingly, soon a new point of contention emerged. Influenced by the ubiquitous presence of statues and paintings of saints in Zurich churches, the issue of images became increasingly prominent; instances of iconoclasm occurred, though most of them were fairly peaceful.[3] In one of the city churches a painting of Jesus mysteriously disappeared, as did a crucifix from another church which wound up in a ditch outside the city, and in yet another the "Eternal Light" was ripped off the wall "while everyone was at supper." Since the Eternal Light was the sanctuary lamp that denoted the presence of the consecrated sacrament, the vandalism was not so much iconoclasm as an attack on traditional eucharistic doctrine.

Toward the end of September, the city council saw the situation as serious enough to appoint a committee to examine the controversial religious issues, chief among them the images in the churches. The committee duly convened, deliberated, and eventually recommended that a disputation be held to address the issues. The city council concurred. The January disputation had been a lame and uninspiring affair, since the advocates of reform dominated; the second disputation, held in October 1523, thus known as the October Disputation, turned into a lively meeting of minds.

3. Lee Palmer Wandel, *Voracious Idols and Violent Hands: Iconoclasm in Reformation Zurich, Strassburg, and Basel* (New York: 1995).

In January the controversy had been between the proponents of the old and those of the new faith, the former represented hardly at all; in October it was a family feud among the partisans of reform. Fierce disagreement came to the fore, though it did not pertain to fundamental theological questions, such as the Mass or images as such. All agreed that both were unbiblical and had no place in a Christian community. The disagreement pertained to timing: since the Mass and images had been found to be unbiblical, when should the Mass be abolished and the images removed from the churches? The conclusion of the majority was to proceed cautiously. The images must first be removed from the hearts of individuals, so the argument ran; then the physical removal would come without turmoil in its own time. This was in line with Zwingli's thinking, as he put it in the course of the debate: "The people must first of all be instructed with the Word of God that neither vestments nor singing is a proper part of the Mass. If presently anyone would celebrate Mass without vestments uproar will result."

Again, the city council concurred. Thus the official sentiment was clear, but by the middle of December the absence of change in the city revived the earlier restlessness. The city council announced that at Whitsuntide, in other words, in about six months, "the whole matter should be taken up again and brought to a conclusion agreeable to God and his holy Word." The council acted with exquisite political prudence when it mandated this strategy. The October Disputation—in fact, the entire course of events in Zurich—had evoked pointed negative reactions among the Swiss cantons loyal to the Catholic Church, and the Zurich council feared adverse political consequences if the city continued on a speedy course of ecclesiastical change. The Catholic cantons would see this as provocation, adding fuel to the fire of an already tense situation.

At long last, on Pentecost 1524, the Zurich city council ordered that the images be removed from the churches "so that all would turn completely from idols to the living and true God." For two weeks the workmen were busy. When they were done, the richly ornamented churches had been transformed into austere, simple houses of worship. The walls of the sanctuary were white, the windows clear, the views unobstructed. Precious works of art, priceless objects of religious devotion, had disappeared under the chisel, the hammer, the paintbrush. What then were meaningful devotional aids, and later generations considered valued treasures of religious art, were gone. But the concern was not about art; it was about true biblical religion.

If the workmen found their work easy, the abolition of the Mass proved to be more complicated. Not until the spring of 1525 did the city council order that the Mass be discontinued and "the remembrance of the institution and the table of God as practiced by the apostles" observed instead. So the rich liturgical splendor of the Mass was replaced by a simple Communion service. For ears and eyes accustomed to the chanting of the liturgy and the ritualistic splendor of the priest at the altar, the new Communion service was a radical innovation. It was simple. After the sermon Zwingli took a place behind a table "covered with a clean linen cloth." Wooden bowls and goblets contained the bread and wine, which were taken by helpers to the congregation. The liturgy was in the vernacular. Although it followed the traditional pattern of the Mass for the most part, one of the Scripture lessons was read by a lay helper, and minister and congregation recited the Gloria and the Creed antiphonally. The mystery of the

Mass had become the communal gathering of the congregation commemorating Christ's death.

What took place in Zurich between 1522 and 1525 was to recur in countless other places: the proclamation of ideas that were vaguely "Lutheran" and thus at odds with the Catholic Church; the agitation for changes in ecclesiastical practice; the intervention and involvement of governmental authority, first with the call for a mediation between the old faith and the new, then with the statutory introduction of ecclesiastical change; finally, the increased role of government in ecclesiastical affairs. The fabric of the one church was torn apart, and a rival form of Christianity established itself against the church represented by the pope.

The question of the ultimate rationale on the part of those who demanded ecclesiastical change was whether they wanted to break permanently with the Catholic Church and go their own way. Some of the changes were marginal to the larger theological issues that agitated so many lives and minds (such as the removal of images from the churches), though even those changes presupposed important theological issues. Others were more crucial, such as the discontinuation of the Mass. But what always mattered was the conviction on the part of the Reformers that they were propounding the true gospel and that this true gospel would be victorious—not in the sense of a defeat of the Catholic Church but of the acceptance by this church of the true gospel. Their boundless enthusiasm may have prompted the Reformers to be a bit naive about the implications of the proposed changes for the future.

Zwingli had delineated his new understanding of the Christian faith in a number of publications, beginning with a commentary on his Sixty-seven Articles, which he entitled *Ußlegen und Gründ der Schlußreden oder Articklen* (Exposition and Explanation of the Conclusions or Articles). The overwhelming themes were the majesty and grandeur of God and the dichotomy of the spiritual and the material. The former brought Zwingli to espouse a predestinarian theology as well as the notion of salvation solely by grace, while the latter was to make it impossible for him to agree with Luther's notion of a real presence of the body and blood of Christ in the elements of bread and wine in the sacrament of the altar.

Chapter 5

THE EMERGENCE OF ALTERNATE VISIONS OF REFORM

Something else happened in the mid-1520s that influenced the course of reform for a long time and in a variety of ways. Reformers appeared on the scene, and reform movements coalesced, that blatantly destroyed any cohensiveness that vaguely existed among those advocating reform. Collectively, this new brand of reformers and the movements they brought about have received a number of designations, of which "Left Wing of the Reformation" and "Radical Reformation" have enjoyed the most extensive scholarly usage. Both terms have problems in that they offer judgments as to what was (theologically) radical or on the "left" in the early sixteenth century, judgments with which one may agree or disagree. The problem is, of course, that subjective theological judgments should not form the basis for descriptive terms for a historical phenomenon.

It seems more appropriate, therefore, to use a term to designate the fact that in addition to the major reform movements there were also marginal manifestations of reform in the sixteenth century. These fringe groups have been interpreted as either ultimate triumph or failure of the broader movement of reform. Scholarly (and theological) interpretations of these groups have differed, but the facts are clear enough. In most centers of Reformation agitation, reformers appeared on the scene, men (and women) who had initially been under the sway of Luther's or Zwingli's teaching, but had grown dissatisfied. They had begun to question, to denounce, to "out-Luther" Luther and to "out-Zwingli" Zwingli, eventually deciding to go their own way. Although their impact upon the broader course of events was modest, they should be neither ignored nor caricatured, the fate that has been theirs ever since the sixteenth century. Some of these fringe reformers were heralds of the modern age, advancing principles that, though fiercely disputed in the sixteenth century, have become the common affirmation of Western society. They insisted on religious freedom and tolerance, for example, claiming that government should not interfere with religion; others argued that most theological disagreements pertained only to secondary matters and could therefore be disregarded.

Doubtless these alternate movements of reform received their incisive stimulus from the mainstream Reformation. Those who subsequently developed their own ideas as to what constituted biblical religion flirted with the Lutheran or Zwinglian programs of reform before they grew disenchanted. The reform movement provided the initial stimulus. Nonetheless, the Reformation hardly suffices as exhaustive explanation for the emergence of Protestant dissent. There were other factors, such as humanism, especially of the Erasmian variety; the mysticism of Johannes Tauler, Thomas à Kempis, and the *Theologia Deutsch* (German Theology); and the enigmatic underground of medieval apocalyptic and philosophical speculation, about which it is easier to offer plausible conjectures than hard facts. Nor must we overlook the import of the Bible, which the dissenting men and women read in the vernacular and with a disarming freshness, and from which they may well have received major insights.

In contrast to the other ecclesiastical groupings in the sixteenth century, the dissenters failed to obtain the support of governmental authority, which in most places was grimly determined to crush all dissenting religious sentiment. The story of these men and women is the story of underground groups and conventicles suppressed with countless mandates, ordinances, and edicts. They were the outcasts of a society that, having closed its ranks against them, offered them neither the opportunity to worship as they desired nor the status of citizenship. Theirs was the story of persecution. Michael Servetus, the Spanish antitrinitarian radical, was burned by Catholics in effigy and by Protestants in reality. Such spectacular demise symbolizes that there was no place for the dissenter in the sixteenth century.

The dissenters formed a company of martyrs. All religious groupings in the sixteenth century supplied the dungeon and the stake and the executioner's block, the Calvinists no less than the Lutherans and the Catholics no less than the Protestants. The Protestant dissenters, however, provided more than any of them, even though the precise number is a matter of conjecture. The several martyrologies written at the time and afterward sought to provide devotional inspirations rather than exact statistical information. A total of some four thousand victims appears a likely estimate for the sixteenth century. Most of them were Anabaptists.

Indeed, the case can be made that most of the dissenters were deliberately martyr-minded. Persecution, martyrdom, and death were for them not accidental misfortunes but the very essence of the Christian confession. After all, Christ, too, had walked the path of suffering and death, and he beckoned his disciples to come and follow him. Often these men and women were ignorant of the subtle points of theological argumentation or the details of biblical interpretation. When they were interrogated, they were often pathetically ill-equipped to match the sophisticated theological learning and wits of their opponents. Still, they were persuaded that they had been called to follow in Jesus's steps, to do as he had commanded them to do, and that was to suffer, even to die. They quoted Jesus's words that the "disciple is not above his master, nor the servant above his lord," and held that the disciple was called upon to be like the master in his rejection, suffering, and death. Martyrdom was a test of obedience, and they were determined not to shrink from it. They were on a pilgrimage and looked beyond the flames of the stake and the executioner's sword to the promised land. In fact, echoing themes that had been sounded in the early 1520s by the likes of Thomas Müntzer or Hans Hut, the Anabaptists made suffering the defining characteristic of the Christian life. It was not until the middle of the seventeenth century, when the Anabaptists—in north Germany now called Mennonites and Doopsgezinde ("baptism-minded")—had acquired striking economic affluence, that this "theology of martyrdom" waned.

One of the most moving documents of such Anabaptist martyr theology comes from a Dutch Anabaptist woman named Elisabeth, who prior to her execution wrote to her infant daughter:

I have . . . borne you under my heart with great sorrow for nine months, and given birth to you here in prison, in great pain. They have taken you from me. Here I lie, expecting death every moment. . . . And I, your dear mother, write you, my dearest child, something for a remembrance. . . .

I must through these lines cause you to remember, that when you have attained your understanding, you endeavor to fear God, and see and examine why and for whose name we both died; and be not ashamed to confess us before the world, for you must know that it is not for the sake of any evil. Hence be not ashamed of us; it is the way which the prophets and the apostles went, and the narrow way which leads into eternal life. . . .

Further, my dear child, I pray you, that wherever you live when you are grown up, and begin to have understanding, you conduct yourself well and honestly, so that no one need have cause to complain of you. And always be faithful, taking good heed not to wrong any one. Learn to carry your hands always uprightly. . . .

Do not accustom your mouth to filthy talk, nor to ugly words that are not proper, nor to lies; for a liar has no part in the kingdom of heaven; for it is written: "The mouth that lieth slayeth the soul." Hence beware of this, and run not in the street as other bad children do; rather take up a book, and learn to seek there that which concerns your salvation. . . .

If it were not the will of the Lord, . . . He could yet easily deliver me out of their hands and give me back to you, my child. Even as the Lord returned to Abraham his son Isaac, so He could still easily do it. He is the same God that delivered Daniel out of the lion's den, and the three young men out of the fiery furnace. He could easily deliver me out of the hands of man. . . .

And now, Janneken, my dear lamb, who are yet very little and young, I leave you this letter, together with a gold real, which I had with me in prison, and this I leave you for a perpetual adieu, and for a testament, that you may remember me by it, as also by this letter. Read it, when you have understanding, and keep it as long as you live in remembrance of me and of your father, if peradventure you might be edified by it. . . . I bid you adieu, my dear Janneken Munstdorp, and kiss you heartily, my dear lamb, with a perpetual kiss of peace.[1]

No other records are extant for this Anabaptist martyr, and so we are in the dark about her beliefs and her role in the Anabaptist movement. A single, touching letter is all we have of someone whose religious faith led her to a violent death. For other Anabaptist martyrs, however, the record is more extensive. For example, the fate of Augustin Würzlburger, a schoolteacher in Regensburg, illuminates the convergence of theological and political concerns behind the surveillance and persecution of Anabaptist dissenters. As the record indicates, Würzlburger, about whom nothing is known except what is found in the interrogation records, had become an Anabaptist and was subsequently reported to the Regensburg city authorities.

The first entry in the records is dated May 22, 1528, and lists the questions that were to be put to Würzlburger, who as yet had not been charged with a crime. The questions examine his beliefs and seek to learn about his connections, contacts, and associations:

1. How he had accepted this unbelief or error? How, or from whom, had he heard, learned, and accepted it? . . .
3. By whom was he baptized and with what words was he entreated to accept it? . . .

1. As quoted in Hans J. Hillerbrand, *The Protestant Reformation* (New York: 1967), 148–52.

5. Who had been baptized with him?

6. The other leaders, directors, preachers, and helpers: who and where are they?

7. The secret assemblies or services attended by him with his fellows: what sign do they use to recognize one another? . . .

9. What were their notions and regulations concerning a community of goods?

10. What were their notions concerning confession, mass, the reception of the sacrament, and church attendance? . . .

12. How often and at what places, here or elsewhere in Bavaria, had he preached? Who had been present at this preaching; also from whom had he heard this teaching?

13. What is the present whereabouts of his associate in preaching and rebaptizing at Oberhaim? Had this associate also preached in Bavaria and whom had he rebaptized?

16. What were his intentions and why had he accepted this preaching and rebaptism? Had he accepted it for the purpose of insurrection and other evil doings? Whom had he baptized in Bavaria, what were their names and residence?

17. Did he revoke this opinion and repent?

Other than the fairly general first question, only question 10 dealt specifically with a theological topic. A great many questions, to be sure, were aimed indirectly at Würzlburger's "rebaptism," but it would appear that the Regensburg authorities saw this not so much as a deviation from universal theological consensus as a secret initiation rite by which the members of a political conspiracy recognized one another.

Würzlburger's second interrogation, which took place three days later, revealed strikingly religious and theological answers to political questions.

In response to the first question Augustin stated that he had been taught the gospel by those who recently had been expelled from Regensburg because of their baptism. He had also read and examined the Scriptures and had found that this teaching was divine truth. Every Christian must be persecuted and suffer, for the world has no friendship with Christians. He thought nothing of his first baptism: "One must not baptize unbelievers. Only after one believes and the gospel has been preached is one to be baptized, if it is desired. . . ."

Concerning the third question he said that he was baptized by Leonhart Freisleben from Prul, one of those recently expelled because of baptism. This was in November and he was baptized, according to God's command in the Gospel according to Matthew and Mark, in the name of the Father, Son, and Holy Spirit. There were four men and one woman who had been expelled from Regensburg because of their baptism. . . .

Fifth: He said that only he was baptized at that time.

Sixth: He said that he did not know any, for he had stayed here and had only traveled to such places in Bavaria, where there were none of them. He knew only one Burkhart Praun, of Ofen, a tall man, about thirty years of age, whom he had met at Regensburg last winter. He was a leader but had told him nothing but what the one who had baptized him had also told him. Since that time he had heard nothing from him. Also, it was true that the congregation at Augsburg had sent one called Hans to Regensburg with a letter. Over a year ago he had been a choirmaster at Regensburg and before that a schoolteacher at Weiden. The letter stated that the congregation had named him or Hans to the office of apostle to preach the gospel. They had cast lots as to who should accept the office, and the lot had fallen to him. For this office he had been given the instruction that he should proclaim the divine truth.

Seventh: That he knew of no secret assembly or gathering, nor of a sign by which they might recognize one another.

One suspects that Würzlburger's responses convinced the Regensburg city fathers that he constituted no danger to the body politic, for nothing happened until June 2, 1528, when the dukes of Bavaria sent the following missive to the Regensburg city council:

> We have received the interrogation records of Augustin Würzlburger. . . . Würzlburger has been shown by his own confession to be a leader and preacher of the heretical sect of the Anabaptists, against the order of the holy Christian church and the imperial edict and mandate. He has also caused several persons to be executed despite their recantations. Therefore, we wish that Würzlburger be sentenced to death according to imperial law because of his confession and evil heretical misdemeanor. You are not to refuse our will nor show any mercy.

That, of course, was heavy medicine for the city council, especially because Würzlburger may have had, through his position as choirmaster in reform-minded Regensburg, friends and supporters. Not surprisingly, the response of the city council was evasive:

> Your letter concerning Augustin Würzlburger, which instructed us to sentence him to death because of his confession concerning rebaptism, has caused us great concern. We do not wish to be disobedient in anything, regarding this or any other matter, and we are grieved indeed by Augustin Würzlburger's error. But, since he has no fault other than that concerning rebaptism and the Christian faith, we cannot understand why we are to put him to death. We want him to desist from his opinion and error. If this should be unsuccessful, we will seek the counsel of other Christian and learned men on how to proceed further.

As matters turned out, the will of the dukes of Bavaria was stronger than that of the Regensburg city council: the Regensburg Chronicle recorded for October 10, 1528, this brief note:

> On Saturday, October 10, Augustin N., a teacher and Anabaptist, was led to the city hall, placed on a bench, where he was charged with having been rebaptized and afterwards rebaptizing others, nine persons all in all. . . . Even though he had deserved, according to imperial law, death by burning, the Council had mercifully ruled that he was to be executed by beheading. This happened . . . the henchman leading him like a butcher leads a calf. He did not say a word even as no one spoke to him.

This vignette reveals the momentum behind the persecution of the religious dissenters in the sixteenth century. Although theological dissent, known as heresy, was distasteful and grounds for the death penalty, according to imperial law, the issue was as much political as it was theological. The authorities were convinced that the Anabaptist dissenters were conspiring to overthrow the established social and political order under the guise of religious belief, just as had been the case when the German peasants rebelled in 1524–1525. To be sure, the theologians almost uniformly fell in line, either appropriating the political charges or being overwhelmed by the theological aberration. Although doctrinal deviation from whatever was the "established" form of religion in a realm entailed grave legal consequences, the kind of questions uniformly asked of suspects of religious dissent suggests that the governmental authorities were out to unmask a political or social "conspiracy." In Germany, in particular, the dreadful memories of the Peasants' War (and, after 1534, the recollection of what had happened in Anabaptist Münster) conveyed to the authorities that religious dissent also had a political ramification.

Most men and women who joined clandestine Anabaptist conventicles or an antitrinitarian congregation were perfectly peaceful. When they talked about the upheaval of society, about catastrophes and conflagration, about a new kingdom, it was because they had imbibed the mysterious language of Holy Writ, the book of Daniel, for example, or the book of Revelation. These writings were for them handbooks and manuals for how God accomplishes his purposes in history, and the more militant of these believers were ready to aid God in this task. Of course, there were the exceptions—men and women who, carried away by biblical fancies and aspirations to create the New Jerusalem on earth here and now, justified the suspicions of authorities that underneath the religious affirmations lurked political insurgency. Indeed, in one respect the authorities' charge of the disruption of law and order was to the point: the dissenters rejected the identity of the political and religious community that had been the legacy of Christendom ever since the days of Emperor Constantine in the fourth century and was universally accepted by Protestants and Catholics alike. The dissenters argued that the religious and the political communities were two different entities, and that to be a citizen of a commonwealth was not tantamount to being a Christian.

Given the lack of formal organizational structures and the reality that the dissenters formed an underground movement, it is hardly surprising that although the number of such dissenters was small, their theological diversity was extensive. In some instances this meant splintering into separate groupings, in others a baffling constellation of affinities, making it harder by far to determine what these men and women advocated than what they opposed: both the Catholic Church and the reform movement represented by Luther and Zwingli, hurling charges of perversion against the former and of compromise against the latter. They wanted a reformation of the Reformation.

This insistence that the Reformation, too, had to be reformed was the common denominator among the dissenters. As the Hutterite *Chronicle* noted, "Luther broke the pope's pitcher, but kept the pieces in his hand."[2] The dissenters were resolved to drop the pieces as well. The Reformers had not gone far enough; they left unquestioned what should have been challenged and affirmed what should have been rejected. However, the specific criticisms differed greatly. The antitrinitarians were concerned about the ancient christological dogma, whereas the Anabaptists focused on the proper understanding of the church (and baptism) and together with the Spiritualists stressed what may be called "practical Christianity." The scriptural statement

---

2. A. J. F. Zieglschmid, *Die älteste Chronik der Hutterischen Brüder* (Ithaca: 1943), p. 43.

"by their fruit you shall know them" served as their motto. The recurrent theme was that the Christian profession had to manifest itself in the daily walk of life.

Dissent seems to have taken its adherents primarily from the lower classes, from the peasants and artisans, which seems to suggest a socioeconomic homogeneity of striking simplicity. The evidence, however, is far from conclusive. Indeed, any definite socioeconomic identification of the dissenters becomes problematic, even though some have argued that Anabaptist conventicles became the haven for disenchanted peasants after the catastrophe of the Peasants' War. The evidence suggests a bewildering reality, indicating that no easily ascertainable economic or social common denominator exists for the adherents of dissent. Because most of what we know about sixteenth-century dissent comes from governmental records of interrogation of alleged dissenters and these records fail to reveal an extensive involvement of the upper classes, the explanation may be that upper-class dissenters were more successful in avoiding governmental suspicion.

Today we marvel at these men and women who defied established religion, old and new, and who accepted social stigma, personal uncertainty, physical hardship, persecution, and death because they had caught a glimpse of a vision of the faith that was at variance with what their contemporaries were willing to accept.

THE REFORM DISINTEGRATES

The preeminent influence in the emergence of the dissenting reform movements was undoubtedly Martin Luther. He had intensified the religious concerns of his contemporaries, and virtually all of the subsequent dissenters owed their real religious awakening to his proclamation. But this proclamation also raised more questions than it seemed to answer. Luther had spoken about the centrality of faith, insisting that faith was the key to the sacraments. That assertion led to the question of the baptism of infants: did infants possess the necessary faith? Another point of uncertainty pertained to the locus of authority. Luther had argued for the centrality of Scripture, stressing that the guidance of the Spirit was necessary for its proper interpretation. Did this mean the Spirit took priority over the letter? Luther had questioned the dogma of transubstantiation. Why had he stopped short of questioning the ancient dogma of the Trinity?

These issues, in particular, were bound to receive further scrutiny, and this they did, first with two reformers who appeared across the sky of the Reformation like comets, burning brightly but disappearing quickly: Andreas Bodenstein Carlstadt and Thomas Müntzer. Though their immediate impact on the scene was slight indeed, their significance for the crystallization of dissent can hardly be underestimated. Carlstadt was an assertive character but also a thoroughly competent and brilliant theologian. A senior member of the Wittenberg faculty, he never avoided controversy; on the contrary, he sought it out. At first reluctant to follow the lead of his junior colleague Luther, he quickly became an enthusiastic partisan and played a significant and vociferous role in the indulgences controversy.

During Luther's stay at the Wartburg, Carlstadt showed himself sympathetic with those who demanded immediate ecclesiastical reform at Wittenberg. After Luther's return he lacked the diplomacy to adjust to his colleague's conservative temper and the flexibility to reconsider his own position. For awhile he continued as dean of the theological faculty, gave well-attended lectures at the university and wrote a torrent of pamphlets but was otherwise outside the current of events. Early in 1523 he went to Orlamünde, south of Wittenberg, where he undertook ecclesiastical reform in the manner that he had desired for Wittenberg. The parish church was stripped of images, communion was observed in simple form, and infants were no longer baptized. Complications arose, for Carlstadt continued to issue prolific propaganda for his brand of ecclesiastical reform. Had he confined his activities to spreading manure as "Brother Andrew," as he did proudly at times, or had he only expounded his evangel to peasants under an oak tree in the manner of the painter Pieter Brueghel, there would have been no problems. But he aimed to change the course of ecclesiastical reform—and this in opposition to Luther.

In September 1524 Carlstadt was expelled from Orlamünde at Luther's urging. For half a year he moved restlessly from place to place, still hoping to influence the course of events. He was unsuccessful, became tangled up in the Peasants' War (how deeply we do not know), and was eventually permitted, after a haphazard recantation, to return to Wittenberg. But the theological and personal estrangement from Luther forced him to leave again. A few years later he found his way to Basel, where he found acceptance. Even though in the heady days of the early 1520s he had resigned his professorship at Wittenberg and asked to be called "Brother Andrew," he died in 1541 a distinguished professor at the University of Basel.

Carlstadt was an important figure in the rise of Protestant dissent. He argued for a speedier and more comprehensive alteration of ecclesiastical life and thought than Luther and most other Reformers were disposed to undertake. His pamphlet *Ob Man gemach faren* (If One Should Tarry) propounded in classical form the argument that biblical insight must at once be translated into actual ecclesiastical reform. Moreover, Carlstadt went beyond Luther in what may be called the "spiritualizing" of the gospel, the move from the material to the spiritual. Accordingly, the sacraments had to be reinterpreted, because they could be only symbols and were not central. He desperately sought to reinterpret Communion so as to deprive it of its sacramental character, and he was sufficiently perplexed by the baptism of infants that he discontinued the practice in Orlamünde.

The other early important dissenting reformer was Thomas Müntzer, a former priest and confessor to cloistered nuns. Born probably in 1489, he too had become a follower of Luther in the course of the indulgences controversy, especially after the Leipzig debate. Afterward, he traveled as a kind of peripatetic evangelist on behalf of the new Wittenberg gospel and with Luther's endorsement assumed an interim pastoral appointment in Zwickau, southeast of Wittenberg. His adamant stance on behalf of reform, together with his rather uncompromising temperament, promptly led to tensions with the other clergy (and the city council), and in the end Müntzer concluded that it was best for him to move on. In a way, his sojourn in Zwickau had proved to be a failure, yet it also had been an important stage in his theological development, for his brilliant mind was ever at work, absorbing ideas, including those of medieval mystics who talked much about spiritual suffering. Müntzer found his way to Bohemia and Prague, undoubtedly sensing a spiritual kinship with Czech Hussites, and on All Saints' Day of 1521 he published a *Manifesto*, a self-conscious and flamboyant ultimatum on behalf of the new faith: if the people of Prague would not accept the new gospel, God would use the Turks to smite them into oblivion.

As matters turned out, the good people of Prague failed to rally to the cause of reform as proclaimed by Müntzer—and found comfort in the realization that the Turks had not smitten them. His failure at Zwickau, his continuing inability to rouse support for a new vision of the gospel may well have prompted him to rethink his calling. That he disappeared from sight for over a year (1522–1523) suggests that he needed a respite. Where he went and what he did we cannot tell, although the historian is tempted to conjecture that he did have contact with Hussite ideas.

In the spring of 1523 Müntzer was appointed minister in the Saxon town of Allstedt. There he had the opportunity to translate his theological theory into ecclesiastical practice. He undertook reforms in the orders of worship, subsequently published *Deutsche Kirchenampt* (German Order of Service), *Deutsch Evangelisch Messze* (German Evangelical Mass), and *Ordnung und Berechnung des Teutschen Ampts* (Order and Description of German Worship), for all practical purposes the first new orders of worship of the Reformation. Though adhering to traditional form, they embodied new content, suggesting a creative change in congregational worship. The Scripture lesson was lengthened, for example, and the entire congregation joined in the recitation of Jesus's words of institution at the celebration of the Lord's Supper. That was a truly striking innovation, the radical application of the principle of the priesthood of all believers that none other than Luther had enunciated in 1520.

Crucial, however, was his increasing theological estrangement from Luther. Early in 1524 Müntzer published two pamphlets, *Vom getichten Glauben* (Concerning Faked Faith) and *Protestation und Erbietung* (Protestation and Declaration), that amounted to a theological declaration of war on the Wittenberg theology. The first pamphlet discussed the nature of faith, while the latter showed how that faith was to be lived in the world. Both were vehement and flamboyant attacks on Luther, to whom Müntzer referred with a biting pun as *"Dr. Lügner"* (Dr. Liar). Müntzer's argument was that one had not only to accept the promise of God's forgiveness, but also to fulfill God's law. In so doing, the believers would experience that the Christian commitment means the "cross" of suffering, both spiritual and physical. Where there is no such suffering, there is no true faith, because true faith calls for obedience and the fulfillment of the law. The true Christian faith, therefore, was diametrically opposed to the "honey-sweet" Christ proclaimed by Luther. The perversion of the true gospel by Christendom at large was best evidenced by the practice of the baptism of infants, who lacked both the suffering faith and the ability to fulfill the law.

Understandably, Luther was more than a bit nervous about Müntzer's preaching in nearby Allstedt; after all, Müntzer's had been a formidable attack, and once again—as had been the case back in early 1522—Luther found it easy to persuade himself that theological deviation was tantamount to the disruption of law and order in society, and would lead to the ultimate failure of reform. The Saxon rulers became leery of developments in Allstedt, and in August 1524 they traveled to Allstedt to inspect things for themselves. They had Müntzer preach a sermon, and even though that sermon on the book of Daniel seems not to have triggered panic on their part, before too long the authorities decided to expel him from Alstedt and Saxony. Müntzer traveled southward and (though the sources are evasive) seems to have come into contact with the peasants' simmering unrest in southwest Germany.

The insurgency of the peasants proved to be Müntzer's destiny. It prompted Müntzer to identify the peasants' cause with his own. The reason is not difficult to ascertain. Müntzer's clarion call for reform had been fatally thwarted by "godless" rulers and authorities, who, as it now turned out, were also oppressing the peasants. His enemies were also their enemies; he and the peasants, therefore, were true allies. One suspects that Müntzer also rallied to the peasants' side because of his conviction that he could offer them the true explanation of how they fit into that overarching divine plan that he had sought, unsuccessfully as it turned out, to outline to the Saxon princes in his sermon on Daniel back in August. He was, in other words, the "Daniel" who enlightened the insurrectionist peasants about their role in the victory of the elect over the godless.

The exact role Müntzer played among the rebellious peasants who set up camp near the village of Frankenhausen in central Germany for the decisive battle against the rulers is not at all certain. Was he a charismatic political leader or merely a chaplain? Historians have frequently assumed that he was the former, although one can just as persuasively argue that he was—no less important—the latter. The peasants went down to disastrous defeat in May 1525 after Müntzer had preached a fiery sermon intimating that divine intervention would overwhelm the enemy. It is not clear if he fought in the brunt of the battle, for afterward he was found hiding in an attic bed, arrested, tortured—it was then that he made the cryptic statement that among Christians "all things should be held in common"—and put to death as an insurrectionist. Müntzer had never voiced such a sentiment about communal living in any of his writings, so one must take this affirmation of communalism with the proverbial grain of salt. As the Hutterite Anabaptist communities were to show but a few years later, a literal recourse to the New Testament would find in the first chapters of the book of Acts a cogent biblical precedent.

A bold individual and a creative theologian passed from the scene who contributed two emphases to the incipient Protestant diversity. He criticized Luther's view of the norm of authority, rejecting the notion of the "paper pope," the Bible, and replacing it with the notion of the Spirit speaking directly to the individual. He also condemned Luther's soteriological view by propounding an alternative: the commitment in suffering to fulfill God's law as a consequence of God's gracious forgiveness.

ANABAPTISM

Those who were dubbed "Anabaptists" (from the Greek, meaning "rebaptizers") by their antagonists were the most dramatic alternate movement of reform in the early sixteenth century. Although it is generally agreed that, in a formal sense, Anabaptism may be said to have begun with the administration of the first recorded believer's baptism (baptism upon confession of one's belief) in Zollikon, a village near Zurich, in January

1525, there is no agreement as to the broader context that led to this act of defiance. Some scholars have challenged the Zurich origins of the phenomenon with the thesis of a "polygenesis" of the Anabaptist movement, a thesis that has found widespread acceptance.[3] They essentially argue that earliest Anabaptism was not a theologically cohesive movement and had different places of origin. Moreover, the Zurich/Zollikon origins of Anabaptism that scholars for most of the twentieth century took for granted have been deprived by these scholars of their theological core with the argument that economic issues in the rural environs of Zurich, in particular the rejection of the tithe, prompted the emergence of a radical reform group among Zwingli's followers.[4] To some extent this revisionist understanding of Anabaptist origins was a reaction against a highly idealized view of Anabaptism as the sole biblical religion in the Reformation.

The polygenesis thesis is attractive but needs contextualization. Surely the issue is not so much where notions of the believer's baptism first cropped up in the early 1520s. In light of Luther's dramatic declaration in his 1520 tract *On the Babylonian Captivity of the Church* that faith was an indispensable element in the two sacraments of baptism and the Lord's Supper, the baptism of infants, unaware of theological issues and lacking faith, was bound to become a topic on the table. That Carlstadt and Müntzer promptly raised questions about the practice of infant baptism and even ceased baptizing infants should not come as a surprise. The reason the Zurich "origins" deserve to be preserved is that what slowly turned into an Anabaptist movement in Switzerland, Austria, and south Germany could be related to Zurich. Given the haphazard means of communication and the reality that whatever communication occurred was underground, not to mention the theological illiteracy of the adherents of the movement who left testimonies, the diversity of the incipient "movement" should not be at all surprising. Important is not so much the heterogeneity of the early phase of the Anabaptist movement, but its quick consolidation.

Theologically, the beginnings of the movement remain shrouded in complexity. The influence of Erasmus of Rotterdam was important, for Erasmus had a vision of the Christian faith that was highly ethical and pacifist, as in his *Paraphrases of the New Testament*. At the same time, both Carlstadt and Müntzer influenced the incipient movement. Nor can one overlook the obvious: the influence of Luther, Zwingli—and the Bible. The Reformers' insistence on the priority of the Word made many seek recourse directly in that text.

The story begins with the growing impatience on the part of some Zwingli partisans about the slow pace of ecclesiastical reform in Zurich in 1523. These disciples of the Zurich reformer included theologically literate and socially prominent individuals, such as Georg Blaurock, a monk, and Conrad Grebel, a learned humanist. During the

3. James Stayer et al., "Monogenesis or Polygenesis: The Historical Discussion of Anabaptist Origins," *Mennonite Quarterly Review* 49 (1975): 83–121. This "revisionist" understanding of Anabaptist history, heavily influenced by categories from social history, has been challenged by Andrea Strübind, *"Eifriger als Zwingli": Die frühe Täuferbewegung in der Schweiz* (Berlin: 2003).

4. John H. Yoder and Fritz Blanke have represented the church-historical approach to the emergence of Anabaptism; see Yoder, *Täufertum und Reformation im Gespräch; Dogmengeschichtliche Untersuchung der frühen Gespräche zwischen Schweizerischen Täufern und Reformatoren* (Zurich: 1968), and Blanke, *Brothers in Christ: The History of the Oldest Anabaptist Congregation, Zollikon, near Zurich, Switzerland* (Scottdale, PA: 1961).

course of 1524, when reform in worship and practice seemed to make little progress in Zurich, these impatient disciples sought to impel Zwingli to action. Unsucessful in this effort, they gravitated toward one another, talked theology and reform, and forged theological rationales for their dissent from Zwingli's strategy to make haste slowly. Their number was modest, perhaps a dozen or so, young, impatient, determined, and overwhelmed with the kind of exuberance typical of all who pressed for ecclesiastical change in those heady days.

The open break with Zwingli occurred over baptism, but underneath lurked an issue of greater importance: the nature of Christian commitment. For the group around Grebel and Blaurock, to be a Christian entailed a voluntary decision to become Jesus's disciple, which found expression in receiving baptism upon confession of faith and a concomitant separation from the "ungodly." There is some foggy record, coming from none other than Zwingli himself, that early on Grebel and others had approached him about establishing a church in Zurich composed only of true believers. Such a strategy had, in fact, been suggested by Luther in his 1523 attempt at a new order of worship, so the idea must have been in the air; but Zwingli's recollection, if accurate, suggests that the notion of the "true" church as small and persecuted, fundamental for subsequent Anabaptism, was a later development, and that early on the future Anabaptists could well envision an established church.

The defiant parting of the ways in January 1525, when a small group administered what they understood as true New Testament baptism upon confession of faith, had an air of Christian primitivism: a peasant house kitchen in the village of Zollikon, a wooden ladle, the desire to be baptized upon confessing the faith, and the simple act of pouring water. Its simplicity notwithstanding, the act defied a thousand years of Christian tradition, ameliorated only by the awareness that many other long-standing traditions of the Christian faith were thrown overboard as well. Those present perhaps assumed that no dramatic consequences would follow. Although their baptism was a flagrant violation of a mandate of the Zurich city council, within two weeks more than thirty men and women had been baptized upon their confession of faith. The Zurich authorities promptly intervened, clearly on the instigation of Zwingli, who saw not only erroneous theology that had long been severely condemned by the church, but also a fateful separation of the sacred and secular community. Everyone known to have been baptized, including Felix Mantz and Conrad Grebel, was arrested. Since most of those recanted, they were quickly released; the few who did not were expelled from Zurich territory.

These expulsions meant that Anabaptist notions were taken by those who had been expelled to other places, mainly to the north and east of Zurich. From the beginning there was an involuntary centrifugal dimension to the Anabaptist movement as it spread from Zurich to other places. The Anabaptist message declared the difference between their view of the Christian faith and that propounded by the Reformers in categorical terms. Theirs alone was the true gospel; the world, while formally Christian, was in spiritual darkness. Therefore, men and women everywhere needed to be challenged to become disciples of Jesus and to signify their commitment with a confession of sin and the reception of adult baptism. Even if there had not been an Anabaptist expulsion from Zurich, the Anabaptist message would undoubtedly have been taken to other places. Governmental suppression made the principle of propagating the message of believer's baptism both necessary and understandable.

Geography influenced the direction of the Anabaptist missionary impulse. The message could be best communicated in German-speaking areas. Moreover, it also was easier to follow the well-established roads to the north than to move eastward across the mountain ranges into Austria, although Anabaptist missionaries did move eastward as well as northward. The Anabaptist missionaries enjoyed an initial period of toleration when they made their appearance in a new community. By the time the authorities moved to suppressive action, the Anabaptist evangelists had created the nucleus of a congregation—and moved on. Persecution forced this new nuclear congregation underground, however, and made further expansion difficult.

Some were ready for the Anabaptist message: spiritually sensitive men and women, dissatisfied with the course of the ecclesiastical reform as pursued by both the Lutheran and the Zwinglian movements, frustrated by the apparent absence of personal commitment on the part of most Christians, bewildered by the increasing theological obsession of the reform movement, which seemed to ignore the commitment to Christian living. The appeal of the Anabaptist message was to all those who were unhappy with the state of things. It is altogether possible that peasants, disillusioned by the catastrophe of the Peasants' War as well as by Luther's seeming abandonment of them, found the emerging Anabaptist conventicles attractive refuge. There may well be something to that, but the Anabaptist appeal was much broader.

The expansion of Anabaptist sentiment had several sources—Zurich, but also Hans Hut, a disciple of Thomas Müntzer, and Balthasar Hubmaier, learned reformer of Waldshut in Austria—and it was unsystematic, sporadic, haphazard, and theologically unsophisticated. It was also modest in its numerical dimension. The network of Anabaptist congregations throughout south Germany and Austria was composed of local conventicles with few members. The missionary, who brought the Anabaptist message of repentance, baptism, and a new walk of life, was not a trained theologian, but a layperson with a striking familiarity with the Bible, from which he gleaned and taught the simple Anabaptist message. To be sure, a few Anabaptist leaders and missionaries were theologically sophisticated, such as Hut, Hubmaier, Hans Denck, and Blaurock, but most of those who spread the Anabaptist message—one thinks of Augustin Würzlburger—were individuals with more enthusiasm and spiritual commitment than theological competence. The consequence was that the Anabaptist message was reduced to its essentials by these evangelists. Subtle points of theological argumentation were ignored, but this proved to be its strength, since the common people might be hardpressed to understand why their commitment violated civic or ecclesiastical mandates.

Not surprisingly, Brueghel's painting *John the Baptist Preaching* has been taken to portray an Anabaptist gathering, for its locale is far from the town, with its impressive church steeple. The huge throng has gathered, hidden in the woods, to hear the preacher's message: only two monks in the lower right-hand corner of the painting express disapproval. Once a nucleus of local believers had been established through baptism, the missionary moved on, and the new congregation was on its own. The baptized believers would study the Bible (one suspects that the German New Testament was easily accessible) and whatever Anabaptist pamphlets came their way. By and large their contacts with the outside theological world were limited; the gathering was like an island in an ocean, part of a universal brotherhood and sisterhood, yet for the most part on its own. In a way, the proclamation of the Reformers had initially encountered the same difficulty, for the exposition of Luther's theology by thousands of well-meaning pastors, all of whom had been Catholic priests, was bound to lead to differences and problems. The pulpits in Lutheran territories hardly propounded Luther pure. Yet the Reformation had the advantage of the dissemination of its ideas on the printed page and an increasingly formal organizational structure. For the Anabaptist movement, this organizational structure and easy accessibility of printed materials was a long time in coming.

Few data are available about the success of this Anabaptist evangelistic effort. There are the official governmental interrogation records of men and women suspected to be Anabaptists, from which one may infer the existence of a network of small Anabaptist conventicles throughout Austria and Germany. The evidence suggests that Anabaptism was anything but a mass movement and that for a long time it was not theologically cohesive. All the same, one must not make too much of the diversity one finds in the extensive governmental records of interrogations. These records pertain, after all, not to the leaders, but to the rank and file of the movement. If a sample of the burghers of Wittenberg or Zurich had been examined about their beliefs, an analogous diversity would be found.

The fragmented expansion of Anabaptists proved a mixed blessing because, lacking an overarching organizational structure, each local conventicle was on its own. Not surprisingly, the need for theological clarification emerged, and in 1527 Anabaptist leaders gathered at no less than three places to seek theological clarity: at Nikolsburg in Moravia, at Augsburg in south Germany, and at Schleitheim on the Swiss-German border. The sources for these meetings are enigmatic, so that the details of the gatherings are unclear; however, the circumstances are obvious. The network of Anabaptist conventicles lacked theological precision and agreement. The three gatherings of 1527 suggest that communication among the local conventicles, though haphazard and infrequent, was not altogether absent.

The meeting at Schleitheim adopted a document entitled *Brüderliche Vereinigung* (Brotherly Agreement) that proved to be the major theological document of Swiss–south German Anabaptism. The very title expressed the reverberations of theological diversity introduced by Anabaptist leaders—Hubmaier, Denck, Hut, Ludwig Haetzer—particularly with respect to the convergence of apocalyptic thought and the peasant uprising. Those in attendance agreed on a "mainstream" document, known as the Schleitheim Confession, which formulated under six headings the theological touchstones for most Anabaptists in the decades to come: baptism of believers upon confession of faith, the ban or excommunication as the hallmark of the Christian community, the Lord's Supper as a memorial meal, the pastoral nature of the ministerial office, nonresistance as expression of the disavowal of the use of force, and the refusal to render oaths.

The former Benedictine prior Michael Sattler was the author of this striking document, which (despite a variety of subsequent scholarly interpretations) may be said to have essentially conveyed the notion that the original Zurich-Swiss Anabaptist vision, no matter how rudimentary, was normative for the movement as a whole. The

Brüderliche Vereinigung had profound societal implications. The rejection of infant baptism meant that the identity of the civic and religious community was rejected, while the refusal to bear arms, occupy governmental offices, and swear oaths meant a further challenge to the established societal order. No wonder, then, that the authorities everywhere, Catholic and Lutheran in intriguing harmony, saw the Anabaptists as potential insurrectionists—and this all the more so because some Anabaptists took their chiliastic anticipation of the end to occur in 1528 or in 1533 at the latest, and marked by the final, bloody showdown between the elect and the damned. This was the vision of Hut, who had imbibed the ideas of Müntzer and proclaimed that the way to God was through suffering in following Jesus. Hut was the key figure of the Augsburg Martyrs' Synod, of 1527, a gathering of Anabaptists from south Germany and Austria, so called because in a short time the Anabaptist leaders present at Augsburg had suffered martyrdom. The Augsburg gathering supported Hut's apocalyptic-chiliastic vision, an indication of the lingering influence of the Peasants' War understood as an end-time event.

Anabaptism was an underground movement. It had no organizational structure, but consisted of more or less autonomous congregations scattered throughout central Europe. Accordingly, its theological heterogeneity should not be surprising, though it may well have been so to the Anabaptists themselves. Until the seventeenth century it possessed no generally binding confessional statements, for the Schleitheim Confession was normative only for south German and Swiss Anabaptists. The situation of Anabaptism was similar to that of Protestantism in France or Scotland during the struggle for official recognition, though Protestants in those countries received support from abroad, notably from Geneva, and they were numerically large enough to establish early organizational structures and confessional standards.

For the Anabaptists this process of consolidation took longer. The absence of organizational structures in Anabaptism had two consequences. First, one can hardly write the history of Anabaptism as a "movement." With the exception of its Hutterite branch, which did possess a measure of organizational cohesiveness (and confessional norms), there was an open-ended complexity to Anabaptist history that makes it difficult to do more than expound the thought of leaders, with glances at specific local churches or the occasional colloquies held between mainstream Reformers and Anabaptists. A second consequence was the persistence of theological differences among the various Anabaptist groups and factions. However, one must not turn this empirical diversity into a theological divergence. It is, after all, astounding how quickly these factions did coalesce into uniformity once the opportunity to do so presented itself in the second half of the century.

Anabaptism was thus a network of loosely knit congregations. Its leaders had no formal theological training. Occasionally a figure of charismatic qualities appeared and through organizational ability or theological exposition put his mark on the movement. Because the theological contribution often took the form of clandestinely printed tracts, it is not surprising that historical nescience has frequently obscured it. The south German Anabaptist Pilgram Marpeck is a good case in point. Although virtually unknown to historians until the beginning of the twentieth century, the discovery of his extensive literary production established him as the most prolific

Anabaptist writer in the first half of the sixteenth century.[5] Remarkably Marpeck held a series of important civic positions in his capacity as engineer, first in Strassburg and then, since 1544 in Augsburg, alongside his determined engagement as an Anabaptist theologian seeking to bring theological cohesion to the disparate Anabaptist conventicles. Marpeck did so in particular by enunciating a biblical hermeneutic meaningful for Anabaptists everywhere. Concerned about the relationship of the Old Testament to the New, Marpeck found their unity to lie in the relationship of promise and fulfillment. In the early 1540s Marpeck engaged in a literary polemic with Caspar Schwenckfeld, one of the spiritualizing dissenters of the Protestant Reformation, who preferred to dismiss such externals as water baptism. Marpeck's *Verantwurtung über Casparn Schwenckfelds Judicium* (Response to Caspar Schwenckfeld's Book Called Judgment) was a weighty tome of some eight hundred pages.

What, then, was the theological core of Anabaptism? The question has been much debated, and for the better part of the twentieth century the notion of an "Anabaptist vision"—the notion, in other words, that the Anabaptists envisioned the Christian faith as the call to discipleship, to follow Jesus, in his suffering, his disavowal of the values of the "world"—dominated efforts at interpretation. Thus the Schleitheim Articles noted that "they that are Christ's have crucified the flesh with its passions and lusts," and identified believer's baptism, the breaking of bread, excommunication, separation from the world, nonresistance, and the refusal to swear oaths as hallmarks of such discipleship. Discipleship, in turn, entailed a public commitment, expressed in adult or believer's baptism upon one's confession of faith.

This turn took place in the context of a society and of churches that were deeply dismayed over the appearance of what Luther promptly labeled the *Schwärmer*, the term derived from the "swarming" of wasps and bees, who in Luther's view shared the same quality of aimless swarming with the likes of Müntzer, Carlstadt, and the Anabaptists. Back in 1521 Luther had nonchalantly told Melanchthon that he had always anticipated Satan to raise the issue of the baptism of infants, and that meant that these "heavenly prophets" did not use the Bible as the source for their teaching. Catholic judgments came easily enough—for Catholics, the Anabaptists were yet another ancient heresy in new disguise—while the Protestant Reformers went out of their way to dissociate themselves from this group that had emerged in their midst.

The spread of Anabaptism throughout Switzerland, Austria, and south Germany was paralleled by a northward expansion into central Germany and the Low Countries. Once more, it is not easy to establish the genealogy of individual congregations and conventicles as they came into existence, but arguably a south German furrier and lay preacher played the crucial role: Melchior Hofmann, at once a sensitive individual ready to suffer for his convictions and a brooding dreamer preoccupied with the arithmetic and imagery of Scripture. Hofmann was obsessed with what he called the "figure," the meaning of the allegorical and figurative parts of Scripture. He had been swayed by the new understanding of the Christian faith that came out of Wittenberg and had become an ardent disciple of Luther, spending time as a traveling evangelist for the cause. Somewhere along the line, however, his story became that of many others: disenchantment

---

5. An important study is Stephen Boyd, *Pilgram Marpeck: His Life and Social Theology* (Mainz: 1992).

with the Wittenberg and Zurich notions of reform. He embraced the notion of believer's baptism and soon became the foremost evangelizer for Anabaptism in the north. In 1531 he extended his activities to Holland, where severe persecution of Anabaptists set in promptly. In itself this turn of events was not noteworthy, for it was merely a painful repetition of what Anabaptists were experiencing almost everywhere. Important in this particular instance, however, was Hofmann's reaction, who interpreted the outbreak of persecution as the obvious sign of the last days and the imminence of Christ's return. He announced that all baptism of believers (the external cause of the persecution) should be suspended for two years, at which time the end would come.

Hofmann became convinced, based on his reading of the Bible, that he would suffer in prison for half a year before God would call him for the restoration of all things. This prediction proved to be crucial, for Hofmann's biblical arithmetic led him to identify the year 1533 as the time of Jesus's Second Coming. He hurried to Strassburg, the "new Jerusalem," to fulfill the prophecy. Upon his arrival he volunteered to be arrested and rejoiced over this turn of events: "And he praised God that the hour had come and he lifted his hat from his head . . . raised his fingers to heaven, swearing to the living God that he would take no other food or drink than water and bread."[6] The words of the Bible had seemingly been fulfilled.

Another prophetic anticipation also seemed to be fulfilled in the town of Münster in northwest Germany, about thirty miles from Holland. A town of some ten thousand inhabitants, not too far from Holland, Münster became the next dramatic chapter in the story of Anabaptism. In Münster the Anabaptists succeeded where they had failed elsewhere: they became the recognized religion of a community and also attained political control. The notion of the persecuted throng of true believers was abandoned in favor of a "New Jerusalem." A strange one it was, at least for outsiders, for it was characterized not only by adult baptism, but also by polygamy and communism. Contemporaries considered these innovations the abomination of abominations, the proof positive that Anabaptists were evil, immoral, and heretical. It mattered little that there were significant differences between the Anabaptists in Münster and those elsewhere. The common affirmation of adult baptism obscured these differences for both the authorities and the Reformers.

A relatively routine transformation of ecclesiastical life in Münster such as was occurring at numerous cities during that time stood at the beginning. Like most cities in the early years of the Reformation, Münster had passed through a period of ecclesiastical tension. Münster did not enjoy the status of an imperial free city but was part of the bishopric of Münster, and the tensions between city council and the guilds, on the one hand, and the Münster bishop, Franz von Waldeck, on the other, were severe enough to keep Waldeck from setting foot in the city. The agitation for religious change received impetus when Bernhard Rothmann, a priest at the convent of St. Mauritz, about three miles east of the city, who had been preaching evangelical notions there since 1524, was twice prohibited from preaching by Waldeck in October and December 1531. Expelled from St. Mauritz Rothmann moved to Münster, where he

---

6. *Bibliotheca Reformatoria Neerlandica*, vol. 7: *Zestiende-eeuwsche schrijvers over de geschiedenis der oudste Doopsgezinden hier te lande* (ed. S. Cramer; Gravenhage, 1910), 7:124.

was welcomed with open arms. At the St. Lamberti Church, the church of the guilds, a stone's throw from the bishop's cathedral, he proclaimed the message of the Reformation. Waldeck appealed to the city council to stop the ecclesiastical innovations, but in May 1532 the city council responded that it was powerless to intervene: the popular support for the new preaching was simply too strong. By that time, Rothmann had acquired the nickname Stutenbernd for his use of ordinary bread (*stuten*) for Communion.

In July 1532 the Münster city council acquiesced to popular agitation and stipulated—with a striking claim to jurisdiction in matters of religion—that all clergy should proclaim the evangelical message and follow Rothmann's lead. The Catholic authorities, concerned about these developments, summoned Rothmann to appear in Cologne to be examined about his beliefs. Not surprisingly, Rothmann saw the handwriting on the wall and refused to appear; he was excommunicated soon thereafter. In August Waldeck ordered, along the lines of the recess of the 1530 Augsburg diet, that all evangelical preaching in the city be stopped and all ecclesiastical changes rescinded until the next diet, meeting at Nuremberg and Regensburg, had rendered a decision about the contested religious issues. At this juncture most loyal Catholics decided to leave the city. Although sixteenth-century statistics are notoriously unreliable, it is estimated that during the sixteen months of subsequent Anabaptist rule some seven thousand people lived in Münster, which would suggest that some three thousand Catholic loyalists had left the city during the early stage of Reformation change. Of the seven thousand, roughly one-third were Münsterites turned committed Anabaptists, one-third were immigrants from Holland and north Germany, and one-third were Münster burghers who had stayed in the city.

Waldeck decided that the time for active intervention had come. To exert pressure on the city he confiscated a herd of oxen belonging to the city and put guards on the main access roads leading to Münster. The city council, in turn, sought to become a member of the League of Schmalkald, but Landgrave Philip of Hesse blocked the request, because he anticipated political complications. Still seeking a resolution of the problem, Waldeck agreed in February 1533 that evangelical preaching could take place in Münster; only the cathedral and the monastic churches in town were to continue celebrating the Mass.

In the fall of 1532 and spring of 1533, the arrival of several preachers from Wassenberg in Holland began a new chapter in the transition of Münster to an Anabaptist city. These preachers were of the more radical sort, especially regarding infant baptism, which they rejected. Münster was divided, with Rothmann increasingly in favor of a Zwinglian, even Anabaptist course, while von der Wieck and other influential city council members advocated a Lutheran stance.

In January 1534 two emissaries of Jan Matthijs, a former baker by trade from Haarlem who had risen to become the leader of the Anabaptists in Amsterdam, arrived in Münster and proclaimed that contrary to Melchior Hofmann's injunction, believer's baptism should be administered. Rothmann and many others—a contemporary chronicler speaks of more than fourteen hundred individuals—were promptly baptized. This baptism made a deep impact upon Anabaptists in Holland and north Germany. Believer's baptism had been suspended upon Hofmann's exhortation that the end was imminent. Hofmann himself lay in a Strassburg prison, patiently awaiting the great day. To Hofmann's followers, the dramatic changes in Münster seemed to be a vindication of the prophet's message that the end was near. Persecution had ceased, the elect went unmolested, the city had changed its face to conform to the vision of the new Jerusalem. Matthijs's exhortation that believer's baptism could again be administered because these were the last days ushered in an atmosphere of spiritual exuberance. Soon thereafter Matthijs arrived in Münster. Elections to the city council brought an Anabaptist majority, a victory for Rothmann and his supporters, and all citizens unwilling to be baptized were compelled to leave the city.

When the last of these men, women, and children disappeared beyond the city walls, Münster had become the "new Jerusalem." The "ungodly" had been driven away and only the "elect" remained. On the face of things, Münster was Anabaptist, but the city had done an about-face from many Anabaptist principles. The notion of true believers as a suffering minority in society was replaced by the assertion of a new identity of church and society. The *corpus christianum* was reestablished.

At about the same time, a siege of the city began. The rulers of the territories surrounding Münster, including the Protestant Philip of Hesse, were unwilling to accept the usurpation of governmental authority in the city. The coalition force that had been assembled by Waldeck included both Catholics and Protestants, an indication that more was at issue than mainstream Protestant religion. As they had been all along, the Anabaptists, now of the Münster variety, were seen as insurgents.

Initally, the siege was unsuccessful. Matthijs, who had risen to be the undisputed leader in the city, died in a skirmish outside the city walls while pursuing the mandate of a dream in which he had engaged the besieging soldiers in open battle. The death of the prophet created only a temporary vacuum. Another Dutchman, Jan van Leyden, took his place. Twenty-four years of age, a tailor by trade, with a keen sense of political reality and an extraordinary spiritual vocation, Leyden was profoundly convinced that God had called him to rule over His elect at Münster and throughout the world. He saw himself as the third David, whose pretentious emblem was a globe with the inscription "King of Righteousness over All."

Major changes occurred in the new Jerusalem. Community of goods, the rejection of private property, was introduced. The precarious economic situation created by the siege of the city was undoubtedly a major factor in this decision, even as the book of Acts provided the biblical precedent. Polygamy was also introduced, again against the backdrop of practical necessity and biblical insight. Estimates are that toward the end of the siege, there were some two thousand men and some five thousand women in the city, of whom many had migrated to Münster from elsewhere. Women outnumbered men in Münster, and because single women were legally without rights, a way had to be found to deal with the problem. The claim to biblical precedent was supported by the patriarchs of the Old Testament, who demonstrated that polygamy was evidently practiced without divine disapproval. Despite the enormous pressures, such as famine, the siege remained unsuccessful.

Then, in the spring of 1535 the besieging forces succeeded in taking the city through treason—committed by none other than the subsequent annalist of Münsterite events. The authority of Bishop Franz von Waldeck was restored in the city, when a terrible vengeance took place. All males were killed; women and children were expelled from the city. Münster was a ghost town until the former burghers, who had fled the Anabaptist regime, were allowed to return one by one. The "king" of the new Jerusalem, Jan van Leyden, the "mayor" of the new Jerusalem, Bernd Knipperdolling, and the chief counselor, Bernd Krechting, were put to death in front of the city hall, their corpses then placed into three iron cages that were hung from the steeple of the St. Lamberti Church, the prestigious church of the Münster burghers and guilds located in the very center of the city. Even today, almost half a millennium later, these cages still hang on the Lamberti steeple, an intriguing memorial to religious strife and intolerance.

The Münster episode showed that the affirmation of believer's baptism could easily turn into an intense eschatological disposition—or vice versa. Most other Anabaptists abhorred the notion that it was biblical to use force and take up arms. The Münster Anabaptists, in their expectation of the imminent end of all things, were convinced that they too could employ force to defend and safeguard their faith.

Afterward, persecution of dissenting religious sentiment intensified in the north (though not everywhere with equal measure), for the fear of the authorities that the Anabaptists were political revolutionaries in disguise had received renewed justification. For the Anabaptists, Münster had been a theological catastrophe. The eschatological frenzy had proved to be a failure: Jesus had not returned in 1534 as Hofmann had predicted, and the establishment of the new Jerusalem had brought immense suffering and bloodshed. Something had gone wrong. The fact that most of the Anabaptists in the north had supported the Münster Anabaptists meant that the local catastrophe had wide repercussions, for, during the brief existence of the new Jersualem, extensive contacts between Münster and Anabaptist congregations in Holland and north Germany had taken place. In March 1534, about the time the siege began in Münster, hundreds of Anabaptists from Holland gathered near Hasselt, today a town in Belgium near the German border, to move to Münster. To their surprise and consternation, they were met not by guides to the new Jerusalem but by officers of the law, who promptly and rigidly dispersed them, raising for them the question of whether they should have defended themselves. These Anabaptists owed their origin to Melchior Hofmann—thus their designation "Melchiorites"—and they were peaceful, committed to the principle of nonresistance. Hofmann's peculiar mix of theological emphases, especially his eschatological predilection, made it easy for some Melchiorites to feel called to defend the cause of the elect with arms. This happened, for example, at the Oldekloster in Frisia, the "old monastery," which was taken over by several hundred armed Anabaptists in March 1535. They too saw themselves as living in the last days, preparing for the final battle of Armageddon. They were able to defend themselves for a week, but most perished in the final assault. Their effort revealed that they were possessed by the crusading ideal—the conviction, in other words, that in the end times the elect of God would rise up and, as prefigured in the books of Daniel and of Revelation, conquer the godless. This motivated a tiny group of Anabaptists in Amsterdam to take over—unsuccessfully, as could be expected—the city hall some six weeks before Münster fell to the besieging forces.

No wonder, then, that the debacle of the "new Jerusalem" caused such consternation. The theological shock was profound. The expected end had not come, the righteous were still oppressed and persecuted, and the godless continued to be in charge.[7] A small group of militants under the leadership of one Jan van Batenburg sought to keep the spirit of the end times alive, but most of the small Anabaptist-Melchiorite conventicles took the happenings at Münster as an indication that they had been in error. As was the case elsewhere, the Anabaptist conventicles and congregations in the north did not possess organizational cohesiveness, so that a variety of emphases, interpretations, and foci characterized the scene. What they held in common, however, was their insistence that both the old, Catholic Church and the new churches of the Reformation had failed to recover the authentic biblical faith, the personal commitment to be a disciple of Jesus, expressed in receiving the initiation rite of baptism.

It was David Joris who became the great consolidator of the Anabaptists in the north. Born around the turn of the century, a glass painter by trade, Joris came under the spell of Luther's teachings in the 1520s and was arrested for disseminating anticlerical publications in 1528. Around that time he came into contact with Hofmann's preaching and was baptized and ordained. At a meeting of Anabaptists in Holland at the time of the Münster siege, Joris spoke poignantly against the use of force by the Münster Anabaptists. The fall of the new Jerusalem vindicated his words of caution. It enhanced his stature, and in the following years he played a major role in redirecting the disillusioned Anabaptists to a spiritual understanding of the topics that had given the Münster Anabaptists such a terrible reputation—the struggle of the elect against the godless, baptism, communism, and polygamy. This mediating, albeit highly spiritual, interpretation of the Anabaptist ethos successfully forged a new unity of the disillusioned Anabaptist groups and conventicles. Joris was the key figure in the theological compromise forged at Bocholt, west of Münster, near the Dutch border, in 1537. In essence, Joris reaffirmed the basic Anabaptist tenets by spiritualizing them. Despair was thus transformed into a new vision.

All the same, a bitter theological controversy with the other Anabaptist leader in the north, the former Catholic priest Menno Simons, together with severe persecutions of his followers, prompted Joris to take the Nicodemite approach—outward conformity to the officially endorsed religion. This eventually took him to Basel, where, without surrendering his convictions but no longer a visible leader of a heretical group, he combined an outwardly respectable (and prosperous) existence with heretical convictions. Joris concentrated on disseminating his ideas through his pen; he wrote some 230 tracts and pamphlets, which were widely and well received. These writings increasingly conveyed a spiritualist understanding of Christianity: believer's baptism as well as the gathering of the true church became less important than the notion of the Spirit-filled believer living the sanctified life. It was not until after his death in 1556 that his true identity as former leader of the Anabaptists in the north

---

7. The best account for the fate of Anabaptists after the Münster debacle are Gary K. Waite, *David Joris and Dutch Anabaptism, 1524–1543* (Waterloo, Ont.: 1990), and Sigrun Haude, *In the Shadow of "Savage Wolves": Anabaptist Münster and the German Reformation during the 1530s* (Boston: 2000).

became evident. In an intriguing manifestation of intolerance, Joris was condemned as a heretic by the Basel authorities, and his corpse disinterred and burned.

By that time, however, the Anabaptists in north Germany and Holland had a new voice and a new leader—Menno Simons—from whose name they received their appellation "Mennonites" in the seventeenth century. Menno, born in Witmarsum, Frisia (in the northern Netherlands), in 1495 or 1496, had been ordained deacon in 1524 and priest seven years later—at an unusually mature age—and served as priest in his native village. Much like Luther, he provided in his later years an autobiographical account of his religious pilgrimage that indicated that soon after his ordination to the priesthood he developed doubts about the doctrine of transubstantiation. He lived with these doubts for several years, surely an indication of a cautious and systematic temperament. News about the execution of a certain Sicke Freerks, an Anabaptist from Leeuwarden, for having been baptized upon his confession of faith prompted Menno to question the practice of baptizing infants. His autobiography makes clear that several factors were important elements in his conversion: the "poor straying sheep" that had taken up arms at the Oldekloster and been killed and to whom he had "disclosed some of the abominations of the papal system," as well as his own "unclean, carnal life, also the hypocritical doctrine and idolatry," which he still practiced "in appearance of godliness."[8]

Menno converted to Melchiorite Anabaptism, and in January 1536, less than a year after the Münster debacle, he abandoned his priestly position and Catholic ties. He was baptized upon confession of faith and ordained by Obbe Philips, who together with his brother Dirk Philips was the leader of the peaceful strand of Melchiorite Anabaptists. Menno began a persistent evangelistic sojourn from Anabaptist conventicle to Anabaptist conventicle in Holland, Frisia, and the Lower Rhine region to assure the Melchiorites, deeply dismayed by the Münster debacle, that according to Scripture Münster had been a fatal error.

A paradigm shift allowed the disenchanted Anabaptists to salvage their faith. Menno focused on the marvel of the Christian's new birth, the sanctified life in Christ who called His disciples to holiness and peacefulness. There are in Menno no striking new theological insights, but wonderfully warm and thoughtful reflections on the new life in Christ. Menno's theological thought was derivative of others, notably Hofmann, expressed, for example, in Menno's appropriation of Hofmann's monophysite Christology: Jesus had not been born of Mary, Menno argued, but in her, passing through her body like water passes through a tube. "Christ Jesus, as to his origin," Menno wrote, "is no earthly man, that is fruit of the flesh and blood of Adam. He is a heavenly fruit of man."[9] As was the case with the monophysite theologians of late antiquity, Menno was persuaded that if Jesus had received his flesh from Mary, he could not have been sinless, and therefore could not have reconciled humans with God.

Menno's intense practical pastoral involvement—while Joris lived affluently in Basel under a pseudonym—with a bounty on his head, moving underground from place to place, constantly running the chance of being detected or betrayed, made him the eminent Anabaptist leader among north German and Dutch Anabaptists. This

8. *The Complete Writings of Menno Simons* (Scottdale, PA: 1956), 670.
9. Ibid., 774.

importance does not mean that Menno was anything like an administrative head of the Anabaptist conventicles in the north. Rather, it meant simply (but importantly) that his particular understanding of the Christian faith was ever more widely embraced by Anabaptists.[10] His understanding focused on the godly life—the emphasis being on what theologians call sanctification. The community of those who committed themselves to this walk of life was the church, which became the very heart of Menno's theology. This church was to be "without spots and wrinkles," and that, in turn, meant conscious separation from all that was worldly. Menno, who successfully gathered the disparate Anabaptist groupings after the Münster debacle into an Anabaptist "mainstream," was later unsuccessful in carrying the day against the more rigorist tendencies expressed in a meeting of Anabaptist leaders in Wismar in 1554.

Menno was the great conciliator, the great evangelist among the north German and Dutch Melchiorite Anabaptists, who little by little succeeded in moving away from Hofmann's intense eschatology, which had been the ultimate cause of the Münster catastrophe. Menno's strength lay in his devotional tone, his persistent reiteration of the theme of the new birth, which made all things new. It is an intriguing manifestation of the changed disposition of Anabaptism in Holland and north Germany that before too long the most contested issue among Anabaptists was how a believing spouse should relate to an unbelieving spouse. The new understanding of the Anabaptist vision in the face of the Münster catastrophe also meant the disavowal of the use of force in any form whatsoever—including military force—by believers. The Münsterite eschatology and the concomitant use of force in "the last days" was repudiated in favor of a patient and peaceful waiting for the second coming.[11]

The Münster debacle made Anabaptists everywhere, especially in the north, more inner directed, eschewing any attempt to impose their ways upon society. Quietism became the hallmark of the movement, which sought to survive in the face of persistent oppression and persecution. In some places, notably Austria, ruthless persecution succeeded in crushing the movement. In others, such as Poland and Moravia, a more tolerant atmosphere allowed the Anabaptists to live a peaceable existence, at least until in the seventeenth century the thrust of the Catholic Counter-Reformation created new and pressing problems. In Holland and Germany the situation was more ambivalent, although the organizational genius and spiritual qualities of Menno allowed the Anabaptist movement to emphasize the principles of peaceful and ethical Christianity. As Mennonites, the Anabaptists of the Reformation era have survived into the twenty-first century.

The overriding issue faced by Anabaptists in the north of Germany was how to establish the church of the true believers. The communion of saints had to be pure, and that meant the exercise of church discipline. The issue came to a head in the late 1540s, when Menno published a tract in 1549 entitled *A Clear Account of Excommunication,* in which he laid down the principles of church discipline, a sentiment echoed a few years later by the Wismar Articles of 1554. An apostate church member had to

---

10. The best introduction to Menno Simons remains Christoph Bornhäuser, *Leben und Lehre Menno Simons': Ein Kampf um das Fundament des Glaubens (etwa 1496–1561)* (Neukirchen-Vluyn: 1973).

11. See also Gerald R. Brunk, ed., *Menno Simons: A Reappraisal* (Harrisonburg, VA: 1992).

be "shunned" or avoided—even within the family. That, of course, was easier said than done, and in 1555 the unresolved issues once more demanded attention, when the Anabaptist leader Leenaert Bouwens excommunicated the husband of one Swaen Rutgers. Swaen accordingly was to avoid all contact with her husband, for, as Bouwens insisted, the heavenly marriage between the believer and Christ was more sacred than any earthly marriage. Herself deeply devout, Swaen demurred at the mandate of "shunning" her husband and was threatened with excommunication.

An almost endless series of internal Anabaptist publications and meetings, from which a great many mutual recriminations and threats of excommunication emerged, sought to delineate a definitive position on the matter.[12] The aging Menno as well as a host of younger Anabaptist leaders in north Germany and Holland participated with vigor in the discussion. In the end, Anabaptists in the North divided into a moderate wing, called the Waterlanders, and a rigorist wing represented by Bouwens. The Anabaptists in south Germany and Switzerland were largely spared the controversy.

In all of this Anabaptists everywhere, north and south, continued to be haunted and hunted by the political authorities at large. They remained an underground movement, with only the loosest organization, which slowly gave way to regional forms of church structure and government. Anabaptists were determined to demonstrate by their piety and commitment to hard work and modest living that they constituted no threat to society. They became the *Stillen im Lande*, the quiet ones in the land, and by the time the century turned, the Anabaptists, in Holland, or *Doopsgezinden*, not only had attained practical toleration, but had also begun to participate in the dramatic prosperity that was seventeenth-century Holland. When Thieleman van Braght published his *Martyrs' Mirror*, the most comprehensive Anabaptist martyrology, in the middle of the seventeenth century, he spent most of his preface bewailing his coreligionists' turn to fancy houses and extravagant living.

THE HUTTERITE EXPERIMENT

By the early 1530s a network of Anabaptist conventicles had been established throughout parts of Switzerland, Austria, and south Germany. About the size of these conventicles we can only make guesses: both adherents of the movement and their antagonists offered figures, but those must be taken with more than the proverbial grain of salt. We simply do not know, and the tally of known Anabaptists in the sixteenth century for German-language areas yields a strikingly low number.[13] As we saw, traveling missionaries, moving from village to village, town to town, established these local Anabaptist communities, then left them on their own, sustained by the Bible and a few tracts from the pens of Anabaptist writers. Larger organizational structures

12. Three years before his death, Menno published two further tracts on the issue—his *Instruction on Excommunication* and his *Final Instruction on Marital Avoidance*. A convenient English translation of all of Menno's writings is found in Menno Simons, *Complete Writings*, trans. Leonard Verduin, ed. John C. Wenger, with a biography by Harold S. Bender (Scottdale, PA: 1956).

13. Claus P. Clasen, *Anabaptism: A Social History: 1525–1618. Switzerland, Austria, Moravia, South and Central Germany* (Ithaca, NY: 1972).

were long in coming, and theological diversity was an understandable consequence. However, this diversity must not be thought of as a principle; it was accidental.

Virtually everywhere these Anabaptist gatherings were underground communities—hidden from the eyes of the authorities, both secular and ecclesiastical, sometimes aggressively pursued by these authorities, at other times barely tolerated or treated with benign neglect. They persisted, but always fearful of sudden governmental intervention.

It was in this situation that word about Moravia began to spread among persecuted Anabaptists.[14] A promised land, it seemed to them, for it was said that toleration prevailed there, in the shadow of Jan Hus's legacy of religious diversity. The Anabaptist message had been taken to Moravia by Balthasar Hubmaier, former priest, doctor of theology, and subsequent reformer of Waldshut, a town some thirty miles north of Zurich. Hubmaier, by all odds the most learned of the early Anabaptist leaders, had put his own particular imprint on the Anabaptist conventicles, notably his assertion, outlined in a tract entitled *Von dem Schwert* (Of the Sword), that a Christian may serve in governmental offices and even be a soldier, a view quite unlike that held by many Anabaptists and found the Schleitheim Confession. As word of the tolerant atmosphere in Moravia spread, persecuted Anabaptists from Austria and south Germany began to flock there. The semi-autonomous Moravian magnates, eager to find toilers for land that had been frequently deserted, were willing to exchange religious toleration for labor. Before long, religious pluralism reigned in Moravia, not only for Catholics and Protestants, but for Anabaptist dissenters as well. That was an important consideration, for, as Caspar Schwenckfeld wrote many years later about Moravia, "no soul agrees with the other in the faith."[15] Seldom in harmony, chronically quarrelling, the divergent Anabaptist conventicles lived uneasily side by side until in the mid-1530s one faction began to overshadow the others. These were the Hutterites, named after Jakob Hutter, the charismatic leader who eventually provided his name for the Moravian Anabaptist conventicles and communities.

Hailing from the South Tyrol, Hutter had been a hat maker by trade (which gave him his name). Born probably in 1500, Hutter joined the Anabaptist movement in 1529 and quickly emerged as leader of the Anabaptists in the Tyrol. Severe persecution by the Austrian authorities and word of the atmosphere of toleration in Moravia prompted Hutter to discover whether conditions were favorable there for the persecuted Anabaptists. At Austerlitz, a village made famous in 1805 through Napoleon's decisive victory over Austria and Russia (not to mention the echoes of that victory in the Austerlitz train station in Paris), Hutter found Anabaptist congregations in Moravia that conformed to his ideal of the apostolic community. These Anabaptists had been expelled from nearby Nikolsburg in 1528, and on the road east to Austerlitz, the homeless, starving, and desolate Anabaptists made the momentous decision to share their resources. In the words of the Hutterite Chronicle, "In light of their

14. Werner Packull, *Hutterite Beginnings* (Philadelphia: 1995).
15. Caspar Schwenckfeld, *Corpus Schwenckfeldianorum*, 17:218. The quote is from the year 1560. Werner Packull, *Hutterite Beginnings: Communitarian Experiments during the Reformation* (Baltimore: 1995), 337; R. Emmet McLaughlin, *Caspar Schwenkfeld, Reluctant Radical: His Life to 1540* (New Haven: 1986).

need, they took counsel with one another and named 'servants of temporal needs.' . . . These men spread a cloak in front of the people. And everyone brought their belongings, freely and uncoerced, so that the needy might be provided for, according to the teaching of the prophets and the apostles."[16] The catalysts for this turn toward a community of goods were economic necessity and the apostolic precedent. It is not altogether clear whether this pooling of resources was meant as a temporary or a permanent measure, though evidently it did not come about after extensive reflection. But the decision took on permanence.

Soon group upon group of Tyrolean Anabaptists found their way to Moravia. Hutter himself stayed in the Tyrol until the governmental persecution became so severe— his sister was arrested and executed—that he too moved to Moravia, where he arrived in August of 1533. He was deeply dismayed at what he found: internal strife, preferential treatment, malnourished children, arrogant leaders, and embezzlement of funds. Internal strife had forced a group of Anabaptists to leave Austerlitz for nearby Auspitz in freezing winter, without food or funds, and the word was that Catholics and Jews showed them greater kindnesses on the way than did their own Anabaptist brethren.

Hutter's arrival and leadership came in time. Though there was apprehension that he too would cause further internal strife and dissension—one Anabaptist leader was urged to "do your best to prevent a root of bitterness from coming up among the servants of God"[17]—Hutter was elected *Vorsteher* (Superior) of the Austerlitz community, and determinedly he undertook to regulate its life. Most importantly, the concept of communal living found both a biblical and an organizational grounding. Each member of the community had a specific responsibility and performed specific assigned tasks. The result was a community both egalitarian and totalitarian. "There was no one who went idle," wrote the Hutterite chronicler; "everyone did what he was instructed and was able to do, no matter whether he had been rich or poor. Even the pastors, who joined our brotherhood, performed manual labor. . . . As in the artistic mechanism of a clock one wheel moves and helps the others and makes them turn, or as in a beehive all bees work together, so it was here. For where there is no order, there is disorder and disruption, where God is absent, everything will soon break asunder."[18] In addition, the charisma of Hutter succeeded in ending the internal strife among the various Moravian Anabaptist communities, each with entrenched leadership, each categorically denouncing the other communities. Hutter received his share of recrimination, was called ambitious, deceitful, and a backstabber, but his leadership remained dynamic and strong.

The debacle at Münster in 1535 had repercussions for the Anabaptists in the Tyrol and Moravia. The Austrian King Ferdinand, for whom the policies of religious toleration of the Moravian nobility were a thorn in the flesh, became determined to crush the Anabaptist heretics. The nobility yielded and expelled the Anabaptists from their lands. A period of restless wandering began, the Hutterites camping out in open fields or deep woods, men, women, and children, many of whom found their way back to Austria and the Tyrol.

---

16. A. J. F. Zieglschmid, ed., *Die älteste Chronik der Hutterischen Brüder* (Ithaca, NY: 1943), 87.
17. Packull, *Hutterite Beginnings*, 223.
18. Zieglschmid, *Älteste Chronik*, 435.

On one of his return forays back to Austria in November 1535, Hutter was arrested (probably betrayed) and taken to Innsbruck, the seat of Ferdinand's government. Even though the Innsbruck authorities had pleaded that the death penalty be carried out with the sword, Ferdinand insisted that as a heretic Hutter had to suffer death by being burned at the stake.

It was to be of enormous importance that a new leader was prepared to lead the Hutterites who returned to Moravia as persecution quickly waned. Peter Riedemann may most be considered the second founder of the Hutterites. Born in 1506 in Silesia, Riedemann became an Anabaptist, was imprisoned, escaped, and moved to Moravia, where he joined the Hutterites probably in 1533. His story became one of a relentless missionary effort, virtually commuting constantly between Moravia and southern Germany. The year 1540 found him in Hesse, where his Anabaptist preaching promptly led to his imprisonment. Landgrave Philip's tolerant attitude toward the Anabaptists meant that Riedemann was essentially under house arrest, rather than languishing in a dungeon. This allowed him to pen the foremost doctrinal statement of the Hutterite Anabaptists—the *Rechenschaft unserer Religion, Lehr und Glaubens, von den Brüdern so man die Hutterischen nannt, ausgangen* (Account of Our Religion, Teachings, and Faith, Issued by the Brethren Called the Hutterites).[19] The *Rechenschaft* shows its theological indebtedness to other Anabaptist theologians, but what is most remarkable is that the confession was written in prison, without access to any writings other than the Bible. The *Rechenschaft* has retained its normative character for the Hutterite communities to this day.

Riedemann's story took a dramatic turn when in 1542 the death of two Hutterite leaders prompted the community to turn to him for leadership. Riedemann faced a moral bind: his confinement in Hesse was so lenient as to make it easy for him to escape, but he was reluctant to violate the confidence of his jailers. In the end, however, he yielded to the entreaties from Moravia. The Hutterites had urgent pled that there was "need of him in great necessity." Riedemann proved to be a thoughtful and competent leader and steered the Hutterite communities through a period of fierce persecution that began in 1545. He died in 1556 at the age of fifty.

PROTESTANT SPIRITUALISM

The signal characteristic of the Reformation was that the notions propounded by an ever larger number of Reformers took on institutional and organizational forms. These new church structures made the Protestant Reformation a chapter in the history not just of theology but of institutionalized Christianity as well. Luther comes to mind as the example par excellence of combining theological insights and practical churchmanship, as do, of course, Thomas Cranmer and John Calvin. Somehow, the ideas of these individuals reverberated with practical consequences.

Alongside these Reformers must be placed other Reformers with demonstrably little, if any interest in practical church matters. Some Reformers delineated their

---

19. One of the few copies of the first edition of 1565 is found in the British Library, London.

notions of what the true Christian faith was all about, attracted followers, but their interest in translating their ideas into practical and organizational reality was limited, if not nonexistent.

They were, in other words, blatantly uninterested in their attempt to sway their contemporaries to their vision of the Christian religion. Or so at least it seemed, for in fact even though success seemingly did not grace their efforts many of their ideas have a remarkable history that extends well beyond the sixteenth century. Arguably, their importance went far beyond their inability to attract many followers and their reluctance to think in terms of establishing new "churches." Their ideas proved to be far more dramatically influential than those of many of the mainstream Reformers.

We are talking about solitary individuals, in other words, who were uninterested in galvanizing their contemporaries and unwilling to establish a "movement." Because these individuals talked and wrote so much about the "spirit" and "spiritual religion" and "spiritual Christianity," scholars have labeled them "spiritualists" or, since that word conjures up modern-day séances, "spiritualizers." These spiritualists eschewed the tangible, empirical manifestations of Christianity, such as water, bread, wine, and church organizations, and preferred to think of Christianity in terms of "spiritual" truths.[20] They were deeply concerned about the Christian faith and found neither the old church nor the new churches authentic manifestations of true Christianity. They were dissenters, convinced that something had gone wrong with the effort at reform. Their focus was elsewhere; their emphases were of a different sort than those of the other Reformers, including the Anabaptists and antitrinitarians. Thus they did not get excited about the prominent points of theological controversy, endlessly argued among Catholic, Lutheran, and Reformed theologians—adult or infant baptism, the relationship of government and the church, the meaning of Jesus's words of institution at his Last Supper. Nor did they take the Trinitarian dogma of the church as the apex of theological perversion. Their point—not utterly novel, because the medieval mystics may be seen as their antecedents—was that these fiercely contested doctrines and theological propositions were external, outward matters that failed to address the core of the Christian faith.

In contrast to the other religious Reformers in the sixteenth century, however, the spiritualists had scant interest in altering or reforming the ecclesiastical status quo. They criticized the existing forms of religion, but proposing new doctrines or forming new churches was not their priority. Sebastian Franck opined, "I am part of the invisible church and I inwardly long for it, wherever among the heathen it may be found. I cannot point to this church but I am certain that I am part of it, where I am and, therefore, I seek neither this church nor Christ in any specific place."[21]

They were individualists; thus they have been, in a manner of speaking, without history. They were outsiders, who lived only in the pages of their writings—if they

---

20. George H. Williams's encyclopedic *The Radical Reformation* (3rd ed.; Kirksville, MO: 1992), remains the most thorough treatment of the phenomenon.

21. Sebastian Franck, *Paradoxa*. English translation: *280 Paradoxes or Wondrous Sayings* (trans. E. J. Furcha; Lewiston, NY: Edwin Mellen, 1986). The original title is *Paradoxa ducenta octoginta, das ist, CCLXXX. Wunderred und gleichsam Räterschafft, auß der h. Schrifft, so vor allem fleysch unglaublich und unwar sind, doch wider der gantzen Welt wohn und achtung, geweiß und waar. Item aller in Got Philosophierenden Christen, rechte, götliche Philosophei, und Teütsche Theologei* (Ulm: 1534).

decided to put their thoughts on paper. Since they considered the empirical forms of the Christian faith to be irrelevant or unimportant, most of them conformed to the expected external religious routine of their respective communities. Only a few were emboldened to testify publicly to their convictions, and whenever that happened it seemed to be mainly by default. These few instances, however, provide the sole evidence we have of their kind, though undoubtedly many thought and believed like them, but lacked the courage or the determination to make their sentiment known.

"In the beginning was the Word": this biblical dictum arguably was the motto of the spiritualists. But theirs was a unique definition of "the Word." They did not mean the "outer" word, the Bible, which they considered an obscure and enigmatic book, where one part disagreed with another and interpretation stood against interpretation. Indeed, they delighted in collecting scriptural passages that, as they claimed, contradicted one another. Their "word" was God's direct communication to humans, conveyed in dreams and visions, prayer and meditation. Scripture was only the external witness and record of this direct communication. This conviction prompted the spiritualists to label all empirical manifestations of religion as peripheral and insignificant. The spiritualists preferred the "living voice" of God to the dead record of Scripture. They considered spiritual baptism more important than the baptism of water at whatever age, and the spiritual union with Christ more meaningful than the eating of bread and the drinking of wine. Outer form was rejected in favor of inner spirituality. The Bible and ceremonies, the sacraments and the church, creeds and ecclesiastical polity were unimportant. The spiritualists' emphasis meant the implicit rejection of a great deal of traditional dogma, or, at any rate, a reversal of priorities, so that the doctrines that were not outrightly questioned were relegated to insignificance. In a way, therefore, the spiritualists anticipated a great deal of the new understanding of religion (and Christianity) that became dominant in the course of the later seventeenth and eighteenth centuries.

Sebastian Franck, a multitalented individual who was a priest, soap maker, geographer, printer, translator, historian, and theologian, deserves the most prominent place in the roster of sixteenth-century spiritualists. After he resigned from the Catholic priesthood, he began a peripatetic life that took him first to Strassburg and then to Ulm. He eked out a living as a maker of soaps but mainly supported himself (and his family) by publishing a large number of works of his own as well as of others. Whenever the unorthodoxy of his writings began to come to the attention of the displeased local authorities, Franck thought it best to leave.

His versatility was characteristic of the spiritualists who came from the ranks of both clergy and laity. They often were theologians of boundless exuberance and endurance. Franck's story is that of a committed yet endless seeker who traversed the full spectrum of religious options of the early sixteenth century. He started out as a Catholic, turned Lutheran, became an Anabaptist, and eventually decided to go his own way. "I do not want to be a papist," he wrote, "I do not want to be a Lutheran, I do not want to be an Anabaptist." He found fault with all.

Franck's was a brief life and, considering the turbulence of the time, a surprisingly tranquil one, but underneath that tranquility there was great turmoil, for he harbored thoughts that offered a radically new understanding of the Christian religion. Franck saw Christianity as the expression of universal religion or, to use language made popular by the English Deist Matthew Tindal two centuries later, "a republication of the religion of nature." Accordingly, religious insight was valid regardless where it was found, within or without the Christian church, within or without the Christian tradition. The great events of the Bible were timeless symbols of God's dealings with humankind. Eternal and universal truth expressed itself in historical form, Franck argued. "The histories of Adam and Christ are not Adam and Christ," he remarked, and he added, "The external Adam and Christ are but the expression of the inward, indwelling Adam and Christ."

Another spiritualist, Sebastian Castellio, was consumed by compassion and made it a theological principle.[22] He paid for it with a life of personal hardship, an early death, and nearly universal repudiation by his contemporaries, but also a place in history. Castellio (or Castellion), a Frenchman, was born in 1515, converted to Protestantism, and in 1540 became principal of a Latin school in Strasburg. An early friendship with Calvin, who was living in Strasburg at that time, led to his move to Geneva. Soon thereafter a break occurred between the two men, and in 1545 Castellio moved to Basel, where he initially lived in dire poverty working for a printing firm until in 1553 he was appointed professor of Greek at the University of Basel.

Castellio expressed his compassion for the antitrinitarian Michael Servetus in an eloquent repudiation of the governmental suppression of dissenting religious opinion. It was entitled *De haereticis, an sint persequendi* (If Heretics Are to Be Persecuted?) and was published in 1553 in response to Servetus's execution in Geneva. Its single theme, repeated with many variations, was that the noblest minds of Christendom through the centuries had been against the persecution of heretics. Indeed, the theologians had understood that persecution was wrong because it contradicted the principles of Christ. Besides, the definition of "heretic" was not simple: "If you are reputed in one town a true believer, you will be reputed in the next town as a heretic. Accordingly, if anyone wants to live today, he must have as many confessions of faith and religions as there are towns and sects, just as a traveler has to change his money from one day to the next."

Although Castellio's prime motivation was compassion as well as horror over the pain and anguish of a fellow human being, he also emphasized the dichotomy of the "external" and "internal" that also was so basic for Sebastian Franck. He argued that differences in the interpretation of doctrines did not touch on the essence of the Christian faith; therefore, such differences should be disregarded. The practice of a moral life was of greater importance than the proper interpretation, for example, of the Trinity. Castellio's Christianity was undogmatic, latitudinarian, and practical, and thus quite different from the eminence of theological norms so universally accepted in the sixteenth century.

If it was the hallmark of the spiritualist sentiment to eschew all external forms of the Christian religion, Caspar Schwenckfeld, a Silesian nobleman, succeeded in forming a "spiritualist" community that has survived until the present.[23] Born of a noble

---

22. Hans Guggisberg, *Sebastian Castellio: 1515–1563; Humanist und Verteidiger der religiösen Toleranz im konfessionellen Zeitalter* (Göttingen: 1997).

23. His voluminous writings are in *Corpus Schwenckfeldianorum*. Published under the auspices of the Schwenckfelder Church Pennsylvania, 19 vols. (Leipzig and Pennsburg, PA: 1907–1961).

family in Silesia in 1489, Schwenckfeld received a university education at Cologne and Frankfurt, and in 1510 became counselor to the Silesian dukes. In the course of the indulgences controversy he became an ardent disciple of Luther, experienced a conversion, and worked as a lay preacher and publicist for the new faith. Soon, however, an alienation took place from Luther: by 1524 his theological studies prompted him to deny the real presence of the body and blood of Christ in the Communion elements. Moreover, he saw Luther's notion of justification as the cause for what he perceived as the moral deterioration in Lutheran lands. A rich period of literary activity followed, mainly on his spiritual understanding of the Christian faith. Eventually, this made it impossible to remain on his parental estate. An unsteady sojourn took him to Strassburg, where the reformers Capito and Bucer (and their spouses) initially welcomed him with open arms but turned suspicious when they learned details of his theology. Leaving Strassburg in 1533, Schwenckfeld moved to just about every south German town that had accepted the Reformation (Hagenau, Landau, Speyer, Esslingen, Ulm, Augsburg, Mindelheim, Kempten, Memmingen, Lindau) until he eventually settled in Ulm. Soon he was expelled and renewed his unsteady pilgrimage. The War of Schmalkald made him a refugee—the Lutheran divines had repeatedly condemned his notions as heresy, and Philip of Hesse's attempt to effect conciliation between Schwenckfeld and Melanchthon failed. He died in Ulm in 1561.

Franck, Castellio, Schwenckfeld, and others serve as examples of what must have been a much larger cohort of contemporaries, men and women, who had neither the capacity to concern themselves with intricate theological questions nor any interest in them. They felt that the competing ecclesiastical factions differed over subtle points of doctrine, and they were persuaded that one of these factions was as good as the other. As the course of events was to show, the future was very much with them.

THE ANTITRINITARIAN DISSENT

Another group of reformers found that the traditional Christian doctrine of the Trinity, as promulgated by the ecumenical councils of Nicaea and Chalcedon, was a major perversion of biblical religion. These reformers became known first as "antitrinitarians," later as Socinians. As their label (again, typically, given by their antagonists) indicates, they found fault with the Trinitarian dogma. Like the Anabaptists and the spiritualists, they were heirs of the late medieval tradition as well as of the Reformation. Antitrinitarian soteriology was not Catholic, though it also was a far cry from what may be called the Protestant consensus. Interestingly, the early representatives of antitrinitarian thought appear to have nurtured their new understanding of the Christian faith while yet in the bosom of the Catholic Church. The Reformation exerted a powerful stimulus, however, both by its questioning of many traditional notions and by insisting on the primacy of the Scriptures as the source for Christian theology. Once many traditional theological points had become exposed to criticism, it was not surprising that the Trinitarian dogma should be similarly questioned.

The antitrinitarians can be classified with the Anabaptists and the spiritualists not only because they shared certain theological similarities, such as the rejection of infant baptism, but also because they denounced the old church and the new as equally perverted and divorced from scriptural truth. Yet there were important differences. Virtually all Anabaptists and spiritualists were orthodox Trinitarians. Most Anabaptists (Menno Simons being a major exception) viewed the person of Christ in completely traditional terms, and although the spiritualists often wrote rather obscurely—one sometimes feels that they had not carried their own theological presuppositions to their logical conclusions—their doctrinal orthodoxy is beyond doubt.

The epic of sixteenth-century antitrinitarianism began with several individuals propounding their critique of the Trinitarian dogma. Decades later came the relatively unmolested establishment of antitrinitarian congregations and conventicles in Eastern Europe. The story ended, temporarily at least, in the first half of the seventeenth century with the disappearance of most of these congregations, and the larger church they constituted, under the impact of renewed Catholic Counter-Reformation vitality. Since antitrinitarianism was a theological phenomenon, it had a lively history of theological discussion and disputes, from the aggressive repudiation of the orthodox Trinitarian dogma to the groping for positive alternatives, which often proved more complicated than the repudiated traditional doctrine. In fact, the antitrinitarians did not advance any essential argument that had not already appeared in the great christological debates of the early church. That they were called "new Arians" aptly expressed their connection with the past. Their ideas were hardly novel; they had been considered by the early church and had been found wanting. Nonetheless, the antitrinitarians were convinced that theirs was the authentic biblical understanding.

Michael Servetus, a Spanish humanist, physician, geographer, and lay theologian, began the Trinitarian discourse of the sixteenth century. Born in Villanueva in Aragon (Villanueva de Sijena) in 1509, Servetus studied law and entered the service of the Franciscan Friar Juan de Quintana, whom he accompanied to Italy in 1529. This Italian sojourn brought a first brush with ideas that prompted him to delve into theology. His first piece of published writing shows him conversant with the biblical languages as well as theology, an indication that his schooling was thorough and extensive. In the summer of 1530, barely twenty years of age, he moved to Basel and there at once began to nettle Johann Oecolampadius, the leading reformer of the town, with bothersome questions about traditional teaching on the Trinity. During his six months at Basel, Servetus worked on a treatise dealing with his Trinitarian views. After moving to Strassburg in 1531, where he befriended the reformers Bucer and Capito, and published this treatise, which he entitled *De Trinitatis erroribus* (Concerning the Errors of the Trinity). Servetus's position was technically Sabellian modalism, which meant Father, Son, and Holy Spirit were the three "modes" or "dispositions" of God. Jesus was divine, indeed the Son of God, but not in the orthodox sense a separate person; nor was he of the same essence as the Father.

The reaction to Servetus's book was predictably negative. Not only did Servetus lose the friendship of Oecolampadius, Bucer, and Capito, but also the city councils of both Strassburg and Basel prohibited the sale of his book. His convictions remained unchanged, however, and in 1532 he published a second treatise, entitled *Dialogorum de Trinitate libri duo* (Two Books of Dialogues Concerning the Trinity), that, despite a few minor retractions (about which he greatly boasted in the preface), reiterated the views of his first book. The adverse reaction to his two books, which should hardly have come as a surprise, prompted Servetus to get out of the limelight. He took on a new identity, called himself Michel Villeneuve, went to Paris, studied medicine, worked as an assistant at a print shop in Lyon, and in 1540 became a physician and and an influential citizen of Vienne, southeast of Paris, having been invited by Pierre Palmier, the archbishop of Vienne. But Servetus had not relinquished his passion for theology and the Trinitarian dogma. Outwardly a faithful Catholic and respectable citizen, he secretly worked on his magnum opus, which he entitled *Christianismi Restitutio* (The Restitution of Christianity), a rather obvious counterpoint to Calvin's *Christianismi Institutio*. Indeed, he began what proved to be a fateful correspondence with the Genevan reformer, assuming that he would convert Calvin to his views.[24]

Servetus's book was published in 1553—anonymously, of course, even though the initials "MS" appeared at the end of the book. Calvin, who knew the identity of the author from the earlier correspondence, saw to it that the Inquisition in Vienne also knew. Within months Servetus was arrested, told the inquisitors a fantastic but believable story, escaped melodramatically, and wound up in, of all places, Geneva. He was brought to trial as a heretic and burned at the stake. Before the flames consumed his body he was heard to cry, "O God, save my soul; O Jesus, Son of the eternal God, have mercy on me." As one bystander remarked, had he placed the adjective "eternal" before "Son," his life would have never been in danger. The flames burned his name indelibly into the annals of European history. Servetus's sentence and death at Champel outside Geneva were orchestrated by Calvin, who has had to accept this blemish, explained neither by the general intolerance of the age nor by the medieval Catholic legacy of the inquisition and persecution of heretics. In the extensive discussion that followed Serevtus's death, Calvin remained adamant. His treatise *Defensio Orthodoxae Fidei de Sacra Trinitate* (Defense of the Orthodox Faith Concerning the Holy Trinity) conveys that the death penalty for heretics was an integral part of his theological thought.[25]

Servetus's execution was not the end of the story. It turned into a cause célèbre, evoking the sentiment of a few voices of dissent, notably Sebastian Castellio's astute and forceful *De haereticis an sint persequendi* and Guillaume Postel's *Apologia pro Serveto Villanovano* (Apologia for Servetus). Servetus, instead of being an epilogue, proved to be the prologue to a lengthy line of critics of the Trinitarian dogma. His ideas were picked up, echoed, and spread by disciples who succeeded, in the end, in translating his theological theory into ecclesiastical practice. The voices of the critics were strikingly similar. They were men of the second generation of the Reformation and had a strong humanist orientation. None was a trained theologian; all were Italian. They eventually found a tolerant atmosphere, and thus a home, in Poland, where in the last third of the century they saw their ideas flourish modestly in a new church, the Minor Reformed Church. Also known as Socinianism (after Laelius Socinus and his nephew Faustus Socinus, the eminent leader of the Minor Reformed Church) this

---

24. J. Friedman, *Michael Servetus: A Case Study in Total Heresy* (Geneva: 1978), esp. ch. 3; see also *Obras Completas Miguel Servet* (Zaragoza: 2003).
    25. *Calvini Opera*, 47:190ff.

tradition, eventually banished from Poland to the Low Countries, survived into the seventeenth century and played an important part in the dissolution of traditional orthodox theology.

The complex theological development of antitrinitarian thought may be seen as proof of the dictum that it is easier by far to challenge traditional points of Christian doctrine than to offer a positive reconstruction. By the early seventeenth century the theological development of antitrinitarian thought reached its culmination. In 1605 a comprehensive theological statement appeared: the Racovian Catechism (named after its place of publication in Rakow, Poland)—*Catechism of the Assembly of Those People Who in the Kingdom of Poland and in the Grand Duchy of Lithuania & in Other Dominions Belonging to the Crown, Affirm and Confess That No Other Than the Father of Our Lord Jesus Christ Is the Only God of Israel; and the Man Jesus Christ of Nazareth, Who Was Born of Virgin & No Other Beside Him, Is the Only Begotten Son of God*. The lengthy title conveyed its basic theological orientation—a kind of adoptionism that held to strict monotheistic affirmation and avoided attributing divinity to Jesus.

The Racovian Catechism was the work of a number of Socinian theologians, with Faustus Socinus clearly the guiding spirit. The catechism's words may not have been his, but its ideas and notions certainly were. The catechism was translated into several European languages, including German (1608) and English twice (the first time in 1614). One Latin translation was dedicated to none other than James I of England, who glanced at the title, detected its heretical bent, and remarked that he sensed satanic authors, the very offspring of Satan, whom he would severely punish if they fell into his hands.[26] By order of Parliament, the catechism was burned in 1614.

The most noteworthy feature of the Racovian Catechism (other than its discussion of the Trinity) was undoubtedly its departure from the customary structure of statements of faith and catechisms. Instead of beginning with the topic of God, the catechism's opening chapter dealt with the authoritative principle: sacred Scripture. This surely must be taken as the catechism's concern about how to relate faith, revelation, and reason. It also echoed the increasing tendency of mainstream Protestantism toward the end of the sixteenth century to see the meaning of Christianity in doctrine.

After an introductory statement—"the Christian religion is the way of attaining eternal life, discovered by God"—the catechism proceeded to affirm the standard Protestant notions of the certainty, sufficiency, and clarity of Scripture. This section of the catechism focused not so much on a positive delineation of the scriptural principle, but on a whole series of responses to possible objections to the central importance of Scripture for the Christian faith. Evidently, for the authors of the catechism, writing in the early seventeenth century, the mere assertion of revelatory truth in the Bible had ceased to be self-evident. The apologetic, almost defensive approach was strikingly novel in the sixteenth century. The truth of the Christian religion was established through the truth of the Christian Scriptures, which was validated by God's acceptance of Jesus and vindicated through miracles and the resurrection.

By far the lengthiest section of the catechism dealt with "The Way of Salvation," with the subheadings of "Knowledge of God" and "Knowledge of Christ." The for-

---

26. Earl M. Wilbur, *A History of Unitarianism*, 2 vols. (Cambridge: 1945–1952), 1:411.

mer affirmed that there was "one God, Father of our Lord Jesus Christ," according to nature and will. That most Christians "commonly hold that not only the Father but also the Son and the Holy Spirit are persons in one and the same Deity" is refuted at considerable lengths; such teaching has no foundation in Scripture.

The section on the "knowledge of Christ" informed the reader that Jesus is "true man by nature"—though he is not a "mere man . . . for he was conceived of the Holy Spirit and born of the Virgin Mary and therefore is from his very conception the son of God."[27] This evidently orthodox language obscured the radical assertion of the catechism that Christ has no divine nature. Christ is described as prophet, king, and priest. As prophet he was the teacher of the will of God, which is found in the Decalogue.

An intriguingly irenic spirit pervaded the catechism and the Polish Unitarians. Faustus Socinus wrote in 1584, "I do not condemn other churches, nor by any means despise them, but acknowledge all as the true churches of Christ . . . even if in certain doctrines which do not relate to the actual precepts (of Jesus Christ), they do not seem to me to think rightly, and whoever keeps the same precepts, I consider to be true members of Christ's body."[28]

The Racovian Catechism constituted the formal profession of faith of the Polish antitrinitarians of the late sixteenth century. Theirs had been a long and tedious path from the first expressions of doubt of the Trinitarian doctrine in Italy and Switzerland, from the first explosive, arrogant pronouncements of Servetus, to the formation of the Polish Minor Reformed Church and the publication of the Racovian Catechism. Strikingly, because their rejection of the common Christian theological tradition past was even more radical than that of the mainstream Reformers, antitrinitarian dissent went beyond Servetus's printed pages and found organizational consolidation in a church. Even more strikingly, the Minor Reformed Church found legal toleration at a few places, notably, in Transylvania and Poland, in both instances growing out of Calvinist settings.

In that way, the Socinians were much like the Anabaptists or Mennonites, who, with the passing of time, found acceptance and legal toleration in north Germany, Switzerland, and the Netherlands. But there the similarity ended. The Minor Reformed Church in Poland eventually became the victim of the resurgent Tridentine Catholicism, and by the end of the seventeenth century, little of that Minor church remained in Poland. The faithful adherents had to emigrate to more tolerant places, such as the Netherlands, where Catholicism did not hold the same power as in Poland.

27. *The Racovian Catechism* (Lexington, KY: 1962), 13.
28. H. John McLachlan, *Socinianism in Seventeenth-Century England* (Oxford: 1951), 16.

Chapter 6

CONSOLIDATION IN GERMANY

The 1521 diet at Worms had marked the beginning of a new phase of the controversy. What had been the voice of a single individual was turning into a widespread chorus, increasingly echoed and reechoed throughout Germany. More importantly, the Edict of Worms had turned Luther's case into an affair of state. Any resolution of the matter had to occur not only in the realm of religion, but also in that of politics.

The German estates were not at all of one mind as to what to do with Luther and the issues he had raised. A considerable number—over forty—were ecclesiastical territories, which could be routinely expected to be supportive of Roman policy and be in favor of strong measures against Luther and his followers. Some rulers were apprehensive that the increasing popular support for Luther might fuel the restiveness among the common people, a fear repeatedly voiced during the deliberations in Worms. The uprising of the imperial knights, led by Franz von Sickingen and Ulrich von Hutten, the latter an early supporter of Luther's, seemed proof positive of an ominous connection between religious and societal reform that might yet draw larger circles.[1] To be sure, the knights' uprising quickly came to an ignominious halt—much like the Peasants' War less than half a decade later—but it indicated a societal restlessness that demanded attention. Luther himself had publicly gone on record as sharing the aspiration of those who carried the banner of the traditional German *gravamina*. His *Open Letter to the Christian Nobility* of 1520 had embraced many of the traditional proposals for societal reform. Others, especially in the cities, were concerned about the role of the church in society and saw the sundry demands for reform as an opportunity to fish in muddy waters. Yet others were convinced of the necessity of church reform and found the emperor's edict against Luther an inappropriate obstacle. Finally, some rulers, such as Duke George of Albertine Saxony and the Bavarian dukes, were solidly committed to the Catholic faith and never hesitated to express their conviction that Luther was a convicted heretic and that they were determined to carry out the Edict of Worms and squelch the Lutheran heresy.

The pivotal role was to be played by the emperor, who symbolically as well as practically had to enforce his edict against Luther. Since the edict was not part of the official recess of the diet, its legitimacy as a document applicable to the empire was doubtful. Strangely, the emperor left Germany immediately upon the adjournment of the diet, which complicated matters greatly, even though the adverse implications of his departure became evident only later. Charles's splendid oratory at Worms, where

1. K. Schottenloher, ed., *Flugschriften zur Ritterschaftsbewegung des Jahres 1521* (Münster: 1929).

he made the uncompromising assertion that he was ready to pledge his life and property to the eradication of the Lutheran heresy, appeared written as on water. Charles's departure for Spain seemed a wise and necessary move, given his dynastic responsibilities in Spain. He had attended, at his first German diet, to the pressing problems in the empire. After some difficult negotiations, a *Reichsregiment* had been installed to exercise a coordinating function in his absence; he had turned over the Austrian lands and the claims to Bohemia and Hungary to his brother Ferdinand; and he had disposed (on paper, that is) of the heretical menace.

In this context, Charles should not be faulted for his instant departure. In May 1521 he had every reason to assume that his edict would prompt the estates swiftly to suppress Luther and his followers. Heresy, after all, had always been crushed or, in the case of the Hussites, significantly contained. One suspects that Charles left Germany with a feeling of accomplishment. Not surprisingly, he directed his attention to Spain, where his election to the imperial throne had been received with ill-concealed apprehension. The prospect of an absentee ruler and higher taxes, the latter a virtual prerequisite for Charles's exercise of the imperial office, was hardly calculated to arouse warm feelings. Moreover, the *comuñeros* revolt, a rebellion of towns against the nobility, had erupted in May 1520, and even though it was quickly suppressed, it underscored deep problems in Spain and the necessity of Charles's presence.

Still, the emperor's departure deprived the Catholic cause of the figure which, despite limited political power, commanded the authority to rally support against the menacing heresy. Accordingly, Charles's absence from Germany was to have important consequences for the subsequent course of events. Two important factors stand out as events unfolded after May 1521: the increasing popular support for reform, however defined, and the inability of the *Reichsregiment*, meeting in Nuremberg beginning in the fall of 1521, to function effectively. Collectively, these two factors meant the practical failure of the Edict of Worms.

The structure of the *Reichsregiment*, meant as a representative body of the estates, was not calculated to make it an effective governing body for complex issues. Its membership rotated every quarter, so long-range policies were difficult to develop and carry out. Some members of the *Reichsregiment* were disposed to stay aloof from controversy and let events run their course. Only the determination of Duke George of Saxony led to a mandate in January 1522 that prohibited all changes in existing ecclesiastical practice.[2] George was well aware of the incipient wave of demand for change and reform. Since the Edict of Worms had, in effect, declared the same, the mandate was gratuitous and—as events were soon to show—ineffective. On the side of the reformers, Hans von der Planitz, the representative of electoral Saxony, became a skillful spokesperson for ecclesiastical conciliation and the need for a church council to address issues of church reform.

When the diet assembled again in Nuremberg in 1523, the papal nuncio, Francesco Chieregati, whose main assignment was to rally the German estates to military action (or at least financial support) against the Ottoman Turks, pointedly reminded the estates of their failure to execute the Edict of Worms—as if the estates

---

2. *Deutsche Reichstagsakten*, 3:21.

needed to be so apprised. The very reason for Chieregati's presence in Nuremberg underscored the complexity of the situation: the unresolved issue of religious reform (and what to do with Luther) was part and parcel of the changes in Europe's broader political picture. Emperor Charles, who should have executed the Worms edict, because only his imperial authority stood behind it, was preoccupied with domestic problems in Spain and the chronic confrontation with France over northern Italy. In Rome, Pope Leo X had died. The new pope, Adrian VI, a Dutch churchman, had been a compromise candidate (he was to remain the only non-Italian pope for almost five centuries).[3] Adrian had been deeply influenced by the piety of the Brethren and Sisters of the Common Life in the Low Countries and was committed to church reform. When his nuncio read a statement to the Nuremberg diet, he caused great consternation—and approval, for he admonished the German estates to execute the Edict of Worms, and, much to the astonishment of those assembled, added sentences that acknowledged the complicity of the church in the existing problem. Because of the sins of "priests and prelates" the church was now in woes, he confessed. Much was taking place in the church that was despicable, even in Rome, and necessary reform had to begin at the top.[4] As matters turned out, Adrian's carefully chosen words (for example, he observed that "possibly" the curia had been the source of abuse) impressed neither those loyal to the church nor the growing throng of reformers. Indeed, if anything, Adrian's well-meant "confession" served only to consolidate those agitating for reform, for they now were able to make a connection between their long-standing grievances and the case of Luther.

A new diet convened in Nuremberg in January 1524. Much had happened since the previous diet had adjourned.[5] Pope Adrian's successor, Clement VII, was to be a supreme pontiff with little empathy for the clamor for reform but with abiding interest in Italian politics and the importance of the Papal States. His legate at Nuremberg, Lorenzo Cardinal Campeggio, had a single assignment: to effect the enforcement of the Edict of Worms. He encountered stiff resistance. The supporters of reform, particularly the cities, demurred.[6] They warned that "much uproar, disobedience, murder, and shedding of blood" would occur if the edict were forcefully imposed, and noted that "the common people everywhere are most eager for the Word of God and the Holy Gospel." Clearly, the house was divided.

Not surprisingly, the recess of the diet was a compromise. The diet proposed that a general council be convened and recommended that a preparatory assembly of the "German nation" take place in November to discuss the "new teaching" as well as the long-standing grievances, the *gravamina* of the German nation. At the same time, the recess called for the enforcement of the Worms edict "insofar as that was possible."[7]

When Charles learned of the recess, he promptly vetoed the proposed German assembly. He was shocked, he wrote, by this incredible scheme proposed by the "pious

3. F. X. Seppelt, *Geschichte der Päpste von den Anfängen bis zur Mitte des zwanzigsten Jahrhunderts* (Munich: 1957), 4:426–37.
4. *Deutsche Reichstagsakten*, 3:397.
5. Ibid., 449.
6. Ibid., 4:507.
7. April 4, 1524, *Deutsche Reichstagakten*, 4:500.

German people." He demanded that the Edict of Worms be strictly enforced and that "all discussion, explanation, or interpretation of the Christian faith" be stopped. Jointly with the pope he would seek to bring about the convening of a general council to deal with issues of reform.

THE UPRISINGS OF 1524–1525

The emperor's injunction appeared to settle the matter. November 1524 came and went, and no German assembly gathered in Speyer. But some Germans did gather, first in southwest Germany, in the Black Forest region, then with increasing intensity and determination in other places, notably central Germany and Austria. Peasants, as well as townspeople, restless and discontented for some time, expressed their grievances against church and society, at first through rioting, then in sporadic acts of violence, and finally through military action. Germany, already in the throes of religious controversy, became the site of the political and social turmoil of the German Peasants' War, perhaps more properly labeled the "revolution of the common man."[8]

This uprising did not come overnight and was not at all novel. Ever since the late fourteenth century Germany (and other European countries) had been beset by periodic peasant and also urban unrest—in Augsburg, Braunschweig, Cologne, Hamburg, Regensburg, Ulm, to name but a few places—as well as the peasant *Bundschuh* ("laced shoe") uprising of the second decade of the sixteenth century. Such restiveness was not surprising, for the lives and livelihood of the peasants had become increasingly marginal. The soil they tilled was not their own but their lords', who claimed most of the fruit of their labors. Johannes Boemus's encyclopedic description of society in the fourth decade of the century, *Omnium Gentium Mores* (1535), called the state of the peasants "pitiable and hard"; described their houses as "huts of clay and wood, rising only little from the ground"; noted their diet as consisting of "inferior bread, oatmeal cereal, and stewed vegetables"; and concluded, in a peculiar juxtaposition of adjectives, that the peasants were "restless, willing to work, and dirty."[9] At the same time, there were tensions in the cities.

In the second decade of the sixteenth century, the *Bundschuh* uprising brought renewed urgency to the plight of the peasants, and at the diet at Worms in 1521 some estates repeatedly placed their determination to get Luther a fair hearing into the context of ominous concerns about the restlessness of the common people. An innocuous event in the Black Forest region in southwest Germany proved to be the catalyst for an ever widening circle of riots and armed insurgency. Most of the peasants' grievances put forward in the late summer and fall of 1524 in numerous local petitions focused on rather tangible economic and social concerns. The grievance documents demanded the restoration of traditional customs and practices. The peasants objected to the new burdens imposed on them by their lords—new taxes and obligations, new

---

8. This is the argument of Peter Blickle's widely discussed monograph, *The Revolution of the Common Man: The German Peasants' War from a New Perspective* (Baltimore: 1985).
9. Joannes Boemus, *Omnium gentium mores, leges et ritus* (Freiburg: 1535).

laws, new judicial procedures, and, above all, the increasingly autocratic tendencies of their lords, including the monasteries, which owned much of the land the peasants worked. While these grievances expressed economic need, the concern that underlay them had to do with a changing societal order that marginalized the peasants in the country and the "common man" in the towns.

When sporadic rioting broke out in southwest Germany in the late summer of 1524, there were a few skirmishes and acts of brutality. Nonetheless, in several instances irenic conciliation was reached between peasants and lords. The riots appeared to be a regional and temporary phenomenon. Six months later, however, the isolated riots in the southwest had turned into widespread insurrection throughout southern and central Germany. Importantly, the uprising was no longer a rural happening: townspeople, even priests and nobility, rioted in demand for the redress of grievances. Rioters in cities were those who felt deprived of participation in the affairs in their communities. The objective was, as for example in Rothenburg, to bring about a more participatory form of governance.

In March 1525 peasants from several regions in Swabia (Lake Constance, the Allgäu, and Ulm) formed a *Christliche Vereinigung* (Christian Union) with a surprisingly moderate political and social program. The programmatic document of the *Vereinigung* became the only statement of grievances that was actually printed and thus enjoyed extensive dissemination. Reprinted no fewer than twenty-four times in the span of just a few weeks, the *Zwölf Artikel Gemeiner Bauerschaft* (Twelve Articles of the Swabian Peasants) offered a view of a society in which the place of the peasants and their obligations to their lords was redefined. Article 9, for example, criticized the avalanche of new laws burdening the peasants, while article 10 complained that common fields and meadows had been appropriated by the lords and could no longer be used by peasants. The demand of the *Twelve Articles* was for the restoration of the old, traditional order.

At the same time, however, the *Twelve Articles* advanced a new demand. The document enunciated a vision of society in which the place of the peasants (and, indeed, of everyone) was determined not by arbitrary human laws, but by the law of God. Thus article 3 demanded that vassalage must be abolished because God had created all people free. This was a startling notion: after all, God had ordered hierarchical society, in which not all were free. Similarly, the peasants asserted that the fruits of creation should be used by all, for God had created them for all. The articles advanced the bold, indeed revolutionary, claim that society should be ordered and reformed according to the principles of the gospel, God's law. And, addressing a religious issue, in a striking departure from economic and social concerns, the *Twelve Articles* insisted that a congregation should be free to elect its own minister, who would preach the "pure Word of God."

This last demand exemplified something extraordinarily important in unfolding events—the link between the peasants' demands and the notions of reform that were being bandied about at the time. Indeed, some of the *Twelve Articles* appeared to come straight from Luther's book. For example, Luther had published a treatise advocating the election of ministers by the local congregation. The *Twelve Articles* focused, however, on something more crucial and pivotal: the criterion by which the peasants' grievances and demands should be measured was the Word of God.[10] The reform movement was thus implicated in the most formidable political disturbance Germany was to experience until the nineteenth century. The situation was all the more serious because the *Vereinigung* called on Luther and Melanchthon, together with Elector Frederick of Saxony and Archduke Ferdinand of Austria, to form a panel of "impartial judges" to evaluate the peasants' demands in light of the divine law. Of course, this "revolution of the common man" might well have occurred without the impetus of the movement of religious reform, for long-standing social and economic grievances had gone unattended for decades. When the uprising did happen, the influence of Luther and the movement for reform was unmistakable.

Much of the pamphlet literature of the early 1520s had called for a reform of society no less than of the church. Although societal reform was not a pivotal issue for Luther, he had supported such notions in his *Open Letter to the Christian Nobility* of 1520 and later had not dissociated himself from those notions. His 1520 treatise had explicitly embraced the traditional grievances, such as the necessity for a reform of university curricula and the curtailment of the import of costly cloth and spices from abroad. In his treatise these topics were as prominent as was the repudiation of what Luther called the "three walls of the Romanists," the theological claim that the church had made excessive claims of authority over secular power.

Add to that Luther's pronouncement in his treatise on the *Freedom of a Christian*, also of 1520, that a Christian is a "perfectly free lord of all, subject to none," and it would seen inevitable that the peasants would take Luther's words as encouragement to insist on societal reforms. Exciting new thoughts and slogans had come out of Wittenberg and other places, such as the "common man" had not heard before. Luther and the other Reformers had asserted that even the simple could understand the gospel and that the high and mighty of the earth had perverted this precious treasure. Luther had proclaimed the priesthood of all believers, insisting that all Christians were spiritual equals. He had also argued that a congregation should be free to select its own minister. In short, there was a connection between the proclamation of Luther and the aspirations of the peasants, who with halberds and sickles went forth to translate their vision of a new society into reality.

No matter how noble (and modern) the aspirations of those who took up arms, militarily and strategically they were no match for the mercenaries of the rulers. In confrontation after confrontation, the peasants went down in defeat, which only made them more determined, more radical, more ruthless. Plundering and atrocities marked their path. The decisive showdown in central Germany took place near the village of Frankenhausen. The peasants' military incompetence led them to set up camp in a valley close to Frankenhausen. The rulers' forces promptly occupied the ridge surrounding the valley, and this strategic advantage led to the peasants' disastrous defeat. But it was no real battle; rather, it was a brutal slaughter of thousands of peasants outside the village on May 15, 1525.

10. M. Brecht, "Der Theologische Hintergrund der Zwölf Artikel," *Zeitschrift für Kirchengeschichte* 85 (1974): 174ff.

The devastation and destruction caused by the uprising; the multitude of peasants killed; the women and children made widows and orphans; the houses, castles, and monasteries burned; the land deserted without hands to till it—all these left little doubt that the toll had been heavy, indeed catastrophic. Some claimed afterward that the number of peasants killed reached one hundred thousand, but that figure, like so many from an age not particularly concerned about statistical accuracy, is undoubtedly too high. But the toll was horrible. Violence and confrontation, not compromise or conciliation, had marked the course of events. Even as the cause of the peasants remained unheard, the cause of the Reformation was profoundly affected.

Luther was deeply implicated, and ever since the summer of 1525 supporters and detractors have sought to justify, explain, or repudiate his role in the course of events. The public manifesto of the *Twelve Articles*, and his identification as one of the "judges" of the peasants' demands, forced Luther, troubled by these events, to clarify his understanding of the relationship of Christianity to the social and political order. He hurriedly composed a tract entitled *Ermahnung zum Frieden auf die zwölf Artikel der Bauernschaft* (Friendly Admonition to Peace Concerning the Twelve Articles of the Peasants). It appeared in April 1525 just before the final showdown at Frankenhausen. Luther wanted to retain his neutrality toward both sides, if not slightly favoring the peasants. He expressed bitterness about the rulers' stubbornness and arrogance, and he seemed to be favorably disposed toward the peasants' demands. These demands seemed right and proper to him, he wrote, although, as a minister of the gospel and not an expert in the law, he was not competent to judge the legal issues of the peasants' grievances. Experts in law and economics had to do this, since these topics contain "nothing Christian."

What evoked Luther's indignation was that the peasants had supported their socioeconomic demands in the *Twelve Articles* with an appeal to the Christian faith. That, he asserted, was an abomination, and he spared no words of vehement denunciation: "And even if they [the demands] were proper and right according to the natural law, you have forgotten the Christian law, since you do not seek to attain them with patience and prayer to God, as becomes Christian men, but with impatience and blasphemy to force the authorities."[11] Luther must have thought that by chiding both rulers and peasants, pointing out that both were in the wrong, his mediating stance would calm the troubled waters; he was mistaken. The uprising continued and increased in bloodshed.

The futility of his first attempt to restore peace prompted Luther to take up his pen again three weeks later. By then, it seemed to some, the uprising had turned into an orgy of lawlessness perpetrated by the peasants. The new treatise, *Wider die räuberischen und mörderischen Rotten der Bauern* (Against the Plundering and Murderous Hordes of the Peasants), was dramatically different in tone from the *Friendly Admonition*. Gone were the sympathetic words about the peasants' plight and the tacit endorsement of their grievances. Gone also was his effort to be a mediator in the conflict, finding right and wrong on both sides. The peasants had turned to violence,

11. WA 18:279–334.

insurrection, and bloodshed; law and order had been disrupted. That was bad enough and deserved repudiation because it was against the divine order. What made it demonic in Luther's eyes was the peasants' recourse to the Christian faith for their socioeconomic agenda. That was a fatal misunderstanding of the gospel, which admonished the followers of Jesus to be long-suffering and to turn the other cheek. It was also a negation of divinely established political authority, which was ordained by God to provide law and order for people. Luther used harsh and almost hysterical language in his pamphlet, and at the end he encouraged the rulers to stab, slay, and kill the peasants as one would kill raging dogs, because nothing on earth was worse than rebellion.[12]

Theologically Luther may well have made a sound case; he did not want to see the Christian faith used (or abused) for political, economic, and social ends. This was hardly a new topic, for the debate over how Christians should relate to the social and political order had been with Christianity from its very beginning. Luther's principle that the Christian faith had no direct bearing on the social and political order was a radical reinterpretation of medieval notions, which had sought to baptize the sociopolitical order with Christian principles.

Luther's treatise came close to being a strategic catastrophe. The peasants saw themselves as betrayed. Understandably, no love was lost between the peasants and the man who wished for their stabbing, slaying, and killing, and there is no way Luther can escape strident criticism. Without doubt, Luther had endorsed a broad definition of reform in his 1520 tract, even as prior to his tracts dealing with the peasant uprising he had not divorced himself from the calls for broader societal reform. His distancing himself from the peasants' goals—his claim that although their grievances sounded legitimate, he was not an expert in these matters—is not completely convincing. He surely was no expert on the importation of costly spices and cloth back in 1520, but he still mentioned it in his *Letter to the Christian Nobility*. Luther even backpedaled on the issue of the election of the minister by the congregation, when it became clear that local parishes were often enmeshed in a myriad of legal and financial arrangements pertaining to their clergy that curtailed the congregation's freedom with respect to its minister, old or new. Perhaps Luther was most upset by the disruption of law and order that the characterized peasants had caused and that to him was their unpardonable transgression. He even may have realized that the peasants would inevitably go down in defeat and did not want the movement for religious reform to be dragged down with them.

The question is whether the reform movement lost significant popular support as a result of events in 1525—not only because of Luther's offensive language and controversial stance, but also because the uprising had made it finally clear that his notion of reform was confined to religion and did not involve societal issues, as one might have expected from the pamphlet pronouncements of the early 1520s. Although in the years to come the reform movement scored significant successes, especially in northern Germany, there also are unambiguous indicators that a great deal of the enthusiastic popular appeal disappeared in the wake of the events of 1525. The Zwickau mayor, Hans Mühlpfort, noted that "Dr. Martinus has experienced formidable desertion both from the common people and the learned as well as unlearned

12. WA 18:361.

ones."[13] The flood of pamphlet literature, which had covered the German-speaking region ever since 1519 with reform pronouncements on societal and religious issues, subsided dramatically.

Marxist historians, who defined the uprisings of 1524–1525, together with the antecedent happenings after 1517, as an "early bourgeois revolution," have rightly understood their pivotal significance.[14] The peasants who took to arms cannot be simply written off as having fatally misunderstood Luther and the Reformation. Rather, they were part of that broad yearning for reform that coalesced into widespread consciousness as result of Luther's Ninety-five Theses. The "revolution of the common man" is thus symptomatic of the inner dynamic of events after 1517—a theological catalyst triggered a public consciousness of reform, which in turn culminated in an insurgency in the name of reform. Events were to show that in Germany, and everywhere else in Europe, reform proved possible only in conjunction with the political authorities, not in confrontation with them.

In the midst of this turbulence Luther had married, prompting Erasmus of Rotterdam, never at a loss for a clever phrase, to remark that what had begun as tragedy had turned into comedy—an apostate monk had married an apostate nun! Luther's bride was Katharina of Bora. Born in 1499 into an impoverished Saxon noble family, Katharina had entered the convent at age sixteen in 1515, and in 1523 she was one of twelve nuns who escaped from their convent in empty herring barrels, aided by a herring merchant and organized by Luther, who subsequently wrote a sixteen-page treatise about the general principle underlying the escape—*Ursach und Antwort, das Jungfrauen Klöster göttlich verlassen mögen* (Reason and Explanation Why Women May Leave Monasteries with Divine Approval). The twelve women came to Wittenberg, where their presence symbolized immense practical issues: the former nuns had to be welcomed back by their families or get married. Katharina became engaged to the son of a patrician Nuremberg family, but the objections of his parents—who can hardly have been enthusiastic about their son's proposed marriage to a former nun—brought an end to the arrangement. Katharina, headstrong as she was, turned down another suitor and eventually conveyed that she would marry only Nikolaus von Amsdorf, Luther's colleague, or Dr. Luther himself. Because of their age (both were forty-two in 1525) neither seemed particularly eligible for matrimony. But no, it happened.

For Luther's partisans, his marriage was a theologically consistent move. His enemies, however, purported to be shocked and dismayed. Thomas More wrote, "Luther not only teaches monks, friars, and nuns to marry, but also being a monk, has married a nun himself and with her lives under the name of wedlock in open, incestuous lechery without care or shame."

Luther had earlier written a friend, "As for what you write about my getting married, do not be surprised that I do not wed," even as he had remarked in a sermon that "happy is the man who does not need a wife." Even though the three reasons

---

13. W. P. Fuchs, ed., *Akten zur Geschichte des Bauernkriegs in Mitteldeutschland* (Leipzig: 1923–1942), 2:436.

14. With the disappearance of the German Democratic Republic in 1990, this Marxist Reformation scholarship ceased to have vocal representatives. For a good example of this scholarship see Adolf Laube et al., eds., *Illustrierte Geschichte der deutschen frühbürgerlichen Revolution* (Berlin: 1974).

Luther subsequently gave for his marriage—his father's eagerness to see grandchildren, his conscience telling him that God had instituted the state of marriage, his determination to spite the devil—may not be (either then or now) the customary grounds for getting married, the union of Martin and Katharina proved to be a happy one. The letters and other documents from Katharina's pen show her a thoughtful and efficient, if at times parsimonious, manager of the Luther household. Luther loved and respected her, and across the dinner table he repeatedly uttered his high esteem, peppered, to be sure, with a great deal of sarcasm, such as his comment that "all my life is patience. I have to have patience with the pope, the heretics, my family, and Katie."[15] Katie and Martin became parents of six children, two of whom died in childhood. Martin's letter on the death of his daughter Magdalena is a deeply touching testimony of parental affection, demonstrating that even in that (for us) distant age, parents, despite (or maybe because of) a shockingly high infant and childhood mortality rate, had deep emotional bonds to their children.

THEOLOGICAL ALIENATION

The year 1525 had fateful consequences other than the uprising of the peasants. It was a year of theological clarification. The controversy between Luther and Erasmus, which had been brewing for some time-revealed that humanist and Lutheran notions of reform were miles apart, while at the same time, the opening salvos were fired in several intra-reform confrontations, which left the movement of reform deeply and bitterly divided.

Desiderius Erasmus, the celebrated intellectual and humanist, had been seen by many, when the indulgences controversy first erupted, as the true instigator of the conflagration. Initially, he had not been indisposed to be so associated with Luther and the other protagonists of reform as long as arguments and issues did not get out of hand. The agenda seemed to be the reform of church abuses. Early on Erasmus wrote Albert of Brandenburg that he had warned Luther "to write nothing seditious, nothing against the pope, nothing in an arrogant or angry tone, but to preach the gospel with sincerity of heart and in all meekness."[16] The elimination of vulgar abuses in the church was for him the issue of the hour, and to the extent to which he saw Luther as a comrade-in-arms toward that end, he was willing to be publicly identified with Luther. However, his careful and subtle neutrality began to give way, after 1520, to increasing concern about Luther's theological reformulations. Though he still saw himself as the grand conciliator who stood above the fray and could bring both feuding parties to their senses, loyal Catholics were suspicious that he secretly sided with Luther.[17] By the early 1520s it had become apparent that Erasmus's notion of the *philosophia Christi*, his intensely moral understanding of Jesus, was at odds with Luther's pessimistic declarations about human sinfulness and justification by grace. Increasingly, too, Erasmus had become concerned about what he perceived to be

---

15. WA TR 2173A; see also WA TR 1656; 3178A. A charming description of Luther's marriage is found in R. H. Bainton, *Here I Stand: A Life of Martin Luther* (New York: 1950), 223–24.

16. *Opus Epistolarum* 103, in Hans J. Hillerbrand, ed., *Erasmus and His Age* (New York: 1970), 145.

17. Later in that same letter Erasmus notes, "I am not accusing Luther nor am I defending him."

Luther's extremist positions and his rigidity, from which Erasmus anticipated general turbulence and a further decline of biblical spirituality.

Egged on to write against Luther, as King Henry VIII of England had done in his *Assertio Septem Sacramentorum* (Assertion of the Seven Sacraments), Erasmus decided to speak out. Characteristically, he did not choose one of the controversial topics in explicit contention between reformers and Catholic loyalists. His topic was subtle: the freedom of the human will toward God. Obviously, Erasmus wanted to have his cake and eat it too: to satisfy those who urged him to take a public stance against Luther and still avoid an engagement with him on a contested issue.

In his *De libero arbitrio diatribe sive collatio* (Colloquy or Conversation Concerning Free Will) of 1524 Erasmus insisted that he meant to raise issues rather than propound certainties. His book was not at all polemical; if anything, it showed itself as the epitome of understatement. He declared himself to be neither judge nor teacher, but "one who argues to find the truth if ever it is to be found."[18] His stated goal was to call attention to a number of biblical passages, fully cognizant that much in Scripture was enigmatic and unclear. What was clear in the Bible, however, were the directives for moral living. Christianity was not ceremonies and dogma but living in harmony with the gospel. Subtly attacking Luther's notion of the utter priority of divine grace, as appropriated by faith, he argued that humans have the freedom to turn to God and thereby be receptive for God's grace. Luther, Erasmus argued, based his notions on a few isolated Bible passages and lacked a clear line of thinking. Luther's teachings gave humans the arrogant notion that biblical moral precepts need not be taken seriously. Thus Christianity lost something from its very center—the gospel mandate for moral living.

Luther knew that Erasmus had challenged him at the theological core and took his time to respond. It was not until almost a full year later, in the fall of 1525, that his answer appeared. Entitled *De servo arbitrio* (Concerning the Bondage of the Will), the book was one of Luther's heavy theological tomes: it delineated several key notions in his theology, outlining his fundamental reflection about Scripture. In contrast to Erasmus, who had argued that much in the Bible was enigmatic, which was good because God wanted it that way, Luther insisted on Scripture's clarity. He cited passage after passage to support his contention that humans were utterly depraved and could do nothing meritorious in God's sight. Indeed, God is described in Scripture as one who condemns or saves almost arbitrarily: according to the Bible, for example, "God hardened Pharaoh's heart."

In contrast to Erasmus's irenic tone, Luther's treatise was sharp, biting, and uncompromising. Erasmus concluded that he could not let this fierce attack go unchallenged and rallied to publish his *Hyperaspistes* (Defense), but by that time it was evident that the encounter of the humanist and the theologian had revealed an unbridgeable gap.

The confrontation between Erasmus and Luther was more than a biting polemic between two theologians. Their exchange revealed to contemporaries, more than anything else, Luther's true objectives. It was no longer possible to see Luther as someone seeking to remedy the abuses in the church. Luther pursued a new and different

18. *De libero arbitrio*, 3.

theology. Humanists everywhere who had earlier been lively supporters of Luther found themselves reflecting on their alignment, and many concluded that their home was with Erasmus and thus with the old church.

The year 1525 also brought theological dissension within the ranks of the reformers to the fore. An early and eloquent partisan of Luther's, Thomas Müntzer, whom Luther called "the arch-devil of Allstedt" after the two had parted ways, had cast his lot with the rebelling peasants and townspeople in 1525 in the assumption that because they and he had a common enemy—the rulers—they shared the same goals. But Müntzer's understanding of a Spirit-filled and suffering Christian faith was not what the peasants wanted; theirs was a strange alliance, and when Müntzer was executed after the battle of Frankenhausen, having joined the peasants probably as their chaplain, his death offered the public spectacle of a reform movement divided.

Andreas Bodenstein Carlstadt, Luther's Wittenberg colleague, had also dabbled on the fringes of the peasants' unrest but had stayed largely out of it, devoting his time and energy to several tracts on the Lord's Supper, specifically to the meaning of the "words of institution." These tracts were published in Strassburg in the fall of 1524 and contained an outright rejection not only of the Catholic dogma of transubstantiation, but also of Luther's notion of a real presence of the body and blood of Jesus in the elements of bread and wine. Carlstadt argued a symbolic, not literal, interpretation of the words of institution. The significance of the occasion for the believer was the confession of the recollection of the death of Jesus and the acceptance of the cross.[19]

Carlstadt suggested that Jesus had pointed at himself when speaking the words, "This is my body . . ."—an interpretation that promptly fell into ridicule because it left unanswered the question of where Jesus had pointed when speaking the corollary words, "This is the covenant of my blood." Yet Carlstadt was not alone in rejecting a literal interpretation of the words of institution, and therein lies his significance at the theological turning point of the Reformation. Other south German and Swiss reformers, notably Zwingli, embraced essentially Carlstadt's spiritualizing interpretation, and Luther's intensely vehement *Wider die Himelischen Propheten* (Against the Heavenly Prophets) of early 1525 heaped scorn and biblical argument on all those who denied the notion of a literal, real presence of Jesus in the elements. This brought Zwingli, whose *De Vera et Falsa Religione* (Commentary on True and False Religion) had anticipated a symbolic understanding of the words of institution, into the fray. A vehement controversy ensued between Luther and Zwingli, aided and abetted by their respective followers. It was to be the issue over which the movement of reform dramatically divided.

THE REFORMATION IN THE CITIES

The course of events in Zurich (as well as the earlier developments in Wittenberg) foreshadowed what was to take place in city after city where the call for reform was voiced.

19. On Carlstadt see Ronald Sider, *Andreas Bodenstein von Karlstadt: The Development of His Thought, 1517–1525* (Leiden: 1974); and U. Bubenheimer, *Consonantia theologiae et iurisprudentiae: Andreas Bodenstein von Karlstadt als Theologe und Jurist zwischen Scholastik und Reformation* (Tübingen: 1977).

In most places, such as both Zurich and Wittenberg, for example, the explanation is to be found in the presence of towering (and overpowering) leaders—Luther and Zwingli. But Zurich and Wittenberg deserve primacy of place, for there the transition from theological pronouncements to religious and societal change was first undertaken, and both communities illustrate that the transition was by no means simple or easy.

In both cities reform meant more than changes in the traditional rites and practices of the church. In Wittenberg a group of burghers presented a set of six articles to the city council; while the first four dealt with ecclesiastical practices (the free preaching of the Word of God, the abolition of private Masses, the celebration of the Lord's Supper according to Jesus's intent, and the distribution of both bread and wine), the remaining two reflected social concerns—the closing of the taverns, "where much drunkenness occurs," and of the brothels, "involving students, priests, burghers, and others."[20] The same insistence on issues of social reform characterized the course of events in Zurich. Tellingly, in 1522 Luther's colleague Carlstadt published a tract with the title *Von abtuhung der Bylder und das keyn Betdler unther den Christen seyn soll* (Concerning the Removal of Images and That No Beggar Should Be among Christians).[21] Carlstadt's tract thus combined an aesthetic judgment based on biblical insight and a mandate of social reform.

Several characteristics defined the course of events in the cities. A dynamic impetus sought to translate theological insight into ecclesiastical practice. Some advocates of reform demanded immediate action, but disagreement in the camps of both the advocates and the antagonists of reform complicated matters. The specific demands put forward were preaching from the pure Word of God and changes in the traditional Mass. The demand for evangelical preaching was, on the face of things, a generic demand: it lacked theological specificity but at the same time suggested that the church had to embrace a new criterion and standard for its message. The intense agitation about the Mass, on the other hand, while seemingly focusing on a secondary issue, namely the private masses, struck at the very heart of Catholic worship.

Wittenberg was one pivotal center of this development, paralleled by Zurich in the south. In both instances, the presence of charismatic theologians not only meant that the theological issues were cogently stated, but in Zurich it also meant a reformulation of the nature of Christian community meaningful for urban communities elsewhere.[22] Reform was understood as the way in which a community, with active participation of the clergy and theologians, reformed all aspects of its corporate life, from worship to the care of the poor. This led, in turn, to a striking phenomenon: the success of the Reformation in virtually all the imperial free cities, prompting the British historian A. G. Dickens to offer the oft-quoted remark that the "Reformation was an urban event."[23]

20. Quoted in Rudolf Mau, *Evangelische Bewegung und frühe Reformation 1521 bis 1532* (Leipzig: 2001), 62.

21. Cited by H. Lietzmann in *Kleine Texte für theologische und philosophische Vorlesungen und Übungen* (Bonn: 1911).

22. B. Moeller's essay, *Reichsstadt und Reformation* (Göttingen: 1962), triggered a flurry of further studies that paid attention to the nature of the success of the Reformation in the cities.

23. A. G. Dickens, *The German Reformation and Martin Luther* (London: 1974), 182.

Of course, it was more than that, but the turning Protestant of the overwhelming majority of the free cities—which were able, despite having the emperor as their overlord, to determine on their own their decision about the Reformation—is surely telling. The banner of religious reform seemed to imply consequences deemed attractive and meaningful for the cities. This striking urban success of the Reformation must not suggest that in all the cities an overwhelming majority of the citizens and óf the ruling elites showed themselves to be partisans of reform. Not at all. The interrelationship of authority and power among elites, citizenry, and clergy were complex and took many forms (for example, a conservative citizenry confronting a reform council and clergy), but eventually the cause of reform almost uniformly won out, sometimes quietly, sometimes after much agitation and restlessness.

A spokesperson and driving agent for reform and change was necessary, someone who had the platform to challenge his community relentlessly to undertake reform. This role was assumed by a local clergy, who thus became the catalyst for change. In Nuremberg it was Andreas Osiander, priest at St. Lorenz, who began to preach the new gospel in 1522, supported by Lazarus Spengler, secretary of the Nuremberg city council and ardent supporter of Luther. In Strassburg the preaching of Matthäus Zell and Martin Bucer led to the city council ordinance of December 1, 1523, that henceforth "solely the holy gospel is to be proclaimed."[24] In Memmingen it was the preaching of Christoph Schappeler; in Schwäbisch Hall, that of one of the most creative of Lutheran theologians, Johannes Brenz. Similarly, there was evangelical preaching in numerous other cities, such as Frankfurt, Ulm, Magdeburg, Bremen, to name but a few: the list of urban communities where reform was preached encompasses just about all of the free as well as many episcopal cities. The ease and speed with which cities formally abolished Catholic worship and theology differed greatly, with some, such as Zurich, acting swiftly, others taking their time. Regensburg, for example, did not introduce reform until 1542, and some cities, such as Cologne, eventually reaffirmed their Catholic loyalties.

But the success of the Reformation in a city depended on more than the presence of a vocal and persuasive minister. A cogent message was necessary. Luther had enunciated it with his clarion call for Christian freedom—"a Christian is a perfectly free lord of all"—and his strident repudiation of what was quickly labeled "works righteousness." On one level, therefore, the new message was attractive because it simplified and eased the demands of religion.[25]

Moreover, the cause of religious reform also showed itself able to speak to civic concerns and issues. Indeed, if there was a common denominator for the "success" of the Reformation in the cities, then it was that the clamor for religious reform was understood to lead to social reform as well. What that meant specifically differed from community to community. It could be a redress of resentment toward the economic prowess of monastic houses within the city walls. It could be the desire of certain dis-

---

24. R. Stupperich, "Bucer, Martin," *Theologische Realenzyklopädie* (ed. Gerhard Krause and Gerhard Müller; Berlin: 1981), 7:259, as quoted in Mau, *Evangelische Bewegung*, 100.

25. This was the thesis of Steven Ozment, *The Reformation in the Cities: The Appeal of Protestantism to Sixteenth-Century Germany and Switzerland* (New Haven: 1975).

enfranchised groups in a community to participate in civic governance. When the message of reform reached Valenciennes, for example, the poignant political differences between the rising merchant class and the ruling magistrates broke out into the open and eventually led the merchants to assume political power and turn the city Calvinist. Something similar happened in Amsterdam.[26]

26. A. C. Duke, *Reformation and Revolt in the Low Countries* (London: 1990), 96.

Chapter 7

REFORM CONSOLIDATED: SPEYER, 1526

The turbulence of the peasant uprising in 1525 had prompted many to consider the violence and bloodshed of that spring and summer a confirmation of the belief, widely held, that these were the last days. Elector Frederick of Saxony, who died that summer, was convinced of it, as was Luther, who had married Katharina of Bora during the height of the peasant uprising to "spite the devil," as he put it, surely one of the more unusual explanations for entering matrimony. When the turbulence was all over, the countless victims and the wanton destruction and devastation of land and people created a ubiquitous sense of despondency.

The Peasants' War had further significance for the subsequent course of events. The territorial rulers, for whom the riots should have hardly come as a surprise, were determined to assure that they were prepared for future uprisings. Discussions among territorial rulers began and quickly focused on an alliance of rulers as the best means of preventing future unrest. Because Luther was seen as the spiritual mentor of the insurgency, his belated criticism of the peasants notwithstanding, the deliberations of the territorial rulers quickly took on a pointed anti-Lutheran edge and could easily be interpreted, especially given the leadership of staunchly Catholic Bavaria, as an ill-concealed attempt to suppress the movement of reform.

This perspective made some of the reform-minded estates uneasy about the Catholic initiatives, and the territories and cities sympathetic to the cause of reform began to promptly explore forming an alliance to ensure that the Catholic territories would not use the pretense of suppressing future uprisings to suppress reform itself. This seemed all the more pertinent because some territories and cities had begun to make changes in their ecclesiastical practices and were thus in public and blatant non-compliance with the Edict of Worms.

The religious controversy took on an ever more pointed political dimension. The two parties of the controversy faced one another not merely as proponents of differing theological points of view, but as antagonists in the political arena. Both sides recognized that a military showdown was altogether possible. The theologians began to move to the sidelines while the political leaders became the spokespersons for the cause of reform. After 1525 two political blocs emerged, the one loyal to the Catholic Church, the other committed to reform. Because people in the sixteenth century understood religion not only as a private but also as a public matter this turn of events was not surprising.

This towering role of the political authorities in the process of introducing (or rejecting) the new faith has led to the suggestion to speak of a *Princes' Reformation*

(*Fürstenreformation*). The term focuses on that phase of the Reformation when the formal decision for or against reform began to be made. The term presupposes the propriety of certain parallel terms, such as "Communal Reformation," "Peasant Reformation," "Urban Reformation," in each instance indicating a particular characteristic of phases or stages of the movement of reform. The Princes' Reformation may have begun as early as 1522, when Elector Frederick of Saxony authorized (or, at any rate, condoned) formal changes in worship and belief, thereby anticipating the trend that the territorial rulers determined the formal religious alignment of a territory, leading eventually to the territorial definition of what constituted the Christian faith.[1]

All the while the emperor, Charles V, whose presence in Germany might have significantly influenced the course of events, was far away, tending to his Spanish interests. In February 1525 he had scored a decisive victory over Francis I of France at Pavia in northern Italy. Francis had been taken prisoner and in January 1526 signed—under duress—the Peace of Madrid. As matters turned out, he had no intention to honor its severe provisions. The document pledged the two rulers not only to oppose the Ottoman Empire, whose forces had reached Hungary, but also to suppress the Lutheran heretics, "who removed themselves from the holy church," an indication that Charles had not forgotten about the unresolved religious situation in Germany. Indeed, he promptly announced that he would presently return there. His arch-foe Francis forced a change of plans, for no sooner had Francis been released from his captivity that he declared (with papal concurrence) his signature to the Peace of Madrid to be null and void because it had been coerced. In May 1526 he formed the League of Cognac, which, also with papal concurrence, committed itself to breaking the Habsburg dominance of northern Italy. Charles's attention was thus once more diverted away from Germany. To complicate matters, his mercenaries in northern Italy, dismayed over not having been paid and left without the opportunity to compensate with the spoils of battle, began to march southward down the Italian peninsula, toward Rome, which they occupied and "sacked."

This *sacco di Roma* was one of the more unsavory aspects of early-sixteenth-century politics. Constable Charles de Bourbon, the commander of Charles's forces in northern Italy, had informed Pope Clement that he was not sure of his ability to contain his restless mercenaries, whereupon the pope offered one hundred thousand scudi protection money, an impressive sum but insufficient to keep the German mercenaries from their southward move. Bribes spared Florence from the onslaught of this undisciplined horde, which was determined to get to Rome (and its riches) and was getting further and further out of control.

The defenders of Rome, few in number and poor in training, quickly sought refuge in the Castel Sant'Angelo, still today one of the architectural highlights of Rome. Originally built as a funeral monument to Roman emperors, it had been turned into a massive fortification—a cylindrical drum with a diameter of some 200 feet sitting on top of a square measuring 270 feet on a side. There the artist Benvenuto Cellini had been placed in charge of the defense, a venture both inexperienced and bound to

---

1. The two noteworthy expositions of the concept are Luise Schorn-Schütte, *Die Reformation* (Munich: 1996), 72; and Peter Blickle, *Die Reformation im Reich* (Stuttgart: 1992), 186f.

be unsuccessful: his charges sought to repel the attackers by throwing statues on them from the ramparts. In the attack on May 6, Constable Charles de Bourbon was fatally wounded. The leaderless mercenaries began to loot the unprotected city for a full week, while Pope Clement, who had found refuge in the Castel—a secret tunnel connected it with the papal apartments—languished there until December, for all practical purposes a prisoner at the hands of the emperor's forces.

When it was all over, the city had been decimated, many of its churches destroyed, most of its shrines looted. The German mercenaries were joined in their plundering frenzy by others, even citizens of Rome. Charles V, understandably, was deeply embarrassed and expressed his regrets to the pope.

The *sacco di Roma* turned into an important episode in the history of sixteenth-century Christianity because it demonstrated that the Christian house was divided. The French king, Francis I, sought an alliance with the Ottoman Empire to defeat Charles, while Charles was too busy to tend to all the challenges and had to watch as his mercenary soldiers occupied and looted the Holy City.

In Germany the Catholic rulers could no longer count on the emperor's imminent return to bring his weight to bear on the resolution of the religious conflict. Indeed, given the complexity of the international situation, it was clear that it would be a long time before the emperor returned. Consequently, some Catholic estates decided not even to bother attending the diet that had been convened to meet at Speyer in June 1526. Their decision proved to be a dire miscalculation.

Foremost on the agenda of the diet was the unresolved religious issue. This meant, of course, the manifest ineffectiveness of the Edict of Worms and the increasing incidence of changes in the ecclesiastical rites throughout German lands—an obvious rupture with the common religious past. When the diet convened, a new atmosphere among the assembled estates became patently obvious. On the day the diet convened, High Mass was celebrated in the Romanesque cathedral of Speyer, as had always been the custom when the high and mighty of the empire came together to deliberate and decide on important affairs of state. But there were new sights. The rulers sympathizing with reform had put the letters *VDMIE* on their coat sleeves, for *Verbum Dei Manet in Eternum* (The Word of God Remains Forever), a quote from Isaiah 40:8, to be sure, but also a rather inflammatory testimonial to the cause of reform. Landgrave Philip of Hesse defiantly had an ox butchered and roasted on a Friday, the day observed by Catholics everywhere by abstinence from meat. Even more important, Philip had met with the new Saxon elector John—Frederick the Wise had died the previous summer—in the central German town of Gotha, and they had agreed to support each other in case either was attacked for reasons of religion. A bit later, this agreement was formalized at Torgau, and several north German estates joined them. In the deliberations of the diet, the proponents of reform stressed the urgency of undertaking reform and vigorously demanded Communion under both kinds, clerical marriage, and an end to private masses. There also was forceful support for the declaration of the Nuremberg diet of 1523 that had mandated that preaching be done from the Word of God.

In the end, however, the deliberations reverted to the fundamental question of what to do with the Edict of Worms. Many of the imperial free cities stated bluntly that this could not be carried out without triggering renewed unrest and turbulence, and they proposed that the emperor be so informed. Their point was obvious: matters had become too complicated to be resolved by the simple enforcement (or non-enforcement) of the edict. Moreover, a crucial matter such as this should not, they argued, be decided in the emperor's absence. Accordingly, the recess of the diet proposed that a delegation be sent to the emperor in Spain to apprise him of the situation in the German lands and to propose that a "free general council or at least a national council" be convened to address the various contentious religious issues. The recess also stipulated how the territorial estates should handle the controversial religious issues at present: "In matters concerning the edict [of Worms] so to live, rule, and act as each estate could hope and trust to answer before God and the emperor."[2]

The proposed delegation to the emperor never materialized, for no agreement could be reached on exactly what the emperor should be told. All the disagreements that had come up during the deliberations at the diet surfaced again. The most important decision to come from the diet was the provision about the Edict of Worms. Here everything depended on the interpretation of the crucial sentence. There is every reason to assume that the majority, which had agreed to this stipulation, understood the provision as a temporary solution, a truce, to be adhered to until the religious issues could be comprehensively addressed. The majority had meant to be sensitive to the demurrers of the cities and territories that, given the situation in their communities, it was impossible to enforce the edict. The majority saw in what might be called the petrification of the status quo a prudent temporizing solution. By no means did the majority (assuredly not the Catholics) understand the provision as a recognition of Lutheran notions or as an acknowledgment of the right of the territorial rulers and cities to do as they pleased. At issue was, plainly and simply, the question of the enforceability of the Edict of Worms, with the majority conceding the current difficulties, which, so it was implied, would be removed before long.

It is equally clear that the reform-minded cities and territories interpreted the provision quite differently, namely as a formal endorsement of their authority to proceed as they found advisable or prudent. Because they were answerable only "to God and the emperor," they understood the provision as acknowledging their authority to undertake whatever religious changes they deemed necessary. They proceeded posthaste to put this understanding into practice, much to the consternation of the Catholic estates, which felt tricked or at least misunderstood.

The recess of Speyer was meant as a truce. Yet the essence of a truce lies in its brevity: if it lasts too long, it becomes unalterable. So it was with the decree of Speyer. The continuing absence of the emperor from Germany, together with the failure of a general council to convene, meant that the premises on which the truce had been based were proving increasingly fickle. Month passed after month, and year after year, and events drifted along. This lack of action made possible the organizational consolidation of new forms of religious life in some territories, such as Hesse and electoral Saxony, and some cities, such as Nuremberg and Augsburg. The history of the

---

2. The recess is found in H. Chr. Senckenberg, ed., *Neue und vollstaendigere Sammlung der Reichsabschiede* (Frankfurt: 1747), part 2, 237ff.

Reformation might have been altered by the emperor's forceful intervention, by his speedy return to Germany, or by the convening of a council. None of these happened, and the truce became a peace.

Thus we are taken back once again to Charles V, the absentee emperor from Spain. The three years between the two diets held at Speyer, in 1526 and 1529, reveal the real tragedy of Charles V for the cause of his church. His absence from Germany during this crucial period, prompted by his complex involvement in Spanish and, indeed, European politics, created a vacuum in Germany and decisively influenced the fate of the reform movement. Charles, if anyone, had the power and authority to stem the tide of the Lutheran heresy. But he was off waging war against his arch-foe Francis I. In 1525 he had won a splendid battle at Pavia, but afterward he lost the peace at Madrid, where he laid down terms for Francis that were as unrealistic as his appraisal of the situation in Germany. During this crucial phase, his concerns were those of the *rey catholico* of Spain rather than of the *Kaiser* of the Holy Roman Empire. We will never know, of course, whether his presence in Germany would have altered the course of events; his absence—undoubtedly much appreciated by the evangelical rulers— certainly did not help to resolve matters nor the Catholic cause.

All the while, the adherents of reform had to assume that the Catholic estates, even in the emperor's absence, might well decide to resolve the religious controversy by using military force against the Lutheran (and Zwinglian) heretics. Landgrave Philip of Hesse was particularly sensitive to this possibility and actively pursued possible courses of action. The tense situation in Germany after the diet at Speyer is best described by a bizarre event that revealed how intensely political the religious situation had become, bringing the opposing religious forces to the brink of war.

In January 1528 Otto von Pack, a Saxon noble and vice chancellor of the staunchly Catholic Duke George of Saxony, confided to Landgrave Philip of Hesse the existence of secret Catholic plans to wage war against electoral Saxony and Hesse.[3] The ensuing course of events had all the trappings of an espionage thriller—forged documents, credulity, miscommunication, and secret agreements. However, it now appears that the secret Catholic plans existed only in von Pack's head, though he may have been privy to conversations in which such an eventuality was discussed by Duke George.

For Landgrave Philip, however, von Pack's revelation was grist for the mill, because he, more than any other evangelical ruler, was adamant that the cause of religious reform had a political dimension and required the support of arms in order to be sustained. He envisioned—much like Zwingli—a European-wide anti-Habsburg alliance directed against the Habsburg hegemony personified by the emperor that would at the same time afford the cause of reform substantive political and military support. Indeed, a strong political alliance of reformers might enable the return of Duke Ulrich back to Württemberg, from which he had been expelled in 1519; might subdue the major ecclesiastical territories; and might even allow one of the evangelical rulers to receive the kingly dignity. This was a grandiose vision that would have committed all of Germany to the cause of reform through military and political means. No doubt Philip, though young and inexperienced, thought big.

3. R. A. Cahill, *Philipp of Hesse and the Reformation* (Mainz: 2001).

Armed with von Pack's secret intelligence, Philip found it easy to persuade the Saxon elector of the urgency of the situation. The two were prepared to go to war against Albertine Saxony and the other estates that were part of the alleged alliance, when, at the last moment, Elector John got cold feet and decided to consult Luther about the matter. Luther was horrified, found that von Pack's revelations were not at all persuasive, and told the elector that a Christian ruler could defend himself only in case he were actually attacked. Those who lusted after war and those who were impatient would not receive divine favor. At this point von Pack's documents were unmasked as forgeries, and Philip's grandiose strategy collapsed. Germany had barely, and at the last minute, stepped back from the brink of armed conflict over religion— even though the Hessian landgrave had astutely noted the intimate connection between religion and political force.

REVERSAL AND PROTEST: SPEYER, 1529

Three years after the diet had adjourned in Speyer, the emperor summoned the estates to meet again in Speyer; but he tendered his apologies that he was detained in Spain. His "proposition," that is, his recommendation of desired action by the diet, had not reached Speyer by the time the diet opened; inclement winds had kept the Spanish vessel carrying the emperor's document in harbor. Charles's brother Ferdinand, who presided over the diet in the emperor's absence, promptly drafted a proposition of his own, declaring it to be his brother's. The document produced consternation among the reform-minded estates because it identified the Turkish Ottoman threat as the principal item on the agenda and called on all estates to do away with religious disagreements, meaning that the reform-minded towns and territories should return to the Catholic fold. That was ominous news.

The deliberations among the estates quickly revealed (hardly to anyone's surprise) disagreement about the contested religious issues. A first draft of the recess of the diet called for the convening of a general council within eighteen months to resolve the religious controversy. Until that time the territories and cities that had undertaken changes should desist from further change. The reform-minded estates and cities voiced opposition, but the Catholic majority, still displeased over the reformers' misreading of the 1526 recess, pursued a tough line. The majority proposed a recess that rescinded that of 1526, renewed the Edict of Worms until a general council, and prohibited any further ecclesiastical changes. Because some half of the estates were ecclesiastical territories, a staunch Catholic majority could be easily mustered in the diet, but even among the Catholics there were those who thought the emperor's alleged "proposition" to be too harsh and proposed, in lieu of a general council, a synod of the German church to restore ecclesiastical unity.

On April 19, 1529, the reform-minded estates, who had taken on the "evangelical" appelation drew up a protest against the proposed recess, to be read to the assembled estates, but Ferdinand and the imperial commissioners ostentatiously left the hall when the reading was to take place; nothing came of a formal protest. Six days later, on April 25, however, the evangelical estates were able to voice their protest against the proposed recess. Because the recess of 1526 had been passed unanimously, it was "honorable, proper, and legal" to rescind it only by a unanimous vote. The evangelical estates would not accept the proposed recess, "since in matters pertaining to the honor of God and the salvation of our souls every person [must] face God and be held accountable so that no one can excuse himself with the decision and doings of others, be they many or few."[4]

That was a startling statement. A minority of five north German territories and fourteen south German cities formally defied the Catholic majority—and the way in which affairs were conducted in the empire. At issue was the status quo. Whether majority opinion could be imposed upon the minority was legally an open question. But more was at stake than legality. The argument that a unanimous decision of the diet could be rescinded only unanimously was arguably a bit phony, since the remainder of the protest set up a criterion—"the honor of God and the salvation of our souls"—that stood outside parliamentary procedure. The implication of the statement was that the medieval world, with its ideal of the *corpus christianum*, the one Christian body, had broken apart. In 1521 a single monk had faced the dignitaries of the empire and demanded freedom to express his understanding of the Bible as dictated by his conscience. Almost to the day eight years later, a group of rulers and representatives of cities echoed his sentiment and thereby challenged the unity of the one Christian body.

There was yet another consequence of the protest at Speyer: it gave the adherents of reform a new label. Their opponents had called the advocates of reform "Martinians" or "Lutherans"; they themselves had preferred "evangelical," meaning "conforming to the gospel." After the protestation of Speyer, however, they began to be referred to as "protesting estates," and before long as "Protestants."

Politically the situation had become explosive. With the diet still in session, several Protestant rulers met to talk about the possible political ramifications of their unwillingness to accept the majority sentiment. In April a plan for a defensive alliance was proposed. If any partner of such an alliance was attacked "for the sake of the Word of God," the others would come to their assistance. Many questions went begging, for not all parties involved understood the significance of the proposal in the same way. The emperor, the overload of the estates, was not mentioned, which meant that the critical issue of what should be done if he were the one to suppress them was consciously avoided.

Everybody anxiously awaited the emperor's next move. Things were going well for Charles. He had scored an important military victory over France and his conflicts with the papacy appeared to be a thing of the past, as spectacularly demonstrated in Bologna in February of 1530 when Pope Clement VII crowned him emperor.

AUGSBURG, 1530

The emperor's next effort to resolve the religious issue came promptly. His summons to the estates for a new diet to meet at Augsburg in 1530 was astoundingly conciliatory. Concerned about the restoration of religious concord for the sake of both religion

4. *Deutsche Reichstagsakten, Jüngere Reihe* (Munich: 1929), 7:1262–65, 1274–88.

and political stability, Charles informed the estates he was eager to "hear, understand, and consider everybody's opinion in love and grace." At the same time, he offered his support "to consolidate all opinions into one Christian truth and to resolve everything that is not properly interpreted by either side."[5] The emperor's language sounded like grand caesaropapism, though it could also be seen as a modification of the rigid line that had characterized the proceedings at Speyer the year before; Elector John of Saxony, at any rate, was confident that an irenic resolution of the controversy was possible.

The emperor's declaration to "hear everybody's opinion" called on the "protesting estates" to formulate their theological "opinion." The problem was, of course, that a gulf existed between Zwingli and Luther over the interpretation of the Lord's Supper. In October 1529 Landgrave Philip convened a colloquy in Marburg to seek conciliation. Even though the opening oration, delivered by a Marburg professor of medicine no less, challenged "the incisive Luther, the magnanimous Zwingli, the eloquent Melanchthon, the brave Bucer" to agree, they did not. Moreover, it had become evident that the reformers disagreed about political strategy. Some wanted Protestant beliefs argued pointedly (the Zwinglian-Hessian approach); others favored treading softly (the Lutheran-Wittenberg approach). Landgrave Philip saw a pan-Protestant alliance as the most viable strategy, while the Saxon Elector John hoped for some sort of rapprochement.

In the end these differing notions meant that "everybody's opinion" put forward at Augsburg consisted of no fewer than three Protestant statements: electoral Saxony, Zurich, and four south German cities. The Catholics responded to the emperor's summons by insisting that inasmuch as they represented the historic faith of the church, there was no need for them to do more than refer to those ancient affirmations.

The confession that proved to be historically most significant came to be known as the Saxon statement: the "Augsburg Confession" or *Confessio Augustana*.[6] Philip Melanchthon had begun to draft sentences in response to the emperor's summons on behalf of the Saxon elector, first in Torgau, then on the way to Augsburg, but they dealt only with areas where the adherents of reform had altered traditional practice and faith—for example, the cup for the laity in Communion, the dissolution of monasteries, and the marriage of clergy. The Saxon notion was that these practical matters would be the foremost agenda items of the diet, and Melanchthon's jottings were meant to express theologically Elector John's political strategy that conciliation of the religious issues was possible. John had been one of the first to arrive in Augsburg, and he shared with the emperor, while still sojourning in Innsbruck, an earlier "Protestant" theological document, known as the Schwabach Articles, to demonstrate the conservative ("Catholic") theology of the movement of reform. Charles's brusque negative response caused John deep consternation, and he considered not attending the diet because conciliation would be impossible.

Then Johann Eck once more poured oil on the fire. He had culled some 404 sentences he thought to be heretical from the Reformers' writings and insisted they be publicly debated. The scope of the conversation shifted dramatically, prompting a

---

5. Karl E. Foerstemann, ed., *Urkundenbuch zur Geschichte des Reichstages in Augsburg im Jahre 1530* (Augsburg: 1835), 1:7ff.

6. H. Immenkötter and F. Wenz, *Im Schatten der Confessio Augustana. Die Religionsverhandlungen des Augsburger Reichstags 1530* (Müster: 1997), is a superb anthology.

change in Saxon strategy: now it seemed essential to submit a more comprehensive confession of faith than had been contemplated. Melanchthon assumed the task; Luther, who as a political outlaw could not be at Augsburg and therefore stayed at the castle of Coburg, at the southernmost tip of Saxon territory some one hundred miles north of Augsburg, received a copy of Melanchthon's final draft. His reaction (to become quite famous in later years) was that it pleased him, "and there is nothing that might be improved or changed. And that would not be appropriate either, since it is not my temperament to be so soft and subtle."[7] "Soft and subtle" opined Luther—"accommodating" might have been the better word.

The Saxon Elector now sought to obtain as many signatories to Melanchthon's document as possible. The emperor's arrival with striking pomp and circumstance in Augsburg on June 15 diverted attention—throngs of soldiers, banners, nobility, clergy high and low, formed a grandiose procession, welcoming Charles to the city. Once he had settled down, Charles wasted no time in making clear his displeasure with evangelical activities and activism in the city. No preaching was to be permitted in Augsburg, he announced, because preachers on both sides had escalated the tensions. But when Charles confronted the four major Protestant rulers, led by the Saxon Elector John, with the statement that he would not allow Protestant preaching as long as he was emperor, especially not in one of his imperial cities, Landgrave Philip rejoined that he failed to understand why the preaching of the Word of God was prohibited. Charles angrily repeated his prohibition, whereupon Margrave George of Brandenburg stepped forward and told the emperor he would rather die than forsake the Word of God. The emperor, taken aback by such determination, reportedly retorted in broken German, "Lieber Fürst, nicht Köpfe ab" (Dear ruler, no heads chopped off).[8] The Protestant sympathizers subsequently refused to participate in the Corpus Christi procession on June 15, when the consecrated host was in procession through the town.

The diet opened on June 21. Addressing the assembled estates, Charles reiterated the two concerns that had prompted his convening of the diet and his presence: to receive support from the estates for military action against the Turks and to conciliate the feuding religious factions. Once more Charles used the language of his original summons to the estates—that he was ready "to hear everyone's sentiment, notion, and opinion." In line with the disposition of the imperial council, the religious issue was the first item on the agenda.

By that time, Melanchthon had turned various drafts explaining the sundry discontinued "abuses" in the church into a comprehensive statement. This document did not emphasize the theological differences between the old and the new faith; its essential argument was that belief and practice observed in Lutheran territories and cities were not only based on Scripture, but also agreed with the teachings of the early church. Thus they could not be labeled heretical. The differences between the two "parties" merely consisted of a few externals, such as the Communion cup for the laity or clerical celibacy. On the contested theological issues, such as the Mass or the episcopacy, Melanchthon employed conciliatory and mediating language. That this Augsburg

---

7. Luther's letter is in WA Br, 5:319.
8. Leopold von Ranke, *Deutsche Geschichte im Zeitalter der Reformation* (Vienna: 1934), 574.

Confession became the classic confessional statement of Lutheranism is, in light of Melanchthon's intentions, highly ironic. For some reason Melanchthon, who did consult with other evangelical theologians present in Augsburg, had not been in touch with Luther during the writing of the final version of the confession. The Saxon councilor Gregor Brück wrote a new, highly political preface which underscored the irenic disposition of the evangelical territories and cities, referred to the recesses of 1526 and 1529, noted that the emperor had repeatedly expressed himself in favor of a general council of the church, and warned that if there was no reconciliation there would be an appeal to such a council.

The confession was publicly presented to the emperor and the estates four days after the formal opening of the diet, though not in a regular session. Emperor Charles had wanted it to be read in Latin, but the estates—probably less to support Luther than to argue the case for the use of the German language in Germany—insisted it be read in German. Five territories (Saxony, Hesse, Brandenburg, Braunschweig, and Anhalt) and two cities (Nuremberg and Reutlingen) had signed the confession; four more signed it within weeks.

The Augsburg Confession had two sections, of which the first outlined the faith of the "new churches" in twenty-one articles. A second section dealt with the removal of existing "abuses" in the church, the topics bandied about for some time—Communion under both kinds, marriage of priests, confession, and monastic vows.

The Catholic estates might have presented a statement of theirs at this point. But they adamantly refused, insisting that they were not a "party" or "faction" but the church universal. Two additional Protestant confessions of faith, prepared for submission to the emperor, did not receive official recognition. One came from the pen of Huldrych Zwingli. Entitled *Fidei Ratio ad Carolum Imperatorem* (Statement of Faith for Emperor Charles), it had been written in a stunningly short time and had intended to summarize the faith of Zurich and other Swiss Protestants. This attempt at a common front had failed, however. Zurich had no intention of going out on a limb on its own, which meant that Zwingli's confession remained his own personal statement. In contrast to Melanchthon's confession, the *Fidei Ratio* was pointedly polemical, both anti-Catholic and anti-Lutheran, undoubtedly because of its author's conviction that he could persuade the emperor with his biblical arguments. Melanchthon opined that Zwingli must have lost his mind, and Eck wrote an anti-Zwingli tirade in which he claimed that the Christian religion had been abolished in Zurich.[9]

A second confession of faith came from the pens of the Strassburg reformers Martin Bucer and Wolfgang Capito. It was a hurried response to the solicitation by the Strassburg representatives at the diet for a statement of the city's faith. On account of the differences about Christ's presence in bread and wine in Communion, Strassburg did not become a signatory of Melanchthon's Augsburg Saxon Confession, so Bucer and Capito wrote the "Confession of the Four Cities" (*Confessio Tetrapolitana*)—Strassburg, Memmingen, Constance, and Lindau—which was accepted by the emperor as a submitted brief. In the negotiations that followed, however, neither Zwingli's statement nor that of the four cities played any role.

9. Mau, *Evangelische Bewegung*, 218.

There was no clarity as to how the diet should proceed after the official presentation of Melanchthon's statement. The Catholic refusal to submit a statement meant, of course, that the emperor hardly found himself in the position of an impartial arbiter. Indeed, he was constantly in touch with the Catholic estates, which resulted, after some deliberations, in the decision to produce a Catholic counterstatement. More than twenty theologians went to work, and within two weeks they had produced a lengthy document that offered the "orthodox" commentary on each of the articles of Melanchthon's confession. It was so lengthy, however, that a shortened version became necessary, the *Catholica et quasi extemporalis Responsio* (A Catholic Response). When the emperor and the Catholic estates saw the document, they quickly concluded that it was far too polemical. A more moderate version was drafted, and this *Confutatio Confessionis Augustana* (Rejection of the Augsburg Confession) was officially read to the diet on August 3. In order to prevent further discussion, the Protestants were not given copies of the document.

This Confutation—surprisingly—acknowledged agreement on a number of theological points, such as Christology and the sacraments, but sharply reaffirmed those ecclesiastical practices where the Protestants had hoped for conciliation—marriage for priests, for example, or monastic vows and the cup for the laity. This strategy fit harmoniously with that of the papal legate, Lorenzo Campeggio, to grant minor concessions to the Protestants and thereby prevent the convening of a general council.

Upon the presentation of the Catholic document the emperor informed the estates that the Confutation had refuted the Protestant confession and ordered the Protestants to return to the Catholic fold "as in his conscience he had to do as Roman, Christian emperor, overlord, and guardian of the holy Christian church."[10] This rather rigid imperial pronouncement was somewhat at odds with the conversations taking place between Catholic and Protestant theologians. Extensive conversations were taking place outside the formal meetings of the diet, and Eck and Melanchthon had discovered considerable areas of agreement, including the issue that had come to epitomize the difference between the two sides, justification. These conversations were particularly trying for Melanchthon, whose conciliatory temperament was not made for the stressful role of spokesperson for the estates that had embraced evangelical theology. Luther's all-too-confident missives from Coburg, which read so well today, may not have helped much.[11] When Melanchthon queried Luther about other possible areas of agreement, Luther retorted that there had been enough compromise.[12] Nonetheless, Melanchthon secretly approached the papal legate Campeggio with the proposition that in return for the Communion cup and priestly marriage, concessions would be possible in the other contested issues—a proposal that, once it became public, caused considerable consternation on the part of the Protestants. The curia responded with a categorical no to these maneuverings.

Early in August a new round of negotiations began among the estates, in a small setting, involving several imperial councilors as well as Eck and Melanchthon. Ironically,

---

10. Herbert Immenkötter, *Die Confutatio der Confessio Augustana vom 3. August 1530* (Münster: 1978), 206.
11. WA Br 5:400.
12. WA Br 5:405.

at this point Eck showed some flexibility, but in the end disagreement carried the day. This was doubly tragic because early in September Campeggio received a communication from Rome that indicated a softening of the curial position—under certain conditions, the Communion cup for the laity and the marriage of priests could be tolerated, even though not officially enjoined.[13] As matters turned out, this dramatic concession came too late to influence the course of negotiations in Augsburg.

Melanchthon had been absent when the diet heard the reading of the Confutation and had been unable to obtain a copy. When he finally did, in October, he was chagrined over its sharp and vehement tone. He promptly responded with a reply, entitled *Apologia* (Apology), that offered a detailed elaboration of the contested issues and thereby brought the disagreement into much clearer focus than had been the case in his original confession.

The emperor's proposed draft of the recess of September 22 reiterated his earlier pronouncement that the Confutation had refuted the Augsburg Confession, prohibited future evangelical publications, insisted on the reestablishment of monasteries and convents that had been dissolved, and the reintroduction of both the Mass and private confession in Lutheran territories. The draft gave the Protestants six months, until April 15, 1531, to accept the Confutation—and return to the Catholic fold. Until that time the recess of the diet at Speyer of 1529 was to be observed. A general council of the church, to be convened within a year, would address issues of church reform. The tenor of the draft recess was, in fact, surprisingly conciliatory. It drew a sharp line between theological issues, where the Protestants were demonstrably in error, and reform issues, where a council would be attentive to Protestant concerns.

Protestant intransigence coalesced quickly. In addition to the signatories of the Augsburg Confession, an increasing number of cities—including Augsburg, right under the emperor's nose, so to speak—indicated their refusal to agree to the recess, forcing the Catholic estates to take further counsel. As more and more Protestant rulers left Augsburg, perfunctory discussions took place about the other major agenda item, the matter of financial support for military defense against the Turks. There was foot-dragging all around, and the emperor received only the agreement that in the case of an actual Turkish attack help would be provided.

Accordingly, the official recess on November 19 dealt mainly with the contested religious issue. The Edict of Worms was affirmed, and further religious changes were strictly prohibited. In particular, the monasteries and convents were to be restored to their rightful owners—and action was threatened against any who disobeyed. A lengthy list of what constituted proper (and heretical) teaching was appended, and the assurance given that the pope would convene a general council within six months to deal with ecclesiastical abuses.

The recess should be seen as the emperor's definitive turn against the movement of reform, nine years after he had first sought to do so at Worms. Having witnessed the continuing disagreement between the two sides, he had become an adamant sup-

13. Gerhard Müller, "Duldung des Luthertums? Erwägungen Kardinal Lorenzo Campeggios vom September 1530," *Archiv f. Reformationsgeschichte* 68 (1977): 159.

porter of the church, which alone suggested unity.[14] The rationale for Charles's sentiment was obvious. He wanted issues of ecclesiastical reform addressed by a council, but he also realized the curia's reluctance to convene one. After all, a council that had addressed reform issues had adjourned just a year before the outbreak of the controversy; to convene a new council could be taken as acknowledgment that the Protestants were right in pressing the need for reform. The fear of conciliarism ran deep in papal bones. On the other hand, Charles was an astute enough politician to recognize (as did the Protestants as well) that he depended on Protestant support for any military action against the Turks.

Both the Turkish threat and the religious controversy were on the agenda of the diet, but the Protestant estates had successfully demanded that the religious issue be considered before the discussion of aid for military defense against the Turks. Thus the possibility of the Protestants' refusal to supply that aid if the religious issue was not satisfactorily settled hung like a cloud over the deliberations of the diet and proved a constant reminder for the emperor to be realistic in his religious policies and pursuits.

The Protestant estates—not surprisingly—rejected the draft, which nonetheless became the formal recess of the diet on November 19, 1530. By that time, however, the diet had turned into a rump gathering composed mainly of the emperor and the Catholic estates, since the "protesting estates" had preferred to leave town once the outcome had become obvious.

The diet had thus ended in discord, with the Catholic majority seeking to force its will on the Protestant minority. But twice in a little over a year the Catholic efforts to force the adherents of the new faith back into the old church and the Protestant efforts to gain acceptance had proved unsuccessful. The Protestant cause seemed doomed; the adherents of the new faith were given a breathing spell of six months. At the same time, Augsburg had seen the first full-fledged effort to achieve theological conciliation. Serious theological discussions had taken place, albeit without success. Interestingly, Augsburg had also demonstrated that there were in fact not merely two parties to the religious controversy—the old, papal church and the new, Protestant churches —but rather four. Neither side was a homogeneous entity; rather, both parties had what we might describe as "hawks," those convinced that the gap between the two sides was unbridgeable, and what we might call "doves," those persuaded that with goodwill and determination concord could be restored. This bifurcation was to become typical during the two decades to follow.

The issue at Augsburg had been whether the disagreement between the two sides pertained to substantive theological issues or mainly to the correction of abuses. Opinions differed. At one point, only the issues of the Communion cup and of clerical

---

14. H. Immenköter, *Um die Einheit des Glaubens: Die Unionsverhandlungen des Augsburger Reichstages im Herbst und Sommer 1530* (Münster: 1974); and *Im Schatten der Confessio Augustana: Die Religionsverhandlungen des Augsburger Reichstages 1530 im historischen Kontext* (Münster: 1997). This is opposed by W. Reinhard, "Die kirchenpolitischen Vorstellungen Kaiser Karls V., ihre Grundlagen und ihr Wandel," in *Confessio Augustana* (ed. E. Iserloh; Frankfurt/Main: 1980), 62ff. John M. Headley, *The Emperor and His Chancellor: A Study of the Imperial Chancellery under Gattinara* (New York: 1983), assesses Gattinara's role.

celibacy remained unresolved, and in the end the directives from Rome were conciliatory even on these issues. Intriguingly, the negotiations failed over the question of "ecclesiastical abuses." The emperor's insistence that a council of the church could resolve the outstanding issues was thus not completely beside the point.

In addition, some of the emperor's advisors were taken by the notion of Erasmus that reform of Christian living was necessary in the church, and they had influenced Charles to think in those terms. At the same time, however, Charles's pursuit of religious conciliation (which he saw expressed in his pursuit of a general council) had powerful political implications. Charles wanted religious peace in the heartland of the empire as a means of assuring the political stability that seemed indispensable for dealing successfully with the Turkish menace in the southeast. A peaceful empire would also allow him the freedom to pursue whatever political or military action he saw appropriate to take against France, with which Spain had been in chronic conflict ever since the last decade of the fifteenth century. Most important, the discussions at Augsburg conveyed that even though both emperor and curia wanted to resolve the controversy, a deep gulf separated the two. Had Charles had the final word in Augsburg, the controversy might have been resolved.[15]

Augsburg revealed an ambiguous situation, more hopeful than some had dreamed, more discouraging than others had feared. The Lutherans had made a point of their theological orthodoxy, yet in the end pointed disagreement as had existed before rendered conciliation impossible. More had taken place than a discussion concerning the viability of the Edict of Worms, as had dominated the two previous diets. There had been serious theological discussion, an indication that the situation was flexible so that the discourse could be taken back to the spring of 1521. To put it differently: the two diets at Speyer had assumed that the theological and political condemnations of Luther and his followers were proper; the diet at Augsburg presumed that these condemnations might be revisited.

THE LEAGUE OF SCHMALKALD

The recess of the diet created a precarious situation for the Protestants. The emperor appeared determined to use force against them after the expiration of the grace period stipulated in the recess, and this danger triggered discussions among the Protestant rulers and the cities. No sooner had as Landgrave Philip of Hesse returned home from Augsburg, that he invited the Saxon elector to meet and discuss the possibility of an alliance as protection against a possible military move of the emperor.[16] Few of the Protestant leaders questioned the political prudence of such a move, which was tantamount, however, to an act of disobedience against the emperor. And that was a theological problem: was it not analogous to what the peasants had done in 1525?

---

15. This is the argument of Gerhard Müller, in *Die römische Kurie und die Reformation, 1523–1534: Kirche und Politik während des Pontifikates Clemens' VII* (Gütersloh: 1969), and "Duldung des Luthertums? Erwägungen Kardinal Lorenzo Campeggios," *Archiv f. Reformationsgeschichte* 68 (1977): 158f.
16. E. Fabian, *Die Entstehung des Schmalkaldischen Bundes* (Tübingen: 1962).

The Wittenberg theologians initially were of little help; they too were concerned about the theological legitimacy of such disobedience. After all, the pronouncements of the apostle Paul in Romans 13 had been for centuries the grounds for unconditional obedience to governmental authority. Luther, in particular, had grave misgivings about a military alliance, not least because early in the controversy he had made the point—as in his letter to Elector Frederick of February 1522, when he was about to return to Wittenberg from the Wartburg—that the gospel should not, and could not, be defended by worldly means. After this initial reluctance, however, Luther affirmed the right of resistance. He was influenced by Landgrave Philip of Hesse, who argued that the constitutional relationship between emperor and territorial rulers meant that the emperor was elected and at his election pledged to carry out certain specified responsibilities, while the territorial rulers inherited their offices. The election of the emperor meant that a bond of mutual responsibility existed between emperor and territorial rulers. If the emperor failed to carry out his responsibilities, it was right and proper for the territorial rulers to oppose him and call him to task. Such was the case if the emperor were to proceed with force against the "protesting estates." The right of resistance of the territorial rulers against the emperor emanated from the exercise of their own authority.

With the theological scruples out of the way, the Saxon Elector invited the signatories of the Augsburg Confession to a meeting at Schmalkald in December 1530. Landgrave Philip of Hesse, Duke Ernst of Braunschweig, and Margrave George of Brandenburg, together with representatives of Nuremberg, Ulm, Strassburg, and Reutlingen, attended the gathering. Those present quickly reached agreement that they would come to one another's assistance in case any were attacked for religious reasons.[17] The draft of a formal alliance was drawn up. Eventually electoral Saxony, Braunschweig, Hesse, Anhalt, and Mansfeld, together with eleven south German cities, including Ulm, Strassburg, Constance, and Reutlingen, formed the alliance. The formal documents of the League of Schmalkald were signed on February 27, 1531, and the league's constitution was approved two years later. The bylaws of the league provided for a common treasury for military defense, mutual military assistance, a common military force of twelve thousand men, and a common supreme war council. The formation of the League of Schmalkald culminated a development that had begun in 1526, when questions about military action for or against the new faith had first arisen and "alliance" had become part of the vocabulary of the Reformation.

The League of Schmalkald was a defensive alliance for protecting the signatories if they were attacked for religious reasons. The members of the league were a heterogeneous combination of political power, and even though Saxony was, on the face of things, the most commanding partner, the real leadership lay with Hesse and Strassburg. But there were problems. Aside from a shared concern about possible military action by the emperor and his Catholic allies, the league had no common purpose. Moreover, as the years passed, the threat of Catholic military action seemed less and less real, and the periodic meetings of the members of the league were increasingly characterized by endless bickering that revealed the complexity of the political situation in

17. G. Haug-Moritz, *Der Schmalkaldische Bund 1530–1541/42* (Leinfelden-Echterdingen: 2002), 41ff.

the empire. There was consensus neither about the religious situation and how it might be resolved nor about a prudent political strategy. Demonstrably, the common religious profession (after all, the raison d'être for the league) did not result in common political goals. Despite its shortcomings, however, the league proved to be a major factor in German politics and religion for well over a decade. Its coming into existence was consequential, for the religious controversy became explicitly entangled with politics. After the establishment of the league, the alternative to the conciliation of the two parties was the use of force to subdue the religious antagonist. For more than a decade, the absence of a military showdown between the religious parties was partly the result of the existence of the league, especially after it became more powerful in the 1530s by admitting additional members and negotiating with England and Denmark about membership.

When April 15, 1531, at last arrived—the deadline set by the recess of the Augsburg diet to reestablish Catholic practices throughout the empire—the political situation had changed so drastically that Charles had no choice but to pretend that no deadline had ever been stipulated. Wherever the emperor looked, there were problems. The pope was reluctant to convene a general council, which Charles thought to be the best means to resolve the religious controversy. The Protestants were determined not to surrender their religious commitment. Rumors were circulating about an imminent Turkish attack on Vienna, and as long as the need for financial support against the Turks persisted, Charles could ill afford to alienate the Protestants. Charles's relations with France continued to be precarious. In a meeting with Pope Clement VII in Bologna 1533, he had succeeded in eliciting a commitment from the pope to convene a general council. Yet it was increasingly obvious that Clement's promise was hardly worth the paper on which it was written. Although Clement did solicit responses from several rulers as to their disposition with respect to a council, he himself saw no need for a gathering of the church, and thus a council was as far off as ever.

Moreover, the formation of the League of Schmalkald had altered the political landscape. It showed that the Protestants were committed not to surrender their religious convictions, and the Saxon Elector's refusal to concur with Archduke Ferdinand's election to the Roman kingship indicated a new intransigence on the part of territorial rulers. Charles's most prudent policy might have been to grant the Protestants coexistence. This was indeed suggested to him by Cardinal Loaysa, who told him that his difficulties were insurmountable and that he should "accept the heretics and have them be subject to your brother as the Bohemians are." The acceptance of religious diversity for the sake of political unity was a fateful suggestion that was to carry the future, but in 1531 Charles would have none of it. He was willing to recognize the status quo temporarily if the Protestants would aid him against the Turks and acknowledge Ferdinand's election as Roman king. He still held two cards, and either might yet prove to be a trump: a peace with the Turks would free his hands for a firmer policy toward the Protestants, while a peace with the Protestants would enable him to pursue an aggressive policy against the Turks.

Then Charles was reminded that one of his best friends was his greatest enemy. In the fall of 1531, his younger brother Ferdinand (1503–1564), to whom he had entrusted the governance of the Habsburg hereditary lands, attacked the Turks in

Hungary in a personal show of force against the town of Ofen and John (János) Zápolya, the leader of the Hungarian magnates, who had sought the Hungarian throne after the catastrophe of Mohács. Ferdinand's move was intended to obtain control of a strategic area—and the prestige of military victory to boot. It was, alas, unsuccessful and served only to increase the tensions between Suleiman II and the West. Suleiman was aware of Charles's determination to fight the Turks as soon as the opportunity presented itself, but he also knew that the religious turmoil in Germany tied Charles's hands. For Suleiman, the opportune hour had struck with Ferdinand's venture. On April 26, 1532, his trumpets sounded, and his mighty military force began to march westward, crossing the Hungarian border in June.

The imperial diet had convened in Regensburg a few days before Suleiman commenced his campaign, and for the first time in a decade the religious issue was not paramount in the estates' deliberations. The ominous Turkish threat dominated the agenda. The emperor hoped to obtain financial aid from the estates, both Catholic and Protestant, to allow him to raise a military force sufficient to deal with the Ottoman menace. The Protestant estates were willing to contribute their share for an anti-Ottoman coalition but insisted on substantial religious concessions in return. They demanded a revision of the Augsburg recess and the formal recognition of the ecclesiastical changes undertaken in their territories and cities. The problem for the emperor was that Catholic territories were rather less enthusiastic about providing military subsidies, which they saw simply as a new form of taxation. This put Charles on the horns of a dilemma. Had he received support from the Catholic estates, Protestant assistance would not have been quite so urgent. The Catholics, for their part, insisted on a strict enforcement of the Augsburg recess and at the same time refused to provide financial support against the Turks. As far as they were concerned, the Turkish threat was not real. They argued, moreover, that the emperor should set an example by supplying troops of his own and observed that Ferdinand's attack on Ofen gave them little confidence in the Habsburgs' ability to handle the precarious situation.

With such divergent views and positions, it is not surprising that the religious negotiations at Regensburg quickly reached a stalemate. With not much happening at Regensburg, the real sites of action were two other cities to the northwest, Schweinfurt and Nuremberg, where secret talks were held between representatives of the emperor and of the League of Schmalkald. The twin issues were the obvious ones—the Protestant demand for religious recognition and the emperor's request for aid against the Turks. Several months of negotiations brought no agreement, but eventually the Protestants became more flexible, demanding mainly the assurance of toleration and the suspension of religious litigation before the *Reichskammergericht*, the imperial supreme court, until a general council could address the outstanding religious issues.

The threat of a Turkish attack still called forth common solidarity. Luther admonished the estates to harmony in such troubled times and, according to an interesting (if erroneous) tradition, intended the first stanza of "A Mighty Fortress Is Our God" as a battle song against the Turks. Luther was deeply perturbed by the Turkish offensive against Vienna, prompting him to translate the Latin antiphon *Da pacem domine* into a German version, "Verleih uns Frieden gnädiglich" (Graciously grant us peace), still used in Lutheran worship today.

The Turks thus hover over the history of the German Reformation as a pivotal, albeit evasive reality. Indeed, the first half of the sixteenth century saw few more portentous realities than the expansionist dynamic of the Ottoman Empire. During the rule of Suleiman the Magnificent (1520–1566), Europe experienced the Turks as a frightening religious and political danger of fatal consequence. Few were able to envision peaceful coexistence with the Ottoman Empire, which represented both a military threat and also a "false" religion. This dual reality of the Ottoman Empire must be kept in mind when listening to sixteenth-century voices about Islam, for the Ottoman Empire and Islam were inextricably linked. Precisely because the Ottoman threat was seen as a religious onslaught on the Christian faith, the church and the pope joined the fray, vociferously advocating military action. It is understandable, however, that the Protestants had problems supporting such a papal initiative, not least because some were convinced that the pope was by far a worse enemy of the true faith.

The aggressiveness of the Ottoman Empire had, in an intriguing way, been a catalyst of the indulgences controversy in 1517. One of the two objectives of the infamous jubilee indulgence had been to raise revenue for military action against the Turks, the other being to obtain funds for the rebuilding of St. Peter's basilica in Rome. Luther adamantly rejected the idea of a preemptive strike against the Turks, which was extensively discussed at the Augsburg diet in 1518. In his *Resolutiones* (Explanations) of his Ninety-five Theses, Luther had argued that to "resist the Turks means to resist the will of God, who chastises us through them"—a remark that promptly landed, as one of Luther's forty-one offensive and heretical sentences, in the papal bull of condemnation. In his *Letter to the Christian Nobility* of 1520, Luther again referred to the topic of the Turks by reminding his readers that the annates, the tax paid to the curia in the amount of the first year's revenue of an ecclesiastical position, were originally meant to finance military action against the Turks but had come to be used for curial expenses.

From the 1518 diet onward, the ominous threat of Ottoman military aggression had hovered like a dark cloud over the deliberations of the German estates. In 1518 papal desire for financial aid against the Turks undoubtedly influenced Cardinal Cajetan's lenient strategy with Luther and Elector Frederick. The death of King Louis of Hungary in 1526 after the disastrous Battle of Mohács dramatized the extreme danger of the empire and made the Catholic estates irenic in their attitude toward the supporters of reform. The same happened in 1530, at the diet at Augsburg, after the Turkish advance to the outskirts of Vienna had once again vividly conveyed the Turkish threat. The relative quiet of the 1530s was disrupted when, in 1540, Suleiman occupied the town of Ofen and dealt Ferdinand a disastrous defeat. A counterattack, led by Joachim II, the Elector of Brandenburg, in 1542, ended in abject failure.

At all of these crucial junctions, most notably in 1530, the Protestant estates adroitly used the Turkish threat as a means to win concessions from the emperor and the Catholic majority. When it came to a choice between solidarity with the empire against the Turks, on the one hand, and solidarity with the adherents of the new evangelical faith, on the other, the answer was clear: the solidarity was with the brethren (and sisters) of the faith. After all, the pope and the Turks were enemies of equal weight for the Protestants. Both suppressed the true gospel and sought to suppress them. The Turks' aggressiveness toward the empire meant that the Protestants were able to utilize them in their scheme for survival. The Ottoman Empire may well have been the cause for the survival of Protestantism in Germany.

At Regensburg compromise was reached. The Protestant estates agreed to financial aid for military action against the Turks, while the emperor promised them the toleration they had demanded. The Protestant estates were to be legally tolerated until the convening of a general council, which would settle the contested religious issues. Also, all religious litigation pending before the *Reichskammergericht* was to be suspended. The agreement reached between the emperor and the Protestant estates is known as the *Nürnberger Anstand,* or Peace (better: Truce) of Nuremberg, because it had been negotiated in Nuremberg. It was a major success for the Protestants, the first move away from the policy of a rigid enforcement of the Edict of Worms. The impetus for the agreement was the political situation, which had forced the emperor's concurrence. The agreement was to have no bearing on the theological differences between the two sides and, above all, was meant to be a temporary solution.

The formal recess of the diet propounded a different version of the matter, for the Catholic majority among the estates was determined to have its way and was unwilling to offer concessions to the Protestants. The emperor for his part faced the uncomfortable alternative of siding with this majority and thus accentuating the religious split and rendering common action against the Turks impossible, or of making concessions to the Protestants and thereby alienating the Catholics. The recess of the diet expressed the sentiment of the Catholic majority, which merely acknowledged, without concurrence, the agreement reached at Nuremberg. The recess also stressed the urgent need for a general council of the church, and asked that such a council convene within six months. Should this not be possible, the diet should convene again to resolve the contested religious issues. Since nothing was said about the recess of the recent diet at Augsburg, it remained formally in force. This made for an ambiguous situation, because the provisions of the recesses of Augsburg and Regensburg could hardly be reconciled.

After the adjournment of the diet, the emperor and his forces proceeded to Vienna to meet the Turks. The emperor, barely recovered from serious illness (which had not prevented him from fathering an illegitimate child), yearned to follow his troops and lead them into battle. He dreamed of a victory by which his name would be forever remembered. "Should I be defeated," he wrote, "I will leave a noble name behind me in the world and enter into paradise; should I be victorious, I will not only have merit before God but will also surely restore the ancient boundaries of the empire and obtain immortal glory."[18] Alas, Charles was thwarted in his aspirations. A small fortress in western Hungary, Güns, resisted the Turkish attack for twenty-one days, sapping the strength of the Turkish offensive. By the time Charles arrived, the Turkish forces were in retreat. No more battles were to be fought, nor were glorious victories to be attained.

Had the emperor returned to Germany to pursue his strategy of resolving the religious controversy instead of being absent for another eleven long years, events might well have taken a different turn. But Charles made his way to Italy, for good reason, so it seemed. As far as he was concerned, a truce prevailed in Germany, an uneasy truce,

18. Quoted by P. Joachimsen, *Die Reformation als Epoche der deutschen Geschichte* (Munich: 1951), 212.

to be sure, but one that had temporarily calmed the situation. The Turks had been repelled, and relations with France, that chronic antagonist of Spain, were tolerable. Only the religious controversy remained unresolved, and Charles was committed to give it priority. He was convinced that short of using force against the Protestants, the only hope for a resolution of the conflict lay in a council. Because the pope was the key to the convening of a council, Charles hoped in a personal encounter to persuade Pope Clement VII to action. "I met with His Holiness," he later wrote in his memoirs, "but without the full success I had anticipated." Charles's retrospective appraisal of the situation was accurate enough, though their meeting in Bologna in February 1533 was amicable and the expressions of papal cooperation were disarming. The pope and the emperor agreed on the need for a council and pledged themselves to secure the cooperation of both France—Spain's mortal enemy—and the Protestants.

Charles had seemingly been successful, but he fatally misjudged Clement VII. The lodestone of Clement's papal policy was the exact opposite—to prevent the convening of a council. There were salient reasons. Not only was there the lingering suspicion about a possible resurgence of conciliar sentiment and the judgment that ecclesiastical affairs could be brought to order without a council. There was also the unlikelihood that the sworn enemies France and Spain would participate as equals in the deliberations of a council. Thus no council was to meet during Clement's pontificate. Because Charles's strategy for resolving the religious controversy in the empire depended on a council, his seeming hour of triumph was in fact the hour of his failure.

POLITICAL CRISIS IN SWITZERLAND

Meanwhile, the atmosphere in the Swiss Confederation had turned no less precarious. The ecclesiastical changes in Zurich in 1525 had triggered a reaction on the part of the Catholic cantons, which insisted adamantly that the Edict of Worms be administered throughout Switzerland. To make sure that their concerns about its administration were taken seriously—more seriously than was the case in Germany—they actively pursued ties with Habsburg Austria. Zurich countered with political moves of its own to assure a balance of political power in Switzerland. The first success came in December 1527, when Zurich signed a treaty with Constance. Soon thereafter Bern turned Protestant, and other towns in Switzerland, such as Glarus, Appenzell, Graubünden, and Basel, were leaning in that direction.

Faced with the growing presence of reform-minded towns and cantons, the five loyal Catholic cantons—Uri, Schwyz, Unterwalden, Lucerne, and Zug—which had allied in 1524, concluded a *Christliche Vereinigung* (Christian Alliance) with Austria in April 1529. They realized that the entire northern part of the Swiss Confederation had turned Protestant, raising the specter of the central cantons being cut off from their important trade with central and northern Europe. The convergence of religion and economics meant a deteriorating situation, especially when, in March 1529, Zurich troops occupied the abbey of St. Gall. Both sides still shrank from armed conflict, but their language was evasive. Zwingli asserted with strikingly timeless words that "the peace so eagerly sought by some is war, and not peace; and the war, for which we so eagerly prepare ourselves, is peace, and not war."[19] He sought to broaden the political muscle of the Swiss reform movement with a European-wide anti-Habsburg alliance. His persistent effort to reach a theological understanding with Luther and the Wittenberg theology faculty concerning the Lord's Supper was undoubtedly influenced by his conviction that a united political front of all Protestants was the best strategy for assuring their survival. Only a politics of strength would safeguard the new faith. Although some Protestant rulers, such as Philip of Hesse, saw things very much the same way, in the end Zwingli's words failed to resonate, especially in Wittenberg, and the Swiss reformer remained isolated.

The recess of the Augsburg diet in 1530, with its ultimatum to the Protestants, had repercussions in Switzerland. The tensions between the Catholic cantons and Zurich took a turn for the worse, and in April 1531 Zwingli implored the Zurich city council to issue a declaration of war against the Catholic cantons—an intriguing illustration of the important role Zwingli played in Zurich political affairs. His notion failed to receive support, however, but within a month economic sanctions were levied against the Catholic cantons to deprive them of essential goods and force them to pursue a conciliatory policy.

The Zurich chronicler reported that in August a fiery comet was seen in the sky over Zurich, and people pondered its significance, as sixteenth-century men and women always did when confronted with unusual natural phenomena. Queried as to its meaning, Zwingli was said to have ominously replied that "many a man of honor, including myself, will be paying dearly."[20] Two months later, the five Catholic cantons, determined to throw off the choking economic blockade, declared war against Zurich, which was militarily ill prepared. The city had over twelve thousand men of conscription age, but on the day of battle a mere seven hundred men constituted its core fighting force, together with some twelve hundred advance troops. There were no horses to pull the cannons, and the morale (and the pay) of the soldiers were low. No fewer than twenty-one military mobilizations had occurred in Zurich between 1524 and 1531, and—like the shepherd boy in Aesop's fable—they were not taken seriously in the end.

On the morning of October 11, 1531, the two opposing forces met for battle. An eighteen-year-old traitor led the Zurich forces into a trap. Zwingli accompanied the Zurich forces with sword and Bible high on a horse. In the afternoon the two armies reached Kappel, a hamlet ten miles south of Zurich, and the skirmish began. Twice the Zurich forces repelled the enemy; then they were overrun. Zwingli, who probably fought in the brunt of the battle, was mortally wounded. "What is it? The body they may kill, but not the soul," were reportedly his last words. Catholic soldiers discovered his corpse on the battlefield, quartered his body, and burned it to ashes—the punishment for a man perceived as a traitor to the Swiss and a heretic to boot. When Luther heard about the battle and Zwingli's death, he vented his exasperation by adding to the vituperative comments he had frequently made about Zwingli by

19. Quoted by O. Farner, *Huldrych Zwingli* (Zurich: 1960), IV:477.
20. *Zwinglis Werke*, E. Egli, ed. (Zurich: 1905), 3:551.

observing that Zwingli had died a sinner and blasphemer—hardly an endearing comment. It prompted Bullinger to pray that God forgive Luther his great sin.[21]

Zurich had suffered an ignominious defeat. By the middle of November peace negotiations were in progress, and toward the end of that month peace returned to the Swiss Confederation. The Peace of Kappel provided that the cantons could determine the religious faith within their boundaries. Any further expansion of Protestantism, however, was declared to be illegal. The new faith was recognized in Zurich and the other Protestant cantons, but that was it. Protestantism was destined to remain a minority religion in the Swiss Confederation. Strikingly, the new faith found legal acceptance almost a quarter of a century before a similar accommodation was reached in Germany; but the dream of a Swiss Confederation, united in the new evangelical faith, had died, like Zwingli, on the battlefield of Kappel.

Yet something else had happened as well. After the theologians had failed to persuade one another, the two factions had marched off to the battlefield, there to resolve their theological as well as political conflict. An ancient Roman adage had spoken of war as *ultima ratio regum,* the final reasoning of kings. The Battle of Kappel offered eloquent proof that in the sixteenth century war could also be the final reasoning of theologians, or, to vary Clausewitz's famous definition, the "continuation of theological controversy by other means." Europe, in the throes of unresolved religious conflict, had surely watched with eagerness.

The cause of the Reformation in Switzerland was not lost, however. The political influence of the Catholic cantons remained strong, even though the economic power of the cantons (Zurich, Basel, Bern) that embraced the new Protestant faith made for a certain equilibrium in the Swiss Confederation. Alongside the broader political impact of Zwingli's death and the Peace of Kappel, there was the reality—only slowly emerging—that Zwingli's death removed a powerful and dynamic influence on the course of the Reformation in south Germany.

A twenty-seven-year-old, Heinrich Bullinger, became Zwingli's successor and was to serve in this capacity for almost half a century.[22] Although Bullinger has stood in the shadow not only of Zwingli but of Luther, Calvin, and Bucer as well, his influence on the Reformation in Zurich and the southern parts of Germany was enormous. Born in 1504, one of several sons of a priest in Bremgarten, Bullinger experienced a conversion to the new evangelical religion in the early 1520s—the outgrowth of reading Melanchthon, Luther, and Erasmus—and between 1523 and 1529 taught the Bible in a Cistercian monastery in Kappel and published biblical commentaries. By 1525 his influence had been a leading force in the monastery's embrace of the new faith. The youthful Bullinger established contact with Zwingli and was present for the several disputations held in Zurich to determine the parameters of the new faith. The defeat of Zurich in the Battle of Kappel forced him and his family to flee to Zurich (he had married a former nun, Anna Adlischwyler, in 1529). In the face of Zwingli's

---

21. See here Brecht, *Martin Luther*, II, 523, and O. Farner, *Das Zwinglibild Martin Luthers* (Tübingen: 1931), 35ff.

22. See Emidio Campi and Bruce Gordon, eds., *Architect of the Reformation—An Introduction to Heinrich Bullinger* (Grand Rapids: 2004).

tragic death at Kappel, the city council and the cathedral chapter elected the twenty-seven-year-old as *pastor antistes*, or head, of the church in Zurich on December 1531. He was to lead this church for forty-four years.

Bullinger promptly demonstrated a stunning measure of activity. His regular preaching responsibilities eventually led to over seven thousand sermons, some of which were subsequently published as devotional works—the famous *Dekaden*. He engaged in prolific correspondence, of which some twelve thousand letters are extant (compared to forty-three hundred of Luther's). He published biblical commentaries, histories, and theological works, writing or editing some 130 books. He was an important figure in the Zurich academy for the training of future ministers that was attached to the Grossmünster cathedral, and his interests and perspectives were European-wide.[23]

Unquestionably, Bullinger's most significant contribution was the adroit (and successful) way he led the church in Zurich (and even Basel and Bern) out of the political catastrophe of Kappel, consolidated it, and placed it on a permanent footing. Zwingli's intimate engagement in Zurich politics, while both tolerated and even endorsed by the two city councils, had meant disastrous political and military consequences for the city. He had led the city into war; the city council became weary of military involvement, and Bullinger found ways to safeguard the public role of the church without seeking to run and dominate secular affairs. Bullinger was the author of city council mandates of 1532 that affirmed Zurich's commitment to the new evangelical faith and ordered the structure of the church and ministry. The ministers had to swear a yearly loyalty oath to the city. Bullinger advocated a pragmatic cooperation of church and state; the ministers were not to involve themselves in political affairs, but they were to offer opinions as general matters of values of importance to the body politic. The pendulum swung in the direction of the political powers. The Zurich church became what later began to be called a "state church"—unlike Calvin's Genevan model, where the church continuously strove for superiority, in matters of morals for example, over the city council.

Theologically, Bullinger's significant contribution was his delineation of what came to be known as covenant theology, first expressed in his treatise entitled *De testamento seu foedere Dei unico et aeterno* (Concerning the Unique and Eternal Covenant or Testament of God), of 1534: God has made, from Adam to the present, a single covenant where his promises are juxtaposed to the human commitment to keep the conditions of the covenant. This view, variously modified, became enormously important in seventeenth-century Reformed theology.

Of equal theological and even political significance were Bullinger's efforts to assure a theological consensus among Swiss Protestants. A first success came in 1549 with the *Consensus Tigurinus* (Zurich Agreeement; the full Latin title was *Consensio mutua in re sacramentaria ministrorum Tigurinae ecclesiae et J. Calvini ministri Genevensis ecclesiae*—Mutual Agreement Concerning the Sacrament), in which Bullinger and Calvin found mediating language concerning the Lord's Supper. Calvin had initially drafted twenty-four brief theses, which went through various redactions, including

---

23. His crucial role notwithstanding, there is not much scholarship on Bullinger. Most comprehensive is Fr. Blanke and I. Leuschner, *Heinrich Bullinger, Vater der reformierten Kirche* (Zurich: 1990).

those of Bullinger, and eventually attained agreement all around. The crucial statement was that in the Lord's Supper the body and blood of Christ are received not by means of a bodily presence of Christ's human nature, which is in heaven, but by the power of the Holy Spirit and the devout elevation of the soul of the worshiper to heaven.[24] The Consensus allowed the merger of the Zurich and Geneva reform movements.

Roughly a decade later Bullinger pursued the same goal of theological consensus with a document that he drafted as a personal confession of faith. This document became known as the Second Helvetic Confession of 1562, the *Confessio et expositio simplex orthodoxae fidei*, which in thirty chapters summarized the common faith of the Swiss Protestants and, in fact, the Reformed tradition as a whole.[25] This Helvetic Confession, which on the contested Communion issue used the language of the *Consensus Tigurinus*, marked a major milestone in the eventual convergence of various south German, Swiss, and Genevan theological strands: the theologies of Zwingli, Bullinger, and Calvin were sharp in their opposition to the Lutheran alternative but were not in total accord when it came to a positive delineation of biblical faith. It is a tribute to Bullinger that under his aegis these three theological strands merged into what came to be called the "Reformed" Protestant tradition.

The Protestant faith in Zurich and Switzerland thus flourished in the decades after Zwingli's death in 1531. It made modest gains, and was strengthened in theology and polity.

THE INSTITUTIONALIZATION OF A NEW CHURCH

By the early 1530s the religious changes undertaken in territories and towns began to be characterized by a sense of permanence. No matter what the professed commitments of all Protestant Reformers concerning unity, the realities of life spoke a language of their own: sermons had to be preached, sacraments administered, ministers educated, congregations organized. In short, a new church had to be brought into being. This was the task of Protestant Reformers in Germany in the 1530s and 1540s.

The formation of new Protestant churches was a slow and haphazard process, which suggests that the break with the Catholic Church was not necessarily understood as a permanent parting of the ways. The first ecclesiastical changes, for example, those in Wittenberg or Hesse in the 1520s, were efforts to assure the continuity of church life. Soon it became evident, however, that the division showed no sign of abatement, or at least that one could proceed as though it did not. This meant comprehensive changes and new organizational structures—in short, the formation of new churches. As matters turned out, while certain external changes were undertaken with relative speed, alterations in disposition were long in coming. The process of Protestantization took the better part of the century.

---

24. *Calvini Opera*, 7:693ff.
25. John H. Leith, ed., *Creeds of the Churches: A Reader in Christian Doctrine, from the Bible to the Present* (Richmond, VA: 1973).

The initial changes undertaken been relatively untheological, moderate, and without revolutionary fervor. They lacked the sense of deliberate confrontation and break, suggesting haphazardness, an unwillingness to risk categorical alienation. What had been avoided, however, turned out to be the reality, and the hopes of the mid-1520s had faded, ten years later, like flowers on a sultry summer day.

The events proved to be different from what the Reformers had anticipated. The Catholic Church had not been open to the kind of change and reform they had desired. The reaction, indeed, had been one of hostility and, before long, even persecution. Nor had conciliation been possible. The parting of the ways, at first unconscious and unreflected upon, became petrified, and no amount of effort seemed capable of bridging the gap. Soon the heavy burden of permanence settled upon the new Protestant churches. The more time passed, the more the likelihood of conciliation was out of the question. The new churches were forced to settle down to everyday routine.

Specific tasks were involved in the organizational consolidation. One pertained to the ordering of the local congregation, its organizational structure and its order of worship. A second aspect was the restructuring of the social functions, such as the care of the poor, which the medieval church had carried out in the past. Finally, there was the matter of the broader organizational pattern of the church. In Germany the question of the structure of the local congregation was greatly influenced by Luther's nonchalance on the matter. He wrote several orders of worship, but his *Deutsche Messe* (German Mass and Order of Service) of 1526 asserted that "in sum and substance this order and all others are to be used in such a way that, if there is abuse, they are promptly abolished and a new one put in its place."[26] Luther sought to emphasize the centrality of the local congregation in ordering its life, from the selection of the minister to the form of the service. He expressed this notion in his 1523 treatise *Dass eine christliche Gemeinde Recht habe* (That a Christian Congregation or Gathering Has the Right and Authority to Judge All Teaching). When a fellow reformer proposed a council to bring about ecclesiastical uniformity among those adhering to the new faith, Luther retorted that such uniformity was neither necessary nor advisable. Structures and forms would issue spontaneously and creatively from the local congregation. In a few instances this actually happened: Thomas Müntzer wrote an order of worship for Allstedt, and Johann Lang one for Erfurt. Not surprisingly, most congregations did not have the necessary creative talent in their own ranks to do so.

Some of the issues could not be solved on the local level. This inevitably placed the governmental authorities in a key role, for they alone could assume broad regional or city-wide responsibilities. Government supervised the external ecclesiastical affairs, the training of the clergy, their remuneration, and the supervision of the faithful. With great reluctance Luther conceded the ruler's role in ecclesiastical affairs. His preface to the *Unterricht der Visitatoren an die Pfarrherrn im Kurfürstentum zu Sachsen* (Instruction of the Visitors for the Clergy in the Electorate of Saxony) of 1527 revealed that he had given up the idea of effecting the building of a new church by way of a

---

26. WA 19, 1112f.

spontaneous evolution of forms, structures, and patterns on the local level.[27] The territorial church was to be built with the help of the ruler. Luther's rationale was that an emergency situation existed. His exhortation was gratuitous and, if anything, showed the clash between theological reflection and political realities. The political authorities were already exercising a considerable role in ecclesiastical affairs, from the scrutiny of the competence and morals of the clergy to the disposition of church property.

The laity's voice in church affairs was modest. Among the Protestant territories, a measure of congregational participation existed only in Hesse, where the organizational structure was less bureaucratic than elsewhere. The same held true for the imperial cities, influenced no doubt by the limited geographic confines and the representative character of the city councils.

Not all of the Protestant clergy were men of achievement, of course, and Protestantism no less than Catholicism had its share of those for whom spiritual commitment was as much a mystery as theological competence. Melanchthon told about a minister who, when asked if he taught the Decalogue, answered that he had not as yet been able to purchase the book. Nor was moral demeanor always the norm. In 1541 the Hessian superintendents requested of Landgrave Philip a radical cure for clerical immoderation: "Whereas there is much complaint about clergy who cause considerable offense by their immoderate drinking and other vices and yet remain unpunished as well as unchanged, we recommend that a jail be established in the monastery of Spisskoppel and the unrepentant clergy be given the option of either leaving their parishes or being confined in that jail with water and bread to bring about their correction."[28]

There also were many dedicated and competent ministers who carried out their responsibilities with proficiency and conscientiousness. They were the field officers of the Reformation, translating Protestant theory into ecclesiastical practice, proclaiming the new gospel, nurturing their congregations, and dealing with the political authorities. In sum, they added religious vitality to theological pronouncements. Though Protestantism had espoused the notion of the priesthood of all believers, in practice it became a *Pastorenkirche*, a church guided by the clergy.

The task of the ministers was to preach and to administer the sacraments. Little difference from Catholicism existed with respect to the reception of the latter, except that it tended to be less frequent. The emphasis upon preaching altered traditional precedent and placed a heavy responsibility upon the minister. There had been a good deal of preaching before the Reformation (that there was none is a stereotyping Protestant misconception), but the sermon had not occupied as important a place as subsequently among the Protestants. This Protestant stress on preaching was easier postulated than put into practice, and it speaks for Luther's practical sense of churchmanship that as early as 1522 he published a church postil to provide examples of biblical preaching. He thereby appropriated the genre of Postils—collections of sermons.

---

27. WA 26:195–240.
28. This illustration (and others) are found in P. Drews, *Der evangelische Geistliche in der deutschen Vergangenheit* (Jena, 1928), 16; see also W. Pauck, *The Heritage of the Reformation* (Glencoe, IL: 1961), 129.

The word itself was derived from *post illa verba* ("after these words," that is, the explanation following the reading of the "words" of Scripture).

In Luther's own lifetime this *Wartburg Postil* saw almost thirty editions, proof of its widespread usefulness. The sermons of the postil were to be used by the ministers as an aid in the preparation of their homiletical exercises or preached as their "own." The zeal for the new gospel was clearly more important than the matter of authorship. Thus the words of Luther or Melanchthon were heard from many a Protestant pulpit in the sixteenth century, even though Luther never darkened the door of that church and the name of Melanchthon was never heard. The people in the pews were edified by such plagiarism, just as they undoubtedly have been whenever the ministry in the pulpit appropriated ideas not exactly their own.

CONTINUED PROTESTANT EXPANSION: CITIES AND TERRITORIES

Emperor Charles V was again absent from Germany for almost a decade, from 1532 to 1541, and the historian ponders anew how events might have unfolded had Charles chosen to spend this time in Germany and resolutely sought to end the religious controversy. Charles's absence, however, made the continued Protestant expansion understandable: without the emperor, the Catholic forces lacked an important symbolic figure, and that at a time when the Protestant movement was formalizing its achievements and consolidating its hold in central and northern Germany (not to mention England and Scandinavia).

The exuberance of the early 1520s was gone, but since the full significance of the movement of reform—its strengths and its liabilities—had become obvious, an impressive roster of territories and cities formally embraced the Protestant faith during the 1530s: Württemberg, Pomerania, Mecklenburg, Dinkelsbühl, Hanover, Nassau, Bremen, Osnabrück, and many others, especially in north Germany. These ecclesiastical transformations did not happen overnight; they were long in coming and were, as often as not, merely the formalization of a state of affairs that had prevailed for some time. Many territories and cities had sat at the sidelines in view of the uncertainty of the recesses of the diets in 1529 and 1530, which made a public acceptance of the new faith both unwise and precarious.

The most striking aspect of this Protestant expansion is the dramatic reality that during this time most of the imperial free cities turned Protestant. Following a brilliant study by Bernd Moeller entitled "The Imperial Cities and the Reformation," which called attention to the fact that the Reformation was accepted by most of the imperial cities, Reformation historians focused a great deal of attention on how specific cities had turned Protestant. Indeed, the Reformation was even labeled "an urban event."[29] A good deal of the exuberance about this pivotal centrality has disappeared

---

29. This quote is from A. G. Dickens, *The German Nation and Martin Luther* (London: 1974); see also Steve Ozment, *The Reformation in the Cities* (New Haven: 1975).

as of late, but the phenomenon remains noteworthy. That virtually all the imperial free cities joined the camp of reform cannot be called into question.

The phrase "joined the camp of reform" calls for amplification. It is tantamount to saying they "became Protestant," but that phrase, too, begs the question. What did being Protestant mean? Surely, it must not be understood as evidence for an overwhelming popular support for the decision to introduce reform. To be sure, the sources tell us of unheard-of numbers of people attending the sermons of reforming clergy; of rioting burghers who insisted on the discontinuation of the celebration of the Mass or on the removal of the images from the churches. But we are without hard statistical evidence that would allow us to turn these happenings into the confident declaration of overwhelming popular support for reform and change. Even as elsewhere in Europe, the formal introduction of the Reformation in a community or territory was an act of state, that is, a decision of the political authorities. In the case of the cities this determination was made by the city council. Indeed, the persisting loyalty of the adherents of the "old faith" throughout Europe, including the German cities, suggests that the Catholic Church was too vibrant and dynamic to make the notion of a wholesale desertion of the faithful a plausible conclusion.

The cities in turn saw themselves more and more as autonomous political and social entities. Increasingly, a spirit of communalism prevailed that suggested to the cities that as a community they should structure all of communal life. This entailed a civic concern for education no less than for the care of the sick and the poor. This raised issues about the place of the church in this communal entity—a church that, while supplying the spiritual needs of the townspeople, was still answerable to a foreign entity in Rome. Whatever religious, psychological, or even social elements prompted a city to turn Protestant, developments in the fifteenth century had a bearing on the situation of the 1520s and 1530s. In many cities where the oligarchies were firmly entrenched, tensions about governance had surfaced in the early sixteenth century. Tensions prevailed, and those outside power were clamoring to seize at least part of it.

The burghers in the cities enjoyed a far greater degree of literacy than did the peasants in the country, who had no means to obtain firsthand information—and make informed judgments—about the happenings in the world beyond their villages. The peasants depended for information on those whose business caused them to travel between town and country and so brought them news.

Not so the townspeople, who had access to the myriad of polemical pamphlets that were being publilshed. While we are unsure about the number of pamphlets that swamped the German countryside after 1519—the size of the editions of specific pamphlets cannot be determined—all commentators have been unanimous in their contention that the number was formidable and, by all odds, probably around one million. The more popular pamphlets, or pronouncements, had numerous reprints. For example, the famous *Twelve Articles of the Peasants* was reprinted no fewer than twenty-four times in no fewer than fifteen cities. There also has been no real clarity about whether these pamphlets had a common theological or social denominator. Probably they did not. The topics of the pamphlets were too diverse, the orientation of the known authors too heterogeneous to warrant the assumption that all sang from the same hymnal. Eberlin von Günzburg published a whole series of pamphlets with the title *Bundtgenossen* (The Covenanters) in which he sought to draw the picture of a new and perfect society.

These pamphlets were cheap, and they were written in the German vernacular. Sixteen or thirty-two pages were the norm, easily printed even by itinerant printers with small printing presses.

Of incisive importance was, in all instances, the role of the leading minister of a town. Whether it was Urban Rhegius in Augsburg, Osiander in Nuremberg, Capito and Bucer in Strassburg, or even Bernhard Rothmann in Münster, the disposition of the minister made the difference. No city turned Protestant over the defiant opposition of its key clergy. To be sure, there were confrontations between clergy and councils, and councils ordered the expulsion of clergy—none other than Thomas Müntzer was expelled from Zwickau—but those instances were few. A number of explanations suggest themselves for this pivotal role of the clergy, for example, that these clergymen had gained the confidence of the burghers and the ruling elites, so that a clergyman's own shift away from the Catholic Church was followed by that of the entire city.

More complicated, and more difficult to identify, are the reasons for the popular support accorded the message of reform. Undoubtedly, these were both religious and other, though whether we are talking about the common folk or the ruling elites, political or economic reasons may have been of importance, whenever one stood to gain from a religious change. Some people surely found themselves persuaded by the new evangelical message of Luther and the other Reformers about grace and faith. Bernd Moeller and Peter Blickle suggested that the new religion emphasized precisely the communal and corporate values that the cities were embracing.[30] Yet others may have embraced the new message because it seemed to them a less demanding religion.

This last suggestion has much to support it. In truth, late medieval religion had come to be encumbered as a religion of works—pilgrimages, indulgences, and fasting—which encumbered the daily lives of the faithful with requirements, demands, and obligations. In contrast, the new understanding of the Christian message called for faith and freedom, as none other than Luther had enunciated in his tract on *Christian Freedom* in 1520. Of course, there is little doubt that a striking simplicity characterized the new message, and it may well be that men and women found this attractive.

At the core there was not so much the acceptance of Protestant tenets on the part of the people, but a change in the ecclesiastical structures and life: the repudiation of episcopal jurisdiction, the dissolution of the monasteries in the cities, the secularization of ecclesiastical property, the discontinuation of the Mass, and the introduction of what was called evangelical preaching.

The Peace of Nuremberg had offered toleration to Protestants. At long last, the formal acceptance of Protestantism by a territory or city at least for the time being no longer entailed ominous political consequences. Quite the contrary: distinct political advantages could be associated with ecclesiastical change, such as the confiscation of monastic property and its use for secular purposes. The Protestantism that emerged from these achievements was self-conscious, political, institutional. Its spokesmen

30. B. Moeller, *Imperial Cities and the Reformation* (Durham, NC: 1992) and P. Blickle, *Communal Reformation in Sixteenth Century Germany* (Atlantic Highlands: 1992).

were the councilors of the League of Schmalkald; it was expressed in the formal church orders that gave form to the changes undertaken. Still, no permanent legal basis for ecclesiastical change existed; obtaining it was the Protestants' objective.

The Protestant expansion created problems: the territories and cities that embraced the new faith after 1532 wanted the provisions of the Peace of Nuremberg also to apply to them. Catholics disagreed, holding that the Peace applied only to those territories and cities that had been Protestant in 1532. The *Kammergericht* (Supreme Court) pursued a staunchly Catholic line and kept the Protestants in legal trouble. Though not serious—the Protestant territories and cities were undertaking whatever ecclesiastical changes they wanted—the lawsuits before the *Kammergericht* were a nuisance and a constant reminder of an unsettled legal issue: the status of church property that had been confiscated by reforming territories and cities and was used as the material basis for the support of churches, schools, and charities. The Protestants argued that the issue of ecclesiastical property was a religious issue over which the court had no jurisdiction.

The decade of the 1530s proved to be a time of dynamic Protestant expansion. In 1534 the duchy of Württemberg, an important territory in southwest Germany, turned Protestant—at about the same time Pope Paul III succeeded Pope Clement VII, while in England Parliament passed ecclesiastical legislation that severed the En-·glish church from Rome.

Two years later the Protestant cause was strengthened by a significant enlargement of the League of Schmalkald—Württemberg and Pomerania as well as the cities of Hamburg, Augsburg, Frankfurt, Hanover, and Kempten became members. The membership of Württemberg made the league a formidable presence in south Germany. Something else strengthened the Protestant cause as well: after more than a decade of intra-Protestant theological strife, a consensus was reached called the "Wittenberg Concord" concerning the contested issues of the Lord's Supper. This was foremost the accomplishment of Martin Bucer, the irenic Strassburg reformer, who ever since the Marburg colloquy between Zwingli and Luther in 1529 had doggedly pursued the goal of theological reconciliation between Wittenberg and Zurich. Bucer did not see their theological divergences as profound, and he was determined to find a mediating formula that would bridge the most blatant disagreement, the one over the Lord's Supper. He himself had come close to the view of Melanchthon that the Supper was spiritual food, in which Jesus was truly present with the elements—"with the bread" rather than "in the bread." While Bucer found little support among the Swiss for his mediating stance, his notions did resonate with key reformers in south German cities. Under his aegis, serious conversations took place in Wittenberg in 1536, in which he advocated the notion of a real presence of Christ in the elements independent of the faith of the recipient, so that even the "unworthy" (*indigni*) received the body and blood of Christ. Eventually, a meeting of theologians from south Germany and Wittenberg in May 1536 brought about a concord—though it was actually a compromise—that was accepted by the reformers of Strasbourg, Frankfurt, Augsburg, Ulm, and Reutlingen. Prompted by Bullinger, the Swiss reformers rejected the agreement. In the wake of this concord, however, a new controversy over the proper interpretation of the words of institution in the Lord's Supper broke out, or, better, a controversy over the Wittenberg concord's interpretation of the words of institution. All the same, the concord allowed the enlargement of the League of Schmalkald into south Germany. In the end the league grew more powerful because of the theological compromise.

At the same time, the European situation changed dramatically. In June 1536 Pope Paul III convened a council to meet in Mantua, in northern Italy. King Francis I of France promptly refused to allow the French bishops to attend (Mantua was situated in the emperor's territory), and the League of Schmalkald likewise declined to send representatives, but because the council never settled down to business, these refusals made little difference. Nonetheless, Paul III's move brought about an important theological document of the Lutheran tradition: the Schmalkald Articles, written by Luther and meant as a summary statement of the new faith. These are the articles, wrote Luther, "on which I must stand and will continue to stand until I die, God willing, since nothing must be changed or yielded." Forty-three theologians, including Melanchthon, subscribed to the document. In 1530, Melanchthon's Augsburg Confession had presented the new faith by emphasizing its agreements with the Catholic Church; Luther's Schmalkald Articles, to the contrary, focused on the distinctly "evangelical" affirmations, finding harsh and aggressive words for the papal religion. The sharpness of Luther's tone raised doubts whether conciliation between the two sides by a council was likely or possible.

The emperor, for whom a council had been the linchpin in his strategy for solving the religious controversy, was forced to confront two new realities: the failure of a council to convene and the political strength of the League of Schmalkald. For a while he tried to forge a Catholic counteralliance, the League of Frankfurt—unsuccessfully, as matters turned out, because several Catholic territories had long-standing treaties with Protestant territories, for example Mainz with Hesse, and there was apprehension about a possible Habsburg power play disguised as concern for religion. Charles also pursued the notion of convening a "German assembly" to take the place of a church-wide council to resolve the religious controversy but then endorsed the notion of theological colloquies of experts to address once more the contested theological questions.

On both sides some were convinced that rapprochement might yet be possible. Perhaps even Charles himself was so inclined, as was, on the Protestant side, the Strassburg reformer Martin Bucer. After more than twenty years of controversy, hope for an amicable resolution of the religious conflict had not subsided. The colloquies got under way in June of 1540, first in Hagenau, then in Worms, and finally—in 1542—in Regensburg. Surprisingly, a great deal of attention was paid during those two years to the legal aspects of church property that had belonged (in the form of endowments or real estate) to the church but had been "secularized" by governmental fiat. The Catholics insisted that according to canon law such property belonged irrevocably to the "Christian church," raising thereby the issue of the identity of this church.

However, there was also a political issue. Several (otherwise quite insignificant) Catholic territories united in the League of Frankfurt were seemingly pursuing bellicose policies, prompting the League of Schmalkald to conclude that a military showdown was imminent. Given this situation, the offer of the Brandenburg Elector Joachim II, an irenic Erasmian, to mediate the disagreements between the two sides received a sympathetic response. Negotiations took place in the fall of 1538 between the League of Schmalkald and King Ferdinand, who represented his absent brother. But the Protestants showed themselves rather stiff-necked and doggedly clung to several far-reaching demands: a permanent "peace," that is, toleration; and the cessation of all religious litigation pending before the *Kammergericht*. As far as the Catholics were concerned, yielding would have amounted to the petrification of the status quo along Protestant lines, and Ferdinand was unwilling to cede that much. Moreover, Pope Paul III, outspokenly unhappy about theological colloquies that were outside official church purview, insisted that they be ended, while the papal legate Aleander opined that the emperor should appear in Germany with Italian and Spanish troops and put an end to the Protestant spectacle. But the emperor had not given up his hope for conciliation and dispatched Johann von Weeze, the exiled archbishop of Lund, to explore if an agreement with the Protestants might be reached.

Indeed, an agreement was reached. On April 19, 1539, the Peace of Frankfurt, or *Frankfurter Anstand*, was signed. It stipulated that no military force would be used against the adherents of the Augsburg Confession, including those who had subscribed after the Peace of Nuremberg, for a period of fifteen months. During that period all religious litigation before the *Kammergericht* was to be suspended as well. In turn, the Protestants agreed not to use force against Catholics and, moreover, to meet shortly to consult about providing financial aid for a military campaign against the Turks. Last, but by no means least, both sides agreed that a theological colloquy should be held to explore the possibility of reconciliation.

The emperor, rather cool to the notion of a colloquy, was initially not at all disposed to support the venture, but the international situation forced his hand. King Henry VIII's matrimonial advances to Anne of Cleves, a niece of Elector John Frederick of Saxony, raised the possibility of England's alignment with the League of Schmalkald. At the same time, France and Denmark were engaged in negotiations with the league, which thus threatened to become—as far as Charles was concerned—a formidable entente of European dimension. To make matters even worse for Charles, his truce with the Ottoman Empire was to end on July 1, 1540, raising the specter of a renewed Ottoman attack on central Europe. Given these realities, Charles could hardly afford to be on a collision course with the German Protestants.

The notion of a colloquy was a rather surprising turn of events. After all, more than twenty years of fierce theological controversy had ensued since Luther's formal condemnation by church and emperor, and new churches had come into being. That a possible theological reconciliation was back on the agenda suggests that the hope for an amicable resolution of the conflict had not evaporated, even after more than two decades. On both sides were men who wished—for whatever reason—for conciliation.

The problem was that the ensuing colloquies did not take place under the aegis of the church and thus lacked authority and ecclesiastical stature. Agreement, even had it been reached, would have amounted to very little. Even if Zurich, Geneva, England, or Sweden, not to mention the German Protestants, had concurred with an agreement, the major consequence would have been a different atmosphere. Such, of course, would have been a noteworthy accomplishment, indeed.

Not everything was pristine purity at Hagenau, Worms, and Regensburg, the sites of the several colloquies. A peculiar mixture of political and religious considerations hovered over the gatherings, and the former may even have been more important than the latter. The emperor considered religious concord in Germany to be of utmost importance for his political objectives, though at the same time his notion of his imperial responsibility as the arbiter of Christendom was an important factor in his thinking. The curia was the uneasy bystander. The possibility of a religious agreement without curial participation was real. In the end, of course, that would have meant no agreement after all.

Into this complex situation burst an embarrassing scandal involving the political bulwark of the German Protestants, Landgrave Philip of Hesse. At issue—not for the first time in weighty human affairs—was sex. Philip was publicly exposed as a bigamist, and the consequences were disastrous for the League of Schmalkald. At the beginning stood (again, not for the first time in the affairs of crowned heads) a *mariage de convenance,* the marriage of Philip and Christina, the daughter of Duke George of Saxony. Philip was chronically unfaithful, though always plagued by religious scruples about his unfaithfulness, so much so that, seeing himself as a sinner, he did not receive Communion for years. To resolve his dilemma, his sister suggested a permanent extramarital relationship. As matters turned out, Philip did not need to look far and wide for an appropriate choice in this regard—Margarete von der Saale, his sister's attractive lady-in-waiting. But Margarete's mother insisted on a proper marriage, and that complicated matters. A divorce was out of question, because the theologians were categorical in their insistence that divorce, except in a few instances, was against divine law. To be sure, canon law allowed the annulment of marriages invalid for a number of reasons, but the Protestant theologians had fiercely repudiated canon law as sophistry, which meant that recourse to its stipulations was hardly a viable option. Events were to show, however, that the remedy offered by Protestant theologians was hardly free of sophistry of its own.

Philip asked Luther and his Wittenberg colleagues for their opinion on the matter. The academicians duly deliberated and eventually drafted a confidential statement that had the hallmarks of a determined effort to remain faithful to their convictions and yet find a solution to the landgrave's problem. The theologians' statement distinguished between "general law" and "special dispensation," between rules and exceptions. Monogamy was general law among Christians, as it had been affirmed by Jesus and was the practice of the church through the centuries. Special dispensation, however, was possible in light of the Old Testament precedent. After all, many of the patriarchs of the Old Testament had several wives. In Philip's case, so the Wittenberg divines concluded, such a special dispensation was appropriate in light of his "nature" and his burdened conscience. This special dispensation was allowed only *in foro Dei,* before the eyes of God; the second marriage had to be kept secret.[31]

Understandably, Philip found the Wittenberg advice eminently helpful, and the wedding with Margarete took place in March 1540. The appreciative bridegroom sent

---

31. The case has been extensively discussed with particular reference to Luther's role. The best study is still, after many years, Wm. W. Rockwell, *Die Doppeleche des Landgrafen Philipp von Hessen* (Marburg: 1904).

Luther a cask of wine and joyously informed him in a letter that his new bride was a relative of Luther's wife, Katie. Luther was not impressed, perhaps even embarrassed, and burned the letter.

Before too long rumors about Philip's second marriage began making the rounds, and the publicity put the landgrave into a precarious situation. He quickly persuaded himself that he had merely followed the advice he had received from Wittenberg, and sought Luther's consent to publish the Wittenberg statement. Luther adamantly refused, declaring that the theologians' statement had been a confidential confessional counsel and as such could not be made public. Philip should simply deny everything with, as Luther put it, a "strong Christian lie." Philip declared himself shocked; lying was sinful, and he would have none of it. As far as he was concerned, it was all the Wittenberg theologians' fault: "If this matter can be defended in one's conscience before Almighty, Eternal, and Immortal God, what does then the damned, sodomite, usurious, and drunken world matter?"[32]

Once the matter had come to light, Philip's position became precarious. The *Constitutio Criminalis Carolina*, the criminal code Charles V had promulgated and the estates had approved at Regensburg in 1532, prescribed the death penalty for bigamists. Under the circumstances, Philip concluded that he had no other option than to seek the emperor's pardon. In June 1541 he and the emperor reached a secret agreement in which Philip agreed not to enter into any alliance with a foreign power nor to support the admission of the Duke of Cleves into the League of Schmalkald. In return, Philip received the emperor's pardon for all violations of "imperial law and order, publicly or privately committed to this day." There was one qualification: the emperor's pardon would not apply in case "war would be waged for religious reasons against all Protestants." This was ominous, for it suggested that the emperor still pondered the feasibility of war as a means to resolve the religious conflict.

The Protestants paid dearly for Philip's marital misadventure, whose agreement with the emperor effectively paralyzed the League of Schmalkald. Theretofore his stance in matters of reform had been informed by his conviction that the cause of reform inextricably linked religion with politics and that the best strategy for safeguarding the cause was to pursue a policy of political and military strength. His secret agreement with the emperor revealed his desperate straits; he was his own worst pupil when he assumed that his concessions pertained only to politics and left religion untouched.

This, then, was the setting of the colloquies that were to be a final effort to find theological common ground. The first colloquy convened at Hagenau in 1540, but the participants could not even agree on an agenda. The second colloquy got under way at Worms in the same year, and this time, after lengthy debates on procedural questions, theological issues were actually discussed. Confidential conversations were also held behind closed doors between Martin Bucer and the Catholic Johann Gropper, both theologians of irenic temperament, congenial choices to pursue conciliation. After the modest success at Worms, the talks were to be continued in the emperor's presence at the forthcoming diet at Regensburg.

---

32. The Wittenberg advisory is found in WA B 8, 636ff., the landgrave's letter in WA B 9, 182ff.

By now a military resolution of the religious conflict was on Charles's mind, but at Regensburg, in the spring of 1541, conciliation dominated. Indeed, Charles was the heart of the conciliatory effort and suggested a last-ditch effort to reach rapprochement with the Protestants. Although representatives of the estates were present at the deliberations, the theologians—Melanchthon, Pistorius, and Bucer on the Protestant side; and Eck, Gropper, and Pflug on the Catholic side—dominated the scene. The basis of the colloquy was a secret agreement reached at Worms, introduced at Regensburg under mysterious circumstances as the *Regensburg Book*. Its scope was broad and included a proper sprinkling of biblical and patristic references, and thus promised a resolution of the disagreements. The mentor was none other than Erasmus, whose *Liber de sarcienda ecclesiae concordia* (Book About Restoring Concord of the Church), of 1533, offered a blueprint how the division might be healed.[33]

Indeed, agreement was reached on several theological points, including that of justification. Though broadly formulated, the theological substance of that agreement was the notion of "double righteousness," the *justitia imputata* and the *justitia inhaerens* (imputed and inherent righteousness), the former freely given, God's declaration of acceptance of the sinner; the latter in humans, love infused into the human heart. In other words, justification was by both faith and works, by grace and deeds of love: "Therefore, it is living faith that in Christ attains mercy and believes that the righteousness of Christ is imputed through grace. At the same time, such faith receives the assurance of the Holy Spirit and of love."

The agreement was enormously significant. For two decades justification had been at the heart of heated disagreement: at Regensburg both sides found it possible to agree on a common formulation. The initial reaction was one of rejoicing. The emperor remarked that "God has been pleased to enlighten" the participants, implying that God generally chose not to inspire theologians. John Calvin, recently reformer of Geneva, found the agreement evasive but accepted it, as did several other Protestant theologians.

Then the wind shifted. From Wittenberg, Luther weighed in with the blunt pronouncement that the agreement was a "vast and patched thing," and even the irenic Melanchthon, on second thought, found it "a hyena and Talmud." Cardinal Contarini, who had stressed the Catholic character of the agreement, discovered that the curia disagreed. As it turned out, these negative voices were decisive, especially because the continuing discussions soon reached an impasse. When the emperor asked the participants of the colloquy in May to provide him with a summary statement, he received two, for no agreement had been reached on most points—except on justification.

The situation turned hopelessly chaotic, because there were actually four factions: the hard-line Catholics and Protestants and the conciliatory theologians on both sides. The specter of a permanent division among Catholics, Protestants, and those who

---

33. Erasmus's *Liber* is found in his *Opera Omnia*, vol. 5, while the text of the Regensburg Book is found in G. Pfeilschifter, ed., *Acta Reformationis Catholicae ecclesiam Germaniae concernentia saeculi XVI. Die Reformverhandlungen des deutschen Episkopats von 1520 bis 1570* (Regensburg: F. Pustet, 1974), 6:24–88. A superb theological analysis is A. Lexutt, *Rechtfertigung im Gespräch: das Rechtfertigungsverständnis in den Religionsgesprächen von Hagenau, Worms und Regensburg 1540–41* (Göttingen: Vandenhoeck & Ruprecht, 1996), esp. 178ff.

accepted mediation hung over the diet and indicated that anything less than an enthusiastic and full agreement was bound to be unsatisfactory.

In June the emperor submitted this meager "result" to the estates. The Catholics rejected the agreement that had been reached, and the Protestants followed suit. The hope, sometimes faint, sometimes strong, that the schism might be healed had disappeared—vanished, one observer sadly remarked, "even as smoke." Hopelessness and confusion followed. The recess of the diet put up a good front, expressed once more the hope for a council and stipulated that a national council should convene if no general council of the church was possible. The Protestants were told to accept the articles on which agreement had been reached. The recess of Augsburg as well as the Peace of Nuremberg were to continue in force until the next diet.

Those were the official pronouncements. Secretly, however, the emperor had entered into several agreements, even as ostensibly encouraging the theological conversations between the two sides. He assured the Protestants that the Augsburg recess would not be enforced and that the Protestants were free to use confiscated church property for salaries for clergy, and for schools and charitable works. In a secret agreement with the Catholic estates, however, the emperor made exactly the opposite commitments. The recess of the diet was thus plainly a farce. Charles meant to temporize and keep his options open. In particular, he pursued plans with respect to the succession in the Duchy of Geldern near the Dutch border. The Geldern estates had named the Duke of Cleves, a Protestant and already a powerful figure in northwest Germany. Charles intervened, insisting that Geldern was part of the Habsburg domain. After a brief military showdown in which the League of Schmalkald stood passively on the sidelines because of Landgrave Philip's deal with the emperor, the Treaty of Venlo in 1543 assured victory for the emperor.

Another diet had failed to resolve the religious controversy. This failure had been the emperor's, for whose rule so much was at stake. But Charles had little time to ponder his situation, because conflict had broken out in another part of his realm. The French king had declared war, the fourth such exercise between the two monarchs. Francis thought he had chosen a perfect time and splendid circumstances. The theater of operations was the Low Countries, which were attacked from three sides: by the French from the south, by the Duke of Cleves from the east, and the Danish navy from the north. But Charles's sister Maria, the regent of Holland, put up a gallant fight, courageously marshaled the defenses of the land, negotiated a treaty with England, and tipped the scales in the emperor's favor. When Charles threw his forces against the Duke of Cleves, victory came quickly. In the Treaty of Venlo of September 6, 1543, the duke agreed to end ecclesiastical reform in his territory. While this provision was a minor aspect of the treaty, Charles's victory strengthened Catholicism in northwest Germany.

THE ROAD TO WAR

Charles's own recollection of events was rather clear and to the point: "This experience opened the emperor's eyes and convinced him that it was not only not impossible, but indeed very easy, to subdue such insolence by force—if done at the proper time and with the necessary means." These words were Charles's own, after his military campaign had ended in success. After Regensburg and Venlo Charles began to wait for "the proper time" and the "necessary means" to wage war against the Protestants. The failure of the negotiations at Regensburg convinced him that no theological compromise was possible. Because the Protestants were recalcitrant, only force remained, and that was how Charles prepared to solve the religious problem in Germany.

Gradually the parts of the emperor's strategy fell into place. In May 1544 his brother Ferdinand successfully negotiated a truce with the Ottoman Turks that served to ensure that waging war against the Protestants would not be thwarted by a Turkish attack. An eighteen-month truce was agreed upon, as was Ferdinand's forfeiting the Turkish-occupied part of Hungary and the payment of tribute to the Turks. By making peace with France at Crépy in September 1544, the emperor eliminated another weighty obstacle to his plans. Only the papacy stood in the emperor's way of solving the German religious problem. Pope and emperor had viewed each other with distrust for both political and religious reasons, but the conciliation between France and the emperor created a new situation for the papacy, and Paul III accepted Charles's offer of peace. The desire to crush the German heretics had become the pope's and the emperor's foremost priority.

A diet meeting at Worms early in 1545 pursued again possible avenues of conciliation. Behind the scenes, however, the emperor concluded negotiations with papal representatives to secure support for the military showdown. Needless to say, the papal response was enthusiastic. The recess of the diet expressed regret about the impossibility of conciliation and announced that another theological colloquy would attempt to reach agreement. One marvels at such language, for it seems evident that neither side truly believed it.

After some delays, that colloquy got under way at Regensburg in January 1546. An air of futility hung over the venture; the emperor was not serious, and the Protestants were hardly optimistic. The two sides went through the routine of trying to settle their differences. Bucer again represented the Protestants. There had been some difficulty finding Catholic participants, but finally Johannes Cochlaeus, together with three lesser-known theologians, agreed to represent the Catholic side. All of them were staunch Catholics and differed greatly in temperament from the irenic representatives who had represented the Catholic Church at Regensburg in 1541. Now, in 1546, disagreement over the agenda was the subject of most of the discussion. Bucer seemed to be the only participant who had not lost enthusiasm and optimism, and he proceeded, quite seriously, to expound the Protestant view of justification. When the Protestants refused to agree to complete secrecy, the colloquy was suspended until the middle of March. In retrospect it is obvious that the emperor's endorsement of the colloquy had been a diversionary maneuver: the decision to subdue the Protestants by force had been made after the peace concluded at Crépy. In a secret codicil to that peace treaty, the French king agreed not only to authorize the attendance of the French bishops at the forthcoming council, but also to provide military support against the German heretics. His involvement, together with the political paralysis of Landgrave Philip of Hesse, dramatically tipped the scales in favor of the emperor.

The emperor had methodically put the pieces of his plan into place. When the diet met in Speyer in 1544 the recess stipulated that a "Christian Reformation" should be undertaken at a forthcoming diet to deal with ecclesiastical abuses. This stipulation was a move calculated to put pressure on Pope Paul III, who promptly complained to the emperor about this move but nonetheless, in November 1544, convened a general council of the church to meet in the town of Trent in northern Italy in March of the following year. The church thereby reclaimed the initiative on the religious controversy, especially because the pope's summons made clear that clarification of the contested theological issues, and not church reform, was to be on the agenda of the council. All the while Charles clung to his strategy of subduing the Protestants militarily and then forcing them to attend a general council (whether as participants or observers was not quite clear) and accept its decisions.

On the face of things, the emperor engaged in a policy of conciliation. At the diet at Worms in 1545, lengthily postponed because of his illness and presided over by his brother Ferdinand, he sought to secure support for a campaign against the Turks; the religious issues, in turn, should be turned over to a general council. The Protestants demurred, stating that they would not recognize decisions of a council. The ensuing stalemate was ended with the agreement to convene yet another theological colloquy to resolve the contested issues. More important than this turn, however, was the arrival of the papal legate, Cardinal Farnese, with whom Charles signed a secret agreement toward the end of June providing massive papal assistance for an armed showdown with the League of Schmalkald—200,000 ducats, 12,500 mercenaries, half of the revenues of the Spanish church, and the authorization to sell off Spanish church property worth 500,000 ducats.

This agreement was big business and suggests that the papacy sensed the seriousness of the hour. The pope and the emperor alike concluded that the golden opportunity to subdue the Protestants had arrived. Outwardly, however, the emperor pursued a policy of conciliation. His agreement to convene a colloquy seemed to underscore his irenic and conciliatory intentions.

Charles's plan was falling into place. He had also cultivated his relations with several Protestant territories, and when the Regensburg diet adjourned in 1546, he had concluded secret treaties with several Protestant territories.

While Catholics and Protestants were seeking to find ways to overcome three decades of strife concerning the proper understanding of justification, the individual who had triggered it all died. There is a bit of irony in the fact that Luther's death came while Bucer, the irenicist among the Protestant theologians, expounded the Protestant understanding of justification at Regensburg. The day was February 18, 1546, and the place—by strange coincidence—Eisleben, where he had been born sixty-two years earlier. Luther's death came when, despite poor health and weakened by congenital heart failure, he traveled in the midst of winter to Eisleben to mediate a feud among the counts of Mansfeld.

He had not been in good health for years, a fact to which some scholars have attributed the irascible character of his later writings. Of course, some had detected such qualities many years earlier—Melanchthon, for example, who had noted in exasperation in 1526, "If Luther just would keep quiet," and who two years after Luther's death wrote to a friend that Luther "frequently expressed his passionate stubbornness, which was not insignificant, more than benefited his person or the common good." Indeed, some of Luther's sharpest (and vilest) polemical writings issued from his pen during the last few years of his life: his intransigent view of the Anabaptists as political revolutionaries who should be hanged as insurrectionists; his invectives against the papacy, which was to him the very incarnation of the antichrist; and his tirades against the Jews, found in his 1543 treatise *Von den Juden und ihren Lügen* (Concerning the Jews and Their Lies).

Jews were a minority community in sixteenth-century Germany (and Europe), periodically subjected to repression, expulsion, and persecution. They did not share the fundamental religious assumptions of society, and so they were considered a community that was strange and bizarre, defamed because of their different manners and their religion, chided for their unwillingness to embrace the dominant Christian religion. Their lack of a homeland and, ever since the destruction of the Second Temple in Jerusalem, their concomitant plight, were taken as proof positive that God had forsaken them.

In the later Middle Ages Jews lived in the towns, especially the free imperial cities, because they legally were subjects of the emperor to whom they had to pay the exorbitant *Judensteuer* (Jews' Tax) in return for a measure of legal and personal protection. Too poor to purchase land and till the soil, too ostracized to become members of an urban guild of artisans, Jews were relegated to earn their livelihoods by being peddlers or small-time bankers. Their modest economic success, together with a kind of chronic scapegoating, led in the fifteenth century to a wave of expulsions—not only famously from Spain in 1492 but also from German lands, with most settling in Poland or Lithuania.

By the early sixteenth century few Jewish communities were left in Germany, though the reiteration of expulsion orders was very much on the agenda. In this setting, Josel von Rosheim, rabbi from the Alsace, the astute, literate, diplomatic spokesperson for the Jewish communities, worked relentlessly to obtain greater legal security. Rebuffed by Martin Luther when he solicited his intervention to forestall expulsion, Josel nonetheless succeeded in getting Emperor Charles to issue a mandate (*Privilegium*) in 1544. This document constituted a major milestone—it prohibited further expulsions, razing of synagogues, and so on.

The existence of Jewish communities in Christian lands was overshadowed by charges that were periodically levied against Jews. Clearly, people saw themselves threatened by the alleged Jewish demeanor and Jewish belief—the former entailing the charge of poisoning wells and, in particular, the charge of the ritual murder of Christian boys to use their blood for bizarre purposes.[34] When the Nuremberg reformer Andreas Osiander published (anonymously) a categorical rejection of this allegation, none other than Johann Eck jumped into the fray to denounce Osiander and affirm the veracity and accuracy of the charges. One suspects that for Eck the particular issue was less important as was his antagonism of anything advocated by Protestants.

Theologians, in turn, saw the Jews as a theological challenge while the populace at large, though not without theological rationales, focused on mundane charges, notably that of Jewish usury. The Reformation controversy seems to have had little

---

34. A thorough study is R. Po-chia Hsia, *The Myth of Ritual Murder: Jews and Magic in Reformation Germany* (New Haven: 1988).

effect on Jewish Christian relations; Luther's literary intervention has the sorry relevance that he was the only theologican of repute in the sixteenth century who took to the pen to write aggressively about Jews.[35]

Ever since ruthless Nazi anti-Semitism in the twentieth century led to the Holocaust and to soul-searching reflection on the historical Christian contribution in sustaining anti-Semitism, this treatise of Luther's has had the sad distinction of being viewed as his most notorious work. Luther had addressed the topic of Jewish-Christian relations earlier. In 1523 he published *Dass Jesus Christus ein geborener Jude sei* (That Jesus Christ Was Born a Jew), in which he condemned Christian hostility toward Jews. "The Jews are blood-relations of our Lord," he wrote, "if it were proper to boast of flesh and blood, the Jews belong more to Christ than we. I beg, therefore, my dear papist, if you become tired of abusing me as a heretic, that you begin to revile me as a Jew."

Twenty years later, Luther's tone had changed. He had been apprised of reports of Christian conversions to Judaism somewhere in southeast Europe, probably Transylvania, and that intelligence (never fully substantiated) prompted an emotional outburst in a vile tract. Two themes characterized the treatise, and they were at once the major themes in the long history of anti-Semitism. The one might be called a "moral" argument—Jews are morally suspect. Wrote Luther: "They are nothing but thieves and robbers who daily eat no morsel and wear no thread of clothing that they have not stolen and pilfered from us by means of their accursed usury. Thus they live from day to day, together with wife and child, by theft and robbery, as arch-thieves and robbers, in the most impenitent security." And: "We let them get rich on our sweat and blood, while we remain poor and they suck the marrow from our bones." At the same time, Luther also advanced the "theological" argument, for example, he claimed that they "misunderstand the divine commandments." While Luther was clearly motivated by religious and theological considerations, his concern was what he angrily labeled the "blasphemy" of the Jews.

The consequences he drew from both his theological and moral arguments were deeply disturbing. The "practical" recommendations toward the end of his treatise that synagogues should be burned down, Jews' houses destroyed, their books burned, and they themselves forced to do manual labor were ominous, foreshadowing what happened in Germany some four hundred years later. Numerous explanations have been offered for Luther's outburst—that he only expressed the general societal consensus of his day; that he was a cranky old man, for whom all of the world, not just the Jews and the papacy and the Anabaptists, had gone awry; that the treatise was little known through the centuries until it was revived in Germany just before the Nazi period. All of these explanations still leave unsettling unease over how a preacher of the gospel was able to exude so much anger. Luther's disciples have tended to ignore this "old" Luther or to confess to be deeply embarrassed by him.[36] If indeed his poor

---

35. See Thomas Kaufmann, "Luthers Judenschriften in ihren historischen kontexten," *Akademie der Wissenschaften zu Göttingen,* 2005, 480–586.

36. The literature on Luther and the Jews has become voluminous. The best access is H. A. Oberman, *The Roots of Antisemitism* (Philadelphia: 1984), a somewhat ideosyncratic book. M. Edwards, *Luther's Last Battles* (Ithaca: 1983) is judicious.

health offers an explanation for his irascible temperament, there also can be little doubt but that other matters weighed heavily on his mind. He had been the catalyst for a fateful division of Christendom, and by the early 1540s it was obvious that the spiritual life of the new Protestant churches was hardly an improvement over that of the old Catholic Church.[37]

Luther had witnessed how his probing of a certain church practice in the fall of 1517 had turned into a formidable conflagration. Assuredly, he had been at first a reluctant revolutionary, and for a long time he saw himself a faithful son of the church even when that church denounced and excommunicated him. The record suggests that he never wavered in his conviction that, like the prophets of the Old Testament, he had been unwittingly called to proclaim the Word of God. Later, Luther witnessed that spirituality was no less at a premium among the new Protestant churches than it had been among Catholics. His very last piece of writing, found at his bedside after his death, suggests both his sense of accomplishment and frustration and is thus a fitting epitaph: "No one can understand Virgil's *Bucolics* and *Georgics* unless he was, for five years, a shepherd or a farmer. No one can understand Cicero's letters, I suppose, unless he has occupied an important public office for twenty years. And no one can adequately understand the Scriptures unless he guided the church, together with the prophets, for one hundred years. There is something most splendid about John the Baptist, about Jesus, and about the apostles. Do not seek to manipulate this sacred Aeneas, but venerate its footsteps. We are beggars, that is true."[38]

Unlike many historical figures, Luther lived to witness the consequences of his ideas and work, and it must have been to him both blessing and curse: the former because his conviction about his faith became ever more definite as the years passed; the latter because he witnessed that the Protestant churches were not exempt from that historical pattern woven with threads of strength and weakness, of vitality and abuse, into one fabric. There seemed to be as little spirituality in Protestant churches as there had been in the old church.

The Regensburg diet eventually opened June 5, and for a while the situation was what it had been for as long as anyone could remember. The imperial proposition spoke of the need for religious peace, but Catholics and Protestants disagreed about almost everything. The prospect seemed to be another stalemate, as had happened so many times in the past. In addition there were perturbing rumors about the emperor's armaments. Alarmed, the Protestants asked Charles for an explanation. The emperor replied evasively: his foremost concern was to deal with disobedient estates as was the responsibility of his imperial office. This begged the question, and the Protestants persistently asked for his definition of "disobedient." This time the emperor's answer was clear: those who under the pretense of religion disregarded law and order were the "disobedient." The handwriting was on the wall.

---

37. G. Strauss, *Luther's House of Learning: Indoctrination of the Young in the German Reformation* (Baltimore: 1978), paints an altogether gloomy picture of the success of the Christianizing effort of the Reformation.

38. As quoted in K. Brandi, *The Emperor Charles V: The Growth and Destiny of a Man and of a World-Empire* (trans. C. V. Wedgwood; London: 1968), 1:471.

On July 20 Charles issued an imperial ban over Philip of Hesse and John Frederick of Saxony, the two bulwarks of the League of Schmalkald, which effectively declared them outlaws and freed their subjects from obedience. This meant war. The ban said nothing about religion, but cited specific violations of law and order, one of which, the Pack Affair, dated back to the late 1520s. The major charge pertained to the feud of Philip and John Frederick with Duke Heinrich of Braunschweig over the city of Goslar, a complex situation in which Philip and John Frederick had used a semblance of legal justification for a blunt exhibition of power politics. In a letter to his sister Maria, Charles was quite candid: "And even though this pretense will not obscure for long that the real issue is religion, it helps for the time being to separate the apostates."[39] Charles's subterfuge was a strategy to divide the Protestant house. He meant to defeat the League of Schmalkald and then force the Protestants to submit to the decisions of the council of the church, which had convened in Trent.

The emperor thought of the war as being fought justly for the cause of true religion. Yet the matter was not quite that simple, for some of his allies were Protestants to whom he had guaranteed the retention of the ecclesiastical status quo until such time as a council would render its decisions. Apparently, the immediate full suppression of Protestantism was not his immediate goal. That it was his ultimate goal, however, is clear; Charles was engaging in the kind of temporizing in which he had become an expert. He hoped to defeat the major Protestant territories first and then deal with his Protestant allies later.

THE WAR

By 1546 the League of Schmalkald had been the political and military arm of the Reformation in Germany for more than a decade. It had been increasingly beset by bickering among its members, because the endless temporizing decisions of diet upon diet seemed to convey that military danger no longer existed. Landgrave Philip's secret agreement with the emperor had done its share to weaken the league. But, once war had been declared, the League of Schmalkald moved with astonishing dispatch, mobilized its troops, and agreed on the general conduct of the war. Only the theologians, who believed that a defensive war alone was legitimate, dragged their feet and advised against precipitate moves.

Military action, however, came slowly. For several months no outright fighting occurred, only insignificant skirmishes here and there. In the late summer of 1546 both sides seemed unsure of their strategy. In the case of the emperor, this uncertainty was an expression of his vacillating temperament; in the case of the members of the League of Schmalkald, a matter of incompetent leadership. Either side, especially the Protestants, could have scored a decisive victory. Their earlier blunders, their naiveté concerning the emperor's intention, even their internal squabbles, could have been things of the past. The prize could have been had for the taking.

39. WA TR 5, 5677.

In the fall the league committed a major strategic blunder that may well have kept it from victory. An acute financial crisis beset the league, and before November had passed, its forces were forced to retreat from the area south of the Danube. The commander of the Schmalkaldian forces, Sebastian Schertlin of Burtenbach, had intended to take his soldiers southward toward the Alps to prevent the papal forces from moving northward into south Germany and joining the emperor. Had Schertlin's move been successful, the emperor's forces would have been too small to confront the league. The council of the league saw things differently, however, and ordered Schertlin back to the Danube, where his forces failed to score an incisive victory and wasted time, as did the emperor's forces, in dilatory maneuvers. This strategy allowed the emperor little by little to subdue the Protestant cities in south Germany.

Enter Duke Moritz of Albertine Saxony, successor to Duke George, that stalwart of orthodox Catholicism. Born in 1521, Moritz had grown to maturity partly in Catholic and partly in Lutheran surroundings and eventually opted for Lutheranism. Scholars still are divided as to whether Moritz possessed deep religious convictions; certainly he possessed none of the religious ardor that marked Philip of Hesse or Charles V. The French would have called him a *politique*, who affirmed religion but subordinated it to the practical demands of political life. Moritz was the prototype of the new type of territorial ruler in the empire, driven by an ambitious determination to enhance his territorial power.

When Moritz in 1541 succeeded to the rule of Albertine Saxony he introduced the Reformation and promptly (and conveniently) pocketed a sizable share of secularized church property. The following year long-standing tensions with electoral Saxony over the bishopric of Meissen led the two Saxon territories to the brink of war. Even though an armed conflict was averted, Moritz came to the realization that electoral Saxony, with its elector, John Frederick, stood squarely in the way of his own expansionist aspirations. He refused to join the League of Schmalkald and for a couple of years pursued an evasive policy, astutely maneuvering in a gray no-man's-land between the emperor and the League of Schmalkald. With the emperor's determination to suppress the league by military force, Moritz found himself in a touchy position. For reasons that historians have tended to associate with moral turpitude, he signed a treaty with the emperor in June 1546 in which he promised to remain neutral in case of an armed conflict between the emperor and the League of Schmalkald. Strangely, he received no concessions from Charles. One suspects that afterward Moritz had second thoughts, for five months later, in November, when the fates of war did not appear to favor the emperor, a second treaty promised Moritz the Saxon electorship and parts of the Ernestine territory in return for his active participation in the war. That was a significant booty but by no means as much as Moritz had hoped for; the emperor, too, could be extraordinarily astute. After signing the second agreement, Moritz attacked electoral Saxony. This forced the Schmalkaldian forces in south Germany to withdraw to the north, leaving Catholic victory (and helpless south German Protestant cities) behind.

The winter months passed without decisive military developments. The emperor consolidated his control of south Germany, and one Protestant territory and city after the other surrendered, exposed and vulnerable without the protecting Schmalkaldian forces. Pleading for the emperor's mercy, they found Charles a harsh and uncompromising victor.

At that point, long-standing tensions between the pope and the emperor came to the fore again. In January 1547 the pope announced the withdrawal of his mercenaries from Germany, and two months later he approved (or instigated) the move of the general council, which had been convened in Trent—a city in imperial territory—to Bologna. Charles was furious, especially because the pope proved less than discreet about the details of the treaty he had concluded with the emperor by publicly acknowledging that "Protestants and Schmalkaldians" were to be subject to the true Catholic religion and obedience to the pope. Since some Protestants, notably Moritz, were in the emperor's phalanx, they were hardly pleased to hear about the true objective of the emperor.

At this juncture the two key allies turned into enemies. Both pope and emperor had viewed each other with ill-concealed distrust, annoyance, and even anger. The pope considered the emperor's various ecclesiastical involvements (aside from that of using force for the unconditional suppression of the heretics) as intrusion, while the emperor was dismayed over papal indifference regarding the resolution of the conflict in Germany. Charles's decision to wage war against the League of Schmalkald had temporarily brought the two parties together, but only for a very brief time. Long-standing disagreements about strategy and power came once more to the fore.

One such point of disagreement (or misunderstanding) was the recently convened council. After years of futile efforts, Pope Paul III's bull *Laetare Jerusalem* had at last summoned a council to meet in the city of Trent in northern Italy in December 1545. The emperor, who for almost a decade had pleaded for such a gathering, found himself in the paradoxical situation of realizing that at this particular juncture he had no use for it—especially if the agenda of the council was to restate an uncompromising Catholic theological position.

As far as Charles V was concerned, the Council of Trent was prepared to do just that. Although disagreements about the agenda were resolved by a compromise stipulating that topics of doctrine and of reform were to be considered concurrently, in fact the council defined several crucial doctrinal issues—tradition, original sin, and justification—within an amazingly short time. Thus the council had, virtually overnight, made explicit the theological differences between Protestants and the church, just as Charles was putting his own sophisticated scheme into action: first to subdue the Protestants militarily by force, and then to bring them to a voluntary return to the Catholic fold by a mediating theological formula and the assurance of ecclesiastical reforms. The last thing Charles wanted in 1546 was the formalization of ecclesiastical and theological differences.

In the early spring of 1547 the hostilities resumed in central Germany. At first the indecisive state of affairs continued. Late in March Charles moved northward to join his forces with those of Moritz and Ferdinand. On April 23 his army reached Mühlberg, a small village on the banks of the Elbe River, and found itself within a stone's throw of the Saxon army. The Saxon elector saw the greenish waters of the Elbe, flowing majestically between the two armies, as an insurmountable obstacle for the emperor's forces, and he failed to craft an active strategy to meet the emperor's threat. Fog hung over the landscape when the emperor's soldiers reached the river that Sunday, but the news that enemy soldiers had been seen on the other side little disturbed the elector. He was attending church and saw no reason to leave, nor to forego a leisurely breakfast.[40]

In the ancient liturgical tradition of Christendom that Sunday was called Misericordia Domini, the Mercy of the Lord, and afterward people found the appellation an apt commentary on the events of the day. Within hours it became obvious that Elector John Frederick was woefully mistaken in his sense of security provided by the river Elbe. A trite incident insignificant in the larger scheme of things but immensely important on the human scale rendered the elector's feeling of safety meaningless. A few days earlier, his soldiers had confiscated two horses from a peasant who now angrily found his revenge by showing the emperor's Spanish soldiers a shallow passage across the river. Led by the Duke of Alba and Charles himself, the Spanish troops crossed the river and fell upon the Saxons. It was the only battle of Charles's thirty-five-year reign in which he himself participated. The Saxons, surprised and stunned, sought their salvation in fleeing, and the fighting was quickly over. Elector John Frederick was taken prisoner. In the formal surrender at Wittenberg on May 19, 1547, he was forced to surrender the title of elector and cede large parts of Ernestine Saxony to Moritz of Saxony, who received the electoral title and dignity. John Frederick steadfastly refused any concession in religious matters. He was charged with heresy and lèse-majesté and sentenced to death, though the emperor had no intention of carrying out the sentence.

Four days after John Frederick's surrender in Wittenberg, a Protestant army scored a victory over Spanish forces near Drakenburg south of Bremen, but this did not turn the military tide. In June Landgrave Philip of Hesse, having realized that the military power of the League of Schmalkald had been broken, surrendered to the emperor. Philip was forced to prostrate himself before the emperor to receive the emperor's pardon, but Charles was stone-faced, as a chronicler reported, "looked at him with a sour face, [and] neither shook his hand nor spoke a single word."[41] Even though the towns of Bremen and Magdeburg continued their resistance, and Magdeburg in particular came to symbolize the Protestant cause, in the larger course of events this made little difference. Charles chose to ignore the inconvenient reality that not all of the Protestants had been forced into submission, and in June he made his way to Augsburg to hold a diet that would deal with the situation created by his military victory.

UNEASY PEACE AND FINAL DECISION

Two concerns were foremost on the emperor's mind as he presided over the gathering of the high and mighty of the empire in Augsburg: a change in the political structure

40. W. Held, 1547, *Die Schlacht bei Mühlberg/Elbe* (Beucha, 1997) tells the story of the battle with great competence.

41. *Wahrhafte Beschreibung, welcher gestalt vor der Röm. Kais. Majestät zu Hall an der Sal Landgraff Philip [. . .] seinen Fußfall gethan* (1547). "Nach [der] Antwort ist der Landgraf ohne Danksagung, aus eigenem Antrieb, aufgestanden; die Kaiserliche Majestät [hat] sauer gesehen und ihm weder die Hand gegeben, noch mit einem Wort angesprochen."

of the empire and the resolution of the religious controversy. Politically, his objective was to strengthen the power and authority of the emperor, a concern that had been on his mind for some time, and he pursued several strategies toward that end—greater influence over a more effective *Reichskammergericht*; an alliance or league of territories and cities with the emperor; and a *Bund*, or league, that would provide for a standing army against the Turks and France. In light of the precarious balance of power in the empire, Charles's strategy was a risky venture from the outset. The territorial rulers had gained substantial power and authority, not least because of the Reformation, and they were hardly disposed to enter into voluntary "servitude," as they called it, to the emperor. Strong opposition from both Protestant and Catholic rulers surfaced immediately and made clear that Charles's goal was not attainable.

The emperor was persuaded that his victory over the League of Schmalkald had put him into a position to resolve the religious controversy in line with his own notions, to accomplish, in other words, what he had first pledged himself in Worms in 1521—to stake "his life, and all his possessions" on the eradication of the Lutheran heresy. But even after his victory, that was easier said than done. At the same time, his relationship with Pope Paul III was anything but harmonious. The pope was concerned about the strategy of enhanced power pursued by the emperor, and the assassination of his son Pierluigi Farnese, duke of Parma and Piacenza, together with the subsequent occupation of Piacenza by imperial troops, poisoned the relationship between the two men. Moreover, Charles's most important ally in the war—Duke Moritz of Albertine Saxony—was a Protestant who would balk at a full and immediate restitution of Catholicism in his territory, even though Moritz's booty from the war had been a hefty part of Ernestine Saxony. Charles was astute enough to realize that after a generation of religious conflict, the restitution of Catholicism had to be pursued carefully. The simple reintroduction of Catholic rites in cities and territories that had abandoned them by becoming Protestant was plainly impossible.

At the diet, which convened on September 1, 1547, Charles was the acknowledged leader—so much so that contemporaries quickly labeled the Augsburg diet the *geharnischte Reichstag*, the armed diet, because of the emperor's heavy hand—an obvious reality, no matter how Charles ventured to soften it. Charles wisely decided to make haste slowly with respect to the religious issue. His objective was to find a temporary, interim solution until the general council, meeting in Trent, had spoken. Thus Charles merged his own objective to bring about an end to the religious controversy with the reform efforts of the church, now at long last manifest in the council sitting in Trent. Ecclesiastical unity might be restored in the empire by guaranteeing the essentials of the Catholic religion while, at the same time, undertaking a determined program of reform and making a few temporary concessions to the Protestants.

Charles's willingness to compromise promptly ran into forceful opposition not only among Protestants but among Catholics as well. In particular, the emperor's confessor, Pedro de Soto, argued for a rigid Catholic stance, without any concessions to the Protestants whatsoever. Such intransigence from one of Charles's closest advisors led to serious tensions in the imperial camp that ended only when Charles bluntly dismissed de Soto.

At Charles's behest, Julius von Pflug had drafted a *Fomula sacrorum emendandorum* as an irenic working brief, but a committee of the diet convened to endorse the draft could not reach accord. Charles then secretly convened another committee, with Johann Agricola as the sole Protestant representative, that promptly—within two weeks—modified the document. When it became public, it was vehemently protested by both Catholics and Protestants. Nonetheless, on May 15, 1548, it was formally issued as *Erklärung, wie es der Religion halber im Heiligen Reich bis zum Austrag des gemeinen Concilii gehalten warden soll* (The Declaration of the Roman Imperial Majesty How Religious Matters Should Be Kept until the Decisions of a General Council).[42] The formal recess of the diet on June 30 incorporated this declaration. The Catholic territories were exhorted to remain faithful to the Catholic faith—but to "steadfastly retain, maintain, and continue nor undertake any changes" in that faith. The concessions made to the Protestants (the Communion cup and the married clergy) were not to apply to Catholics. In both cases, the changes introduced in Protestant territories were to be tolerated, subject to papal approval, until the council had rendered its decision.

The lengthy document summarized the basic tenets of the Christian faith in some twenty-six articles. It tenor was clearly Catholic, especially with respect to the sacrifice of the Mass, the papacy, veneration of the saints, and episcopal jurisdiction. Its "conciliatory" orientation lay in the effort to accommodate Protestant concerns on justification without surrendering Catholic doctrine. Sections 4 to 8, on justification, used Protestant terminology to express Catholic sentiment, essentially along the lines of the compromise forged at Regensburg: God draws individuals "not as a dead boulder but with their will" (article 6). The seven sacraments and the traditional ceremonies were to be retained, while efforts should be made to explain them to the common people and to do away with everything that might give reason for abuse. Until the decisions of the council (and in anticipation of papal approval), the Communion cup was to be allowed for the laity, and the same was to be the case with married priests. One might label the document a true compromise, and it was a pity that neither the representatives of the old church nor those of the new were willing to accept it.[43]

On July 9, 1548, the emperor issued a parallel document for his Catholic subjects, entitled *Formula Reformationis per Caesarem Majestatem statibus ecclesiasticis . . . proposita*.[44] No less lengthy than the emperor's *Erklärung*, the document dealt with such issues as the reform and education of clergy, the spiritual responsibilities of the bishops, the need for visitations, and diocesan synods.

Charles's efforts were well meant and sprang from a deep concern as well as anguish over the divided Christendom and the concomitant threat to a cohesive body politic. But when the documents were made public, opposition came from all sides. The Catholics objected not only that concessions had been made to the Protestants, but also that the emperor had usurped ecclesiastical prerogatives and ventured into a realm where only the church had authority. The documents, after all, had been issued by a political and not an ecclesiastical authority. Protracted negotiations with the curia about Charles's *Erklärung* eventually led to papal concurrence: a papal bull of August

42. See M. K. Th. Hergang, ed., *Das Augsburger Interim* (Leipzig: 1855), 20–155.

43. L. Schorn-Schütte, ed., *Das Interim 1548–50: Herrschaftskrise und Glaubenskonflikt* (Gütersloh: 2005).

44. J. Mehlhausen, ed., *Das Augsburger Interim von 1548. Nach den Reichstagsakten* (Neukirchen-Vluyn: 1970).

18, 1548, authorized the various dispensations along the lines of the *Erklärung* and the *Formula Reformationis*. The Communion cup was allowed under certain circumstances, as were a number of provisions pertaining to clergy. Even the manner by which the new owners of formerly ecclesiastical lands and property could reach accommodation with the church was eased. Putting rivalries and jockeying for power aside, the pope realized in the end that the emperor's strategy might well be the best way to achieve conciliation and eventual reunion.

On June 30, 1548, the so-called Interim became law as part of the recess of the diet, but owing to the vigorous objection of Bavaria, it was to apply only to Protestants.[45] The document seemed to be the death warrant for German Protestantism, but not surprisingly there was an immediate resurgence of opposition in Protestant regions. Only the presence of the emperor's troops in south Germany allowed the forceful introduction of the Interim there. The Protestant clergy were uncertain how far to take their opposition or when to resign or be dismissed. In Württemberg some four hundred pastors were dismissed from office. In Hesse a meeting of clergy and rulers in September 1548 led to the acceptance of the Interim because they "understood that they were permitted to preach the Word of God freely and purely and that both Communion under both kinds as well as the married clergy were permitted, for which they were grateful. As far as external ceremonies were concerned, they had no complaint and they would wear the alb, surplice, and other vestments. With regard to several other matters they requested further information."[46] Many of the leading reformers who had labored in their communities to introduce the new faith—Johann Brenz in Schwäbisch Hall, Martin Frecht of Ulm, Martin Bucer of Strassburg, and Andreas Osiander of Nuremberg—resolutely rejected the Interim and were dismissed from their posts. Together with the large throng of other clergy, their names and identities are long forgotten but all of them had been adamant in their opposition to the Interim. Eventually they brought it down.

The situation was different in the north, where the political authorities in Protestant territories and cities generally supported the opposition of the Protestant pastors. In some instances, opposition to the Interim was politically motivated—to assure that the emperor's harsh measures against the Lutherans were not concealed efforts to enhance imperial power—and in some instances there may have been economic considerations. The emperor's sister Maria, the regent of the Low Countries, advised her brother not to be too harsh with the Lutheran heretics, because they might take their trade to Hamburg rather than to Antwerp. But the common denominator was opposition, and it was based on the conviction that the stipulations of the Interim grossly violated the new-found understanding of the Christian faith.

---

45. The text is found in Hergang, ed., *Augsburger Interim*, 232–72.

46. G. Franz, ed., *Urkundliche Quellen zur Hessischen Reformationsgeschichte* (Marburg: 1955), 3:65, nr. 651, "Die Predicanten haben sich vernehmen lassen, dieweil sie verstanden [haben], daß sie das Wort Gottes noch lauter und rein predigen dürfen, und daß die Communion in beider Gestalt und die Priesterehe nachgelassen [erlaubt] würden, wollten sie solches dankbar annehmen, sich auch in dem, was äußerliche Ceremonien seien, nicht beschweren, desgleichen Chorrock, Meßgewand und anderen Ornat antun. In einigen Punkten bitten sie um weitere Auskunft."

Affairs were particularly complicated for the new Saxon elector, Moritz. Given the strong Protestant orientation of his acquired Ernestine territories—which included Wittenberg—not to mention his own (albeit somewhat modest) Protestant commitment and his determination to pursue policies that he deemed best, Moritz could not accept the Interim. In fact, he had voted against the recess at Augsburg and sought for a compromise acceptable in his territory. Extensive negotiations followed in which the Wittenberg theologians were pressured to accept a modified form of the Augsburg Interim. Melanchthon and his Wittenberg colleagues had voiced their concerns about the Augsburg document, but further negotiations between them and the Saxon councilors led to agreement concerning the so-called middle things, *adiaphora* in Greek, concerning which agreement should be possible because they did not touch on the fundamentals of the faith. Agreement was reached at Torgau, but when the Saxon estates met in Leipzig, they rejected the document, which was subsequently published by the staunch and intransigent Lutheran theologian Matthias Flacius as the "Leipzig Interim," as a blatant illustration of the fickleness of the Wittenberg theologians, foremost among them Melanchthon.[47] The Wittenberg divines were determined to be uncompromising with respect to doctrine but willing to compromise on adiaphora. This meant the reintroduction of Catholic rites, such as extreme unction, the ordination of pastors by bishops, and the use of vestments (rather than the black professorial gown) in services, especially the Mass. The Leipzig Interim, too, was a compromise—between Lutheran theology and Catholic rites.

The storm of protest was extensive. Moritz, overwhelmed by this grassroots opposition in his own territory, could not afford to give the Leipzig agreement the force of law. In July 1549 he issued a section of the Interim dealing with topics of practical churchmanship—the so-called Small Interim—as a kind of compromise that would satisfy the theologians and give him what he most wanted, support for his political maneuvers against the emperor.

Electoral Saxony thus echoed what was happening elsewhere in Protestant territories and cities: resolute opposition, unwilling acceptance, partial success, and blatant failure. Importantly, however, the ventures of Elector Moritz triggered an intra-Lutheran conflict that reverberated long after the immediate issues at hand had been resolved: what was the true Lutheran faith and what were its nonnegotiable elements? Melanchthon and the other Wittenberg theologians had provided one answer: there were "adiaphora" concerning which one could be flexible. But there was another answer, given with increasing intensity by a widening chorus of Lutheran theologians but especially by a theologian of the younger generation: Matthias Flacius.

Born in 1520 in Albona, across the bay from Venice, at the head of the Adriatic Sea, Flacius was appointed professor of Hebrew at Wittenberg in 1544 over Luther's objections. That problem notwithstanding, the young professor quickly made a sufficiently positive impression—the rector of the university observed that Flacius was "young, learned, and poor."[48] Flacius began to publish—his first theological writing

47. *Corpus Reformatorum*, 7:258–64.
48. O. K. Olson, *Matthias Flacius and the Survival of Luther's Reform* (Wiesbaden: 2002), 52.

was entitled *De Voce et Re Fidei* (Concerning Voice and Substance of Faith)—and was destined to live his life as a professor of theology.

Then came the War of Schmalkald, the disastrous defeat of the Protestants, the ignominious negotiations at Augsburg and Torgau, and—to top it all, as he saw it— his colleague Melanchthon's concessions in the Leipzig Interim. Flacius became deeply dismayed over the compromises accepted by many of the Lutheran theologians and began a literary campaign (under various pseudonyms) against the interims of Augsburg and Leipzig. This triggered tensions and conflict between him and Melanchthon, prompting him to realize that Wittenberg was not the best place for him. He resigned his professorship, went to Magdeburg and Hamburg, then returned to Magdeburg, the important town on the Elbe River that had defiantly refused to surrender to the emperor in the war. The town's resistance had attracted a throng of reformers from every part of the empire, such as Nikolaus von Amsdorf and Erasmus Alber, and it had become a valiant bully pulpit for opposing the emperor's imposition of a religious settlement. Flacius's major work, *De Veris et Falsis Adiaphoris* (Concerning True and False Middle Things), published in 1549, contained the striking thesis: "nihil est adiaphoron in casu confessionis et scandali"—nothing is a middle thing if there is a scandal and in the case of [defending] one's confession.

Defiant Magdeburg was the perfect site for Flacius's activities, which he pursued with vigor, determination, and humorlessness. It was in large measure his doing that Lutherans became involved in an intense theological controversy, the adiaphoristic controversy. Perhaps the fundamental conviction in Flacius and his comrades-in-arms was their insistence on the freedom of the church from the involvement of the state. Before the lasting vigor of the resistance could be measured, the course of political events speedily provided the answer to the question of the success of the emperor's solution of the religious problem.

In March 1550 Charles convened a diet to meet at Augsburg. But it was a changed man who came to that south German city, which ranks so prominently in the history of the German Reformation. Three years earlier Titian had painted the emperor as the victor of Mühlberg: high on a horse, clad in shining armor, a lancet in his right hand, confident and determined. In 1550 Titian painted the emperor again, but this time in a painting of the Last Judgment, in which the emperor appeared as one of many who stood before the judgment throne of God. Astutely, the artist captured the change: then the pride of the victor, resolutely determined to impose his will upon the conquered; now the dejection of failure, turning increasingly to spiritual concerns.

The imperial proposition made much of the papal willingness to reconvene the Council at Trent and decried the widespread disregard of the Augsburg Interim and its provisions for ecclesiastical reform. The recess of the diet of February 1551 ordered the continued administration of the Interim but agreed that the objections against it would be considered at a future date. Charles's intent to suppress Protestantism had alienated his Protestant allies and angered his Protestant foes. His intent to restructure the relationship between the emperor and the territorial rulers had precipitated even greater difficulties.

At this point Moritz, for Protestants the "Judas of Meissen," who had seemingly betrayed the Protestant cause in the war, was facing new troubles. The city of Magdeburg, a member of the League of Schmalkald, had defied the emperor's plea to surrender, and Moritz had commenced a siege on the emperor's behalf, a move calculated to alienate him further from the Protestant estates. But he could ill afford to have the emperor or anyone else besiege the city—which held enormous importance for north German affairs—and afterward keep it as a prize. His move meant that he took to the field once more against the Protestants, which added to his infamy.

Somewhere along the line, Moritz must have realized that his future lay neither with the Catholics nor with the emperor. Continuing to ally himself with the Catholic estates meant that further expansion of his territory in the direction of surrounding Catholic ecclesiastical territories was impossible. In February 1550, three Protestant rulers entered into an informal agreement for the protection of the faith, actively pursuing the involvement of France. Moritz at once saw dire consequences: the defeat of the emperor would inevitably mean the restoration of the status quo ante, for Moritz the loss of those lands (and the dignity) that had come to him after the war. The emperor's position weakened further, when France concluded peace with England in March 1550, which meant that it was free to turn to the old archenemy, Spain, and the emperor.

Moritz had on one occasion remarked that he was always eager to find out "where all the winds blow," and now the winds clearly blew against the emperor. He promptly explored military ties with France and in 1551 entered into an agreement with several Protestant rulers for the purpose of securing the release of Landgrave Philip of Hesse, who had been the emperor's prisoner since 1547. In October 1551 Moritz, Duke Albrecht of Mecklenburg, and Landgrave Wilhelm of Hesse concluded a treaty with France. The common foe was Charles V, who was aware of the gathering storm but seemed incapable of facing the facts of political life, in part because he took Moritz to be incompetent and unstable. Unable to act decisively (his health was poor at the time) he exhausted himself in verbal antics, such as that he would have Philip of Hesse cut to pieces.

Charles's sentiment notwithstanding, Moritz's scheming meant failure of the emperor's goals and saved the political stature of Protestantism in Germany. It is difficult to say whether Moritz's allies were deeply concerned about religion. Territorial interests were foremost on their agenda, and Protestantism served them better than the emperor.

In March 1552 Charles asked his brother Ferdinand to represent him in negotiations with Moritz and the other "conspiratorial" rulers. He gave Ferdinand little room to negotiate, however, and allowed the release of Philip of Hesse only as a bargaining point. This meant Ferdinand's freedom of action was rather severely curtailed: there were to be no legal concessions on the disputed religious issues and no acknowledgment of the need for political reform in the empire. When the talks began in Passau in April, Moritz demanded the immediate release of Philip and a permanent religious peace, with full legal recognition of the new Protestant faith. Understandably, Ferdinand objected. The two sides decided to adjourn.

Moritz concluded that only a spectacular demonstration of the resurgent strength of the emperor's opposition would break the deadlock—and he undertook to do precisely that. In May 1552 he abruptly moved his troops southward across the Bavarian Alps toward Innsbruck, where the emperor was staying. As matters turned out, Charles had left Innsbruck well before Moritz's mercenaries reached the town, but the embarrassment and humiliation of his flight conveyed that the Protestants had regained the strength they possessed before the War of Schmalkald. Negotiations with Moritz resumed, but no breakthrough resulted; both sides simply reiterated the demands made at Passau. Yet neither side was prepared to quit the negotiations, and in the end their persistence carried the day. Agreement was reached.

Part of the emperor's rationale was that no useful support had come from the council of the church that was meeting in Trent. The Protestant territories were ready to face a new military showdown with the emperor, especially since he had his hands tied in a new conflict with France. The agreement reached at Passau stipulated that no territory or city should be attacked for religious reasons and a new diet should attempt a definitive resolution of the religious issues. Moritz had persistently demanded a permanent religious peace but had not received it. All the same, the Passau agreement noted that if a definitive settlement could not be reached at the next diet, the peace should be extended indefinitely.

After almost thirty years of temporization, the situation in Germany demanded a resolution. The emperor's military tour de force against the Schmalkaldians had ended in failure, while the resurgent Protestants ever more forcefully demanded the formal recognition of their faith. The emperor, while unwilling to concede failure, did sign the Passau agreement, though his heart was not in it: "Solely the consideration of your particular situation, your realm, and your lands have prompted me to do so," he told his brother.[49] Charles's health had deteriorated (his valet blamed it on the emperor's habit of drinking cold beer upon rising in the morning) and he was deeply despondent. He did convene a diet to be held at Augsburg to seek a solution and asked Ferdinand to represent him there. Ferdinand should approve only such decisions as he could accept in good conscience. Later Charles himself protested "against everything that would offend, hurt, weaken, or endanger our true old Christian and Catholic religion," and subsequently refused to offer an opinion about the ongoing negotiations.

The contested issues at Augsburg were many, but one stood out: the permanence of the settlement. The two other important questions were ecclesiastical jurisdiction and church property. The Catholics could acknowledge neither the abrogation of the former nor the secularization of the latter without surrendering important affirmations of their faith. The Protestants, on the other hand, saw the acknowledgment of ecclesiastical jurisdiction as the retention of ecclesiastical authority contrary to that of the ruler. The problem was that in many instances the boundaries of a diocese went through a territory that had turned Proestant. Ecclesiastical property, in turn, had been used in Protestant territories and cities for the support of education and religion,

---

49. K. Lanz, ed., *Correspondenz des Kaisers Karl V.* (Leipzig: 1846), 3:483.

and its restitution was practically impossible. The Protestants accordingly demanded the acceptance of the secularizations.

On September 25 the estates in Augsburg agreed to "a permanent peace"—permanent, that is, unless a future council brought conciliation.[50] The fundamental provision was the right of the territorial rulers to determine the official religion within their territories. Before the end of the century the famous phrase *cuius regio, eius religio* (he who rules determines the religion) had been coined to describe the significance of this provision. Subjects who disagreed with the official religion of their territory had the right to emigrate. The so-called *reservatum ecclesiasticum* provided that the religious conversion of an ecclesiastical ruler after 1552 (in other words, the acceptance of Protestantism by a ruler who exercised political authority by virtue of his ecclesiastical office) was a "personal" conversion only and would not affect the ecclesiastical and political status of that territory. The Protestants yielded at this point, but they were paid well for their concession. All ecclesiastical changes up to 1552, including the secularization of church lands, were formalized, and the "ecclesiastical jurisdiction" in Protestant territories was "suspended" until a future conciliation.

Few events in the Reformation were more significant than the document promulgated in Augsburg on September 25, 1555. To be sure, it was a haphazard document, and all the flowery oratory of the occasion could not obscure the fact that tedious negotiations, unavoidable compromise, and stubborn determination had produced a complicated document. Almost forty years of religious and political conflict had defied a consensus resolution. Other strategies and scenarios had been tried—theological reconciliation, armed force—but they had failed. Only the formal legal recognition of Lutheranism remained, because neither of the two religious parties was politically strong enough to force its will upon the other.

The peace established the legal recognition of Lutheranism and thereby the religious division of Germany. For sixty-three years—until the Thirty Years' War broke out in 1618—peace would prevail in Germany, and even when war came, it had other, more pertinent causes than religion. Not until after World War II did the German lands enjoy such a lengthy period of peace. In the second half of the sixteenth century, Germany was spared the kind of religious-political turmoil and bloodshed that would characterize France and the Dutch provinces.

Full religious freedom had not been achieved for Lutherans or Catholics. Only the territorial ruler had this right; his subjects had to accept his ecclesiastical decision or pack their belongings and emigrate. Accordingly, German ecclesiastical life developed along territorial lines, as did the political life of the empire. It was deeply significant that both pope and emperor were absent from the deliberations at Augsburg. Karl Brandi, Charles V's biographer of a generation ago, was prompted to call this "the most perfect expression for the dawn of a new era." Both had lost their authority and power to influence events in Germany. On paper the traditional concepts of universal church, emperor, and pope were still invoked, but they had lost much of their

50. E. Walder, ed., *Religionsvergleiche des 16. Jahrhunderts* (Bern: 1960), 68ff.

meaning. The territorial ruler assumed new responsibilities. He was politically auto-cratic and ecclesiastically important, powerful over church no less than state.

The real climax of these events came a few weeks after the adjournment of the diet. On October 25 Emperor Charles announced his abdication. On that occasion he reviewed his life from the day, forty years earlier, on which he had been declared of age—his successes and his failures—and lamented his failing health and the absence of peace. Stark symbolism lay in Charles's selection of his birthplace, Brussels, as the site of his abdication. He had returned to the beginning.

The following August, Charles left Brussels for Spain. Toward the end of Novem-ber he saw for the first time the palatial house built for him at the foothills of the Castillian Sierra de Gredos, adjacent to the monastery of San Jeronimo de Yuste. From February 1557 to September 1558 it would be his home. The former emperor had reached the end of the road and found his sole solace in his religion and the things of the world to come. To be sure, his life at San Yuste was by no means ascetically sim-ple. He had attendants, counselors, cooks, physicians, and all the rest, but these made little difference to a man who had left behind the turbulence of the world.

There are many legends about Charles's months at Yuste—that he occupied him-self with synchronizing his many clocks, or that he ordered his own Requiem Mass to be celebrated in his presence. No legend is ever without some truth, and though not fully accurate, these stories convey something of his temper. Reportedly, in his final weeks he often sat in front of Titian's monumental *Gloria*, which depicted humankind appearing before the judgment seat of God. Titian had included Charles and his late wife in the huge throng, Charles's head bare of the imperial crown. Perhaps he pon-dered his appearance before the divine judgment seat, perhaps he trembled about being acquitted. On September 21, 1558, he died. In his last hour the archbishop of Toledo placed a crucifix into his hands and reminded him of Jesus's death as the foun-dation of all grace—an exhortation that later led to trouble for the archbishop.

Charles's life and rule were inextricably linked to the course of the movement of reform, and with uncanny irony his public life paralleled the years of the German Reformation: in 1519, when he was elected emperor, the case of Luther was slowly turning into an *affaire d'état*, and in 1555 his abdication came in the wake of the for-mal recognition of Lutheranism in Germany at the Diet of Augsburg. But more had happened than chronological proximity. Charles exemplified the interaction of reli-gion and politics that characterized so much of the Reformation era. He was both a Catholic and the emperor, and he was convinced—influenced by the vision of his chancellor, Gattinara—that these two functions could be in harmony. It turned out that they were not, and that proved Charles's tragedy. Had he been less a dreamer of noble visions and aspirations, less a devout Catholic, less a disciple of Charlemagne, he might have been more a man of resolute action. As matters turned out, Charles failed at what mattered most to him: to advance his religion and Christendom, a fail-ure that seemed all the more blatant because his was an age where others were rich in achievements—Gustavus Vasa, for example, or even Henry VIII. Charles was pos-sessed of noble intentions, but they did not grant him success in his endeavors. He meant so well. Perhaps he was one of those "pure of heart" who according to the Scriptures are said to inherit the kingdom of heaven but whose sojourn on this earth is shrouded by defeat and failure.[51]

LUTHERAN TURMOIL

The coterie of sympathizers who helped turn Luther's theological pronouncements into a movement also created a problem that was to haunt Lutheranism for decades until the year 1580 finally brought a resolution. There was pointed disagreement as to what Luther taught with respect to certain theological topics.

The reason for such disagreement, alas, lay in none other than Luther himself. No matter how profound and insightful, Luther was one of those theologians in Christian history (St. Augustine comes to mind as another) whose genius prompted them always to address topics and issues in polemical contexts, with the inevitable consequence of overstatement, rigidity, and caricature of the opponent. This is how Luther delineated his views of human nature in his controversy with Erasmus, and how he defined his understanding of Communion in his controversy with Andreas Carlstadt and Huldrych Zwingli.

Luther's followers latched on to different aspects of the reformer's pronouncements and came to different conclusions about what was authentically Lutheran (and therefore, in their understanding, authentically biblical) teaching. These disagreements surfaced periodically during Luther's own lifetime. Luther, for his part, either ignored them as insignificant (as indeed they were in the larger scheme of things) or was goaded to take sides, which he generally did with uncommon grace.

Related to these polemics was a widespread concern for order and clarity. The exciting storm and stress of the first decades of the Reformation controversy were past, and a seemingly irreparable schism existed between those who stayed loyal to the Roman Church and those who found their allegiance to the new interpretation of the Christian gospel. What initially had been unthinkable had in fact happened: a new church had come into existence, indeed, a number of churches, as well as the host of practical issues that attend any new structure or organization.

What was the faith of the new Lutheran church? On one level the answer was fairly simple: it was the confession of faith transmitted to the emperor at Augsburg in 1530, though it existed in two versions (unaltered and altered) and had an appendix, Apology, attached. There was also a second document, which Luther had drafted for the League of Schmalkald, the Schmalkald Articles. And beyond these formal statements was the thought of a host of theologians, committed followers of Luther, who eagerly provided their own addenda and asterisks to these statements and to other theological topics. The situation grew more tense after Luther's death, and as a result no fewer than seven controversies beset German Lutheranism between 1548 and 1580. The antinomian controversy, triggered by Johann Agricola, pertained to the question of

---

51. The best of the recent biographies is A. Kohler, *Karl V: 1500–1558: Eine Biographie* (Munich: 1999).

whether the law had a place in Christian preaching. Related to antinomianism was the Majoristic controversy, named after Georg Major, a pupil of Melanchthon, who argued that good works were necessary for salvation. Major insisted that salvation itself was by faith alone but afterward good works had to follow. They did not assure salvation but were the indispensable outcome. Major's argument drove the so-called Gnesio-Lutherans ("authentic" Lutherans) to the barricades, for they saw in Major nothing but an awkward return to the Catholic notion of salvation by faith and works.

A third controversy, dubbed the Adiaphorist controversy, surfaced after Emperor Charles had promulgated the Augsburg interim, in the wake of his victory over the League of Schmalkald in 1547. The bone of contention was none other than Melanchthon, who appeared to be willing to accept the provisions of the Interim because they pertained, so he argued, only to "indifferent issues" (Greek *adiaphora*). In a way, the underlying contention was that Melanchthon had surrendered to the emperor's wiles, and the Gnesio-Lutherans would have none of that.

Chapter 8

THE REFORMATION IN ENGLAND

On June 22, 1527, one of those rare pleasant English summer days, King Henry VIII of England apprised his wife Catherine of Aragon of his conclusion—rather stunning for Catherine—that the two of them were not truly married in the sight of God, that they had been living in sin for eighteen years, and that they must separate. Not surprisingly, on hearing this news Catherine burst into tears. Henry temporarily relented but afterward quickly regained his composure and determination: he repeated his conviction that he was living in sin and that his ties with Catherine must be dissolved.

King Henry had succeeded to the English throne in 1509–eighteen years of age, handsome, energetic, highly educated—and because his father had increasingly become gloomy and suspicious, young Henry's succession was received as a welcome turn. Initially, no one was disappointed, especially since the youthful king much preferred to travel the countryside hunting, leaving governance in the hands of trusted advisors, a role played before too long by Thomas Cardinal Wolsey. But also, before too long, another side of the king came to the fore—egotistical, alarmingly self-confident, adventuresome. His subjects were to get plenty of demonstration of this aspect of Henry's character, especially in the realm of religion.

The king's determination to free himself from his marriage bond with Catherine marked the intriguing beginning of an unraveling of events that in the end not only separated Catherine and Henry, but also divorced the English church from its Roman matrix and brought reform to England. Whatever is to be said about the complex interplay of political, dynastic, and religious forces in England, until his death in 1547 King Henry VIII stood in the middle of things. Hans Holbein's famous painting depicts the king's temperament and qualities in addition to his outward appearance—Henry looks straight at the viewer, his hands confidently at his hips, an individual bold, determined, resolute, fully aware of his qualities and power.

The Reformation in England is unthinkable without this king. Whatever the popular religious sentiment, however lively the theological discourse, however strong the Catholic sentiment, the English Reformation was an act of state and had to do with the king. Thomas More, for a brief and unhappy time the king's chancellor, once counseled the ambitious Thomas Cromwell to tell Henry always "what he ought to do, but never what he is able to do; so shall you shewe your self a true, faithful servant and a right worthy Counselor; for if a lion knew his own strength, hard were it for any man to rule him."[1]

---

1. N. Harpsfield, *The Life and Death of Sir Thomas More* (ed. E. V. Hitchcock and R. W. Chambers; London: 1932), 147.

The advice was gratuitous; Henry did know his strength, and events in England derived their momentum from this reality. Even in faraway Germany, Luther assessed the king astutely when he observed that "Harry [Henry] is Pope, and the Pope is Henry in England."[2]

Scholars have endlessly discussed the nature of the religious change in England in the 1530s. Was it carried out by a resolute king who imposed his will on the land and it thus came about by dynastic accident rather than by religious or theological determination? Or did the call for religious change surface when Catholic belief and practice were diminishing in England, when criticism of the church was rampant, and when reform notions highlighted ideas whose time had come? Both perspectives have been forcefully expressed, most recently with the contention that there was little popular support for religious change in England, even though an ardent group of zealous "gospellers," as the reformers came to be called in England, persistently clamored for change in the religious discourse and the culture of England.

Of course, the same questions hover over the course of events in German lands, and not only there but also elsewhere in Europe, suggesting that events in England may well have followed the continental European pattern: dissatisfaction with the fiscal and political engagements of the church, criticism of the clergy, new religious and theological messages, zeal for reform, and consolidation of a new church.[3] It all comes to the question if the church in England was, in the opening decades of the sixteenth century, flowering and dynamic or were there indications of theological and religious restiveness? Did the religious changes in England come from below and grow out of popular support, or were they imposed from above by the king acting in Parliament?

However much the English course of events may be seen very much as paralleling the events on the Continent, those who advocated change in England (including, for reasons of his own, the king) did not succeed in accomplishing what had occurred in Germany—the creation of public consciousness of a deep societal crisis. In England events centered too much on the king's "great matter," and that was hardly to be understood as entailing a crisis for anyone other than the king himself—and those standing in his way.

The uniqueness of English events lay in the reality that ecclesiastical change occurred not merely once but—depending on how one counts—no fewer than six times between 1529 and 1559. First, at other places in Europe, such as France or Poland, prolonged uncertainty about the final outcome of the agitation for change characterized the course of events. In England official determinations were made again

---

2. Quoted in Basil Hall, "The Early Rise and Gradual Decline of Lutheranism in England," *Humanists and Protestants: 1500–1900* (Edinburgh: 1990), 216.

3. The current debate was triggered by A. G. Dickens's magisterial *Reformation in England* (New York: 1964), which argued the case both for the meaningful survival of Lollardy into the early sixteenth century, the essentially religious character of the reform movement in England, and the extensive acceptance of Protestant ideas by the common people. A whole slew of recent studies has defended and rejected Dickens, with important contributions by Rosemary O'Day, *The Debate on the English Reformation* (London: 1986); the most ardent revisionist has been Christopher Haigh, *The English Reformation Revisited* (New York: 1987); and also his *English Reformations: Religion, Politics, and Society under the Tudors* (Oxford: 1993). An almost lyrical portrayal of Catholic religion and piety in pre-Reformation (and Reformation) England is Eamon Duffy's *The Stripping of the Altars: Traditional Religion in England 1400–1580* (New Haven: 1992).

and again. Second, there was the role of Henry VIII, made intriguing by Henry's own conservative theological bent, which under ordinary circumstances would have hardly disposed him to initiating ecclesiastical change of any sort. But these were not ordinary circumstances. By temperament and conviction the English king was pre-destined to excel other sovereigns of Christendom in his jealous zeal for the Catholic faith. Yet the story of English Christianity in the sixteenth century took rather unex-pected turns.

While Henry provides the cue for the desertion of the English church from Rome, his ecclesiastical maneuvering would not have been possible without a congenial atmosphere in the land. To be sure, Henry encountered stiff opposition, but it was more isolated than pervasive. There was also support, tacit as well as overt, which allowed the king to move ahead with his schemes for ecclesiastical change. Moreover, one surely cannot isolate the English course of events from the religious upheaval on the Continent (though historians have had a tendency to do precisely that). By 1529 Henry was well aware of the developments and changes that were taking place in the empire and elsewhere in Europe and of the pivotal role played by the secular author-ities, for example, Gustavus Vasa in Sweden, in confronting the church.

In addition to the king's heavy hand, two factors were significant for the course of events in England: the religious ferment in the land and the Continental precedent. It is doubtful if these forces would have prevailed against the king, and what can be said about the Continent surely applies to England as well: nowhere did religious change occur against the will of the ruler, and in fact it occurred everywhere with the ruler's consent. When an English parson later in the century explained that the Lord's Prayer was so called because "it comes from our Lord, the king" (presumably the teenaged Edward VI), his biblical ignorance took him to a profound political insight.[4]

A striking feature of religious reform in England was that official religion changed several times in the course of the century, and each time the common people no less than the clergy had to adjust to the change newly ordered by the king, the queen, or Parliament. Of course, the episcopal hierarchy, the bishops, had to do the same. Robert Joseph, novice master of the Benedictine monastery at Evesham, grieved about the preaching of the reformers in a letter in 1531. "O saeculum corruptissimum," he wrote (oh, the most corrupt of centuries), praying that God would put an end to it all posthaste. Joseph left his monastery when it was dissolved nine years later, became chaplain and then vicar at All Saints in Evesham, adjusted to the changes under Edward VI, then to those under Mary, and finally to those under Elizabeth I. He even-tually obtained a vicarage in Worcestershire, where he died in 1569. His is, in short, a story of exquisite adaptation, undoubtedly emulated by thousands of others.[5] Nowhere else in Europe were people exposed to such repeated alterations of the offi-cial religion in the land.

The evidence for the state of early-sixteenth-century religious and ecclesiastical affairs in England is not particularly extensive. It would appear that there prevailed the same intriguing mixture of spiritual vitality and ecclesiastical criticism found in

---

4. "Bishop Hooper's Visitation of Gloucester," *English Historical Review* 19 (1904): 102.
5. Robert Joseph's story is told in Norman Jones, *The English Reformation* (Oxford: 2002), 6ff.

Germany. The church might have weathered the storm and stayed its traditional course, as happened in Spain, for example. A catalyst was necessary to rally the forces of reform. In Germany it was a particularly atrocious sale of indulgences; in England it was a vexing martial problem facing the king. As in Germany, the issue in England was less how much vitality flowered—to be ruthlessly mowed down by Henry and his reforming cohort—but whether those who wanted change, for whatever reason, were able to create a new consciousness in the land that made reform possible.[6] That was a major difference between England and Germany. In Germany the catalyst was a religious concern (the practice of indulgences), which subsequently became embroiled in economic and political machinations. In England the situation was the reverse: a political and dynastic issue—"the king's great matter"—stood at the beginning and promptly took on a religious dimension.

England had a history of strong religious dissent: John Wycliffe's long shadow continued to fall over the land, and from the last decades of the fifteenth century till the first decades of the sixteenth the incidence of Lollard conventicles appears to have increased. John Foxe, the English martyrologist, spoke of a "secret multitude of true professors," and despite his apologetic intentions, he probably was an accurate historian.[7]

The first formal recognition of the presence of Lutheran ideas in England came from none other than the king himself. Henry had read Luther's 1520 treatise *The Babylonian Captivity of the Church* with considerable indignation, and, theologian as he saw himself, had published a response, entitled *Assertio Septem Sacramentorum* (Assertion of the Seven Sacraments). Though hardly one of the searching theological publications of the early sixteenth century, the *Assertio* was a competent restatement of the traditional Catholic doctrine of the sacraments—so much so that the very learnedness of the book promptly raised doubts about its authorship. Some suspected the gifted and ambitious Thomas More.

These demurrers about authorship notwithstanding, a special copy of the book was presented to Pope Leo X in September 1521. In return, the pope expressed his admiration for the king's erudition and orthodox faith; one month later he conferred the title *Defensor Fidei* (Defender of the Faith) upon Henry, a title that British monarchs continue to use even though the faith they nowadays are called upon to defend has long ceased being that of the popes—or, for that matter, of the Reformation.

Luther was sufficiently challenged by the king's foray into theological learning to write a caustic response—tact was never one of Luther's finer qualities—entitled *Contra Henricum Regem* (Against Henry, King of the English), which deserves pride of place as the most vitriolic and insulting publication ever hurled by a theologian against royalty. Luther sort of apologized in 1525, when he was told that the English king might join the ranks of reform, but neither the apology nor theological (or political) considerations swayed the king. In fact, Henry wrote Luther that he despised him for his cowardice as he had formerly hated him for his heresy.

---

6. Duffy, *Stripping of the Altars,* forcefully and eloquently argued the case for the vitality of the English church before the Reformation. His stance is that Protestantism expanded very slowly in a country whose people continued to be devoted to the Catholic Church.

7. S. R. Cattley and G. Townsend, eds., *The Actes and Monuments of John Foxe* (London: 1843–1849), 4:218.

The king's valiant venture into the realm of theology notwithstanding (Henry also saw himself as an accomplished composer; he composed a little piece called "Pastime with Good Company"). Lutheran ideas continued to find their way to England through commercial travelers and books and pamphlets. As early as 1519, Luther had been told that his writings were admired in England. John Foxe, the chronicler of the Reformation in England, reported later that the Lutheran hotbed was the university at Cambridge, a not surprising claim—many universities were hotbeds of reform—but that assertion is otherwise unsubstantiated. To be sure, many of the future leaders of the Reformation in England were at Cambridge during the 1520s—such as Hugh Latimer (1485–1555), William Tyndale (ca. 1494–1536), Thomas Bilney (1495–1531), and Thomas Cranmer (1489–1556)—and they likely first imbibed reform notions at the Cambridge White Horse Tavern, as Foxe so exuberantly reported. Also in Cambridge at that time, however, were future ecclesiastic dignitaries, future bishops as well as future Protestant martyrs. Not all clerics in Cambridge at that time became reformers, and they probably were more excited by Erasmus's vision of a moral Christianity than by Luther, though soon the group was tellingly dubbed "little Germany." The latest theological fads were a frequent topic of discussion, and London merchants, particularly Germans living for commercial reasons in England, began to be interested in the ideas wafting over from the Continent. Soon also came the first burnings of Lutheran books, dutifully presided over in London by Thomas Wolsey, cardinal, archbishop of York, and lord chancellor of England. Robert Barnes (1495–1540), an Augustinian friar and student at Cambridge, where he received his doctorate in theology in 1523, was the leader of the Cambridge group, having been converted to Luther's ideas by Thomas Bilney.[8] He was not particularly gifted, but he was likable and witty, and when he became a reformer, he found his calling. On Christmas Eve, 1525, he preached a fiery sermon in Cambridge and early the following year was promptly summoned to appear before Cardinal Wolsey, who needed to demonstrate that he could be counted on when it came to the suppression of heresy. Barnes was a convenient heretic to punish, and so he was charged for having preached "before the butchers of Cambridge" and for holding to heretical doctrine (the former undoubtedly as offensive as the latter). Barnes's views had a hefty dose of anticlerical sentiment—he had preached that the church should not have temporal possessions, that the bishops were the successors of Judas Iscariot, and that the church sold spiritual benefits the way peasants sold cows and oxen, hardly notions calculated to endear him to Wolsey, who if anything was committed to the good and prestigious life. Barnes formally recanted and in penitence walked around the pyre outside St. Paul's, where a number of heretical books had been committed to the flames. But for Barnes this formal recantation did not mean a change in his views, which were pure Lollard and Luther. He went to rather extravagant lengths to fake suicide in the Thames—with a sealed note to be found even before his body could be retrieved from the Thames—but his real intention was to leave the country. After he did he eventually found his way to Wittenberg.

8. N. S. Tjernagel, *Robert Barnes and Anglo-Lutheran Relations, 1521–1540* (Ph.D. diss., University of Iowa), 1955.

William Tyndale (ca. 1494–1536), another member of the Cambridge group, came to be a most remarkable figure of the early English Reformation.[9] He had taken a master of arts degree at Oxford and exuberantly imbibed Erasmus, whose *Enchiridion* he translated into English. He then turned to Luther, became tutor and chaplain, and somewhere along the line became proficient in Greek. His lifelong passion was to make the New Testament available in the English language, and he pursued that goal with an impressive single-mindedness of purpose, though it also had a way of making him self-righteous and difficult. Given the church's disapproval of vernacular translations, Tyndale had to pursue his goal of translating the New Testament in clandestine fashion—first as part of the household of a London merchant, where he labored for six months, hardly ever pausing to sleep, then on the Continent in Cologne and Worms, where his translation was completed and eventually published. By March 1525 copies of his English New Testament found their way across the Channel and began to influence religion in England more than any other sixteenth-century publication. Like Luther, Tyndale used Erasmus's Greek New Testament as his source, and like Luther, he had an exquisite flair for language. The early-seventeenth-century Authorized, or King James, Version of the English Bible, normative for English-speaking Protestants for centuries, derived most of its translation of the New Testament from Tyndale. And for good reason: Tyndale's simplicity and directness survived the ravages of fads and ideology. Like all translations, Tyndale's work also offered interpretation, for example, when he used "congregation" rather than "church" as a translation of *ekklesia* or rendered the Greek *agape* of 1 Corinthians 13 as "love."

Driven by zeal to make the Bible available in the language of the common people, Tyndale could not resist adding his own glosses and commentary to his translation. His extensive prefaces to the books of the New Testament were pure Luther, taken almost verbatim from Luther's introductory notes to the German translation of the New Testament. Tyndale's later editions, including that of the Pentateuch of 1530, added extensive marginal notes that brimmed with crude attacks on priests, the church, and the pope, and insisted on his utter fidelity in translating: "I call God to record against the day we shall appear before our Lord Jesus Christ to give a reckoning of our doings, that I never altered one syllable of God's Word against my conscience."[10]

While working on his translation in London, Tyndale had become acquainted with the Society of Christian Brethren, an enigmatic enterprise that distributed religious books, even heretical ones, from the Continent. Whether this meant the conscious colportage of Lutheran ideas is another question. Historians who so argued may have used imagination rather than evidence.

The dissemination of the vernacular Scriptures in England was truly revolutionary. The common people (if they were literate) could read the Bible themselves, form

---

9. Donald Dean Smeeton, *Lollard Themes in the Reformation Theology of William Tyndale* (Kirksville, MO: 1986); C. R. N. Routh, *Who's Who in Tudor England* (London: 1990); Christopher Haigh, *English Reformations: Religion, Politics, and Society under the Tudors* (Oxford: 1993); Christopher Hill, *The English Bible and the Seventeenth-Century Revolution* (London: 1993); David Daniell, *William Tyndale: A Biography* (New Haven: 1994); *Selected Writings: William Tyndale* (ed. David Daniell; Manchester: 2003).

10. New Testament, Preface. *The newe Testament as it was written, and caused to be written, by them which herde yt. To whom also oure saveoure Christ Jesus commanded that they shulde preache it unto al creatures* (Worms, 1526).

an opinion, and decide which side was right or wrong in the theological controversy. They may have been mistaken in their conclusions; because they lacked theological training they probably often were. But their lack of education did not keep them from proffering their marginalia to the Sacred Writ. The Protestants castigated the Catholic notion that Scripture could not be understood by simple men and women.

Alongside the vernacular Bible, a host of other publications conveyed new religious and theological ideas to English readers. Tyndale not only translated the Bible but also wrote theological tracts, such as *A Briefe declaration of the sacraments* or *The obedie[n]ce of a Christen man and how Christen rulers ought to governe* (Antwerp, 1528), a striking appeal to the English king. Tyndale had many comrades-in-arms. John Frith published *A Pistle to the Christen Reader: The Revelation of Antichrist* (1529) and *A Letter unto the Faithful Followers of Christ's Gospel* (1532). George Joye wrote an *Answer to Ashwell* (1531), a discussion of justification by faith. From the pen of William Barlow came *A Dyaloge Descrybyng the Orygynall Ground of These Lutheran Faccyons* (1531), and William Roy published *A Proper Dyaloge betwene a Gentillman and an Husband Man* (1530).

Some forty books advocating reform were published between 1525 and 1533. While this figure is too modest to warrant the assertion of a widespread impact, it is sufficient to suggest the intrusion of the new theological currents into the country. The English religious scene was certainly more turbulent than it had been ten or fifteen years earlier, with assuredly an increase in "evangelical" sentiment in the land.[11]

There is evidence that Lollardy, the heretical movement going back to John Wycliffe, had survived into the early sixteenth century, but also that its various groups and conventicles appear to have increased in number. Whether the Lollards constituted a noticeable element in the English ecclesiastical scene in the early sixteenth century is difficult to say; however, their existence signified the continued religious restlessness.

Then there was the influence of Erasmus in England, which he visited frequently, more so than any place else. This meant Christian humanism which stood in more than chronological proximity to the Reformation, and the line between the humanist critique of ecclesiastical abuse (real or imagined) and the Protestant repudiation of Catholic religion was so thin that many contemporaries never perceived the difference. In England (as elsewhere), humanism supplied both defenders and opponents of the Catholic Church, an indication that it had no specific theological propensity. Some, such as Stephen Gardiner or Thomas More, criticized church life until they realized that they were only encouraging defiance of the church. Then they stiffened in their attitude, became unwilling to acknowledge any ecclesiastical shortcomings, and were indisposed to explore new avenues of theological reflection. Others, such as Robert Barnes or John Hooper, turned into ardent Protestants.

In sum, the religious scene in England in the 1520s was lively and exciting. Its main ingredients—Lollardy, Erasmian humanism, and new theological ideas coming from Germany—indicated that religious life might undergo turbulence, if not change.

---

11. A. G. Dickens vigorously defended his not "from above" but "from below" understanding of the English Reformation in "The Early Expansion of Protestantism in England, 1520–1558," *Archive for Reformation History* 78 (1987): 187ff.

Events and forces were disparate, religious and political, and marked by a great deal of serendipity. Whether the forces of reform might have carried the day was rendered moot, however, by an unexpected turn of events. A middle-aged king's determination, matched by the determination of his queen, who felt profoundly betrayed, was to create an altogether new situation.

"THE KING'S GREAT MATTER"

King Henry's announcement to Catherine on that June day in 1527 that they were not truly husband and wife was astounding news for the queen, who had taken for granted that they had been duly married for seventeen years—even though she had not remained unaware of her husband's periodic marital escapades during those years. Henry's quest for a "divorce" was to overshadow the foreign and domestic affairs of England and eventually led to the separation of the English church from Rome.

Catherine had come to England from her native Aragon in 1501 to be married to Henry's elder brother, Arthur, the heir to the English throne. Not surprisingly, diplomatic considerations rather than even a semblance of romantic disposition prompted the match: political ties between England and Aragon would minimize, for both, any French threat. Barely five months after Arthur and Catherine's nuptials, in April 1502, Arthur died of consumption, making the sixteen-year-old Catherine a widow. The notion of a Spanish-English alliance, cemented by a marriage, persisted, of course, even after Arthur's unexpected death, and Henry was called upon to take his older brother's place.

The problem was that canon law, which regulated marriage law, prohibited marriage with the widow of one's brother, though it was possible (under certain conditions) to receive a papal dispensation. Such a dispensation was sought for Catherine and Henry and they received it, with some uncertainty as to the exact legal grounds on which it was issued. The dispensation seemed to presume that the marriage between Arthur and Catherine had not been consummated—a striking premise, since the two, though teenagers, had been married for five months, and Arthur had boasted rather gleefully about his sexual exploits. Later, when Henry began to share with the world his spiritual scruples about his marriage to Catherine, she insisted vigorously to have been a virgin when she married him.

The papal dispensation removed the impediment of affinity between Henry and Catherine and allowed a marriage contract to be signed in June 1503. Since the final portion of Catherine's dowry was not forthcoming, however, the wedding itself was postponed. When Henry eventually succeeded his father, Henry VII, in 1509, the marriage between Henry VIII and Catherine was promptly solemnized. Curiously, the day before the wedding, Henry recorded a protest against his marriage, asserting that he had been forced into it. At the same time, he also petitioned the pope for help in mollifying Catherine's "excessive" piety, hardly a good omen for the marriage to come.[12]

The young couple was meant to live happily ever after. At some point, Henry began to have doubts about the legitimacy of the papal dispensation (and thereby his mar-

12. The sources are in J. J. Scarisbrick, *Henry VIII* (London: 1968), 9.

riage). What prompted these scruples is difficult to say, but a number of considerations suggest themselves. Politically by the mid-1520s Spain was no longer England's obvious choice of a continental ally, and if anything it had come to be in England's interest to join a European-wide anti-Habsburg alliance against the seemingly all-powerful Charles, king of Spain and emperor of the Holy Roman Empire.

The absence of a male heir may also have set Henry pondering; it undoubtedly became the factor of major importance. Catherine had become pregnant eight times during the first ten years of her marriage, but only a daughter, Mary, had survived infancy. In the end, neither Henry's vow to lead a crusade against the Turks nor the counsel of Spanish physicians, considered experts in the matter, was able to alter the simple reality that there was no son. Henry had sired a bastard boy, so the evidence put the responsibility for the state of affairs on Catherine. As matters stood, the royal succession would fall on his surviving child, his daughter Mary, a dreadful and ominous prospect because a queen was thought not to be able to exercise a strong and vigorous rule. Henry may well have shuddered when pondering the future of England after him.

Henry himself provided a pious reading of the matter. The study of Scripture had convinced him, so he claimed, that he was under a divine curse for having violated the law of God. "My conscience was incontinentlie accombred, vexed, and disquieted," he observed, "whereby I thought myselfe to be greatlie in danger of Gods indignation. Which appeared to be (as me seemed) the rather, for that he sent us no issues male: and all such issues as my said wife had by me, died incontinent after they came into the world, so that I doubted the great displeasure of God in that behalfe." Leviticus 20:21 ("And if a man shall take his brother's wife, it is an unclean thing: he hath uncovered his brother's nakedness; they shall be childless") told him that Catherine and he were under a divine curse.

Another version was offered by Reginald Pole, the ardent Catholic, who later in Queen Mary's reign was elevated to Archbishop of Canterbury. Pole charged that Henry's "passions for a girl" had been the reason. The "girl" was the young and vivacious Anne Boleyn.[13] The Venetian ambassador reported that "madam is not one of the handsomest women in the world," and, judging from her portrait, Anne was no beauty, though—again relying on the rather wooden portraits of Catherine and Anne—Henry must have seen her vivaciousness and youth as an improvement over his utterly solemn wife Catherine. Then there was her age—Anne was barely twenty in 1527, while Catherine was forty-two, seven years older than Henry. No matter: the king fell madly in love with Anne, who, in contrast to her sister, Henry's former mistress, kept him at arm's length. One suspects that in the beginning Henry had no idea of the interminable complications facing his amorous fancies. Whatever the ultimate reason for his determination to break the marriage bond with Catherine, he knew that he needed papal concurrence. All too confidently (as matters turned out) he was persuaded that the pope would routinely grant his request for an annulment of his marriage with Catherine, or, to say it more precisely, for rescinding the papal dispensation that allowed the marriage. After all, less than a decade earlier Henry had jumped into

13. See the most recent study of Eric Ives, *The Life and Death of Anne Boleyn* (London: 2004).

the theological fray with his pronouncement on the sacramental structure of the church, which feat and services had earned him the title of "Defender of the Faith."

But there were complications. Practically, Henry wanted to be "divorced" from Catherine; technically, he wanted the pope to declare that according to canon law a marital impediment had existed between him and Catherine. Consequently, the papal dispensation that had allowed the marriage had to be rescinded. This, of course, was tantamount for the pope to say that his predecessor had made a mistake. The problem was that Henry's desire for an annulment of his marriage ran counter to the consensus of a formidable array of canon lawyers who claimed that, given certain conditions, a dispensation to marry one's brother's widow might be issued and did not conflict with either natural or divine law. Henry's case was by no means unique—with generations of canonists exploring every aspect of marriage law, it hardly could be— so for the pope to acquiesce to Henry meant to go contrary to virtually unanimous legal opinion. Henry's case was further weakened because certain peripheral uncertainties and ambiguities (for example, whether the marriage between Arthur and Catherine had actually been consummated) had been summarily removed by a second dispensation, which validated Henry's marriage with Catherine even in that case.

However inadvertently, Henry's request for an annulment of the prior dispensation had raised the fundamental issue of ecclesiastical authority. His petition to have the pope withdraw the dispensation meant, in fact, that he called upon the pope to declare that his predecessor had acted erroneously. Clearly, Pope Clement VII could not do that. Moreover, Henry's case, feeble in light of canon law, was further weakened by the political situation. Almost to the day of Henry's dramatic announcement to his wife Catherine, the emperor's plundering German mercenaries had marched southward from northern Italy to Rome and taken and looted it (contemporaries talked about the "sack" of Rome). Pope Clement VII sought refuge in the Castel Sant'Angelo, originally a tomb, then a fortress, close to the Vatican and the Tiber River. The castle was connected in the thirteenth century to the Vatican by the famous safe passageway that runs along the top of the encircling wall of the Vatican. The efforts of the emperor's mutinous troops to storm the castle failed; but Pope Clement was hardly a free agent. The emperor, nephew of Catherine of Aragon, was vitally interested in the "divorce" for political reasons and used every conceivable pressure to sway the decision in Catherine's favor. This put the pope in a difficult position, aggravated by his temperamental inability to make decisions. Henry's "great matter" provided the pope with a splendid opportunity to demonstrate his tendency to procrastinate. "I have never seen him so slow," wrote Stephen Gardiner, who was the chief negotiator with Pope Clement in "the king's great matter" and later received the bishopric of Winchester. Clement must have thought that by postponing a decision the matter (perhaps nothing more than a middle-aged male's infatuation) would take care of itself, though he entertained little doubt about the seriousness of the issue. There is no evidence that he was ever willing to make an uncanonical decision, even though Charles and Henry, each in his own way, pressured him to do precisely that. In faraway Rome the conviction may well have prevailed that the middle-aged king's romantic fling would come to an early end. Little did the papacy realize the depth of the king's dynastic concern and of his amorous passion for this "girl."

Cardinal Wolsey, the king's chancellor, was first called upon to solve the matter in line with the king's desire. Wolsey, a man of humble origins, could look back on a distinguished career in church and state that had made him the alter ego of the king for the better part of two decades.[14] But his extraordinary administrative skills and his powerful position in the church as both cardinal and archbishop, not to mention his savvy, failed him in "the king's great matter." At the outset, Wolsey took it for granted that, given his legatine authority, he himself could pronounce judgment on the king's marriage. Then he was persuaded, all too confidently, that Henry's pursuit would encounter no serious obstacles on the part of the pope. After a year or so, however, Wolsey (and Henry) had to realize that there was no help from that quarter. At Henry's behest Wolsey traveled to France to secure Francis I's support to free the pope from the fangs of Charles's troops. The strategy was that the pope's gratitude would induce him to honor Henry's request for the annulment. Wolsey failed in his mission, and this meant the king's displeasure—undoubtedly he was influenced by Anne Boleyn. In early October 1529 Wolsey was deprived of his position as lord chancellor (and the role of Henry's alter ego) and made to surrender the Great Seal of the realm. For awhile it appeared that Wolsey would be allowed to retire to his archbishopric of York, but in November he was indicted for violation of the fourteenth-century statutes of praemunire. Known by this Latin term, which simply means "strengthen," these statutes vaguely prohibited the English from acknowledging any foreign power. Wolsey was indicted for having acknowledged the pope. Eight days later he lost the chancellorship and just about all the worldly dignities and possessions he had accumulated during his spectacular career. In February 1530 Wolsey received the king's pardon and retired to York province; for the few months he was yet to live he carried out his episcopal responsibilities in an exemplary manner, something his worldly pursuits in the king's service had never allowed him to do. There were signs of Henry's benevolence, but in the end Wolsey's enemies (which included Anne Boleyn) and his own scheming to return to power did him in. In November 1530 he was charged with treason—"both in and out of the kingdom." As happened frequently during Henry's reign, the nature of the charges was not exactly clear. On the way to the London Tower, his penultimate destination, Wolsey died on November 29, having told William Kingston, "Master Kingston, I see the matter against me now it is framed; but if I had served God as diligently as I have done the king He would not have given me over in my gray hairs." No matter how brilliant a statesman and administrator, no matter how deep his loyalty to the king, and, no matter how blind he was to the need for judicious reform in the church, Wolsey, the loyal if self-assured servant, never quite understood the intensity of the king's determination to end his marriage with Catherine, nor that Henry's wrath had fallen so heavily on him. As Jonathan Edwards was to say in a famous sermon, "The wrath of kings is very much dreaded."

Wolsey's successor as lord chancellor was a choice both obvious and strange: Thomas More, a distinguished humanist, successful lawyer, member of the King's Council, and speaker of the House of Commons in the early 1520s. More had patiently

---

14. A. F. Pollard, *Wolsey* (London: 1929), continues to be the most detailed (and judicious) account of the cardinal.

if ambitiously waited in the wings for a long time for higher office. But More, a devout Catholic who hated heretics with a humorless vengeance, was also known to oppose the king's "divorce," and later, when "the king's great matter" had become the foremost topic in the realm, More asserted that at the time of his appointment he had shared his scruples with the king and Henry had agreed that More would not be involved. This meant, of course, that the king's highest official remained aloof from the major issue of the day. Absent from any involvement in "the king's great matter," More conducted the affairs of state competently, though never rising to the level of influence and royal confidence that had characterized Wolsey's tenure. Indeed, a year after More assumed office, a competitor had emerged who perhaps more than rivaled him in sharpness of mind and clarity of purpose—Thomas Cromwell, who shaped policy throughout the 1530s.

Sadly, Thomas More's tenure as lord chancellor was also characterized by a ruthless persecution of Protestant sentiment in the land. John Foxe remarked in his *Book of Martyrs* that More was "a bitter persecutor of good men, and a wretched enemy against the truth of the gospel." Indeed, More continued in his relentless pursuit of Protestant heretics even when it was clear that the king's pursuit of his "divorce" meant that Protestants were beginning to be seen as the king's allies.

In November 1529 Henry convened Parliament, which had not met for years. The business at hand seemed routine, though several bills dealt with ecclesiastical matters and were stridently anticlerical in tone. These bills restricted probate fees of mortuaries and prohibited pluralities of benefices as well as all efforts to secure papal dispensations for such pluralities. This provision placed an English statute over papal prerogatives. The language of the act was cautious, all the same, for only the effort to obtain a dispensation was prohibited; nothing was said about papal authority.

By that time another development was in the making. Thomas Cranmer, an otherwise undistinguished Cambridge don, had observed that the real issue of the king's divorce was theological: it was not the canonists of bygone centuries that mattered, but Scripture. Thus the battle cry of the continental Reformation was heard in England with the notion that theological consensus based on the Bible set aside papal edicts. "The king's great matter" was to be decided on the basis of the Bible—not on church tradition or even by the pope. When reported to the king, Cranmer's suggestion fell on fertile ground. The Cambridge don, so said the king, "hath the sow by the ear." The grateful king began to shower the young Cranmer with attention and preferments. When, in the summer of 1532, William Warham, the unhappy archbishop of Canterbury, died, Henry saw to it that Cranmer was consecrated as his successor.

Cranmer's suggestion prompted a grandiose canvass of the European citadels of higher learning. Oxford and Cambridge were sounded out first, and the situation there proved paradigmatic of things elsewhere. There was no clear-cut response; accordingly, the ambivalence of the academics had to be resolved by royal intimidation. As a rule the sentiment of a university depended on its geographical location: Spanish universities decided in favor of the papal dispensation; French universities, against it. In the end the results of the "opinion poll" were impressive but inconclusive. Henry could comfort himself that broad theological opinion favored his "divorce," but the sentiment was by no means unanimous. Moreover, when all was said and done, the university opinions rendered were worth no more than the parchment they were written on—of little influence in the harsh world of an arrogant king determined to have his way.

By 1530 three long and indeterminable years had passed since the king first voiced his pangs of conscience. He had engaged in legal maneuvering, had pleaded and pressured. A deadlock prevailed, and the overriding question was whether a way could be found to break it. That most of the English bishops offered their support in the king's quest for an annulment did not seem to be of any help; indeed, when Henry twice suggested in 1530 to nobles that he might proceed without the pope, he encountered staunch opposition.

Then the king tried blackmail. In the summer of 1530 the attorney general filed charges against eight bishops and seven other prominent clergy; in December the indictments were broadened to encompass the entire English clergy. The exact nature of the charges was not altogether clear: were the clergy indicted for having accepted Wolsey's legatine authority, or for their violation of the praemunire statute, that is, the recognition of a foreign authority (the pope)? On the face of things, the charges were accurate, but the church had been operating that way as long as anyone could remember—and, as part of the church universal ruled by the pope in Rome, had to operate that way. The clergy were stunned but, quickly regaining their equilibrium at the convocations of Canterbury and York in January 1531, they undertook to deal with this preposterous situation by bribing the king. In return for their pardons, they offered substantial "subsidies"—Canterbury pledged £100,000 and York, £18,840—as grants to the king in gratitude for his defense of the faith. Henry graciously accepted and allowed the convocations to pay off the subsidies in five annual installments. But he needed more. His new vision of his royal role, suggested to him by Cromwell, was that he was responsible not only for the temporal but also the spiritual well-being of his subjects. Church courts and a set of laws not under his jurisdiction constituted an infringement of the sovereignty of the crown. The king wanted the clergy to acknowledge his authority as "singular protector, supreme lord and only supreme head of the English church and clergy." According to tradition, John Fisher, the aged bishop of Rochester and a stalwart of the conservative anti-"divorce" faction, proposed the insertion of the phrase "so far as the law of Christ allows."[15] In fact, however, the phrase was added through Cromwell's shrewd intervention in order to soften the blow to the clergy. Events were to show that the phrase made little, if any, difference in the course of ecclesiastical events, for it became quickly clear that even the determination of "the law of Christ" was the prerogative of the king.

With this modifying phrase the Canterbury Convocation accepted the document, though some of the lower house, perhaps as many as a third, insisted that the concession did not touch on the unity of Christendom or the authority of the Holy See.[16] Bishop Fisher was not the only one who worried, however, about to what the convocations had agreed. The ardent Catholic Reginald Pole, though safely in Italy, observed:

---

15. D. Wilkins, ed., *Concilia magnae Britanniae et Hiberniae,* 4 vols. (London: 1737), 3:742.
16. The document is in the Staatsarchiv in Vienna, as cited in Scarisbrick, *Henry VIII,* 276.

"The king standeth even upon the brink of the water and he may yet save all his honour, but if he put forth his foot but one step forward, all his honour is drowned."[17]

The acknowledgment of a royal headship of the church was nothing more than the continuation of trends involving the ever greater political control over the church. Indeed, several of the earliest English reformers had explicitly called upon the king to take the lead in reforming the English church. As John Fisher's insertion (and the dissenting sentiment of the clergy of the Canterbury Convocation) suggests, so long as the limits of claimed royal prerogative acknowledged papal authority, Catholics could live—however apprehensively—with this reality. By the same token, under the tutelage of Cromwell, Henry became increasingly convinced of a rather absolute sense of royal authority that allowed for no ecclesiastical independence. There was talk, startlingly new, about the ancient privileges of the English church and about the true nature of Henry's "imperial" office as it related to the church. Henrician caesaropapism developed parallel to but distinct from the quest for the marital annulment.

The years 1529–1532 were thus a time of transition. The tools for a revolutionary change in policy were close at hand, but Henry, a staunch if conventional Catholic, grappled for more traditional means of resolving the deadlock over the divorce. In 1531 even an indefatigable optimist had to admit that the king was no closer to his goal than he had been in 1527. Time was running short, and Henry was growing impatient.

The final effort to force the hand of the papacy—on its weakest point, namely, money—came in January 1532, when Parliament passed the Conditional Restraint of Annates. This prohibited the payment of annates, the first-year revenue of an ecclesiastical position, to Rome. Henry meant to tighten the financial screws and deprive the pope of his English revenue. The lesson was unambiguous: no annulment, no money. The king's bill had rough sledding in Parliament, and Henry had to do the unusual: go to the House of Lords no fewer than three times to cajole, and in the House of Commons to insist on a division of the house, with those supporting the bill on the one side and the opponents on the other.

In March Parliament presented a supplication to the king that had all the appearances of a grievous sigh of a people oppressed by the church. The twelve complaints included both the sublime and the ridiculous—that minors were given benefices and that there were too many holy days, especially at the harvest time, "upon which many great, abominable, and execrable vices, idle and wanton sports be used and exercised." The *Supplication against the Ordinaries* reeked of the anticlerical spirit of the Hunne affair, which had perturbed London early in the century. But the heart of the matter was stated at the beginning of the *Supplication*. The clergy make laws, so the king was told, "without your knowledge or most royal assent," none of which were "declared unto them in the English tongue."

The clergy in convocation, when confronted with this charge, realized the gravity of the situation and decided to fight back, prompting Henry to call the response "slender" and "sophistical" and to tell Parliament, "Their answer will smally please you."[18]

17. J. Strype, *Memorials of the Most Reverend Father in God, Thomas Cranmer, Sometime Lord Archbishop of Canterbury* (London: 1694), appendix 1.
18. Henry Gee and William John Hardy, eds., *Documents Illustrative of English Church History* (London: 1896), 154ff.

The *Answer of the Ordinaries,* much of which was written by Bishop Stephen Gardiner, sharply argued the case for the traditional spiritual independence of the church from the political powers in a way that evoked the memory of the clash between Thomas Becket and Henry II. Although Gardiner's document seemed to outdo itself with obsequious encomia for the king, its message was unmistakable and clear: the way things were was the right way and must not be changed.

The king was undeterred. He informed the speaker of the House of Commons and other dignitaries that he had discovered the English clergy were "but half his subjects," because alongside their fealty to him they also swore an oath to the pope in Rome: "They seem to be his subjects and not ours."[19] While the House of Commons was pondering this open challenge to papal loyalty, Henry demanded, rather abruptly, that the bishops grant him veto power over all ecclesiastical legislation and the right to revoke existing canons that stood in conflict with royal authority. The bishops were put on the spot. On May 15, after several of them had chosen to absent themselves, the upper house of the Convocation of Canterbury submitted to the king. "Having our special trust and confidence in your most excellent wisdom, your princely goodness and fervent zeal to the promotion of God's honor and Christian religion, and also in your learning, far exceeding, in our judgment, the learning of all other kings and princes," the bishops agreed to obtain royal assent for all new constitutions, canons, and ordinances. The following day Thomas More, pleading ill health, resigned from his office as lord chancellor. Something dramatic had happened. Chapuys, the Spanish ambassador, reported that there was "a new papacy made here." The clergy were now inferior to shoemakers, he said, for these latter could at least make their own statutes.

The man who implemented this Henrician revolution was Thomas Cromwell. He had been Wolsey's secretary and, somewhat unexpectedly, weathered the fall of his master. After attracting the king's attention for his competence, he quickly rose to prominence and served for ten years or so as the king's right-hand man. Cromwell possessed the genius of mind and the singleness of purpose that enabled him to be the preeminent figure of the 1530s.[20] He stepped into a vacuum: no all-powerful Wolsey was around, and More had relinquished the office of lord chancellor. Henry wanted to rule himself in the important affairs of state, and Cromwell filled the role of brilliant administrator splendidly. His particular counsel to Henry was that as sovereign of an "empire" he exercised supreme authority in both church and state. Two conflicting concepts of church-state relations were thus put on the table—the one medieval, characterized by the ultimate ecclesiastical supremacy over secular authority, and the other modern, characterized by the ultimate supremacy of the positive laws of the state over any law of nature, God, or the church. Cromwell proved to be a brilliant proponent of the latter view, seeing in Parliament the full manifestation of the English nation and grasping the possibilities this new perspective offered.

19. Edward Hall, *Hall's chronicle; containing the history of England, during the reign of Henry the Fourth, and the succeeding monarchs, to the end of the reign of Henry the Eighth, in which are particularly described the manners and customs of those periods. Carefully collated with the editions of 1548 and 1550* (London: 1809), 205.

20. Geoffrey Elton relentlessly pursued this notion. See, for example, his *Politics and Police: The Enforcement of the Reformation in the Age of Thomas Cromwell* (Cambridge: 1972).

Henry's patience, strained by the inconclusiveness of the "divorce" proceedings, was obviated by a scheme that offered a solution to his problem, and those who had ominously prophesied that it would be all over with the pope's authority in England if the king's request were denied could comfort one another with the accuracy of their prediction. It was an obvious consequence of Cromwell's premise that there could be no legal appeals to any authority abroad.

The Act of Restraint of Appeals accordingly prohibited, with sundry allusions to historical precedent, any appeal abroad by declaring England to be an empire whose king could adjudge all spiritual and temporal matters in his realm. Practically, the act kept "the king's great matter" in England; theoretically, it culminated the delineation of a new concept of government. A perfunctory trial, presided over by Cranmer, declared the marriage between Henry and Catherine invalid. A week later Anne Boleyn was crowned queen of England. She was already with child, the king's child.

Alas, the king and his new bride were not to live happily ever after. Anne ended her life on the executioner's block, accused of adultery, but the real reason for her tragic end was her failure to bear the king a son. And she no longer fit the king's pleasure, sensual or otherwise. Thus continued the king's marital adventures, which made him husband no less than six times, surely a true testimonial to his commitment to marriage! Sadly, he had two of his wives executed (Anne Boleyn and Catherine Howard), on charges of adultery, while two actually survived him (Anne of Cleves and Catherine Parr). Although all of Henry's marriages were an intriguing mixture of sensuality, quest for a male heir, and political considerations, there also was religion. After Henry's "divorce" from Catherine of Aragon, the Catholic religion could hardly be sustained in England; and Anne Boleyn proved, indeed, a measured but headstrong advocate of reform, her conviction aided by self-interest and leading to her fall. Henry's marital adventures can hardly be divorced (if that be the proper term) from his religious policies and political initiatives. Jane Seymour, the third queen to share the king's bed, did give birth to a son—christened Edward—yet her death in childbirth leaves open the question of whether she and Henry would have lived happily ever after. Henry's fourth wife, Anne of Cleves, was very much a political dalliance and, given the king's strong opinions on such matters, a catastrophe; Holbein, who had been commissioned to paint Anne's portrait, had yielded to artistic freedom and improved on her features. That Anne could not speak English and Henry did not speak her German dialect hardly helped matters. Cromwell, who had engineered the match also to buttress England's Protestant leanings and ties with the League of Schmalkald, paid for Anne's failure to gratify the king with his head, but when the Catholic party at court, led by Bishop Stephen Gardiner, procured the nineteen-year-old Catherine Howard as the king's new wife, it was Archbishop Cranmer who assiduously compiled proof of Catherine's rather checkered background. Henry's sixth wife, Catherine Parr, godly and sober, impressive and agreeable, had clear sympathies for the reformers, such as Coverdale and Latimer. She was well versed in matters of theology and engaged Henry in serious theological conversation, greatly to the pleasure of the king, who saw himself as a theologian extraordinaire. Now it was the Catholic faction that sought to undo Catherine, even to the point of charging her with heresy. When Henry informed Gardiner that it was "a thing much to my comfort, to come in mine old days to be taught by my wife," Gardiner rejoined that the queen was full of heresy and that he could convince the king "how perilous it is to cherish a serpent within his own bosom."[21] The distracters failed in their effort to use the one or the other of the six queens to achieve their own ecclesiastical purposes. But try they did.

The preoccupation with "the king's great matter," as Henry's pursuit of a "divorce" was euphemistically called, and the introduction of ecclesiastical change by parliamentary statute must not lead us to assume that England was bereft of Reformers and theological reflection. Neither the pursuit of the "great matter" nor the parliamentary fiat would have been so smooth had there not been a concomitant religious restlessness and anti-Roman agitation. England had its reformers, men who had accepted the new interpretation of the gospel and propagated it. One must not impute staggering theological creativity and brilliance to these men, but they ostensibly played an important role in the course of events, bringing about religious ferment and making their role in the English Reformation an indispensable one.

Initially the reformers' message consisted of a vague echo of Lutheran commonplaces, those sweeping assertions propounded by reformers everywhere with disarming self-confidence: the sole emphasis on Scripture and salvation by faith alone, the rejection of works righteousness and human traditions. This was followed in England by a more sophisticated delineation of the new theology, though the king's own theologically conservative temper, witnessed by the Six Articles Act of 1539, tended to keep Protestant sentiment in check.

In an intriguing way, the cause of ecclesiastical reform was advanced by the king, who needed propagandists to make sense out the new form of Christianity that he had enjoined. For example, in an interesting propaganda pamphlet *A Remedy for Sedition* of 1536 (with the interesting subtitle "wherein are conteyned many thynges, concernyng the true and loyall obeysance, that commens owe unto their prince and soveraygne lorde the kynge"), Sir Richard Morrison offered the priceless sentiment that "religion is that which keeps subjects in obedience."

After 1534 anti-Catholic propaganda was not only tolerated but actively encouraged in England. Previously, Protestant tracts had to be printed on the Continent and smuggled to England; now they could actually be printed in England. A tract entitled *Of the Olde God and the New*, probably by Miles Coverdale, was prohibited at its first publication in 1529—and officially endorsed five years later. Protestant propaganda moved freely, though an element of precariousness remained. Henry wanted antipapal propaganda and support for the notion of royal supremacy. At the same time, he was firmly Catholic in his own theological orientation, and the propagation of salvation by faith alone or a non-Catholic understanding of the sacraments was to him an abomination; he would have none of it.

To propound theological notions in Henry's England after the "king's great matter" had triggered the break with Rome was rather like walking a tightrope. The argument had to be both antipapal and pro-Catholic, a combination that required an exquisite measure of theological versatility. Still, a multitude of writings—several hundred theological books, devotional tracts, primers, plays, and poems—were issued from the

---

21. Scarisbrick, *Henry VIII*, 478.

printing presses during the last dozen years of Henry's rule. The tenets of the Protestant Reformation, such as the centrality of Scripture, were widely expounded.

Since the king himself seemed sure of the direction of his ecclesiastical policy, but not so sure how it should be carried out, royal encouragement (or repudiation) of specific theological views remained haphazard. Indeed, for a while the key word was ambiguity, as the sequence of official theological documents, from the Bishops' Book to the Six Articles and the King's Book, made abundantly clear. England steered a middle course between Henry's staunch Catholicism and his repudiation of the papacy and the Roman Church.

The Christian humanism of Erasmus seemed to supply the necessary solution, for it not only strove to return to the sources of earliest Christianity but it also combined a hefty dose of anticlericalism with a moral understanding of Jesus's message. Although the official endorsement of Erasmianism did not come until 1547, when it was stipulated by the king that the clergy should study the *Gospel Paraphrases* of Erasmus, his informal influence was felt long before then. Several of his treatises were published in England in the early 1530s, notably his *Exhortation to the Diligent Study of the Holy Scripture*, which was subsequently included in Tyndale's 1536 edition of the New Testament. These efforts were necessary because Catholicism in England, as on the Continent, contined to command the loyalty of many, even though it seems one-sided to suggest that a flourishing and dynamic Catholic church life was nipped in the bud by an arrogant king. What is clear is that neither in England nor on the Continent was anticlericalism a major force. The Venetian ambassador to England, after having been in the country for three years, observed that there were not many true Catholics in the land and all those were over thirty-five, while Bishop Edmund Bonner of London, a formidable Catholic stalwart despite his support of the royal supremacy, thought that there were three religions in the land: Catholic, Protestant, and "the third is a neuter, being indifferent."[22]

In the changes occurring at the higher levels of church and society in England, the common people in England could discern little difference in the churches where they worshiped. To be sure, their king had a new queen (whom many despised as a harlot) and a new title, "Supreme Head of the Church," and the pope's authority had been repudiated. But the people in the pews who faithfully (or not so faithfully) attended divine services were neither asked to believe anything different or new concerning the faith nor confronted with a different form of worship. They still had the same minister, and aside from a few subtle changes, the same prayers were offered and the same affirmations made as before. Yet for a few men and women these subtle changes were either too radical or not radical enough, and they were the ones who suffered the king's wrath. In the main there was little opposition to the changes, and the king and Parliament were not particularly stern in the enforcement of whatever theological position constituted orthodoxy after 1534.

There were, however, spectacular incidents of opposition and vengeful persecution, notably those of Thomas More and John Fisher. Both highly learned, both committed to the ideals of Erasmian Christian humanism, they risked no open opposition

22. Philip Hughes, *Reformation in England* (New York: 1963), 3:60.

and preferred to be silent witnesses to the king's turn from the full Catholic faith. But Henry, habitually insecure and yet cognizant of the treacherous path down which he was leading the English church, was aware of their opposition. When the affair of the Nun of Kent broke, a simple peasant woman who claimed to have visions predicting the king's death were he to leave his wife Catherine, both Fisher and More, while not really implicated were taken to the executioner's block, the former lord chancellor of the realm and the aged bishop, because of the king's vindictiveness—as the adage from the book of Proverbs had it, "The wrath of the king is death." The irony of More's trial was that he appealed to the same ultimate principle as did Luther at the Diet of Worms: the existence of an objective divine order, which was the obligation of all individuals to accept. The issue, in other words, was not subjective dissent, but the acknowledgment of the compelling truth of that order, which could no more be denied than that the sky was blue and the grass green.

Ecclesiastical life in England continued as it had been. The familiar prayers were offered, the traditional services performed, the Catholic faith expounded and confessed. Recent scholarship has suggested that the majority of the English people continued to be loyal to the old church, with the Protestant reformers a minority. Indeed, while both Parliament and Convocation showed themselves astoundingly pliable in the face of a determined king, there was opposition, especially to Henry's "divorce." Importantly, the king cajoled the support of both the bishops and the nobility. The leaders of the church offered no real resistance to the king's alterations, while the nobility in Parliament was by and large supportive of the king. So was the new archbishop of Canterbury, Thomas Cranmer, who was consecrated in March 1532 under rather incompatible circumstances: in private he foreswore the oath of canonical obedience to the pope, while publicly, at his installation, he swore it. His pivotal role as archbishop (he had been a mere archdeacon prior to his appointment) supported the purposes of the king and enhanced reform in England.

The ties with Rome had been cut. The repudiation of papal jurisdiction over the English church meant that ecclesiastical authority in England had to be newly defined. With stunning self-confidence in ecclesiastical matters, Parliament in 1534 undertook to legislate the new church. The Ecclesiastical Appointment Act dealt with making ecclesiastical appointments; the Dispensation Act placed all authority for dispensations with the archbishop of Canterbury; the Act of Submission of the Clergy transformed into statute the earlier acknowledgment of convocation not to legislate without the king's consent; and the First Act of Succession vested the English crown in children of Henry and Anne Boleyn and thereby bestowed parliamentary sanction on the king's "divorce." Finally, and most importantly, the Supremacy Act transformed the acknowledgment of convocation that the king was the supreme head of the church into a parliamentary statute, while the corollary Treasons Act made it high treason to question the king's titles or to suggest that he was a heretic. The language of the Act of Supremacy is worth noting:

> Be it enacted by the authority of this present Parliament, that the king, our Sovereign Lord, his heirs and successors, kings of this realm, shall be taken, accepted, and reputed the only Supreme Head on earth of the Church of England . . . and that our said Sovereign Lord, his heirs and successors, kings of this realm, shall have full power and authority from time

to time to visit, repress, redress, reform, order, correct, restrain, and amend all such errors, heresies, abuses, offences, contempts, and enormities, whatsoever they be.[23]

Truly, this was a revolutionary pronouncement, already rehearsed, to be sure, many times on the Continent, where it had been verbalized (and carried out) with greater hesitancy and less boldness. Of course, those who knew of the history of Christianity also knew that ever since the days of Emperor Constantine the arm of secular government had ventured into the religious realm, seen to the appointment of bishops, and countered the absolute claims of the church with absolute claims of its own. Throughout the Middle Ages the monarchs of Europe, especially the emperors, had claimed jurisdiction in the spiritual realm as well. Luther had viewed the involvement of the secular authorities as temporarily unavoidable, but Henry VIII ventured forth with greater brazenness and stunning self-confidence, arguing to his last days that the role he had defined for himself (and his successors) was the most appropriate way to safeguard true religion. One may argue, looking at the European Reformation as a whole, whether the doctrine of royal headship was a more radical religious revolution than any form of continental Protestantism, but it assuredly received more extensive theological justification in England. Stephen Gardiner's *De vera obedientia* (Concerning True Obedience) made an elaborate case for the submission of the faithful to the ecclesiastical pronouncements of the king.

A further act of Parliament stipulated that the traditional "First Fruits" and the "Tenths" were to be paid to the king, "upon whom and in whom dependeth all their joy and wealth."[24] Although subsequent modifications of this act mollified its stringent provisions, the financial burden of the English clergy increased dramatically.

By 1536 the need to have a formal statement of the doctrinal stance of the new English church became obvious, if for no other reason than that negotiations were under way with the German Lutherans about a possible membership of England in the League of Schmalkald. Henry directed the convocation to undertake this task. The result was the Ten Articles, which on every page showed the influence, even as regards the structure, of the Augsburg Confession. The document mentioned only three sacraments—baptism, the Lord's Supper, and penance. Article 4 on the Lord's Supper was pure Lutheranism: the body and blood of Christ were "corporally, really and in the very substance exhibited, distributed and received."[25]

Additional statements of faith were promulgated as well. *The Institution of a Christian Man* (1537), also known as the *Bishops' Book* because bishops had a heavy hand in its drafting, exuded a more conservative theological bent. It restored, for example, the four sacraments that the Ten Articles had omitted. But still it proved not to the king's liking. Henry had commissioned the statement, and the bishops had tried hard but unsuccessfully to get the king's endorsement before the book went to print. Knowing what it meant to evoke royal displeasure, the bishops noted cautiously in the preface that "we have none authority either to assemble ourselves together for any pretence

---

23. *Statutes of the Realm*, 3:492.
24. Ibid., 493.
25. Charles Hardwick, *A History of the Articles of Religion. To Which Is Added a Series of Documents, from A.D. 1536 to A.D. 1615: Together with Illustrations from Contemporary Sources* (London: 1888), 1:217ff.

or purpose, or to publish anything that might be by us agreed on."[26] And how right they were! When Henry eventually got around to giving the document his theological appraisal, he made rather extensive changes in the text, including a rather self-confident rewriting of the First Commandment.

About that time, Henry's rule was to be put to its most severe domestic test. Certainly, by the mid-1530s it was clear (to the imperial ambassador Chapuys, at least) that the exuberant advocates of reform were a minority in the land and those who were able (and willing) to follow Henry's exquisitely subtle notions of ecclesiastical reform were fewer yet. On the other hand, there were those who were dismayed, bewildered, and afraid about what had been taking place in England—and apprehensive about what might yet come. Clearly, the king had brought disunity to the land. As early as 1534 rumor was rife that an uprising was in the making, and in October 1536 rebellion did break out in the northern part of the country—Lincolnshire and Yorkshire, foremostly, as well as other places in the north. These uprisings have been given the collective label "Pilgrimage of Grace," perhaps an oversimplification, for they were numerous and diverse, in focus and intent, with diverse leadership, though Robert Aske was assuredly most prominent.[27] Economic and social grievances were responsible for the unrest, much as in the uprising of the German peasants and their town allies in 1524–1525, but at its heart—certainly in Lincolnshire—was a quintessentially conservative rebellion against the religious changes in England that had been promulgated ever since 1532.

In December the rebels, or "pilgrims," drew up a list of grievances, which included a condemnation of the king's divorce. Henry, who had initially paid little attention to the affair, empowered the Duke of Norfolk to negotiate, including the promise of a general pardon and a convening of Parliament to adjudicate the pilgrims' grievances. As it turned out, the pilgrims made the big mistake of trusting the duplicitous king's words: Robert Aske instructed the pilgrims to disperse, after having removed the pilgrims' badge from his clothes with the words, "We will wear no badge or sign but the badge of our sovereign lord."[28]

Henry had no intention of honoring the commitment made, however, and with bloody vengeance he dealt with the rebellion and its leaders. Aske and others were condemned by a servile judiciary to die. So, by the summer of 1537 England was tranquil again, the symbolic plebiscite in the north of England about the king's policy a thing of the past. What was so striking about the uprisings and rebellions that are clustered under the heading of the Pilgrimage of Grace was that they were a conservative, backward-oriented insurrection, a conservative revolution. Although they shared with the German Peasants' War the intriguing admixture of political, social, economic—and religious—grievances, they differed from the German peasants' insistence on the principles of "divine law" as a guide for the conduct of both the church and the body politic. Quite the opposite in England, where the demand was to restore what had been changed and abolished.

26. C. Lloyd, *Formularies of Faith put forth by Authority during the Reign of Henry VIII* (Oxford: 1856), 27–28.

27. A thorough and impressively detailed study, with an assessment of Aske, is R. W. Hoyle, *The Pilgrimage of Grace and the Politics of the 1530s* (New York: 2001).

28. *Letters and Papers*, XII, I, 43ff., as quoted in Scarisbrick, *Henry VIII*, 345.

At about the same time, Henry had tired of his second wife, Anne Boleyn (or tired of her failure to give birth to a son). He began to flirt with Jane Seymour, saw to it that a compliant Cranmer declared the king's marriage with Anne to have been invalid, and sent Anne to the executioner's block, the executioner having been brought from Calais. The king embarked religiously on a Catholicizing trend. In 1539 he asked Parliament to pass the Six Articles Act; he, the eccentric Catholic at heart, had become concerned about the spread of Protestant notions in the land, and the act marked a swing in the direction of the theological climate. The theological ambiguities of earlier theological pronouncements were removed, as was the Protestant flavor of both the Ten Articles and the *Bishops' Book*. The pendulum swung in the direction of theological conservatism, influenced by the king's own religious temperament and perhaps by his shrewd awareness that the country still preferred the old way. The points of doctrine affirmed in the Six Articles Act (transubstantiation, Communion under both kinds, celibacy, vows of chastity, private masses, and auricular confession) pertained to the major controversial issues between the old church and the new, and the theology of the Six Articles was decidedly Catholic. Henry had taken it on himself to improve the draft of the act with his own theological emendations. Protestants promptly dubbed the act the "whip with six strings." Once again, however, the preamble to the act related the king's supremacy to the conservation of the "true, sincere, and uniform doctrine of Christ's religion."[29]

The practical significance of the Six Articles must not be overstated, for the Articles hardly heralded a conservative reaction during the last few years of Henry's reign. Understandably, the Six Articles proved a profound shock to the gospellers in England and their comrades-in-arms on the Continent; their aspirations to instigate true reform in the church in England seemed to have come to naught. Even Cranmer, who had gotten married, felt sufficiently apprehensive to return to a state of practical celibacy by sending his wife back to her native Germany.

The chronological connection between the Six Articles and Cromwell's fall suggested a broad scheme, perhaps even a plot, to eradicate Protestantism in England. One doubts Henry intended such a complete reversal of his ecclesiastical policy. He had become concerned about the barrage of Protestant propaganda, and, good Catholic that he was, viewed this development with dismay. The Six Articles were meant to stabilize the religious situation in England based on the kind of religion the king envisioned: Catholic in its theology, yet autonomous from Rome. The articles were to be a word of counsel for all would-be reformers. Intriguingly, no additional measures of anti-Protestant suppression followed, and the act's ferocious penalties (the death penalty was prescribed for the denial of transubstantiation or marriage by one who had vowed chastity) were not enforced.

A full year passed almost to the day between the promulgation of the Six Articles and Cromwell's fall. His conservative foes of long standing, notably the Duke of Norfolk and Stephen Gardiner, had been able to persuade the king that he was responsible for Henry's ill-fated marriage with Anne of Cleves, that non-entity among Henry's wives. Of course, Norfolk and Gardiner cared not so much about the king's marital

---

29. Gee and Hardy, eds., *Documents Illustrative of English Church History*, 303.

bliss as Cromwell's policy of aligning with the German Protestants. A court camarilla that despised him, as did Norfolk, because he was an upstart without noble birth, and that detested him, as did Gardiner, because he favored Protestant ideas, succeeded in gaining the king's ear and brought about his fall. "I crye for mercye, mercye, mercye," Cromwell wrote to his king from the Tower, but he went unheard (one of the witnesses at his trial was Richard Riche, who had already distinguished himself by perjurious service to the king in More's trial) and was condemned to die at the scaffold.[30] Gratitude and mercy were not part of the king's vocabulary.

Later, John Foxe, the martyrologist and creator of a genus of Protestant martyrs, called Cromwell a "valiant soldier and captain of Christ" and provided a moving, though apocryphal, account of Cromwell's last moment: "He patiently suffered the stroke of the axe, by a ragged butcherly miser, which very ungodly performed the office."[31] In his last words Cromwell protested his orthodoxy and offered a prayer for the king. Soon afterward the reformer Robert Barnes was executed, and the irony of that occasion was that on the day of his execution two other Protestant sympathizers were burned and three priests were hanged, drawn, and quartered for having denied the king's supremacy. "What a country England was to live in," a foreign observer remarked, "when they hanged papists and burned antipapists."[32] The execution of an equal number of Protestants and Catholics on a single day was a bizarre manifestation of the ecclesiastical via media Henry was disposed to travel.

The king continued his careful maneuvering between the conservatives and the Protestants, temporarily moving in one direction but then reverting to the other. The last doctrinal pronouncement of the reign, the *Necessary Doctrine and Erudition for Any Christian Man*, was issued in 1543. It is known as the *King's Book*, because Henry had not only called for its drafting but also contributed the preface, for him a splendid opportunity to demonstrate once again what he deemed to be his theological competence. Not surprisingly, it was a theologically conservative document. That same year a law with the exquisite title of An Act for the Advancement of True Religion removed the authorization to read the Bible from the "lower sort" and restricted it to the upper classes of society. A parallel note in the *King's Book* observed that the reading of the Bible had led some "to sinister understanding of Scripture, presumption, arrogancy, carnal liberty, and contention." Of course, the king would have none of this.

A revision of the service books was ordered in 1543, and a book of homilies (a collection of sermons to be read from the pulpit) was submitted to convocation but not published. In 1545 a book of vernacular prayers was authorized, while an act of Parliament empowered the king to seize the last bit of ecclesiastical property, the so-called chantries, and use it to pay for the war with France. That same year Henry made what proved to be his last appearance in Parliament. He had words of commendation for his loyal subjects (after all, Parliament had "nationalized" the chantry endowments), but also biting criticism: "Charity and concord is not amongst you, but discord and dissensions beareth rule in every place." The king continued harshly:

---

30. J. S. Brewer, ed., *Letters and Papers, Foreign and Domestic*, 21 vols. (London: 1862–1910), 15:824.
31. Foxe, *Acts and Monuments*, 5:402.
32. Ibid., 5:438.

One calleth the other Heretic and Anabaptist, and he calleth him again, Papist, Hypocrite and Pharisee. I see and hear daily that you of the clergy preach against each other without charity or discretion. Some are too stiff in their old "Mumpsimus," others are too busy and curious in their new "Sumpsimus." . . . Thus almost all men be in variety and discord and few or none preach truly and sincerely the word of God, according as they ought to do. You of the temporality be not clean and unspotted of malice and envy, for you rail on bishops, speak slanderously of priests, and rebuke and taunt preachers. . . . Shall I now judge you to be charitable persons who do this? No, no, I cannot do so. Alas, how can the poor souls live in concord when you preachers sow amongst them in your sermons debate and discord? They look to you for light and you bring them darkness. Amend these crimes, I exhort you, and set forth God's word truly, both by true preaching and giving a good example, or else, I, whom God has appointed his vicar and high minister here, will see these divisions extinct, and these enormities corrected, according to my true duty, or else I am an unprofitable servant and an untrue officer.[33]

Henry had never been at a loss of words, but on that occasion his eloquence was exquisite as he spoke about his own role in the course of events. To be sure, he consulted the church, represented by Archbishop Cranmer and the two convocations, but in the end he did what he pleased, and the church made no formal ratification. Yet one must be careful, for the English church accepted the king's entreaties and the parliamentary statutes, and so by quiet acquiescence it did "formally" embrace the manifestations of the king's authority as supreme head of the church promulgated by the king and Parliament.

What was on Henry's mind during the last months of his life, when sickness ever more burdened his worn-out body, is impossible to know. He knew that his purse was empty and the government virtually bankrupt—a damper on anyone with grandiose ideas and hopes. Perhaps Henry was concerned to ward off a possible attack on England by Charles V after the emperor had successfully concluded his war against the League of Schmalkald. Perhaps he intended a full introduction of Protestantism in the land, such as John Foxe suggested, when he wrote that "most certain it is and to be signified to all posterity, that his full purpose was to have purged the state of the Church." On the other hand, Henry may well have been convinced that his hybrid of ecclesiastical complexities, which continually astonished those around him but not himself, could survive as a stable creature. He may well have seen the solution precisely in the continuation of his own policies; after all, he was always, while self-confident and vain, an astute politician.

The odd composition of the Council of Regency that was to rule during the minority of his son Edward complicates all conjectures, though the most obvious explanation is that Henry was concerned to thwart a submission to Rome, in which event his son, Edward, would have been considered a bastard and the Tudor dynasty removed from the English throne. On the other hand, to allow the Protestants to triumph would have been squarely against Henry's own theological temper.

One thing is clear—the establishment of the Reformation in England was the king's doing, from beginning to end, perhaps even with more consistency than has customarily been accorded him. But it is clear that Henry was able to take advantage

33. Ibid., 5:534–36; Bernard, *op. cit.*, 588.

of fortuitous circumstances, not the least the religious turmoil on the Continent. At his death, he took the secret of his future plans for the realm with him. What is more, he may well have been aware that kings do not rule from the grave. The two tutors of his son (who had been inconspicuous humanists) turned into ardent Protestants, and, most important, the Council of Regency did not retain the balance between conservatives and "gospellers" that Henry had wanted.

Henry died in the early morning hours of January 28, 1547. His last request had been to see Thomas Cranmer. When the archbishop arrived, he found Henry in the throes of death. The king stretched out his hand and for the last time the two men, so unlike in character, locked hands. Cranmer asked the king for a sign of his trust in Christ, and the king pressed his hand. So died one of the most eccentric figures of the entire century. Few rulers in the sixteenth century pursued policies, ecclesiastical and otherwise, more erratic and bizarre, more brilliant and strange. Yet when the lord chancellor announced his death to Parliament, there were tears in his eyes.

If the elements in the English religious scene in the 1530s are obvious enough, their importance for ecclesiastical change is enigmatic. The king's "divorce" has often been singled out as the factor of primary importance, which suggests that Henry's determination to free himself from Catherine of Aragon at all costs brought about the ecclesiastical breach with Rome. One may also cite the religious ferment in England (either of indigenous origin or imported from abroad) and argue that the Henrician Reformation by statute formed only the legal foil for deep religious changes. One may also assert the priority of constitutional considerations in the king's growing awareness of the proper scope of the royal office with its notion that kingship included authority (and power) over church as well as state.

One does best to emphasize the interplay of these factors. All of them were present, and collectively they forced—as well as thwarted—the course of events. Had one or the other of them been absent, there would undoubtedly have been other expressions of a confrontation between king and pope, but they would have been resolved amicably; religious agitation, but no outright introduction of the Protestant faith; a desire for a "divorce," but a shying away from its grave consequences.

Still, if any factor was decisive, it was the "divorce" that provided the element of urgency and inescapable pertinence. That Henry did not enjoy the full prerogatives of kingship could be pondered and then forgotten; that some reform was called for in England likewise could be ignored. Only the absence of a male heir was a cruel reality, which assumed greater urgency and relevance with each passing day.

THE REFORMATION ENFORCED

With the trials of Thomas More and John Fisher, the curtain had fallen on the first act of religious change in England. It might have been the last. Though theological ambiguities existed, further religious changes did not appear to be in the offing, and the general pattern of ecclesiastical life might have continued. But there was a second act, even more spectacular than the first, which prompted Nicholas Harpsfield, a contemporary chronicler, to reflect that the king could no more keep from further changes "than it is possible for a man to roll a millstone from the top of a high hill and afterward to stay it in the midst of its course." By parliamentary fiat, the English monasteries were dissolved.

Henry's financial problem was the main cause for the religious houses' dissolution. The cost of government had risen substantially during his rule because of several factors, not the least of which was his extravagant involvement in European power politics. The Restraint of Annates had diverted into the royal exchequer moneys that had theretofore gone to Rome, but this was only the proverbial drop in the bucket. More was to be had from the church for the asking. A simple statistic indicates the relationship of monastic wealth to the king's pecuniary troubles: at the end of Henry's reign the annual rental value of the monastic lands was more than double the annual expenditures of government. The confiscation of monastic wealth promised to end the Crown's financial embarrassment. Cromwell's scheme was to use the property as a permanent endowment.

In the summer and fall of 1535 representatives of the king undertook a visitation of the monasteries. Upon its completion, the visitors produced a report that depicted the monasteries as iniquitous dens of vice, corruption, and superstition. The king himself appeared before Parliament to relate the sorry tale, and his performance must have been impressive. Hugh Latimer recalled many years later that "when their enormities were first in Parliament house, they were so great and abominable that there was nothing but down with them." The king told Parliament that the monasteries were wealthier than necessary and that many no longer served a spiritual purpose.

To disentangle fact and fiction in the visitors' report is virtually impossible, though there seems little doubt that English monastic life was hardly a paragon of spiritual vitality in the fourth decade of the sixteenth century. This state of affairs did not make the monasteries dens of iniquity, however; in all likelihood, most monasteries were fulfilling their functions in about the same way they had for some time.[34]

Early in 1536 Parliament passed the Act for the Dissolution of the Lesser Monasteries, those with an annual income of less than £200. Intriguingly, not the number of the religious in a house nor in specific monasteries, but the "clear yearly value of two hundred pounds" marked the dividing line between those houses "wherein (thanks be to God) religion is right well kept and observed" and those abounding in "manifest sin, vicious carnal and abominable living." The act provided that the property of the monasteries was to go to the Crown. The religious had the choice of transferring to larger monasteries, serving as secular clergy, or surrendering their clerical vocation. However, in 1539 the larger monasteries were dissolved as well.

The impact of the dissolution was far-reaching. By 1540 an institution that had been at the heart of the English religion for centuries ceased to exist. Thousands of monks and nuns became homeless and without vocation. Enormous wealth changed hands. The composition of the House of Lords was altered by the disappearance of the monastic abbots. There were social and economic consequences, since the monasteries had provided, especially in less populous places, lodging for the traveler and alms

---

34. The dissolution of the monasteries continues to generate interest—even in the realm of mystery novels. See C. J. Sansom, *Dissolution* (New York: 2003), which places a murder in a monastery in the early 1530s in the context of high politics.

for the poor. On the other hand, the dissolutions brought a benefit to learning, since some monastic funds were used for educational purposes, such as endowments of professorships or the establishment of cathedral schools. Cromwell's scheme to keep the monastic lands in the hands of the Crown did not materialize, for pressing fiscal needs (caused by the wars against France and Scotland) forced their sale, which, in turn, created a group with a vested interest in the retention of the break with Rome.

The summer of 1536 brought much rain in England, and an age disposed to regard anything unusual as an ominous foreboding of the future promptly offered its interpretation: rains were God's vengeance on behalf of the victims of Henry's religious policy. The first month would, so the prophecy went, "be rainy and full wet, next month death, and the third month war." There was war; an uprising occurred in the north. It was quickly subdued, but others occurred in places many miles apart.

There were differences among the various uprisings. In Lincoln the townspeople were the banner bearers; in York, the gentry. The grievances were a motley assortment of economic, social, and religious concerns. The common motif, with the exception of the uprisings in Cumberland and Westmoreland, was indignation over the recent religious changes in the land: the royal supremacy, the new bishops, and the dissolution of the monasteries.

The uprisings came to naught. By matching shrewdness with dishonesty, Henry survived the most serious crisis of his rule. The northern uprisings revealed the extent of discontent in the land. It was not only that the king had broken with Rome. Catherine of Aragon had been a popular queen, and her shoddy dismissal in favor of a "fair wench" hardly endeared Henry to the people. The trials of Fisher and More, the other executions, and the attack on the property of the church helped arouse discontent and prompt restlessness among the people.

The task of guiding the new church in England fell to Thomas Cromwell. As the royal viceregent he looked after ecclesiastical affairs and demonstrated his administrative competence. At the same time he showed himself to be a skillful proponent of the king's ecclesiastical cause by launching an extensive propaganda effort in which he was joined by Cranmer, the archbishop of Canterbury. The king was never far away, though. He was erratic and unpredictable, and his concern with theological matters oscillated between active interest and nonchalance. Cromwell was efficient because his policies agreed with those of the king.

The initial official statements concerning ecclesiastical policy (aside from the cluster of parliamentary acts promulgated in 1533 and 1534), the First and Second Royal Injunctions, were doctrinally vague and addressed themselves to matters pertaining to the broader social involvements of the church. Of far-reaching import was the stipulation of the Second Injunction that "the very lively word of God," which everyone must "embrace, believe, and follow, if he looks to be saved," be read, and, moreover, that "one book of the whole Bible of the largest volume, in England," be put into all parish churches. This was a new development. A few years earlier Henry had issued a proclamation that had denounced "the divulging of this Scripture at this time in English tongue," insisting that to do so would be more to "further confusion and destruction than the edification of their souls." By 1538 the situation was different, and the influence of the Protestant gospellers was evident.

The stipulation called for an official version of the English Bible, and Cromwell entrusted Miles Coverdale with the task. Coverdale, who had published an English Bible in 1535, knew no Hebrew and only a little Greek, and simply translated from German and Latin. What he could not get from Luther's translation or the Zurich Froschauer version, he lifted out of Tyndale. Neither a biblical scholar nor even a translator, he was nonetheless a gifted stylist who knew how to turn a smooth phrase. The result of his efforts was the so-called Great Bible, first published in April 1539 and republished six more times before the end of 1541. The title page pompously stated that it was "the Byble in Englyshe of the largest and greatest volume," and the ornamental woodcut placed the king in that gloriously prominent center place theretofore reserved in similar title pages for God, who now found a place—a small place—near the top of the page. The practical problems thwarting the general use of the English Bible were many. The price was high and, of course, one had to be literate to make use of it. The provision that a copy of the Bible was to be put into all parish churches overcame certain practical difficulties.

THE EDWARDIAN REVOLUTION

"The trumpets sounded with great melody and courage to the comfort of all them that were present." So the chronicler reported the scene at the king's passing and the succession of a new king. Henry's nine-year-old son, born of his third wife Jane Seymour, succeeded to the throne, the sixth English king to bear the name Edward. He was a handsome youth, with an angular face that resembled his mother's. His literary remains show that he was intelligent and devout, though also more than a bit perplexed by what was going on about him. As Jane Seymour's son, Edward's succession was not hailed by conservatives. Protestants, on the other hand, saw the opportunity for further religious reform in England that the eccentric ecclesiastical policies of Edward's father had precluded. At Edward's coronation Archbishop Cranmer likened him to King Josiah, of the Hebrew Scriptures, who destroyed idolatry and properly worshiped God, an association expanded a few months later in the *Book of Homilies* to include none other than Henry VIII, said to have had "the lyke spirite unto the moste noble and famous prynces, Josaphat, Josias, and Ezechyas."

The change in England's rule could not have been more dramatic. The crown passed from a strong even charismatic ruler to an innocent youth. Power in the land was vested in a group of councillors, sixteen in number, designated as Council of Regency. Henry had provided for religious equality on the council, but the Duke of Somerset, the young king's uncle, promptly secured his appointment as lord protector, and within two months the council had been transformed into an advisory group to Somerset. People called Somerset the "good duke," and indeed he was conscientious, intelligent, and able. But he also was enormously egotistical, autocratic, and contemptuous of the fellow members on the Council of Regency. The country was beset by a host of problems—a precarious financial situation, restlessness among the peasants, and uncertainty about religion—and Somerset demonstrated an almost compulsive zeal to set everything right. In the process he alienated his fellow council members and injured their self-esteem. Solving the problems required more tact than Somerset could muster.

The continuation of Henry's often unpredictable ecclesiastical policy seemed the most viable strategy. Such was, indeed, the official stance: the new religious policies were to be but the continuation of what Henry VIII had been planning. Somerset paid wonderful lip service to this approach when he announced that "he would suffer no innovations in religion during the king's majesty's young age."[35] The deterrents to further "innovations" existed on the Continent as well as at home. On the Continent Charles V, in whose eyes Catherine of Aragon's daughter, Mary, was the legitimate heir to the Tudor throne, had at long last undertaken to wage war against the League of Schmalkald, and the outcome was bound to influence things in England. At home, there was the disheartening realization that support for Protestant reform was limited to those who had benefited from the sale of monastic property, to academic Cambridge dons, to some of the lower clergy and of the nobility at the court. These supporters of reform had lived with an uneasy truce between outer conformity and inner persuasion during Henry's rule and now yearned for meaningful religious change. The bishops, on the other hand, were hardly inclined to be active participants in the burial of the religion that had taken them to prestige and power. They had an able and forceful leader in Stephen Gardiner, bishop of Winchester, whose influence remained formidable. For the time being, Henry's Six Articles Act continued in force.

The first indication of a new religious direction came barely six months after Henry's death. In July 1547 a book of homilies was published entitled *Certain Sermons or Homilies Appointed by the King's Majesty to Be Declared and Read by All Parsons, Vicars, and Curates*. Although without legal standing, the homilies conveyed what Somerset, Cranmer, and others saw as the proper religion of the realm.

Most of the homilies shared a highly moralizing understanding of the Christian faith. They inveighed "Against Swearying and Perjurie," "Against Whoredom, and Adultery," and "Against Strife and Contencion," spoke "Of the Declinyng from God," and delivered "An Exhortacion against the Feare of Deathe" while stressing the importance of the "reading of Holy Scripture." Archbishop Cranmer wrote the homily "Of the Salvacion of All Mankynde," which gave the book a distinct Protestant ring: he expounded justification by grace alone through faith, the cardinal Protestant assertion, with striking clarity and uncommon emphasis. The rhetoric of the homilies deserves admiration. For example, the Homily "Of Good Woorkes" questioned the excessive number of holy objects used by Catholics in their devotional lives: "And all thinges which they had were called holy: holy coules, holy girdels, holy pardoned beades, holy shooes, holy rules, and all full of holynesse. And what thyng can be more foolishe, more supersticious or ungodly then that men, women and chyldren should weare a friers coote to deliver them from agues or pestilence, or when they dye, or when they be buried, cause it to be caste upon them in hope therby to be saved."[36] However, the *Homilies* had nothing to say about the Lord's Supper, a lacuna best

---

35. John Foxe, *Acts and Monuments*, 6:106.
36. *Certain Sermons or Homilies (1547) and a Homily against Disobedience and Wilful Rebellion (1570)* (ed. Ronald B. Bond, Toronto: 1987), 110.

explained by the fact that Cranmer was by that time beginning to move from a Lutheran understanding of the real presence of Christ in bread and wine to the Zwinglian (Calvinist) notion of a spiritual presence. To acknowledge this openly would have played into the hands of the conservatives, whose support was both wanted and needed. Bishop Gardiner eventually gave his grudging public support to the book but made a point of focusing on the obedience owed the king in "An Exhortacion to Obedience." Importantly, the parliamentary injunctions, which ordered the use of *Certain Sermons and Homilies*, also stipulated that all clergy should obtain within three months "the New Testament both in Latin and in English, together with the paraphrase upon the same of Erasmus."[37]

Parliament met in November 1547 and dutiful repealed the Six Articles Act and the statutes against heretics and Lollards, and removed all restrictions on the printing and reading of Scripture. Catholics, previously under the threat of the Treason Act, and Protestants, previously under the threat of the acts against heretics, could breathe more easily. Aside from testifying to Somerset's own religious commitments, this parliamentary move was an effort to still the waves of religious excitement. The easing of legal restrictions unleashed a torrent of Protestant propaganda, surely an indication that people were eager to discuss the ideas that had perturbed and divided the Continent for three decades. Richard Smith, an Oxford don, reflected on the situation with uncommon (for the English) overstatement: "The nation was everywhere afflicted with so great miseries, shaken with so many differences of sects, tossed with so many waves of diverse opinions, as scarcely any country ever before was."[38]

A royal visitation, which like the late medieval episcopal visitations was charged to assess the spiritual and fiscal condition of individual parishes, was begun in the summer of 1547. Bishop Gardiner protested, as did his London colleague Bonner, with the result that both wound up in jail. This visitation proved the most comprehensive attack on traditional religion yet, and it was accompanied by a series of iconoclasms that destroyed stained glasses in churches and other objects of devotion. In 1548 ashes on Ash Wednesday and candles at Candelmas were prohibited, while clerical marriage was officially approved. At the same time, Somerset and Cranmer restricted the number of those who were authorized to preach, an obvious albeit awkward effort to control what was preached from the pulpit. The *Book of Homilies* was deemed to be the more reliable (and controllable) medium of instructing the faithful from the pulpit. In September 1548 preaching was prohibited completely—an intriguing manifestation of the commitment of the gospellers for the preaching of the Word.

As on the Continent, the Mass turned out to be a major point of controversy. In particular, the withholding of the cup from the laity was a visible symbol of biblical error. The Act against Revilers and for Receiving in Both Kinds introduced Communion under both bread and wine. Subsequently, Parliament appointed a committee, composed of Cranmer and other "bishops and learned men," to draft a new liturgy for the English church, since the Mass was no longer acceptable. As matters turned out, Cranmer was the driving force on this committee. In January 1549 Parliament

---

37. Gee and Hardy, *Documents*, 417–18.
38. J. Strype, *Ecclesiastical Memorials Relating Chiefly to Religion* (Oxford: 1822), 265.

endorsed the committee's draft report and passed the First Edwardian Act of Uniformity, which ordered the introduction of the draft, now labeled *The Booke of the Common Prayer and Administration of the Sacraments* as the legal form of worship in England. A further act, one year later, ordered the destruction of all old service books.

The Book of Common Prayer is surely, next to the venerable King James translation of the Bible, the most famous piece of writing in the English tongue. While its theology is not always unambiguous, the polish of its prose has rarely been matched. In the Book of Common Prayer, over centuries and oceans, the adage *lex orandi, lex credendi* (the law of prayer is the law of belief) found expression. The beautiful cadences of its prayers have expressed the piety of Anglican Christianity and indeed of English-speaking Protestantism. Since the words of the Book of Common Prayer were spoken in the English vernacular, the common people worshiping could understand and speak them. As had happened on the Continent, the mystery of the ancient office, spoken in Latin by the priest, was replaced by the translucency of the vernacular.

The sources of the Book of Common Prayer were many and heterogeneous: the Sarum Breviary, widely used in England and based on the Salisbury liturgy; the divine office of Francisco de Quiñones, the great liturgist of the early sixteenth century; and several Protestant German church orders. But the whole was here greater than its parts. Cranmer succeeded in fusing his sources into a creative whole. While the medieval liturgical tradition provided the basic outline for public worship, everything resembling Catholic ritual was omitted—exorcism in baptism, the use of incense and holy water in burial, the consecration of oil for the anointing of the sick. A few traditional practices remained, such as the prayers for the dead and extreme unction. The most dramatic change occurred in Communion, where the prayer of consecration was followed by general confession, offered by one of the communicants. But all references to the sacrifice of the Mass were omitted. The promulgation of the Prayer Book had been preceded by a debate on the Lord's Supper, attended by bishops and important laity, that revealed expected disagreements on the topic but did not keep Parliament from approving the book.

Promulgation of the Act of Uniformity precipitated another uprising, the causes of which—like those of the Pilgrimage of Grace—reached back into the early part of the century. Not all was well in English society. Prices had risen drastically in the course of the century; according to some observers they tripled in the first half of the century. Population had increased much faster than had productivity. One particular problem was the so-called enclosures, the effort on the part of landlords to deprive tenants of their land and convert it into sheep pasture (English wool was a highly sought commodity in Europe), thereby jeopardizing the peasants' livelihood.

Social reformers, the "Commonwealth Men," appeared on the scene and offered their remedies for the alleviation of the increasing social ills. Though in fact the sheep enclosures were quite insignificant, except in the Midlands, the noise made by the pamphleteers drowned out the economic realities. People took the enclosures to be a grave problem, and their perceptions made all the difference. Hugh Latimer, John Hales, and Thomas Smith represented the sentiment, eloquently embodied in the *Discourse of the Commonweal of This Realm of England,* written in 1549 by William Stafford but not published until 1581 under the stupendous title *A Compendious or*

Briefe Examination of Certayne Ordinary Complaints. The call was for a greater concern for the welfare of the "common man."

The uprising occurred in the summer of 1549, in Devon and Cornwall to the west and in Norfolk to the east. The demands of the rebels, formulated in fifteen articles, revealed a curious mixture of economic and religious issues. The Mass was to be reinstituted, and the Six Articles restored, as was the use of Latin in Scripture and the divine service. Cornishmen, it was argued, could not understand English any better than Latin.

Within weeks of the suppression of the rebellion, Somerset was arrested, blamed for the uprising, and sent to the Tower by order of the Council of Regency. This ended the first phase of Edwardian rule, and John Dudley, Earl of Warwick, the main instigator of Somerset's fall, became the dominating figure. Dudley was an opportunist, prepared to engage in whatever intrigue seemed advantageous to him. Henry VIII had beheaded his father for conspiracy: the son may have been congenitally predisposed to walk the path of intrigue and scheming. In all likelihood Dudley was without religious conviction, though before his death on the scaffold he confessed that he had always been a Catholic, a surprising statement from the lips of a man who took England on a distinctly Protestant course. He had profited from the religious change, and its revocation would have had disadvantageous consequences for him. Moreover, he was an individual greedy for power, and he may have sensed that only the consolidation of Protestantism would thwart Mary's accession to the throne—a most serious threat to his power.

Under Dudley's influence religious policy in England became pronouncedly Protestant. Dudley favored the two ardent Protestants John Hooper and John Knox, together with Cranmer, whose ever evolving theology took him from a moderate to a pointed Protestant view. With the assistance of Nicholas Ridley and Martin Bucer, Cranmer undertook a revision of the Book of Common Prayer. In March 1552 Parliament passed the Second Act of Uniformity, which called for the introduction of the revised prayer book. The new edition had commendable words for the old, calling it "agreeable to the Word of God and the primitive Church," but this was an instance where the left hand (the preface) claimed not to know what the right (the book) was doing, for the changes, particularly in the section on Holy Communion, were drastic. The words "Mass" and "altar" were discarded. There was no specific consecration of the elements, and the ministers were to take the unconsumed wine and bread home for domestic use after the service.[39] In the first prayer book the minister, in distributing the elements, was to tell the communicants, "The body of our Lord Jesus Christ which was given for thee preserve thy body and soul into everlasting life." In the second prayer book this was changed to the exhortation: "Take and eat this in remembrance that Christ died for thee and feed on him in thy heart by faith with thanksgiving." The emphasis was now on "remembrance," the theology that of Zwingli and Calvin.

The new prayer book had already been approved and was at the printers when the Scottish reformer John Knox appeared on the scene and complicated matters. Knox

---

39. C. Buchanan, "What Did Cranmer Think He Was Doing?" *Grove Liturgical Studies* 7 (1976): 22.

was unable to accept the prayer book as biblical: to kneel when receiving the sacrament, as the book enjoined, was for him idolatry. In a sermon he aroused the conscience of the young king in this matter. Since the book was in press, the Solomonic solution was to add an appendix, the "Black Rubric" (with the prayer book already in press it was too late to print the insertion in red, as all the other such instructions in the book had been). It explained that kneeling did not mean adoration but gratitude. Happily, the Black Rubric safeguarded tender consciences as well as theological integrity.

The new prayer book did not lend itself to the same breadth of interpretation as the first, but an atmosphere of tolerance in England remained. Knox's intervention, as well as the row involving Bishop Hooper's unwillingness to be consecrated in traditional vestments, suggest that there were printed differences among the reformers. Those who wanted a "reformed" church then and there combated others who, like Cranmer, thought it possible to combine Catholic structures with evangelical reform. The second Act of Uniformity was stricter than the first, but still sufficiently vague to let many matters stand where they had been three years earlier. Church attendance was enjoined upon the people, since many "following their own sensuality, and living either without knowledge or due fear of God, do willfully and damnably" refuse to attend divine worship. That, however, was the extent of religious regimentation.

After six years of Edwardian rule, Protestantism had come to be firmly established in England. Some of this had been accomplished by foreign divines come from the Continent, notably Bucer, but many native reformers spread the Protestant tidings where they counted most—among the people. From 1548 on, a flood of Protestant writings rolled over the English countryside. Some writers, such as Peter Moone or John Ramsey, were obscure and hardly brilliant. Others, for example, Hugh Latimer and Richard Cox, were respectable as well as profound. Their theological tracts and devotional works, such as Latimer's famous *Sermons on the Plough*, disseminated the Protestant faith in the land.

Then on July 6, 1553, barely six years after he had succeeded his father to the throne, King Edward VI, the "godly and virtuous imp," died. For four days his demise was kept secret while Dudley desperately plotted to influence the course of events. Next in the line of succession stood Edward's half sister Mary, but her accession spelled disaster for the ambitious Dudley. His solution was to remove both Mary and her half sister, Elizabeth, from succession (since both could be viewed as bastard children of Henry VIII). The children of Frances Brandon, a niece of Henry VIII, were declared to be the rightful successors to Edward. This placed Jane Grey next in line. Edward had agreed to this scheme, and four days after his death Jane was proclaimed queen. But the very next day Mary asserted her rights to the crown, and within another two days Dudley's scheme, in which Cranmer had been an eager participant, had tumbled. Dudley had failed to arrest Mary, who was welcomed by the people with spontaneous and enthusiastic support, while the supporters of Jane Grey had fumbled step after step. The Protestant divines at Cambridge had offered fervent prayers for Dudley's success, and even Cranmer was feverishly supportive and active in the scheme, but no intervention came forth—unless, that is, Mary's success was to be so considered.

THE MARIAN REACTION

What Henry VIII had striven with such determination to avoid did come to pass in July 1553, when Mary, daughter of Catherine of Aragon, succeeded to the English throne. It was as if that unfailingly self-confident king had merely been teased with the prospect of a lengthy rule of his son Edward. Mary was thirty-seven years of age when she received the crown, and those years had left their imprint upon her. Her father had once boasted, "This girl never cries," a telling characterization of her temperament. Though by nature gentle and simple, Mary also possessed a harshness of spirit that may have grown out of life experience. She had been a teenager when her parents' marriage was declared by Parliament to be invalid and she had been made to accept the taint of being a bastard. Rejected by her father, mistreated by her half brother Edward and his council, hers had been an unhappy life, which found comfort in her religion. Understandably, it was the Catholic religion of her mother, and Mary was forced to witness how that faith was repudiated in the land. It would have taken a work of supererogation for her to overcome such years of rejection and affront with grace and gentleness; Mary clearly saw no reason to rise to the occasion.

Consigned to the shadows, Mary had been aloof from the English scene for more than two decades. As a result, she failed to understand that by mid-century the religious changes wrought by her father and half brother had become accepted by the English people and that a sizable number of important individuals had benefited from the religious changes. She was mistaken when she took the wave of popular enthusiasm that greeted her succession to the throne as an endorsement of her Catholic faith.

Mary ascended the throne at a time when, after two decades of incessant religious turbulence and never-ending change, the English people yearned for tranquility. Had Mary understood this and ruled accordingly, she would have been seen as a good ruler. But history has given her the ugly name "Bloody Mary," an ironic term, for Mary possessed deep personal piety and integrity and professed to noble ideals, an uncommon accumulation of qualities for any ruler. Epitaphs are written, however, by posterity, and in Mary's case posterity appeared on the scene all too quickly. One may well conjecture that if Mary had lived as long as her half sister, Elizabeth, English religious and political history would have taken a different turn. After all, in the sixteenth century rulers succeeded, given time, in determining the religious loyalties of the people. Mary undoubtedly could have done the same. This is not to underestimate the strength of Protestantism, but to point to a fundamental characteristic of the Reformation: only by obtaining or influencing political power did Protestantism attain formal success. In the end, however, the trouble with Mary's rule was not so much her religious policy as its brevity. Five short years could not assure the meaningful reestablishment of a lasting Catholicism in England.

Still, Mary committed more than her share of blunders. She failed to translate her noble personal qualities into policies congenial to the English people. She approached policy issues like a surgeon performing an operation, determined to bring about improvement. The English people had forsaken the Catholic faith, and she was going to rectify this evil. This she saw as her foremost task, even though her initial statements about religion showed a magnanimity uncommon in the sixteenth century. She was going to leave all free to follow whatever religion they chose, she said. One suspects that she was convinced that the English people would easily return to the Catholic fold, and the few who would not could be ignored. She mistook the English temper, however, and as soon as she recognized this, her policy changed. The Protestant bishops who had been appointed during the rule of her father and half brother were deprived of their sees; some were arrested. The adamant Protestants—about eight hundred in all, many of them capable and important figures—emigrated to the Continent. Upon their return to England in the 1560s, they were known as the "Marian exiles," major players in the establishing of the Church of England.

The queen's helpmate in carrying out reconciliation with Rome was Reginald Pole. An Englishman of royal blood—he was a cousin of Henry VIII, who actually paid for his schooling at Oxford and Padua—Pole vigorously opposed the king's quest for the marital annulment and claim to supremacy. In 1536 Pole received the cardinal purple and was instructed to go to England, since "the king's great matter" was reaching its decisive phase. Pole got as far as the Low Countries when he learned that he had been convicted of treason in England and that a spiteful king took terrible revenge on his family. After he had almost been elected pope in 1549, Pole came to England in November 1554 upon Mary's succession. Mary's marital negotiations with Philip of Spain caused the delay in his return. He became the queen's trusted confidante and, in 1556, Archbishop of Canterbury, the last Roman Catholic to hold that office.

Parliament met in October 1553 and dutifully passed several bills of repeal pertaining to religion and worship. The act that had annulled Henry's marriage with Catherine was rescinded, as were the definitions of heresy promulgated under Edward. According to the latest version of the law of the land, Mary was again the legitimate offspring of a proper marriage. The queen's intention clearly was to take the country back to where it had been in 1529, when Henry VIII's pursuit of his "great matter" had first begun to sever the cord between England and Rome. There was considerable resistance in Parliament to the proposed repeals. One-quarter to one-third of the members dissented, telling evidence of the extent of Protestant sentiment among its members. On the delicate matter of the restoration of papal supremacy Parliament balked outright, and there were also strong indications that the restitution of monastic property would run into formidable opposition. For some, the two were causally related.

Mary carried the title of "Supreme Head of the Church," even though her official documents bear the nondescript "etc." in its stead. The former lands of the church continued to be in secular hands, and the pope's sentence against England stood. Upon Mary's succession, Pope Julius III had appointed Reginald Pole legate to England to bring about reconciliation. When Pole arrived in England, he proved to be a tough customer, for he was adamantly rigid on the trickiest issue, the restitution of the church lands. But the matter had turned complex: some of the lands had changed hands, and the question of who should make the restitution defied easy answer.

This problem was the main stumbling block in the formal return of England to the religion of the forebears. Once it was clear that the formal restitution of Catholicism did not mean the return of these lands to the Church, no significant resistance remained in Parliament. As soon as the new owners of church lands realized that their property would remain untouched, they became willing to accept the latest ecclesiastical change in the land. Having gone through no fewer than three such changes in the official religion (including the two undertaken under Edward, from the first to the second Prayer Book), the English people had tired of the religious controversy and theological squabble and were willing to accommodate themselves to any policy. The most adamant Protestant partisans were on the Continent, a fact that had bearing on the ease with which Mary's ecclesiastical changes were accepted in England; the men of ardent Protestant conviction had left the country.

The formal restoration of the Catholic religion did not mean a persuasive popular commitment to Catholicism. The former came easily enough; the latter proved nearly impossible. Parliament considered reconciliation with Rome toward the end of November 1554, and on the last day of that month came the moment for which Mary had been waiting for more than twenty years. Pole addressed Parliament, gathered at Whitehall, and after having praised the queen as "a virgin, helpless, naked, and unarmed," he expressed with warmth and forgiveness—"touching all matters that be past, they shall be as things cast into the sea of forgetfulness"—the Roman Church's wish for the English church to be reunited.[40] The lords of the realm fell to their knees and, speaking for the English people, declared themselves "very sorry and repentant of the schism and disobedience committed in this realm." Pole then pronounced the official pardon of the church.

England was Catholic again. Parliament promptly passed several bills to provide the legal basis for the religious restoration, though not without some pointed opposition in the House of Commons. It revived the ancient law against heresy, and later, in January 1555, it repealed all of Henry VIII's ecclesiastical legislation, from the Statute of Restraint of Appeals to the Supremacy Act, explicitly providing, however, for the protection of the new holders of church lands. Even though Mary did not at all concede that Parliament had a legitimate voice in ecclesiastical affairs, Parliament had to be involved—after all, the separation from Rome had occurred through legal acts of Parliament, and so new acts of Parliament had to formalize the separation's repeal.

Soon thereafter the persecution of the Protestants began and did not end until four years later, when Mary's reign came to an end. The instigator was the queen herself, who may have thought she was doing penance for the heresy of her father and half brother. She showed herself thereby a true child of the age, for in the sixteenth century religious diversity was a pill too bitter to swallow. Diversity entailed the disruption of order, which was feared as much as the possibility that the dissenters might infect others with their heretical venom. Since in the sixteenth century criminal law was severe and capital punishment all too common, the Marian persecutions were neither unique nor particularly ruthless. The number of victims was fewer than four hundred. There were several prominent figures—Thomas Cranmer, Hugh Latimer, Nicholas Ridley—but in the main the victims of the Marian persecutions were simple folk, artisans, and their wives.

Later, the pen of John Foxe added a spectacular glow to the persecution; his book describing it would not have been so successful if it had not been touching sensitivities. Born in 1516, educated at Oxford (where he was said to have shown "good incli-

---

40. C. Erickson, *Bloody Mary* (New York: 1978), 390.

nation and towardness to learning"), and elected fellow of Magdalen College, Foxe embraced Reformation ideas early on, was accused of heretical leanings, and was expelled from Oxford.

Upon the succession of Queen Mary, Foxe became one of the Marian exiles who left England for the Protestant Continent. Returning to England in 1559, Foxe completed work on a book which he had begun even before his continental exile—a Latin folio of some 750 pages that told the story of the true church from Wycliffe to Cranmer. His book had the fairly nondescript title *Rerum in Ecclesia Gestarum,* which might be loosely as "What Has Happened in the Church," though the very last phrase of the subtitle was a portentous omen of things to come: "Part One: The story continues especially with the horrendous persecution under recent Queen Mary."[41]

Foxe became single-mindedly focused on, even obsessed with, his project of telling the story of the church as the story of the martyrs of the faith. He translated his Latin tome into English, added voluminous material, and four years later published the fruit of his work. Entitled *Actes and Monuments of These Latter and Perillous Dayes, Touching Matters of the Church,* it promptly became known as the *Book of Martyrs.* Swollen to a seemingly unmanageable compass and comprising almost 2,500 folio pages, it covered the early Christian martyrs, the church in the Middle Ages (with particular emphasis on Wycliffe and his movement), the Protestant Reformation, the history of both Henry VIII and Edward VI, and finally the suffering of the faithful under Mary. The book offered no fewer than four dedications: to Jesus, Queen Mary, the learned reader—and to the "persecutors of God's truth, commonly known as papists."

Foxe's book was a work of passion—rage and fury flowed from his pen, and castigation and condemnation triumphed over historical accuracy and empathy. His deep indignation is never far away, nor are the multitude of invectives for which he undoubtedly holds a record. The criticism of his work—much of it justified—led him to publish a "corrected" edition in 1570, and within the next hundred years there were no fewer than seven further printings. The influence of Foxe's book was not only a matter of style and content. The book was also officially enjoined: in 1571 convocation ordered that copies of the book be kept in all cathedrals.

Foxe was far away on the Continent when the Marian turmoil was taking place, but he went about collecting his material with indefatigable diligence. Published first in Latin at Basel in 1559, his story appeared in an expanded English version four years later. The title of Foxe's work set the tone for its content, for it was meant to be not a cool and neutral report of fact, but a passionate defense of a great cause: *Actes and Monuments of These Latter and Perillous Dayes, Touching Matters of the Church, Wherein Are Comprehended and Described the Great Persecutions and Horrible Troubles That Have Bene Wrought and Practised by the Romishe Prelates.* In the preface came the inevitable apology to the reader who might feel—together with the author—that in light of the "infinite multitude" of books another publication might be "superfluous and needeles." Foxe's implication was, of course, that it was not superfluous, for he meant not to be a historian but to score a point. He was little concerned, for example, about the

---

41. *Rerum Ecclesia Gestarum* (Basel: 1559), title page, "In primis de horrenda, sub Maria nuper Regina persecutione narratio continetur."

details of "the king's great matter," but lengthily narrated how it led to the spread of the gospel. Like that of other sixteenth-century martyrologists, Foxe's credibility has been questioned, though research has vindicated his generally judicious handling of the facts.

For several hundred years the *Book of Martyrs* was a second Bible for the English people, frequently chained alongside the Great Bible in English parish churches. Such fame was hardly only theological. The content made it fascinating both for those who sought spiritual edification and for those who thrilled to read about martyrs writing their defiance in their own blood on the walls of their dungeons, or about persecutors with "monstrous making and misshapen fashion of feet and toes."

The Marian persecution hardly endeared the Catholic faith to the English people, who were shocked by the ruthless suppression of a religious sentiment on the part of those who themselves had shared it a few years earlier. The country was perturbed by the executions and burnings, and there was public sympathy for the victims; the most illustrious of these was Cranmer, who on Mary's succession had been deposed as archbishop of Canterbury and indicted for his complicity in attempting to get Jane Grey on the English throne. Brought to trial, he first confessed to his Protestant convictions boldly but soon began to waver. A brief recantation acknowledging the pope to be the head of the Church of England "so far as the laws of God and the laws and customs of this realm will permit" marked the beginning, and five additional and increasingly far-reaching recantations followed. In the last one he confessed that he had misused his office and authority, had exceeded Saul in malice and wickedness, was a blasphemer, a persecutor, and contumelious.

Whether Cranmer was sincere in his confession or grasped at recantation in hopes of saving his life will never be known. He had been catapulted to public prominence much against his wishes. At his trial he recalled that upon receiving word in Germany of his nomination to the archbishopric of Canterbury he delayed his return to England for weeks, hoping the king would forget about him. Henry did not, and Cranmer became archbishop and rose to be the king's trusted ecclesiastical advisor. Cranmer was a scrupulous scholar, ever willing to follow new insights. He was persuaded that by divine ordination a sovereign exercised authority in the external affairs of the church and that the people were called upon to render obedience. When Mary ascended the throne and demanded his obedience, he found himself on the horns of a dilemma, created by his temperament and theological perspective—his willingness to change and to be submissive.

March 25, 1556, was a rainy day, and the gray clouds that hurled rain onto houses and roads in Oxford forced the sermonic exhortation, a standard element of the execution of heretics, into St. Mary's Church. The news of Cranmer's recantation must have made the rounds, and so those present in the church waited to hear the condemned heretic revoke his involvement in the Reformation from his own lips. But after Cranmer had risen from a prayer that he himself had written and began to speak, his words were unexpected. Every man hoped to give an exhortation at the time of his death, he said, and that was what he, too, wanted to do: "I come to the great thing that troubleth my conscience more than any other thing that I ever said or did in my life, the setting abroad of writings contrary to the truth." He renounced everything that he had written since his degradation: "And forasmuch as my hand offended in writing contrary to my heart, therefore my hand shall first be punished. For if I may come to the fire, it shall be first burned."[42] Amid the ensuing uproar Cranmer was silenced and hurried off to the stake. When the fire had started, he stretched out his right hand, according to a bystander's report, "and thrust it into the flames, and held it there a good space."

It matters little that Cranmer was Protestant and his judges Catholic. If the ecclesiastical labels had been reversed—as they were at other places and other times during that eventful century—the story would raise the same provocative questions. The lesson of the religious persecutions of the sixteenth century might well be that people then killed for religious reasons as they today kill for political ideals, but also that, in the end, an individual's integrity is a treasure beyond price. Matthew Parker, archbishop of Canterbury under Queen Elizabeth, offered another commentary. In the margin of *Bishop Cranmer's Recantacyons*, the account of his trial and martyrdom, Parker wrote two words: *homines sumus*—we are all human beings. Cranmer, a man of high achievements and distressing shortcomings, serves thus as a reminder that history is made not only by heroes but by human beings, simple and complicated, courageous and weak. Ever since that rainy day in 1556, men and women have thought about Cranmer, and indeed there is much to ponder about a man who seems to have changed theological opinion and ecclesiastical sentiment like a weathervane in a storm.

England was holding its breath. The north country was conservative and thus more congenial to the Catholic religion (most of the victims of the persecution came from the southeast), but even there minor annoyances—about married clergy or monastic lands—cropped up with almost predictable regularity. The English people went about their daily chores showing little enthusiasm for the old religion. There were few zealous Catholics in the land, no eloquent Catholic pamphleteers, no gifted Catholic preachers. The Catholic faith was imposed from the top.

In November 1558, after long delays and great reluctance, Mary consented to name Elizabeth as her successor. An air of resignation overcame her, and her mind seemed somewhere else. A few days before her death she remarked, "what good dreams she had, seeing many little children like angels play before her, singing pleasing notes." In the early morning hours of November 17, 1558, she died and forty-three years of an unhappy life came to an end. Her chief advisor, Cardinal Pole, who, intriguingly enough, had been charged with heresy in Rome because of his teaching concerning justification, also passed away that day, as if one star had governed both their destinies, or perhaps as if the one was not to face the future without the other.

A little more than five years had passed since Mary had come to London. The cheers that had greeted her then had faded, and the joyful brightness of that August morning had given way to the dreary cold of November. The English people shed few tears to grace her departure. She had ventured to accomplish great things *ad majorem Dei gloriam*, and outwardly it seemed that she had accomplished them. Her religious zeal had proved a poor guide in the affairs of state; she had pushed too hard too fast. Perhaps this was because of her dogmatic disposition, perhaps because of her awareness that she was living on borrowed time. Failure in her religious policy was the end,

---

42. Thomas Cranmer, *Miscellaneous Writings and Letters* (Cambridge: 1646), 564–65.

for even though the Catholic faith had been formally restored in England, the hearts of the people had not been won.

In history the seal of success is often the permanence of accomplishment, even as the seal of failure is immediate rejection. Mary Tudor's failure was that her half sister, Elizabeth, was to repudiate what she stood for. Were it not for the sad fact that she committed the blunder of making martyrs, her name would be written, as one must reluctantly conclude, as on water.

THE ELIZABETHAN SETTLEMENT

Mary was succeeded by another woman: her half sister, Elizabeth, twenty-five years of age, tall, full of poise, with reddish hair, not particularly attractive, though with striking eyes. Rather like Mary, Elizabeth too had had a trying youth. At her birth her father could hardly hide his disappointment that his wife had not borne a son. Soon thereafter her mother had lost the king's favor, and Elizabeth—as did Mary—experienced the consequences of being considered a bastard. Mary had despaired over her experience; Elizabeth learned the art of diplomacy, a bitter process that enabled her to rule England superbly for some forty-five years. When she died England was more powerful for her reign. "I pray God save her Grace, long to reign over us, to the glory of God," a contemporary wrote when she came to the throne.[43] And so she did. The English people welcomed her warmly, pleased to be rid of the Spanish influence that had led to higher taxes at home and to military defeat abroad, notably at Calais, which after many years as an English outpost on the Continent was lost to France.

The pressing problem facing the new queen was what to do about religion. When Edwin Sandys wrote to Heinrich Bullinger in Zurich upon Pole's death, "We have nothing to fear . . . for dead men do not bite," he expressed the sentiment of the gospellers, who felt the time ripe for a change. Whatever her religious conviction in 1558, Elizabeth acted as a good Protestant, though perhaps mainly because of circumstances. As Anne Boleyn's daughter, she was, of course, illegitimate in the eyes of the Catholic Church, and at the news of her succession Pope Paul IV plainly if undiplomatically expressed himself along such lines. Understandably, she would hardly embrace the religion that so labeled her. And what began as political expedience may well have settled as personal habit, though the queen never became a Protestant zealot. Scholars have disagreed about her religiosity, some seeing her as a bulwark of the Protestant faith, others suggesting that she was what the French called a *politique*, an Englishwoman first and a religious partisan second. The evidence is inconclusive. During Mary's reign, Elizabeth had requested Catholic books to read and Catholic theologians to converse with her, attended Mass, and acted like a loyal Catholic. She even seemed to indicate that she accepted Mary's religious settlement.

Everything changed when she became queen. William Cecil, whom she named her secretary of state, was known for his Protestant sympathies, and at the Christmas Mass in 1558 she prohibited Bishop Oglethorpe of Carlisle from elevating the host and the

43. *Journals of the House of Commons* (London: 1803), 52.

wine, walking out when Oglethorpe refused her instruction. She also walked out of her own Coronation Mass on January 25, 1559, when the bishops welcomed her on her arrival at Westminster and took the oath of allegiance, but refused (with the exception of Oglethorpe) to participate in her coronation and the Mass. Later, Elizabeth kissed the Bible in public, but she was a good actress and may well have done this for the gallery. She spoke favorably of the Augsburg Confession, and a charmingly simple verse, perhaps apocryphal, was said to express her view of the Lord's Supper:

> 'Twas God the word that spake it,
> He took the Bread and brake it;
> And what the word did make it,
> That I believe and take it.[44]

If Elizabeth's personal circumstances, her background and religious convictions, were one factor in disposing her to venture yet another alteration of the official ecclesiastical state of affairs, the temper of the English people undoubtedly was another. The fiber of Catholicism in England had been damaged. For almost a generation England had not really known the Catholic faith (excepting, of course, the five years of Marian rule), and dynamic Catholic leadership was absent. No enthusiastic and youthful partisans had come to the fore during the five years of Catholicism restored.

The impossibility of Catholicism as the official religion of the realm left open the question of the form of Protestantism to be introduced. Elizabeth, in other words, had a number of options. Clearly, she intended to reverse the religious policy of her half sister, but this need not have meant more than the return to the ancient religion of her father. To do more was hazardous, and she must have known it. Elizabeth told the Spanish ambassador that she wanted to restore religion to the state in which her father had left it. The bishops of the English church were Catholic, and the international situation, in light of the conflict with France, was precarious. The ardent English Protestants were abroad, and even though the English people were weary of the religious persecution under Mary, formal Catholicism continued strong.

The settlement Elizabeth chose to have Parliament promulgate was neither the only nor the self-evident one. She wanted a settlement at once limited and conservative that would allow further changes at a later date. The meager evidence suggests that the House of Commons wanted the comprehensive reestablishment of Protestantism. The outcome was a compromise in which neither side got all it wanted, but each was granted more than the other side originally was willing to concede.

Elizabeth's first Parliament met the end of January 1559. A bill was introduced to "restore the supremacy of the Church of England, etc., to the Crown." The evidence concerning this bill and what happened in Parliament is enigmatic. Obviously royal supremacy was to be reintroduced, but Elizabeth seemingly was content to let the details of a religious settlement rest until a later time. Such a circumspect policy would allow her to settle her political problems before the religious one.

When the Protestant House of Commons received this bill it added enough Protestant riders to turn it into a comprehensive instrument for religious change. Then the

---

44. S. Clarke, *The Marrow of Ecclesiastical History* (London: 1675), 2:94.

conservative House of Lords changed the bill back into its original form. The Commons diplomatically passed the bill; simultaneously, however, they approved another bill reestablishing Protestant worship. The Commons had made their sentiment plain. They wanted more than supremacy and the possibility of additional changes in the future: they wanted the introduction of Protestantism right then and there.

At this point the Convocation of Canterbury decided to flex its muscle, and by the end of February it had drawn up five articles "for the disburdening of their consciences and a profession of their faith," the first four of which upheld traditional Catholic teachings of the Mass and papal supremacy. The fifth insisted that spiritual authority "hath hitherto ever belonged, and of right ought to belong, only to pastors of the church . . . and not to laymen." This was a not-so-gentle slap in the face to both the new queen and her father and might well have triggered a confrontation between the convocation and Parliament. But nothing happened; Elizabeth and Nicholas Bacon, lord chancellor, decided simply to ignore the clerics and have Parliament enact the desired ecclesiastical settlement.

On Wednesday of Holy Week, March 22, 1559, both houses of Parliament passed the original bill, which needed the queen's assent to become law. Elizabeth seems to have had every intention of assenting but then changed her mind. Parliament, instead of being dissolved, was adjourned until after Easter. The queen had been informed of the peace concluded at Cateau-Cambrésis between France, Spain, and England. The international situation had cleared, and Elizabeth could face the domestic issues without regard to possible complications abroad.

Elizabeth may also have come to realize that there was no likelihood that English Catholics would ever agree to any change from the status quo, no matter how conservative. The fierce declaration of Convocation in its five articles, while an extraordinary departure from thirty years of ecclesiastical silence and all-too-willing concurrence with varying royal decrees concerning religion, made this quite evident. The bishops of the church would not fall in line. The queen was caught in a dilemma: the Catholic hierarchy was intransigent, unwilling to accept the supremacy, while the Protestants in Commons were adamantly clamoring for change. In the end Elizabeth arguably found it the lesser evil to move in the Protestant direction.

Upon reconvening, Parliament considered two new bills, one dealing with supremacy, the other with uniformity. The bishops in the House of Lords put up formidable resistance, the bishop of Chester asserting that the faith must depend on more than the whims of Parliament, but eventually both houses of Parliament approved both measures; in the House of Lords it passed by the rather narrow margin of twenty-one to eighteen. All the ecclesiastical members of the the the House of Lords voted against both bills. In substance, the Act of Supremacy undid Mary's repeal of Henry VIII's ecclesiastical legislation: the Act of Annates, the Statute of Appeals, the Consecration of Bishops, and the Submission of the Clergy. In addition, Queen Mary's submission to Rome was rescinded.

For the second time within thirty years England had cut its ties with Rome, and the church in England was once again the Church of England. The ecclesiastical clock was set back to 1547, with a few changes. The queen was not "Supreme Head on Earth under Christ of the Church of England," but the "Supreme Governor, as well in all spiritual causes, as in temporal." One may argue whether this was merely semantic subtlety—whether the change of words amounted to a difference without a distinction—but that is too simplistic a view. The problem was, of course, that that age was not willing to concede that a woman might be the "head" of the church, though, of course, Elizabeth was indeed the head of the body politic. Importantly, however, Elizabeth was not the self-confident theologian her father had seen himself to be. She was a partner of Parliament, and her "governorship" was indirect at best. The new title lacked the theological significance of the old, and, as it turned out, both the theory and the practice of Elizabeth's ecclesiastical rule were different.

The Act of Supremacy also redefined heresy, or rather, it repealed, to put it more exactly, the act of Mary's Parliament that had revived the old heresy laws. Scripture, the decrees of the first ecumenical councils, and Parliament, acting with the consent of the convocation, were declared to be the bases on which heresy was to be judged.

The new Act of Uniformity reintroduced the second Edwardian Act of Uniformity that had accompanied the prayer book of 1552. A few changes were made in the new edition. In the litany the priest's petition, "From the tyranny of the Bishop of Rome and all his detestable enormities, Good Lord, deliver us," was omitted, and the "Black Rubric" also disappeared. The new edition added a rubric to Morning Prayer prescribing the use of vestments, and two years later the prayer book was amended by the addition of a number of saints' days and festivals.

The most significant change of the new prayer book concerned the Lord's Supper and consisted in the juxtaposition of the words of distribution of the two earlier 1549 and 1552 editions. The minister now informed the faithful that "the bodie of our lord Jesus Christ, which was geven for thee preserve thy body and soule into everlastinge life: and take and eate this in remembraunce that Christ died for thee, feede on him in thine heart by faith, with thankesgevynge." Theologically, this meant a juxtaposition of the Lutheran view of the real presence and the Zwinglian view of a spiritual presence of Christ in the Communion elements.

Although the settlement of religion was arguably the result of accident and compromise, not to mention an act of state, it promptly was seen as a wise resolution. In effect, it was a minimalist settlement: it bound the church in England only to two standards—the role of the monarch in ecclesiastical affairs and a common order of worship. Within those two parameters, great latitude prevailed, tempered eventually by the *Thirty-nine Articles* of 1563. Through the centuries the Elizabethan settlement has shown an amazing ability to be many things to many people, admixing Protestant substance with Catholic principle. Indeed, it delivered what some of the early continental reformers had promised: a reform confined to the recent and blatant abuses of the church.

With the statutory settlement of religion out of the way, the theological definition of the Elizabethan church remained an unresolved issue. Of course, sixteenth-century England had a tradition of theological nonchalance: Henry VIII had waited until 1539 before promulgating the Six Articles, and during Edward's rule the Forty-two Articles were not issued until 1553. The Convocation of Canterbury, which, through the removal of all but one of the Marian bishops, had become a body favorable to the religious settlement, addressed the issue in 1563 and produced a revision of Cranmer's

Forty-two Articles. After extended discussion seven of these articles were omitted, the wording of others was changed, and four new articles were added, bringing this theological revision to the Thirty-nine Articles.

The official title of the articles was "Articles of Religion, Agreed Upon by the Archbishops and Bishops of Both Provinces and the Whole Clergy, in the Convocation Held at London in the Year 1562 for the Avoiding of the Diversities of Opinions, and for the Establishing of Consent Touching True Religion." Theologically the articles advocated a moderate Protestantism and may be said to have focused mainly on the basic affirmations of the Christian faith and the major differences with Rome—even though in the nineteenth century John Henry Newman, in his famous Tract 90, sought to give the articles a Catholic interpretation.

The Thirty-nine Articles rejected Anabaptist views on community of goods and the oath, though they omitted the condemnation of the extreme forms of Protestantism in the Forty-two Articles (antinomianism, chiliasm, and universalism). Predestination was defined rather loosely without reference to the touchy question of reprobation. Superogation of merit, transubstantiation, and the sacrifice of the Mass were rejected, while the centrality of Scripture and justification by faith in Christ's merit were affirmed. Clergy were allowed to marry, and both bread and wine were to be distributed to all in the Lord's Supper. Calvinist influence may be seen in the article on baptism, which speaks of the rite as a "sign of regeneration," and in that referring to the Lord's Supper, which states that "the body of Christ is given, taken, and eaten, in the Supper, only after a heavenly and spiritual manner."

The person guiding the English church through this turbulent time was Matthew Parker, the new archbishop of Canterbury. While a student at Corpus Christi College in Cambridge, Parker had become an early enthusiast of the Wittenberg gospel, had been appointed chaplain to Anne Boleyn in 1535 and to the king two years later—a fact that did not prevent his indictment as a heretic yet two years later. During the reign of Edward VI Parker gained further honors, and during the short rule of Mary Tudor he managed to live unobtrusively, devoting his time to scholarly pursuits. William Cecil, later Lord Burghley, Queen Elizabeth's advisor, recommended Parker to the queen as archbishop, but Parker had observed enough of the turbulence attending that office during his lifetime to decline the honor. "I would rather die" was his initial response, and only Cecil's plea of duty and responsibility made him relent.[45] His formal consecration in 1559 did not follow the traditional Catholic rite, which had bearing on the question of whether the historical episcopate was retained in the English church.

Parker's scholarly expertise and practical savvy steered the discussion of the new articles of faith in the direction he considered important and proper: to form a church that came as close as possible, in worship and theology, to the teachings of the early church, a hallmark the Anglican communion has continued to claim for itself. Parliament approved the Articles of Religion in 1571, but Elizabeth declined to give her assent. She soothingly asserted that the articles contained the faith "she doth openly profess" but added that she could not approve them because she disliked their form.

---

45. Cited in G. R. Elton, *Reform and Reformation—England, 1509–1558* (Cambridge, MA: 1977), 300.

Obviously, she had more than stylistic scruples. Her formal approval would have formalized the theological character of the settlement of religion in England, and she was concerned about international repercussions.

Elizabeth's official approval came in 1571. By then the settlement, though severely tested by a determined and highly articulate minority, had begun to shape religion in England. The papal bull of excommunication, hurled against Elizabeth in February 1570, had made clear that no rapprochement with the papacy was possible. For obvious political reasons the papacy had waited to take that final step, hoping that the queen's conservative stance would bring England back into the Catholic fold. When it became obvious that it would not, the cord was cut. The ways of Rome and Canterbury parted, and Elizabeth was free to make the Thirty-nine Articles official. Subscription to the articles was made mandatory for the clergy.

Back in 1562, when it was not completely clear (or obvious) whether the settlement of 1559 would stand the test of time, John Jewel, bishop of Salisbury, had taken it on himself to write a grand apologia for the newly established church, and his *Apologie or Answere in Defence of the Churche of Englande* proved to be the most pointed theological apologetic for the Church of England until Richard Hooker penned his *Laws of Ecclesiastical Polity* at the end of the century. Jewel argued pointedly that the reforms undertaken in English church affairs since the 1530s had successfully established a truly apostolic church. In learned and irenic prose he argued that the English church had returned to the authentic teachings of the early church. "We are come as near as we possibly could, to the church of the apostles and of the old Catholic bishops and fathers, which church we know hath hithertounto been sound and perfect . . . and have directed according to their customs and ordinances not only our doctrine but also the sacraments and the form of common prayer."[46]

This was assuredly confident language; it explains the self-confidence of the Anglican tradition when it was challenged soon after the settlement of religion—and through the centuries.

THE PURITAN DISSENT

On June 19, 1567, the sheriffs of the City of London paid an official visit to the Plumbers' Hall. They found a group of some one hundred men and women, described to them as a wedding party. The sheriffs arrested the leader of the group and threw him into jail. When asked the following day why the group had met, the answer was that they objected to the use of the surplice by the clergy—it was called "idolatrous gear"—and, moreover, that the English church raised the authority of the ruler above that of Scripture. This incident marked the first public manifestation of dissatisfaction with the official settlement of religion.

The Act of Uniformity promulgated by Parliament in 1559 evoked opposition. As a matter of fact, the settlement of religion was promptly attacked from two sides. Only one of the sitting bishops had given his assent to the settlement, indicating that

---

46. J. Jewel, *An Apology for the Church of England* (Ithaca, NY: 1963), 121.

Catholic sentiment remained (at least in some quarters) strong. On the other side, the adamant Protestants were no less unhappy, for the settlement smacked to them of papal religion. The attacks from both Catholics and ardent Protestants provided the backdrop for the delineation of the theological and ecclesiastical identity of the Anglican Church.

Who were the dissenters? Before long, they were called "Precisionists" because they determined to be "precise" in following the mandates of the Bible, but the label that stuck lastingly was "Puritans." It was, like many other terms, a label coined by opponents. There are people, wrote someone in 1567, "who call themselves Puritans or unspotted lambs of the Lord." The dissenters were determined to rid religion in England of all of its "popish" remnants, thereby making it "pure." "The hotter sort of Protestants are called puritans," was the verdict of one contemporary. Others called the Puritans the "reformers of the Reformation," for the Puritans were persuaded that in order to realize the biblical ideal, the Reformation itself (in this instance the Elizabethan settlement) had to be reformed. The Puritan William Fuller pointedly wrote to the queen that "but halflie by your Majesty hath God bene honoured, his Church reformed and established." The desired reforms yet to be undertaken pertained to matters of practical churchmanship and to theological issues, though even the practical matters entailed theological presuppositions. On the face of things, and not for the first time in Christian history, the Puritan controversy seemed to be about embarrassing trifles. When the Puritans sought support from their continental brethren, such as Bullinger, Zwingli's successor in Zurich, they discovered that Bullinger did not think the points of contention serious enough to warrant schism.

Much has been written about the Puritan temperament which may be said to have been a timeless phenomenon in Christian history. Periodically through the centuries, some of the faithful insisted on a "pure" or "purified" church, divested of human additions and unbiblical impurities. That one of the medieval heretical movements used the very name (the "Cathari") is surely telling. William Haller's comment that it is difficult to say who was the first and who may prove to be the last Puritan underscores the universality of the phenomenon.[47]

"Puritanism" as it emerged in the second half of the sixteenth century and "Puritanism" as it characterized the English scene in the seventeenth century differed significantly. The former, to be described on these pages, was devoid of the sectarian propensity (most sixteenth-century Puritans wanted only to reform the established church and did not consider leaving the established church). At issue were issues of biblical interpretation and worship. It was without that kind of sour-faced drabness and dedication to the proposition that anything enjoyable is sinful that the historian of seventeenth-century Puritanism so ubiquitously encounters. In the seventeenth century moral issues dominated the discourse. Nor did sixteenth-century Puritanism have the political involvement it was to have in the seventeenth century.

Many suggestions have been made about Puritan origins—the Lollard heritage, the influence of the vernacular Scriptures, the flourishing of learning, and the continen-

---

47. William Haller, *The Rise of Puritanism; or, The Way to the New Jerusalem as Set Forth in Pulpit and Press from Thomas Cartwright to John Lilburne and John Milton, 1570–1643* (New York: 1938).

tal Reformation, particularly of the Calvinist variety.[48] The best explanation would take all these factors into consideration and conclude that indigenous (and timeless) sentiment was strengthened by continental influence. Nonetheless, the pivotal influence of Calvinism must be noted. The first intellectual leaders were men who had preferred a residence abroad to the hazards of Marian England, who in Geneva, Strassburg, or Frankfurt had encountered a resolute, comprehensive, dynamic religious reform, a far cry from what they had known in their native land. They had also found in Calvin's thought a biblical theology that demanded their intellectual admiration. Both faith and life of the church had been reformed, and the result was, as far as they were concerned, impressive.

The Elizabethan settlement of religion stands at the beginning of Puritanism, for that settlement was the thorn in the flesh of all those who became convinced that it had not introduced biblical religion. Those who later became known as "Puritans" argued that too many vestiges of popery remained in the English church, and they would have none of it. Impatiently they sought to change the settlement. The range of dissatisfaction emerging during the next few years was wide. The dissenters did not like the prayer book of 1549, which was the substantive basis of the settlement. They were further dismayed that the higher clergy lived in pomp and circumstance, that wafers were used in Communion, that the host was elevated, that the service was ritualistic and assigned an inferior place to the sermon, that saints' days were observed, and so forth. In the Convocation of 1563, those who urged reform beyond the Act of Uniformity wanted a reduction in the number of saints' days, the elimination of clerical vestments, the end to kneeling when receiving the Lord's Supper, and an end to emergency baptisms, not to mention the removal of organs from churches. In short, a bundle of demands was brought forward, and at least in part the dissent was a reaction to the lukewarm commitment of those who had approved the Act of Uniformity.

The Puritan debate engrossed England for the better part of a century, attesting to, if nothing else, the intensity with which religious views were held and the measure of religious freedom prevailing in the land. By and large the Puritan dissenters were able to keep their heads on their shoulders and their pamphlets on the printing presses, though neither assignment was particularly easy. In its initial thrust Puritanism was a clerical movement, spearheaded by the clergy exiles who had returned to England upon Elizabeth's succession. Naturally, they found support among the laity, especially the nobility, as suggested by the persistent agitation in the House of Commons for further ecclesiastical change beyond the stipulations of the Act of Uniformity and the establishment of numerous lectureships of Puritan disposition. Still, the preponderance of the clergy as leaders of the opposition and the importance of clerical issues must be noted. Questions about vestments and polity would naturally exercise (or excite) men of the cloth (they had to wear the vestments), though, of course, laypeople saw what was going on at the altar.

The first clash did indeed occur over vestments. The Royal Injunctions of 1559 had stipulated the wearing of "seemly habits, garments, and such square caps" for the

---

48. For a summary of the discussion, see Patrick Collinson, *The Elizabethan Puritan Movement* (London: 1967).

clergy. Those who saw these as unbiblical abominations protested. Vestments were a natural point of controversy, for the daily officiating of the clergy irritated those who abhorred everything reminiscent of Rome. The need for additional change seemed nowhere more urgent than here.

By the end of 1564 the anti-vestment cause had its spokespersons: Thomas Sampson and Laurence Humphrey, both from Oxford. Archbishop Parker, in turn, wrote several articles aimed at achieving conformity among the clergy. These "Advertisements" indicated, among other things, the proper "apparel for persons ecclesiastical"; they prescribed an oath for the clergy, exacting the laudable promise to read one chapter from the Old and New Testaments daily, and demanded conformity to the wearing of proper vestments for the divine service. The latter was the sticking point for the dissenters, who had seen the gospel preached in Strassburg or Geneva by men of God wearing the plain black professorial gown. Thomas Sampson called the required vestments the "dumb remnants of idolatry."[49]

They were unwilling to yield. Worship services were disturbed, and a literary controversy began. A host of pamphlets issued from the printing presses, often distinguished more by zealous devotion than by incisive argumentation. The author of *A Briefe Discourse against the Outwarde Apparell and Ministring Garmentes of the Popishe Church,* for example, thought that the issue lent itself to poetic consideration:

> The Popes attyre, whereof I talke,
> I know to be but vaine:
> Wherefore some men that wittie are,
> to reade mee will disdaine.
> But I woulde wishe that such men shoulde,
> with judgment reade me twise:
> And marke how great an evill it is,
> Gods Preachers to disguise.[50]

The showdown came with surprising resolution and determination. In April 1566 Archbishop Parker observed that there were some people who "do profess openly, that they will neither communicate nor come in the church where either the surplice or the cap is, and so I know it is practiced."[51] In August Bishop Grindal wrote to Swiss colleagues that there was talk among some dissenters of withdrawing from the official church and establishing private worship meetings in place of the official services of the church. Soon there were indications that separatist conventicles were forming at some places. One wonders whether those who gingerly or resolutely concluded that the official church was no longer their spiritual home intended to separate permanently and categorically from the official church. Probably not, though it was inevitable that the dissenters would seek out one another's company. The Puritans harbored the hope that the settlement of 1559 was not the final word but could—and would—be changed and modified.

49. *Zurich Letters Comprising the Correspondence* (Cambridge, 1842), 1:67.
50. As quoted in J. H. Primus, *The Vestments Controversy* (Kampen: 1960), 108.
51. *The Correspondence of Matthew Parker. Comprising Letters Written by and to Him, from A. D. 1535, to his death, A. D. 1575* (Cambridge: 1853), 270.

In 1572 the smoldering fire burst anew into flames. The new issues were church polity and church discipline. In June *An Admonition to the Parliament* appeared anonymously, a fiery and devastating catchall of assorted anti-settlement polemic. Not much of the polemic was new, not all was profound, but everything was advanced with a cocksure conviction that acknowledged no contrary argument. John Field and Thomas Wilcox, two young London clergy—youth was as much a common denominator of Puritan sentiment as was the desire to "purify" the church—had collaborated on this *Admonition*, whose fundamental assertion was clear: "We in England are so far off from having a church rightly reformed, accordying to the prescript of God's word, that as yet we are not come to the outward face of the same." The document demanded that ministers be "called" by the congregation, that all clergy be equal, and the "titles, livings, and offices, by Antichrist devised," such as archbishop, bishop, and dean, be abolished. The church should be governed by a simple ministry of ministers, elders, and deacons.

Discontent thus had received a new focus: the episcopal form of church government. A new leader appeared, Thomas Cartwright, professor of divinity at Cambridge. In the spring of 1570 Cartwright lectured on the Book of Acts and found ecclesiastical practices in England, measured by that biblical standard, sorely wanting. He proposed that the offices of archbishop and bishop be abolished; that deacons and ministers lead the congregation, the former caring for the physical and the latter for the spiritual needs; and that congregations elect their own ministers.

When broadminded and thoughtful Archbishop Matthew Parker died in 1575, Lord Burghley, the queen's trusted advisor and himself of Puritan leanings, recommended the former bishop of London and present archbishop of York, Edmund Grindal, to succeed him. He was truly learned and competent, and internationally known; a committed Puritan, deeply influenced by Bucer, Grindal thought the settlement of 1559 to be open to modification. Though known to be sympathetic to the Puritan cause—Grindal had not supported Parker in the enforcement of clerical vestments—the strategy was to have him win over the moderate Puritans.

Grindal promptly got into difficulties with the queen, particularly when she ordered him in 1576 to suppress the "prophesyings" (rather tepid Bible studies rather than subversive cells) and achieve uniformity in worship. Grindal twice refused his queen's instructions, for he saw them as inappropriate interference in ecclesiastical affairs. When in 1577 Elizabeth asked him to reconsider his position, his response was vehement, if lacking in decorum. In language the queen probably had never heard before—and was not to hear again—he replied: "I am forced, with all humility, and yet plainly, to profess, that I cannot with safe conscience, and without the offence of the majesty of God, give my assent. . . . Bear with me, I beseech you, Madam, if I choose rather to offend your earthly majesty than to offend against the heavenly majesty of God. And although ye are a mighty prince, yet remember that He which dwelleth in Heaven is mightier." If that were not enough, Grindal reminded his sovereign that she would have to answer for actions before the judgment seat of God— words hardly calculated to endear the archbishop to the self-confident queen. Not surprisingly, Grindal was suspended from office and placed under house arrest.

John Whitgift, his successor as archbishop, had earned his spurs with his anti-Admonition tract, *An Answere to a Certen Libel Intituled, An Admonition to the Parliament*.

As far as he was concerned, "God be thanked, religion is wholly reformed, even to the quick, in this church." Once appointed to the archiepiscopal office, he lost no time in stilling the waves of ecclesiastical discontent. He sought to achieve uniformity with a set of articles that required the clergy to affirm that the Book of Common Prayer was consonant with the Bible, obligating them to use it in worship. The Puritan divines refused to subscribe to the articles. Suppression of Puritan sentiment now became more widespread, and suspensions of nonconforming ministers more frequent.

Deep in the hearts of the dissenters was the conviction that they could somehow or other persuade the church to revise the settlement of 1559 and accept a biblical norm for the church. Conventicles of dissenting clergy discussed how this might be achieved. In 1584 a bill in Parliament sought to replace the prayer book with the Genevan liturgy, but the effort failed. Two years later another concerted effort, embodied in the Book of Discipline, ventured a transformation of the polity of the Church of England through the establishment of parish consistories and panels of clergy and elders. Although there was support, it proved to be haphazard. Another two years later a series of pamphlets known as the Marprelate Tracts advocated with unheard-of shrillness a radical change in English religion. The shrieking tone of the tracts—they spoke of "dunghill ministers," "vipers," and "scorpions"—suggests that the dissenters were getting desperate. Toward the end of the century, Archbishop Richard Bancroft inaugurated the most severe crackdown against the dissenters. The clergy conventicles were dissolved, leaders such as Thomas Cartwright were imprisoned, and some—such as the separatist ministers John Greenwood and Henry Barrow—were executed as seditionists. The same year the queen issued an act "to retain the queen's subjects in obedience." To attend meetings of "conventicles" was declared incompatible with the affirmation of the queen's supremacy. Offenders were given a period of grace in which to conform; if they refused, they had to abjure the realm.

By that time, however, a new phenomenon, marginal at first, had become important: separation from the established church. In a way, the notion entailed acknowledgment of defeat—it had been found impossible to reform the church in England. As the years passed and the idea of comprehensive reform proved increasingly illusory, some dissenters were ready to take the step of breaking away from the church altogether. Robert Browne ("dissent incarnate," as he had been called) illustrates the kind of soul-searching and meandering vacillation that characterized those who made the radical break. Twice arrested for nonconformity, he eventually left England and crossed the Channel to the Netherlands with a group of faithful followers. There he published in 1582 his famous pamphlet, *A Treatise of Reformation without Tarrying for Anie, and of the Wickedness of Those Preachers Which Will Not Reforme till the Magistrate Commande or Compell Them.* His point was simple: the Church of England was so corrupt and unbiblical that true believers had no choice but to go their own way, "be they never so few." Browne denounced the ministers of the English church as "dumbe dogges, destroiers and mutherers of soules," indeed, "pope's bastards," and he joined in the denunciation of the polity and the discipline of the Anglican church.

The ecclesiastical climate in England had become severe: In 1593 three adamant Puritans were hanged for sedition. But there is no need to follow the course of the Anglican-Puritan debate beyond this point. Neither the legal provisions just noted nor the gallons of ink spilled in the publication of Puritan and anti-Puritan tracts must mislead into thinking that the controversy touched the marrow of Elizabethan society. Nothing could be further from the truth. Undoubtedly many laypeople were drawn into the debate; its main protagonists, all the same, were the men of the cloth, for the bones of contention were esoteric and of little concern to most people. The debate was a squabble among theologians. Only in the seventeenth century did this change—but by then the controversy had ceased to be merely theological. Ostensibly still religious, it was a political matter and as such dominated the English scene for several fateful decades.

THE CLOSE OF THE REIGN

While the Puritan attack on the official religion in England may well be said to have dominated English affairs in the closing decades of the sixteenth century, there were other developments as well. The Act of Uniformity of 1559 had provided a fine of one shilling (quite an amount in those days) for any absence from church services on Sunday. That was more than most Englishmen earned and may well indicate that unexplained absences from Sunday services had increased, and that religious uniformity, as enjoined by statute, was nothing but a pious wish. Five years later the penalties became even more severe, with the forfeiture of all of the person's goods. Those who refrained from attending church received the label "recusants." While initially meant for all who did not attend church services, eventually the term become the prerogative for nonattending Catholics.

Their story is an important one for Elizabethan England. Catholic sentiment was surviving in the land, despite various and repeated efforts to suppress it. Not surprisingly, the Catholic Church, focused and self-confident as the result of the Council of Trent, undertook measures to strengthen the loyal Catholic remnant in England and indeed to enhance it.

But being Catholic in Elizabethan England meant not only religious dissent; it at once also became part and parcel of the increasingly intense political conflict between England and Spain, which culminated in the defeat of the Spanish Armada in 1588. Queen Mary had married Philip II of Spain in 1554 under circumstances that were the epitome of a dynastic marriage, except that Mary did fall in love with her husband, who was eleven years younger than she and who found it appropriate to complain, upon meeting her, that she lacked eyebrows. After Philip's succession to the rule of Spain and the Netherlands in 1555, his distancing himself from her did not prevent his dragging Mary into the continental conflict. The enthusiasm with which Elizabeth was welcomed by the English people may not have been an endorsement of her anticipated Protestant religious policy; it assuredly was the disavowal of Mary's Spanish alignment.

There are two perspectives on the place of Catholicism in Elizabethan England: that of the extent of Catholic sentiment in the land, and that of the government's policies toward Catholics. With respect to the former, the evidence is ambivalent, though it suggests that staunch Catholics were few in number. They included the hierarchy and many priests; there is a record of some two hundred priests (out of a total of about nine thousand) refusing the Oath of Supremacy when in 1559 a royal commission traversed the land administering it, but those records are evasive. The Northern Rebellion of 1569, which combined social and political concerns with a devoted commitment to the Catholic Church, failed to rouse the English people.

Catholic sentiment and commitment was revived a decade or so later when some of the Catholic exiles on the Continent began to strategize how their native land might be returned to the Catholic fold. William Allen, formerly principal of St. Mary's Hall in Oxford and eventually a cardinal of the Catholic Church, Robert Persons (1546–1610), and Edmund Campion (1540–1581), both also from Oxford, were the key figures who epitomized the intense effort to restore Catholicism in England. In 1568 Allen had established a college in the small town of Douay in northwestern France, some twenty miles south of Lille and not too far from the English Channel. The town had a sizable English Catholic refugee population, and here, under the tutelage of men who had held key posts at Oxford and Cambridge, Catholic missionaries were aggressively trained to return to England, to strengthen those who had remained faithfully Catholic, and to restore those who had renounced their Catholic faith.

During the last three decades of Elizabeth's reign, wave upon wave of Catholic missionaries found their way to England, not only seminary priests from Douay but also, increasingly, Jesuits. While the English clergy with Catholic sympathies were content to conform externally to the religion of the prayer book and to celebrate Mass in secrecy, the priests who came from the Continent showed a grim determination to make England Catholic—or die. Audaciously they traveled the English countryside, and neither imprisonment nor death figured in their thinking. Some 160 Catholic missionaries died for their faith and its propagation during Elizabeth's rule. Constantly at risk of being discovered, concealed in strange places, hidden in secret attics, these priests were indefatigable in their efforts and aggressive in their cause. When discovered and apprehended, tried, and in the end burned at the stake, they gloried in their suffering.

Campion returned to England in 1580, the news of his return barely a secret. Clandestine mobile printing presses made it possible to print Catholic literature: from Campion's pen, an open letter to the lords of the Privy Council (later dubbed "Campion's Challenge"), and *Ten Reasons*, written for students at Oxford. This intriguing combination of living underground and yet being a public figure aroused the authorities; betrayal eventually put him into the hands of the law. In November 1581 he was tried on charges of treason. He acquitted himself nobly, acknowledging that the queen was his lawful sovereign; but to renounce *Regnans in Excelsis*, the papal bull that excommunicated the queen and her loyal subjects, he could not. Torture had made it impossible for him to hold up his wrenched right arm, but a fellow defendant kissed the arm and then raised it for him. The sentence was death by hanging, drawing, and quartering. On the scaffold, he prayed for "your Queen and my Queen." Two other Jesuits were hanged the same day at Tyburn, and eleven more were hanged the following year.

The Jesuit missionaries and seminary priests labored in the broad setting of the political tensions between England, Scotland, France, and Spain, with Mary Queen of Scots a pawn who might be elevated to be queen also of England. Understandably, the widespread sympathies that existed for things Catholic, especially in the northern counties, were dissipated. The Armada played a role as well: Allen collaborated with Spain in the overthrow of Elizabeth and the invasion of the country. In 1602 Elizabeth made clear that she had never entertained the notion of allowing the exercise of Catholicism in England. Jesuits were ordered to leave the country within thirty days, while those in the secular clergy, Catholic at heart and yet opposed to them, were given a more leisurely three months.

The government thus reacted with increasing severity to the Catholic proselytizing efforts: a catena of statutes were enacted to suppress Catholic sentiment. In 1563 the defense of papal supremacy was prohibited on pain of praemunire (forfeiture of property). Priests who celebrated Mass were condemned to death. Later laws imposed numerous penalties and fines for nonattendance at Anglican services, and Catholics were effectively barred from inheriting land, entering the professions, or taking up civil or military office. They could not be loyal subjects if they refused to accept Elizabeth as head of the church. In 1571 it became a treasonous offense, punishable by death, to call the monarch a heretic or schismatic. In 1581 to convert someone or to be converted to Catholicism was made treasonous; a fine of £20 per month was levied for recusancy. In 1585 it was made treasonous for Jesuits or seminary priests to enter the country. In 1587 suspected recusants who failed to appear for trial incurred guilt, and in 1593 recusants were restricted to within five miles of their homes.[52] The flavor of governmental action is seen both in the titles of the bills—"For the assurance of the Queen's royal power over all estates and subjects within her majesty's dominions"; "the Act against bringing in and executing papal bulls"; "the Act against receiving absolution from the See of Rome"; "the Act against Jesuits"—and in typical language:

> For the better discovering and avoiding of all such traitorous and most dangerous conspiracies and attempts as are daily devised and practised against our most gracious sovereign lady the queen's majesty and the happy estate of this commonweal, by sundry wicked and seditious persons, who, terming themselves Catholics, and being indeed spies and intelligencers, not only for her majesty's foreign enemies, but also for rebellious and traitorous subjects born within her highness's realms and dominions, and hiding their most detestable and devilish purposes under a false pretext of religion and conscience, do secretly wander and shift from place to place within this realm, to corrupt and seduce her majesty's subjects, and to stir them to sedition and rebellion.

These words make clear that for Elizabeth the issue was not just something on which all of her contemporaries agreed: that the cohesiveness of a commonwealth required that all people be bound to the same values, religious and civic, and therefore that they be commanded to worship the same way. It was that the purpose of the Catholic missionaries was not to evangelize but to stir the English people "to sedition and rebellion." In other words, behind the effort of seminary priests and Jesuits to re-Catholicize the land stood a political agenda.

---

52. In the eighteenth century, active discrimination of Catholics was largely allowed to lapse, although formal Catholic emancipation did not come until 1829.

The papal condemnation that Pope Pius V had hurled against the queen in the bull *Regnans in Excelsis* in 1570 not only excommunicated her but also deposed her from the throne.[53] The pope's hope that Spain and France would put their political (and military) muscle behind the ecclesiastical verdict proved to be a vain one. A committed Catholic, John Fenton, who smuggled a copy of the papal bull into England and affixed it to the palace of the bishop of London, paid with his life for the deed. The charge was treason, understandable in light of the bull's exhortation to the English people not to recognize Elizabeth as their queen.

The official stance was soon successful: the word "Jesuit" conjured up feelings of fear and dismay, and the official contention that the Jesuits were but the advance contingent of a Catholic invasion of England was widely accepted.

ANGLICANISM ESTABLISHED

If the relentless Puritan debate shaped the face of religious dissent in Elizabethan England, it also shaped the Church of England. By the time the century turned, English Christianity had found its identity—vis-à-vis both Rome and the Wittenberg-Geneva axis. Until Cranmer's Forty-two Articles, the reformed English church had no statement of faith, the Six Articles having been a restatement of traditional Catholic belief. Although the prayer book, with less than full subtlety, conveyed a new understanding of the "Mass" as the Lord's Supper and a spiritual presence of Christ in the elements, it was not until the Forty-two Articles were recast into the Thirty-nine Articles that the English church had a theological creed. This document lacked theological crispness, however, thus continuing the qualities of ambiguity so characteristic of the course of events in England.

It was Bishop John Jewell who made the case for the Church of England in his *Apologia Ecclesiae Anglicanae* for the English church.[54] The warrant for the English church lay in its polity, particularly the role of the monarch as "supreme head of the church of England," and in its conservative liturgy. Theologically, there was little uncertainty: until a revisionist mood began to prevail in the mid-seventeenth century, the conviction held that the English church had succeeded in removing the abuses of the Roman Church by sharing the basic Protestant tenets. The key affirmation was the insistence that the English church had successfully reestablished the church of late antiquity. This meant, among other things, that even before the first "Puritan" appeared on the scene, the place of bishops in the early church vindicated their continued place in the Church of England. While Jewel and other early apologists for the English church left open the question of whether the office of bishop existed by human or divine right and institution, by the time the century ended and Richard Hooker had begun to write his magisterial *Of the Laws of Ecclesiastical Polity*, the fronts had hardened with the insistence on the part of those who defended the 1559 settle-

---

53. The bull is found in Charles Dodd, *The Church History of England: From the Year 1500 to the Year 1688, Chiefly with Regard to Catholicks* (Farnborough, Hants, Eng.: 1970), vol. 2, app. li.

54. John Booty, *John Jewel as Apologist for the Church of England* (London: 1963).

ment that the office of the bishop in the church was given by divine law. This recourse to the early church, which created the Nicene Creed, an important element in Anglican theology, proved to be the hallmark of the new Anglican religion.

In early 1603 Elizabeth had reigned as queen no less than forty-five years. In religious matters a remarkable harmony had been achieved in the land. The defiant resistance of the Puritan activists to the settlement of 1559 had seemingly spent itself; the radical Puritans were well on their way to separate from the Church of England, but that church exuded self-confidence and stability. In March of that year Elizabeth, who had been in splendid health all her years, deteriorated quickly in energy and spirit. Archbishop Whitgift, when called to her bedside, admonished her to prepare her soul for God. She replied, "That I have done long ago," and in the early morning of March 24, 1603, just as the first buds were beginning to appear on trees with their promise of new life, she died.

Chapter 9

THE ROMAN CATHOLIC CHURCH

The sixteenth century marked no less an important epoch for Catholic Christendom than it did for the new Protestant churches. It was, by all odds, the most turbulent of centuries for that Church, which at the beginning of the century was self-confident, yet challenged, and by the end was battered, yet self-confident. The sixteenth century was the time of both the greatest crisis and the greatest triumph for the Roman Church; perhaps, one suspects, the latter would not have been possible without the former.

About the depth of the crisis there can be little doubt. Never before had the Western church been confronted with such formidable desertion—apostasy, in the eyes of the church; never before had the church had to face such flagrant challenges and blatant disregard of its teachings. The church that claimed to be the seamless robe of Christ, outside of which there could be no salvation, was torn apart. Men, women, monks, nuns, priests, even bishops renounced the faith they had pledged to uphold. Statues and shrines, revered by the faithful, were removed from churches and many were destroyed. Religious endowments that had comforted the living in their concern for the dead were dissolved and used for purposes greedy as well as communal. Monasteries and convents in which devout men and women had sought to live pious and spiritual lives were shut down and dissolved.

Country after country repudiated the authority of the Catholic Church and pledged loyalty to new forms of the Christian religion. Some of the losses suffered by the Catholic Church in the course of the century were countered, to be sure, by impressive gains, particularly overseas, and when the sixteenth century ended, the Catholic Church—what was left of it, mainly in southern Europe—was assuredly stronger, more dynamic, and more self-confident than it had been at the beginning of the century when Luther's Ninety-five Theses triggered the first defection from its ranks. Just as the shrines and images destroyed could not be restored, however, the apostasy from the church and the rejection of papal authority turned out to be irreparable to this day.

Early in the nineteenth century the German historian Leopold von Ranke employed the term "Counter-Reformation" to describe the major impulse of Catholic life and thought in the sixteenth century and to argue that the entire epoch, roughly from the Peace of Augsburg to the Peace of Westphalia, 1555 to 1648, was dominated by these Catholic anti-Reformation impulses.[1] Following Ranke, other historians, mainly Protestant, used the term "Counter-Reformation" to describe Catholic history

---

1. Leopold von Ranke's suggestion, in his *Deutsche Geschichte im Zeitalter der Reformation,* was taken up by Moriz Ritter, *Deutsche Geschichte im Zeitalter der Gegenreformation* (Stuttgart: 1895).

in the sixteenth century. The Catholic reaction against the Protestant Reformation became the dominant theme of sixteenth-century Catholic historiography.[2]

The term maintained a sacrosanct place in Reformation historiography until, in the 1930s, Catholic scholars pointed out that sixteenth-century Catholic history cannot be viewed exclusively as a reaction against the Protestant Reformation. Such a perspective ignores or minimizes those Catholic reform impulses in the sixteenth century that had little, if anything, to do with the Reformation challenge.[3] Accordingly, the term "Catholic Reform" (or "Catholic Reformation") was introduced to make reform, both autonomous and triggered by the Protestant Reformation, the hallmark of sixteenth-century Catholicism. But Ranke's ghost lingered, and "Catholic Reform" was then bundled with "Counter-Reformation" into the somewhat cumbersome appellation "Catholic Reform and Counter-Reformation" to denote the dual characteristic of sixteenth-century Catholicism—its indigenous self-renewal and its reaction against the Protestant Reformation.[4] While clumsy, the term assumed (the point is important) that sixteenth-century Catholicism was characterized by certain features that allowed loyal laypersons, conscientious priests, and sensitive members of the hierarchy to work for the revitalization of their church. A parallel argument insisted that in the fifteenth century medieval Christianity gave way to a new form of the Christian religion—spiritual, intellectual, individualistic—and that the Roman Church and the Reformation were different strands of the same new religion.[5] This church continued to command allegiance and supplied the people's spiritual needs.

Protestant propaganda argued that the Catholic Church was unwilling (or unable) to undertake needed reform in the late fifteenth and early sixteenth centuries. Nothing could be further from the truth. To be sure, the pursuit of reform in the fifteenth century was haphazard and sporadic. Alongside the vigorous quest for monastic reform, the reform proposals drawn up by Nikolaus of Cusa for Pope Pius II were never implemented. However, the Fifth Lateran Council, convened by Pope Julius II under political pressure from Germany and in session from 1512 to 1517, dealt extensively with reform issues, proof positive that the church wanted to put its house in order, although there was disagreement and even lack of full understanding what that exactly meant. The Reformation intensified the sense of urgency for Catholic Church to undertake and implement reform, even if some of the trickiest aspects of ecclesiastical reform—episcopal residence and pluralism—continued to defy resolution. Thus, the impact of the Reformation upon Catholicism, directly and indirectly, was strong. The Council of Trent, which set the direction of the Catholic Church for centuries, is unthinkable without the threatening reality of the Protestant challenge—but it also bespeaks the continued self-confidence of the Catholic Church that the council fathers gathered at Trent saw no reason to explore possible theological compromise with the Protestants.

---

2. A detailed account of the relevant historiography is in John W. O'Malley, *Trent and All That: Renaming Catholicism in the Early Modern Era* (Cambridge: 2000).

3. Hubert Jedin, *Die Erforschung der kirchlichen Reformationsgeschichte seit 1876* (Darmstadt: 1975).

4. O'Malley, *Trent and All That,* has proposed "Early Modern Catholicism" instead. However, his term raises the question if Catholicism remained a cohesive entity during the time generally understood as "early modern," i.e., 1500 and 1789.

5. John Bossy, *Christianity in the West, 1400 to 1700* (New York: 1985).

During the first years of the indulgences controversy, the church and the curia faced a problematic situation. Neither the nature of the information reaching Rome about Luther nor the disposition of those entrusted with the examination of his teaching (such as Sylvester Prierias or John Eck) made for the likelihood of a fair assessment. To be sure, Cardinal Cajetan heard Luther's notions about authority, penance, and indulgences firsthand at Augsburg, and he was learned and fair-minded, but that ill-fated encounter hardly sufficed for a full appraisal of the concerns of Luther and those who were rallying around him. Moreover, considerations of European politics (notably the election of a new Holy Roman emperor) preoccupied the curia for almost all of 1519, and afterward a sense of urgency seemed to override deliberate reflection on the most prudent course of action. Those in Rome who knew their history also knew that heretical challenges had always been contained by the church. If anything, the lesson of history seemed to be that the sharper the quick response, the easier the heretics' containment.

Thus the course of curial action was hardly surprising, and, given the circumstances, it could hardly have been otherwise. An altogether different perspective, however, came from the lips of none other than Pope Leo X. The controversy in Germany, he remarked early on, was nothing but a squabble among monks. He did not mean this as a positive statement, of course, nor did he seem to appreciate the theological differences that subsequently came out into the open. But it was an uncannily shrewd remark—that the happenings in Germany could be ignored and that they required as little curial attention as did a thousand other "monkish squabbles." For all his congeniality, his preoccupation with art and learning in Rome, and even his view of the papacy as a secular monarchy, Leo's remark was more astute than most remarks made at the time. Had its implication been followed, Martin Luther might well have died a Catholic saint.

From the very outset the ensuing controversy had an inordinately sharp tone. Undoubtedly, the cause of this intriguing turn was that from the beginning the formal ecclesiastical proceedings against Luther hung like the sword of Damocles over the course of events. And the formal ecclesiastical verdict against Luther and his followers was issued less than three years after the controversy had erupted. In the great debate that followed, the Catholic Church found itself at a disadvantage, if for no other reason than that its protagonists had to be on the defensive. It was the Reformers who propounded novel and startling ideas, requiring the defenders of the status quo to reiterate what has been said and written a thousand times. Henry VIII's *Assertio Septem Sacramentorum*, that spirited defense of the sacramental teaching of the Catholic Church, is a good case in point. If it was a mediocre work, as most commentators seem to think, then because it was well-nigh impossible for Henry to say anything strikingly new on a subject that the theologians had discussed for centuries.

Moreover, the heat of controversy had a way of triggering extremist statements that, in a more circumspect atmosphere, might well have remained unsaid. Not surprisingly, in their effort to put Luther and the other Reformers in their place quickly and bluntly, the Catholic protagonists made all sorts of dubious pronouncements. The *Dialogus* of Sylvester Prierias, for example, argued that any criticism of churchly practices was in itself heretical. Perhaps, as has been suggested, the Catholic protagonists themselves did not always understand the authentic Catholic position. More likely, however, the tensions of the polemics misled them. They were disposed to degrade Scripture, denounce its use in the vernacular, or reject the need for reform, precisely because the Protestant antagonists emphatically affirmed all that. In so doing, they unduly narrowed the Catholic position, lost friends, and influenced few people. The matter of ecclesiastical reform graphically expressed the two horns of the dilemma. If the need for reform was conceded, it could be understood as acknowledgment that the advocates of reforms were correct—the church was indeed in desperate straits. After all, they boasted after Pope Adrian VI's confession that it confirmed what they had been saying all along. If, on the other hand, Catholics denied the need for reform, they were likely to be chided for dishonesty in the face of indisputable evidence. The dilemma was real.

Of even greater importance was the lingering uncertainty over the nature of the controversy. There was no end to persuasive or even prophetic pronouncements in this regard, especially after Luther had been joined by a host of other Reformers, all of whom argued for reform. The multitude of suggestions was bewildering. Some thought that at issue were ecclesiastical abuses that needed to be corrected to restore peace and tranquility in the church. Others pointed to certain practices, such as the withholding of the Communion cup from the laity, while yet others focused on theological disagreements, though precisely what these were remained enigmatic and uncertain. The bull *Exsurge Domine* seemed to suggest that Luther's errors pertained to the doctrines of indulgences and penance. In 1524 Erasmus singled out anthropology as the crucial point of contention, while Melanchthon was persuaded at Augsburg in 1530 that conciliation would be possible if only the Communion cup were offered to the laity and priests were allowed to marry. Luther, in turn, declared that the controversy was all about the proper understanding of Christ. Somewhere along the line the concept of justification crept into the picture and decades later became the article of faith "on which the church stands or falls." There was no dearth of suggestions.

It is hardly surprising, therefore, that the theological controversy remained inconclusive, though such was not the case with respect to the official posture of the Catholic Church, which had been painfully evident ever since *Exsurge Domine*. The theological debate which then took place was a grandiose free-for-all, and subsequent generations of scholars have claimed to understand the contested issues better than did the contemporaries.[6] Martin Bucer, by all odds the most irenic of the Protestant Reformers, remarked in 1541 that "both sides have erred, ours by defending some matters all too vehemently; yours by not removing many abuses."[7]

This was the burden of all Catholic apologetics in the early years of the controversy, of Johann Eck, Thomas Murner, Johannes Cochlaeus, Thomas More, and all the others. They differed in theological insight, religious acumen, and literary skill, some arguing more incisively, others enjoying considerable popularity. All of them shared the rhetorical disadvantage of having to defend the status quo. They had to counter bold and sweeping generalizations, for the Reformers were, in a way, the *sim-*

---

6. The illustration par excellence is, of course, the Lutheran-Catholic agreement on justification, the *Common Declaration on Justification*, signed in 1999.

7. L. v. Pastor, "Correspondenz des Cardinals Contarini," *Historisches Jahrbuch* 1 (1880): 337.

plificateurs terribles whose imprint on the course of history the nineteenth-century historian Jakob Burckhardt so resoundingly bewailed.[8] In short, the Catholic handicap was real and the difficulties staggering.

The situation changed only after the initial mood of desperation (and righteous indignation) had given way to a calmer reflection on the nature of the controversy. Then, and only then, did Catholic writers (Peter Canisius is one of the eminent illustrations) adapt their ways. They supported the vernacular Scriptures, wrote popular catechisms, and denounced the life and thought of the new churches, for they had enough empirical evidence before their own eyes to garner a devastating polemic.

Two recurrent themes were heard again and again from the lips of the protagonists: the call for reform and the call for a council. In both matters, as in all other Catholic affairs in the sixteenth century, the key lay in the papal office. The popes labored under the handicap of the immediate past. The Renaissance popes, from Nicholas V to Julius II, had been concerned (successfully, as it turned out) to transform Rome, the center of the Christian religion, into a center of art and culture. They had also engaged in power politics, seeking to preserve the integrity of the Papal States against aggressive encroachment from other Italian states. When, in the course of the sixteenth century, the character of the papacy changed, it was difficult to turn over a new leaf. Only gradually did the popes become pointedly focused on ecclesiastical affairs and matters, and even then they continued to be caught as though between two millstones in politics, notably the fierce struggle between France and Spain. Because ecclesiastical pronouncements invariably entailed political ramifications, there was no easy way to proceed. Thus the relatively simple issue of Henry VIII's "divorce" from Catherine of Aragon became an important matter in European power politics, and Pope Clement VII had to rule on the canonical regularity of the marriage in an intensely political context. To side with the English king meant to provoke the hostile reaction from the emperor. To side with the emperor, in turn, meant to trigger a confrontation with the English king. In turn, the notion of a general council was as vehemently rejected by Francis I as it was advocated by Charles V, and both were eminently guided by political considerations. The popes were caught between the proverbial rock and the hard place.

The seven popes in the half century between 1513 and 1565, from Leo X to Pius IV, were (with one exception) utterly upright and competent successors to the apostle Peter. Some, such as Adrian VI, were deeply spiritual. Understandably, each had his views of the nature of the crisis (or absence thereof) besetting the church, and each prescribed the remedies he deemed most appropriate and necessary.

The brevity of papal reigns in the sixteenth century affected the church as well. The popes ruled, on the average, for about seven years, all too brief a time to initiate and carry out important and far-reaching policies. If we omit the three lengthiest pontificates, those of Clement VII (1523–1534), Paul III (1534–1549), and Gregory XIII (1572–1585), the tenure of their predecessors and successors shrinks even more. At the same time, Charles V and Elizabeth I ruled for a generation, and England had only five sovereigns during the entire century.

---

8. Jakob Burckhardt, *Weltgeschichtliche Betrachtungen,* translated as *Force and Freedom: Reflections on History* (ed. James Hastings Nichols; New York: 1943).

The rule of Leo X, during which the controversy erupted, was burdened by that pope's somewhat easygoing and secular disposition. Although not too much should be made of that and no blame, if that is even the right word, should be laid on him— most of his diversions from spiritual and ecclesiastical affairs were innocent (nowadays surely nobody would see in the pope's watching a movie an indication of a blatant lack of spirituality). Far more consequential for the ensuing course of events were other factors, such as the cursory knowledge of the nature (and extent) of the controversy north of the Alps and the sense of accomplishment after the adjournment of the Fifth Lateran Council, which had promulgated a great many reform measures. From the perspective of the reform movement, it seems futile to ask whether the reform decrees of the Lateran Council lacked seriousness of purpose or were haphazard; the plain fact is that, whatever the intent, the conciliar legislation never had a chance. No sooner had the council adjourned that the indulgences controversy began to excite the land, and with it came new issues and challenges. The Lateran Council was rather like a fruit that ripened out of season: it sought to achieve its goals in terms of one epoch, but it was judged by another.

After Pope Leo X's death came the tedious election of Adrian VI in January 1522. Adrian's election was a compromise, the last effort to find a successor to Leo before the cardinals would have to agree not to agree. Adrian, the last non-Italian pope until Pope John Paul II in the late twentieth century, was a devout and spiritually minded individual who saw the reform of the church, and especially of the curia, as the foremost goal of his pontifical rule. That he was not Italian but hailed from Utrecht may have given him a more realistic perspective of the religious and theological turmoil in Germany. During his brief pontificate he was an outsider in Rome, unfamiliar with the workings of the curia and suspicious of his advisors. Importantly, however, his pontificate was breathtakingly short; he died less than two years after his election. When he ventured forth boldly, such as with his famous "confession," which his nuncio Francesco Chieregati conveyed in January 1523 to the German diet, he assuaged neither friend nor foe. Tellingly, his epitaph bewailed, "Alas, how much depends even for the best of men on the times."[9]

The eleven years of the pontificate of Clement VII (1523–1534) brought little change, leading Leopold von Ranke, who was not easily given to dramatic pronouncements, to call Clement "the most catastrophic pope ever to occupy the throne of St. Peter." In part this verdict was prompted by Clement's temperamental inability to make decisions, though it might be more appropriate to say that he sought to postpone decisions he knew were bound to be catastrophic. Clement talked much but decided little.

Importantly, however, Clement had to face serious political issues that consumed a great deal of his interest and energy. The struggle between France and Spain reached the Holy City in 1527, with the spectacular "Sack of Rome," and made Pope Clement temporarily a de facto prisoner of the emperor. The divorce of Henry VIII at the same time put Clement into a position where any decision was bound to have fateful polit-

9. L. v. Pastor, *History of the Popes* (St. Louis: 1915), 9:217.

ical and ecclesiastical consequences. No wonder Clement sought to avoid the confrontation. That he eventually decided against the English king (it surely was the more fateful choice and the greater of two evils) speaks for his integrity. If all of these were not sufficient problems, the persistent resistance of Francis I to a general council made concerning a council an impossibility.

Thus little happened during Clement's pontificate: no council, no reform. Predictably, England deserted the Catholic ranks, as did Sweden and a number of German territories and towns. But these realities tend to offer a one-sided picture. The desertion of England and Sweden from the Roman Church would not have been thwarted either by a council or by ecclesiastical reform. Only in Germany might effective reform measures have made a difference, though theological differences rather than concerns about practical reform seemed increasingly to occupy center stage.

Under Pope Paul III, who succeeded Clement in 1534, the several streams of Catholic vitality burst into the open. The years of Paul's pontificate marked the turning point of Catholic history in the sixteenth century. A vigorous pope led the comprehensive effort to regain both vitality and self-confidence in the church. This last point is particularly important. Pope Paul III was not only committed to convene a general council; he also understood the necessity of reform. During his pontificate, "reform" became part of the official vocabulary and policy of the papacy. In 1537 Paul convened a reform commission comprising nine cardinals, among whom three eminent and reform-minded individuals made their mark: Gasparo Contarini, Reginald Pole, and Gian Pietro Carafa, later to become Pope Paul IV, all three deeply devout, but not necessarily deeply orthodox, Catholics. Chaired by Contarini, the commission, which met constantly between November 1536 and March 1537, hammered out a reform document that was formally presented to Paul III on March 9, 1537.[10] Entitled *Consilium delectorum cardinalium et aliorum praelatorum de emendanda ecclesia* (Counsel . . . Concerning the Reform of the Church), the document insisted that an exalted view of the papal office together with plain ordinary greed were at the root of the evils besetting the church. At the same time, the document called for a radical change in the practice of the dispensations and exemptions offered by the curia and demanded greater care in priestly ordinations. The vision of a triumphant and self-confident church was beginning to be recaptured, even though the practical consequences of the document were modest indeed. The deeply entrenched bureaucracy of the curia rose in defense of their livelihood, and the pope himself became anxious about the potential loss of a major revenue stream.

If the *Consilium* had only modest consequences, Paul III did move energetically on another issue—the residency obligation of bishops and priests, by all counts a major cause of the shortcomings of the church. At issue was that scores of bishops had never set foot in their dioceses and that thousands of priests had never celebrated Mass in parishes in which they were the canonical incumbents. The root problem was that the legal and financial emoluments did not necessarily accrue to those who performed the actual tasks and bore the real responsibilities of a particular position. Thus bishops

10. The text is in *Concilium Tridentinum* XII, 131–45.

received the revenue from their dioceses while a substitute fulfilled their canonical obligations. In the diocese of Lincoln, England, some 247 priests of a total of 1,088 were absent during a 1518–1519 visitation.[11]

The three remaining popes of the sixteenth century were vigorous, spiritually minded, and highly competent. Each of them in his own way left a permanent mark on the church: Pius V (1563–1572), Gregory XIII (1572–1585), and Sixtus V (1585–1590).

Pius V was canonized by his church in 1712 in recognition of his deep spirituality and a far-reaching ecclesiastical importance. His eminent achievement was his vigorous implementation of the decrees on the Council of Trent which he approved in January 1564 in the bull *Benedictus Deus*. This was a striking convergence of conciliar and papal authority, both parties contributing to the effectiveness of the document. Nonetheless, both the bull and Pius's policies made clear that Pius V saw the papacy as an active agent and as more than merely the executor of the decisions of the council. In March 1564 he issued a new index of prohibited books and, in November of that year, the Tridentine profession of faith.

With Pope Gregory XIII, the centralization of the church (meddling, as Archbishop Borromeo of Milan saw it, in the affairs of local bishops) became ever more pointed. Gregory was seventy years of age when he was elected, but he took charge of the affairs of the church with a gusto that would have left much younger men breathless, and his pontificate turned out to be one of the longest in the sixteenth century. Gregory utilized special papal representatives, nuncios, as papal commissioners for supervising reform in particular areas. Above all, Gregory recognized the potential of the Society of Jesus for vitalizing the church. He used the Jesuit missions to bring the Christian message to such faraway places as China, Japan, and the Philippines, although, when asked about his foremost achievement, he mentioned the establishment of a university, the Gregorian University in Rome.

The pontificate of Sixtus V, finally, takes us to the emerging world of the baroque, which has been taken as the epitome of the triumphalist Tridentine church, a new world of utter self-confidence and brilliance. Born Felice Peretti in 1521 into a poor family, he took the papal name Sixtus in memory of the last pope who had been a Franciscan monk, though the fifth Sixtus to be pope seemed anything but a disciple of St. Francis: Sixtus was authoritarian, rigid, unyielding, and given to violent outbursts of temper—though he could also be generous, thoughtful, and pious.

Sixtus relentlessly pursued three goals, which clearly defined him as a churchman molded by the temper of the Council of Trent. At issue was the defense of the Catholic faith, further reforms in the church, and the enhancement of the authority of the pope. In 1588 Sixtus undertook a comprehensive realignment of the administrative structure of the Roman curia. He created fifteen "congregations," or "departments," six of which were responsible for the affairs of the Papal States, while the remaining nine administered the global affairs of the church. Of these, the congregation supervising the doctrinal fidelity of the faithful—the Roman Inquisition—proved not only most important but also most powerful.

11. Ph. Hughes, *The Reformation in England* (New York: 1963), 1:103.

THE COUNCIL OF TRENT

The notion that an ecumenical council should address the contested issues of church reform and renewal was a rallying cry that hovered over the course of the conflagration almost from its beginnings.[12] The chief advocate of a council was Emperor Charles V, who saw such a council addressing matters of reform as the best means to stem the Protestant menace. On the other side, the Protestant Reformers also agitated ardently for a council—Luther did so in the early stage of the controversy, and other Reformers followed suit. In a way, the emperor and the Protestants were allies; but it only seemed that way, for their respective views of the objectives of such a council differed greatly. The emperor wanted a council to address moral reform in the church in order to revitalize it and thereby diminish the appeal of the Protestant heretics. The Protestants, on the other hand, wanted a council to take the church theologically back to what they saw as its biblical roots and, on that basis, bring about conciliation between the two sides.

Charles was driven to his advocacy because he understood his role not merely as sovereign of a part, albeit the major part, of Europe. He viewed his imperial role as constituting guardianship of all of Christendom, the pope's counterpart as guardian of the Christian faith, whose responsibility included the well-being of the church. A council was to him the best guarantee that a catastrophe resulting from the relentless controversy might be avoided. Charles doggedly persisted in his pursuit of a council, despite the opposition of Rome and France, and it may well be that his persistence eventually brought it about.

Early on, Charles's great antagonist was Pope Clement VII. As his role in Henry VIII's "great matter" suggests, Clement was the great procrastinator, who did not wish to make decisions unless absolutely necessary. Although he could hardly oppose Charles outright in his pursuit of a council, he could (and did) make haste slowly, so that even though he promised, in 1531, that he would convene a council, he never vigorously pursued it. Clement sided with those in the church who thought a council unnecessary; the theological positions of the church had been variously affirmed, and whatever reform was needed could be undertaken without a council.

Clement's successor, Paul III, on the other hand, proved to be Charles's ally; he was committed to a council but thought it prudent to wait for the judicious moment to convene it. In June 1536 he convened a council to Mantua, in northern Italy, to meet the following May, but the opposition of both France and the German Protestants meant failure to that effort. Understandably, the success of a council depended on the largest possible participation of bishops and heads of monastic orders; political rivalries, notably those between Spain and France, needed to be resolved before such participation was likely and a council could gather successfully. Peace had to prevail between Spain and France, which had waged war intermittently ever since the last

---

12. On the prehistory of the Council see H. Jedin, *A History of the Council of Trent* (London: 1957), 30ff. The decisions of the Council, in form of Canons and Decrees, are found in *Canons and Decrees of the Council of Trent*, ed. H. J. Schroeder (Rockford, IL: 1978). See also P. Prodi and W. Reinhard, eds., *Das Konzil von Trient und die Moderne* (Berlin: 2001).

decade of the fifteenth century. Peace finally came in 1544, and Paul III promptly acted.

The identity of modern Catholicism was molded at Trent. The council's doctrinal pronouncements, which repudiated the Protestant Reformation, formed the face of the Catholic Church, aptly called Tridentine Catholicism, for centuries. Their objective was to sharpen Catholic identity, for the council affirmed various Catholic teaching by appropriating medieval positions and drawing out their consequences, especially where the challenges of the Reformers had pointed to ambivalences in existing formulations.

The First Phase of the Council

When the council formally opened in Trent on December 13, 1545, widespread skepticism reigned whether serious discussions and decisions would in fact materialize. The external circumstances were not exactly harbingers of good things to come: only 31 bishops were present, a rather minute flock given the large number of bishops, heads of monastic orders, and abbots making up a general council of the church. Subsequently, the attendance increased to 187. Even then, however, the geographic distribution of the council fathers, only two of whom came from France and only one from Germany, hardly reflected the geographic diversity of the church.

The site of the council had prompted an extensive discussion between pope and emperor, and several possibilities were considered: Verona, Bologna, Mantua, even Mainz and Cologne. At issue was neither climate nor comfort, but politics. Trent, a town in northern Italy, at the southern foothills of the Alps, was chosen as a compromise between the emperor, who demanded that the council convene somewhere in the empire so as to minimize papal influence, and the pope, who feared that a council meeting on German soil would be a puppet of the emperor. Both the emperor and the pope were correct in their fears, and so a compromise had to be found. Trent was that acceptable compromise.

In January the council fathers tackled their first item of business—a "decree concerning the manner of living during the council," a practical manual exhorting the council fathers to proper decorum while in Trent. That assignment proved easy enough. Three cardinals, Giovanni del Monte, Reginald Pole, and Marcello Cervini, presided over the sessions of the council and stayed in constant touch with the curia, even though the council proved anything but a pliant tool of the papacy.

At the outset, the council fathers faced the crucial decision concerning the agenda of the council: should topics of church reform or of theology be first on the agenda? These two scenarios were no mere formality; the alternatives reflected different notions as to what was of foremost necessity—to reform the church or to counter the Protestant heresy. Pope Paul wanted a theological agenda; the emperor, an agenda of reform. The council fathers decided on a compromise, the first of many, all intra-Catholic compromises, rather than compromises with Protestants. The authority of the pope was acknowledged from the beginning; clearly, this was not going to be a runaway council, defying papal authority with conciliar notions.

The council fathers agreed that the various Protestant theological positions had been properly condemned, either as old heresies in new disguise or as new deviations from the faith, and were unacceptable. Accordingly, the council quickly reached decisions on several controversial issues that had agitated the church for a generation—the relationships between Scripture and tradition, between sin and justification, and the nature of sacraments. Issues of practical church reform proved to be less tractable; a triangle of financial, legal, and power issues seemed to render reforms impossible.

The diverging notions of pope and emperor brought about a suspension of the council. Charles, determined to be victorious over the League of Schmalkald, sought to exert greater influence on the deliberations (and decisions) of the council—a prospect viewed by the pope with obvious dismay. The pope, while eager to suppress the German Protestants, was aghast at the possibility of a politically and ecclesiastically stronger emperor after a victorious war. In January 1547 he withdrew his mercenaries from Charles's forces, and in March the council fathers voted to move the deliberations "for health reasons" (the plague had reportedly broken out in Trent) to Bologna, located in the Papal States. Charles was furious—in April he scored a decisive victory over the League of Schmalkald in the Battle at Mühlberg and he threatened to see to a continuation of the deliberations at Trent.

Pope Paul III did the wisest thing he could do—he suspended the council in February of the following year. The council fathers were able to go home. Much had been accomplished, even though the rankling between pope and emperor had meant that the discussion on the important topic of the Eucharist was not concluded.

The Second Phase, 1551–1552

Half a decade passed before the council reconvened, and a great deal happened during those intervening years, notably the election of a new pope upon Paul III's death in November 1548. Paul's successor was Giovanni del Monte, one of the three presiding legates at Trent, though it had taken the conclave three months to elect him in February 1550. Taking the name of Julius III, he called the council back into action in May of the following year. Wisely, he determined that the council should return to Trent. The emperor's victory over the League of Schmalkald meant that a number of Protestant representatives, including from electoral Saxony, were strong-armed by Charles to appear in Trent. Their presence proved to be irrelevant, however, for the council fathers were of no mind to accept the Protestants as equals.

Charles, on the other hand, had a different notion as to what the council should accomplish, and his tensions with the new pope were of the same sort as those he had had with Paul III. Although several important theological decrees were passed by the council (on the Eucharist, penance, and confession), the shifting political fortunes in Europe brought the council to a halt in the spring of 1552. France had allied with the rebellious German territorial rulers against Charles V, who barely escaped being captured. Voices in Rome reiterated the argument that a council was unnecessary to affect reform in the church. Just as Pope Julius III was beginning to work on a comprehensive reform document for the curia, he died.

The Third Phase, 1562–1563

The council's work was thus left in abeyance. The seventy-nine-year-old Gian Pietro Carafa was elected as Pope Paul IV in May 1555—about the same time the German diet, meeting at Augsburg, provided legal recognition for the Lutheran territorial and city churches in Germany. Paul's was a determined commitment to church reform but also considerable reluctance to trust the council. He fought with Charles V's successor, Philip II, and denounced Emperor Ferdinand for his acceptance of the Peace of Augsburg. Paul felt that, rather than wasting time in conciliar deliberations, strengthening the Inquisition and relentlessly pursuing every inkling of heresy were the best means of setting the church in order. He had no interest in reviving the council.

Paul's determination to ferret out heresy was grim indeed. No matter how high the position held, the shadow of suspicion could fall on anyone. Cardinal Giovanni Morone was arrested under the suspicion of heresy, the Jews of Rome were forced into a ghetto and obliged to wear a mark on their clothing, and the Index of Prohibited Books, now formally issued, sought to control the access to the printed page. Among the included books were, for example, the writings of Erasmus. It is hard to know whether to admire Paul for his unflinching determination to rescue the church from mortal danger or to denounce him for instituting an atmosphere of fear in the church. There is no way of telling how the church would have fared had his pontifical reign lasted longer.

Paul's successor, Pius IV, was elected to the throne of St. Peter in December 1559, a perilous time for the church. The conclave, in which the conflicting influences of Spain and France were paramount, was in session for more than three months before white smoke issued forth from the chimney of the Sistine Chapel: Gianangelo Medici, elevated to the cardinal purple in 1549, was elected and took the name of Pius IV. Hardly a church reformer, Pius faced a difficult situation. The Peace of Augsburg had come to be accepted as a fait accompli; in England the new queen, Elizabeth, predictably would take her country onto a Protestant course. In France issues of regency were about to push the country to the brink of a religious civil war in which the French Protestants would show their political and military prowess. When Pius IV began to warm up to the notion of completing the council that had been meeting in Trent, he faced formidable obstacles: Philip II of Spain insisted that the decrees and canons of the preceding sessions be affirmed, even though they had not received papal confirmation. Germany and France, on the other hand, demanded a new council, for they were convinced that the pointedly orthodox decrees would make the domestic political situation more difficult.

The papal bull of November 1560 that convened the council was ambiguously worded, calculated to alienate neither Spain nor Germany nor France. Nonetheless, difficulties continued, and it was not until more than a year later, on January 18, 1562, that the council actually began its work—109 cardinals and bishops, 4 abbots, and 4 heads of monastic orders had gathered. The presiding cardinals had thought to finesse the issue of the nature of the convened council (was it a continuation of the previous meetings or was it a new council?) by submitting for consideration a twelve-point reform document. A vehement debate erupted over its first article, the residency oblig-

ation of bishops. The disagreement sharpened over the question of whether the obligation was *divinum jus*, by divine law, or by church polity.

The Significance of the Council

The Council of Tent was to clarify a number of theological topics and issues of the
practical life of the church and in so doing condemn Protestant teaching. No doubt,
Trent was successful in this, especially because the papacy fell in line and made the
decrees and canons of the council its own.

Foremost in the theological achievements of the council was the clarification of the
relationship of Scripture and tradition. From the very beginning of the Reformation
controversy, the Reformers' rejection of the dogmatic significance of church traditions
had been a major point of contention. The Reformers' stance of "Scripture alone"
meant the rejection of a crucial element of Catholic teaching; at issue was the principle of authority and the nature of the church.

This slogan of the Reformers had initially triggered baffled silence on the part of
those loyal to the Catholic Church. What chagrined them was the Reformers' insistence that Scripture and tradition could be at odds, could in fact be in tension with
one another. For their part, the Catholic protagonists argued the essential harmony
of the two.

The council fathers at Trent quite appropriately undertook to counter the Protestant scriptural principle with a restatement of the traditional Catholic position that
there was not (and could not be, since the church was promised the guidance of the
Holy Spirit) any tension between Bible and church, between divine revelation and the
traditions in the church. At the same time, the council's decision laid the basis for
future reflection. In the end, the press of time and the disposition of the council members prompted them to table the pivotal topic of ecclesiastical authority, even though
the affirmation that apostolic teaching was retained in the church provided a hint
about the thinking of the council fathers.

Some council fathers saw tradition as referring to liturgical or disciplinary matters;
others argued that tradition was an autonomous source of revelation. The latter view
meant that the truth transmitted by Christ to the apostles and through them to the
church was partly found in Scripture and partly in tradition. The council instead
favored the notion that truth was found both in Scripture and in tradition, leaving
thus unspecified the exact significance of tradition. The council declared that the
source of all truth (dogmatic, moral, and ecclesiastical) was the gospel revealed by Jesus
and proclaimed by the apostles. It was transmitted in two ways: through the written
books of the biblical canon and through the oral traditions of the church. Thus both
a "partly-partly" and a "both-and" understanding of the relationship between Scripture and tradition could be read into the council decree. Both were of equal importance, since both contained the gospel. Importantly, the council's decree meant that
tradition was declared a possible basis of doctrine because it had been retained authentically in the church. The church became the decisive locus of authority, holding the
monopoly on both Scripture and tradition.

The Tridentine council decree on the biblical canon also declared the Latin translation of the Bible, the Vulgate, to be authoritative for liturgical and theological use. It prohibited all interpretation of Scripture other than that promulgated by the church. In short, the council countered the Protestant scriptural principle with a distinctly Catholic perspective. By discussing the topic of grace and justification early in their deliberations, the council fathers wanted to clarify the orthodox Catholic position on the topic that ranked so centrally in the Reformation controversy. This was needed because no normative church teaching was in place. Luther and the other Protestant Reformers had been free to proffer their opinions and views.

When the council fathers turned to the topic of original sin, a crucial aspect of the broader topic of justification, the council fathers affirmed the anti-Pelagian decision of the Synod of Orange, of 529, which held to the priority of grace in the process of salvation. Adam's sin had affected human nature through the loss of original righteousness. The act of baptism, however, removed the stain of original sin from the individual so that sin remained only as potential, as concupiscence or desire, not as inescapable, actual sinning. It was a pointed encouragement of spiritual living.

The council further declared that justification was based on Christ's act of atonement, and it had two aspects. One was the initial justification of the godless individual in conversion and baptism because of the merits of Christ, leading to the state of grace. The other was the pious walk of life in faith. Theretofore there had been no clear definition of tradition, and particularly its relation to the written revelation found in the Bible.

CATHOLIC RENEWAL AND COUNTER-REFORMATION

The Council of Trent was the catalyst for the two most salient developments in sixteenth-century Catholicism: response and renewal. By defining the parameters of Catholic theological teaching, Trent provided the tools for an aggressive response to the Protestant challenge. The topic of ecclesiastical reform, so easily and even glibly talked about, was more complicated, though both council and papacy were committed to it. Few guidelines existed for how bishops and clergy might be reformed, and as matters turned out, the meaning of reform differed from country to country and from diocese to diocese. There was great success in reform wherever the political authorities lent a supporting hand and aided the reform efforts. The education of priests and the enhancement of preaching became important topics. In addition, new monastic communities came into being (through the centuries always a telltale indication of Catholic vitality), and new forms of piety emerged that emphasized Catholic spirituality in contrast to Protestant notions.

In short a revitalized Catholic Church began to reassert itself in the 1560s and 1570s finding expression in a forceful counter-reform (or Counter-Reformation) against Protestant heresy. The forces in the church advocating rigidity increasingly dominated, and irenic sentiment disappeared. Indeed, advocates of an irenic disposition toward Protestantism were suppressed, haunted, and persecuted.

All of northern Europe had become Protestant. Catholic efforts concentrated on southern Europe (with some attention paid to Germany, the Netherlands, Switzerland, and England). The Catholic Church took on the qualities of Mediterranean spirituality—Italian, French, and Spanish forms of mentality and culture—and increasingly displayed the exuberance of feeling, color, and movement that we tend to associate with the Baroque.

THE IMPLEMENTATION OF TRIDENTINE REFORM

Reform, as implemented after Trent, meant the structural pursuit of doctrinal and religious uniformity within the Catholic Church. The agents in this process were the papacy, bishops, and the secular authorities. Trent envisioned the bishops' pivotal role in the process of undertaking reform, though it was clear that, for reform to be successful, the support of the political authorities was indispensable. The reform efforts focused on attempts of uniformity in liturgy, law, instruction, piety, preaching. This was achieved through the promulgation of uniform missals, rituals, prayer books, catechisms, as well as the control of books and of the clergy. It found expression in use of Latin (instead of the vernacular) in worship, Bible, law, and theology. Thereby, the Catholic Church attained an inner cohesiveness that provided striking vitality. New catechisms—notably the *Catechismus Romanum* of 1566 and (since the Jesuits had their own ideas about what constituted the best catechism) the "Canisi," the German-language catechism of Peter Canisius—offered the guidelines for the religious instruction of young and old.[13] Entitled *Catechismus, sive Summa doctrinae Christianae* (Cologne, 1560), Canisius's catechism outlined the Christian faith under the twofold heading of "wisdom" and "justice." Afterward Canisius published a Smaller Catechism for early adolescents and also a Smallest Catechism (*Der klain Catechismus: Sampt kurtzen gebetlein für die ainfeltigen*) for young children to instruct them in prayer.

Two initiatives, one old and the other new, became the guardians of Catholic uniformity: the Inquisition and the *Index librorum prohibitorum* (Index of Prohibited Books) of 1574, the latter following earlier efforts to censor unorthodox books. Both were determined to suppress, sometimes harshly, religious dissent within the ranks of the church and also society, and both were successful as long as secular government supported church action. Two years after the adjournment of the Council of Trent, subscription to the *Professio Fidei Tridentina* (1564), a combination of a statement of faith and a loyalty oath, was made mandatory for all clergy, bishops, and teaching theologians. For over four hundred years, this subscription meant loyalty and uniformity, until the Second Vatican Council in 1967 ordered the discontinuation of the practice.

A telling sign for the resurgence of Catholic self-assertion and self-confidence was the calendar reform undertaken by Pope Gregory XIII in 1582, which replaced the hopelessly erroneous and out-of-synch Julian calendar. The unwillingness of Protestant territories to accept Gregory's venture until the eighteenth century indicated the depth of the great divide between Catholicism and Protestantism as well as the strength of

13. J. Oswald, ed., *Petrus Canisius: Reformer der Kirche; Festschrift zum 400. Todestag des zweiten Apostels Deutschlands* (Augsburg: 1996).

Protestant self-confidence (even in the face of an obvious calendar problem). Gregory also promulgated a new authoritative edition of canon law.

NEW FORMS OF CATHOLIC SPIRITUALITY AND RELIGIOUS LIFE

While secular authorities sought to engage their realms in modernization processes and the Catholic Church sought to confessionalize society, the foremost task at hand was to strengthen those forms of piety that expressed Catholic distinctiveness and underscored the difference to Protestantism. These efforts encompassed the obvious: pilgrimages, crucifixes, candles, holy water, and so on. In an intriguing way, they entailed the sacralization of the daily world by carrying religious structures and customs into the world, expressed in the frequent tolling of bells, in roadside crucifixes, or in statues of holy women and men.

Alongside the doctrinal separation from Protestantism and the emergence of new forms of Catholic spirituality, strong mystical tendencies came to the fore. Especially in many places in southern Europe small circles of individuals sought ways to deepen religious commitment within the church. Their example, their popular literature, their preaching, their charitable works—first most modestly, then with larger consequences—began to affect church and society.

The vitality of the Catholic Church derived from these individuals and their growing number of adherents and followers. All affirmed their loyalty to the church, and this mystical Catholicism had a way, by emphasizing the mystical elements of Christianity, of gelatinizing the dogmatic differences to Protestantism.

Alongside the Council of Trent, the establishment of new religious orders marked the other important feature of sixteenth-century Catholicism. Both council and monastic orders shared the twin goals of defining authentic Catholic doctrine and accomplishing reform.

Through the centuries, spiritual vitality and monastic vitality have been closely linked in the Catholic Church, and one may well have been the barometer for the other. Sixteenth-century Catholicism vindicated this relationship as new and forceful religious orders emerged. Importantly, these new orders grew more out of the concern for vitalizing the Catholic Church than a determination to combat Protestant heresy.

All religious orders in the Roman Catholic tradition spring from the spiritual vision of their founders, charismatic leaders no matter how much they themselves sought to fit into the background; they were organizational geniuses with spiritual priorities. The sixteenth-century founders of new monastic orders had overpowering conversion experiences, which turned them from secular pursuits, often quite lucrative and prestigious, to lives of committed religious devotion. Ignatius of Loyola, for example, had not only a religious conversion during his convalescence in 1521 but also an overpowering religious experience on his way to Rome, when at the shrine of La Storta, some nine miles from the city, he "experienced such a change in his soul and saw so clearly that God the Father placed him with Christ his son." The vision told him "ego vobis Romae propitius ero" (I will be supportive of you in Rome).

An officer in the Spanish army, Ignatius (his full name was Iñigo Lopez de Oñaz y Loyola) was severely wounded in the defense of Pamplona against the French in May 1521—about the same time Luther stood before Emperor Charles V and the diet of the empire in Worms. His injury effectively ended his military career and his year-long convalescence afforded ample time for reflection and soul-searching, triggering his resolve to serve the Virgin Mary and the church. Together with his brother Peru Lopez, he went to the monastery of Montserrat, inland from Barcelona. The location of a famous statue of the Virgin, called the Black Madonna for its color, Montserrat was an important pilgrimage shrine. There, in March 1522, Ignatius gave away his military garments, his mule, and all his worldly possessions, dedicating his sword to the Virgin. Then he made a general confession, a sign that a new chapter in his life had begun. Ignatius continued then to Manresa, where he spent several months in reflection; the groundwork for his famous *Spiritual Exercises* was laid at that time.

The new orders had their beginnings in Italy and Spain, an intriguing geographic indicator that the Protestant heresy played a minor role in the new Catholic religious fervor. First in chronology were the Theatines, founded by Gaetano da Thiene (1480–1547), scion of a Vicenza family of nobility. His career in law, which included high offices in the curia in Rome, ended abruptly when a conversion led him to the priesthood and charitable work in northern Italy. In association with Gian Petro Carafa, later to become Pope Pius IV, di Thiene turned to Rome (a "Babylon" in his eyes) to help alleviate the social ills of the Eternal City. The two found followers and in 1524 Pope Clement VII formally approved the new order. The Theatine order represented the best of Catholic reform concerns prior to the Council of Trent. The order sought to reform the church by reforming the priesthood, especially through greater education, while not neglecting the more traditional monastic concerns of engaging in pastoral care and care for incurables.

There was vitality in the Catholic Church before Pope Paul: the work of individual bishops, the Oratory of the Divine Love together with its monastic offspring, the Theatines. Under Pope Paul III, however, the little springs became a river. In 1535 the Regulars of St. Paul, or Barnabites, were approved, and one year later, the Capuchins. In 1540 came the approval of the Society of Jesus. Although the Jesuits and their founder, Ignatius of Loyola, were to overshadow most other expressions of the resurging Catholic spirituality in the sixteenth century, they were but a small part of a much larger picture. Indeed, their real impact was not felt until many decades later. At mid-century the Jesuits were only a handful of men, at Ignatius's death just about one thousand.

Initially, Ignatius and his companions had to endure a good deal of opposition and persecution from high and low places, an indication that not all were ready for new ways to foster spirituality and serve the Catholic Church. Ignatius, rather like Luther, had experienced a spiritual crisis, but in contrast to the German reformer, he had found the answer in the church. Thus he indicates that the Catholic Church did possess the vitality and spirituality needed in the early sixteenth century: the story of Luther will always need to be juxtaposed to that of Ignatius of Loyola.

The story of Ignatius is the story of an individual committed to serving his church. The reality and the spread of the Protestant "heresy" played only an insignificant role in this resolve. Undoubtedly, Ignatius was aware of that heresy during his Parisian student days, but by that time his spiritual commitment had been made, his spirituality formed, and his priorities delineated. Ignatius of Loyola would have walked his path even if the world had never heard of Luther and the other Reformers. He symbolizes indigenous Catholic vitality in the sixteenth century and illustrates how such vitality could be turned to combat the Protestant Reformation. By the time the century ended, the Society of Jesus had turned its attention to the suppression of Protestant heresy and had become the signal expression of the Counter-Reformation.

Ignatius did not wrestle, as did Luther, with the perturbing question of a gracious God. He knew that upon his confession and his works God was forgiving him. The core of the issue for Ignatius was how to live a spiritual life and serve God to the fullest. His military experience had taught him the value of discipline, and more than any other founder of a monastic community, Ignatius imposed the principle of discipline on the community that he created, a notion superbly expressed in his Rules for Thinking with the Church. His famous devotional guide *Spiritual Exercises*, by the same token, not only underscored this commitment to discipline; it also expressed the deep Jesus mysticism of Ignatian spirituality.

If Ignatius of Loyola personified one strand of such renewed Catholic vitality in the sixteenth century, Teresa de Cepeda y Ahumeda, known for her hometown as Teresa of Avila, represented another. One of ten children of Alonso de Cepeda, a Toledo merchant, and Beatriz de Ahumada, Teresa was born in Avila, Spain, a pilgrimage center, on March 28, 1515. To this day Avila is an impressive town with a massive wall over a mile in length surrounding the town, punctuated by no less than ninety towers. Even in her childhood years, Teresa was devoted to spiritual matters. At the age of seven she resolved to go to the Moors with her brother Rodrigo, there to suffer martyrdom for Jesus—surely, an exquisite manifestation of piety on the part of someone of such youthful age. Sister and brother were thwarted by their uncle, who met them as they were leaving town and promptly returned them to their parents.[14] The youthful dream of martyrdom gave way to the role of the obedient daughter.

Early on Teresa determined to become a religious, but plagued by various physical ailments as she was, she doubted if she had the vocation to be a nun. To complicate matters, her father did not look kindly on her plans. Eventually, in November 1535, at the age of twenty, Teresa entered the Carmelite Monastery of the Incarnation in Avila (an order dedicated to meditation, prayer, work, and penance). She received the habit the following year.

Teresa soon began to have visions, and she was endlessly perturbed about their authenticity. She was told by her spiritual counselor that her visions were nothing but the doings of the devil and she should respond by laughing, advice Teresa did not find particularly helpful.[15]

Teresa was convinced that the true spiritual life called for living in utter separation from the world. Accordingly, in September 1560, several Carmelite nuns gathered in Teresa's convent cell and pledged themselves to establish an eremite convent.

14. Ephrem de la Madre de Dios, *Tiempo y Vida de Sta. Teresa* 142–43.
15. Ibid., 295.

Relatives of Teresa's provided help as they bought a house in Avila for this purpose, pretending that it was for their own use. It took two years to iron out the difficulties with the authorities, but on August 24, 1562, a new convent dedicated to St. Joseph was established; it proved to be the beginning of the Discalced Carmelite Order.[16] During the next several years, Teresa was not only a tireless organizer but also as an equally tireless author. During this time she wrote works that became classics of Western spirituality: *Camino de perfección* (*The Way of Perfection*), which explained the Lord's Prayer as a vehicle for understanding prayer; and *Las Moradas del castillo interior* (*The Mansions of the Interior Castle*), which describes the seven steps leading to mystical union with God. The "interior castle" is the soul, and in its center is the Trinity. Through prayer—the progressive journey through the mansions of the castle from the outside to the center—the individual enters into ever deeper communion with God. Teresa's notion of interior prayer grew out of her christological understanding of God: in the human being Jesus, God encounters the faithful, loving soul as friend.

Teresa described her spiritual journey in the *Libro de la vida* (*Book of Her Life*), written when her activities aroused the suspicion of heresy. In April 1567, however, the head of the Carmelite Order approved Teresa's work and even authorized her to establish additional convents. Thus began the famous "Teresian" reforms, which aimed at reestablishing true Carmelite life for women religious. Teresa served as prioress at the convent in Avila, initially with a great deal of opposition from the community, for the people of Avila seemed unaccustomed to such a resourceful woman. During the last few years of her life Teresa established additional convents, bringing the total she founded to no less than eighteen.

Teresa, who died in 1582, was beatified by Pope Paul V in 1614, and three years later, in 1617, the Spanish parliament proclaimed her the Patroness of Spain. Pope Gregory XV canonized her in 1622 together with Ignatius of Loyola, Francis Xavier, and Philip Neri. Teresa's hallmark was not only her organizational talent, which triggered monastic reform and new religious houses, both male and female. Teresa also was a keen theologian, who molded her own spiritual experience into a cohesive theological framework. Over four hundred letters from her pen testify to her organizational and pastoral skills. She was chronically concerned about the authenticity of her mystical experiences, and she used Augustine's *Confessions* and writings of medieval German mystics as both inspiration and validation. Radical poverty and intensive contemplation were the mainstays of her thought.

Teresa of Avila had a kindred spirit in Juan de Yepes y Alvarez, who called himself Juan de la Cruz, John of the Cross. Born in 1542, John studied at Salamanca and became confessor to the nuns of the Convent of the Incarnation, where Teresa was abbess. Suspected of heresy for his intense religiosity, his reform efforts ran into opposition from the ecclesiastical establishment. For a short while he was imprisoned. Eventually he found a place, modest to be sure, in the network of reformed Carmelite houses. He died in 1591, isolated and misunderstood—until centuries later, in 1726, the Catholic Church canonized him and in 1926 declared him to be a "teacher of the church."

16. Ibid., 32.9.

Several of John's writings belong to the best of Western mystical literature. In his *Subida del Monte Carmelo (Ascent to Mount Carmel)* and *Nocche oscura del alma (Dark Night of the Soul)*, both of 1579, John described the purification of the soul from all worldly burdens. His goal was that of other mystics in the Christian tradition—the "ascent to Mount Carmel," the union of the soul with God, after having gone through the "dark night of the soul," the despair over the alienation from the source of all being.

Carlo Borromeo, the third major figure in sixteenth-century Catholicism, made a different contribution to the dynamic vitality of the church. Born to a noble family at Rocca d'Arona (near Lago Maggiore) in northern Italy in 1538, Carlo was destined, as a younger son, for an ecclesiastical career. At the young age of seven he received the monastic tonsure and his first benefice.[17] Subsequently, he studied canon and civil law at the University of Pavia, where he received the doctorate in December 1559, just before his uncle, Cardinal Giovanni Angelo dé Medici, was elected Pope Pius IV. Soon thereafter, Pius created him a cardinal and made him his secretary. At the curia Carlo was an effective and diligent administrator. The death of his elder brother, Federico, triggered a spiritual transformation as he increasingly adopted an ascetic lifestyle. In 1563 he was ordained to the priesthood and consecrated bishop at the same time. His spiritual commitment made him aware of his obligation to reside in his diocese (a matter much discussed at the recently adjourned Council at Trent), and having resigned all his curial offices except membership on the new Congregation of the Council, which was concerned about clergy, he moved to his diocese Milan in September 1565.

Once in Milan, Borromeo began to pursue reform measures in line with the decrees of the Council of Trent which he had so heavily influenced. Within a month of his arrival he convened a provincial synod, the first held in Milan since 1311. Subsequently he held five more councils at the three-year intervals prescribed by Trent. There were also no less than ten diocesan synods between 1568 and the year of his death. The degrees of these gatherings regulated the deportment of the clergy, administration of the sacraments, liturgy, Lenten observances, funerals, the construction and furnishing of churches, and the management of parochial property. Through the publication of the decisions of these synods as well as Borromeo's pastoral letters, the impact of the reforms in Milan went far beyond the borders of his diocese.

Borromeo became a tireless visitor of the parishes, monasteries, and institutions of the diocese. He spent part of each year in making pastoral visits, which often required long and arduous journeys in his extensive territory. Further observing the Tridentine injunctions, he established a seminary in his diocese. He reorganized the diocesan administration, made use of the religious orders, especially the Jesuits, Barnabites, Theatines, and Capuchins, and founded a congregation of diocesan priests, the Oblates of St. Ambrose. He controlled the printing and selling of religious books. In 1575 he received papal authorization to restore the Ambrosian rite in the churches

---

17. The literature is not that extensive. See, however, the detailed biography of De Roo, André. *Saint Charles Borromée. Cardinal Réformateur, Docteur de la Pastorale (1538–1584)* (Paris: 1963), and the useful collection of papers edited by John M. Headley and John B. Tomaro, *San Carlo Borromeo: Catholic Reform and Ecclesiastical Politics in the Second Half of the Sixteenth Century* (Washington: 1988).

and monasteries subject to his diocese. He set an example of preaching for his clergy, enjoined their practice, and provided preaching aids.

In his reforming zeal, Borromeo was accused of rigorism. Conflict arose with the political authorities, where he insisted on the complete autonomy of the church as indispensable for the pursuit of his goals. He sought to base his policies on the law of the church and the traditions of the diocese of Milan. Understandably the civil authorities refused to recognize them. The archbishop claimed the right to his own police force and the right of clergy to bring laypeople before ecclesiastical courts in civil cases. Borromeo excommunicated the Milanese governor for disregarding the prohibition of entertainments on religious holidays. Only in his last years did he enjoy the collaboration of the civil authorities.

Borromeo was canonized in 1610. He came to be venerated by Catholics throughout Europe and the New World not only as an exemplar of uncommon sanctity but also as the model of a bishop. As such, he was enormously influential in subsequent centuries.

Chapter 10

JOHN CALVIN AND THE REFORMED TRADITION

In March 1536 a six-chapter book was published under the nondescript title *Institutio Religionis Christianae* (*Institutes of the Christian Religion*). The somewhat elusive word *Institutio,* loosely translated as "the main points," expressed the author's intention to offer a summary introduction to the Christian religion, in the format of a catechism, as understood by the proponents of the Reformation. The book numbered several hundred pages, 514 pages to be exact, no mean achievement for its author, a twenty-seven-year-old Frenchman by the name of Jean Cauvin, or John Calvin, an unknown in the firmament of Protestantism.

The origins of the young author's book had been simple. Early in 1534, Calvin—one of the group of reform-minded students in Paris—had accepted the invitation of one Louis du Tillet, a friend and canon at the Angoulême cathedral in the south of France. There young Calvin became something of a local celebrity among those similarly interested in reform; and, admired for his evident learning and intellectual brilliance, they asked him to preach. Calvin complied, and these homiletical ventures prompted him to jot down reflections on aspects of biblical religion. While the multitude of Reformers had written a multitude of books and pamphlets, there was as yet no summary and cohesive elaboration of the new evangelical religion. "All I had in mind," Calvin wrote in the preface, "was to hand on some basics by which anyone with an interest in religion might be formed to true godliness. I labored over this task particularly for our French countrymen, for I observed that many were hungering and thirsting after Christ."

Written in Latin, the book was "about the whole sum of piety and whatever is necessary to know in the doctrine of salvation." It was structured along six chapters on the Ten Commandments, the Apostles' Creed, the Lord's Prayer, the true sacraments, the false sacraments, and the relationship of the civic and the religious authorities. The book offered a thoughtful summary of the new Protestant understanding of the Christian faith. It gained attention, but hardly more so than dozens of other Protestant theological writings published at that time. Nonetheless, despite such somewhat inconspicuous beginnings, its author was to dominate the theological discourse of the Reformation until his death in 1564—and beyond. The final edition of the *Institutes*, revised, enlarged, and edited at a time when Calvin's health had begun to deteriorate and he was in severe physical pain, appeared in 1559, with a French translation published the following year; the first French translation had appeared in 1541.

Calvin arguably became the most influential of the Reformers, especially in the Anglo-Saxon world of Old and New England. While partisans (and scholars) will disagree as to whether Calvin does indeed deserve the accolade of having been the foremost Protestant theologian in the sixteenth century, about his influence there can be no doubt. His thought has often taken to be synonymous with the Protestant tradition. He became the great theological system builder of the Reformation—logical, systematic, in contrast to Luther, who rambled through the theological thicket with the vigor of an exuberant genius, neither fearful of paradox nor hesitant of overstatement, often leaving his followers baffled and disunited. Calvin's thought was clear and systematic, and while the Calvinist tradition also had its share of internal theological disagreements, especially in the seventeenth century, Calvin's systematic thought had the virtue of clarity that spared it intense disagreements and controversy.

Two factors, in addition to the systematic quality of his thought, made for Calvin's historical significance. One was the site of his activities (the town of Geneva on the border between Switzerland and France), while the other was his active involvement in a grandiose missionary effort to spread the Protestant gospel throughout Europe and especially in France.

Compared with the real urban centers of economic or political power in England, Spain, Italy, or France, Geneva was a modest city indeed. What took place in that small commonwealth, even with regard to ecclesiastical change, was quite unimportant in contrast to the dramatic significance of happenings in the Holy Roman Empire or England or Italy. Although histories of the Reformation have a way of recounting the course of events in Geneva in detail, there is no more justification for doing so than for narrating the events in Strassburg, Basel, Augsburg, Nuremberg, or any other of the towns in central Europe in similar fashion.

The history of the Reformation in Geneva might be justifiably slighted—except for Calvin, who spent most of his adult life in the city. On his deathbed he recalled the struggles with his opponents during his years at Geneva, and told the city councilors, the pastors, teachers, and deacons present that "the Lord our God so confirmed me, who am by no means naturally bold (I say what is true), that I succumbed to none of their attempts." A surprising statement—"who am by no means naturally bold." Surely, no description of Calvin sounds more unbelievable. We envision him as a cold, stern, determined even tyrannical individual. Perhaps Calvin himself sensed the astounding tenor of his words, for he added, "I say what is true." What he meant to say with this comment was that he never saw himself as a forceful leader. He was a theologian, an exegete of Scripture. His natural disposition was alien to the demands of his formal practiced responsibilities in Geneva. Moreover, Geneva was not his home; he was a stranger in the city; he never intended to spend his life there. But he became persuaded that God had called him to Geneva, and he was going to do God's work. That was his vocation.

Through his writings, correspondence, contacts, not to mention his teaching at the Genevan Academy, Calvin transferred his vision of the Christian religion from the small town on Lake Geneva to the four corners of Europe, to France no less than to Scotland, Poland, Hungary, and Holland. Calvin was himself a refugee, Geneva was not his home, he was a stranger there, and his heart lay in the mission to propagate the true gospel in his native land. Calvin's thought had a kind of centrifugal quality that made it the normative vocabulary of those who adhered to the new faith. Throughout

Europe, Calvin's beliefs took on flesh and blood. His followers established churches, suffered deprivation and martyrdom, and went into exile because they were persuaded that Calvin, who had never taken a formal course in theology, propounded the authentic Christian message. In several countries, notably in Scotland, France, and the Low Countries, the fabric of Calvinist thought interwove intricately with certain political aspirations so that the cause of the Reformation (which was Calvin's Reformation) became inextricably linked to the broader political course of events. When Calvin wrote to Protestants languishing in French prisons, he evoked the vision of a spiritual battlefield to which God had summoned the faithful: "You serve God with your blood vindicating his truth. It is necessary for you to experience conflicts. . . . If God pleases to use you even to death in his battle, he will sustain you with his mighty hand to fight courageously and will not allow your blood to be shed uselessly."[1]

Like his reforming counterparts, Calvin had a penchant for work. His literary output, especially in the form of biblical commentaries, was enormous. In addition, Calvin was actively involved in the administration of ecclesiastical affairs in Geneva, corresponded prolifically with recipients all over Europe, and preached countless sermons from the pulpit of St. Peter's Church. Most of these sermons perished early in the nineteenth century, when eager Genevan archivists got rid of them for scrap paper. Some two thousand sermon manuscripts are extant, preached over a ten-year period, which accounts for the highly impressive average (especially in light of the thoughtfulness of their content) of two hundred sermons a year. These activities, coupled with a persuasive theology, carried Calvin's message far beyond Geneva.

Other factors contributed to the significance of Calvin's work. During Calvin's ascendancy in the 1540s, German Lutheranism was engaged in a bitter life-and-death struggle for its survival, Emperor Charles V having decided to force the Lutheran heretics into submission by military might. At the same time, Lutherans were also forced to cope with theological dissension within their own ranks. Luther's somewhat unsystematic mind had allowed his disciples to offer divergent interpretations of his thought. The result was disagreement, controversy, and an inward preoccupation.

Calvinism found itself in a quite different situation. Calvin's French background, coupled with the geographical proximity of Geneva and France, made France the ideal missionary field for those who embraced the Genevan gospel. Calvin's aspiration was to lead his native land to the true understanding of the Christian faith. Alongside his deep emotional involvement was the linguistic affinity—the language of his tracts and his letters of counsel, inspiration, and exhortation was, as a rule, in French. He spoke directly to the French people in their language, the way Luther had been able to speak to the Germans; the geographic location of Geneva added its own particular significance.

The sites of vigorous Calvinist expansion in Europe were also places of political and constitutional turbulence, and this had profound consequences for the history of Calvinism. Virtually all Reformers had agreed on the right of the lower magistracy to resist the upper magistracy. In Germany this line of thought had provided the theological rationale for the founding of the League of Schmalkald. Elsewhere in Europe, notably in France, the issue was considerably more complicated, for there a prolonged

---

1. *Calvini Opera*, 14:423ff.

and complicated struggle took place for the legal recognition of the Protestant faith, pursued in the face of intermittent persecution, but also in the presence (at several places) of a serious constitutional crisis. This precipitated reflections on the relationship of the Christian faith to the secular authorities, and Calvinist theologians offered some striking answers to make their views congenial to places of political upheaval. Calvinism, in other words, was at the right time and place when certain political issues arose and demanded an answer. That was its destiny and its historical significance.

Calvin himself was a complex individual—timid and stern, modest and aggressive, an unusual combination of opposites. He could be aggressively vindictive, always in the service of the greater religious good, as he himself claimed. Above all, he was a man driven by a purpose. The second generation of the Reformation may have called for individuals of this type, and Calvin brought impressive credentials, foremost a profound mind. Much has been written about his theology and there can be little doubt that it was one of the eminent achievements of the century; one can say this without engaging in the kind of parochial hagiography that so often inflates denominational founding fathers to bigger-than-life stature of historical prominence. Compared with the other eminent Reformer, Luther, Calvin was more systematic and less paradoxical.

Several themes occupy important places in Calvin's theological thought. The assertion of divine sovereignty is one; predestination is another; the righteousness of faith, yet another. The difficulty lies not so much in the acknowledgment that these were important themes, but in the assessment of their relative significance. One way of identifying a common thread among the themes of Calvin's thought is to understand his theology as a systematic delineation of the theological ramifications of justification by grace alone. The spectrum of Protestant opinion in the sixteenth century shows that this principle lent itself to a variety of expressions, and Calvin's exposition was therefore not the only one.

A telling question in Calvin's dedicatory epistle to King Francis I in his *Institutes* put it all into simple words: "How does the kingdom of Christ come to us and remain among us?" The question presupposed that the establishment of God's kingdom was indeed most important. The majesty of divine sovereignty overwhelmed the Genevan reformer and may well be taken to be the leitmotiv of his theology. God's sovereignty— over little things as well as big ones, over good as well as evil, over damnation as well as salvation—forms the running theme of Calvin's *Institutes*. Both the natural universe and humankind point to this sovereignty and thus to the glory of God.

Intriguingly, Calvin discussed the topic of predestination in his *Institutes* in the context of soteriology and not in connection with his elaboration of the topic of God. Predestination does not tell us about the nature of God, Calvin seemed to say, as about God's gracious dealing with humans. This was Calvin's notion of predestination, sometimes referred to as double predestination, because it spoke to both the fate of those predestined to salvation and to those predestined to damnation. God did not merely allow the fall of Adam and the damnation of some of humankind; God actually willed it. And Calvin was persuaded that this doctrine was found in Scripture, and he gloried in the redemption of the elect.

Predestination was the radical application of the notion of justification by grace alone, which itself was an expression of God's sovereignty. To the Protestant assertion that redemption is effected by God's grace, and not by human works, Calvin added that God is utterly free to bestow this grace upon whomever he pleases. While other Reformers, such as Luther, essentially shared Calvin's notion but chose not to emphasize it, Calvin did not hesitate to explicate this teaching and, indeed, to consider it crucial for the Christian faith.

Calvin pointedly distinguished predestination from foreknowledge. The two were not identical. Thus he observed in his *Institutes*,

> We say rightly that [God] foresees all things, even as he disposes of them; but it is confusing everything to say that God elects and rejects according to his foresight of this or that. When we attribute foreknowledge to God, we mean that all things have always been and eternally remain under his observation, so that nothing is either future or past to his knowledge: he sees and regards them in the truth, as though they were before his face. We say that this foreknowledge extends throughout the circuit of the world and over all his creatures. We call predestination the eternal decree of God by which he decided what he would do with each man. For he does not create them all in like condition, but ordains some to eternal life, the others to eternal damnation.

This, in short, was Calvin's notion of predestination, the teaching that God had eternally elected those who were to have everlasting life. Needless to say, Calvin understood this to be a biblilcal teaching, growing out of a sharp delineation of the notion of divine sovereignty and power. At the same time, however, Calvin's exposition of the topic in the *Institutes* makes clear that for him the doctrine was supported not only by Scripture and the understanding of divine sovereignty, but also by empirical reality. It is noteworthy that Calvin began his discussion of predestination in his *Institutes* by calling attention to an obvious fact: not all humans are exposed to the preaching of the Christian gospel, and not all of those who are exposed to it do accept it. Since the gospel is necessary for salvation, it followed for Calvin that not all humans have equal access to salvation. This, Calvin argued, poses the question as to why large parts of humankind are deprived of the salvatory word of the gospel. His answer, of course, was to assert that God had so willed it.

Calvin saw this as the clear and self-evident teaching of Scripture, but he conceded the difficulties in comprehending it. Quite aptly, he wrote in the *Institutes*, "We ought not to seek any reason for it because in its greatness it far surpasses our understanding." Calvin asserted that the teaching guaranteed an individual's redemption as nothing else could. The certainty of redemption was related to the certainty of election, which, in turn, was the consequence of Christ's redemptive work. And this redemptive work—the death on the cross of God's Son—was as impenetrable a mystery as was the mystery of predestination. If one interprets election as a consequence of divine sovereignty, it would follow, as it did indeed for Calvin, that God did not merely allow the fall of Adam—God actually willed it.

An important corollary of Calvin's doctrine of predestination was the question if God's eternal election might be discernible in individuals. Calvin was reluctant to speak about a possible verification of election in oneself or in others. Wrote Calvin, "To determine safely of others if they belong to the church or not, to separate the elect from the damned, is not our office. It is the singular right of God to know who are his own." Yet at the same time he cautiously suggested that there were signs, fallible to be sure, but signs nonetheless. Calvin identified three of these: proper belief, proper faithfulness in worship, and proper walk of life. There were approximations by which the identity of the children of God and the children of darkness may be inferred. "Led by loving benevolence we must consider as elect and members of the church all those who through confession of faith, walk of life, and participation in the sacraments confess the same God and Christ with us, even though a good part of imperfection remains in their character."[2]

To be sure, in later years Calvin somewhat modified his language by paying greater attention to an individual's allegiance to the church, which meant, for example, that excommunication of an individual rendered a judgment about this person's eternal destiny. An important aspect of Calvin's understanding of the Christian faith surfaced here: the walk of life as evidence of election. This did not mean that moral propriety by itself was understood as the telling evidence of election. It meant that those men and women characterized by morally impeccable lives were more likely to be among the chosen elect than those who were not. And the church took it upon itself to monitor the morals of the faithful.

Calvin's notion had consequences. Wherever Calvin's understanding of the Christian religion found entrance, serious determination prevailed to follow the rule of Christ. Perhaps the other Reformers gave in a bit too easily in their advocacy of the pursuit of the godly life, or they were overcome by theological scruples about the use of the magistracy to achieve moral reform. Calvin, however, saw his goal and pursued it relentlessly. No wonder that John Knox found Geneva "the most perfect school of Christ since the days of the Apostles." Indeed, Geneva was distinctive, and those who went there were quite aware of it. Whether all the people were different is impossible to say, though the reports (such as the one by Knox) were uniformly exuberant. Clearly, however, the civic authorities endorsed the Calvinist ethos and helped put it into practice.

One of the more fascinating interpretations of Calvin's impact on European society had to do with economics, and for almost a full century the topic turned into one of the more controversial topics in the study of the impact of the Reformation. A century ago, the German economist and sociologist Max Weber argued in a lengthy essay entitled "The Protestant Ethic and the Spirit of Capitalism" that Calvin's notion of predestination, as it merged with Luther's concept of vocation, led to the emergence of a capitalist "spirit." In effect, Weber sought to make a point not so much about religious belief, Protestant or other, but about the ethos of practices that derive from such belief.[3]

Calvin's notion was that the believers' "walk of life" offered a hint of their eternal election. Additionally he emphasized that all human endeavors and jobs were divine "vocations" and that the gospel mandated frugal and simple living. This meant that the Calvinists were told to pursue their daily work as a divine calling, to work hard, and yet to spend little. The wealth acquired beyond what was needed to maintain a frugal lifestyle could then be put to ever new economic use.

---

2. Ibid., 1:75: "et fidei confessione et vitae exemple et sacramentorum participatione."
3. The best brief summary of Weber's argument and the controversy surrounding it is found in the article by William H. Swatos Jr., "Protestant Ethic Thesis," *Encyclopedia of Religion and Society* (ed. William H. Swatos Jr.; Walnut Creek, CA: 1998), 379–82.

This has been called the "Protestant ethic," which expressed not merely the divine calling to work but also the commitment to a modest lifestyle. This work ethic flourished among late sixteenth- and seventeenth-century Calvinists, especially of the Puritan variety in Old and New England. Richard Baxter, for example, insisted that God rewarded his elect in this life—if they lived according to his laws, which meant that they were diligent in their use of time and talent, lived frugally—and used the "capital" that accrued from their frugal lifestyle for new investments.

Weber agued that the "Protestant work ethic" arising from such theological and moral considerations facilitated the breakthrough of the spirit of modern capitalism as a comprehensive social and economic system. He was well aware that there had been centers of early capitalism, such as Florence, that long antedated those of Calvinist orientation, and his argument attained its cogency by the question why those older centers eventually failed to flourish, while the (newer) Calvinist North American colonies succeeded. Weber did not argue (as most of his critics who seem not to have read him thoroughly insisted) that Protestant/Calvinist doctrines caused modern rational capitalism. Rather, his thesis was that Protestantism facilitated a convergence of factors that provided the elements for the spirit of modern capitalism. This dynamic convergence flourished in the seventeenth century, well after the period of the Reformation. We make note of it, however, since the origin lay in the theological affirmations of Calvin (and Luther) in the sixteenth century.

Related, though not particularly argued by Calvin, was the reality that the church governance he delineated had a democratic propensity since the presbyteries on the local level allowed for lay involvement. This conveyed to the emerging class of burghers, merchants, in the second half of the sixteenth century a new kind of confidence and self-assurance.

CALVIN'S LIFE

Jean Cauvin, son of Gérard Cauvin, secretary to Charles de Hangest, bishop of Noyon, and procurator of the cathedral chapter of the town of Noyon, located some fifty miles north of Paris, was born the fourth of four sons on July 10, 1509. Both the year of his birth and his family background are important: Jean Cauvin belonged to the second generation of Reformers who appeared on the scene after the initial battles of the Reformation had already been fought. He reached theological maturity when the period of reforming *sturm und drang* had passed. In 1509 Luther was well on his way to the theological doctorate; in 1517, when the indulgences controversy broke out, Jean Cauvin was barely eight years old; in 1536, when he published his first theological treatise, the Reformation had been introduced all over south Germany and Switzerland.

Jean Cauvin spent his youth in the urbane and cultured setting of a French cathedral town and was exposed, through his father's professional prominence in town, to the *haut monde* of ecclesiastical and social life. His father's successful career (he was successively registrar of Noyon, secretary to the bishop, and finally procurator of the cathedral chapter) afforded him a social standing with access to the powerful town elites, an environment altogether different from the austere monastic cell that was Luther's home for almost two decades. Jean Cauvin's aristocratic tastes and manners differed sharply from his uncouth and earthen Wittenberg counterpart.

When time came for young Jean to pursue university studies, Gérard Cauvin manifested the timeless sentiment of parents to harbor great ambitions for their offspring. Given his relationship to the bishop, Gérard secured several benefices for Jean (who received the first when he was barely twelve years old). Perhaps there was a bit of self-interest involved, since these benefices allowed Jean to study without heavily drawing on his father's resources.

Accordingly, in 1523 Jean Cauvin, fourteen years of age, went to Paris to pursue the customary course in the liberal arts. He latinized his name to "Calvinus" and studied first at the Collège de la Marche and then at that citadel of orthodoxy, the Collège de Montaigu. While eminent intellectually, the college was also a bizarre mixture of otherworldly neglect, authoritarianism, and orthodoxy. Erasmus, who also had been a student there, as later John Knox and Ignatius of Loyola, described it in his *Colloquia* as "a barrack, filthy, bleak, inhospitable, reeking with the foulest smells, clotted with dirt, brayed with noises, where the dinner would be stale bread and half a herring. Here, at four in the morning, a small wretch of fourteen would begin his lessons . . . until seven in the evening."[4] Sentiment will differ as to the productivity of such a pedagogical approach.

After completing the customary course in the liberal arts, Calvin received the degree of master of arts, probably in 1529, at which point in time his father intervened, insisting that his son study law rather than theology, as he himself had first proposed. "Ever since I was a child," Calvin wrote many years later, "my father had intended me for theology; but thereafter inasmuch as he considered that the study of law commonly enriched those who followed it, this expectation made him incontinently change his mind."[5] Even in those days the law was a highly lucrative and prestigious profession, but there is reason to conclude that such paternal intervention was related to Gérard Cauvin's conflict with his bishop over the bishop's demand that he turn over the accounting books for the cathedral. Gérard had refused to do, and it is not clear to this day if he had something to hide or felt his integrity impugned. At any rate, Gérard was excommunicated by the bishop, hardly the proper setting for his son to study theology.

Nonetheless, young Calvin's years at Montaigu were of deep importance and consequence. He encountered eminent teachers—the Nominalist theologian Johann Major, for example, and Guillaume Cop, personal physician to the king, father of Nicolas Cop, who was to deliver the famous speech at the University of Paris in 1533. Calvin received not only a thorough exposure to the liberal arts but also the rudiments of the theologians of the early church.

In deference to his father's wishes John moved to Orléans for the study of law. Not much is known about his religious views at the time, though it does appear that during his stay in Orléans he was increasingly exposed to humanist notions and thought;

---

4. François Wendel, *Calvin: The Origins and Development of His Religious Thought* (New York: 1963), 18. Erasmus's tirades against Montaigu are in his *Colloquia*, the "Fish Diet." See C. R. Thompson, ed., *The Collected Works of Erasmus: Colloquia* (Toronto: 1997), 715f.

5. *Calvini Opera*, 32:32.

Orléans, together with a brief sojourn in Bourges, were to prove significant in that respect. The fatal illness of his father ended, altogether unexpectedly, John's studies at Orléans. He hurriedly returned to Noyon, where he and his brother Charles became promptly embroiled in a dispute with the cathedral chapter over the lifting of their father's excommunication—John Calvin's views of the church may well have been shaped by that incident. His eventual return to Paris, for further humanist studies, was aided by the awareness that his father's dictum to study law was now no longer relevant.

In following the humanist pattern of producing commentaries on works from classical antiquity, his main preoccupation during that time was writing a commentary on Seneca's treatise *De Clementia*. It was published in April 1532. "At length the die is cast," he wrote a friend with an intriguing mixture of self-confidence, modesty, and ambitiousness. "My commentaries on the books of Seneca, *De Clementia*, have been printed, but at my own expense, and have drawn from me more money than you can well suppose. At present, I am using every endeavor to collect some of it back."[6] Calvin, much like all authors of all times, expected his book to make a major impact, perhaps even give him European renown—none other than Erasmus had published the book twice, inviting his readers to improve on him (doubtless with only half-hearted sincerity)—but, alas, the book did not catapult him to the intellectual prominence he had hoped.

One must not read too much of the future reformer John Calvin into this first work, though scholars have tended either to ignore it or bestow great importance onto it. Calvin's future notion of natural law undoubtedly was derived from Stoic thought, and the exegetical approach of the commentary (using grammar and parallel passages) laid the foundation for his later mastery of biblical hermeneutics. Nonetheless, one will have great difficulty in finding the subsequent reformer in this work.

Sometime after the publication of his Seneca commentary Calvin became a follower of the new evangelical understanding of the Christian religion as well as a despiser of papal superstition. The sources for this turn of events are scant, however, and the details of Calvin's turning away from traditional religion remain altogether enigmatic. This is in contrast to Luther, who was given to talk about his "conversion" so often that scholars have found themselves confused and almost as incapable of understanding exactly what happened, as they are in the case of Calvin. The most pertinent source for Calvin is a scant sentence in his *Commentary on the Psalms* of 1557: "God by a sudden conversion subdued and brought my mind to a teachable frame."[7] It would appear that both Luther and Calvin experienced their religious "conversion" at once as a break with the Roman Church.

In May 1534 Calvin traveled to Noyon to surrender his ecclesiastical benefices. Undoubtedly, something of importance must have compelled him to cut his ties with the church, and there is reason to believe that the conversion mentioned in his Psalms commentary was the precipitating factor. Roughly a year earlier, in August 1533, Calvin had attended a meeting of the cathedral chapter in Noyon, assisting with the organization of a procession against the plague, but later that year he was already suspect as a

---

6. *Corpus Reformatorum* (hereafter *CR*), 38:13.
7. *CR* 59:21.

"Lutheran" in Paris. His friendship with Nicolas Cop, whose speech on All Saints' Day on the text of the Beatitude "Blessed are the poor in spirit" had been a mélange of Erasmian and Lutheran notions, including Luther's distinction of law and gospel, raising the likelihood of being arrested as were other of Cop's friends. Indeed, Calvin may well have contributed to Cop's speech.

A time of unsteady meandering in France followed. Calvin's new Protestant conviction increasingly made his stay in France dangerous. In the fall of 1534 he moved to Basel, where he preoccupied himself with theology by reading extensively in theological works, mainly those of Luther, and began to correspond with reformers as well as with old friends (here the imperious tone so characteristic of his later correspondence made its first appearance). Mainly he worked on a catechism of the new evangelical faith he subsequently entitled *Institutes of the Christian Religion*. Completed in August 1535, the book was published in March of the following year.

Later that summer Calvin returned to his native France and Noyon. King Francis I had proclaimed an amnesty for all Protestants abjuring their belief, but Calvin most probably returned to settle matters pertaining to his father's estate. He found occasion to visit Paris briefly, and was then on his way eastward to Strassburg, where he planned to settle as a private scholar-theologian. The renewed outbreak of hostilities between Francis I and Charles V made it impossible to travel directly eastward to Strassburg. He was forced to make a southerly detour, which in April 1536 took him to Geneva, where he planned to stay overnight and then continue northward to his destination, Strassburg.

Geneva had by the 1530s lost some of the importance it had enjoyed in the fifteenth century, though its strategic location at the crossroads of important trade routes continued to make it a significant commercial center. The woodcut in Sebastian Münster's *Cosmographey* of 1564 shows its modest size, though prominently depicting the steeples of a dozen or so churches. Formally part of the Holy Roman Empire (though not of the Swiss Confederation), Geneva was ruled by its bishops, which rule had practically turned into the rule by the dukes of Savoy, since the Genevan episcopal see had become what might be called their wholly owned subsidiary. The Genevan elites, by the same token, had persistently striven to gain independence from the dukes and had sought ever closer ties with the important town of Bern.

In the opening decades of the sixteenth century, especially after 1519, when Fribourg and Bern formed a compact to enhance Swiss importance, Geneva was beset by severe internal tensions between supporters of Savoy, mainly the old patrician families which had come into wealth in the fifteenth century, and those of the Swiss Confederation, mainly new citizens. Gradually, the latter gained in influence, and Genevan city council assumed jurisdiction over the affairs of the city (taxation, judiciary, currency) and one after the other, priests left the town. The supporters of ties with the Swiss carried the day, which meant the end of Savoy rule. The last episcopal visit to Geneva occurred in 1533.

The close political ties with Bern, which had turned Protestant by that time, exposed Geneva to Protestant influence. Protestant sentiment reached Geneva fairly early through Lambert d'Avignon, later the principal figure in the Hessian Reformation. One suspects that Lambert's preaching impacted the town, but no significant agitation for reform ensued. Intriguingly, the concrete signal for the introduction of reform in Geneva came over the issue of indulgences. When, early in 1532, an indulgence was announced in Geneva, handbills were found in the city that had this to say: "God, our heavenly father, promises forgiveness of all sins to everyone, requiring only repentance and a living faith." When a canon of St. Peter's removed one of these handbills from the sanctuary, a young man quietly picked up the shreds and posted a new handbill. The two promptly got into a fistfight, joined by bystanders in what must have been an intriguing way to resolve theological differences. The city council promptly reprimanded the participants in this theological free-for-all, but at the same time exhorted the Genevan clergy to preach the "gospel and the epistles, only the divine truth, without adding fantasies, legends, or other absurdities." The slogans of the Reformation had found their way into the city.

A small group of evangelicals persistently agitated for religious change, and when a hesitant city council failed to take sides they resorted to public provocation: marchers in a religious procession were hooted with the catcall "feed thistles to those braying asses."[8] In the fall of 1532, Guillaume Farel came to Geneva to preach the new evangelical message but was blatantly unsuccessful, barely escaping unscathed when pursued by a frenzied Catholic mob; cries "au Rhosne, au Rhosne" (into the Rhone, into the Rhone) left no doubt about their intentions.

Farel, a Frenchman, who had studied in Paris with the humanist Jacques Lefèvre d'Étaples, joined the reforming circle at Meaux, but finding it not radical enough moved to Basel in 1523. There he and Erasmus developed mutual hostility, which undoubtedly was the cause for his expulsion from the city. A peripatetic evangelistic activity in Switzerland followed. His unsuccessful debut in Geneva did not dissuade him from further visits to the city and efforts to spread the new evangelical message there. He found a compatriot in Pierre Viret and together these two sought to stem the ecclesiastical tide in Geneva. Catholic sentiment continued to be strong—Viret barely escaped being poisoned (with spinach, no less)—and a disputation in June 1535 that dragged on for weeks did not lead anywhere until an outbreak of iconoclasm brought the provisional abolition of the Mass in August and the formal repudiation of Catholicism one year later on May 21, 1536. With raised arms, the Genevan citizens voted for the new faith, to live henceforth "according to the holy law of the gospel and the Word of God" and to "abandon all Masses and other ceremonies, papal abuses and other idols."

By turning Protestant the city of Geneva followed the course of events in numerous other cities and communities throughout the empire and, indeed, Europe. In Geneva, as elsewhere, the Mass was the symbol of a perverted church that needed to be abolished; and in Geneva, as elsewhere, the government usurped authority and power to have a say in religious affairs. Geneva was different, all the same, in that no extensive preaching and proclamation of the "new gospel" had occurred in the city prior to turning Protestant, and the struggle for religion was, in a way, only pretense for the political power struggle between those in the city who wished to remain under Savoyan rule and those who wished for Genevan independence. Religious preference in the city was thus hardly clear.

8. Philip Benedict, *Christ's Churches Purely Reformed* (New Haven: 2002), 80.

In turn Guillaume Farel was a firebrand with an explosive and ebullient Gallic temper; he knew neither weakness nor patience, only a zealous pursuit of the things of God. "At no time did any man preach the Sacred Word of God purely without being persecuted and denounced by the world as a rogue and an impostor," he said on one occasion; his life provided abundant illustration for his contention. Compared to Calvin, Farel seems to have been less talented and insightful—though of course few would fare well in such a comparison. But there was something charismatic in him, for after all he succeeded in persuading an utterly reluctant Calvin to make his domicile in Geneva. After he had become Protestant, Farel turned into a homeless refugee for the faith; he had served as clergy in Basel, Montbeliard, Strassburg, and Bern, and even published two important theological treatises, *La manière & fasson*, a church order, and *Summaire & briefve declaration*, a summary catechism on the Christian faith. The monument erected in his memory in front of the cathedral of Neuchâtel, where he was to spend most of his life, shows him with arms raised high, holding a Bible—Farel could be Moses hurling the Ten Commandments against the golden calf, and the similarity is more than coincidence. Wherever he was, the spirits divided; he left traces of tension, strife, and acrimony. Some would have called him a rabble-rouser, of the ilk of Thomas Müntzer, Matthias Flacius, or John Knox.

In Geneva Farel's agitation was successful. In March 1533 it was noted that "the number of those who desire the Word is very great," and at the end of that same month the Genevan council, with curious ambiguity, ordered that nothing be said publicly against the sacraments, that the good burghers of Geneva live in peace and harmony, and that the ministers not preach anything that cannot be proven from Scripture. Pierre de la Baume, the Genevan bishop, decided to leave the unfriendly city, assuring everyone that he would return shortly. He never darkened the streets of Geneva again.

Calvin passed through Geneva for an overnight stay two months after the formal declaration of the city to join Protestant ranks. Before the day was over his life had been altered and Geneva had become the site of his destiny. He had planned to stay overnight, but Farel had learned that the youthful author of the recently published *Institutes* was lodging in town, visited him, and pled with him to stay. Calvin later recalled that he pointed out to Farel "that I had several studies for which I wished to keep myself free," and then noted that Farel responded by uttering "an imprecation that God would curse my retirement, and the tranquility of the studies which I sought, if I should withdraw and refuse to give assistance, when the necessity was so urgent. By this imprecation I was so stricken with terror that I desisted from the journey that I had undertaken."[9] To be sure, one will not go amiss in seeing a bit of drama in Calvin's own recollection of the encounter—the biblical precedence of unwilling (and terror-stricken) prophets when hearing God's voice springs to mind.

Farel wished for Calvin's presence in Geneva as his assistant. Not surprisingly, therefore, the very first official mention of Calvin in Genevan records in the minutes of the city council for September 5, 1536, did not not even identify him by name: "Master Guillaume Farel points out the necessity of the lectures begun by that Frenchman at St. Peter's and requests that he be retained and supported. He was told that

9. *CR* 59:25.

such support would be taken under advisement."[10] Hardly an exuberant expression of welcome—and support: Calvin had agreed to stay in Geneva without being assured of his livelihood.

The lectures mentioned were Calvin's first activity in Geneva—the exposition of the Epistles of the apostle Paul, done, according to a contemporary note, "with great praise and profit." Calvin, who could combine personal humility and striking arrogance, promptly called himself "professor sacrarum literarum in ecclesia Genovesiensis," a rather high-sounding title that obscured his modest role in the ecclesiastical affairs of the city, correct only if the root meaning of the Latin *professor* was employed. Nonetheless, the title and lectures expressed Calvin's self-understanding as a teacher rather than as a pastor. The insights and erudition of his lectures, as well as his spectacular participation in a theological disputation about the new faith in Lausanne, propelled him into a pastoral role, and by 1537, the twenty-seven-year-old had become one of the leading clergy in Geneva. The combination of his legal background and theological erudition were tailor-made for a community that was seeking to find its way theologically and politically. His youthfulness notwithstanding, the members of the city council quickly came to respect him, while the much older Farel never hesitated to draw upon his younger colleague's theological and intellectual erudition.

Calvin threw himself into church affairs in addition to his biblical expositions in the Genevan cathedral. He drafted a church order that dealt with the frequency of the celebration of the Lord's Supper and worked on a brief statement of faith that was to be subscribed by all wanting to receive Communion, "so that it can be seen who agrees with the gospel and who would rather belong to the kingdom of the pope than of Jesus Christ." The document also included provisions for church discipline to monitor those coming to Communion so that the clergy could prevent unrepentant sinners from receiving Communion.

A provision in the church order stipulated that all Geneva citizens should publicly subscribe to this confession. In March 1537 the two city councils approved most of the provisions of the document drafted by Calvin, except that Communion should be celebrated only four times a year. The subscription by the Genevan citizenry to the proposed confession of faith, however, proved to be a different matter. Most burghers balked, were recalcitrant, and refused to subscribe, whereupon the city council issued a mandate that no one should be denied access to the Lord's Supper. The clergy, including Calvin, were aghast.

The elections to various municipal offices in February 1538 resulted in a striking victory for the opponents of the recent ecclesiastical changes. Tensions between the city council and the clergy increased, Calvin calling it a "most miserable situation," forgetting that in part it had been caused by his rigidity in forging ahead with extensive religious change when the Genevan citizens and the council were not ready. At this point, Farel's rashness and Calvin's inexperience precipitated a fateful development. The city council, concerned about the deep-seated tensions in the city, ordered that some ecclesiastical practices, abolished in Geneva, but still retained in Protestant Bern, should be reintroduced in Geneva. The council was undoubtedly prompted by

10. *CR* 49:204.

a desire to reduce tensions in the city by removing some of the most radical innovations, while at the same time strengthening ties with Protestant Bern. Specifically, the council ordered that unleavened bread rather than ordinary bread should be used in Communion and that four religious holidays, previously abolished, be reintroduced. Farel and Calvin conceded that these were insignificant matters, but voiced adamant opposition to the decision of the council. At issue, for them, was the interference of secular government in church affairs.

Communion was to be celebrated on Easter. Farel and Calvin made clear that they would not follow the Bernese form and were promptly ordered by the city council to conduct the services along Bernese lines. Farel and Calvin responded by not serving Communion at all. "A holy mystery would be profaned," said Calvin.[11] Two days later Farel and Calvin were ordered to leave the city. Calvin's involvement in public ministry, reluctantly begun but vigorously pursued, had ended in failure. Farel found a home at Neuchâtel, while Calvin continued the journey to Strassburg that had been so unexpectedly interrupted two years earlier and accepted an invitation to serve a congregation of French refugees there. For three important years Strassburg was his home; indeed, it was more than that. It was his school of theology and ecclesiastical leadership. His friendship with Martin Bucer, the Strassburg reformer, his participation at the Colloquy of Regensburg, not to mention the publication of the French edition of his enlarged *Institutes of the Christian Religion*, together with his intense pastoral responsibilities made this a rewarding and enriching period in his life. In Strassburg he also married Idelette de Bure, widow of an Anabaptist, though it seems —judging from remarks in a tract on celibacy—that his main objective in marrying was to be relieved of the burdens of everyday domestic life: "I know not if I shall ever marry. If I did so, it would be in order to devote my time to the Lord, by being more relieved from the worries of daily life."[12] Idelette, of whom a few portraits are extant, seems to have been regal and aristocratic but unlike Katharina of Bora, who married Luther, only scarce comments tell us about her married life. In July 1539 Calvin received Strassburg citizenship; without doubt he had every intention of making the city his permanent home.

Meanwhile Genevan ecclesiastical affairs were in trouble. Calvin's supporters (and he had many) were deeply discontent. Ami Perrin, scion of an old Genevan family, led a faction that called themselves Guillermins, after Guillaume Farel's first name, who both opposed a treaty concluded with Bern in the summer of 1530, which gave Bern extensive legal rights in some outlying villages, and also advocated—in view of the dire state of ecclesiastical affairs in Geneva—Calvin's return. The Genevan pastors, faced with the enormous challenge to win the populace over to the new faith, seemed paralyzed and inept. No strong leader was on the scene and the clergy were characterized by a striking inability to measure up to the challenge of the situation. The Artichauds, who approved of the "articles" of the treaty with Bern, began to lose influence, because it became evident that Bern wanted to extend its political influence over Geneva. Early in 1540, the Guillermins succeeded in obtaining the majority on

11. *CR* 49:225.
12. *Calvini Opera*, 10 a, 228.

the Small Council. In June riots occurred in the town, and shortly thereafter one of the leaders of the Artichauds was executed in an enigmatic exercise of justice.

When Jacopo Sadoleto, bishop of Carpentras, prompted by the situation in Geneva, published an appeal to the city council to return to the Catholic fold, he offered a persuasive plea for the unbroken tradition of the Catholic Church, which—no matter how extensive and formidable the abuses—laid claim to the divine promise of the continuing presence of the Holy Spirit. His argumentation was neither novel nor particularly brilliant, though it did demonstrate that theological learning was not an exclusive Protestant prerogative. For Sadoleto the alternatives were simple: to believe either "what the church throughout the whole world has approved with general consent for more than fifteen hundred years or the innovations introduced during the last twenty-five years by crafty or, as they think of themselves, wise men."

When none of the Genevan clergy rallied to respond, it was left to Calvin, writing in Strassburg at the behest of the Genevan council, to make the cogent case for the new faith. Polite in tone, and therefore a bit unusual for much of the Reformation polemic, Calvin rejected the charges of personal dishonesty of the Reformers and countered Sadoleto's stress on tradition with the "threefold ground" of the true church: doctrine, discipline, and the sacraments. Calvin's cogent defense prompted some Genevans to think wistfully of him. His return began to be advocated by the Guillermins, and in September 1540 the city council issued its invitation, dispatching an official delegation to Strassburg on October 20, 1540. Calvin hesitated. He could not have been less interested: "I would prefer a hundred other deaths to that cross."[13] But eventually he yielded: one suspects that the assurance of the Zurich city council that it would support him in Geneva was a factor of considerable importance.

One full year after he had first been approached and solicited, on September 2, 1541, Calvin began his journey back to Geneva. His future was unknown. In his pockets he carried a letter from the Strassburg city council, giving him a six-month leave. Perhaps he intended to stay only until calm and order had returned to the church in Geneva; the six months stretched into twenty-three years. More than once during this long time Calvin surely pondered the wisdom of his decision to return. The Genevan city council provided a house for him on the rue de Chanoines, where he was to live until his death in 1564, and provided him with a salary double that of the other pastors.

His erstwhile colleague and mentor Guillaume Farel chose to stay in Neuchâtel.

CALVIN AND THE GENEVAN CHURCH, 1541–1564

At thirty-two years of age Calvin was still youthful when he returned to Geneva in 1541. In contrast to his previous appointment, he returned as acknowledged leader of the Genevan church and occupied a position different from the subordinate role he had filled three years earlier. The Genevan city council had ventured to make Calvin's decision easier by pointing out that, given the strategic location of Geneva, his influence would be enormous not only in the city but in Switzerland, France, and Italy as well.

---

13. *CR* 39:214.

Geneva offered Calvin the opportunity to translate his theology into ecclesiastical practice. To be sure, even in Geneva the real tended to fall short of the ideal, and Calvin's relationship with the city and its political elites was never more than a *mariage de convenance* where neither partner was particularly happy, but both found the relationship valuable. Calvin was too one-sidedly concerned about religion to be fully appreciated by the Genevan citizenry, and Geneva was far too worldly to gain Calvin's full respect.

When Calvin, who was rarely given to flamboyance, stood for the first time in the pulpit of St. Peter's after his return, he simply continued his scriptural exposition where it had been interrupted three years earlier, a telling indication that he sensed the importance of symbolism. Now the leader of the Genevan church, his work in Geneva took place in the setting of the formal adoption of the *Ordonnances* and the support of his ministerial colleagues. The Genevan pastors were competent men, and their commitment to Calvin's vision offers an important explanation for Calvin's own accomplishments, even though it promptly turned out that they too were not free from human weakness and foibles. Their corporate unwillingness—Calvin excepted—to minister to the dying during the plague of 1542, since "God had not yet given them the grace" to go to the sick, is well known.

Calvin wasted no time on his return to Geneva. On September 13, 1541, the very day of his return, Calvin asked the city council to convene a commission to promulgate a new church order. The council agreed, and Calvin feverishly went to work drafting such an order. He left little doubt that this was foremost on his mind, and that the abject failure back in 1538 had not led him to change or modify his views. A first draft was completed within a week, at which point the city council offered demurrers: new pastors were not to be installed with the laying on of hands, as in Strassburg, but with a simple prayer; Communion was not to be celebrated every month but only four times a year. The city council was concerned about the provision for the appointment of new pastors and about the "company of the pastors" assuming judicial roles. The most serious objection pertained, however, to Calvin's proposals for a consistory, to comprise the pastors and twelve lay members nominated by the city council with the concurrence of the pastors. This body was to have the right to censor, even excommunicate, any citizen whose faith or walk of life violated correct doctrine and proper morals. The city council saw this consistory as an intrusion into the jurisdiction of government, and said no. Yet, as far as Calvin was concerned, the right to monitor the lives of the faithful, indeed if necessary to excommunicate, was the very linchpin of church discipline. Calvin had learned this in Strassburg, and he intended to put this into practice in Geneva. Despite the council's opposition, he held firm; the council eventually acquiesced but insisted on the addition of a new article, placed at the very end, which stipulated that after the exercise of church discipline had run its course—so "that the civil power remains in its entirety"—the consistory was to refer the matter to the council, "which upon their relation will decide to order and do justice according as the case requires." Understandably, here was the seed for future conflict. On November 20, 1541, the council representing the people of Geneva approved the new order. No opposition to this new understanding of church and society was voiced; the opponents chose to remain silent.

The *Ordonnances ecclésiastiques,* as the church order was entitled, were Calvin's contribution to the issue of practical churchmanship.[14] Heavily influenced by Bucer and his treatise of 1538 on *True Pastoral Care,* no less than by his own practical experiences in Strassburg as pastor of a congregation, Calvin formulated both his vision of the church and of the proper ecclesiastical structure. As far as he was concerned, the New Testament contained an explicit paradigm of the four ministries of the church and how the church should be structured. This was a new vision of the ministries, derived from Bucer in Strassburg. The *Ecclesiastical Ordinances* stipulated that there were four congregational offices: ministers (*pasteurs*), teachers (*docteurs*), elders (*anciens*), and deacons (*diacres*). The ministers of the Word, collectively known as "venerable compagnie des pasteurs," were responsible for preaching and the administration of the sacraments. The teachers provided for the religious instruction of the congregation, taught the young, and trained future ministers. The elders supervised the congregation to assure proper Christian demeanor. The deacons, twelve in number, cared for the sick and the poor.

Of these four offices, that of the elders was undoubtedly the weightiest. "Their office," said the *Ordinances,* "is to take care of the lives of everyone," surely a rather weighty assignment, about which the city council had severe reservations since the assignment seemed to impinge on the judicial prerogatives of secular government. The council agreed only when the appointment of the elders was made a prerogative of the council.

Together with the pastors, the elders made up the consistory, which was the heart of the *Ordinances,* the instrument, as Calvin observed, for "the supervision of the congregation of the Lord so that God might be honored purely." In effect, it was a mixture of governmental social discipline and theological orthodoxy. It met weekly and considered the cases brought before it—a large variety of offenses, such as theological deviation, blasphemy, sexual misconduct, dancing, swearing, nonattendance at church —some major, others not. The minutes of the meetings of the consistory fill volumes, and there is a lot of pathos, sadness, even humor in the records; for example, the case of a femme fatale who, cited because of improper dress, retorted that those who did not want to see her that way should close their eyes. Or, Claude Morel, a mason, who when cited to appear before the consistory for failing to attend church, offered a response that surely must be considered timeless commentary on hearing sermons: "On Sunday he was at the sermon," he answered, "and Calvin preached. Does not know what he said at the sermon, and could not say it, and this was at the morning sermon, before dinner."[15] One of the more intriguing instances occurred when the consistory heard the case of an individual who had failed in his attempt to commit suicide. Since suicide was considered murder, the poor fellow was to have been sentenced to the gallows; only when it occurred to members of the consistory that that was exactly what the fellow wanted was his punishment changed to expulsion from the city.[16]

14. They are found in *CR* 38:5ff.
15. For Geneva the records of the consistory are immense. Robert M. Kingdon has provided a succinct glimpse into the operation: *Registers of the Consistory in Geneva at the Time of Calvin* (Grand Rapids: 2000).
16. Jeffrey R. Watt, *Choosing Death: Suicide and Calvinism in Early Modern Geneva* (Kirksville, MO: 2001).

Once the *Ordinances* had been approved, the consistory swung into action. In its first full year of operation (1542) it heard no less than 320 cases, and within eight years that number had increased to 584 per year. In 1550 only 86 cases involved doctrinal deviation, while 238 cases had to do with interpersonal disputes and some 160 with sexual improprieties. Some 38 individuals were cited before the consistory for having spoken ill of the clergy.[17] In the early years of the consistory, the main topic seems to have been failure to attend church—which must have involved a large number of individuals telling on their nonchurchgoing neighbors. A careful and intrusive ecclesiastical supervision of the citizens was thus established in Geneva—and also wherever Calvinist congregations were established. In a way, the institution of the consistory may be seen as part and parcel of the larger exercise of social discipline in sixteenth-century Europe: authorities everywhere seemed to be concerned to mandate rigidly certain forms of behavior. Such efforts at supervision were hardly new, for public regimentation of morality was a characteristic of late medieval society. Neither Lutheranism nor Anglicanism was devoid of a religiously motivated supervision of morals, challenging the notion that supervising the lives of the faithful was a distinctive Calvinist characteristic.

It can also hardly be said that Calvin's notion of church discipline was unvaryingly put into practice elsewhere in Europe where Calvinist congregations were established. Extant records suggest notable variations over time and place, indicating that while the principle of monitoring the lives and beliefs of the faithful was affirmed, its practice depended on local circumstances. With respect to Geneva, one cannot speak of a clerical tyranny, for the consistory was not a clerical body. The majority of its members were elders, laymen. The uniqueness of the Genevan situation was that a body that spoke for both the ecclesiastical and the political community administered the regimentation of the faithful. The prerogative of the church to supervise the lives of its members was forcefully asserted, even though there were long and difficult, but successful battles to establish that prerogative. The opposition came from the secular authorities, who objected to what to them was an ecclesiastical usurpation of civic jurisdiction.

Alongside the activities of the consistory, there was an equally intense social legislation that, seemingly endless, structured and ordered the life of the faithful. No gambling, dancing, singing of "dirty" songs, or lounging in the streets during regular worship hours. Some of the penalties were draconic, such as the death penalty if adultery involved two married persons.

The presence of Calvin and the activity of the consistory changed much that was familiar to the Genevan burghers. Taverns were closed, though for a short time a harmless version that would have won the approval of a league of teetotalers was unsuccessfully tried. Theaters were shut down, gambling was prohibited. In the main, the Genevan citizens accepted the changes with a mixture of approval and resignation. This is noteworthy and cannot be solely explained by the passivity that characterizes many common folk. The acceptance of the new order suggests that Calvin was seen as a charismatic figure, and to envision him as a haggard and sour-faced ecclesiastical tyrant fails to do justice to his contribution to Geneva.

17. Benedict, *Christ's Churches*, 97.

Indeed, Calvin functioned as more than a member of the Genevan clergy. He aided in the revision of the Genevan constitution, a task for which his legal background proved to be of great value. He was helpful in a variety of other ways as well, for example, in the drafting of regulations for the Geneva fire department and the keepers of the city gates. He also was the chief architect of a treaty concluded with Bern in February 1543, which asserted Genevan rights without diminishing those of Bern. Yet, no matter how well accepted by the Genevan citizenry, the work of the consistory evoked negative repercussions. This was particularly true after 1546, when the consistory sought to regiment morality in Geneva even when no criminal acts had been committed.

Several instances became causes célèbres. One concerned Pierre Ameaux, member of the city council, but also—and more importantly—a manufacturer of toys and playing cards. Calvin's new morality meant that his business was drifting toward bankruptcy. His wife, a veritable *femme scandaleuse*, had been engaged in illicit affairs, and though Ameaux had sought a divorce, his request had been turned down. He suspected that Calvin was responsible for this adverse decision. At a dinner party in January 1546, Ameaux carelessly made disparaging remarks about Calvin. He called him a wicked individual, a Picard who preached false doctrines and stifled the education of youth. To add insult to injury, Ameaux added some uncomplimentary words about his fellow council members, whom he described as spineless henchmen of the "Picard."

Ameaux had said all this in the privacy of his home, among friends, but within twenty-four hours the word had leaked out about his castigations of Calvin. Ameaux was arrested. The city council was willing to settle the matter with a gentleman's agreement with one of its members. Ameaux was to appear before the council and apologize in Calvin's presence, but Calvin bluntly informed the council that this was unacceptable. Not he had been offended, but God, and this required a drastic punishment. Weeks of tension followed, including a public insult of Calvin by a pastry baker during a sermon. The Genevan citizens uniformly sided with Ameaux, but eventually Calvin had his way. Ameaux, scion of a patrician family and member of the city council, was sentenced to walk through the streets of Geneva, dressed in a penitent's garb, carrying a torch, kneeling at appointed places, beseeching God for mercy. The sight of a member of the city council walking through the streets of Geneva in penitence conveyed that the consistory was no respecter of rank and standing.

If nothing else, this episode should have taught the Genevan citizens to be careful about what they said both in private and in public. It failed to do so, evidenced by one of the pastors confiding to an acquaintance that Calvin was "impatient and vindictive. If he gets his knife into you, you are lost." Those words, too, promptly reached the city council, and the pastor was dismissed. Yet hardly had the commotion died down than another case was in the making, this time involving the very paragon of Genevan society. At a wedding in March 1546, Ami Perrin and Amblard Corne had danced. Elsewhere a harmless activity, dancing was strictly forbidden in Geneva. Perrin, a syndic, had been one of Calvin's earliest supporters and had voted against his expulsion in 1538; Corne, in turn, was a member of the consistory. Both men had to spend a time in jail and then apologize. For Perrin the experience meant a change of heart; he increasingly became one of Calvin's bitter opponents. Perrin's family got into trouble as well. His father-in-law had been excluded from Communion because of immorality, and Perrin's wife was twice reprimanded by the consistory for dancing. This made no difference to her, however, for with a tongue befitting Xanthippe she called a member of the consistory a "great pig."

In May 1547 Perrin was sent to Paris to transmit the congratulations of Geneva to the new king, Henry II. As it turned out, he conducted some private diplomacy on the side to obtain French support in case of an attack of Emperor Charles V, who was then, after his victory over the League of Schmalkald, at the apex of his power. There was nothing treacherous about Perrin's conversations, except that they were conducted in secrecy, and when they became public Perrin was in trouble. Fortunately, a fellow Genevan, Laurent Maigret, had also negotiated with France with Calvin's knowledge and concurrence, and this meant that either Calvin was implicated as much as Perrin, or neither one was. After some political maneuvering, in the course of which Bern came to Perrin's aid, both were released from prison and Perrin was reinstated in his position as syndic.

There were other difficulties during this time, for example, when in June 1546 a small handbill, written in Savoyard dialect, was found in the pulpit of St. Peter. It contained a bitter indictment of Calvin and the Genevan clergy. "You and your colleagues had better be quiet. If you persist in infuriating us, nothing will keep you from being silenced." The uneasy question about the document was not so much its content as its implications. Was it the manifesto of an individual dissatisfied with the state of affairs in the city and unhappy about the stern hand of the consistory? Or was it the voice of a whole faction waiting for the right opportunity to strike? The authorities swung into action and within hours arrested one Jacques Gruet, an eccentric bachelor with many connections to Savoy.

The search of his house revealed various incriminating documents, for example, the draft of a petition to the city council against Calvin, and papers with vague references to a possible French intervention in Genevan affairs. No connection to the handbill could be established. The Genevan authorities (and Calvin) suspected that Gruet was part of a huge conspiracy and interrogated him under torture. Gruet's pain brought the confession that he had indeed been the author of the handbill, but he denied to the end that he had had accomplices. He was found guilty and in June 1547 beheaded. The whole affair, with Calvin the driving force, was a blatant miscarriage of justice. Gruet had been charged with blasphemy and sedition, but neither could actually be proven in his trial. Three years after his execution, workers remodeling his house found a manuscript under the floor boards. It called Jesus an impostor, Mary a prostitute, and the apostles rogues. At long last, the charges against Gruet seemed justified.

The election to the city council in 1548 revealed the extent of the unhappiness over Calvin's ecclesiastical and civic policies, since his supporters stood on one side and his antagonists on the other. The two factions were different in composition. Many of Calvin's supporters were Italian and French refugees who had left their native lands for religious reasons. They had not exactly been welcomed in Geneva with open arms and were frequently branded as outside agitators. The distinguished old families of Geneva, led by Ami Perrin, were among Calvin's opponents. They were called Libertines, to suggest thereby that they wanted to be free from all restrictions and discipline. The label was biased; the Libertines themselves preferred to be known as patriots. They were staunchly Protestant but resented what they saw as the inquisitorial supervision that Calvin had established in Geneva. The election brought a victory for Calvin's opponents, and for five years Calvin had to labor under trying circumstances. Genevan burghers found "Calvin" an appropriate name for dogs, and the minutes of the council record numerous complaints of Calvin about maltreatment and humiliation.

Calvin must have often pondered the wisdom of his staying on in Geneva. But he did, persuaded that he had been placed there to lead the forces of light against darkness. At the end he won, despite all the opposition. The explanation points not only to his abilities and talents, but also to the fact that throughout his first fifteen years in Geneva crucial incidents threatened his authority but were weathered by him so successfully that they enhanced his stature in the city. Jerome Bolsec serves as a case in point. He had been a Carmelite monk, but had doffed the habit to pursue various activities neither very spiritual nor very proper. For awhile he was a spy at the court of the duchess of Ferrara; he then settled in Geneva, practicing medicine. In October 1551 he became embroiled in a controversy over predestination. During a Bible study conducted by Calvin, he made the point that the notion of faith as a divine gift made God into a tyrant. Calvin responded with a lengthy defense of the predestinarian position. At other places, such disagreement over a subtle theological issue might have been the end of the matter, but not at Geneva. Jerome Bolsec, doctor and amateur theologian, was arrested at the doors of the church and thrown into jail. He was indicted on no less than seventeen points, to which, on all accounts, he gave a splendid defense—not altogether original, but reiterating the classic arguments against predestinarian theology. He so perplexed the Genevan city council with his arguments that the opinion of the other Swiss Protestants was requested. The responses from Basel, Zurich, and Bern were lukewarm at worst and cautious at best, for in good Lutheran fashion they called the topic a mystery that should not be pursued too deeply.

Yet Bolsec had raised a fundamental issue: either his views or those of Calvin were to be accepted in Geneva. Since the council was not prepared to break with Calvin, the ax fell on Bolsec, in surprisingly mild form. In December 1551 Bolsec was banished from Genevan territory. This might well have ended the story, but Bolsec was not one to forgive and forget. Many years later, in 1577, after he had returned to the Catholic fold, he published a biography of Calvin that turned into a diatribe of venom and calumny.[18] To be sure, today Bolsec's work evokes little more than antiquarian interests. At the time of its publication, however, the book was an enormous success and proved, as its numerous editions indicate, a welcome arsenal for all anti-Calvin polemic.

Calvin promptly demanded that the Genevan pastors and the two city councils subscribe to the *Consensus Genevensis*, a detailed formulation of the doctrine of predestination. He had his way. But it was a pyrrhic victory, since the extent of the opposition in the city became evident. The new spokesperson for the dissenters was Jean Trolliet, a former monk, who in the summer of 1552 invoked the authority of Melanchthon to denounce the teaching of Calvin's *Institutes* on predestination. In

---

18. Hierosme Hermes Bolsec, *Histoire de la vie, moeurs, actes, doctrine, constance et mort de Iean Calvin* (Lyon: 1577).

November the council assured Calvin that this book was biblical, but at the same time told Trolliet that he was an honorable man. Calvin's situation had become precarious.

For the span of two decades Calvin relentlessly sought to order the Genevan church. His measures and policies were hardly borne by widespread and universal enthusiasm; the steady influx of French Protestant refugees contributed its share of the tensions in the city. In a way, Calvin's story paralleled that of other reformers—Martin Bucer in Strassburg, Urbanus Rhegius in Augsburg, even Luther in Wittenberg. All of them pursued the dual task of shepherding the local congregation to a better understanding of the faith, while at the same time paying attention to broader developments and issues. In the case of Calvin this meant the evangelizing of his native France.

Calvin's time in Geneva needed over a decade to become normal. At issue was Calvin's insistence on church discipline and the magistrates' insistence on authority over ecclesiastical affairs. Both provoked seemingly endless challenges and disputes. The twist in Geneva was Calvin's assertion that civil government had to serve as the church's handmaiden to transform Geneva into a holy city. The decision, in 1545, to discipline moral transgressions more severely in Geneva led to the emergence of a faction of so-called Libertines who resented ecclesiastical and political censorship.

Things came to a head in 1553. Theological strife beset the city, since Calvin was as much concerned about doctrinal orthodoxy as he was about godly living. Earlier the young humanist teacher Sebastian Castellio had triggered a conflict with Calvin by venturing forth in 1543/44 about his unorthodox views of certain scriptural passages. He promptly found himself expelled from Geneva on Calvin's insistence and decided to settle in Basel to the north. The following year, after Calvin had published a treatise on predestination and renewed controversy had broken out over the topic, the Genevan council ordered that no one was to criticize or disagree with Calvin.

Then, unwittingly the case of Michael Servetus brought things to a head. The details of the Servetus trial have been recounted elsewhere and will not detain us here. Importantly, however, his trial took place in the setting of severe tensions between Calvin and his Libertine opponents. The fall of Servetus spelled disaster for Calvin's opposition. The Libertines sought to use Servetus—who himself may have been quite innocent of their maneuvering—to inflict a decisive defeat on Calvin. The trouble was that they supported the wrong man. Servetus's theological dissent was so radical that Calvin emerged as the champion of the traditional Christian faith against stark heresy and unbelief. There is a faint possibility that Servetus stopped at Geneva cognizant of the problems and tensions, hopeful to fish in muddy waters. Once there and once tried at court, he saw himself as leader of the attack on Calvin. His boldness at his trial might bear this out.

After Servetus's arrest, the libertines, who held the majority on the large council of the two hundred, interceded for him, and tensions increased during the trial when Philibert Berthelier requested to receive Communion. Berthelier had been excommunicated by the consistory the year before, but now the city council decided to grant his request. Calvin retorted that he would not offer the elements to an unworthy person, but the council exhorted him to obedience. The day when Communion was to be observed, September 3, 1553, fell during the final phase of Servetus's trial. Berthelier had been counseled not to come to church, and thus a confrontation with Calvin in front of the Communion table was avoided. Still, Calvin's stand made an impression. The council's case had been ill chosen, for Berthelier had been properly condemned by the consistory, and, if anything, the lapse of time had sanctioned the propriety of the verdict. Calvin outlined once more to the council the functions of the consistory, and the council decided in the middle of September that the stipulations of the *Ordinances* must be followed. Servetus, at his trial, contributed his share both to his condemnation and to the defeat of the opposition by an embarrassingly insolent demeanor that irritated everyone and alienated the few friends he had. Perrin made a last-minute effort to have the case decided by the council of the two hundred rather than the Small Council. He was turned down, and from then on there could be no doubt about the verdict.

The trial of Servetus marked the turning of the tide about Calvin's place in Geneva. Calvin became the unchallenged spokesperson for the faith, but the question of the consistory's right to excommunicate remained unanswered. In November 1553 Berthelier requested again permission to receive Communion, and after some consultation the council of the two hundred decreed that no one should be excommunicated without a hearing before the council. A year passed in a constant turmoil and tension. Berthelier was in and out of prison, and acted submissively and arrogantly toward the consistory; the council alternately was determined and hesitant to assert itself against the consistory. In January 1555 at long last the two councils decided that the "mandates must be obeyed."

On the face of things, this was an evasive statement, but its meaning was beyond doubt. The right of the consistory to excommunicate had been conceded. Desperately the Libertines grasped at a straw. In May Perrin introduced a resolution at the city council that French newcomers to Geneva be not permitted to vote for ten years, since they might conspire with France. His argument was hardly persuasive, and Perrin was informed that refugees who had been expelled from France at the threat of death were unlikely to conspire to bring Geneva under French control. Later that same month a riot occurred in the city, mainly occasioned by the abundance of wine that Perrin had made available to his supporters. In the ensuing tumult Perrin wrested the mayoral staff from the syndic Aubert. This civic disobedience, indeed, smacked of rebellion, even though Perrin told Aubert, who was a rather short individual, that he simply wanted to raise the staff to show it to the crowd and thereby restore order. From this distance it is difficult to say exactly what happened. Perhaps it was merely a public demonstration, perhaps an insurgency. Be that as it may, the council acted ruthlessly. Four of the participants in the tumult were executed; Perrin, Berthelier, and Pierre Vandel, one of their compatriots, escaped. Sternly, the council ordered that all those interceding for the emigrants be beheaded. This turn of events had repercussions in Geneva's relationship with Bern, which had supported Perrin with Geneva asserting that this was a domestic matter, not a Bernese affair. In 1556 Bern rescinded its treaty with Geneva, only to renew it two years later, showing that internal strife in Geneva had diplomatic ramifications. The relationship between the two cities was strained, and from then on Bern scrupulously prevented Calvinist sentiment from taking root in Bernese soil.

A new chapter of the Genevan Reformation began in 1555, the groundwork having been laid with the adoption of the *Ecclesiastical Ordinances* fourteen years earlier.

Only after 1555 was Calvin unchallenged in Geneva, though even then he was hardly a "pope" and Geneva hardly a theocracy. He always had to submit his manuscripts to a censor, and this fact alone should suffice to discount any dramatic characterization of his influence. Geneva was molded by Calvin's ideas rather than by his hand. It was hardly an ecclesiastical dictatorship. Most Genevan burghers accepted Calvin's ideas. The establishment of the right of the consistory to excommunicate was a major accomplishment, though even then some difficulties were by no means over. Calvin himself continued to be convinced that the city was far too lax in its pursuit of Christian morality. Three times between 1555 and 1558 he voiced his protest against the inadequate opposition to immorality in the city. "The evil has increased," he observed on one occasion, "the city has been greatly contaminated, and above all God has been insulted."

The sixteenth century was hardly characterized by Victorian prudery, and the ostentatious show of luxury in dress and apparel, or the culinary extravagances of food and drink, would be found offensive by most of us today. Calvin's death brought no disruption of affairs in the city, no virulent uprising, no unleashed reaction. It was a smooth transition from him to his successor, Theodore Beza. Yet the "man of Geneva," as Calvin was frequently named in diplomatic correspondence, remained a stranger within the gates of the city, for not until December 1559 did the Genevan council offer him citizenship. Calvin had never requested it, and the council never made the offer, perhaps fearful that citizenship would constitute an irreversible reality. When citizenship was awarded—recognizing "the many valuable services shown to our republic by him since the Christian reformation"—Calvin made a point of emphasizing that he had not requested it, so as to avoid the suspicion of some.

Calvin's eminent achievement of these years was the founding of the Genevan Academy. Initial plans had been formulated in 1556, but three years passed before the academy, or Collège de Genève, was formally established. The realization of Calvin's dream was no easy matter, for Geneva was a small town and not overly prosperous. The academy was conceived as an ambitious undertaking, to include not only a school of liberal arts, but also a school of theology for training ministers, a school of law for preparation for government service, and a school of medicine for training physicians. A phalanx of capable teachers joined the faculty, most notably Theodore Beza and Pierre Viret in theology. The star, of course, was Calvin himself, who offered exegetical lectures that he had given earlier at St. Peter's. Calvin's academic involvement was more cursory, though a constant educational concern pervaded Calvin's activities in Geneva, from his first Bible study as "ille Gallus" in 1536 to his courses at the academy.

Since theology was the queen of the sciences, the impact of the academy was especially significant in theology. Students came from many European countries—France, Holland, Scotland, Hungary, Poland, from wherever Calvin's message had raised its banner—to study and prepare themselves for the proclamation of the Genevan gospel. At stake was nothing less than its future. Who was to provide for the continuity of proclamation? The problem was serious. Most of the early Reformers possessed theological training, be it on account of their formal academic background or—as in the case of Calvin—their rigorous self-discipline. Most of the Protestant clergy had been Catholic priests, and this too meant the semblance of competence in matters religious.

But what about the future? Where were the future clergy to come from? The Genevan Academy provided the answer for the Calvinist Reformation.

"Send us wood, and we shall send you arrows." These words Calvin had written to the French Protestants, and thus it happened. In all, 162 students were enrolled in the academy in the first year, and some not-so-well-meaning friends thought that the ambitious undertaking would fail for lack of students. But within five years the number had swelled to over 1,500. Calvin himself drafted the statutes of the academy, a competent constitutional statement, perhaps partially copied later in the century by the Jesuit General Aquaviva in his delineation of the principles of Jesuit education.

If the Genevan Academy was one facet of Calvin's activities extending beyond the walls of Geneva, his ecumenical efforts were another. He had grown to theological maturity during the time of the colloquies of Worms, Hagenau, and Regensburg. While his theological realism made him skeptical about the possibility of Catholic-Protestant concord, he was deeply concerned about the doctrinal divisions within Protestantism. Not even the Swiss Protestants were in full doctrinal agreement, and a consensus increasingly demanded itself as an act of theological prudence. The foremost differences pertained to Communion. Luther's *Kurzes Bekenntnis vom Abendmahl* (Brief Confession Concerning the Lord's Supper) of 1544 had renewed the controversy, after the publication of Zwingli's writings the previous year had extended what must have been an irresistible challenge. Both Calvin and Farel negotiated with Bullinger, and though agreement was difficult, a consensus was reached in May 1549. This was the Consensus Tigurinus, which stretched Calvin's and Bullinger's theological magnanimity to a bursting point. Yet it was a genuine agreement, and hardly any event had greater significance for the Calvinist tradition, for it brought the union of Swiss Protestantism, the merger of Zwingli's tradition with that of Calvin.

Calvin died in the early evening hours of May 27, 1564; and Theodore Beza, his successor as senior pastor in Geneva, recorded that "as the sun went down, the greatest light in this world was taken up into heaven."[19] The funeral was simple, for so Calvin had wanted it—no hymns, no eulogies, no tombstone. This expressed his conviction that his person possessed no significance. As one contemporary said, "No man knoweth his resting place until this day," a testimonial to the way Calvin had understood his role in Geneva. No cult of personality here—a temptation that the Lutheran tradition could never quite resist when it came to Luther.

Three hundred years later the citizens of Geneva, in filial piety, erected a monument in honor of the Reformation. It is a short walk from the university, the successor of the Genevan Academy, along the Promenade des Bastions. Statues of John Calvin, Guillaume Farel, Theodore Beza, and John Knox, the four leaders of the Calvinist Reformation, symbolize the events of the sixteenth century and the tradition that Calvin founded. Looking closely, one notes that the statue of Calvin is only slightly taller than that of the others, a striking expression of the way he himself wanted his place in Genevan affairs understood.

19. *CR* 21:49, 168.

What a strange man he had been, timid and stern, aggressive and modest. His temperament seems to suggest kinship with none other than Ignatius of Loyola. The second generation of the Reformation called for men of this type, brilliant, determined, cool. There was an abiding purpose in Calvin, and to achieve this purpose Calvin brought impressive theological credentials. Much has been written about Calvin's theology, and there can be little doubt that it is one of the most eminent achievements of the century—and one can say this without engaging in the kind of parochial hagiography that so often inflates denominational founding fathers (and mothers) or even *viri obscuri* to positions of historical prominence.

Chapter 11

CHANGES IN EUROPE

The turbulence that profoundly beset Germany in the first half of the sixteenth century did not remain confined to German lands; the Reformation movement quickly became a phenomenon of European dimensions. Virtually all European countries experienced periods of agitation and turbulence comparable to those in Germany, and the basic characteristic was always the intriguing intertwining of religion and politics.

Students of the Reformation have probed if these European events are to be seen as shock waves of what happened in Germany. Most scholars have answered this question affirmatively, and so reform throughout Europe tended to be measured by German, which meant Lutheran, criteria.[1] Understandably, non-German historians have begged to differ. They have argued the distinctiveness of reform in their countries. Particularly as regards the question of origins they have insisted on sources of reform independent from Germany. While acknowledging the importance of Luther, these historians maintained that the course of reform events in their countries had independent origins and causes, even as reform unfolded in particular and distinctive ways.[2]

This European Reformation was a religious phenomenon, just as had been the case in Germany. People throughout Europe heard, read—and accepted the new interpretation of the gospel. Often unwittingly they thereby broke with the church. They developed new forms of religious life, with new hymns, new liturgy, new literature. Some became the normative religion in the land, while others succumbed to the use of force. Successful or not, theirs always was the story of a religious movement. This "religious" Reformation, however, must be placed into the context of certain societal forces, that ambiguously political world of parliaments, councillors, edicts, and ecclesiastical litigation, of power politics, of long-standing social or economic grievances. The cause of religious change and renewal intersected society, even the haut monde of diplomacy, and religion became part of societal history. Obviously, these two facets were interrelated. They were not necessarily the two sides of the same coin, for one could well be divorced from the other: the Anabaptists illustrate the exclusive preoccupation with religion, and Gustavus Vasa of Sweden, the preoccupation with politics. Most of the time, however, the Reformation was both.

---

1. For European historiography on the Reformation, the volume by A. G. Dickens and John Tonkin, *The Reformation in Historical Thought* (Cambridge: 1985), is the best introduction.
2. Lucien Fevre's famous essay, "Une question mal posée: les origines de la réforme française et le problème des causes de la réforme," *Revue historique* 161 (1929): 1–73, is, even after two generations of scholars, still worth reading.

Scholars have minimized outside influences on the emergence of reform and stressed the indigenous elements. This perspective would make the Reformation in Europe the simultaneous expressions of reform, precipitated by the state of ecclesiastical affairs in European countries in the early sixteenth century. In France, for example, the reform efforts of Bishop Briçonnet at Meaux have been cited as "the cradle of the French Reformation." Briçonnet took his episcopal responsibilities in Meaux with utmost seriousness. Focusing his attention on preaching and inaugurating a comprehensive system of preaching throughout his diocese, he promptly ran into conflict.

To focus on Briçonnet and his Meaux circle as the beginnings of reform in France means to employ a particular definition of "reform." While there may have been instances in which concern for reform was paramount well before 1517, the aim of the Protestant Reformation was not so much "reform" as "reinterpretation" of the gospel, characterized by an increasingly inimical stance toward the church. This Reformation built on earlier expressions of reform sentiment; in the end, however, the Reformation introduced an element of discontinuity, which found foremost expression in the self-consciousness of those who pursued reform that they were, indeed, onto something new.

Luther's ideas made their way from Germany to the four corners of Europe, and his name became a household word in France, England, and Sweden. This dissemination of his ideas was made possible by the flow of commerce and people—as well as broadsides, pamphlets—throughout Europe, which allowed a student in Oxford to know what was happening at Basel, or apprised a cleric at Strassburg of happenings in Wittenberg. Academicians, especially humanists, engaged in lively correspondence in which the communication of the latest academic news was often an important content. In March 1518, for example, Erasmus sent Thomas More a copy of Luther's Ninety-five Theses, and in April 1519 he wrote John Fisher extensively about the Wittenberg professor.

News and ideas were disseminated by people who traveled professionally across borders. Foremost were the merchants, about whose role England offers particularly conclusive evidence. There also were students, especially those who studied in Germany, who brought news about the progress of religious reform, sometimes as mere reporters, sometimes as newly converted partisans of the new faith. The printers must also be mentioned; economic interest or religious conviction (or both) made them eager to ship the pamphlets propounding the new faith abroad.

There is extensive evidence for the colportage of Luther's books outside Germany. Zwingli propagated their distribution in Switzerland, Erasmus noted that they were read in the Low Countries, while in England they were publicly burned. In February 1519 the Basel printer Froben shipped six hundred copies of Luther's pamphlets to Spain and France, assuredly a business and religious enterprise of major proportion. About that time a student at Paris wrote that Luther's writings were received "quite openly," and Luther himself recorded that his writings were read by the doctors of the Sorbonne.

The impact of Luther's writings in such places as France or England, for example, was decidedly different from that in Germany. Only Luther's Latin writings could meaningfully communicate his notions abroad, while in Germany his vernacular pamphlets were the major source for his impact. Most of his early writings, addressed to specific topics, were general in nature and did not express a "Lutheran" propensity. Thus, during the early years of the Reformation, Luther did not publish an exposition of his understanding of justification, and of his views on the Lord's Supper only the basic outline (the repudiation of Catholic sacramentalism) was clear. The label "Lutheran," so freely placed upon the proponents of the new theology, was misleading. "Lutheran" was only the affirmation of the primacy of Scripture in the formulation of Christian truth, the repudiation of the primacy of the pope, the minimal value placed on external rites and observances, and the important postulate of Christian freedom.

The Reformers' tracts had to be in Latin in order to break the linguistic barrier between German lands and the rest of Europe. This meant, of course, that Luther's appeal underwent an important modification. In Germany Luther had been able to speak directly to the common people in their language. He had done so successfully, as the number of reprints of his vernacular tracts shows. Such direct communication was impossible elsewhere in Europe; accordingly, the popular response to the Lutheran proclamation found in Germany could not materialize easily in other countries. The transmission of reform ideas had to focus on essentials and on catchy slogans: Scripture versus "man"-made traditions, salvation by grace versus salvation by works.

Despite this handicap, the new theology found active propagators throughout Europe. Its spread was little dependent upon outside influence but utilized the efforts of indigenous colporteurs who shared the characteristic of youth and Erasmian propensity, men such as Bilney, Tyndale, Barnes, Biros, Wishart, or Petri. Some of them, for example, Olaus Petri of Sweden, had been in Germany and had savored the new theology firsthand. Others, like William Tyndale of England, traveled there after their "conversion" to the new faith. All of them were little known and certainly not part of the academic or ecclesiastical "establishment."

Each country had such indigenous Reformers, men who ventured to proclaim the new theology and did so against great odds and at great personal danger. Several paid for their faith with their lives and thereby testified to the intensity of their commitment: the first Protestant martyrs, burned in Brussels in 1523, came not from Germany but the Low Countries. The local Reformers assured the spread of the Protestant faith in their lands; their efforts transformed the ideas from abroad into a message congenial to the new environment.

The propagation of the new theology took the form of an amalgamation of basic notions of Luther's theology with elements from the local Reformers. This synthesis explains the immense variety of theological emphases that characterized the scene, making the Reformation in Hungary different from that in Sweden or that in Poland. One would hardly expect these Reformers to have adopted all of Luther's thought, especially since the "Lutheran" notions reaching them were, as already noted, so general as to require further delineation. Moreover, the Reformers who carried the Protestant message forward in the various European countries had pondered theological issues before they encountered Luther. While this encounter proved to be of considerable importance in their theological development, it did not do away with prior theological reflection and autonomy. In other words, Luther was only one of several factors. The transmission of Luther's ideas was thus twofold: it occurred through his writings as these were read in European countries, and it took place through the native Reformers who had absorbed some of his ideas.

In Germany the reform movement reached its high point by the late 1520s, at a time when the Reformation in the rest of Europe was only getting under way. In a way, the German Reformation ended before the European Reformation began. This time lag meant that the defenders of the ecclesiastical status quo had advance warning. The defenses could be strengthened and the counterattack prepared. The kind of blitz so successful in Germany was impossible elsewhere in Europe.

This time lag may help to explain the important transition of the new theology from a vague Lutheranism to a distinct Calvinism. While the Reformation in Germany was Lutheran, in the rest of Europe it was Calvinist. Did this mean that Calvin's thought was more persuasive or that Luther's was too Teutonic? An explanation seems needed, and the time lag between the two Reformations affords a clue: at the time Protestantism vied for acceptance in Scotland, England, the Low Countries, and France, Calvinism was the ascending star in the firmament of the Reformation, while Lutheranism was beset by serious internal strife.

The Protestant goal was to spread the new gospel; it was as simple as that. At the same time, the Protestants wanted the right to live their faith, to worship publicly without legal restriction. Thus they strove for the official acceptance of their faith, a legal matter to be decided by the governmental authorities. Naturally, therefore, the Protestant quest was to obtain a favorable governmental decision. In many instances they were successful: in many German territories and cities, in Sweden, and in England. In other places, notably in France, they made a persistent effort to sway the ruler's sentiment. They were unsuccessful, but this very failure prompted another approach in the quest for legal recognition: alignment with a political faction in the land in order to force the ruler's hand. In France, Scotland, Poland, and the Low Countries, the Protestants sought to achieve the goal of legal acceptance by allying with the nobility against the ruler. The situation differed from country to country, not only with respect to the ultimate outcome of the struggle, but also with respect to its characteristics. In France, for example, the Catholic cause, and thus the opposition to the Protestant efforts, was supported not by the king but also by some of the nobility. Accordingly, the struggle was between rival factions, with the king occupying an uneasy position between them. In Scotland and the Low Countries another variant can be observed. There the rulers were foreign, and the struggle against them took the form of opposing foreign influence. The Protestant cause became embroiled in a complex political picture and ceased to be a purely religious phenomenon.

Our purview here will focus on six countries where events seem to have been more significant. Each of these countries, of course, had its own particular history of reform, each its particular story of Protestant success or failure. These histories have been variously written. To relegate them to collective nescience is not to minimize their importance, but to assure that the multiplicity of events does not obscure the common lines.

While important in their own right, the histories of the Reformation in these countries are primarily significant for their paradigmatic confirmation of general trends of the period.

FRANCE

In France the Reformation almost succeeded and then fatally failed. The simple explanation is that reform efforts in France never succeeded in obtaining the political backing that was the quintessential ingredient in the successful Reformations throughout Europe. In fact, France splendidly illustrates that popular support itself did not suffice to bring about a change in the ecclesiastical affiliation of a country. In France Protestants did enjoy political support but not where it counted—in the king's court.

The story of the Reformation in France is thus mostly a religious and theological story, with heavy politics thrown in for good measure. The French story may be told in several ways: as the influx of Lutheran ideas into the country, as the account of a religious movement, or as the struggle between competing factions for political power —not to mention the eventual emergence of Calvinism as the prominent Protestant faction. These aspects describe the same historical reality, even though differing emphases open up different perspectives.

In France the Protestant movement became involved in a fierce political power struggle. The better part of the century was necessary to demonstrate that Protestantism could not be victorious in France, and the stations along the way were marked by persecution, wars, and bloodshed. In retrospect, the historian can see the options clearly enunciated from the beginning. Given the saturation of the land with Protestant ideas, the task was to convert the monarch to the new faith; it was as simple, or as difficult, as that. Aside from the possibility that the ruler experienced a religious conversion, as variously happened in Germany, the raison d'être for a change of ecclesiastical loyalties could have been tangible political or financial rewards, Henry VIII being the spectacular, if unsavory, case in point. In France no political advantages existed for supporting religious change—nor, for that matter, did any of the French rulers in the sixteenth century find themselves in the kind of personal predicament that led Henry VIII to sever the ties with Rome.

The Pragmatic Sanction of Bourges, promulgated in 1438, had established a number of important privileges of the crown in the ecclesiastical realm. The sanction caused a running battle between crown and papacy that was not resolved until the Fifth Lateran Council in the second decade of the sixteenth century, when it was finally declared null and void. But this was a pyrrhic victory since a new concordat between the curia and the French crown, concluded at the same time, granted to the crown virtually the same rights enjoyed before, including the right to nominate bishops, abbots, and priors. The French kings thus possessed extensive power over ecclesiastical affairs, which provided them with substantial revenue, and they could hardly be lured to break with Rome for the mundane reasons important elsewhere in Europe.

The Protestants had to force the king to undertake ecclesiastical change because the people wanted such change—and the French Protestants tried to do precisely that. Zwingli dedicated one of his major works to King Francis I, and Calvin followed suit with the dedication of his *Institutes* to Francis. The Protestant program was to achieve the legal acceptance of evangelical worship in the land.

Another option was to seek a change through political means. In the end this is what happened, though it took several decades for this strategy to surface. The course of ecclesiastical change became embedded in politics. The cause of religion was con-joined to the cause of politics, and the proponents of the one saw advantages in becoming advocates for the other. Protestants saw their cause strengthened by politi-cal power, while those concerned with issues of political power embraced the cause of religion for the political advantages that would bring.

The simplest explanation of the origins of the Reformation in France is to see it as the extension of Luther's proclamation. There is evidence of an early influx of Lutheran ideas into the country. An impressive phalanx of French scholars has dissented from this view of Lutheran origins, arguing that a reform movement existed in France before Luther, evidenced by the widespread propagation of the Bible toward the end of the fifteenth century and the reforming attitudes of Marguerite d'Angoulême or Jacques Lefèvre d'Étaples. There is no doubt that in France, as elsewhere throughout Europe, humanists and Christian humanists propagated notions of reform, of returning to the *fontes*, the true sources of the Christian faith, well before anyone had ever heard of Mar-tin Luther. Lefèvre was, much like Luther, a serious student of the apostle Paul and an ardent advocate of the pivotal centrality of the Scriptures.

In a way, the divergence of opinion hinges on different definitions of the terms "Reformation" or "reform." In a general sense, these terms may describe the rich variety of reform impulses evident (albeit by no means overwhelmingly so) in the early sixteenth century. In that definition, the origins of the French Reformation do indeed lie on native soil. The terms "Reformation" or "reform" can be used in a more restricted fashion, how-ever, to mean a theological reorientation that entailed a conscious break with Rome. If used in this latter sense, we cannot speak of an autonomous French Reformation. How-ever much Lefèvre deviated from medieval scholasticism or however close his biblical commentaries came to a view of justification embraced by the Reformers, he was not a Protestant arguing the sola fide or the sola Scriptura. A humanist, Lefèvre was critical of the church, but always its loyal son, a fact illustrated by his continued faithful allegiance to the church after the Lutheran controversy had begun to divide people.

Thus the Reformation in France should be said to have had its beginnings when Luther's writings first found their way into the land. In August 1521 a mandate pub-lished "with the sound of the trumpet and the town crier," "à son de trompe et cri publique," called for all of Luther's writings to be confiscated, and in November a royal ordinance prohibited the publication of all writings "favoring and defending the books of Luther." Luther was grouped with such heretics as Wycliffe and Hus, and his *Babylonian Captivity* was compared to the Koran. Lutheran notions were becoming known in France.

The defeat of King Francis I at Pavia in 1525 and his subsequent imprisonment by Charles V had repercussions for the ecclesiastical situation. In order to gain the sym-pathies (and political support) of the pope, and thereby help effect the release of the king, no doubt could exist about the orthodoxy of the French church. The Parlement of Paris and the Sorbonne—the one the political, the other a theological authority—strove to outdo each other in the suppression and persecution of Lutheran heretics.

Francis himself was religiously moderate, but for political reasons he could not afford to be sentimental about the protection of the religious innovators. He needed the support of the papacy against his archenemy Charles V, which meant, in turn, that he had to show himself a faithful and loyal son of the church. Francis might well have supported the church even if the political situation had been different. As matters stood, however, the political situation gave him little choice. Politics intermingled with religion from the outset, and in contrast to other places, such as Sweden or England, political prudence mandated the perpetuation of the ecclesiastical status quo. In short, Francis was bound to see no advantages in repudiating the allegiance to Rome.

Francis opposed dissent within the French church, not only because he wanted to remain in the good graces of the papacy, but also because his struggle with Charles V made a tranquil domestic situation mandatory. His concern was not so much doctrinal deviation but the disruption of unity in the land. He was indisposed to surrender control of the church for the sake of questionable doctrinal adventures that offered little except risks and pitfalls.

Two harmless events precipitated the showdown between the old church and the new faith. One was a speech of a distinguished academician, the other a one-page broadside posted on the door of the king's bedroom. In both instances the consequences were dramatic.

The speech, a *concio academica*, was given on All Saints' Day, November 1, 1533, by Nicolas Cop, distinguished physician and rector of the University of Paris.[3] It began with an encomium for the Virgin Mary, and continued with a mélange of Erasmus, Lefèvre, and Luther, theologically quite harmless, yet startling, for Cop remarked that those who sincerely follow Christ are not necessarily heretics. Moreover the speech was delivered at an official occasion and had the aura of academic approval. Loyal Catholics were in an uproar and demanded action against Cop, who preferred to flee unceremoniously to Switzerland. Afterward Francis I enjoined the Parlement of Paris to take measures against the Lutheran heresy. During the next twelve months numerous arrests, convictions, and executions followed; France proved to be an inclement climate for the new faith.

The broadside was posted at the churches and public buildings in Paris and provincial cities on October 18, 1534. It was entitled *Articles véritables sur les horribles, grandz et importables abuz de la Messe papalle* (Veritable Articles Concerning the Horrible, Enormous, and Insufferable Abuses of the Papal Mass) and called for the abolition of the Mass, the abomination of abominations, "through which the world, unless God has mercy, will be completely devastated, destroyed, ruined." A pamphlet written by one Antoine Marcourt, an exiled reformer living in Neuchâtel, had been the source for the broadside, and hundreds of copies were smuggled into France.[4] The problem with the broadside was not only its theology but with its postings—which included the door to the king's royal apartments in the castle of Amboise.

The Protestant propaganda effort was understandable, though hardly prudent. Since the handbills were posted in five provincial towns all at the same time, an organized group was thought to be behind the coup. Francis had to ponder the disquieting thought that the religious innovators had been able to reach the door of his own royal apartments.

3. The text is found in *Calvini Opera*, 9:873ff., with an English translation in *Institutes of the Christian Religion* (1536 ed.), ed. and annotated by Ford Lewis Battles (Grand Rapids: 1975): 363–72.

4. Gabrielle Berthoud, *Antoine Marcourt* (Geneva: 1973).

He was livid. The Affair of the Placards, as the incident came to be called, brought an end to the king's policy of benign neglect of reform and reformers and the beginning of a ruthless suppression of religious dissent. In January 1535 Francis, carrying a candle, bareheaded, and dressed as for a funeral, participated in an impressive procession from the Louvre, the royal palace, to the church of Notre-Dame. All of the venerable relics were removed from their shrines and carried the short distance from palace to church. At the end of the celebration of the Mass Francis spoke. The heretics who had committed this despicable act were not France, he said. They were vile and had to be dealt with like a disease.

Within a month seven individuals had been sent to the stake and a stern mandate ordered full censorship. At the same time, Francis could hardly alienate his potential allies in his struggle with Charles V, the Protestants in the League of Schmalkald; political prudence prevented him from more drastic measures. In July 1535 Francis signed the Mandate of Coucy, which freed the imprisoned Protestants and allowed Protestant refugees to return to France—the amnesty, incidentally, that gave Calvin the opportunity to return to his native land for one last time. During the next two years Francis was preoccupied with foreign affairs, but afterward he turned again to domestic affairs. Additional mandates against Protestants, in 1539 and 1540 made the suppression of heresy an affair of state.

The nature of the reform impulses in France during the 1520s and 1530s are enigmatic, though clearly things were in a state of flux so that one must be careful with the use of the term "Protestantism" or even "Reformation." Thus we have conservative bishops supporting radical clergy, for example, or we have conservative bishops, such as Briçonnet, under suspicion of heresy. In other words, no cohesive "movement of reform" existed. Reform sentiment centered in the cities and towns, especially among the artisans, and as in Germany, economic deprivation or social discontent must not be taken as key elements in people's openness to religious change. In France as elsewhere in Europe the touchstone for those who found the church lacking in biblical fidelity was the Mass. After Calvin's French translation of his *Institutes of the Christian Religion* appeared in 1542, a phase of consolidation began, where clarity of what it meant to be Protestant became the overriding issue.

In March 1547 the reign of Francis I ended—and as far as the religious conflagration was concerned, it did so quite differently than the way it had begun. The king's ambivalence about how to deal with the various reform initiatives had been replaced by a determined effort to retain Catholic uniformity. But, when Francis died, success in this effort was far from complete. The new king, Henry II, continued the policy of suppression with even greater determination and ruthlessness. During Henry's reign the various streams of reforming sentiment—Waldensians, followers of Lefèvre, Lutherans, Zwinglians, Calvinists—merged into a homogeneous French Calvinism. Local Calvinist assemblies cropped up, though in clandestine fashion and in constant danger of exposure to persecution: in Picardy, the Champagne, Normandy—the list could almost be a roll call of French regions and municipalities. Everywhere the "secte lutherienne," those "who corrupt the youth," made its appearance. Calvin himself participated in the affairs of the French church. He wrote letters of exhortation, comfort, and instruction; the Genevan church unremittingly sent pastors to France, men learned, determined, eager, zealous—thirty-two of them, for example, in the year of Henry's death. Protestantism continued to expand.

Henry II resolutely opposed the French Protestants from the very beginning of his reign. He possessed little of his father's empathy for an Erasmian kind of religious reform (if anything his religion was that of absolutism), and he was deeply persuaded that Protestantism constituted a mortal danger for the realm. On the occasion of his coronation, Cardinal Guise charged him to become the savior of the church, since "the heresies of a single man had brought turmoil not only to Germany and France, but also to the entire world." There was little need for this exhortation, for Henry was himself determined to crush the Protestants. That his mistress, Diane de Poitiers, who not only dominated his love life but at times his policies, had little sympathy for the stern Protestant religion also intensified the situation. One of Henry's first measures was to establish a new judiciary body, the so-called *chambre ardente* (fire court), which was entrusted with the function "to counter the blasphemous and heretical disturbers of the peace and tranquility of this most Christian kingdom." The *chambre ardente* in Paris rendered over five hundred verdicts in the two years of its existence from December 1547 to January 1550, most of them death sentences. By the same token, the chamber hardly had universal support, especially from the church, which resented that a secular body had usurped the traditional prerogatives of the church.

In 1551 Henry issued the Edict of Chateaubriand, which sought to make the persecution of heretics more effective. The edict spoke of the "common malady of this contagious pestilence that has infected many noble towns," and its forty-six articles provided for the judicial treatment of heretics. The property of fugitive heretics (those who had fled to Geneva) was to be confiscated. Informers, even if they had themselves attended heretical gatherings, were to go free. All communication with French refugees in Geneva was prohibited. The importation of printed materials with heretical ideas was outlawed. Persecution intensified, yet success eluded the king. Some of those who had earlier advocated severity against the Protestant heretics began to have second thoughts, pondering what was to be done if the persecution did not accomplish its goal, whether it were possible to continue the policy of persecution indefinitely, and if not, what kind of rapprochement was possible between the Protestants and the king.

France faced a difficult situation during those eventful years in the middle of the century. What should be done if continuing persecution did not accomplish its goal? Was it meaningful to continue the policy of persecution indefinitely? If not, what sort of rapprochement was possible between the French Protestants and the king? This was the time when Emperor Charles V faced the same questions in Germany, answering them with the Peace of Augsburg. In France the situation was different than in Germany, where the new faith had for some time assumed a political dimension, and the emperor had to confront not merely religious sentiment but concrete political power that incisively forced his hand. Henry II's response to this situation was one of determination to eradicate the Protestant heresy.

Henry was a victim of circumstances. Had he been able to devote all his attention to the religious problem at home, events might have taken a different course. But he faced enormous problems abroad. Unlike his father, who never missed an opportunity to make up his mind, Henry listened to his advisors. They complicated matters by not providing the same counsel. Anne de Montmorency, elder statesman of France, counseled one way, the members of the Guise family another. At issue was war against Philip II of Spain. In October 1555 Pope Paul IV had declared war upon Spain, and even after the Truce of Vaucelles had temporarily thwarted dreams of Italian splendor, he continued to work for a resumption of the conflict. Henry was torn between the irenic counsel of Montmorency and the belligerent advice of the Guises.

In the end, Henry could not resist the temptation to settle—presumably once and for all—his accounts with Spain. In the spring of 1557 his forces invaded northern Italy. But his papal ally was no match for the forces of the Duke of Alba, and in August the French troops were defeated at Saint-Quentin in the Netherlands. The war continued for another year, but Saint-Quentin had been decisive.

Understandably, Henry could hardly attend to the dramatic religious problems in his realm during this time of war. When he did, however, his policies continued unchanged. On July 24, 1557, he issued the Edict of Compiègne, which sharpened the already existing means of suppressing the Protestant heresy. The death penalty was made the standard punishment for heretics. The king asserted that so to proceed was his divinely ordained office, "for the honor of God, the preservation of the Christian religion, and the welfare, tranquility, and peace of our subjects."

At that time Cardinal Carafa came to France to supervise the establishment of the Inquisition, which had proved so successful in crushing heresy in Spain and Italy. Yet even his intervention did not halt the determined expansion of French Protestantism. Within weeks of the Compiègne Edict a mob of Parisians attacked a Protestant congregation. Over three hundred Protestants had gathered, and since the meeting was in the evening and in a home, it was bound to gain the attention of neighbors. A riot broke out, and most of the Protestant worshipers were arrested. The attack of the mob revealed the intensity of the Catholic sentiment among the people; but the size of the Protestant congregation also showed that Protestantism had passed the stage where Protestants numbered only a handful. The Protestant congregation at Paris had its own minister, held regular services, and celebrated Communion. This situation was multiplied throughout France where well-organized Protestant congregations worshiped underground. Congregation was linked to congregation. It made the French Protestants (unlike, for example, the persecuted Anabaptists in Germany) more than islands in a vast ocean, but part of an extensive network with its own identity.

About this time the French Protestants submitted several bold petitions to the king. They sought the cessation of persecution, but their hope was plainly for more than mere toleration. They wanted a sweeping change of the existing ecclesiastical order: church property was to be confiscated and used for charitable and educational purposes; the king and the people should accept the Protestant religion. The petititons included the thinly veiled threat that if the king failed to do so, God would take his crown from him. One suspects that the French Protestants would have willingly settled for less, but their programmatic petitions are of immense importance for understanding their self-confident temper at the time. Their program was radical, and no matter how much they denounced the charge that they meant to revolutionize society, that is precisely what they were out to do. But what if the course of events did not bring the realization of their aspirations? The French Protestants had to face a burning question about the future, even as the king did. The Protestant answer was to embrace a program of political engagement that was to incisively influence the subsequent course of events.

An acute financial crisis of the government forced Henry II to convene the assembly of notables for January 1558. The Protestants hoped that this occasion might bring a discussion of the religious question, but they were mistaken. The king saw no reason to alter his policy of persecution. And the more doubtful its success, the greater his determination. The Protestants began to realize that in their quest for the recognition of their faith the support of the nobility might render invaluable service. Calvin sought to intervene from Geneva by writing to King Antoine of Navarre, who had married a daughter of Marguerite d'Angoulême. He asked that the Protestant teachings be examined in order to remove, once and for all, the charges leveled against them. Several Protestant ministers visited the king to strengthen the Protestant case, but they were no more successful than the Genevan reformer. Nor was the intervention of several German Protestant rulers with the French king any more fruitful, for Henry bluntly told them that the Protestants were disturbers of law and order and enemies of Christian unity and peace. Henry was unwilling to forsake his determination to free his land from the heretical pestilence. Still, he realized that his foreign policy was bankrupt, that his dream of conquests abroad, especially in Italy, would not materialize, that governmental finances were in a desperate state, and that his army was hardly equipped to launch a major attack upon Spain. Peace talks were initiated, and after six months of negotiations with Spain a treaty was signed at Cateau-Cambrésis on April 3, 1559.

On the face of things, this peace was by no means a disaster for France, which received Metz, Toul, and Verdun from Germany. Still, a new epoch began on April 3, 1559, for the history of Europe no less than that of France, but above all for the history of the French Reformation, for from then on the French king was able to devote his attention to the suppression of the Protestant heresy. Quite aptly, a French Protestant wrote Calvin that the king was about to throw "his entire might" against the Protestants. Indeed, Henry wasted little time. A mandate of June 2, 1559, ordered all officials to "undertake the expulsion, punishment, and correction of the heretics in the entire realm." Eight days later the king was present when the Parisian Parlement discussed the contested religious issues. One member, Anne du Bourg, spoke freely about the doctrines of those "called Lutherans," and he so annoyed the king that he was arrested afterward, together with several other eminent Protestants.

Then, unexpectedly, on July 10, 1559, the king died. During a joust a splinter of a lancet had entered a slot in his visor and penetrated his skull. The French Protestants uttered words of relief upon hearing of the king's demise, for a ruthless enemy of their cause was gone. The twelve years of his reign had been a constant, unyielding, uncompromising effort to crush the Protestant sentiment—unsuccessful, as it turned out, for the Protestant cause had experienced a spectacular advance.

The heir to the throne was Francis II, fifteen years of age, hardly capable of heading the affairs of state. Was a regency necessary? And who should be the king's advisors? These questions should have been explored but they were hardly discussed, for Charles Cardinal Guise (of Lorraine) simply took over the reigns of government. The

Guise maneuver evoked the vehement protest of the Bourbons, the other influential family in French affairs, who argued that the king was a minor and that a council of regency should be formed, headed by the elder Bourbon, Antoine of Navarre. Antoine himself was hardly an improvement, a weak figure, concerned only about the increase of power of his own realm. His younger brother Condé, on the other hand, was ambitious, driving, and astute, though perhaps too much so. His religious conviction was not deep and he was hardly a shining light on the religious firmament. In his politics he had to accommodate his vacillating older brother, which meant that his own actions were modest.

This constitutional situation had repercussions for the history of French Protestantism, especially since there were religious overtones to the tensions between the Guises and the Bourbons. The Bourbons sympathized with the Protestants, while the Catholic Guises advocated a policy of severe suppression. Thus the constitutional problem assumed a religious connotation, and the French Protestants were drawn into this political battle, the outcome of which was to have a lasting effect on the future of Protestantism in France. The French Protestants supported the Bourbon claims to the regency, agreed that the Guises were usurpers from abroad (most of the Guise lands were in Lorraine) and that Cardinal Guise was a puppet of the pope. The theological rationale for this political involvement came from Calvin's doctrine of the right of resistance of the *magistrats inférieurs*, which held—parallel to Luther's thinking on the matter—that the *princes du sang* (the princes of the blood, the higher nobility) had the right to oppose the unconstitutional moves of the Guises in order to guarantee a proper constitutional government in France. Calvin provided the theological support, but he did more than that. The victory of Antoine of Navarre over the Guises promised toleration for the Protestants, and Calvin was determined to exert his utmost influence. He instigated a delegation to Antoine that went to great lengths to emphasize his constitutional right to oppose the Guises and held before him the suffering of the church (*ecclesiae calamitates*), which would increase if the Guises had their way. Antoine made some half-hearted promises but left no doubt that he would retire to Navarre if he encountered problems. The response of the clergy deserves to be recorded, for it could hardly be superseded in boldness: "You intend to yield to the opponents? To tolerate this infamy? To disappoint the hopes of the realm? Will any prince be more despised than you?"

By that time the French Protestants had become Calvinists, Calvin working tirelessly for the conversion of his native land to the new faith. His efforts had been graced by a measure of success; Calvinist minorities could be found everywhere in France, especially in the south and the north, and they came from all classes of society. Many of the urban centers had a Protestant majority or at least a substantial Protestant minority by the early 1560s. Only the countryside remained steadfast in the traditional Catholic faith. Initially, the French Protestants had been unfocused theologically (much akin to the early situation in Germany and elsewhere), but a progressive imposition of strict Calvin's tenets in the 1550s turned them into ardent Calvinists.

The Huguenots, as the French Protestants came to be called (there is no agreement as to the origin of the word), saw themselves as a religious elite, committed to the high standards of the godly Christian life, viewed Catholic practice and belief as abominable superstition, and were prepared willingly and defiantly to accept martyrdom. Moreover, they were superbly organized—Calvin's notion that there was a biblical paradigm for the external ordering of the church meant strict clarity regarding local congregations and embedded faith and life of the church in local, provincial, and national synods. A first national synod in 1559 (convened without Calvin's endorsement) drew up a confession of faith and declared that all doctrinal matters in local congregations should be brought to the national synod.[5]

A word must be said about the political reflections of the French Protestants. The minister who subsequently reported the conversation of the Protestant clergy with Antoine to Calvin offered a suggestion: if the king should prove to be a disappointment, could they resort to arms against the tyrant since they had suffered injustice? The remark was significant, for here first appeared—almost symptomatically for the state of French Protestantism at the time—the notion of disobedience, which from then until the Edict of Nantes (1598) turned into an important element in the history of the French Reformation. Scholars have variously interpreted the significance of this notion, reflecting if it was a radical departure from previous views or the proper extension of Calvin's ideas. Catholics, as a rule, have argued the latter, and Protestants the former. The truth probably lies somewhere in the middle: Calvin's own connection with the changing temper of French Protestantism was indirect, and "radical political tendencies" were present in French Protestantism long before 1559. This observation notwithstanding, the face of French Protestantism changed after Henry II. Theretofore, the adherents of the new faith had been committed, above all, to a new form of the Christian religion. They risked their lives to read the forbidden books coming from Geneva and to attend the meetings of the Protestant congregations. After Henry II this began to change. French Protestantism, firmly established and a force in the life of the country, increasingly found its recruits among individuals who had other than religious reasons to follow its banner. Prior to 1559 the French Protestants tended to be martyrs; after 1559 they were rebels.

Calvin and Theodore Beza watched the development intently, increasingly concerned about the trend of events. They counseled, pleaded, warned. "Let us pray to God," Calvin wrote, "that he might still the turbulent waves through his wonderful wisdom and goodness." Beza asked his French coreligionists if they possessed the *certa vocatio* (the certain vocation) that God had called them to do what they were doing. Yet the Genevan reformers failed to influence the course of events. The *huguenots de religions* and the *huguenots d'état* came together to pursue common action.

The Showdown

The winter of 1559–1560 was in France a winter of discontent that brought an attempt to change the political situation by force. The soul of the attempt was Condé, the actual leader of La Renaudie, a member of the lower nobility. The goal was an attack on the royal court, to "liberate" the king from the influence of the Guise, and

5. N. M. Sutherland, *The Huguenot Struggle for Recognition* (New Haven: 1980); and H. Jahr, *Studien zur Überlieferungsgeschichte der Confession de foi von 1559* (Neukirchen: 1964).

to convene an assembly of the estates to reform the country. The Duke of Guise learned about this conspiracy in February, and speedily the royal court settled at the castle of Amboise, prepared to withstand any attack behind its formidable walls. Catherine de Medici sent for Gaspard de Coligny, leader of the French Protestants, who told her that the situation was the fault of the king's advisors. The persecutions should cease and a general council deal with the religious question. On March 2 an amnesty, the so-called *Edit d'Abolition* of Amboise, was promulgated. Excluded from its provisions were the clergy and those who conspired against the king. However, shortly thereafter the conspirators struck. They failed miserably and the revenge of the Guises was frightful; the corpses of the victims grotesquely decorated the towers and walls of the castle of Amboise. The Protestants had been uninvolved in the conspiracy, and even Coligny, by his presence at Amboise, had indicated his aloofness. Suspicion fell at once on Condé, who emphatically protested his innocence.

Whatever the rationalization for the conspiracy, on the face of things it had clearly been insurrection. The consequences were fatal for the Bourbons—and thus for the Protestants. Anne, First Duke of Montmorency, abhorred the use of force and, despite being Coligny's uncle, went over to the Guises. Although his position as constable of France was somewhat inconspicuous, he was head of the Montmorencys, an influential noble family. Any Bourbon attempt to win control of the state was bound to fail, for the alliance of Montmorency and the Guises was most powerful.

Religiously, however, the future seemed favorable for the Protestants. In May 1560 a new mandate allowed personal freedom of religion but prohibited public assemblies. This was an impossible solution, for the prohibition of corporate meetings, if observed, meant the death blow to the French Protestants. A violent protest greeted the concession, which was, all the same, a complete departure from previous policy. The mandate was reluctantly issued, but the number of Huguenots left the government no other choice. It was a case of too little too late.

Toward the end of August Catherine and Michel de L'Hôpital succeeded in convening an assembly of notables of the realm in Fontainebleau to discuss the religious state of affairs in the country. The deliberations concerned the need for a general council or, if such a council were not possible, a national synod of the French church. Some members of the hierarchy recognized the need for ecclesiastical reform. Thus the bishop of Valence joined the call for a council and distinguished between two categories of Protestants: those who pledged allegiance to the king while adhering to the new doctrines, and those who sought to strengthen their cause with the force of arms. The latter should be punished as revolutionaries and the former allowed to hold to their personal religion. Public Protestant worship, however, should be prohibited. Admiral Coligny supported the call for a council and demanded that religious persecution cease until such a council could meet. Moreover, he demanded that the royal guard, which had been established by Francis Guise, be discharged. He was the advocate of a new policy, neither the suffering and martyrdom advocated by Calvin nor the open insurrection and revolution proposed by Condé. His aim was conciliation between the French crown and the new faith. If the Calvinists thought mainly of religion and little of the affairs of state, and Condé mainly of the affairs of state and little of religion, Coligny thought it possible to combine the two to the advantage of both. This is what he must have had in mind when he wrote: "What I desire most is that God will be served everywhere and principally in this realm, in all purity and according to his laws, and then this realm will be preserved." Perhaps Coligny should be seen as the French counterpart of Thomas Cromwell, deeply Protestant and at the same time concerned about the proper synthesis of religion and the body politic. Cardinal Guise vehemently opposed the Protestant requests, which indicated his unwillingness to make any concession to the heretics. The cardinal knew that any concession was tantamount to a recognition of sorts, and as a loyal Catholic he could not recognize a heretic except on pain of eternal damnation. Moreover, if matters of ecclesiastical reform were to be considered, then the church should do so without any regard for the notions of the Protestant heretics.

The deliberations of Fontainebleau led to the convening of the general estates at Orléans on December 13, 1560. Since they had not met for many years, the gathering portended a difficult situation. After the adjournment of the meeting of Fontainebleau a host of *cahiers* (petitions), tracts, and pamphlets were published, airing the issues and problems at hand. The nobility demanded the curtailment of royal power, and the common people wanted changes in taxation and the judiciary. The *cahiers* also expressed the Calvinist demand for the secularization of church property, the freedom of public worship, and the enforcement of standards of church discipline throughout the country.

Everything hinged on the attitude of the government, which lost little time in determining action. It negotiated with Spain, which agreed to amass troops along the border of France and Navarre. This tied the hands of Antoine of Navarre. Condé, who had traveled with his brother to Orléans to join the royal court, was arrested for his participation in the conspiracy of Amboise.

Francis II's unexpected death after a brief illness in December 1560 changed the political picture overnight. Cardinal Guise had ordered the faithful to participate in expiatory processions and prayed that the king's life be spared "at least until heresy has been extinguished." Francis himself echoed the sentiment and observed that the only reason for living was to crush the Protestant heretics. He had to leave that chore to others.

His successor was Charles IX, eleven years of age, second son of Henry II. This time there was no question that a regent was needed; Antoine of Navarre should have asserted his rights as a *prince du sang* and claimed the office of regent. The royal court was in a state of paralysis and confusion, even to the point of disregarding time-honored etiquette for the late king's funeral. All attention focused on who would govern France during the new king's minority. Calvin, deeply concerned about the developments in France, entertained little hope that Antoine would rise to the occasion. He proved to be correct. Antoine yielded to Catherine de Medici, who assumed the regency.

Catherine, widow of Henry II, emerged as the key figure in French political and religious affairs, who pursued, together with the new chancellor Michel de L'Hôpital, a policy of compromise. Catherine was not deeply interested in the religious questions that perturbed the time. Niece of Pope Clement VII, she possessed outstanding qualities, but piety and erudition were not among them. Her strength lay in her political astuteness. She had a good deal of feminine charm that brought success where a man might have failed. As was L'Hôpital, Catherine was convinced that judicious church reform would bring the French Calvinists back into the fold. Moreover, she thought that once the two sides talked face-to-face, their differences would prove to be minor. Catherine's charm and persuasiveness overwhelmed Antoine. Subsequently a few administrative changes were made in government that decreased the influence of the Guises somewhat, but Francis retained control over the armed forces.

The die had been cast. Antoine's failure to bid successfully for the regency meant that the last chance to introduce the Reformation with the help of the political author-ities had been lost. Eight days after Francis's demise the general estates met at Orléans. The fiscal bankruptcy of the government dominated their deliberations, but in the background lurked the religious issue. Even before Francis's death some anti-Guise pamphlets had demanded that a national assembly appoint a regent for the time of the minority of the king. Unwilling to accept Catherine de Medici's fait accompli, some estates reiterated this demand, but Antoine's unwillingness to support them led to the failure. In a lengthy speech to the estates, L'Hôpital emphasized his conviction of the importance of an irenic religious settlement, which he believed could be effected by a general council. Contrary to the precepts of the gospel, religion had become the pretext for the disruption of law and order. "Let us replace those satanical words 'Lutherans, Huguenots, Papists' by that beautiful name 'Christians,'" he said. Here was the voice of Erasmus, tempered by the insights of a wise statesman, who aptly included in his address the ancient dictum *une foi, une loi, un roi* (one faith, one law, one king). Unless the religious question was satisfactorily settled, there would be no tranquility in the land.

The petitions submitted by the three estates were so numerous and comprehensive that the government adjourned the assembly for several months. The amnesty of March 1560 was reaffirmed on February 22, 1561, and at the same time an end to religious persecution was ordered. Nothing concrete had taken place at Orléans, except that Catherine's regency was now firmly established and the persecution of the Protestants ceased. An uneasy truce prevailed in the land. No clear solution of the reli-gious question was in sight, however, aside from L'Hôpital's well-meant proposal to trust the possibilities and wisdom of a general council. This was hardly realistic—as the deliberations at Trent were to show—for a new kind of Catholicism was begin-ning to make its appearance, less than ever before willing to solve the religious prob-lem by conciliation.

Catherine was convinced that the tranquility of the realm depended on the pre-vention of the Bourbons or the Guises from attaining too much power. This convic-tion became the cornerstone of her policies, and for awhile she was successful. But on Easter 1561 an important alliance was formed when François of Guise, Anne de Montmorency, and Jacques d'Albon de Saint-André pledged, upon receiving Holy Communion, that they would protect the Catholic religion, the crown, and their own possessions. The equilibrium of power, so carefully sought by Catherine, had been dis-turbed. The Guises had become strong enough to defy the queen regent.

Catherine had a clear notion how the religious problem should be solved. Con-vinced of the strength of Protestantism (perhaps it was her fatal error to have over-estimated that strength), she was persuaded of the futility of continued persecution and thought it possible to clear the air with a truce. Afterward a council, either national or general, might effect conciliation between the two sides. In short, hers was the program of L'Hôpital and exemplified the same weakness. The staunch Catholics were hardly receptive to such a course of action and neither were the militant Calvinists. Catherine might have learned a lesson from the futile efforts of Emperor Charles V, whose mediating policy satisfied neither party. The weakness of her notion also lay in her inability to find supporters; its strength was an astute understanding of the realities of the state of affairs. France could not be pacified with a substantial segment of the populace in opposition, and Catherine was aware of this more than anyone else.

Thus she pursued her plans for a national French council, and in September 1561 she succeeded as a first step in bringing the two parties of the conflict together for a colloquy at Poissy. The gathering was referred to as a "colloquy," and for the first time, the two religious factions did talk with one another—albeit not with the success that Catherine had hoped for. The participants showered one another with tirades and grandstanding in the public sessions, showing a bit more empathy and understanding in private conversations.[6] Theodore Beza had come from Geneva and Peter Martyr Vermigli from England to lead the Reformed cause; they faced a formidable throng of cardinals, bishops, and theologians. Cardinal Guise spoke for the old faith. L'Hôpital's opening remarks that those present should accept the Protestants as fellow Christians expressed the queen's sentiment. L'Hôpital felt compelled to underscore the legitimacy of the colloquy as a means to restore peace and concord to the realm.

The agenda for the negotiations was restricted, and obviously the colloquy was not the venue for solving all the issues that had perturbed Christendom since the beginning of the Reformation controversy. It was only to find a suitable resolution of the religious strife in France. Beza was suave, eloquent, and conciliatory—at least he approved of the colloquy. He asserted that the Protestants were obedient to the crown and had nothing in common with those who resisted the king under the pretext of religion. Cardinal Guise, on the other hand, was unconciliatory and plainly disinterested in the whole venture. He pointed to the disagreements between the various Protestant factions—which he said proved persuasively the need for the teaching authority of the church—and he added that there was no point in talking with the heretics about conciliation as long as they did not agree with one another.

After the colloquy had gotten under way, the Catholic participants demanded that the Protestant heretics accept the understanding of Communion and the church as outlined by Cardinal Guise, or the colloquy should be adjourned. When Diego Laynez, the new superior general of the Jesuits, appeared at Poissy, delegated by the pope, he left no doubt about his disapproval of the whole undertaking. "From my reading and my constant experience," he said, "I am persuaded that it is most dangerous indeed to deal with or listen to persons who have separated themselves from the church." Laynez told Catherine that she had no authority in ecclesiastical matters, which were decided only by the pope. A council of the church was presently in session and the Protestant heretics should be sent to Trent to be instructed in the true Catholic faith, "not by women, soldiers, and others" as at Poissy, but by the council fathers assembled at Trent.

6. D. Nugent, *Ecumenism in the Age of the Reformation: The Colloquy of Poissy* (Cambridge: 1974).

For a short while an agreement on Communion seemed possible, but when Beza outlined the Calvinist position of the meaning of the Lord's Supper, insisting that the body and blood of Jesus were as far from the bread and wine as the heavens were from the earth, there were gasps in the huge audience, and it became clear that the gulf between the two sides was formidable. Laynez's intransigent attitude brought eventual failure. After the colloquy the Catholic clergy voted to grant a subsidy of seventeen million livres to the crown and indicated thereby that the church was not beyond coming to the rescue of the government. Poissy revealed that the queen's religious policy had suffered bankruptcy. Conciliation between the two religious parties had failed. Were there any alternatives?

The Catholics were increasingly perturbed by Catherine's efforts to solve the religious problem by making concessions to the Protestants. They left little doubt about their position. When the queen asked François of Guise what he would do in case the king turned Protestant, he retorted that he and his friends were strong enough to defend the ancient faith of the French kings by force.

Michel de L'Hôpital, Catherine's confidante and fellow-in-arms, sought to be her helpmate. A man of impressive abilities and talents, Catholics had stereotyped contempt for him, while Protestants showed awe. L'Hôpital is said to have been part of the growing faction of the politique, composed of moderate adherents of both religious factions, who were persuaded that the country needed, above all, a strong monarch to end the religious strife. L'Hôpital would have betrayed himself had he relegated religion to an inferior place. But his faith was neither staunchly Catholic nor aggressively Protestant; it was of that evasive, yet powerful, version propagated by Erasmus. It consisted of simple precepts and essentially was a way of a godly life. L'Hôpital thought that this religion was the answer to the religious problem facing France. He was persuaded that the use of force against the heretics was bound to be unsuccessful and that the Catholic Church should concern itself with the Calvinist charges and answer them. His goal was irenic accord.

His portrait shows a sensitive face, noble forehead, and gracious eyes. He has had his share of ambiguous fame, characteristic of so many historical figures. L'Hôpital was a man of talents, but hardly a great man, and certainly not a hero. That he never forgot to look after his own affairs must not be charged against him, particularly since this did not prevent him—contrary to widespread practice—from being scrupulously honest in his conduct of governmental affairs.

L'Hôpital is said to have been a Frenchman first and a Christian second; but this is hardly correct. He was persuaded that the bonds of religion were more intimate than any other human affinity. Unfortunately, his understanding of religion was outdated by the time he proposed it, for both Catholics and Protestants found it too vague. Yet, whatever the weakness of his suggestion and the failure of its realization, the fact remains that no viable alternatives were suggested by others at the time. L'Hôpital at least tried.

The efforts of Catherine and L'Hôpital resulted in the convening of the notables of the realm to discuss the state of the country. This meeting took place at Fontainebleau at the end of August. The Bourbons were not present and the gathering was dominated by Admiral Coligny, who acted as the spokesman for the Protestants. Gaspard de Coligny was an outstanding political figure in sixteenth-century France and also an eminent representative of French Protestantism. He had distinguished himself in the last military campaign of Francis I and had quickly attained a position of prominence in the French army, which he reorganized. By 1553, when he was in his mid-thirties, he was admiral of France (the commander-in-chief of the French fleet) and governor of the Île-de-France. Other honors followed, until in 1557 Coligny, defending Saint-Quentin in the course of another war with Spain, was forced to surrender and was taken prisoner. The time of enforced leisure brought about a preoccupation with the Bible and religious books, and subsequently his conversion, which led to his resignation from his military offices and the hope of a quiet life of spiritual contemplation on his country estate. He was eventually again placed in the public limelight, as the leader and spokesman of the French Protestants. A noble figure, he possessed a deep spirituality, but was above all, a statesman and politician rather than a theologian.

The country could not be pacified with a substantial segment of the populace in opposition. In 1562 the Huguenots had 2,150 congregations with money and men, and Beza remarked to the royal envoy that persecutions are futile and that the Reformed church "was like an anvil on which many hammers have been broken."[7]

In the fall of 1561 the Catholic nobility began to leave the royal court, which was characterized by an ever more open display of Protestant sentiment. The queen leaned heavily upon the advice of Coligny. In November rumors of an imminent attack by Spain and the papacy were making the rounds and added to the tensions. One month later the triumvirate of François of Guise, Montmorency, and Saint-André scored a decisive triumph. Antoine of Navarre joined their ranks after having been persuaded (though not much persuasion was really necessary) that he should assert his claim to the regency and be assured of their support of his claim. Antoine' s defection from the Protestant side tipped the scales in favor of the Catholics.

The country, in the meantime, neared chaos. The Protestants attacked Catholic churches, and Catholics assaulted Protestant services. In January 1562 Catherine issued the Edict of St. Germain, the "January Edict," which granted the Protestants the right to worship, except in fortified cities. This was a dramatic concession, not unlike what had been promulgated in the empire at Augsburg in 1555. Catherine had written to Rome that it was impossible "to reduce either by arms or law those who are separated from the Roman Church, so large is their number." After some forty years of struggle and persecution, the French Protestants received the right to public worship. The notion of only one recognized religion in the realm, so central to the medieval world, ended. No longer was it possible to speak of *une foi, une loi, un roi,* since two faiths were recognized. That the French crown was willing to suspend (at least temporarily) the notion of the *corpus christianum,* a society where church and state were one, was revolutionary. To be sure, the preface of the edict spoke of "reunion and return to one fold, which is all that we desire," suggesting that the edict was to be temporary. We need to recall that even the Peace of Augsburg sought to propagate the pious fiction of the temporary character of its provisions, even though everyone knew that conciliation was impossible and the peace for all practical purposes was permanent.

---

7. Theodore Beza, *Histoire ecclésiastique des églises reformées au royaume de France* (1580).

Issuing the edict, Catherine had no notion, of course, what the future would bring. Her decision was a manifestation of realpolitik, the recognition that those who supported the old faith were simply not strong enough to impose their will on those who clamored and agitated for change. The success of the edict depended on the willingness of both sides to be content with less than full success. In the end, neither side was willing to acknowledge this—and more bloody conflicts ensued. According to French legal procedure, the edict had to be endorsed by the various parlements throughout the country. This turned into a tedious affair that especially in Paris fanned Catholic tempers. At the same time, the Duke of Guise negotiated with the Duke of Württemberg to prevent German Protestant support of the French Huguenots. France was ready for domestic peace.

The edict did not mark the end of the religious turbulence in the realm. Indeed, for the remainder of the century the French countryside was filled with the sound of battle and the sights of destruction. In the spring of 1562, armed conflict began, the first of the Wars of Religion, which lasted intermittently (there were further wars in 1567, 1568, 1572, 1574, 1577, 1580) until the end of the century. After theological arguments no longer persuaded and diplomacy no longer restrained, the battlefield was to render the final verdict. Such had been the case in several places where the Protestant faith sought legal recognition—in Switzerland, Germany, the Low Countries, and Scotland. France followed this pattern, though there the ensuing conflict lasted longer, and was more disastrous, than anywhere else. Moreover, in France religion was only the veneer in those wars: men exploited the sacred in order to pursue the profane. To be sure, the lines were always neatly drawn, with Catholics on one side and Protestants on the other, but often neither Catholics nor Protestants were greatly concerned about religion. Other factors impinged upon the action and made lip service to one brand of religion both easy and prudent.

The catalyst for the outbreak of the first War of Religion came on February 29, 1562 (just about a month after the January Edict) when François, Duke of Guise, ordered his governor in the Dauphine, the southeast province around Vienne, to arrest the Protestant clergy and hang them on the nearest trees. The next day was a Sunday and François was on his way to Paris. Passing through the small town of Vassy in the Champagne, François wanted to hear Mass, but instead his soldiers encountered a group of Huguenots worshiping in a barn. The Edict of Toleration had made such worship legal but Vassy was in the duke's realm, and he was not of the disposition to allow heretics to worship publicly.

Historians still have trouble sifting through the highly charged emotional accounts of the event to know what really happened. François, who was himself assassinated barely a year later, claimed that his soldiers had first been shot at by the assembled Huguenots and "the inconvenience that happened at Vassy took place against my will, since I went there with no intention to do them any harm." It is clear, nonetheless, that François rejected the Huguenots' claim to worship and his representatives began to argue with the worshipers about the legality of the service. Tempers rose, stones were thrown, the Huguenots put up barricades, and the duke's soldiers began to fire into the crowd of defenseless men, women, and children. When the hour of bloodshed was over, over seventy men, women, and children had been killed, and many more wounded. When the news reached Condé, he demanded that François be punished and ordered that all armed Huguenots should convene at Orléans. Other incidents followed at other places, with Catholics and Huguenots vying for the greatest atrocities. A national Huguenot synod meeting in Paris appealed to the prince de Condé to become the "Protector of the Churches." Condé agreed, a fateful decision, for Huguenot leadership, which had been exercised by the pastors, turned to the noble "protector." Political considerations entered the picture; the Protestants became more militant in tone, and Condé acted decisively.

Both sides appealed for support from abroad, the Guise to Spain and Savoy, Condé to England and the German Protestants. The choices were made for religious reasons, which meant a change in the traditional political alignments. Spain, long the arch-foe of France, turned into a potential ally. Needless to say, political considerations also continued as an important factor. England's Queen Elizabeth aimed for more than the intangible satisfaction of aiding her despicably radical and disobedient coreligionists in France. A staunch anti-Catholic stance served her well at home, as her ambassador to France shrewdly advised: "It standeth your Majesty, for the conservation of your realm in the good terms it is in, to countenance the Protestants as much as you may." In September 1562 Elizabeth agreed to supply English soldiers, mainly to guard Le Havre, which after the hostilities was to be exchanged for Calais—a rather painless way for England to regain the city. Elizabeth had driven a hard bargain; Condé's willingness to accept it showed his desperation, the fact of the treaty his foolishness.

The summer passed with continued violence on both sides. Though efforts had been made to agree on a truce, the atmosphere was one of distrust: concessions of one side were taken as subterfuge by the other. Afterward the war began in earnest. The massacre at Vassy was the emotional catalyst, but in a real sense the outbreak of hostilities was related to the failure of the crown to assert itself against the two religious factions. The Protestants thought themselves too strong and the Catholics saw themselves too threatened to enter upon the path of compromise. The actual outbreak of hostilities was by no means deliberate, determined, or planned. The transition from peace to war turned out to be surprisingly smooth, an indication perhaps that both sides, including the Huguenots, anticipated an armed showdown. The country became engaged in a fratricidal conflict before the country was aware of it.

The intensity of the ensuing conflict showed once more that fraternal conflicts have a way of being incomparably brutal and ruthless. Excesses abounded on both sides. In April a Huguenot assembly in Sens was attacked by a frenzied mob, and virtually all Huguenots died in a merciless slaughter. According to one chronicler, children dragged a Protestant corpse through the streets, shouting, "Bring out your swine! Here is your swineherd!" But Catholics held no monopoly on cruelty. Not all of those who fought on the Protestant side were of deep religious commitment. Before the war, Calvin had counseled his French compatriots against the use of military force lest their impatience bring the cause of the true gospel to naught. His exhortation to suffer martyrdom resonated little among the increasingly frenzied and radical Protestant rank and file.

The only outright battle was fought at Dreux and was a Catholic victory. But neither side was able to score a decisive victory, and soon a plague seemed to be upon both houses. Condé was taken prisoner and François of Guise was assassinated in February 1563. Thus the leaders of the two factions were gone, much to the advantage of Catherine, the queen, who was able to reassert her role in the course of events. On March 19, 1563, she brought about the Peace of Amboise.

The Huguenots were deeply disappointed in the Peace. Condé had demanded the reinstatement of the Edict of Saint-Germain, but the Catholic opposition laid open the division in the Huguenot ranks: the Huguenot nobility showed itself unconcerned about those not of noble rank and failed to rally behind the goal of an affirmation of St. Germain. Accordingly, the Peace of Amboise granted religious freedom to the Huguenots, which meant that no one could be forced to attend the Mass, but worship services were confined to the households of the nobility and to a limited number of towns, though the actual site had to be outside the towns. No Protestant worship was allowed in Paris. Both Calvin and Coligny (admiral of France and a moderate Huguenot leader) voiced their protest against the Peace, since it discriminated against the common people.

The assassination of the duke of Guise placed a bad mark on the Huguenots. The assassin was a young Huguenot noble, Poltrot de Méré, who was arrested and confessed under torture that Condé had hired him to kill the duke. Now torture is hardly ever an infallible means to ascertain truth, and there has always been grave doubt about Méré's confession, especially since he himself subsequently revoked it. Coligny, too, denied the charge but admitted that he "did not dissuade him from it" and added—with insuperable bad taste—that the duke's death was "the greatest good that could have come to the realm and to the church of God and especially to myself."

The Peace of Amboise ended the hostilities but did not end the underlying problem of an aggressive Calvinism and a country politically and religiously divided. Catherine, for one, saw Condé and the Huguenots as outright insurgents, and she would have none of it. Her strategy of trying to mediate between the two sides gave way to siding with the Guise and the Catholic faction. Moreover, the war had shown most Frenchmen still to be good Catholics, but the determination and commitment of the Huguenots continued to be formidable.

Catherine was now more firmly in control than she had been for some time. In 1564 she undertook a lengthy tour of the country, mainly to give her young son Charles, the king, a dose of public exposure. The trip would have been recorded as a routine publicity tour, were it not for an event that illustrates the impact of serendipitous and freakish happenings in the course of history. During June and July 1565, Catherine and her entourage stayed in Bayonne, on the English Channel, where she met the Duke of Alba, with whom she talked about various matters of state, such as the threat of heresy and the possibility of an alliance between the empire, Spain, and France. It was all talk, however, and no decisions of any sort were reached.

It was common knowledge that Alba was on his way to the Netherlands, sent by Philip II to restore order, arrest dissidents, and eradicate heresy. Those who did not know what had taken place at Bayonne—and that included almost everybody—drew ominous conclusions. Rumors that the meeting had been about a treaty against the French Protestants promptly made the rounds and filled the Huguenots with terror. Of course, France would have welcomed such an alliance with Spain and the empire, but Catherine was unwilling to be drawn into a complicated political reality. When, in the summer of 1567, Alba marched with his soldiers from Italy to the Netherlands to crush the Protestants (in fact, by that time peace had already been restored there), the Huguenots, still unsettled by Bayonne, feared that Alba might decide on a prearranged stopover in France to crush the French heretics. Catherine shared the concern about Alba's scheme and hired soldiers as defense against a possible attack, but her move only intensified the Huguenot concerns and worries. The seond "war" of religion broke out in 1567, the Huguenots this time disinguishing themselves with their acts of cruelty— in September some eighty Catholic priests were massacred at Nîmes. In the spring of the following year, hostilities ended with the Peace of Longjumeau, which reinstated the Peace of Amboise. Nothing had been gained by either side.

Between the wars, when each side realized its inability to subdue the other, edicts of pacification were issued, granting some measure of religious freedom to the French Protestants. However, these edicts settled little, except that people became more fanatical and frenzied anti-Huguenots. Disorder ruled throughout the land, riots were commonplace, and economic problems found religious expression.[8]

Before too long another round of hostilities broke out, each side surpassing the other in cruelty, even to women and children. Both factions must have become convinced that this was the final call to arms, the battle of Armageddon, as one Huguenot remarked: "We fought the first war like angels, the second like men, and the third like devils"—hardly the appropriate characterization of those who claimed to fight for eternal verities. Exhaustion set in soon, and both sides recognized that neither was strong enough to impose its will fully on the other. In August 1570 the Peace of Saint-Germain ended the conflict. The Huguenots were authorized to hold four fortified places and the right to public worship in more communities than had been previously the case. Also, a general amnesty was declared. No wonder that the pope expressed his dismay that the heretics had been afforded legal recognition and King Philip II called the treaty nothing less than "shameful." In part, the peace came about because Catherine de Medici had taken even more to the conviction that some sort of rapprochement was called for—and that the influence of the Guise family had to be curbed.

The treaty of Saint-Germain gave the Huguenots as much legal standing as they ever would (as matters turned out), and the only way to fan the religious fires was to repudiate the treaty; wisely the Huguenots chose not to, and religious issues moved to the background. Catherine de Medici became intensely concerned about marrying her son Henry to Queen Elizabeth, but the English queen demonstrated once more her uncanny ability to ward off her suitors and turn marital misadventure into diplomatic advantage so that nothing came of this marital venture.

The political aspect in the winter and spring of 1571 was the prospect of an anti-Spain alliance, advocated by Admiral Coligny, who continued to exert a powerful influence on the young king. Coligny had arrived at the royal court in September 1571, was well received, and fiercely argued the case for war against Spain—a catastrophic policy that could end only in failure since France would have to wage war without allies, with neglible chances of success. The increasing Protestant influence in high places—symbolized by Coligny as well as by the king's mistress, Marie Touchet—was bound to have

8. Barbara Diefendorf, "Prologue to a Massacre: Popular Unrest in Paris, 1557–1572," *American Historical Review* 90 (1985): 1067ff.

repercussions. Another civil war, on the heels of a conflict with Spain, would surely take the country to the verge of disaster. None realized this more than Catherine, who was unwilling to watch idly as the country drifted into disaster. The solution was clear: to remove Coligny and his fateful influence on the king.

The queen's determination was the prelude to one of the most infamous happenings of the century. The heat of partisan strife, both at the time and since, has clouded the event, though about Catherine's complicity there can be no doubt. She did not need to look far for accomplices. The Guises, convinced that Coligny had been responsible for the murder of Duke François, were willing to lend their hand.

On August 22, 1572, Gaspard de Coligny was shot on his way home from a meeting of the council by a Catholic fanatic. The unsuccessful assassination had been carefully planned. The assassin used the ground-floor window of a house with a rear exit, which allowed him a speedy escape. But something went wrong. The assassin missed his target and Coligny was only wounded. When the king heard of the attempted assassination, he burst into tears and vowed to punish the culprit. This might have spelled disaster for the queen, for an investigation would have revealed her involvement. Frantically she sought a way out of a possible catastrophe and embarked on a precarious scheme. With the help of two accomplices she told the king of a Huguenot plot to murder the dignitaries of the realm and establish a Protestant commonwealth. For two hours she worked on her doubting son, seeking to persuade him of the existence of the plot and of the need to eliminate the Huguenot nobility as promptly as possible. At long last Charles was convinced and gave his permission to execute the supposed "conspirators." "Kill the lot! Kill the lot!" were his frantic words as the meeting ended.

The occasion for executing the plot was splendidly chosen, so much so that it seems to prove the premeditation of the whole venture. The wedding of Catherine's daughter Margaret to Henry of Navarre in August had brought many of the Huguenot nobility to Paris and provided a convenient opportunity to eliminate the Huguenot leaders with one stroke. Early in the morning of August 24, Saint Bartholomew's Day, the tocsin sounded. Coligny, the first victim, was murdered in his bedroom and his corpse thrown from the window. Elsewhere in Paris a terrible slaughter began—in the streets and the squares, the houses and gardens. The previous evening a list of Huguenot leaders in the city had been compiled that became the systematic reference book for the slaughter. Even the king himself participated in the event, it was said, shooting at Protestants from a window in the royal palace.

The massacre seemed to have accomplished its goal, for only a few of the Huguenot leaders survived. What is more, what began as the elimination of the Huguenot nobility in Paris turned into an indiscriminate slaughter in other cities, whence it spread into the provinces. The number of victims was high, the figures ranging from two thousand to ten thousand in Paris, and ten thousand to thirty thousand in the provinces, where the killings went on for weeks. Whichever set of figures one decides to accept as authentic, the Massacre of Saint Bartholomew's Day was wholesale murder, such as the sixteenth century had not seen. Despite apparent evidence to the contrary, it may well have been unpremeditated, but once the decision was made there was a ruthless quality to the extermination. The massacre was by no means the only act of brutal violence occurring during the Wars of Religion. The Protestants promptly charged that the meeting at Bayonne had planned the massacre, a version that finds support in Catherine's words, quoted by the papal nuncio, that it took place in accord "with a long-conceived plan." Still, the general course of events, as well as the direct evidence, suggests that the massacre was unpremeditated and a spontaneous decision on the part of Catherine. It was indeed an act becoming the impulsive Catherine, for no matter how temporarily successful, it was a most serious blunder.

Not surprinsgly, the Catholic world was delighted. Philip II exclaimed that this was the "best and most cheerful news" he had received for some time; Venice and Tuscany extended congratulations. Pope Gregory joyfully informed the college of cardinals and then attended a Te Deum Mass. A commemorative medal struck by the pope showed an angel raising a cross with one hand and slaying a Huguenot with the other: *Hugunotorum strages* (the death of the Huguenots). The prayer on the occasion deserves to be remembered: "Almighty God, who rejectest the proud and blessest the humble, we offer Thee the tribute of our most fervent praise, because, taking heed of Thy servants' faith, Thou has granted them a splendid triumph over the treacherous enemies of the Catholic people; and we humbly beg Thee in Thy mercy to continue what Thou hast in Thy faithfulness begun, for the glory of Thy name." The impressive cadences of this prayer reflected more the official French report, which spoke of the suppression of a revolution, than the actual facts. For the time being at least, the Catholic Church had reason to rejoice. Protestantism was paralyzed; its leaders were gone. Of those who survived, some left the country, and others returned to Catholicism.

Momentarily, at least, French Catholicism seemed to have crushed the Protestant heresy. The Huguenots were confounded and leaderless. Only two of its leaders, Henry of Navarre and Henry of Condé, had survived the massacre; both were princes of the blood, but the bloodshed paralyzed their determination and courage. Subsequent events, however, showed that Protestantism in France possessed rich religious resources. The Huguenot clergy rose to the challenge and strengthened the weakhearted. Deprived of those who had been only fellow travelers, French Protestantism lost in numbers but gained in vitality. The slaughter had also deeply disturbed Protestant Europe, which provided the French Protestants considerable moral as well as financial support.[9] The loss of political power was made up by the pen, a weapon even more powerful and formidable. A host of pamphlets appeared and ably argued the Huguenot cause—a new cause, as it turned out.

Influenced by a variety of sources, including, of course, Calvin, but molded by the sequence of political events from the constitutional crisis of 1559 to the Massacre of Saint Bartholomew's Day in 1572, the thinking of French Protestants underwent a striking development. A few impatient ones all along had groaned under the persecution and longed to repay in kind, taking to force to obtain the victory of the gospel; but most French Protestants were moderate, influenced by Calvin, who incessantly counseled that God had called them to patience and suffering rather than the use of force. The Genevan reformer pointedly rejected those who, as he put it, sought "to convert the universe in an instant." But the chronic persecution, the constitutional crisis,

9. Robert M. Kingdon, *Myths about the Saint Bartholomew's Day Massacre, 1572–1576* (Cambridge: 1988), presents a fascinating summary of the propaganda war that ensued after the massacre.

and especially the Massacre of Saint Bartholomew's Day reoriented the Protestants. Theretofore, French Protestants had emphasized loyalty toward royal authority. The new pamphlets argued differently, and many of them hardly espoused religious concerns. Sharply antiroyalist in tone, they saw royal power not as absolute, but as dependent upon its legitimate exercise. François Hotman's *De furoribus gallicis* (1573) offered an account of the massacre and a vehement indictment of the crown. His *Franco-Gallia*, of that same year, showed that in the past the people had exercised sovereignty and that the absolute exercise of royal power was a recent development. The theme of an anonymous Latin tract, published in 1557 under the pseudonym of Junius Brutus, but attributed to Philip du Plessis-Mornay and entitled *Vindiciae contra tyrannos* (*Defense of Liberty against Tyrants*, or *Concerning the Legitimate Power of a Prince over the People, and of the People over a Prince*), was the proper attitude toward authority: whether commands of a sovereign have to be carried out, even if they were contrary to the law of God, and whether resistance against such a sovereign were permissible. Question 2 in the book put it this way: "Whether it be lawful to take arms for religion?" The tract asserted that the *officiarii regni* (officials of the realm) had the right and the responsibility to resist a king who violated the law of God. Kings were not above the people: "Seeing that the people choose and establish their kings, it follows that the whole body of the people is above the king, for it is a thing most evident, that he who is established by another, is accounted under him who had established him." Even more pointedly: "Subjects are the king's brethren, not his slaves." A tract entitled *Du droits des magistrats sur les sujets*, by Theodore Beza, argued that an unfaithful king had to be removed from office, and another tract, *La France-Turquie*, drew ominous parallels between Charles IX and the Turkish sultan. The French Protestants resolutely opposed the absolutist tendencies of the king.

Since the French Protestants failed to yield politically, another armed conflict (now the fourth) was inevitable. Military action centered mainly on the powerful city of La Rochelle, an important Huguenot stronghold on the Atlantic coast, north of Bordeaux. The Duke of Anjou, brother of the king, began the siege in February of 1573, after he had encountered considerable problems in raising the necessary finances. The indecisive siege, which might have gone on indefinitely, ended when Anjou was elected king of Poland. The Peace of La Rochelle, concluded in June 1573, and confirmed by the Edict of Bologna in July, restored the provisions of the Treaty of Saint-Germain. This meant the concession of liberty of conscience for the Huguenots rather than freedom of worship.

Not all Huguenots recognized the Peace of La Rochelle. Sancerre, on the banks of the Loire, another Huguenot stronghold, held out for eight months until famine in the city forced surrender; by then, soup made of parchment had become a luxury. In the southern part of the country, where the Huguenots were strong, a series of demands were hurled against the king, demanding especially the rehabitation of the victims of the Massacre of Saint Bartholomew's Day and unconditional freedom of worship. A meeting at Montauban in August 1573, led to a first move to establish a Protestant confederation, while a gathering at Millau in December drew up plans for an instrument of government that dealt with finances, religion, and administration. These were clearly plans for a state within the state—a rival government that effectively would assume royal authority. A second meeting at Millau in July 1574 demanded the release of Henry of Navarre and the Duke of Alençon, freedom of worship, and the convening of the general estates. Damville, governor of Languedoc, was given the command of the Huguenot forces.

By that time France had a new king. Charles IX died on May 30, 1574. His reign had been an intriguing episode on the French throne. His pathetic involvement in the Massacre of Saint Bartholomew's Day has tarnished his historical image, tending to make him into a royal monster, but all descriptions of the king during his earlier years are full of praise and commendation—though part of that may be discounted as the gratuitous and professional flattery of courtiers. With growing years and declining health, Charles accumulated an array of negative character traits and increasingly became neurotic and unbalanced. He had a weird obsession to shed blood (his treasury constantly had to pay indemnities for butchered animals), which may well be taken as more evidence of an unstable mind.

After Charles's death, Catherine de Medici reappeared on the scene, detained Francis of Montmorency and Alençon, and thus conveniently exercised the regency until the new king arrived from Poland. She had a good reason to move against the two men, as well as a number of others, for a conspiracy had been in the making to get Alençon away from the court. The situation was crucial; in the absence of the new king, law and order might be disrupted, vengeance for Saint Bartholomew's Day might raze the country. The heads of two gentlemen of Alençon's entourage had to roll, and according to a contemporary chronicler they were carried away by their mistresses—with a kind of selfless devotion that one might not otherwise expect in the members of the oldest of professions. The conspiracy had involved some politiques, who were of a liberal Catholic propensity, more concerned about politics than religion.

The new king took the name of Henry III and was hardly an improvement over the old. He was the darling of Catherine (she called him "my dear eyes"), and her doting maternity clouded her otherwise astute sense of politics. Henry was a bon vivant who preferred the diversions of wine, women, and song to his royal responsibilities. He was not meant to be king, especially not at so treacherous a time. As a contemporary put it, Henry inclined to the life of a country gentleman with plenty of money, and the Venetian ambassador remarked that he delighted "in the domestic chase." Henry was the prototype of a Renaissance sovereign—cultured, learned, immoral, and at the same time sanctimoniously religious. Henry spent enormous amounts of money breeding poodles but also joined the flagellants. He was undoubtedly competent, capable, and astute; and the historian, even as the contemporary, wishes that Henry would have chosen to give more evidence of these traits. Henry returned to France in September 1574, and the ensuing months demonstrated that he was hardly capable of dealing with the political situation. The Huguenots had found support for some time, both among the politiques and the moderate Catholics, the former angered by Catherine's assumption of the regency without consultation of the estates and demanding sweeping changes in government. In the south, Huguenots and politiques worked hand in hand to establish provincial assemblies. They wanted complete religious freedom, the reduction of taxes, the convocation of the general estates, and the elimination of foreign influence in the country. No longer was religion the major concern, but *du bien public* (the public good). Henry rejected these demands and left little doubt that he would seek to suppress both the Protestants and the politiques. This was far from easy, however. Though Henry hired Swiss mercenaries, who plundered the countryside "to make a Christian man's heart bleed," and even achieved sporadic success, the Protestants held the fortified cities. The Catholic attempt to take them proved unsuccessful.

The conflict had ceased to be over religion. There were still mostly Catholics on one side and mostly Protestants on the other, but the matter had actually turned into a feud between the Guises and the Montmorencys, the former staunchly standing for Catholicism, the latter advocating political reform and religious toleration. The king supported the Guises but faced powerlessly those, who like Henry of Navarre, were ready to unite for religious freedom and political reform. A manifesto promulgated at Nîmes in April revealed that the conflict had turned on the absolutist tendencies of the king. Much of royal authority was to be exercised by a representative body rather than by the king. Henry called the demands "hard," yet was willing to consider them. His unwillingness to concede religious toleration brought the matter to naught. The conflict dragged on for another year while the king cut a remarkably weak figure, spending endless hours discussing philosophy and poetry rather than the affairs of state. The climax came in May 1576 with the Peace of Beaulieu, or Monsieur, since Alençon played a major role in its realization. It brought a real victory for the Huguenot cause. Its seventy-three articles stipulated various political reforms but also the rehabilitation of the victims of Saint Bartholomew's Day and freedom of religion for the Protestants. Only Paris was excepted from this latter provision. Afterward, however, Henry had second thoughts about his concessions. So did the militant Catholics who formed the Catholic League, an increasingly important and powerful instrument for the crown as well as for Catholicism. Henry, who had actually been left out of its formation, finally gave in by shrewdly utilizing the league. He concluded the Treaty of Bergerac in September 1577, which was less favorable to the Protestants than the previous one but assured several years of peace.

Coexistence at Last: The Edict of Nantes

In 1584 the country, already beset by constitutional woes, was faced with a new issue: the problem of the successor to Henry III, who was childless and (after the death of his younger brother) the last of the Valois. Next in line of succession, after the death of duke of Alençon, the last surviving brother of Henry III, stood Henry of Navarre, who, as leader of the Protestants, was bitterly opposed by Catholics. The prospect of a Protestant king rallied Catholics to action. The Catholic League, formed in 1576, now received dynamic impetus—its members committed themselves to the eradication of heresy and, more pointedly, to the notion that only a Catholic could be king of the realm. The league allied with Philip II of Spain, while Pope Sixtus V provided spiritual support by excommunicating Henry and depriving him of all claims to the French crown. In 1585 the legal toleration of Protestants was rescinded and the last of the Wars of Religion broke out. More than the fraternal conflicts, that war demonstrated the confusion of religion and politics. Henry III resented the power and influence of the Guises, so much so that he instigated the assassination of Duke Henry of

Guise and Cardinal Louis of Guise in December 1588. Not to be outdone, the following summer a fanatical Catholic sought revenge by assassinating the king.

On his deathbed Henry asked the army to swear the oath of obedience to Henry of Navarre as his royal successor, who took the appellation of Henry IV. With Henry of Navarre the Wars of Religion and the French Reformation reached their end. Though a Protestant and a leader of the Protestants, Henry IV was hardly religious. Beyond following the expected religious routine, especially before and after battles, he gave no evidence of religious conviction, except a coolness—surprisingly, considering his leadership of the French Protestants—toward rigorous Calvinism. Had he lived in Geneva, his problems with the consistory would probably have been unending; he was hardly a model Calvinist Christian. His goal was to be a Frenchman, and his conversion to Catholicism was less a traitorous default of the Protestant faith than a wise political move.

In July 1593 Henry abjured his Protestant beliefs and professed the Catholic faith, uttering, according to tradition, "Paris is well worth a mass." The quip, if authentic, was well taken: Paris was the heart of French Catholicism, Henry could never hope to rule the city as a heretic, and Paris was France. Henry understood that with the Protestants in the minority, he could pacify the country only as a Catholic. Decades of indecisive civil strife provided ample evidence. All the same, Henry's embracing Catholicism did not change the political picture overnight. A long struggle took place before he finally controlled the country. His conversion brought the more moderate Catholics into his camp, even as it freed the country from the threat of war with Spain. An astute use of force, persuasion, and money brought the nobility to his side. The Protestants, though shocked by his ecclesiastical turnabout, remained his loyal subjects, and the antiroyalist sentiment that had become so prominent among them during the days of Charles IX and Henry III disappeared.

On April 13, 1598, the king took the decisive step of settling the religious problem in the country. He promulgated the Edict of Nantes, the last of the long string of edicts and mandates that began with the Edict of Chateaubriand in 1551 and sought to pacify the country. With certain limitations, the edict granted freedom of worship to Protestants. They were allowed to worship in places where they had been authorized to do so in 1596 and 1597; elsewhere, Protestant worship was restricted to one place in a bailiwick. Paris continued to be forbidden to Protestants, as were episcopal and archiepiscopal seats. The edict decreed the full equality of Protestants in governmental offices, and guaranteed them one hundred places of safety for a period of eight years. This last provision was particularly noteworthy since it revealed the character of the edict: though issued by the king, it was essentially a contract between two political powers.

The Edict of Nantes marked the end of the Reformation in France. As in the Peace of Augsburg of 1555, the notion of religious freedom was anchored in a document of state. As in the Edict of Saint-Germain, the Edict of Nantes repudiated the principle of the *corpus christianum*, and in so doing it departed from over a thousand years of European history, during which each man, woman, and child had been, by the fact of citizenship, a Christian of the kind prescribed by the sovereign. The Edict of Nantes ended this organic union of church and state, paralleling a development that had found legal expression in Augsburg in 1555 and that eventually encompassed all of Europe. In France, however, this declaration of religious freedom was soon reversed. In 1629 the political and military provisions of the Edict of Nantes were rescinded, and in 1685, three years before the Toleration Act in England, Louis XIV revoked its religious provisions as well. The notion of national unity, even in religion, was victorious once more—though, as matters turned out, only for four years short of a century, when a revolution removed religion from the public square. At the time of the Edict of Nantes, the Protestants probably made up about one-tenth of the population, far too few to force their will upon the land. The edict afforded them the maximum that could be attained under the political and religious circumstances.

The country had come a long way since that day in August 1523 when the Parlement of Paris and the theological faculty of the University of Paris had joined hands to suppress Luther's books and ideas. The ensuing seventy-five years had brought the failure of those efforts, and Protestantism had come to be a vital force in the country. The Edict of Nantes safeguarded the Protestant accomplishments, yet disallowed what they so determinedly strove for: to convert the country to the new faith. Part of the explanation undoubtedly is that the decisive battles, theological as well as military, were fought in the second half of the century, when a Catholic Church invigorated by the Council of Trent confronted the Protestants. But more important surely was that none of the several French kings in the sixteenth century ever wavered in the support of the old church. To be sure, an economic crisis beset France from mid-century onward and the Protestants sought to use the constitutional issue of the regency to rally support. They succeeded in triggering the seemingly endless Wars of Religion, but in the end they were neither politically nor religiously strong enough to carry the day—and the country.

SCANDINAVIA

In the end, all of Scandinavia was Protestant, even though the course of reform had a distinctive pattern. At the beginning of the century the Catholic Church was lively and little popular criticism was voiced. The Renaissance prelate, the immoral monk, or the absentee bishop was an unfamiliar figure in Scandinavian lands. The monasteries were centers of spirituality as well as places of learning. All the same, the ecclesiastical transformation took place in the Scandinavian countries with breathtaking speed. It succeeded in achieving quickly what elsewhere took tense and tedious developments. The explanation for the distinctive Scandinavian pattern of reform must not be sought in the religious or moral bankruptcy of the old church—but neither in the forcefulness of the Protestant proclamation.

By the early sixteenth century, the Union of Kalmar, formed in 1397 and uniting Denmark, Norway, and Sweden (with Finland), was showing increasing signs of stress and seemed to be on the verge of breaking up. The incumbent on the throne was King Christian II, one of the more remarkable sovereigns of the century. A typical Renaissance ruler, Christian was literate, learned, and cultured, but also arbitrary, ruthless, and egotistical. In Denmark he opposed the higher clergy and nobility, though it is hard to say if he was guided by a progressive temper or by absolutist tendencies. One of his main political objectives was to bring Sweden into closer submission to Denmark. In so doing, he supported the pro-Danish faction in Sweden, represented by the archbishop of Uppsala, Gustav Trolle. This led to bitter conflict with Sten Sture, the administrator, or *rigsforstander*, in Sweden. In 1517 the Swedish estates, convened by Sture, deposed the archbishop, whose influence with the curia in Rome led to Sture's excommunication and the interdict placed over Sweden.

Understandably, Christian was not disposed to accept this turn of events. In January 1520 he invaded Sweden under the pretense of defending the traditional rights of the church. Sture was defeated. Christian magnanimously announced an amnesty for the nobles who had fought against him and invited them to join him in the coronation festivities in Stockholm. Unsuspecting, the nobility accepted the invitation, but a scheme, concocted by Christian and Trolle, brought their downfall. The archbishop announced that the royal pardon had not affected the ecclesiastical censure, and he requested Christian to punish the nobles on behalf of the church. Christian dutifully complied. Over eighty nobles and clergy were executed.

This "Massacre," or "Blood Bath," of Stockholm had grave repercussions. Archbishop Trolle's involvement caught up the church in the Danish-Swedish political strife, and did so on the side of those who represented Danish rather than Swedish interests. But despite his seemingly decisive victory, Christian's success proved short-lived. Gustavus Eriksson Vasa, scion of the Sture family, garnered the support of the remaining nobility as well as the peasants, and set out to throw off the Danish yoke. His first success came in 1521 with his defeat of Trolle; two years later he was in control of most of the country save Stockholm. That same year Christian II himself was deposed by the Rigsrådet, the Danish Council of State, since he had also attempted to weaken the influence of the Danish nobility—unsuccessfully, as it turned out, as had been his Swedish venture. Stockholm now surrendered to Gustavus Vasa, who was elected king of Sweden and Finland.

In Sweden the customary assurances at his coronation in 1523 about upholding the "privileges, persons, and possessions of the holy church," but there was a hollow ring to this assurance, since this church had sided with his political opponents. His reassuring words conveyed exceptional magnanimity vis-à-vis a church that was, in effect, leaderless: most of the bishops had been supporters of Christian II and felt it prudent to leave the country upon Gustavus's accession to the throne.

In the spring of 1523 Gustavus nominated the papal nuncio John Magnus, a conscientious but weak figure, as archbishop of Uppsala. He also nominated four additional churchmen to episcopal sees, all loyal Catholics, but politically on his side. In September he requested the papal confirmation of these nominations, asking, at the same time, that payment of the customary annates be suspended. The war of independence had been expensive, and Gustavus apprised the curia that the country was too destitute to pay but he would pledge "greater obedience" in all other matters.

Pope Adrian failed to comply. He continued to support Trolle and, moreover, elevated a foreigner to one of the vacant sees. Gustavus found that appointment unacceptable and threatened that, if necessary, he would procure the confirmation of his nominees "by the only high priest, Jesus Christ." His threat was obvious, yet Pope

Clement VII, Adrian's successor, showed himself unwilling to become involved in this kind of ecclesiastical blackmail. He confirmed only one of the royal candidates and turned down the request for the suspension of the annates. As matters turned out, this was the last official communication between the curia in Rome and Sweden.

Gustavus's religious convictions were enigmatic, but he understood that the new evangelical teaching could be utilized to touch the wealth and societal influence of the church. He supported the reform sentiment in Stockholm by appointing the reform-minded Laurentius Andreae, archdeacon at Strengnäs, as his chancellor and Olaus Petri as major clergy in Stockholm. Later, Gustavus unilaterally named Laurentius archbishop.

Andreae became the king's key ecclesiastical advisor. An astute politician in addition to being a competent theologian, he persuaded the king that the acceptance of the Lutheran faith offered benefits without liabilities. His was a vision of a national church. In a letter to the Vadstena monastery Andreae argued that the church had to serve the public good and that its wealth was to serve the nation. A mandate of January 1525 that stipulated that the income of the church was to go to the king was the first legal manifestation of this new sentiment. One month later, Olaus Petri got married in a public ceremony and the following year he published his translation of the New Testament into Swedish and his *Een nyttwgh wnderwijsning* (A Necessary Instruction), largely a translation of one of Luther's pamphlets—a sign that plagiarism was less important than the dissemination of the new gospel.

The country, however, continued in a state of fiscal crisis. Gustavus was hard pressed by his foreign creditors, yet he had no money and increasing taxes was out of the question. Gustavus appeared unperturbed and sought to arrange a theological disputation—by that time a well-established strategy of reform-minded authorities to pursue reform diplomatically—where the king's preferences came through rather pointedly: Olaus Petri was allowed to present his answers to ten questions Gustavus had formulated, while the proponents of the old church were instructed to submit their response in writing.

The discontent among the peasants about their tax burden and the various ecclesiastical reform measures led to the Daljunkern's Revolt in 1527. In June of that year Gustavus convened a diet at Västerås, where he confronted the assembled estates with the news that the country was on the verge of bankruptcy. This announcement was hardly novel; what was new, however, was the king's insistence that the property of the church should be used to solve the fiscal crisis. One of the bishops retorted that to touch the property of the church was to touch the authority of the pope. Gustavus seemed impressed by the argument and told the estates that under the circumstances it would be best for him to abdicate. He "would move on his way," he said, "never to return to this unreasonable, perverted, and ungrateful fatherland."

After some hesitation the estates agreed that they had nothing to lose from the king's proposed action—nothing, that is, except their faith. Gustavus announced his intention to abdicate three more times to the assembled estates before he agreed to change his mind. The recess of the diet accordingly handed the episcopal castles and lay fiefs over to the king, who, in effect, was given the authority to decide the needs of the church and the body politic. Moreover, all property given to the church after

1454 could be reclaimed by the families of the donors. All clergy were placed under the authority of civil courts for civil offenses. The recess also stipulated that the "pure Word of God should be preached" and that the Scriptures should be read publicly in churches and schools. Gustavus rather coyly noted that his foremost concern was the true Christian faith, since—as he put it—he knew no Lutherans. A royal *ordinantia*, issued with the recess, spelled out the relationship between the spiritual and the temporal realm. The existing structures of the church were retained, though the authority of the bishops was restricted and replaced by that of the king. The bishops, who had put up valiant resistance against the manipulations of the king, eventually yielded and formally acknowledged the king's authority.

The Diet of Västerås marked the beginning of the Swedish Reformation. Royal authority in ecclesiastical affairs was strengthened and the ties with Rome were cut. Otherwise, however, ecclesiastical life in Sweden continued largely unchanged. The bishops continued their episcopal functions even as the clergy continued their accustomed round of activities. Only the stipulation of the *ordinantia* that the Word of God be preached introduced a new, if vague, element. The ties of the Swedish church with Rome were repudiated, as were the numerous legal prerogatives that the church had enjoyed. But the new church could hardly be labeled Protestant, and quite a few years were to pass before that changed. The obvious parallel of Swedish events with those in England under Henry VIII comes to mind, for both sovereigns acted in response to specific needs against the backdrop of reform impulses. A national synod that convened in Örebro in January 1529 agreed on a few modest changes in church life, notably the abolition of several saints' days.

The royal usurpation of ecclesiastical power (and property) hardly evoked repercussions, Gustavus's position was stable, and his decision to be crowned was the outward expression of this consolidation of power. A few days before his coronation in 1528, Petrus Magni, bishop of Västerås, the only bishop confirmed by Pope Clement VII in 1524, ordained three bishops, and this provided for formal historical episcopal succession in Sweden. Since Petrus himself was anything but a Protestant, he had the three episcopal candidates assure him, perhaps somewhat gratuitously, that they would seek papal confirmation at the earliest opportunity. Not surprisingly, nothing of the sort ever happened.

One year later, however, peasant discontent led to revolt, and the grievances were both political and religious: the peasants, now joined by gentry and nobility, demanded an end to the religious changes. Gustavus, sensing the threat to his rule, promised indeed not to undertake further religious reform. This turn of events brought religious reform in Sweden to a halt. Gustavus was concerned about potential international repercussions, particularly from temporarily recatholicized Denmark. Reform came to a standstill, but for a brief time only. Once Denmark had definitively embraced Protestantism in the late 1530s, Gustavus resumed his efforts to create a Swedish national church with power the diet vested in him. In this he was astute enough to rely on the established structures of the church to propose changes, but when the synod at Uppsala insisted on the use of the Swedish language in all divine services, he quickly interfered with the dictum that the Swedish clergy had no authority to order changes in the life and faith of the church in Sweden. Andreae and Petri began to fall out of the king's graces. At a meeting of the estates at Örebro in December 1539, Gustavus issued a mandate for the Swedish church, which defined him as "the protector of the Holy Christian faith," and the nonreligious administration of the church was handled by laymen.

The ecclesiastical transformation in Sweden was thus haphazard, erratic, yet at the same time smooth and undramatic. There was no sudden drastic change, no abrupt upheaval; Catholicism just faded away. The monasteries were not forcibly closed, as was the case in England. Deprived of their economic base, they decreased in significance until they dissolved on their own accord. Church services were in the vernacular, but they closely followed the Catholic practice. Two explanations have been offered for the character of the Reformation in Sweden—Gustavus's utter lack of religious interest and conviction, and the absence of popular support for reform, expressed in the two conservative uprisings against religious change. Of these, the former undoubtedly was the major factor, since popular support was by no means the inevitable prerequisite of the formal introduction of the Reformation; England under Henry VIII is a perfect case in point. Rather, the clue lies in Gustavus, who would not tolerate the powerful institution of the church as an independent force in the realm, and thus was driven to Protestant tendencies, and yet had to make haste slowly as long as his hold on the Swedish throne had not consolidated.

The Swedish church that emerged from the Reformation did not adopt a Protestant church order until 1571 and theological statement until 1593. Interestingly enough, the statement of faith then adopted was the Augsburg Confession of 1530, not any of the subsequent confessional Lutheran documents, such as the Schmalkald Articles or the Book of Concord. By adopting the Augsburg Confession, the Swedish Lutheran Church made clear its disposition to ignore some of the contested theological legacies of Luther which at that time were bitterly dividing the Lutheran churches.

The Swedish Reformation, then, is a paradigm for formal religious change in a country without extensive popular support for reform. Except for the vocal and highly partisan German community in Stockholm, no extensive support existed. The crucial decisions from the top were made between 1525 and 1530.

In Denmark the course of reform events had its own momentum. King Christian II had ventured a reform of the Danish church that entailed a weakening of the power of the bishops. In his attempt to lessen the power of church as well as of the nobility, both opposed to the enhancement of royal power, Christian had welcomed the notions of reform emanating from Wittenberg, and he had invited members of the Wittenberg faculty, as Andreas Carlstadt and Martin Reinhardt, to Denmark to proffer support. His removal from the throne in 1523 halted his efforts but did not remove him completely from the Danish scene. He repeatedly sought to reverse the decision of the Council of State. As brother-in-law of Emperor Charles V, Christian also had crucial European connections, which evoked the specter of Habsburg military intervention to restore him to the Danish throne. In the meantime, he wound up in Wittenberg, where he quickly established a friendship with Luther.

Christian's uncle and unexpected successor, Frederik I, owed his succession to the support of nobility and the church, which meant that he could hardly afford to continue his predecessor's effort at reform. Indeed, in his coronation charter he had to distance himself from Christian's reform effort by pledging "not to allow any heretics, disciples of Luther or others, to preach and teach, either openly or secretly, against God, the faith of the Holy Church."[10] Such flowery language notwithstanding, reform preaching increasingly made headway in Denmark, aided by the internal weakness of the church (the archbishopric of Lund, for example, had no less than five incumbents between 1519 and 1536). By 1526 the evangelical cause had found an eloquent spokesman, Hans Tausen, member of the Order of Saint John. Tausen had studied at both Louvain and Wittenberg and had clearly found the new Wittenberg theology more persuasive than what he had learned at Louvain. That same year, a diet at Odense stipulated that bishops no longer needed confirmation by the pope and that the customary annates and other fees traditionally paid to Rome would henceforth go to the king. At key places, such as Viburg, Malmø, and—by the end of the decade—Copenhagen, the new preaching was vocal and persuasive. In 1530 Frederik sought to convene a colloquy to render a verdict on the ecclesiastical norms for the country, but renewed agitation by Christian II for his return and the unstable situation in Germany created by the recess of the Augsburg diet precluded the event. The towns' support of Frederik (against Christian) was rewarded by the king with a charter that allowed them to introduce the new evangelical religion.

Frederik's death in the spring of 1533 triggered a string of complex events, in which religion and politics, nobility and towns, merged and clashed, leading in 1534 to an outright uprising. Within a month, however, the revolt collapsed; all sides were willing to support the evangelical cause. Duke Christian, who had been victorious in the uprising, promptly had the Catholic bishops arrested. A diet, meeting in October 1536, endorsed the creation of a Lutheran church in Denmark. Johann Bugenhagen, recently installed by Luther as "superintendent" or "bishop" of Magdeburg, drafted the church order that formally made Denmark a land of the Reformation.

Consolidation in Sweden

Gustavus Vasa, one of the few crowned heads in history whose rule was a shining success, died in 1560. He had faced tensions and difficulties, but he had risen to the challenges and overcome them; his reign was a spectacular achievement. Sweden was a different country in 1560 than it had been in 1521, when Gustavus first sought to rally the Swedish people against Denmark. Personally, he was domineering, unreasonable, and of a quick temper; but he had a propensity for statesmanship that made all the difference. Another Swedish king and namesake, Gustavus Adolphus, observed a century later that he "was the instrument by which God raised up again our fatherland to prosperity." In many ways, Gustavus Vasa was the prototype of the new kind of ruler who made his appearance all over Europe during the sixteenth century: competent, autocratic, calculating, and determined.

Yet no matter how great his achievements in the realm of politics, in religion Gustavus did not match them. Personally he possessed only a modicum of religious commitment, not more, perhaps, than what one might conveniently expect from any

---

10. A Pettegree, ed., *The Early Reformation in Europe* (Cambridge: 1992), 104.

sixteenth-century individual. His religious policy had severed the Swedish church from its Roman matrix, had discontinued certain Catholic practices, and introduced others that obviously grew out of Reformation notions. The ecclesiastical transformation in Sweden was smooth and undramatic. There was no drastic or dramatic change. There were no martyrs, neither of the old nor of the new faith. No formal confession of faith guided the emerging Swedish church, which in most respects, for example, retaining archbishoprics, closely followed the Catholic precedent. The Swedish people must have thought the theological differences minimal. Monasteries were not shut down as in England; deprived of their economic base, they slowly decreased in significance until they faded away.

As matters turned out, Gustavus's lengthy rule gave him some thirty-five years to alter the ecclesiastical landscape of Sweden. He could thus well afford to move cautiously. His greatest virtue may well have been patience, a virtue that so many of his royal peers failed to possess.

Gustavus was succeeded by his son Eric, the fourteenth Swedish monarch to carry that name. Eric was as capable and brilliant as his father, but he lacked the mental equilibrium that distinguishes the genius from the insane. Eric XIV could have been a textbook case for the psychiatrist. He ruled for nine stormy years, until the nobles decided that they had had enough and deposed him. Part of the problem was that Eric had decided to marry his mistress, a beautiful woman, but the daughter of an army corporal; Eric's marital decision was taken as definitive evidence of insanity. He was kept imprisoned for eight years, until death mercifully freed him in February 1577, probably with the help of poison. Next in line of succession, upon Eric's deposition, was Gustavus's second son, John III, hardly a rousing improvement over Eric, but his reign at least showed some important successes. During his rule, the religious problem demanded renewed attention. A Protestant of the kind officially recognized in Sweden, the new king was married to a Catholic. For a variety of reasons (some theological, others not) he had ambitions to resolve the religious disagreement between the old and the new church. He was a humanist at heart and was touched by the irenic and conciliatory notions of Erasmus.

John III was undoubtedly intrigued by the possibility that his son Sigismund, who was brought up Catholic, might unite Sweden and Poland—if Sweden would leave the Protestant ranks. Like other crowned heads of the time (one thinks of Henry VIII), John III considered himself an insightful theologian, and he drafted a church order in 1575, the *Nova Ordinantia*, an amplification of the church order of 1571, that had been written by Archbishop Petri. In 1577 John III drafted a liturgy, the *Liturgia Suecanae Ecclesiae*, and felt confident that he had cut the Gordian knot of the complex theological disagreements between Protestants and Catholics. The liturgy, known as the Red Book for its reddish-brown parchment cover, followed the Roman Missal at several crucial places and thus had a distinct Catholic flavor. The clergy objected to the book, as did the nobility, but the king persisted in insisting on its use. To complicate matters, he secretly dispatched an emissary to Rome to establish contact with the curia and invited Jesuit missionaries to Sweden, requesting Rome to allow Communion under both kinds, marriage of the clergy, and the vernacular Mass.

In all likelihood Pope Gregory never seriously intended to grant these requests—he had earlier turned down the Swedish queen's request for Communion under both kinds—but the king's attitude opened vistas of restoring Sweden to the Catholic fold. Gregory dispatched Antonio Possevino, secretary to the general of the Jesuits, as papal nuncio to Sweden. Wearing secular clothes, Possevino arrived in Sweden in December 1577, and at once set out to persuade the king of the truth of the Catholic faith. Since John III had a high opinion of his own theological erudition, this was no easy task. All the same, after several months Possevino's persuasive skill began to wear down the king, who received absolution and declared himself ready to accept the Tridentine confession of faith. He attended Mass, exclaiming (according to one contemporary), "I embrace the Catholic Church forever." If John actually said those words, he defined "forever" in a strikingly new way.

The formal acceptance of Catholicism in Sweden depended on the papal response to John III's earlier quest for concessions. The pope's response was essentially negative. The king, in addition to his opinion of his own theological astuteness, was too sagacious a politician not to know that Catholicism without these concessions was impossible in Sweden. The papal refusal to accede to the king's requests meant the end of the efforts to restore Catholicism in Sweden.

Nonetheless, unabashed by his failure with Rome, John III sought to impose his theological notions on the Swedish church; again, he ran headlong into trouble. Though some moderates were willing to go along with his proposal, the die-hard Lutherans were not. They found support in the king's younger brother Charles (Karl), who pointedly rejected the proposed liturgy and offered his protection to all clergy who found themselves on the receiving end of John III's determined, if aggressive, ecclesiastical policy. Indeed, the opposition was strong enough to thwart the king's efforts, and the outcome of the matter was bad feelings between the king, Charles, his council, and the clergy.

When John III died in 1592, he was succeeded by his son Sigismund III, who had been elected to the Polish throne five years earlier. This election turned out to be a mixed blessing, for Sigismund had promised to turn over Estonia, a part of Sweden, to Poland, but this he found impossible in light of vehement Swedish opposition. He himself was a committed Catholic, and what he may have lacked in devotion to the church was more than amply compensated by his wife, Anne of Habsburg. Thus his succession to the Swedish throne increased the specter of recatholicization to a serious level. Boldly, Charles, the late king's brother, moved to action. The controversy over the introduction of John III's liturgy had left the Swedish church divided and theologically confounded. Charles realized that only a united church could successfully oppose Sigismund's efforts to restore Catholicism. In March 1593 he convened a meeting at Uppsala, attended mostly by clergy, but also by members of the council and nobility. After several weeks of deliberations the gathering reached an agreement about the nature of the Swedish church. The liturgy of John III, the cause of many of the problems, was denounced for its superstition. The Bible was declared the sole authority of the faith, and the three ancient creeds (Apostles' Creed; Nicaea; Chalcedon), together with the Augsburg Confession, were said to be its proper interpretation. The church order of

1571 was declared to be mandatory. The teachings of Zwingli and Calvin were condemned. Charles, a Calvinist at heart, did not object to signing the condemnation: "Write them all down that you know to be of that kind, and do not except the devil in hell, for he is also my enemy." Other provisions prohibited services other than those in conformity with the accepted faith and called for the reestablishment of the University of Uppsala for the education of the Swedish clergy. Sigismund III was to accept these stipulations as a prerequisite for his coronation. The *Uppsala Möte*, as this gathering is known, may well have been the most significant event in the history of the Swedish church during the sixteenth century. "Sweden has become one man, and we have all one lord and one God," Andreas Björnram, archbishop of Uppsala, who chaired the meeting, exclaimed after the adoption of the document. He was a bit exuberant, for the official adoption of the confession said little, if anything, about the true sentiment in the land. Yet the point was well taken. The period of doctrinal uncertainty, prevailing ever since the ties with Rome were severed, had ended. The Swedish church had become Lutheran—vaguely Lutheran, to be sure, for Lutheranism in Germany had long found the Augsburg Confession insufficient to define its theology. In Sweden, however, the Augsburg Confession was satisfactory to give to the Swedish church its needed identity.

The documents of Uppsala were widely circulated and almost universally accepted, a sure indication that the sentiment expressed was congenial to the faith of the people. Sigismund III was still in Poland when the news of this fait accompli reached him. He refused to approve the decisions of Uppsala, and when, with the papal nuncio Germanico Malaspina, he reached Stockholm in September 1593, he had Mass celebrated. This was a bad omen but also a rallying cry for the Protestants. Sigismund's coronation took place at Uppsala in February of the following year, but in the preceding negotiations the estates declared they would boycott the occasion unless the king agreed to the Uppsala document. On the very day of his coronation Sigismund III formally agreed to this demand, even though he had beforehand sent a secret protestation to Rome, stating that he had made the concession under duress and that he would not feel bound to honor it once he exercised full control in the country.

Subsequent events showed that he was prepared to be true to his words. The Mass continued to be celebrated. Soon political issues added impetus to the general discontent. Sigismund III violated his coronation agreement by appointing deputies for the provinces directly responsible to him rather than to the council. Charles forced a meeting of the Swedish diet at Söderköping in October 1595 that decided that he should act as regent during the king's absence and that the direct communications between the king and the provincial deputies should cease. Moreover, all Catholic priests were to be expelled from the country and the Mass prohibited. Sigismund III was hardly going to accept this turn of events willingly. After Charles's position had been weakened by serious tensions with the council, Sigismund III, at the head of Polish troops, landed in Sweden in the summer of 1598, prepared to take control of the country. A military defeat in September forced him to negotiate a truce with Charles, in which he agreed to rule Sweden according to his coronation agreement. He then left for Poland. Charles convened a diet at Stockholm in July 1599 that deposed Sigismund III and appointed Charles regent for the king's minor son, who was to be reared in the Protestant faith. This move, however, was unacceptable to Sigismund III, and after an interregnum Charles himself became king in 1604. The diet of Söderköping of the same year prohibited all Catholics from the realm.

Charles made final the victory of Lutheranism in Sweden at a time when the fortunes of Protestantism throughout Europe had become precarious. The Counter-Reformation was prying piece after piece from the Protestant edifice. In Germany several territories returned to the Catholic fold; in Poland Protestantism was increasingly suppressed. Sweden, quite to the contrary, was a shining light on the Protestant horizon.

SCOTLAND

Nestled along the perimeter of European civilization, Scotland was in the European backwaters in the early sixteenth century. Two centuries earlier it had won its independence from England. Since then it had been repeatedly defeated in battle but had always succeeded in retaining its independence. Unlike England, Scotland boasted no strong sovereigns dominating the realm. Instead, a restless nobility vied with the church hierarchy for power in the land. The Scottish population numbered about a half-million, some three thousand of whom were clergy and members of religious orders. The church owned a considerable share of the wealth of the country, and its annual revenues were double that of the crown.

The formal acceptance of Protestantism in Scotland was the final success of the new faith in Europe. Afterward Protestants failed to score further successes, and a new era brought mainly spectacular accomplishments of a revitalized Catholic Church. Protestant success in Scotland came very late and took place against a church that might have gotten sufficient cues from the Continent to deal successfully with the Protestant challenge. It missed that chance. In Scotland the Lollard tradition provided the same semi-indigenous backdrop as it did for the course of ecclesiastical change in England. Although its impact upon Scotland has not been explored as thoroughly as it has been for England, Lollardy had survived into the sixteenth century in Scotland. The principal cause of the initial religious ferment was Luther, whose writings were disseminated in Scotland as they were elsewhere in Europe.

At first, it seemed that Scotland, like Ireland, would be spared the agitation of the Reformation. In 1526 Pope Clement VII felt it appropriate to congratulate the people of Scotland since they were "without injury from the perfidious Lutheran heresy," adding "unlike the nearest country," a none-too-subtle reference to neighboring England.[11] Indeed, around the middle of the century Archbishop John Hamilton, papal legate and primate of the Scottish church, father also of three children, with a long-standing relationship with Lady Grisel Sempill, showed himself very much a reform-minded church dignitary, issuing a catechism in 1552 and *Ane Godlie Exhortation*, of

---

11. As quoted in James Kirk, "The Religion of Early Scottish Protestants," in *Humanism and Reform: The Church in Europe, England, and Scotland, 1400–1643: Essays in Honour of James K. Cameron* (ed. James Kirk; Oxford: 1991), 361.

1559, known as "The Twopenny Faith" because of its cheap price (though it only comprised four pages!). While the catechism denounced clerical immorality, there is little evidence of ecclesiastical corruption, even less of disdain for Catholic teachings, even though the *Complaynt of Scotland*, of 1549, asserted that "the abuse and the sinister ministration of thy office is the special cause of the schism and of divers sects that trouble of Christianity."[12]

In 1525 the Scottish Parliament passed an act against heresy, renewed in 1535, that prohibited Lutheran books. The next three decades brought little Protestant activity, if the sparsity of Protestant treatises published in Scotland is taken as cue, even though there was an influx of vernacular Bibles from England.

The banner of reform was first carried by Patrick Hamilton, a young relative of the king, who in the mid-1520s began to proclaim a message of reform. With "Master Patrick Hamilton," so John Knox wrote in his *History of the Reformation in Scotland*, "our history doth begin." Hamilton had been abroad on the Continent, studied at Wittenberg, and imbibed enthusiasm for the new gospel according to Wittenberg. While there he defended several Latin theses, which he subsequently entitled *Loci Communes* and then published in an English version under the title *Dyvers Frutful Gatheringes of Scrypture Concernying Fayth and Workes*. They became known by their shorthand title *Patrick's Places* and found their way into John Foxe's *Actes and Monuments*,[13] an imposing exposition of the new faith. Hamilton wrote that "faith makes God and man friends," or that "the faith of Christ is to believe in him; that is, to believe his word and to believe that he will keep thee in all thy need and deliver thee from evil." Even though he had been given a professorship at the newly established university at Marburg, Hamilton decided to return to his native Scotland, where his reform preaching triggered his arrest, trial, and conviction of heresy. On February 29, 1528, he walked to the stake. John Knox recorded his execution and recalled Hamilton's gracious gesture to his servant, to whom he gave his clothes: "These will not profit in the fire; they will profit thee. After this, of me thou can receive no commodity, except the example of my death, which, I pray thee, bear in mind; for albeit it be bitter to the flesh, and fearful before men, yet it is the entrance unto eternal life, which none shall possess that denies Christ Jesus before this wicked generation." Knox added that in "St. Andrews, yea, almost within the whole realm (who heard of that fact), there was none found who began not to inquire: Wherefore was Master Patrick Hamilton burned?" Knox reported that Cardinal Beaton was told that "if you will burn them, let them be burnt in deep cellars, for the reek of Patrick Hamilton has infected as many as it blew upon."[14] Burning of heretics was unknown in Scotland; only two had been put to death for over a century.

After Hamilton's death, the evidence for Reformation activity in Scotland remains scant, though one John Gau published *The Richt Vay to the Kingdome of Hevine*, a thoroughly Protestant treatise, in 1533. Indirect evidence for clandestine Protestant activ-

---

12. As quoted in Alec Ryrie, *The Origins of the Scottish Reformation* (Manchester: 2006), 23.
13. The text is found in James Edward McGoldrick, *Luther's Scottish Connection* (Madison, NJ: 1989), 74–100.
14. J. Knox, *History of the Reformation in Scotland*, W. C. Dickinson, ed. (Edinburgh: 1949), 1:76–78.

ity came from the duke of Norfolk to Thomas Cromwell in 1539, "daily there are come to me gentlemen and clerks who flee out of Scotland, as they say, for reading the Scriptures in English."[15] But some eighteen years passed before another prominent Protestant reformer appeared on the scene, and a martyr to boot. George Wishart, in his thirties, "comely of personage," had studied at Saint Andrews, had probably witnessed Patrick Hamilton's burning, and had become a parish priest. After a decade his Protestant convictions forced him to flee to England. But he had to discover painfully that England was not a safe place for a zealous Protestant who publicly denounced prayers offered to the Virgin Mary; Wishart was sent to the stake. A recantation saved him, prompting him afterward to flee to the Continent. By 1543 he was back in his native land, however, and the following year he began to proclaim the Protestant gospel. His return to Scotland had been prompted as much by political reasons as by his zeal to spread the new evangel.

The death of King James V, in December 1542, threw Scotland into a state of crisis. Quite aptly, the king's last words had reportedly been, "All is lost." True enough, the country had suffered a disastrous defeat in battle at the hands of the English. The future was uncertain. After the king's death, David Cardinal Beaton produced a document to show that James had named him regent for his infant son. But Beaton was hated and his document was at once labeled a forgery. Early in January 1544 the convention of estates named James, Earl of Arran, regent and had Beaton arrested as conspirator against the realm. In March Parliament confirmed James's appointment and at the same time authorized the use of the vernacular Bible. James had Protestant inclinations and favored closer ties with England. But French influence in Scotland continued strong, and James was too weak a figure to counter it. Moreover, to complicate matters, his own legitimacy hinged on the validity of a divorce granted by the pope to his father. Thus there was a limit to James's Protestant leanings.

In the ensuing struggle for power Cardinal Beaton emerged victorious. The tie with England—in the form of the marriage treaty between Mary Stuart and Henry VIII's son Edward—was voided, the alliance with France renewed, and Beaton made chancellor. The English party had been defeated. In this setting George Wishart proclaimed the Protestant gospel; given the political situation, his proclamation strengthened the pro-English party. Wherever Wishart moved in the Scottish countryside he attracted large crowds of people, but eventually this popular response precipitated his arrest. "In the end of those days that are called the Holy days of Yule," in the year 1545, Wishart went to Haddington, not more than twenty miles from Edinburgh. There he was arrested, taken to Beaton's castle at Saint Andrews, and on March 1, 1546, burned as a heretic.

Before too many weeks had passed, however, a group of Scottish noblemen under the leadership of one Norman Leslie provided a sequel to Wishart's execution. In the early morning of May 29, 1546, they walked across the drawbridge of Beaton's castle, north of Saint Andrews, where the rocks drop almost vertically into the sea. It was a mighty castle—John Knox called it Babylon—and an even mightier symbol of the

---

15. William Clebsch, *England's Earliest Protestants, 1520–1535* (New Haven: 1964), 82.

cardinal's power. Before the guards realized what was happening, the men had disarmed them and continued on their way to the cardinal's quarters. Beaton made a futile effort to barricade himself in his room, but the noblemen stormed in and, while he shouted, "I am a priest, I am a priest, ye will not slay me," he met his end—as John Knox observed in his *History*, "without *Requiem aeternam*, and *Requiescat in pace*, sung for his soul." The conspirators decided to remain in the castle. They were besieged, a slow and tedious affair, which dragged on for months. Mary of Guise sought support from across the sea in France, while the noblemen hoped for help from England. At first only a handful, they finally numbered about 150.

One of them was John Knox, who thus made his entrance into the spotlight of history. "Nane have I corrupted, nane have I defraudit, merchandise have I not made of the glorious Evangel of Jesus Christ." Such words were Knox's self-description in his last will and testament, and an apt description it was. To be sure, Samuel Johnson called him one of the "ruffians" of the Reformation, and true enough there was an uncouthness about him that has prompted a biographer to speak of him as the "thundering Scot." An even more eloquent tribute came from the regent of Scotland who, standing at Knox's grave, remarked, "There lies one who neither flattered nor feared any flesh." His long beard—"black, flecked with grey, thick, falling down a hand and a half"—and lean, angular face gave him a stern and austere look and conveyed the impression of an ascetic and determined individual. But such he was not, at least not in his personal life, where he could be warm and jovial. He went to plays, bowled (then a favorite pastime), and enjoyed wine.

To speak about the Reformation in Scotland is to speak about John Knox. Even as Luther personified the Reformation in Germany, Calvin that in Geneva and France, so did Knox represent the ecclesiastical transformation in Scotland. Much like his Swiss counterpart Farel, Knox seemed to possess the temper of a prophet of Hebrew Scripture. That God had chosen him to proclaim his message constituted the marrow of Knox's life. Had there been no Calvin in the sixteenth century to stress the profundity of God's election, Knox would have taken his place, for the conviction of God's omnipotent rule was real and deep for him.

Born about 1513, Knox was quickly recognized for his intellectual acumen and went to study at Saint Andrews, without taking a formal degree. He became a priest but seems never to have performed parish responsibilities. Instead, he occupied various legal positions and served as tutor of children of the nobility. The years passed without particular distinction, and not until he met Wishart did his life dramatically change.

There are encounters of fateful consequence in life, when one mind exerts an inescapable imprint upon another. Such happened when Knox encountered Wishart, for Wishart taught Knox about the new evangelical gospel.

Later, after Cardinal Beaton's assassination, Knox contemplated going to Germany, that haven of peace for English Protestants, but went to Saint Andrews instead to continue his tutoring. The nobles told him that this would give him the protection of the castle and their children the benefit of his teaching. Knox was persuaded by that argument, and by Easter time he was at Saint Andrews. His presence, however, took an unexpected turn. As he engaged in his everyday instruction in "their grammar, and other humane authors," in the catechism and the New Testament, his religious commitment and learning became increasingly evident, and—much to his surprise—the congregation of Saint Andrews elected him to be their preacher. "Whereat the said John, abashed, burst forth in most abundant tears, and withdrew himself to his chamber." The "foresight of trouble to come" made him hesitate, but in the end he accepted the charge. Knox possessed no real qualifications for the office except a burning devotion to evangelical religion. What he lacked in formal competence he made up in exuberance. "Others shed the branches of the Papistry, but he strikes at the root, to destroy the whole," wrote one observer.

In June twenty-one French galleys appeared on the waters beyond the castle and soon afterward the queen's forces arrived by land. A siege began and on the last day of July the castle was forced to surrender. The terms of surrender were honorable, but they were not kept. The leading conspirators were imprisoned in France and the others—among them Knox—sent to the galleys. In those days a ditty made the rounds: "Preasts content you now; Preasts content you now; For Normond and his company has filled the galleys fow [full]."

Thus Knox came to serve an apprenticeship as in Dante's *Inferno*. His galley bore the name of *Our Lady, Notre Dame*, and as he sat chained to his bench, rowing day upon day, endlessly across the North Sea he had ample occasion to reflect on the idolatrous religion that provided the name. Nineteen months are a long time to be chained in a galley, rowing endlessly across the North Sea between Scotland and France. In later years Knox rarely spoke about his experience, but when he did his words abounded in pangs of sorrow. "I know how hard the battle is betwixt the spirit and the flesh, under the heavy cross of affliction," he remarked at one time, "where no worldly defence but present death doeth appear. I know the grudging and murmuring complaints of the flesh; I know the anger, wrath and indignation which it conceiveth against God, calling all his promises in doubt and being ready every hour utterly to fall from God." In his *History*, Knox related how he was asked, while serving on a French galley, "if he thought that ever they should be delivered," and he recorded his answer: "God would deliver them from that bondage, to his glory, even in this life."

Released in 1549, Knox became the minister at Berwick, an English town near the Scottish border. It was a rough place, unruly and chaotic, full of homeless people, refugees, mercenaries, and others attracted to such places. There was "better order among the Tartars," said one contemporary, than in the town. It was, no doubt, an arduous assignment, but Knox handled it well: "God so blessed my weak labours that in Berwick (where commonly before there used to be slaughter by reason of quarrels that used to arise amongst soldiers), there was as great quietness all the time that I remained there as there is this day in Edinburgh." It was an arduous assignment, but Knox was persuaded that he handled it well. Afterward followed a lengthy sojourn on the Continent, mainly at Geneva. He was impressed with what he saw there, prompting him to offer the famous and exuberant eulogy that Geneva was "the maist perfyt school of Chryst that ever was in the erth since the dayis of the Apostillis; in other places, I confess Chryst to be trewlie preachit; but maneris and religioun so sinceirlie reformat, I have not yit sene in any uther place."

In the meantime the political situation in Scotland was deteriorating steadily. The country was divided between the Regent Mary of Lorraine, who pursued a pro-French policy, and the Scottish nobility, who favored close ties with England. The marriage treaty between Henry VIII's son Edward and Mary Stuart, concluded in 1543, had been voided, to be replaced by a new marital agreement with the French dauphin Francis. Their marriage in 1558 seemed to make the Scottish ties with France permanent. Again, religion and politics converged: the pro-French policies of the regent were of course also perforce pro-Catholic policies. Those of the nobility who wished for political change saw the new Protestant faith as a convenient handmaiden.

In 1558 Knox decided to intervene in the political controversy. He published a vehement tract entitled *The First Blast of the Trumpet against the Monstrous Regiment of Women*. His point was simple: Mary should abstain from idolatry and turn to the true biblical religion. Alongside finding the occasion to reiterate traditional prejudices against women in the public sphere, there was more on Knox's mind, for beyond this simple exhortation there also was a startling argument in the tract: Knox asserted that a ruler who persecuted true religion (as did Mary) could not legitimately claim the loyalty of her subjects.

Knox had written this treatise on "godly rulers" during his stay at Dieppe, and at the urging of the Genevan printer Jean Crespin he published it—anonymously, and without an indication of the printer. He had sought counsel (and concurrence) from Calvin and Bullinger who were unwilling to join Knox's stricture: "By the curse and malediction pronounced against women, by the mouth of St. Paul, who is the interpreter of God's sentence and law, and finally by the minds of those writers who in God's church have been always holden in great reverence that it is a thing most repugnant to nature, to God's will and appointed ordinance . . . that a woman should be appointed to dominion and empire, to reign over man, be it in realm, nation, province or city."

On December 3, 1557, a group of Scottish Protestant nobles had signed a covenant that began with the dramatic words, "We, perceiving how Satan, in his members, the Antichrists of our time, cruelly doth rage, seeking to overthrow and to destroy the evangel of Christ and his Congregation, ought, according to our bounden duty, to strive in our Master's cause even unto death." The document challenged the clergy to promote "'the most blessed Word of God" and pledged to defend these ministers, "the whole Congregation of Christ and every member thereof at our whole powers and waring of our lives, against Satan and all wicked power that does intend tyranny or trouble against the aforesaid congregation." Not only had the Protestants asserted themselves publicly with this covenant, they also had given themselves a name—the "Congregations" of Christ. Protestant congregations began to be formed. When Walter Mill, eighty-two years of age, was burned in April 1558 as a heretic, Protestant determination was intensified. Said Mill or Myln: "As for myself I am fourscore and two years old, and cannot live long by the course of nature; but in a hundred better shall I arise out of the ashes of my bones."

The turbulence of the times and Mill's execution raised the fear of further persecution of Protestant clerics. The covenant made its way around the land and even more men signed it. Disturbances occurred and images were destroyed. In Edinburgh an angry crowd burned the image of Saint Giles and the council refused to replace it. When several ministers were summoned to Edinburgh to explain their preaching, they were accompanied by throngs of supporters. In the audience with the queen regent, one of the gentry who had come to support the ministers spoke these ominous words: "They trouble our preachers, and would murder them and us: shall we suffer this any longer? Nay, Madam, it shall not be." The occasion must have been striking, for, in the chronicler's words, "and therewith every man put on his steel bonnet." The nobility meant business and were ready for battle. Parliament met in November and December and had it not been for the regent's delaying tactics, the Protestant lords would have registered a protestation asking for religious freedom and ecclesiastical reform.

The year turned. On the first day of 1559 the Beggars' Summons, nailed to "the gates and posts of all the friars' places," called upon the monks, in the name of the "blind, crooked, bedrels, widows, orphans, and all other poor," to leave their houses in favor of the poor. "If ye fail, we will at the same time, with the help of God and the assistance of His saints on earth, of whose ready support we doubt not, enter and take possession of our said patrimony, and eject you utterly of the same." Of course, the broadside was not written by "beggars" but most likely by Knox.[16]

As at other places of turmoil, religion and politics were strangely mixed in Scotland. In April 1559 the Peace of Cateau-Cambrésis ended at long last the Habsburg-Valois struggle, which allowed France to devote its attention to Scotland. With French support the queen regent began to pursue a strong Catholic policy. Archbishop John Hamilton made a last-minute effort to counter the Protestant tide by publishing a vernacular catechism, but it was not enough.

In February 1559, the regent issued a rather harsh proclamation that made any violation of ecclesiastical policies—such as eating meat during Lent—punishable by death; Protestant preachers were labeled outlaws. Clearly, Mary was forcing a showdown, and she felt confident in doing so since the Peace of Cateau-Cambrésis freed France to intensify its preoccupation with Scotland. A provincial synod, called by Mary in March, was to goad the church to self-reform, but failed to get the bishops to move to action.

Then, all of a sudden, word began to spread in early May that "John Knox, who was new come out of France, had been all night in that town. At what news they rose suddenly from the board where they sat and passed forth to the yard, altogether abashed." Knox back in Scotland? Indeed, he had returned, but more than a man was back: Knox was the symbol of the cause to which the Protestants were rallying. Slowly, Knox began to make his way through the Scottish countryside—Dundee, Stirling, Perth, Saint Andrews, Saint Giles. At Perth, Knox preached a fiery sermon in the morning, and when a priest tried to say Mass in the afternoon—boxing a man's ear who spoke out against it—a storm broke loose. By evening time the "rascal multitude" had stripped the town of everything that smacked of Catholic idolatry. Knox himself provided a description of how the monastery of the Grey Friars was cleansed: "The Grey Friars was a place so well provided, that unless honest men had seen the same, we would have feared to have reported what provisions they had. Their sheets, blankets, beds, and coverlets were such as no Earl in Scotland hath the better: their napery

---

16. J. H. S. Burleigh, *A Church History of Scotland* (Edinburgh: 1960), 143.

was fine. They were but eight persons in convent and yet had viij puncheons of salt beef (consider the time of the year, the eleventh day May), wine, beer, and ale." This iconoclasm dramatically polarized the situation and prompted a military showdown. Neither the church nor the regent, the one previously pursuing active reform, the other strikingly tolerant of the Protestants, was willing to make the accommodations now called for.

Scotland was at the brink of civil war. To be sure, there was a political issue—the regent's ties with France—but the rebellion also involved religion. The Protestants, who called themselves "the Congregation," received the tacit support of the political class, not the least for the increasing suspicion of France. On June 29 the Protestants occupied Edinburgh—peacefully, even as they had taken hold of most of the country, without firing a single shot. Still, the outcome of the confrontation between the queen regent and the nobility, between the old and the new faith, depended upon the success of either side to get reinforcements from England or France. In July the Protestant lords appealed to Elizabeth for help. The English queen saw the dangers of a French-dominated Scotland, though she also must have realized the risk of a break with France. Knox came forth with the proposal that Elizabeth provide troops whom she might publicly declare rebels once they had joined with the Scots. He does not seem to have been overly burdened by the propriety of his suggestion, given his conviction of the unbiblical character of all "monstrous regiments of women," assuredly another indication that at times all individuals yield to the temptation to be more concerned about the means than the end. Elizabeth's situation was touchy. To aid the Scottish nobility meant supporting rebellion against a duly instituted authority. It also meant supporting Knox, whose *Blast of the Trumpet Against the Monstrous Regiment of Women*, while directed against the queen regent, had decried all female rulers. Knox made a futile effort to eat his words, but Elizabeth remained unconvinced. The regent meanwhile fortified Leith, which was situated on the Firth of Forth and thus provided a strategic link with France. Toward the end of July 1559 a truce was signed that required the Protestants to evacuate Edinburgh and accept the regent's authority, while the regent agreed to let Edinburgh decide its religion and promised not to molest any Protestant minister. Parliament was to consider a permanent religious settlement.

At long last England provided financial assistance for the Protestants, even though Secretary William Cecil argued that the wealth of the Scottish prelates would suffice to end all financial problems in the land. French troops arrived in Scotland and the Protestants once again marched on Edinburgh, demanding that the regent send the French troops back. The regent refused and the Protestant lords formally deposed her on October 24. Disaster then fell on the Protestants. Early in November they attacked Leith but were routed back to Edinburgh. For a second time they had to withdraw from the city. In the cold of winter the faithful, carrying the heavy burden of defeat, made their way out of Edinburgh. "The despiteful tongues of the wicked railed upon us, calling us traitors and heretics: every one provoked the other to cast stones at us. One cried, 'alas, if I might see,' another, 'Fie, give advertisement to the Frenchmen that they may come, and we shall help them now to cut the throats of these heretics.' And thus, as the sword of dolour passed through our hearts, so were the cogitations and former determinations of many hearts revealed."

A few days afterward Knox preached at Stirling to the shattered remnant of the Congregation. His text came from Psalm 80: "How long wilt thou be angry against the prayer of thy people?" As far as he was concerned, the answer was obvious and the lesson clear. The Protestants had put their strength in men rather than God. "When we were few in number . . . when we had neither earl nor lord to comfort us, we called upon God; we took him for our protector, defence and only refuge . . . we did only sob to God." But their attitude had changed and they were more concerned that "this lord will bring these many hundred spears; that man hath the credit to persuade that country: if this earl be ours, no man in such bounds will trouble us." This was a good piece of critical inventory and only time would reveal whether it could bring about a cure.

The new year brought England's naval intervention, and in February a treaty was signed at Berwick between England and the Protestant lords. Soon thereafter English troops crossed the border and, together with the Protestants, began a siege of Leith. France, the hope of the queen regent, was beset by internal difficulties (notably the Conspiracy of Amboise) and was threatened by Spain, which was unwilling to condone French imperialism in Scotland.

On June 10, 1560, the queen regent died, and with her an era. Mary of Guise had tried valiantly to maintain order in the country and to thwart the advance of Protestantism. Her qualifications had been impressive and admirable, but failure still had been hers. Within one month England and France decided to withdraw their troops from Scotland. Parliament was to meet in August. A new structure of governmental authority vested power in a council on which the Protestant nobility had a majority. Nothing was said in the treaty about the religious question, but the sentiment in the land and the withdrawal of French influence made the Protestant prospects hopeful. In retrospect Knox marveled: "What was our number?" he asked, "Yea, what wisdom or worldly policy was in us, to have brought to a good end so great an enterprise?" The changes were hardly dramatic and the solution of the religious question by no means obvious. Parliament met on August 1, and Knox preached a sermon on the prophet Haggai. The rebuilding of the temple provided for Knox the biblical parallel to events in Scotland, and Knox minced no words to call for resolute action: idolatry—including papal authority—had to be abolished and ecclesiastical discipline as well as the proper use of the sacraments restored. A petition was drafted and Parliament showed itself duly impressed. The Protestants were asked "to draw, in playne and severall heidis, the summe of that Doctrine, quilk thay wald menteyne, and wald desyre that present Parliament to establische, as hailsome, trew, and onlie necessari to be believit, and to be resavit [received] within that Realme." On August 17 Parliament adopted almost unanimously the confession of faith drawn up by Knox and his ministerial colleagues, and several days later statutes were passed against the Mass and papal jurisdiction. What just a little over a year earlier had been a small, outlawed minority had been victorious in a bloody civil war and had succeeded in establishing a Protestant commonwealth.

A great many problems remained unsolved. Though the celebration of the Mass was prohibited, more than that could not be done. The political situation in the land did not lend itself to the legal imposition of any uniformity, nor to the deprivation of the bishops. The Scottish Reformation showed that even political maneuvering needed popular support. During the deliberations in Parliament the bishops, including Archbishop Hamilton, gave no indication of resolute opposition to the Protestant confession and thereby set the precedent for the lower clergy. Indeed, five of the bishops joined the Reformation, three working actively for the cause of the new faith.

The chroniclers of events must be careful, however, lest they wax too lyrical about the accomplishments of 1560. Parliament had not been authorized to deal with the religious question; thus it was a dubious route to the formal introduction of Protestantism in the land. Not until 1567 did the crown finally give legal sanction to the new church. For seven long years there was, as one of the Protestant leaders remarked, "nothing of our religion established, neither by law nor parliaments." There is always great danger in oversimplifying historical developments, and the customary assertion that with the decision of the Scottish Parliament in 1560 Scotland became Protestant begs the important question of precisely how this occurred. What happened in 1560 was simply that a new church was recognized, while the structure of the old church was left intact. The years 1558 and 1559 had been tumultuous—Archbishop Matthew Parker prayed, "God keep us from such a visitation as Knox hath attempted in Scotland, the people to be orderers of things"—and the formal establishment of Protestantism took place quietly. The key characteristics were continuity and gradual change, a somewhat unexpected feature in light of the aggressive character of Knox's Protestantism. Monasteries were not forcibly dissolved in Scotland; rather, they faded away. Nor did Scotland impose, at least for several years, any deprivations on those religious who decided to remain Catholic. Mass could no longer be celebrated, and thus the major spiritual function of the Catholic Church disappeared. But there were no executions or burnings in the Scottish Reformation. One can think of no finer tribute to it.

Afterward Knox and several other ministers went to work on a church order. The result was the so-called *First Book of Discipline*, first drafted during the siege of Leith in April 1560 and presented to Parliament in January of the following year. It was a splendid and comprehensive effort to order the life both of the kirk and of society at large. On certain points, such as the sacraments, the book was refreshingly simple; at others, it was concerned with tedious detail, such as its provisions for the widows of clergymen or the three universities. Even professorial stipends were set. Theology was truly the queen of the sciences in those days: the professor of philosophy received £100, the professor of medicine and law £133, but the theologians £200.[17]

There were serious discrepancies of emphasis in the *Book of Discipline*. While it dealt in great detail with the procedure of electing superintendents, it said hardly anything about their functions. Such unevenness was undoubtedly unintentional, for the book did not benefit from extensive and careful revision but was speedily adopted. The *Book of Discipline* suggested some stringent ways of altering the financial structure of the church. Ecclesiastical discipline was outlined, as was an interesting distinction between "crimes capital"—such as blasphemy, adultery, and murder, which did not fall "under the censure of the Church" since they were to be punished by the civil sword—and "drunkennesse, excess (be it in apparel, or be it in eating and drinking, fornication, etc." Another interesting feature was the office of superintendent.

17. The *Book* is found in D. Laing, ed., *The Works of John Knox* (Edinburgh: 1855), 2:183–260.

For all practical purposes the superintendent performed the functions of a bishop. He was addressed as "my lord superintendent" instead of "lord bishop," and his emoluments were in keeping with episcopal precedent.

When Mary Stuart, the young queen, returned from France, the religious decision had been made. Knox's account combined meteorological observations with theological judgments: "The very face of heaven, the time of her arrival, did manifestly speak what comfort was brought unto this country with her, to wit, sorrow, dolour, darkness, and all impiety. For, in the memory of man, that day of the year was never seen a more dolourous face of the heaven than was at her arrival. . . . That fore-warning gave God unto us; but alas, the most part were blind."

Mary has always baffled observers and has incited little measure of scholarly controversy. Her fatal error was that she overestimated her own abilities and underestimated the power of the nobility. Scotland could not be ruled autocratically, as she wanted, and that was her failure. Had she taken the counsel of her half brother James Stuart, a lot of things might have gone differently, and she might have retained her crown. When she was succeeded, in 1567, by her infant son and his Protestant regent, Scotland steered onto a more distinctly Protestant course, though not until January 1573 were all holders of benefices required to subscribe to the confession of faith. For a short time (five or six years) ecclesiastical life in Scotland increasingly conformed to the English pattern.

Then a change occurred. The stimulus came no doubt from Geneva and Calvin's successor, Theodore Beza, who bombarded the British Isles with epistolary exhortations warning Knox emphatically not to subject the Scottish church to the "plague" of episcopacy. Andrew Melville, principal at Glasgow, widely renowned as a scholar, became the Scottish prophet of the new evangel. Melville had spent five years in Geneva before returning to Scotland in 1574. He had never been a pastor, was a man of purely academic propensities, but sounded the clarion call for a number of younger men who, as Regent Morton had it, disturbed the peace of the church "by their conceits and overseas dreams, imitation of Geneva discipline and laws." In 1578 the agitation reached its climax. A general assembly decided in June of that year that no bishops should henceforth be elected. Scotland was on its way to a truly presbyterian polity. Scottish Protestantism was strongly Calvinist, both in theology and polity, and lastingly influenced Anglo-Saxon Protestantism at large.

However, in Scotland as elsewhere in Europe, Protestantism was "successful" because it gained the victory of parliamentary fiat. Officially and legally, Scotland in 1560 became a Protestant country with a Protestant (Calvinist) church established by law. As just noted, however, it took some time for a Scottish Reformed Church, distinctive in polity and theology, to take on form. As elsewhere in European countries turning Protestant, the majority of the people either were indifferent to religion and religious issues or still were loyal to the old faith. Also, in Scotland no less than elsewhere, the Protestant cause was advocated not only by reformers driven—as was John Knox—by a commitment to the message of the Bible. There were also those who sought mainly political or economic gain, goods, and grandeur. While the former were mainly drawn from the towns and the lesser nobility, the latter came from the upper nobility for whom old pursuits of power merged with new political goals. That the label was "Lords of the Congregation" is surely telling.

John Knox, whose determination and vision had played such an important role in the events leading up to the success of the Scottish Reformation, lived to see the fruits of his labor. He enjoyed esteem and importance, not to mention domestic tranquility: in 1564, he married a second time; his wife, Margaret, some thirty-three years his junior, gave birth to three daughters. Knox died, not quite sixty years of age, on November 24, 1572. On his deathbed he observed that "I know that many have complained much and loudly . . . of my great severity; but God knows that my mind was always free from hatred to the persons of those against whom I denounced the heavy judgments of God. . . . Therefore, I profess before God and his holy angels, that I never made gain of the sacred word of God, that I never studied to please men, never indulged my own private passions or those of others, but faithfully distributed my talent entrusted to my care for the edification of the church over which I did watch."

And at his funeral the Earl of Mortoun, the regent of Scotland, observed: "Here lyeth a man who in his life never feared the face of man, who hath been often threatened with dagger, but yet hath ended his dayes in peace and honour."

The legalization of the Calvinist faith in Scotland marked the first (and last) formal establishment of Calvinism anywhere in Europe. The movement was formidable in many places—the Netherlands, France, Hungary—but only in Scotland did it score full success.

EASTERN EUROPE

In Eastern Europe, particularly in the two most important countries in the East, Poland and Hungary, the movement of reform was every bit as important as in the West.[18] In the East the Protestant faith flourished. This was due in part to the tolerant attitude of the rulers, but far more important was the role of the nobility, whose pursuit of religious change influenced the course of events. This explains the involvement of political factors, just as the general decline of Poland's political importance was attributable to the kings' inability to assert themselves against an increasingly powerful nobility. The atmosphere of governmental toleration meant that the religious map of Eastern was far more checkered than that of Western Europe. Whereas in the territories and cities of the empire or in France eventually one faith dominated and fought off competitors, greater equality prevailed in the East. This made Lutherans, Calvinists, Anabaptists, antitrinitarians, and even Bohemian Brethren more or less equal partners in the attempt to proselytize the land. Poland, Lithuania, Hungary, and Transylvania exhibited the picture of a religiously pluralistic society, where—in contrast to the countries of the West—government was not used to establish a normative religious tradition. The consequences of this situation were twofold. For one, it created an atmosphere of mutual affinity (what we today might call ecumenical temperament), of which the Consensus of Sandomierz was the most eloquent expression. The Anabaptists and the antitrinitarians, however, stood outside this fraternal unity of Protestants, thus leaving a divided house after all. Moreover, the absence of

18. K. Maag, ed., *The Reformation in Eastern and Central Europe* (Aldershot, England: 1997).

strong Protestant sovereigns made the countries in the East targets of the Counter-Reformation. Indeed, the divisions within Protestantism turned out to be a major point in Catholic polemic, which argued that because truth was always one, Protestantism, variously divided, could not be truth.

Catholics sought to utilize governmental support in their effort to crush the Protestant heresy. But there was far less central power in Poland and Hungary than in the West, and that meant more reliance on theological arguments and issues of ecclesiastical reform. Eventually, the Catholic efforts were successful, and both Poland and Hungary returned to the Catholic fold. Thus the story ended about where it had begun. Because for most historians—as for the capitalist entrepreneur—success is an important criterion for the importance of events, ideas, and individuals, the history of the Reformation in the East seems uninteresting and inconsequential. But there must be little doubt that the Reformation in Eastern Europe was characterized by an exciting pattern of its own, which was only in part similar to that prevailing in the West.

In the early sixteenth century Poland, situated to the east of the Holy Roman Empire but very much part of Europe, teemed with intellectual excitement—and political problems. Renaissance and humanist notions were firmly established, making places such as Krakow lively intellectual and cultural centers. At the same time, however, the distribution of power and authority between the nobility, the *szlachta*, and the king was neither settled nor resolved, creating the same kind of ambiguity that prevailed in Germany. When the message of reform reached Poland, it benefited from but also was thwarted by this lack of political stability.

Poland was the one country, with the possible exception of France, where the Reformation failed after it had almost succeeded. The early spread of Protestant ideas, unsupported by governmental edict, was as successful as anywhere else in Europe, surely evidence of the new theology's persuasiveness. Then came the collapse. The decline of Protestantism is doubly noteworthy because Protestants did not suffer any determined or systematic religious persecution. Neither the religious commitment of the Protestants nor their political strength was apparently sufficient to force the permanent recognition of their religion. Had the Protestants been able to entice the king to their side, the story might have had a different ending. But they had not. Nor was the Protestant nobility, the lower *szlachta* and the higher magnates, prepared to oppose the king. They possessed the power they wanted and had little political reason to take up the cause of religion and combine it with political interests, as happened, for example, in France.

On the map of early-sixteenth-century Europe, Poland was an impressive spot of color. Yet appearances were deceiving. The greater part of what appears as Poland was Lithuania, including the Ukraine to the east, which was ruled by the Polish king as grand duke of Lithuania. The Polish king exercised little political power; that was increasingly held by the nobility, who dominated the Polish diet. In contrast to the situation in the empire, the cities—the few of them there were—had no representation in the diet. With a series of weak kings, disaster was inevitable. Good fortune had it that the first two Polish kings in the sixteenth century, Zygmunt (Sigismund) I, who ruled from 1506 to 1548, and his son Zygmunt Augustus, who ruled from 1548 to 1572, were strong monarchs, which meant that the catastrophic decline of royal authority in Poland did not come until after the sixteenth century.

Such was the setting for the religious events when Luther's writings first appeared in Poland. In 1525 Albert of Hohenzollern, the grand master of the Knights of the Teutonic Order, renounced the Catholic faith and secularized the lands of the order, the first official repudiation of Catholicism anywhere in the sixteenth century. Albert's edict demanded that the pure and simple gospel be preached in the land—the nondescript but portentous wording that everywhere introduced the Reformation. He declared himself the hereditary ruler of the lands, which extended from eastern Prussia to the Finnish Sea, and obtained the approval of the Polish king for this step—an important matter, for the lands of the order were a Polish fief. The pope protested, but his voice went unheeded.

The form of Protestantism reaching Poland was Lutheranism. Only after 1548 did Calvinism make its appearance in the land, quickly emerging as the principal form of Protestantism. We need not adduce such explanations for Calvinism's prominence as Poland's antipathy toward Germany, the Germanic character of Luther's message, or even the congeniality of the more democratic form of the Calvinist church government for the temper of the Polish nobility. The simple fact is, as has been observed elsewhere, that Calvinism was the most aggressive form of Protestantism in the middle of the century, and Calvin the shining star in the Reformation firmament. The success of Calvinism was thus unsurprising. Although Lutheranism always remained restricted to those regions where the German element was strong, Calvinism spread all across the land, to Great Poland no less than Little Poland and Lithuania.

When King Zygmunt I died on April 1, 1548, the spread of Protestant ideas in Poland had reached the point where the political authorities had to decide how to deal with the movement. The new king, Zygmunt Augustus, initially seemed to lean toward Protestantism. He was devout, committed to reform, and enlightened about ecclesiastical dogma. He had followed the theological controversy in Germany and elsewhere with unusual interest and corresponded with Melanchthon and Calvin, who twice challenged him to introduce the true gospel in Poland. But that hope was premature and Protestant rejoicing groundless, for Zygmunt remained a faithful son of the Catholic Church. Perhaps he was a Catholic at heart, or perhaps he realized that Protestantism was not strong enough in the land to allow him to become a Protestant. Moreover, there were marital complications. His bride, Barbara Radziwill, had been actively opposed by many of the Protestant nobility, and the main support for the marriage had come from the bishop of Krakow, who also was the king's chancellor. A few days after the queen's coronation in December 1550, Zygmunt Augustus publicly announced that he would remain a faithful Catholic and that the heretics would be expelled from the country.

But no action followed. An important factor was the strong Protestant orientation of the *szlachta*, who demanded at the diets of Piotrków in 1547 and 1548 that the Word of God be preached freely in the land. They got nowhere, but the very vigor of their demand was indicative of the atmosphere in Poland. Indeed, even the Catholic hierarchy lent support to the Protestant cause. Not only did some insist on vigorous ecclesiastical reform, but they also described this reform in a way hardly compatible with Catholic principles. Thus some demanded a married clergy, the Communion cup for the laity, and the suspension of ecclesiastical jurisdiction until the convening of a national synod. Over the next several years the Protestants continued to exert political pressure to secure legal recognition. They hoped to achieve it at a diet in 1555. At that time negotiations were taking place at Augsburg that gave a measure of religious freedom to the German Lutherans. Determined to attain the same, the Polish Protestants demanded religious liberty. The bishops voiced their opposition, but negotiations brought an agreement to convene a national synod.

The king set out to obtain papal approval for the synod, at the same time requesting also a married clergy, the vernacular Mass, and Communion under both kinds. As might well have been expected, the response of the curia was negative. Perhaps this response—as well as the dispatch of a papal legate to Poland—caused Zygmunt Augustus to have second thoughts about the Protestant demands, for in 1557 he prohibited the further expansion of the new faith. The prohibition, however, was one thing; its implementation, another.

At the Diet of Piotrków in 1562–1563 the *szlachta* demanded the end of ecclesiastical courts once and for all. Evasively, the king ruled that no member of the nobility should be tried by an ecclesiastical court without a prior conviction by a secular court. Most of the ecclesiastical litigation came to a standstill, but there was no formal statement, which allowed the king in 1564 to announce that the traditional rights of the clergy should never have been curtailed.

That same year, 1564, Zygmunt formally accepted the decrees and canons of the Council of Trent, yet another indication of his Catholic orientation. To make matters even more complicated, the Diet of Piotrków in 1565 declared all decisions of ecclesiastical courts null and void. This decision meant a victory for Protestantism in Poland. Yet the situation continued to be ambiguous, because religious freedom was restricted to the nobility. Only people living in the estates of the Protestant nobility were able to embrace the new faith.

Up to this point the generic term "Protestant" was used for the expressions of reform in Poland. In fact, however, striking diversity characterized the scene: Lutherans, Calvinists, Bohemian Brethren, and even antitrinitarians feuded and competed with one another. But the Lutherans who had witnessed the legal recognition of their faith in Germany by the Peace of Augsburg were unwilling to embark on a risky venture of close affinity with the Calvinists, who, in Germany, had been explicitly refused recognition in the Peace. Even the Bohemian Brethren were little willing to surrender their own confession in favor of a more ecumenically oriented agreement. The decision of the diet of 1565 allowed Protestants to practice their faith for several years free from repression, though Protestantism hardly flourished during this time. It did become firmly established and found distinct organizational forms. Protestant printing presses busily poured out propaganda; as a matter of fact, the desire for Protestant literature immensely increased the number of printing presses in Poland. In 1558 Nikolaj Rej published a widely read book of homilies. In 1563 a Polish Bible appeared, though the Protestants had been beaten to their favorite project by the Catholics. Two years earlier, Catholics had published a Polish translation of their own, which illustrates that a new Catholicism had arisen, revitalized, bold, aggressive, that countered Polish Protestantism during the most crucial phase of the effort at reform in Poland.

One can only make intelligent guesses at the reasons for Protestantism strength at that time. Almost half the members of the upper house of the Polish diet, excluding the bishops, were Protestant in 1569. These were the great landholders, the higher nobility, and the percentage indicates the distribution of Protestant sentiment among that segment of the population. No comparable figures are available for the lower house, the chamber of representatives, though one may well assume because of action taken at several diets that most of the representatives of the nobility were strongly Protestant. The death of Zygmunt Augustus in July 1572 confronted Poland with the problem of its dynastic future, for the king had been the last male of the Jagiellon dynasty. From then on the Polish kingship became an elective office, dominated and manipulated by the nobility.

We need not pursue the details of the story of Polish decline except where it had a bearing on ecclesiastical events. The key factor was the nobility (from all accounts, the common people were little affected by the religious controversy), who were little willing to burden themselves with a strong monarch. The Union of Lublin, in 1569, enhanced their prerogatives against the king. Thus, even though the *Consensus Poloniae* of the following year brought the three major Protestant factions—Lutherans, Calvinists, and Bohemian Brethren—to recognize one another as orthodox and thereby made Protestants, with the exception of the antitrinitarians, a unified front, the nobility had achieved its political goals and saw no more need to side with the Protestants. In the deliberations following King Zygmunt Augustus's death, the diet agreed to the Confederation of Warsaw of January 28, 1573, which granted religious freedom to the nobility (much like what had happened at Augsburg in 1555), though the language used was sufficiently vague and raised immediate doubts about whether the antitrinitarians were included in the provision. The confederation was also unclear about whether the Protestants were merely assured personal religious freedom or legal recognition was given to their churches and thereby their right to public worship. Politically, however, the document made clear that the nobility had achieved its goal of independence from the crown.

The successful candidate for the Polish throne was Henry of Valois, whose explicit willingness to accept the Confederation of Warsaw with his *articuli Henriciani* (Henry's Articles) had a great deal to do with his election. When a Polish delegation traveled to France to accompany Henry to Poland, the Protestants told Henry quite plainly "nisi id feceris, rex in Polonia non eris" (if you do not subscribe, you will not be king in Poland). At his coronation, however, Henry had second thoughts and sought to circumvent a formal recognition of Polish Protestantism. Dramatically, two noblemen participating in the solemn ritual refused to proceed with the coronation— and Henry gave his approval.

He might have spared himself the trouble, for his reign in Poland was short-lived. Henry unexpectedly returned to his native France. After a brief interregnum, Stefan Batory was elected king; he ruled from 1576 until 1586. His religious policy was ambivalent but in the main favored Catholicism. Stefan's successor, Zygmunt III, whose rule extended to 1632—almost half a century—pursued a staunchly Catholic policy, and when he died, Poland was once again a Catholic country. But it was also a weak country, for its political significance had diminished drastically during his reign.

This revitalization of Catholicism took place, like the earlier spread of Protestant sentiment, without the active exercise of royal power. Batory was fond of the Jesuits and favored them in a variety of ways; Zygmunt III was a Catholic through and through. Yet neither Batory nor Zygmunt persecuted the Protestants. Protestantism just faded away, sapped of its inner vitality and strength. Why? The reasons were many. For one, Polish Protestantism was never a popular movement; it was mainly restricted to the nobility. Still, what people thought and felt in sixteenth-century Europe—whether in England or Poland, Germany or Italy—made little difference; the common person was scarcely even a supporting actor on the stage of history in those days. This was particularly true in Poland. But the absence of popular support alone did not fatally harm the Protestant cause. Other factors proved to be decisive.

For one thing, the Catholic Church was too strong—not so much in terms of the religious vitality of Catholicism in Poland but in the strength of the hierarchy that exercised political power—was supported by the king, and withstood the initial Protestant assault with little defection from its ranks. Furthermore, the Protestant base was not broad enough to consolidate political power. Very few towns in Poland might have provided a reservoir of strength for the Reformation. The towns had no political voice in Polish affairs, and therefore their religious sympathies could find no political expression. Finally the kings never wavered in their Catholic conviction. Protestant sentiment was mainly restricted to the magnates and the *szlachta*, which meant that the attitude of these two groups was crucial for the cause of the Reformation. If either defected from the Protestant cause, the Reformation in Poland was lost. And this is just what happened. Because the nobility had little to gain by embracing the Reformation, the decision about ecclesiastical alignment was governed solely by religious considerations. And here the situation was none too favorable for Protestants, for soon a vital and attractive Catholicism, rejuvenated by papal refom and the Council of Trent, confronted a divided Protestantism. Moreover, the odium of antitrinitarianism weighed heavily upon the Protestants and helped to discredit their cause. The Polish Minor Church never stood a chance of dominating the coutnry's religious fate. Lutherans and Calvinists feuded with one another but joined hands to denounce the Bohemian Brethren, despite the glowing affirmations of the Consensus of Sandomir. Elsewhere in Europe the several forms of Protestantism also competed with one another, but one always possessed governmental recognition. Poland's situation was quite the contrary—Lutherans, Calvinists, and Bohemian Brethren were equal partners and used this equality to create hopeless confusion. Also, none of the Protestant traditions was able to boast of a preeminent leader. John Lasco passed from the scene quickly, and of the other leaders (relative unknowns such as Gliczner, Lismanini, and Turnovius come to mind) none was outstanding or possessed a charismatic character.

The Catholics, on the other hand, could claim such a man, and his impact upon events was far-reaching. He was Stanislas Hosius (Hozjusz), eminent theologian and outstanding churchman. Born in 1504, he had studied at Krakow, Padua, and Bologna. He entered government service in 1533. In 1549 he was appointed bishop of Chelmo (Kulm), and two years later he received the diocese of Ermland. In 1560 he served as papal nuncio to negotiate with the German emperor about the continuation of the Council at Trent, and in 1561 he received the cardinal's purple. Afterward he assisted in curial affairs and was appointed grand penitentiary of the Sacred College, recognition both of his expertise and of his service to the church. Pope Gregory

XIII, who had so honored him, described him as a "great saintly cardinal, a pillar of the church, the jewel of the sacred college, and the fame of the papal court."[19]

Gregory might well have added that Hosius saved Polish Catholicism. Combining theological astuteness and practical churchmanship, Hosius molded the temper of the Catholic Church in Poland, despite the brevity of his actual presence there—from 1549 to 1558, and then again from 1564 to 1569. Hosius embodied a new type of ecclesiastical prelate. Competent, conscientious, and devout, he was also a Catholic of strong conviction; Protestantism for him constituted utter evil and perversion. "The Lutherans," he wrote on one occasion, "are assuredly no Christians, for they do not derive their name from Christ. They have cut themselves from the body of Christ through the most abominable blasphemy of the sacred." The struggle between the old and the new faith was for him a clash between light and darkness, and he left no stone unturned to spread this message and carry out his program. He vigorously supported the work of the Jesuits in Poland and founded a Jesuit school at Bramsberg that received his name, Lyzeum Hosianum. Other Jesuit schools followed, and the pedagogical work of the Catholic Church in Poland was significantly strengthened. This made for a more literate clergy, and though greater literacy is surely not to be equated with greater godliness, the Polish Catholic clergy did become more spiritually sensitive.

Hosius's major contribution was literary. His magnum opus, written in the space of a few days in 1551, was a statement of faith entitled *Confessio fidei catholicae*. In the span of three decades the book saw almost forty reprints as well as translations into several other languages—telling proof of the work's appeal. The author's theological acumen was solid, sound, and unoriginal, though one might add that for his polemical purposes originality was hardly necessary. Hosius meant to expound the fundamentals of the Catholic faith rather than engage in theological polemics, and in an uncommon manifestation of authorial modesty he had others read his manuscripts before committing them to print, which undoubtedly improved his work but obscured whatever creativity he himself possesssd. No opponent of Protestantism in Catholic ranks was as bitter and hostile toward Protestants as Hosius. While he could be quite mild-mannered, as a rule he was not.

An important factor was the strong Protestant disposition of the *szlachta*. At the diets of Piotrków in 1547 and 1548 the *szlachta* demanded that the Word of God be allowed to be preached freely in the land. They got nowhere with their demand, but the very vigor of their demand was indicative of the atmosphere in Poland.

Protestants were legally protected in Poland until the eighteenth century. Even though there were many ways in which life could be made difficult for them, Protestants remained—with the exception of the Socinians, who were denied the appellation of Christians, and in the seventeenth century were expelled from the country. Religiously speaking, Poland passed through the Reformation era in a strangely ambivalent state.

---

19. The literature on Hosius is mainly in Polish. In English there is H. Kowalska, "Stanislaus Hosius," in P. G. Bietenholz, ed., *Contemporaries of Erasmus: A Biographical Register of the Renaissance and Reformation* (Toronto: 1986), 2:206–7.

Catholicism and Protestantism stood side by side, the one vigorous and aggressive, the other impotent and listless.

The Reformation in Poland failed, above all, because Protestantism failed to make its political case. Catholicism succeeded, however, and that made all the difference. In Poland the Jesuits scored their most smashing success, largely, if not completely, through the intensity of their devotion and their vision. They busied themselves with establishing an educational system wherein a new generation of Poles, especially the offspring of the *szlachta*, was educated along Catholic lines. Taking to the pulpit, the Jesuits succssfully propounded Catholic claims. Piotr Skarga, a Jesuit, combined administrative skill, theological erudition, and folksy eloquence, as the court preacher of Zygmunt III and attained fame through his "sermons to the diet," in which he chided the power elite for their disunion and advocated a strong monarchy as well as the religious unity of the country. Skarga was a crucial participant in the discussions that led to the Union of Brest of 1596, which united the Orthodox bishops of Poland with the Catholic Church.

HUNGARY

The story of the Hungarian Reformation cannot be told without speaking of the country's larger political situation. The spread of Protestantism took place without governmental support, for the authorities were if anything hostile to the new theology coming from Germany. The presence of a large German segment along the northern fringe of Hungary may have had something to do with the ease with which the new faith was received. Conversely, some of the hostility may have been due to political and ethnic, rather than religious, considerations.

Within such a setting, the Reformation scored a virtually comprehensive victory. By the end of the century Hungary was, practically speaking, Protestant: a secret report to the curia conceded that among a thousand Hungarians only one Catholic could be found. Most of the bishoprics had been vacant for decades, and the efforts of the Jesuits to establish a bridgehead had failed.

Yet this Protestant success was replaced eventually by failure. The absence of strong political support of the Protestant faith was a major reason for its eventual downfall, which came when the king used force to reestablish Catholicism in the land. This recatholicization of Hungary, which was never fully successful, lies outside the chronological scope of our narrative, yet it must be mentioned to show that in some instances the seventeenth century brought dramatic reversals.

On the face of things, Hungary was a rather inclement climate for the new evangel. The preponderance of the German element in the land—George of Brandenburg was the guardian of the youthful King Louis II—had evoked anti-German sentiment and Hungarian nationalism. In Hungary, unlike Germany, nationalism could not be a contributing factor in the popularity of the Reformation; if anything, it was an obstacle. The country was in the throes of a deep financial and political crisis, and the search for a scapegoat pointed conveniently to German elements.

This much was true. The royal court at Buda was open-minded with respect to reform, though this meant the advocacy of Erasmian principles of ecclesiastical renewal. Queen Maria, the granddaughter of Emperor Maximilian, was an Erasmian at heart, a candidate ripe for the Protestant faith, which may have prompted Luther, who could be quite political, to dedicate one of his tracts to her.

Then came 1526 and the catastrophe of Mohács, where on August 29 the Turks decisively defeated the Hungarian forces. The toll was dreadful: the king, two arch-bishops, five bishops, and a host of others lay dead on the battlefield. Two thousand Hungarian heads, the chronicler reported, were lined up in front of the sultan's tent. "With all these murderous swords stretched out to lay hold of the garment of life the plains seemed like a friend with a thousand arms," wrote a Turkish observer after the battle. Hungary had lost more than a battle. It had lost, within the span of a few short hours the leaders of church and state. Hungary fell into hopelessness and confusion. The southern and central parts of the country lay destitute and defenseless before the Turkish enemy, causing a Polish diplomat to write: "The whole country is dreadfully devastated; everywhere is misery and lamentation." Naturally, people sought an expla-nation for the disaster. Expressing the general tendency to find a kind of metaphysi-cal significance in the military disaster, a broadside attributed the defeat to the "idolatry, transgression, cruelty, falsehood, and evil lives" of the people. Luther's ded-ication of his *Four Psalms of Comfort* to the widowed queen made the same point, and the argument was persuasive enough to silence the contention that divine vengeance had befallen Hungary on account of the spread of the new faith. In fact, the disaster of Mohács gave new impetus to the Protestant proclamation, which saw the catastro-phe as a divine judgment on a perverted church. Protestant sentiment prevailed in high places. George of Brandenburg, an uncle of the late king, was a Protestant, as was the queen's confessor, Conrad Cordatus.

The catastrophe had robbed the Catholic hierarchy of its leaders. But even if it had not, the Catholic Church would hardly been able to withstand the Protestant onslaught. Humanist mentality had penetrated its clerical ranks—the prelates spoke more of Plato and Virgil than of Christ, remarked one observer, and Renaissance practices characterized clerical life. Catholicism in Hungary did not possess the vitality to counter the challenge of the Reformation. No eminent figure rallied the Catholic Church to polemical battle. After Mohács came a time of transition, both religiously and politically, in which a vacuum enabled the further spread of the new faith.

The king's death brought Ferdinand I of Austria and John (János) Zápolya into competition for the Hungarian throne—or whatever remained of it after the Turkish victory. Each sought to outdo the other in suppressing the Lutheran heresy—Zápolya persecuted Protestants while he himself was excommunicated by the pope—but they failed to crush the movement. If nothing else, their rivalry prevented a unified reli-gious policy and made success for them impossible. Both men needed the support of the nobility to achieve the undisputed right to the throne, and when the chips were down, neither Ferdinand nor Zápolya was willing to risk losing that support because of a too rigorous pursuit of a Catholic policy. Ferdinand, in particular, despite his deep Catholic commitment and his ruthless persecution of Protestants in Bohemia and

Austria, demonstrated that he knew very well how to distinguish religious zeal from political prudence.

Hungary consisted of three areas: a narrow strip in the northwest under Habsburg rule, a large section of the country under the domination of the Turks, and, in between, Transylvania in the northeast. Protestantism was strongest in the northwest, but elsewhere, too, the Protestant message was spread, often by the nobility. No force was used in the propagation of Protestantism. The nobility could appoint the clergy in their domains, and Protestant magnates naturally chose Protestant ministers. On the other hand, Protestantism spread even where it was opposed by the nobility. It was strong in the areas under Turkish rule, for the Turks showed little interest in intra-Christian rivalry; from their vantage point, both versions were wrong. If anyone aided the Protestant cause, it was the Turks, for they tended to favor the Protestants rather than the Catholics, who were ruled by a foreign power, the pope. The Turkish domination also aided the Protestants in another way, for the Protestants could argue for spiritual renewal in the face of a divine scourge. By the early 1530s Protestantism was widespread in Hungary.

There were quite a few reformers on the scene. Matthias Dévai Bíro deserves to be mentioned first, for he has been called the "Hungarian Luther."[20] Originally a Franciscan monk, he came to Wittenberg in 1529 to study and fell under Luther's influence. Upon his return to Hungary, he proclaimed the Protestant message and published a series of theses entitled *Rudamenta salutis*. Promptly arrested, he had an opportunity for two years to ponder his Protestant convictions behind bars. Then followed the restless life of a minister of the new evangel: thrown into jail, always harassed, but never intimidated. His theological position was akin to that of Melanchthon, especially with regard to Communion. When the Protestant clergy met for the first Protestant synod at Erdöd in September 1545, Bíro's theological temperament dominated the gathering.

István (Stephen) Szegedi Kis, another Hungarian Reformer, possessed greater theological erudition and acumen than did Bíro and even appears as a figure of European renown. Born in 1505, he studied at Krakow and Vienna, favorite and convenient institutions of higher learning for Hungarian students. In 1543 he went to Wittenberg, where he earned a doctorate in theology. Back home, he became an evangelist for the new faith, first in the central region of the land and, after 1551, in the area occupied by the Turks. In 1554 he was elected superintendent of the Protestant churches. Though always viewed with suspicion by the Turks, Kis forcefully guided ecclesiastical affairs until his arrest in 1561. Charges of spying were brought against him. He languished in prison for over a year until an exorbitant ransom secured his release.

Kis resumed his efforts at once, and until his death in 1572 he continued as leader and organizer of the Protestant faith in the Danube region. Szegedi Kis's fame rests not only on his achievements of practical churchmanship; he was also a theologian of exceptional ability. He wrote several theological works that appeared in print after his

---

20. On both Bíro and his fellow reformer Melius see A. S. Unghváry, *The Hungarian Protestant Reformation in the Sixteenth Century under the Ottoman Impact: Essays and Profiles* (Lewiston, NY: 1989).

death, though not in his native Hungary but in the centers of Protestantism in Europe, in Basel, London, Zurich, and Geneva. One was a history of the papacy entitled *Speculum romanorum pontificum*; another, a book of biblical homilies, *Tabulae analyticae*; a third, a comparative theology, *Theologiae sincerae loci communes*. Szegedi Kis's most astute theological work was a defense of the Trinitarian dogma against the Transylvanian antitrinitarians, *Assertio vera de Trinitate*, published by Theodore Beza in Geneva. Most widely known was the systematic theology with the title *Theologiae sincerae loci communes de Deo et homine*, a work a bit stuffy and tediously scholastic, but what it lacked in warmth and sparkle it made up in erudition.

Szegedi Kis's theological home was Switzerland, and he exemplified the theological reorientation of Hungarian Protestantism at mid-century, for which he himself was in large measure responsible. Because he had earned his doctorate at Wittenberg, his Calvinist reorientation is a bit astounding. Initially Luther's influence had been paramount, but Hungarian Lutheranism was not pure Wittenberg, for Melanchthon occupied a more prominent place than Luther. The Synod of Erdöd, for example, accepted the Variata version of the Augsburg Confession, surely anathema to all good Lutherans.

The second half of the century brought a contest between Lutherans and Calvinists in Hungary. Gone was the fraternal concord of the earlier years, though it returned toward the end of the century when a resurgent Catholicism called for a common defense. The influx of Calvinist ideas meant the doctrinal clarification of what up to then was vaguely called Protestantism. At most places the adherents of the new faith were called "Lutherans," a legitimate but misleading label. Their ideas were those of the Wittenberg Reformer, but they were the Protestant commonplaces, such as the assertion of the superiority of Scripture over tradition, or the righteousness of faith. Only the coming of Calvinist thought sharpened doctrinal sensitivity among the Hungarian Protestants. Besides Stephen Szegedi Kis, it was also Márton Kálmáncsehi who oriented Hungarian Protestantism along Calvinist lines. A former priest active in Debrecen, the largest town along the upper Tisza, Kálmáncsehi had drunk deeply from the wells of Zwingli. He did not acknowledge Christ's bodily presence in the sacrament and held that a simple wooden table sufficed for an altar. Until his death in 1557, he fought long and hard against the Lutherans, mainly over his rejection of the altar and his view of Communion.

Two years after his death an agreement was reached at Marosvásárhely between "Christian teachers from all of Hungary and Transylvania" concerning a view of Communion that was essentially Calvinist. The terse objectivity of the Lutheran view was given up, and faith was made the prerequisite for the reception of Christ's body and blood.

The overwhelming figure during this period was Peter Melius, youthful, zealous, and competent, who published over thirty tracts, practical and devotional in character, that firmly embedded the Protestant faith in the land. Melius sought to spread the Protestant faith among the common people: for him, their involvement was an important expression of the Reformation. "Each believer, bestowed with God's grace, may teach in his circle," he wrote. In 1562 he helped to draft the major Hungarian confession of faith, which carried the title of *Confessio catholica*, or *Confessio Debrecinensis*.

Toward the end of the century the victory of the Reformation in Hungary was virtually complete, even though a handful of Catholics were left here and there. Some three hundred priests were still in the country, and virtually all the bishoprics were vacant. Had the provincial diets taken the proper steps to abolish the bishoprics, a decisive blow would have been dealt against Catholicism. As matters went, Catholicism astoundingly asserted itself again. An initial expression of resurgent Catholicism had already come in 1548, when King Ferdinand demanded that the heretics (the Sacramentarians and the Anabaptists) be suppressed and Catholic worship restored. The omission of any reference to the Lutherans suggests that in Hungary as in Germany the same fine line was drawn that considered only the Lutherans worthy of ecclesiastical recognition. The provincial diets dutifully renewed this law for several years, without noteworthy practical consequences. Ferdinand refrained from using force, and his successor, Maximilian II, was actually benevolent toward the Lutherans, though he hated the antitrinitarians and threatened them with the stake. Maximilian's successor, Rudolf II, who ruled from 1576 to 1608, sought to crush both Protestantism and the nobility. At long last the Catholics had several competent literary spokesmen, notably Nikolaus Telegdi, who wrote in the vernacular and knew how to turn a Hungarian phrase. Telegdi had learned his lessons from the Catholic polemic of the time. All the ills of the day were blamed on the Protestants, who had disrupted and disturbed the good old days.

Toward the end of the century the suppression intensified. Rudolf II sought to enforce Catholicism under the legal pretense that the cities were his property. There were sporadic acts of violence throughout Hungary, notably at Kaschau in 1599. The Protestant ministers were expelled from the city, the Protestant churches were turned over to the Catholics, and Protestant worship was prohibited. At long last the Protestants—the Lutheran cities and the Calvinist nobility—recognized the seriousness of the situation. They decided to make the formal recognition of freedom of religion the prerequisite for any deliberations of other issues at the forthcoming diet. The king's representative played the game shrewdly by putting the religious issue on the agenda—though at the end. The Protestants thought themselves safe, but before the last point of the agenda had been reached, the diet was adjourned, and, adding insult to injury, a stipulation was included in the recess that renewed the former laws protecting the privileges of the Catholic Church.

The Protestants finally roused themselves to action. Meeting at Gálaszécs in September, they announced that they would not recognize this addition to the recess if the free exercise of religion were restricted.

Into this tense atmosphere fell the uprising of Stephen Bocskay, one of the most powerful and wealthy men in eastern Hungary. Bocskay had originally pursued a strong pro-Habsburg policy but had increasingly realized that Habsburg was interested in Hungary only for the sake of strengthening the Habsburg domain. He was persuaded that the strengthening of Transylvania was the only means of safeguarding Hungary against the Turks. He became involved in some political scheming, and in 1604 hostilities began with Barbiano, Rudolf's commander-in-chief. In April 1605, after several impressive military victories, the Hungarian diet elected him king of

Hungary. But Bocskay had no political aspirations and wanted only to safeguard Hungarian rights. Among these was freedom of religion, a right that the Peace of Vienna, concluded in 1606, gave to most Hungarian Protestants. Two years later this peace was made the law of the land, and Protestantism was thus formally recognized. Protestants could worship, organize their congregations, and even occupy important offices of state. Although the new faith had failed to score a complete victory, its accomplishments were legally safeguarded in 1608.

THE LOW COUNTRIES

The Low Countries, comprising present-day Netherlands and Belgium (though with the exception of Flanders), were part of the Habsburg domain, and even in the sixteenth century their people were prosperous, proud, and important—qualities that were to make the Dutch Empire the foremost political might in the early seventeenth century. There were important cultural and political differences among the several Dutch provinces, and the Low Countries' common bond was Habsburg rule.

Dutch merchants shipped fine cloth to the four corners of the compass, while Antwerp increasingly rivaled Augsburg as the banking center of Europe. The European westward expansion into the American continent no less than the southward expansion along the coast of Africa were crucial geopolitical factors in this striking Dutch development, coupled as they were with the increasingly precarious trade and commerce in the eastern Mediterranean.

The church was dynamic, greatly marked by the lay movements of the Modern Devotion, the Brethren and Sisters of the Common Life, the fourteenth-century Dutch quasi-monastic movement whose members eschewed the formality of the monastic profession but nonetheless wanted to life lives of devotion to the love of God and neighbor, humility, and simplicity. Particularly strong was the influence of the Christian humanism of Erasmus, who had himself been influenced by the Modern Devotion. Cornelius Gropheus remarked in 1521, "Everywhere the arts and letters are being restored, the gospel of Christ is reborn and Paul is again alive."[21]

The origins of the Reformation in the Low Countries are not difficult to establish: the influx of Lutheran ideas coupled with the rich presence of Erasmian notions and ideas. The principle "the enemies of our enemies are our friends" (referring to the scholastic theologians) made for kinship between the disciples of Erasmus and those of Luther. Lutheran notions were found among the Augustinian friars—not at all surprising, because three of the major Augustinian monasteries (Antwerp, Dordrecht, and Ghent) were part of the Saxon province and there was much communication between them and Wittenberg. The monastery in Antwerp was labeled a hotbed of Lutheran heresy. Luther's appeal seems to have consisted of his denunciation of works righteousness and his appeal to Christian freedom—understood as revolutionary by his contemporaries in the Dutch provinces no less than elsewhere.

---

21. *Biblotheca Reformatoria Neerlandica*, 6:38, as quoted in A. C. Duke, *Reformation and Revolt in the Low Countries* (London: 1990), 13.

Emperor Charles V deserves credit (if this is the proper word) for demonstrating how this Lutheran menace was to be dealt with: in the spring of 1521 he ordered the burning of Luther's books. Persecution of those suspected of Lutheran heresy followed, and eventually some two thousand Protestants were martyred. Efforts at suppression were more rigorously carried out than elsewhere in the empire, where Charles depended on the goodwill of the territorial rulers to join him in his strategy of dealing with the Lutheran ideas. The first Reformation martyrs—Henricus Vos and Johannes von der Eschen, two Augustinian friars—were burned in Brussels on July 15, 1523. Their martyrdom moved Luther to write one of his finest hymns, "Aus tiefer Not schrei ich zu Dir ("Out of Deep Distress I Cry to Thee").[22] Though Reformation sentiment could thus exist only as an underground movement of small circles, by 1525 Luther was a household word in the Dutch provinces and his followers acquired a name: *Luytrianen.*

In the late 1520s and early 1530s reform notions of a dissenting sort made their way into the Dutch provinces. Melchior Hofmann introduced his brand of eschatological Anabaptism there, and his teaching of the imminence of the end and of Christ's return appealed to some people. When some of his Dutch converts reported the severe persecution they were suffering because of believers' baptism, Hoffmann announced a "moratorium" on all baptisms. The end was at hand, so there was no need to endure unnecessary suffering. Although some of the Dutch converts to the Anabaptist cause migrated to the "new Jerusalem" of Münster in 1533, including the two subsequent Münster leaders Jan Matthijs and Jan van Leiden, the small, clandestine Anabaptist conventicles in the Dutch provinces were the Reformation's only manifestation in the Low Countries. The conventicles formed an underground movement, chronically and severely tested by oppression and persecution. Tieleman van Braght's moving account of early Dutch martyrs in *Bloody Mirror* did its part in making this reality widely known. The first decades of the reform movement in the Dutch provinces were, therefore, hidden years. In the words of De Hoop Scheffer, an eminent Dutch historian of a few generations ago, "The history of Anabaptism is the history of the Reformation in our fatherland."[23]

Around the middle of the century a change occurred with the steady influx of Calvin's ideas into the country. Calvin's evangelizing disciples made their way from France northward, first to the Walloon region and then into the Dutch provinces. While Calvinist ministers went on their spiritual errands to the Dutch provinces, new Dutch disciples traveled southward to Strassburg and Geneva to imbibe Calvin's vision of the gospel. Catholic suppression peaked. Charles V issued two edicts in 1550 that were so brutal—the mere suspicion of Protestant heresy was deemed sufficient to bring the accused to the stake—that no one was willing to administer them.

In 1550 Calvin's name appeared for the first time in an official list of heretical books, and before long clandestine Calvinist congregations had sprung up everywhere in Holland. It is puzzling that Lutheranism, whose centers were geographically much closer to the Dutch provinces than were Strassburg or Geneva, was not able to be the

22. WA 35:91ff.
23. J. G. De Hoop Scheffer, *Geschichte der Reformation in den Niederlanden* (Leipzig: 1886).

dynamic catalyst of reform in the Low Countries. One might conjecture that Calvin's view of the Lord's Supper, with its notion of a spiritual presence of Jesus in the elements of bread and wine, was more acceptable in a land where the Sacramentarians (*Sacramentariërs*), individuals who in the 1520s began to deny that bread and wine became the true body and blood of Jesus in the Mass, continued strong.

Not surprisingly, there was also a political angle to reform in the Low Countries. It became pronounced soon after the succession of Philip II, when the efforts to make the Dutch provinces a more pliant tool in the hands of this Spanish overlord took on new dimensions. Philip's attempt to bring the Dutch provinces into line by reducing the traditional rights and privileges of nobility and townspeople and by centralizing power created deep resentment and opposition. This situation suggested to the Dutch the desirability of a religious faith other than that accompanying Philip's policies. Lutheranism at the time was not only beset by severe theological controversies but also had been privileged by the Peace of Augsburg into an establishment religion. Calvinism, on the other hand, nowhere politically recognized, could provide the answer in its insistence on the right of subjects to take up arms against immoral or illegitimate political authority.

The theological consolidation occurred in 1561, when Guy de Brès, the staunch Calvinist pastor of the congregation at Tournai, wrote a confession of faith, the Belgic Confession, "for the faithful scattered everywhere through the Netherlands." Brès had become a Protestant in 1547. Persecution as well as a desire to learn made him a globetrotter for the new faith, and he found his way to England, Brussels, Frankfurt, and (of course) Geneva, where he was ordained pastor. In 1561 he returned to the Low Countries and quickly began work on a confession. Translated into Dutch, his work, entitled *Confession de foy*, quickly became the norm of faith for the Dutch Protestants—somewhat against the wishes and sentiment of Calvin, who failed to see the purpose in yet another statement of faith. De Brès modeled his confession after the French Confession of 1559, though expanding the section on the Lord's Supper— still a hotly contested internal point of controversy among Protestants. The theological orientation remained the same: "that we receive through faith . . . in our hearts the true body and the true blood of Christ, our only Savior."

De Brès sent a copy of his confession, together with a covering letter, to Philip II. His intention was to show that the confession vindicated the theological orthodoxy and peaceful character of the Protestants. He challenged the king to cease all religious persecution. Philip was hardly impressed, and de Brès paid for involvement in the Reformation with his life at the stake in 1567. Three years earlier, in 1564, Philip II had ordered the decrees of the Council of Trent be administered in the Low Countries and the decrees against heretics fully enforced. In 1566 a group of young nobles drew up a petition that combined religious and political concerns: abolition of the Inquisition, softening of the laws against heretics, refraining from administering the decrees of Trent, and calling an assembly of the Estates-General. When Philip's regent in the Low Countries, Margaret of Parma, asked her advisors what to do with the petition, she was told not to fear "those beggars" (*ces gueux*), and the appellation became the rallying cry for all who opposed the Spanish rule. A riotous fury broke out, and Calvinist preachers, thoroughly trained in Geneva, egged the people on.

By the early 1570s the northern provinces were strongly Reformed. There has been much discussion about how this happened, all the way from the allegation of a corrupt Catholic Church to the heavy hand of the political authorities and the failure of that church to provide for the care of souls. In all likelihood, however, it was because the Reformed message meshed more harmoniously with local political agitation. Throughout Europe religious strife was accompanied by political strife, and the fate of religion depended on which of the two options, Catholic or Protestant, was better able to relate to the political issues of the day. William of Orange, who did his best to pacify the country not only religiously but also politically, nonetheless faced political limitations. His peacemaking efforts in 1566 (after civil war had broken out), 1572, and 1578 were no more than efforts at achieving a truce; he wanted "freedom of religion for both Reformed and Catholic religion."[24]

By the late 1570s the Dutch Calvinists had appropriated the standard Protestant theory of the right of resistance against political authority acting unlawfully. Dutch Calvinist political thought, as it found expression in the Revolt of the Netherlands, took much of its ideological argument from the French monarchomachists (opponents of princely absolutism), who, in turn, had imbibed the whole tradition of Protestant reflection on the right to resistance. The struggle for sovereignty was also the struggle for a new faith. Calvinism benefited immensely from this coalescing of concerns, and when the northern provinces attained their independence in 1581, Calvinism was established as the dominant religion.

CONCLUSION

The attempt to introduce formal religious reform was successful in two countries, while the outcome in the other three remained in doubt for a long time. Might this suggest different patterns of popular Reformation appeal? Or the presence or absence of charismatic leadership in particular countries? We must ask whether any generalizations emerge from these diverse responses to the Reformation challenge. The two countries that turned Protestant were in northern Europe, and it is tempting to conclude that the farther away a country was from Rome, the more likely it was to become Protestant. One might also ponder a chronological pattern (because the Reformation gained momentum as the years passed) of some sort—but although Sweden turned Protestant in the mid-1520s, it was 1560 before Scotland did so.

We have already variously noted the pivotal role of politics in the process of ecclesiastical change. Each of the six countries (with one exception) suffered serious political problems. The challenge of the Reformation came not to stable societies but to societies undergoing political turbulence. The coming of the Reformation meant that these six societies experienced religious challenges as well; but the relevance of these problems to the unfolding of ecclesiastical events was limited, contrary to what one might expect. The same must be said about social or economic conditions where impact on the religious transformation was indirect.

24. As quoted in A. C. Duke, *Reformation and Revolt*, 203.

In Sweden the political issue was its recently won independence from Denmark and the financial needs of the crown. Gustavus Vasa found himself in dire financial exigency, and the wealth of the church suggested itself as a remedy for his fiscal worries. Moreover, the church had been an active, even partisan participant in the struggle between Sweden and Denmark and, had unfortunately been on the losing Danish side, which hardly endeared the Swedish church to the new king. That the confiscation of ecclesiastical property and the royal usurpation of ecclesiastical prerogatives were not followed by confessional changes or liturgical modifications supports the contention that the king's initial intent was not to cut the ties, theological and ecclesiastical, with Rome. Gustavus's primary concern was to remedy his fiscal distress and at the same time to assure that the Swedish church remained beyond the slightest suspicion of disloyalty. There was little theological agitation, and the ecclesiastical transformation effected by the king was smooth. Unlike Henry VIII of England, Gustavus did not take his country on a complicated path of personal vindictiveness and ecclesiastical idiosyncrasy. Thus Sweden saw little of the turbulence that afflicted England between 1527 and 1558.

France and Scotland, in turn, experienced a different political situation. There the attempts at ecclesiastical change had initially failed (in both countries because of the crown's adamant support of the old church). Nonetheless, in both countries Protestant agitation for reform continued for decades, and competing factions strove for political power. In Scotland the contest was between the nobility and the queen regent, though underneath lurked the resentment of the Scottish people against the French influence in Scottish political affairs. In France the contest was between competing factions of the nobility, with a king in the middle who lacked the ability (or the power) to prevent the two factions from dragging the country into bloodshed.

These political tensions existed independently of the religious turbulence and the efforts at ecclesiastical reform. Indeed, they predated the coming of reform, even though they may have been weightier in substance. The tensions had a bearing on the course of the Reformation because political issues could easily be given a religious rationalization and meaning. Generally the conservative forces, the proponents of the political status quo, favored the Catholic faith. This was true in the case of the queen regent in Scotland and the king in France, who felt prompted to suppress the emerging manifestations of Protestantism. Rough support for Catholicism, in turn, made it prudent for Protestants to support those in political opposition, for the opponents' enemies were also the enemies of the Protestants. Political opposition seemed to assure the realization of their own religious and ecclesiastical goals.

If those intent on religious reform aligned themselves with a political faction because they saw religious advantages to so doing, those concerned about politics could similarly discern the advantage of supporting the Protestants' religious goals, if for no other reason than to acquire additional political strength. Thus the marriage of politics and religion seemed to offer advantages to both sides. Neither Catholics nor Protestants in Scotland and France introduced politics into the arena of contest for the acceptance of the true gospel; the political issue had been on the table well before Protestants made their appearance.

In Poland the situation did not differ in its outcome from what had happened in France; both countries withstood the Protestant challenge and remained in the

Catholic fold. An important difference existed with respect to the turmoil that accompanied Protestant agitation. France suffered bitter civil war and immense bloodshed, while Poland escaped them. The reason for this must not be sought in either Catholic religious commitment or Protestant numerical strength. Rather, it is to be found in indigenous political issues present in one country and absent from the other.

The Protestant nobility in Poland may have forced the issue of the formal introduction of Protestantism at the death of Zygmunt (Sigismund) II, when the Jagiellon dynasty ended and the election of a Protestant king was a possibility. Apart from the desire of the Protestant nobility to have a Protestant king, there was no real reason to compel such an agenda. Traditional prerogatives and constitutional liberties were not endangered, and Protestant rigidity and determination might have thrown the country into civil strife, as happened in France, with no obvious advantages.

The developments sketched here and the comparisons drawn pertained only to external considerations—to the way the Protestant religion got caught up, willingly and unwillingly, in the power play for formal recognition. They say nothing about the theological persuasiveness of the Protestant message, nor do they speak to the intensity of piety that did (or did not) characterize the internal history of Protestantism (or Catholicism) in these countries. Although the story of legal recognition and political deals assuredly does not suffice as the full history of Christianity, it is important in that it shows how spiritual conviction became a part of the harsh realities of power politics.

Politics and religion were so intimately connected in the Reformation that religious aspirations were seldom free of mundane entanglement. This was a consequence of the long shadow of the medieval notion of the *corpus christianum*, of Christendom, that fell over the sixteenth century, and the subsequent two centuries as well. It was the conviction that church and society were but two sides of the same reality: that membership in the body politic meant membership in the church, and that the foremost task of a ruler was the support of the Christian religion. This was why the history of the Christian churches in the sixteenth century became part of the political history of the time.

Chapter 12

THE PROTESTANT VISION: THE THEOLOGIES

Whatever else may be said about the events in the sixteenth century described as "the Reformation"—namely, that they included a heavy dose of politics, traditional political rivalries, and social and economic issues—there can be little doubt that the controversy also involved, significantly and dramatically, theology. Stark theological disagreement divided Western Christendom, and bitterly.

The new Christian tradition called Protestantism rivaled both Eastern Orthodox and Roman Catholic Christianity in significance and numerical strength. However, Protestantism was never a single theological or organizational entity; rather, it was divided into several ecclesiastical traditions and churches, each of which determinedly argued (as did the Catholic Church) that it was in sole possession of Christian truth. It was Catholic polemic that lumped the diverse streams of anti-Catholic sentiment in the notion of a single phenomenon called the "Reformation." The various Protestant streams insisted that they had little in common.

This Protestant diversity makes it difficult to outline and summarize common Protestant theological affirmations. Any attempt to do so runs the risk of offering generalizations and common denominators that defy historical (and theological) reality. Nonetheless, several common affirmations stand out—not too surprisingly, for theology was what much of the conflagration was all about. To be sure, the push for reform had begun as a quest for deeper spirituality, but underlying theological assumptions of this spirituality quickly came to the fore, and the "Catholic" Luther, about whom some Protestant theologians wax so lyrical, disappeared. At the same time, political and economic interests came to the fore, and religious and theological concerns were hijacked to serve secular power plays. Nonetheless, one cannot understand the turbulence of the sixteenth century without paying tribute to the central importance of the theological discourse.

The fundamental characteristic of all Protestant theologies was the categorical disavowal of the primacy of the Roman pontiff. No matter what else is to be said about Protestant theology, one fact is clear: all Protestant churches, without exception, renounced their allegiance to the pope in Rome. That was the common bond. A pope, who held judicial and theological primacy, was neither needed nor wanted.

Several theological affirmations were shared by all Protestants. They are often identified by three Latin phrases—*sola scriptura, sola gratia, sola fide*, by Scripture alone, by grace alone, by faith alone. It was the modifier *sola* (alone) that constituted the incisive Protestant affirmation, for Catholic theology has, of course, always affirmed Scripture, faith, and grace; the charge that it did not has been Protestant propaganda.

Protestants argued a focus *solely* on Scripture, grace, and faith. The Protestant polemic in the sixteenth century had it that Catholics relied on tradition and minimized the importance of sacred Scripture. None other than Luther claimed that he had never seen a Bible until late in his study of theology—an assertion that, if true, was surely the consequence of the economics of publishing rather than the church's theological position. In their anti-Catholic polemic, the Reformers offered what may be at best described as a caricature of Catholic thought—that Catholics disavowed the Bible in favor of tradition, and grace and faith in favor of good works.

None of this was true. Catholics did affirm the Bible, grace, and faith—but with a difference. Scripture was juxtaposed to church tradition; faith and grace were juxtaposed to merit and works. Church theology and dogma sought to balance competing claims.

After 1519, when Luther began to insist on the sole authority of Scripture, he dissented from a long and honorable tradition. He turned the affirmation of Scripture into the *sole* affirmation of Scripture and, by so doing, rejected those competing sources of authority that had become normative in the Roman Church: tradition, pope, and council. The delineation of the Reformation principle of authority was thus, above all, negative. It entailed the repudiation of other sources of authority. The Reformers held that tradition, pope, and council had in the past usurped authority to promulgate unbiblical doctrine and teaching. Luther and the other Reformers provocatively and with great gusto added the modifier "human-made" to the word "tradition." Traditions were "human" traditions, and they stood in sharp contrast to the Word of God.

Protestant theology rejected this balance in favor of Bible, grace, and faith alone. Accordingly, it was the Bible alone that constituted the source of Christian truth, unmitigated by church practice or church tradition. It was grace and faith alone that were the bedrock of salvation. All Protestant Reformers waxed eloquent about the absolute primacy of the Word. Thus Luther wrote, "The Word of God is both original and authoritative. It is God's word and is not the word of the church, which has here only the role of receiving and transmitting," while Calvin observed, "Scripture, gathering together the impressions of Deity, which, till then, lay confused in our minds, dissipates the darkness, and shows us the true God clearly."[1]

Positively, this meant the enunciation of *sola scriptura*, the formal principle of the Reformation. There is a bit of uncertainty as to when and how Luther came to insist on *sola scriptura* (though he never used the phrase). His much-maligned colleague Andreas Carlstadt may well have been the catalyst. At any rate, Luther's Catholic antagonists found the new perspective baffling—after all, the initial disagreement had been over the priority of the authority of pope or council, and now Luther rejected both. Luther, in turn, increasingly realized that the matter was not quite that simple. When his German translation of the New Testament, the September Bible, was published in 1522, he included a preface to apprise the reader how to understand Scripture (virtually all translators of the Bible in the sixteenth century deemed it necessary to tell their readers in prefaces how to understand the sacred Word, even though in different contexts they affirmed that the Word was self-explanatory). Luther's preface, with its illuminating heading, included a strident comment about the Epistle of James,

---

1. See, respectively, WA 30.2:682, Calvin, *Institutes* 1.6.1.

which Luther described, with his characteristic flair for language and theological judgment, as an "epistle of straw with which I would prefer to heat my oven."[2]

The Reformers opposed the assertion that there had to be an authentic interpreter of Scripture, namely the church and its traditions. As Johann Eck had put it in the Leipzig debate, "Scripture is not authentic without the authority of the church." The Council of Trent, in reviewing the Protestant assertion, consistently affirmed that "all saving truths are contained both in the written books and in unwritten traditions."[3] Of course, Protestant theologians affirmed tradition (except for the antitrinitarians, all Protestant theologians adamantly embraced the ecumenical creeds of early Christianity), but they did so in their own particular way by insisting that tradition must always be measured by Scripture: "Fathers and councils," wrote Calvin, "are of authority only insofar as they agree with the rule of the word."

For Catholic theologians this was a rather puzzling argument. How could a learned theologian doubt that Scripture and church, for which Jesus had promised the presence of the Holy Spirit, were not in harmony? The pronouncements of the Reformers were so incomprehensible to the Catholic polemicists that they were initially stunned into silence. At the Leipzig Disputation Johann Eck first called attention to this tricky situation, and a bit later, in 1521, Jacobus Latomus (subsequently labeled by John Foxe "an enemie to the Gospell") published his *Articulorum Doctrinae Fratris Martini Lutheri . . . Ratio ex sacris literis & veteribus tractatoribus* (Explanation from Sacred Scripture and Ancient Writings), in which he used scriptural citations to make the case for traditional Catholic positions. Luther promptly retorted, first in his *Rationis Latomianae pro incendiariis Lovaniensis scholae sophistis redditae Lutheriana confutatio* (A Lutheran Refutation of the Latomonian Explanation) (1521) and then in the preface to his German translation of the New Testament, that not all Scripture was of equal spiritual value. As Luther put it, the Epistle of James, which Latomus had cited to make the case for the Catholic insistence on the importance of good works, did not merit inclusion in the New Testament. The exchange between Latomus and Luther was a forewarning that the topic of scriptural authority was more complex than Luther and the other Reformers had recognized.

The underlying presumption of the Protestant argument was that the meaning of scriptural passages was clear and self-evident. Luther made a point of this when he wrote that Scripture was "most certain and open, as well as clear as could be, since it interprets itself."[4] Or, in his Genesis lectures, "The Holy Spirit is not a fool or a drunkard to express one point, not to say one word, in vain."[5] In 1521 Luther had written against Hieronymus Emser: "I cannot stand it that they slander and blaspheme Scripture and the holy Fathers this way. They accuse Scripture of being dark . . . and they give the Fathers credit for being the light that illumines Scripture, even though all the Fathers confess their own darkness and illumine Scripture only with Scripture."[6]

2. WA TR 5:5443, 5854.

3. H. Denzinger, *Enchiridion symbolorum: definitionum et declarationum de rebus fidei et morum* (Barcinone: 1963), 783, "in libris scriptis et sive scripto traditionibus."

4. WA 7:97.

5. WA 54:39.

6. WA 7:639.

Scripture's clarity about matters pertaining to eternal salvation was the indispensable premise. If Scripture were vague on this point, some adjudicating entity (the church) would indeed be necessary to interpret the biblical text. The Reformers saw the "Word" as a sacrament in the Catholic sense—it conveyed its truth (and its spiritual benefits) objectively, was clear in its meaning. The phrase used by Luther in his famous response at the Diet of Worms, "My conscience is *captured* by the Word of God," expressed this objectivity.[7]

A host of Protestant statements echoed Luther's sentiment. The Belgic Confession of 1561 noted in article 7: "We believe that those Holy Scriptures fully contain the will of God, and that whatsoever man ought to believe, unto salvation, is sufficiently taught therein." Likewise the seventeenth-century Westminster Confession in article 8: "The Old Testament in Hebrew (which was the native language of the people of God of old), and the New Testament in Greek (which, at the time of the writing of it, was most generally known to the nations), being immediately inspired by God, and, by His singular care and providence, kept pure in all ages, are therefore authentic; so as, in all controversies of religion, the Church is finally to appeal unto them."

It followed that the text of the Bible had to be available to the faithful in the vernacular, for otherwise they could not appropriate the teachings of Scripture, nor would they be able to render valid theological judgments. No wonder, then, that wherever Reformation ideas became institutionalized, one of the foremost agenda items was to make the Bible available in the vernacular. Of course, vernacular Bibles existed before the Reformation. The novel turn was not only that the invention of movable type had made books cheaper and thus more available, but also that the Reformers insisted on the utter centrality of the Bible for Christian faith and life. In all countries in which Protestantism gained a foothold, the vernacular translation of the Bible proved to be not only a major religious but, as matters turned out, also a literary feat.

There was yet another practical ramification to the insistence on the Bible as sole norm of the faith. For the principle of *sola scriptura* to be practically meaningful, the people had to be able to read. (That reading would lead to diverse interpretations was beyond the understanding of the Reformers, because according to them the text had one clear and obvious meaning.) The need for literacy meant that Reformers everywhere argued for the establishment and maintenance of schools. Needless to say, they did not provide education for the general purpose of edification or learning or personal advancement; they provided education so that men and women could read the sacred Scriptures for themselves.

This universal Protestant affirmation of the Bible as the sole norm of authority was predicated on the notion that Scripture was divinely inspired and therefore the reservoir of salvation. About that there was no dispute—not between Catholics and Protestants nor between Protestants and Protestants, including even the antitrinitarians (Socinians) of the sixteenth century. This consensus is noteworthy, especially because less than two hundred years later it began to be roundly rejected. The thinkers of the Enlightenment treated the Bible as they did any other book from antiquity and promptly identified a myriad of problems. How could the author of a book (at issue

---

7. *Deutsche Reichstagsakten, Jüngere Reihe*, 2:581.   1643 - 46

Westminster Divines

were the biblical books ascribed to Moses) describe his death? Did not the logistics of the passing of the multitude of Israelites through the Red Sea defy common sense? Were there not fatal inconsistencies in the four Gospels' descriptions of the life of Jesus? Earlier theologians and churchmen, well aware of these issues, had offered supernatural explanations. The Bible was, after all, divine revelation.

Toward the end of the sixteenth century, Protestant theologians began to address the question of how the nature of the inspiration of Scripture was to be understood, a novel pursuit in Christian theology but deemed necessary because Protestant theology put so much emphasis on the authority of Scripture. This pursuit must also be seen in the context of the outcome of the Reformation: the coexistence of no fewer than five traditions and churches, each of which claimed to be the sole possessor of Christian truth. This meant that doctrine, not practical Christian living, came to dominate the debate, and in the end everyone came to define Christianity as doctrine: Catholics as the church defined it, Protestants as Scripture revealed it. The effort of Protestant theologians to explain the manner of the divine inspiration of the Bible was thus the effort to buttress the truth claims put forward by each tradition. Luther had understood Scripture as the document of divine revelation, but the true source of faith was not any human appropriation of its truths. It was direct divine action, embodied in the oral proclamation of the gospel.

Toward the end of the sixteenth century, however, Protestant divines began to turn Scripture into a pool of proof texts for doctrine. Scripture became the comprehensive norm, and from the late sixteenth century onward all systematic theologies began with a chapter on Scripture; for example, the first chapter of the Wittenberg theologian Leonhart Hutter's *Compendium Locorum Theologicorum: Ex Scriptis Sacris, & libro Concordiae . . . Collectum* was entitled "De Scriptura Sacra." The Calvinist-Reformed tradition moved along a parallel track, which is hardly surprising because that tradition was exposed to the same considerations as were Lutheran divines. The first chapters (canons) of the *Formula consensus ecclesiarum Helveticarum reformatarum,* declared the Bible as fully inspired.[8]

The eventual outcome of this type of Protestant reflection was the notion of the verbal inspiration of Scripture—an altogether novel understanding, for previous theologizing had never been forced to think through the issue; the divine authority of the church, manifest either in pope or council, rendered it moot. The verbal inspiration of Scripture meant that each word, indeed, each letter, including the Hebrew vowel marks, of the Bible was divinely inspired. Not surprisingly, the Belgic Confession of 1561 devoted its first seven articles to an explanation of the primacy and sufficiency of Scripture, and the same emphasis was also found in the antitrinitarian Racovian Catechism.

A second area of common Protestant consensus pertained to the doctrine of the church. Luther had at one time rather boisterously noted, "Thank God, even a child of seven knows what the church is," but that had proved to be an all-too-exuberant judgment, as was his winsomely simplistic addition, "namely, the holy believers and the sheep who hear their shepherd's voice."[9] The matter was not quite so simple, in

8. Published Zurich, 1714.
9. WA 50:250.

large measure because the word lent itself to a variety of definitions: "church" could mean the local assembly of believers as well as the community of all believers in all times and places. In his *Von dem Abendmahl Christi, Bekenntnis* (Confession concerning the Last Supper of Christ), Luther focused on the latter: "I believe that there is a holy Christian church on earth, that is, a community or throng or assembly of all Christians on earth, the single bride of Christ and his spiritual body."[10]

An essential insight of Luther's about the Christian faith came into focus here—his notion that the spiritual is always embedded in the physical. Or, as his "theology of the cross" expressed, there is an empirical and a spiritual way of perceiving things: the crucifixion of Jesus as the execution of a Jewish revolutionary outside Jerusalem, or the atoning death of the Savior of the world. Thus the church must have both an empirical and a spiritual dimension, just like baptism or the Lord's Supper. There is a church that can be empirically seen, even as there is a church that can only be apprehended in faith. "Invisible, spiritual is the church, only to be perceived by faith,"[11] or "whatever is believed is neither corporeal nor visible."[12] For the latter, Luther drew his inspiration from Augustine and medieval nominalism. To be sure, Augustine's distinction was different: the invisible church was God's predestinarian mystery. Augustine never did what Luther did, namely, connect these two churches. The affirmation "I believe that there is a holy Christian church on earth" entailed for Luther an existential affirmation. This church, though invisible, was real, gathered by God through the ages, composed of a small throng of men, women, and children whom God had called.

Luther never tired of emphasizing the communal nature of the church. The *communio sanctorum*, the communion of saints, was a "gathering of hearts," a fellowship, a bond. This view was a far cry from the hierarchical church, with its division of clergy and laity, its hierarchical organization from the pontiff in Rome down to the parish priest. And as vindication of the authenticity of this spiritual church, God has given it external signs—baptism, the Lord's Supper, indeed, the Word—that vouchsafe truth.

By making this distinction between the spiritual and the empirical church, the former in its own way every bit as real as the latter, Luther posed for himself the question of whether there was a way to gather truly spiritual Christians together. Both in his *Formula Missae et communionis* (1523) and in his *Deutsche Messe* (1526) Luther advocated that "those who seriously want to be Christians, confessing the gospel with hand and mouth," should gather separately from the larger group of Christians. This was but another instance in the endless challenge to gather the "true" or the "committed" Christians—monasticism did that, as did the sixteenth-century Anabaptists or the eighteenth-century Methodists. The notion fit poorly with what was so incisive about Luther's main point: the connection between the empirical and the spiritual.

Eventually, the church which embraced Luther's theology came to be called "Lutheran." Luther himself had grave misgivings about this nomenclature, and initially other appellations, such as "Martinians," had seemingly carried the day, even though an early and obvious label—"evangelical"—had fallen into discredit through

10. WA 28:507.
11. WA 7:10.
12. WA 6:300.

the Anabaptists' use. Luther's followers were "those related to the Augsburg Confession," a rather bland designation that eventually did give way to the combination of "evangelical" and "Lutheran" that made history.

The other Reformers emphasized different aspects of the church, but there was consensus among them about what Luther had enunciated. Both the Anabaptists and Calvin, however, were committed to gathering in the empirical, visible church those who gave evidence of their serious Christian profession; membership in the "visible" church was integral to obtaining eternal salvation. To be sure, for Calvin such salvation came through God's mysterious judgment in predestination. But Calvin conveyed that faithful adherence to this visible church and a proper walk of life were signs of one's eternal election. And although the Anabaptists stayed away from anything that smacked of predestination, they too put great stock in the visible gathering of believers as the true church.

AFFIRMATIONS AND DISAGREEMENTS

But there were also stark theological disagreements among the various Protestants, for the Reformation movement promptly became a house divided. Not only did Protestant divines propound a multiplicity of theological interpretations, but differing theologies also had organizational consequences. Distinct Protestant churches came into existence, an unintended yet consistent development, for that seemed the only way to assure the integrity of theological positions held. The role of the secular authorities, city councils, and territorial rulers became more and more powerful. Nonetheless, theological considerations were not the sole forces operative in the emergence of the several Protestant traditions. As is characteristic of the Reformation in general, the story was one of multiple forces and factors; politics no less than personalities had a way of playing important roles. Thus, when all was said and done, several stark theological differences marked the sixteenth-century Protestant scene.

These theological disagreements among the Reformers triggered two kinds of responses: that of Martin Bucer, for example, who for reasons both theological and political endlessly pursued a strategy of irenic conciliation between Wittenberg and Zurich; and that of Martin Luther, who did not seem to be able to yield an inch—at the Marburg Colloquy Luther refused a fraternal embrace with Bucer and told him categorically, "You have a different spirit."[13]

The Lord's Supper

Perhaps not surprisingly, the most adamant internal Protestant disagreement was over the two sacraments that Protestants had retained from the seven sacraments of the Catholic Church—the Lord's Supper and baptism. The disagreement over both sacraments surfaced in the early 1520s and agitated Protestantism until the end of the century and beyond. Only various ecumenical agreements of the twentieth century have

13. W. Köhler, *Das Marburger Religionsgespräch* (Leipzig: 1929), 129.

sought (more or less successfully, one fears) to render these sixteenth-century dis-agreements moot.

Early on in the indulgences controversy, in his 1520 tract *Babylonian Captivity of the Church,* Luther had made a frontal assault on the Catholic Church's sacramental system, questioning its nature and function, as well as on a number of the traditional sacraments. Luther argued that in a sacrament a divine promise (the forgiveness of sins) was attached to a visible sign. Accordingly, he rejected five of the traditional sacraments because either the empirical sign (for example, in marriage) or the divine promise of forgiveness (as in ordination) was missing. Luther further departed from the medieval consensus with his argument that a sacrament, in order to be effective as a vehicle of divine grace, required faith on the part of the believer. This was contrary to the traditional Catholic affirmation, which held that the efficacy of the sacraments occurred *ex opere operato,* from the proper performance of the rite. Luther's declaration raised questions with regard to the Lord's Supper and, even more, baptism. As for the Lord's Supper, Luther's position seemed to suppose a subjectivity that denied the reality of Jesus's presence in bread and wine, while the baptism of infants became a dubious matter because one could not accept the notion that they possessed the requisite faith.

The traditional teaching of the Western church regarding communion, formalized by the Fourth Lateran Council in 1215 and subsequently expounded by Thomas Aquinas, is commonly referred to as "transubstantiation." It rested on the Aristotelian distinction between the "substance" of things, their essential being, and their "accidents," their outer appearance. This distinction made it possible to speak of bread and wine in the mass in a twofold way: their "accidents," that is, their composition of flour and water, and of alcohol; and their "substance," that is, their being bread and wine. The doctrine of transubstantiation held that the consecration of bread and wine by the priest changed ("transferred") their substance from bread and wine to the body and blood of Christ while leaving their accidents, that is, their appearance, unchanged. This was an empirical happening, independent of the faith (or absence thereof) of those who partook of the elements. Thus the Lateran Council decreed that "His body and His blood are truly contained under the species of bread and wine, upon the substantive change through divine power of bread into the body and wine into the blood."[14] A corollary affirmation was the notion that the (consecrated) host as the true body of Jesus may be said to include his blood as well, for which reason the laity were offered only the bread, with the insistence that receiving only the bread still made for a complete reception of the sacrament. This traditional view was based on the notion of the actualization of the death of Jesus on the cross through the action of the officiating priest and the sacrificial offering of Jesus to God the Father through the priest. The rejection of both notions by the Reformers mandated a reflection on the meaning of the rite.

Luther and the chorus of the other Protestant Reformers charged that the doctrine of transubstantiation employed Aristotelian philosophical categories in order to explain a biblical happening—and they would have none of it. But beyond this com-

---

14. Denzinger, *Enchiridion symbolarum,* 430.

mon repudiation of Catholic doctrine stood a diversity of Protestant views. All Reformers agreed that there was a dominical command to perform the act, and Luther saw the benefits in making concrete and tangible the divine promise of forgiveness for those who believed.

At the core of Luther's view stood a literal interpretation of Jesus's words of institution, "this is my body" and "this is the new covenant of my blood." Quite in line with tradition, he argued that these words entailed the real presence of Christ in bread and wine, with forgiveness of sins as the meaning of the sacrament. Given the importance of the doctrine of transubstantiation and its concomitant, the Mass, it is not surprising that the discussion in the sixteenth century of the meaning of the Lord's Supper focused on the interpretation of the words of institution with a neglect of other aspects of the sacrament.

A letter in the early 1520s of the Dutch humanist physician Cornelis Hoen turned the Reformers' common repudiation of the Catholic understanding of the mass into a painful and fierce intrareform controversy. Hoen suggested that Jesus's words of institution should be understood symbolically. In other words, Jesus had conveyed to his disciples that bread and wine at the Last Supper were symbolic of the body and blood that were about to be given and shed for them. The (Latin) words "hoc *est* corpus meum" (this *is* my body) should be understood as "hoc *significat* corpus meum" (this *signifies* my body), making the believers' remembrance of Jesus's sacrificial death on the cross the key of the celebration. Although Luther promptly rejected this interpretation, Zwingli and other reformers were impressed.[15]

Andreas Carlstadt, Luther's colleague at Wittenberg, shared Zwingli's misgivings about the traditional literal interpretation of the words of institution. Carlstadt suggested that Jesus had pointed at himself when speaking the words—an intriguing interpretation that failed to win supporters because it raised the question of where Jesus had pointed while saying "this is my blood." An unsympathetic critic of Carlstadt surmised Jesus might have had a nosebleed. Because the renderings of Paul's account of Jesus' last supper has Jesus say, "This is the new covenant of my blood," Carlstadt might have deserved a bit more respectful hearing, but at this point in 1524 Luther had concluded that he was an unreliable theological troublemaker.

It was Zwingli who emerged as the cogent spokesperson for a "symbolic" interpretation of the words of institution, and in so doing he became Luther's most vocal and persuasive critic—and adversary. Zwingli embraced the notion of a spiritual presence of Jesus in the bread and wine. The faithful, in other words, were spiritually partaking of Jesus's body and blood in the sacrament. Thus, Zwingli wrote, "his body is eaten, when we believe that he died for us."[16] He found the scriptural confirmation for a spiritual eating in the passage of the Gospel of John 6:26ff., where much is made of the distinction between the spirit and the flesh; but Luther categorically denied that this passage had any relevance to what happened in the sacrament. Wrote Zwingli in his *Fidei Ratio* (Principle of Faith), submitted to Emperor Charles V at Augsburg in

---

15. Hoen's treatise is well discussed by B. J. Spruyt, *Cornelius Henrici Hoen (Honius) and His Epistle on the Eucharist: Medieval Heresy, Erasmian Humanism, and Reform in the Early Sixteenth Century Low Countries* (Leiden: 2006), esp. 168ff.

16. *Zwinglis Werke*, 3:347.

1530, "to eat the body of Christ spiritually means trusting with heart and soul in the mercy and goodness of God through Jesus Christ, that is, to have the assurance of faith that God will grant us the forgiveness of sins." In that same "confession," Zwingli noted that the "true body of Christ is present through "the contemplation of faith" (*fidei contemplatione*).[17] For him, the supper was a meal of thanksgiving and gratitude, of mutual exhortation and covenant of those partaking of bread and wine.

Both Luther and Zwingli were aware that there were christological ramifications to their positions. According to the Apostles' Creed, Christ sat at the right hand of God the Father and therefore could not be physically present in the innumerable sacramental acts performed in Christendom. Luther found the explanation for the sacramental happening in the concept of the pervading omnipresence (ubiquity) of God. The hallmark of God was ubiquity, a notion for which Luther found the scriptural basis in the book of Psalms—God was in every tree, leaf, blade of grass, indeed, the uttermost ends of the earth, but God had so ordered things that only in the sacrament of the altar was he to be apprehended and appropriated. This concept of the all-pervasive presence of God made it easy to appropriate the true and real body of Jesus in bread and wine. "Even though he is in all creatures and I may find him in a stone, in fire, water, or even a rope, he does not want me to seek him there without the Word and jump into the fire or water or hang myself on a rope. He is everywhere, but he does not want me to seek him everywhere."[18]

Luther, whose insistence on the centrality of faith in the sacrament may be said to have triggered the controversy, clung to the traditional notion of the real presence of body and blood of Jesus in bread and wine. He rejected the Catholic notion of transubstantiation as a philosophical construct, but did not find it easy to explain how exactly the real presence of Christ in the sacrament was to be understood. He was not at all bothered, as was Zwingli, by the intrusion of material considerations into spiritual matters. At the Marburg Colloquy Luther pointedly asserted that the issue was faithfulness to Scripture. Indeed, if God were to command him to eat manure, he said, he would do it, confident that it would be to his eternal salvation. "Let not the servant be above his master," he added, while Martin Bucer, representing the Zwinglian view, retorted "but where is it written that we must walk with closed eyes through Scripture?"[19]

For Luther, who had not at all wanted to participate in the colloquy and who appeared, strangely enough, in the attire of a Saxon councilor, the issue was a touchstone for the assertion that Scripture was clear and needed no interpreter. If the simple phrase "this is my body" did not have a self-evident meaning, the principle of *sola scriptura* was in jeopardy.

Calvin appropriated the basic contours of Zwingli's thought by rejecting the notion of the real presence of body and blood of Jesus in bread and wine. Like Zwingli, Calvin insisted that the supper was more than a memorial. It was "spiritual eating." Indeed,

---

17. This is the theme in Zwingli's discussion of the Supper in his *De vera et falsa religione commentarius* (Comments on True and False Religion): *Zwingli's Werke* 3:628ff.

18. WA 19:492.

19. As quoted in Hans J. Hillerbrand, *The Reformation* (New York: 1965), 160.

Calvin observed that "it happens through the incredible power of the Holy Spirit that we commune with the body and blood of Christ; the secret power of the Holy Spirit is the bond of our connection with Christ."[20]

The other Reformers of the sixteenth century took their positions closer either to Luther or to Calvin—Melanchthon, for example, who in the Variata edition of the Augsburg Confession of 1540 noted that the body and blood are not distributed but "exhibited" in the form of bread and wine. Indeed, Melanchthon was much closer to the Zwinglian position than he let on at the 1529 Colloquy at Marburg, when he chose to remain silent, refusing to speak even when Luther challenged him to do so.

The English Reformation's views on the meaning of the Lord's Supper were a reflection of Thomas Cranmer's theological development as it came to be embodied in the two editions of the *Book of Common Prayer* of 1549 and 1552. Although the first edition of the prayer book clearly affirmed Luther's notion of a real presence of Christ in the elements of bread and wine, the second edition, three short years later, embraced the Zwinglian or Calvinist notion of a spiritual presence.[21] When, in 1559, the Elizabethan settlement of religion had to go on record as to which sort of Protestantism was to be reestablished in England, the sage members of Parliament, once they had concluded that a full restoration of Protestantism as it had existed toward the end of Edward's reign was not possible because of Queen Elizabeth's strategic reluctance, decided to juxtapose the 1549 and 1552 editions of the prayer book, leaving open the question of the precise teaching of the English church.

The Anabaptists in their various groupings, finally, had little problem with seeing the Lord's Supper as a meal of memory and community as well as an expression of mutual love. Thus the letter of the Zurich group to Thomas Müntzer noted that "the bread is nothing but bread. In faith it is the body of Christ and the incorporation with Christ and the brethren. Although it is simply bread, yet if faith and brotherly love precede it, it is to be received with joy." And the Schleitheim Confession stated, "All those who wish to break one bread in remembrance of the broken body of Christ, and all who wish to drink of one drink as a remembrance of the shed blood of Christ." Both Peter Riedemann's *Account of Our Religion* and Menno Simons's influential writings echo the notion that the supper was a simple memorial and fellowship meal— even a kind of eschatological meal—partaken of by committed disciples.

Baptism

If the intra-Protestant controversy over the Lord's Supper was triggered in large measure by Luther's 1520 insistence that the sacraments receive their salvatory meaning through the faith of the recipient, the controversy over baptism was triggered by him as well, and for much the same reason. Luther's view remained the majority opinion among the Protestant Reformers. Thus on the one hand stood an impressive phalanx of Reformers (as well as some from the old church) who forcefully insisted that the practice of baptizing infants was biblical. On the other hand was a small cadre of dissenters,

20. Calvin discusses the nature of Christ's presence in the *Institutes* 4.17.32–34.
21. P. N. Brooks, *Thomas Cranmer's Doctrine of the Eucharist* (Basingstoke: 1992).

promptly named "Anabaptists" (or "rebaptizers" by their opponents), who found no biblical support for the traditional practice.

The Anabaptist rejection of infant baptism not only touched on the core initiation rite of the Christian community; it also related to a fundamental premise of medieval society that affirmed the identity of the secular and the religious realm. Everyone, except the Jews who had been allowed to live in Christian Europe, was both a member of the body politic and a baptized member of the church, part of both the temporal and the spiritual realms—a notion that allowed the government to stake out claims of sovereignty over certain aspects of church life, such as the appointment of bishops. Moreover, because the Latin term *sacramentum* (sacrament) also means "oath," the sacrament of baptism was easily understood in a civic sense as an oath of fealty to authority, both civic and heavenly. A refusal to have a newborn infant baptized was thus also a challenge to the existing political order. In the sixteenth century, only the Anabaptists and a few other individual dissenters were able to envision a society in which church and state were not synonymous.

The first reservations concerning the baptism of infants were expressed in late 1521 to Melanchthon by three visitors to Wittenberg from Zwickau, and subsequently by Müntzer and Carlstadt. Undoubtedly, Luther's declaration about the necessity of faith for the beneficial reception of the sacraments triggered questions about the biblical validity of a centuries-old practice in which the infant to be baptized could hardly be presumed to have the necessary faith. Questions about the practice were thus in the air in the early 1520s, and there is sporadic evidence of parents failing to present their newborn infants for baptism. It was in January 1525 that some of Zwingli's supporters in Zurich performed the first believer's baptism in the sixteenth century. Later they charged—evoking a somewhat weak response from Zwingli—that they had been pushed in this direction by none other than Zwingli himself, who seemingly had conceded that there was no clear evidence for or against the baptism of infants in apostolic Christianity.

The argument of Zwingli's followers was simple. As Balthasar Hubmaier declared in his *Von der christlichen tauf der Gläubigen* (On the Christian Baptism of Believers), instruction through the Word of God stands at the beginning of the Christian life, which leads to the recognition of sin, purifying the human heart in faith and trust. The believer then testifies to this acknowledgment of sin and faith through baptism, which seals the confession. The baptism of infants was not biblical; there was no parallel, as Zwingli and especially Calvin argued, to Old Testament circumcision. Baptism in anticipation of a future faith, wrote Hubmeier, was tantamount "to mak]ing a judgment at Easter about that year's wine, which is to be made in the fall, without anybody knowing if hail, frost, or other thunderstorms might destroy the grapes."[22] Only the conscious decision to be a disciple of Jesus, born of remorse over one's sinfulness, should lead to the decision to receive baptism. Since infants were incapable of such a decision and therefore lacked the requisite faith, their baptism was unbiblical.

---

22. Hubmaier's rhetorical gifts are also evident in his remark that Jesus did not tell his disciples "go into all the world and baptize young infants, teaching them some years later." See here R. Armor, *Anabaptist Baptism: A Representative Study* (Scottdale, PA: 1966), 28f.

Only adults were able to make the decision to be baptized. The Schleitheim Confession of 1527 stated the matter clearly and simply: "Baptism shall be administered to those who have learned repentance and amendment of life, and who believe truly that their sins are taken away by Christ, and to all those who walk in the resurrection of Jesus Christ, and wish to be buried with Him in death, so that they may be resurrected with Him, and to all those who with this significance request baptism of us and demand it for themselves." The theological establishment, both Catholic and mainline Protestant, promptly labeled the advocates of adult baptism "rebaptizers" or "Anabaptists," a label that (like all labels created by antagonists) distorted the concern of these men and women. They claimed, with a felicitous mixture of facetiousness and truth—that they were incapable of remembering if they had, in fact, been baptized as infants. This puzzled the authorities and eventually led to the universal introduction of parish registers (medieval churches had been fairly haphazard in this regard) in which births, baptisms, marriages, and deaths were duly recorded.

The Christian Life: Church Discipline

When Calvin returned to Geneva in 1542, he created something startlingly new in the history of practical Christian living. His famous *Ecclesiastical Ordinances*, the price the Genevan city council had to pay for his return from Strassburg, not only conveyed Calvin's understanding of the biblical model of church organization. It also made church discipline a centerpiece of church life. The ordinances were embodied in the institution of the consistory, a body composed of pastors and elders, clergy and laity, and charged with the supervision of the life and faith of the people of Geneva.

Much has been written about church discipline in Geneva and, earlier in Zurich, the *Ehegericht,* the marriage court, and about the absence of parallel of this kind of discipline in early Lutheranism. The rigid exercise of church discipline in Geneva (and wherever Calvinism gained a foothold) became the defining characteristic of Calvinism. Importantly, the introduction of church discipline in Geneva must be seen as part of a larger European phenomenon. Ever since the late fifteenth century governmental authorities had sought to introduce social discipline—a comprehensive effort to make life orderly and more disciplined—in their communities. The impetus for social discipline came from those who exercised political power and wished to exercise it in all spheres of communal life and all aspects of society. In a way the widespread disposition of political authorities to introduce the Reformation in their jurisdictions may be seen as an increasing desire to exercise power.

In short, life in the early decades of the sixteenth century was far more structured—and disciplined—than it had been a hundred years earlier. One can discern this trend in many aspects of societal life, from the sharper regulation of prostitution to the stricter ordering of the guilds and the poor. What began to be called the "French disease," syphilis, did its share in creating a demand for greater structure, as did the increasing flight of the poor into the cities, confronting the civic authorities with new problems and issues that called for regulations, control, and discipline. However, this exercise of social discipline must not be viewed as an externally imposed regime that was accepted by the rank and file of the people with stoic disengagement. Nothing could be further from the facts: the common people accepted disciplinary control freely and willingly, which is precisely why it proved so successful.

This, then, is the context within which we must see Calvin's consistory. It comprised six clergy and twelve "elders," the latter chosen by the Genevan magistracy. Calvin and the other pastors were merely consulted by the small council when it made its determination, surely an indication of the heavy hand of government (to which the twelve elders reported) in this ecclesiastical arrangement. The consistory met weekly on Thursdays. Generally, alleged offenders were hauled before it by the police. In one way the consistory was a truly democratic institution, for it judged rich and the poor, old and young, male and female, supporters and enemies of Calvin. Its intent was to assure a godly community, and the magistracy's interest in social control and Calvin's commitment to church discipline went hand in hand. The strategy was that by dealing with individuals—their absences from divine worship, their unruly or offensive behavior, and so on—the larger community could eradicate broader societal evils, such as dancing, theater, and games of chance. That the Genevan city council had curtailed dancing well before Calvin's arrival underlines the magistracy's interest in a well-disciplined community. The heavy involvement of the magistracy in determining consistory membership might be interpreted as a determination not to let the clergy have free rein—to be a loose cannon.

Calvinism's emphasis on godly living did not mean that sixteenth-century Lutheranism, on the contrary, cared nothing about Christian living. In fact, Lutheran catechisms frequently showed kinship with Catholic publications.

Lutheran Turmoil

The coterie of supporters and sympathizers who helped turn Luther's religious and theological pronouncements into a reform movement also helped create a problem that was to haunt Lutherans for decades, until the year 1580 finally brought a resolution. At issue was stark uncertainty and disagreement about Luther's teaching on certain theological topics.

The reason for such disagreement, alas, was Luther himself. Although profound and insightful, Luther was one of those theologians in Christian history (Augustine comes to mind as another illustration) whose genius prompted them to address topics and issues always in polemical contexts. The inevitable consequence was overstatement, rigidity, and caricature of his opponent. Thus Luther delineated his anthropology in his controversy with Erasmus, his views on justification in his confrontation with Gabriel Biel, and his understanding of Communion in his controversy with Carlstadt and Zwingli.

Luther's followers latched on to different aspects of the reformer's pronouncements and came to different conclusions about what was authentically Lutheran (and thereby, of course, authentically biblical). These disagreements surfaced periodically during Luther's own lifetime. Luther, for his part, either ignored them as insignificant (as indeed they were in the larger scheme of things) or was goaded to take sides, which he generally did with uncommon gracefulness (for him).

Related was undoubtedly a widespread concern for order and clarity. The exciting storm and stress of the first decades of the controversy were gone. A seemingly irreparable schism had occurred between those who stayed loyal to the Roman Church and those who transferred their allegiance to the new interpretation of the Christian gospel. What initially had been unthinkable had in fact occurred: a new church had come into existence, and with it the host of practical concerns and issues that attend any organization.

What was the faith of the new church? On one level, the answer was fairly simple: for Lutherans, at any rate, it was the confession of faith transmitted to the emperor at Augsburg in 1530. There was also a second document that Luther had drafted for the League of Schmalkald, the so-called Schmalkald Articles. But beyond these formal statements was the host of theologians, devout and committed followers of Luther, and they eagerly provided their own addenda and asterisks to these statements and to other theological topics. The situation became tenser after Luther's death, and no fewer than seven controversies beset German Lutheranism between 1548 and 1580. The antinomian controversy, triggered by Johann Agricola, pertained to whether the law had a place in Christian preaching. Related was the Majoristic controversy, named after Georg Major, a pupil of Melanchthon, who argued that good works were necessary for salvation. Major insisted that salvation itself was by faith alone but good works had to follow. They did not assure salvation but were the inevitable outcome of true faith. Major's argument drove the so-called Gnesio-Lutherans ("authentic" Lutherans) onto the barricades, for they saw in Major but an awkward return to the Catholic notion of salvation by faith and works.

If these skirmishes were not enough to keep German Lutherans inner oriented, a third controversy, dubbed the Adiaphorist controversy, surfaced after Emperor Charles V had promulgated the two interims, of Augsburg and of Leipzig, in the wake of his victory over the League of Schmalkald in 1547. The bone of contention was none other than Melanchthon, who appeared willing to accept the provisions of the Augsburg Interim because they pertained, so he argued, only to "indifferent issues" (*adiaphora*) that had no bearing on such fundamental issues as justification or the nature of the church. Opposing him were those for whom these "indifferent issues" were simply the tip of the iceberg, manifestations of underlying fundamental differences. Ever since the late 1530s, when Melanchthon had been party to an unofficial revision of the Augsburg Confession (the so-called *Confessio Augustana Variata*), he had labored under theological suspicion. Now the sentiment became widespread that Melanchthon had weakly surrendered to the emperor's wiles, and the Gnesio-Lutherans would have none of it.

Matters became even more complicated when Moritz, the newly created Saxon elector, conveyed to the emperor the impossibility of carrying out the Augsburg Interim in his newly acquired territories, and the staunchly Lutheran city of Magdeburg not only defiantly refused to submit to the emperor's forces, but in so doing turned into a formidable propaganda center for the Reformation, with a flood of publications not unlike those of a generation earlier in the early 1520s. "Nihil est adiaphoron in statu confessionis" (nothing is indifferent when the faith is at stake) was the battle cry, and the bitter controversy subsided only when the two interims had become moot.

In one respect, one must not make too much of these Lutheran theological disagreements; from earliest Christianity to the twenty-first century the history of Christian thought has been full of controversies, disagreements, and debates. The problem was that important energies that might have been utilized to make the case to the world at large for the Lutheran understanding of the faith were consumed by intra-Lutheran feuds. These lingered until the early 1570s, when the rulers of Lutheran territories stepped in to force the theologians to reach consensus on the disputed issues. The Formula of Concord of 1577 and the *Book of Concord*, which contained the Formula, together with the ancient creeds, Luther's Small Catechism, the Augsburg Confession, and Luther's Schmalkald Articles, were the outcome.

Chapter 13

CONCLUDING REFLECTIONS

Scholars of the Reformation have both told the story of the course of events and also have addressed what we have come to call "master narratives," the grand picture, the meaning, the underlying forces. Discerning the meaning of it all seems more difficult than telling the story itself.

Fundamental questions continue to hover over sixteenth-century events and have engaged historians: Was the Reformation, as a formal acceptance of the new theology, imposed from the top or did it come about through pressure from below? Should we distinguish between an "urban," a "princes'," and a "communal" Reformation? Was there contuinity between theological currents in the fifteenth century and the theologizing of the Reformers? Was the movement of reform in the 1520s cohesively Lutheran?

Most pointedly, were the primary forces operative in the Reformation movement religious in nature or secular? Two responses are possible, and the diverse perspectives have had (and continue to have) ardent supporters. In recent times, all the same, the number of those who wish to minimize the place of religion in the sixteenth century altogether and of those who find nothing strikingly new in Reformation thought has noticeably grown, certainly in North America.[1]

Of course, the Reformation may be understood in altogether nonreligious terms— as a manifestation, sometimes blatant, sometimes subtle, of power politics, economic greed, or social change at the beginning of the sixteenth century. The evidence supporting this contention is obvious. The consolidation of political power and authority was ubiquitous throughout Europe in the early sixteenth century, and the German tradition of divisive particularism explains in great measure why territories and cities were able to introduce the Reformation despite the emperor's high-handed determination to crush the Lutheran heresy. With this religious decision came political aggrandizement that conveniently led to economic gain. Whatever is to be said about the religious conviction of such rulers as Gustavus Vasa, Henry VIII, or Philip of Hesse—probably not much, for we cannot be privy to the feelings and convictions of sixteenth-century individuals—all of them, without exception, became wealthier and more powerful as the result of the ecclesiastical changes they introduced in their respective domains, though these rulers may not have anticipated this undoubtedly

---

1. For example, see the anthology *Early Modern Europe, Issues and Interpretations* (ed. James B. Collins and Karen L. Taylor; Malden, MA: 2006), in which religion (not to mention the Reformation) does not appear at all as either an "issue" or an "interpretation."

welcome turn when they made their ecclesiastical decisions. Lest the role of the political rulers in the course of events be seen as all too obvious, however, we should note that they (not to mention the city councils of the towns that turned Protestant) took considerable risks in siding with a new faith. Only afterward did it become evident that rulers' moves had not had dire, even catastrophic consequences for them. A few, such as Philip of Hesse or Elector John of Saxony, did pay for their Protestant alignment with the loss of their dignity and power. Nonetheless, cynics will find this harmony between spiritual truth and pecuniary gain a telling counterargument against the postulate of the primacy of religion; it may well have been that for the Protestant rulers, as for capitalist entrepreneurs, success was the mother of all things.

Economic and social forces played a similarly important role in the course of events. In Germany conflicts between peasants and their lords, between artisans and patricians in the towns, and between territories and towns were a crucial part of the early-sixteenth-century scene, as was the emergence of new modes of production in silver and copper mining and textile manufacturing, not to mention a creeping inflation that was deeply unsettling for many. Marxist historians, in particular, have been fond of emphasizing these aspects of the early sixteenth century to make the case for a crisis in German (or European) society, especially since the new holders of economic power sought political power as well.[2]

By the same token, the main perspective on the Reformation has been that it was an authentically religious phenomenon. Protestants have so argued through the centuries, at times invoking metaphysical reflections, always pitting the "good guys" on the one side against the "bad guys" on the other in a kind of "Western novel" mentality where the lines between the good and the bad were always sharply drawn.

To label the Reformation a religious event leaves unanswered, however, how this religious characteristic is to be understood. It has been suggested that the Reformation was a phase of the quest for reform that accompanied the Catholic Church from the twelfth century onward. According to this view, the Reformers echoed the cry for a reform of the church "in head and members" propounded from the councils of Constance and Basel to Nicholas of Cusa and Erasmus of Rotterdam, an illustrious line of progenitors sometimes referred to as "pre-Reformers." Luther becomes a sort of sixteenth-century Hus or Wycliffe, his distinction being the brilliance of his theological insight or the ripeness of the time.

A variant of this explanation sees the Reformation as a reaction—a "counterreformation"—to the theological climate of the fifteenth century, particularly the nominalism of such theologians as Gabriel Biel. This approach sees late medieval nominalism as the consistent development of earlier theological trends or as an odd theological confusion, foreign to the proper spirit of medieval theology.[3] In either

---

2. A vigorous application of this Marxist understanding is A. Laube et al., eds., *Illustrierte Geschichte der deutschen frühbürgerlichen Revolution* (Berlin: 1974).

3. This was one of the many thought-provoking suggestions from the pen of the late Heiko A. Oberman. It presupposes also the notion of an extended "epoch" of reform, extending from the fourteenth into the seventeenth century. See Heiko A. Oberman, *The Two Reformations: The Journey from the Last Days to the New World* (New Haven: 2003).

view, the Reformation becomes a "counter"-phenomenon, an understandable though, in light of its "heretical" deviation, ironic phenomenon.

The perspective presented in these pages has sought to eschew a unitary explanation of events, arguing that the Reformation had different characteristics at different times. When the controversy commenced in 1517 over Luther's Ninety-five Theses, its public dimension concerned a revival of spirituality. At that stage, well before the "Luther affair" coalesced into a movement, theology did not overpower the public discourse—notwithstanding the eagerness of a few academics for a good theological bout, particularly with an upstart from that new university in Wittenberg. There were surprisingly few laments about prevailing ecclesiastical abuse. The plea of Luther and those who stepped to his side was for deepened spirituality, for greater inward commitment rather than mere external observance, for reliance on God rather than on human-made rules, a call that had been voiced by Erasmus with more wit but perhaps with less personal engagement. Luther and the other Reformers did not hesitate to step on the toes of the ecclesiastical establishment or reminding it, sometimes angrily and sometimes sarcastically, that it had moved in the wrong direction. Certainly Luther's early concern was within the family, so to speak, and the Reformers' challenge of the church and its teachings was rather like that of a little girl announcing in angry parental defiance that she will leave home forever—without ever doing so.

Precisely for this reason was it possible for loyal Catholics to concur with the message and walk a precarious balancing act: to support the message of the centrality of the Word, on the one hand, with loyalty to the Catholic Church, on the other. Initially, the Reformers did not see their pronouncements as an unbridgeable confrontation, indeed a break, with the church. Over time they were forced increasingly to recognize that their theological views were condemned by the church as incompatible with church teaching. Yet they remained stubbornly confident that they were on the side of the angels and eventually would win the hostile church over to their side. Although their denunciations left little doubt about their conviction that in the Catholic Church the true gospel was perverted rather than obscured, and therefore not properly proclaimed, some of the Reformers remained indefatigable optimists, believing that the Roman Church would eventually see things their way.

Here, then, is the key to understanding the impact Luther and the other early Reformers had on their contemporaries. Surely most of those who thronged to them and supported their cause did not see themselves in resolute opposition to the Roman Church, even if they entertained a variety of misgivings and grievances; they simply longed for a deeper understanding of the Christian faith. The resolute mood of separation came much later. The Reformation began as a call for deepened spirituality; the filial revolt came later. Dissent and loyalty, defiance and obedience, combine to explain the popularity of Luther's cause, even as they explain the partial disintegration of his movement, which occurred the moment the church demanded submission. Some prized loyalty to the church, while others risked the consequences of disobedience rather than give up what they had come to call the gospel.

The Reformers assumed that their theological affirmations could somehow be subsumed under the broad mantle of a church truly catholic—even to the point of the church coming to see the errors of its ways. After all, the one increasingly pivotal issue in the theological controversy (other than such corollary topics as clerical celibacy, the Communion cup, or episcopal residency), justification, remained dogmatically undefined by the Catholic Church until the Council of Trent issued a decree on the topic. Some individuals of keen theological insight thought it possible, even after two decades of controversy, to engage in conciliatory negotiations in order to overcome the breach. That the scene was crowded with well-meaning self-styled diagnosticians convinced that they knew exactly where the fatal breach was in the first place hardly helped matters. The tirades hurled between Ingolstadt and Wittenberg by agitated if self-confident academics could be seen as other instances of theologians quarreling about issues of small import to the spiritual lives of the common people.

In the end, both the Catholic Church and the Reformers understood that the controversy had brought to the fore theological disagreements that could be ignored only if either ignorance or bias were allowed to take the place of sharp analysis. While Protestants simply wished to be left in peace with their view of the gospel, the Catholic Church called upon them to return to the Catholic fold—which they refused to do. In the moment of truth, the Reformers rejected the notion that the church was infallibly right. The depth of their own personal religious experience—something Luther, Zwingli, and Calvin had in common—goes a long way toward explaining such obstinacy. The course of events persuaded them that their concerns had been rejected out of hand by the church and never given a hearing. Luther, for one, outdid himself initially with subservient expressions of loyalty to the Roman Church during the first years of the controversy (witness his letter to Pope Leo X that introduces his tract on Christian freedom) before he came to realize, much to his dismay, the depth of the gap between the church and his understanding of the gospel.

An intriguing constellation of factors catapulted the Luther affair far beyond its expected dimension. What might well have been but another "squabble among monks" became an affaire d'état embedded in the financial wizardry of the curia and the tensions between imperial and territorial power in Germany—with significant consequences. An otherwise fairly innocuous matter was catapulted to overwhelming importance, especially because at the very outset of the conflagration Albert of Brandenburg inserted an official component into what could easily have remained an academic controversy. Albert insisted in early December 1517 that the curia formally ascertain Luther's orthodoxy. Had religious or theological issues been the sole ingredient in the Luther affair, a different and less dramatic course of events would surely have ensued.

It is beside the point, in this context, to cull from the multitude of medieval theologians those whose views were akin to Luther's and the other Reformers, label them "pre-Reformers," and conclude that there was nothing new in the sixteenth century—at present a rather popular sentiment among scholars. Similarities undoubtedly existed, including disparagement of tradition and hints of the sole authority of Scripture. Jacques Lefèvre d'Étaples's views on justification were certainly closer to those of Luther than to those subsequently canonized by the Council of Trent. Yet even if there were far more than these isolated instances of "Protestant" theology before the Reformation, they would not challenge the radical newness of the Reformation. The point is that Luther succeeded in bringing his theological notions into the public consciousness.

Whatever the insights of the pre-Reformers, they never entered ordinary people's lives, never enthralled the intellectual and political elites, never succeeded in framing a movement. The Reformation brought a new message—because contemporaries understood and accepted it as new and made it a battle cry.

The conclusion is as simple as it is far-reaching. No single factor was responsible for the Reformation, neither theological profundity nor the personalities of the controversialists, neither the state of the church nor that of society. Any or all may well have been of incisive importance (thus the frequent references to Luther in this book), but the controversy turned into a movement and the movement into a schism because these and other forces meshed in a striking way; a slight difference along the way would have precipitated a different course of events. No single factor, party, or person deserves eminent credit or blatant blame.

And what about the common people in the story? The current interest in social history has brought about a new interest in the common people as players in the events. No narrative of the sixteenth century can bypass a consideration of the role of the men and women in the pews. To be sure, as regards the larger course of events, whether in the empire, France, or England, the crucial decisions concerning religious change and fidelity to Rome were made by the powerful elites. The statutes passed by Parliament in England the Uppsala Assembly, or the Peace of Augsburg promulgated in Germany by the imperial diet, were decisions made by secular authorities. Indeed, a provocative study of the English Reformation made the point that in England a resolute king with the help of Parliament (hardly an ecclesiastical body) imposed a break with the Roman Church on a people deeply loyal to that church.[4] Everywhere in Europe the formal decision for or against the reform movement was made by political authorities.

This does not mean that the men and women of the "common sort," as they were called at the time, were altogether absent from the course of events, and recent scholarship has sought to determine exactly what role they played. One thing seems to be clear: the common people provided the context for whatever change did or did not occur. Also, they arguably supplied the martyrs for the cause of religion. There were a few martyrs of societal eminence, such as Thomas More and John Fisher in England; but most of those who died for their faith were simple men and women, such as Elizabeth Barton, the nun of Kent, as the rosters in the sixteenth-century martyrologies clearly show.

Recent scholarship has offered a lengthy list of interpretations of popular religion both on the eve of the Reformation and afterward. Some have argued that at the turn of the century people were anything but Christianized: they combined an embarrassingly low level of theological literacy with a crude fondness for magic and superstition.[5] The course of the sixteenth century brought about a change as the common people acquired a higher level of theological conversancy and supernatural beliefs began slowly to wane.[6] But this assertion has not been uncontested, and despite several insightful

4. Eamon Duffy, *The Stripping of the Altars* (New Haven: 1992), has much to say here.
5. Jean Delumeau, *Catholicism between Luther and Voltaire* (London: 1977) (originally: *Catholicisme entre Luther et Voltaire* [Paris: 1971]).
6. The most vigorous effort to associate the Reformation with the decline of magic in a kind of Weberian sense was Keith Thomas's magisterial *Religion and the Decline of Magic* (New York: 1971).

local studies (for example, for Brandenburg), we still lack a cohesive picture—did acculturation take place in the sense that the intellectualizing of the elites was eventually appropriated by the common people, or did the retention of ritual eventually influence the ruling elites? The provocative studies published in recent years leave unanswered for many the question of whether their findings lend themselves to broad generalizations.[7] In all of this, one theme cannot be sounded too often: the common people were almost universally illiterate when the great conflagration began, though by the time the century ended significant change had taken place in this respect.

There is no evidence—not even for England, which appears to be a patent instance of political intrusion into ecclesiastical affairs—that a new form of the Christian religion was unilaterally imposed on people who showed absolutely no inclination for it. Henry VIII was able to proceed on his path in England precisely because of his awareness that change resonated among some of his subjects—in Parliament, in London, out in the country. In a way, the deeply religious character of the Reformation, which resonated with a segment of the common people, harmonized with the deeply religious character of the late Middle Ages—a time characterized by the ubiquitous reality of canon law, the equal ubiquity of the sevenfold sacramental system, the societal power of the hierarchy—and common people who entrusted to the church, without fully understanding the theology, their eternal salvation and destiny. The Protestant Reformation may be seen as the replacement of one all-embracing religious system by another, with little discernible difference as far as the common people were concerned, but with decisive difference among the representatives of a new social class.

It may be instructive to attempt to throw light on the sixteenth century by having recourse to the twenty-first: it is surely safe to say that even today most church members, whatever their denomination, have little interest and even less competence in any serious engagement in current theological feuds and disagreements. Take the Joint Declaration on Justification, signed in 1999 between the Lutheran World Federation and the Vatican's Pontifical Council for Promoting Christian Unity. When the draft of this declaration became public, a fiercely negative reaction of German theologians and church historians ensued, and in the end, approximately 250 (which meant some 98 percent of all German Lutheran theologians) of them signed a letter dissenting from the key conclusion of the joint declaration that "a consensus in basic truths of the doctrine of justification exists between Lutherans and Catholics." In other words, the experts dissented. Needless to say, the implications of the joint declaration were revolutionary in light of the fierceness of the theological controversies in the sixteenth century, but what is relevant here is that the Lutheran synods in Germany all endorsed the declaration and that the laity showed no discernible interest either in the joint declaration or, for that matter, in the dissenting theologians.

---

7. See such studies as William A. Christian Jr., *Local Religion in Sixteenth-Century Spain* (Princeton: 1981), or Marc Foster, *Catholic Revival in the Age of the Baroque: Religious Identity in Southwest Germany, 1550–1750* (Cambridge: 2001).

CONSEQUENCES

Not surprisingly, partisan judgments have clouded the assessments of the meaning of the Reformation.[8] Protestants have seen the Reformation as the recovery of authentic biblical religion, while Catholics have judged it a heretical perversion. Protestants affirmed the keen biblical insights offered by the Reformers into all areas of personal and societal life, while Catholics, especially in their post-Enlightenment polemics, found that all the ills of modernity, particularly disrespect for authority and an emphasis on individual rights, could be laid at the feet of the Reformation. Secular observers, too, have chimed in and asserted their views of the connection between the ideas of the Reformation and the rise of modernity. During and after World War II books made Luther an ancestor of Hitler.

Needless to say, these are treacherous waters because so much is at stake. However, several conclusions about sixteenth-century events are uncontroversial and even widely endorsed. They should stand at the beginning of any exploration of the impact and consequences of the Reformation.

The most spectacular consequence of the Reformation was the division of Western Christendom. This division shows no signs of abatement—periodic efforts at reconciliation (especially in the twentieth century), intermittent Protestant conversions to Rome, and enthusiasm about such ecumenical agreements as the 1999 Catholic-Lutheran Joint Delaration on Justification, a theological topic that sixteenth-century Lutheran theologians had asserted was the article "on which the church stands and falls."[9] In the sixteenth century, the disunity of the Christian church, already a painful reality after the split between East and West, was accentuated by a split right through the heart of Western (Latin) Christendom. The unity of the Western church became a thing of the past, and that division has had far-reaching consequences—a quarter of the two billion adherents of Christianity worldwide are Protestants.

To be sure, there had been schisms before. Most prominent was the one that separated Eastern and Western (Greek and Latin) Christianity, but there had been others: the pathetic, albeit temporary schism between the rival papal factions of Rome and Avignon in the fourteenth century, and the intermittent heretical challenges to the Western church by the Waldensians and Cathari and by the Lollards and the Hussites. These divisions, though modest in their challenge of the Roman Church—and they hardly entered the consciousness of the faithful—rendered dubious the notion of a "catholic" church and a seamless robe.

---

8. A new twist in the reflections on the Reformation asks the question of the continued viability of the Reformation in the twenty-first century. See Mark Noll and Carolyn Nystrom, *Is the Reformation Over? An Evangelical Assessment of Contemporary Roman Catholicism* (Grand Rapids: 2005).

9. However, that over 250 German Lutheran theologians (just about all of them) signed a protest against the declaration suggests that ecumenical agreements are just as tricky today as they were back in the sixteenth century. Nonetheless, it was reported that when Mark Hanson, the presiding bishop of the Evangelical Lutheran Church in America, had an audience with Pope John Paul II, he stated with tears in his eyes that it was his most profound wish to be able to share Communion in 2017, the anniversary year of Luther's Ninety-five Theses.

At the dawn of sixteenth-century Europe, the Christian religion in the West was one, bedazzling in its complexity and impressive in its structure. It was personified by the bishop of Rome, the successor to the apostle Peter, the prince of the apostles. The pope was called vicar of Christ on earth, the "servant of the servants of God," and his splendor and authority staggered the imagination of the faithful. This holy Catholic Church commanded universal allegiance and claimed the ancient attributes of being holy, catholic, and apostolic. Even those who in the early sixteenth century were uneasy about the state of the church, such as the humanists, and wished for less political involvement of the papacy or less emphasis on financial matters were fiercely loyal to it.

By the twilight of the sixteenth century, everything had changed. The unity of Western Christendom had vanished, relegated to a melancholic dream. Christendom in the West was divided—not into two factions, Catholic and Protestant, but into no fewer than six: Catholics, Lutherans, Calvinists, Anglicans, antitrinitarians, and Anabaptists. The coexistence of these churches was an uneasy one, because each determinedly claimed to be in sole possession of truth, denouncing its rivals with intense self-confidence.

To what extent this division of Christianity was a nagging consciousness of the sixteenth century (or even the seventeenth century) is difficult to say. Despite a few exceptions here and there, within the borders of a commonwealth or city only one faith was officially recognized, and all—men, women, and children—had to conform to it in a kind of pragmatic, if artificial, universality of truth. There were exceptions. In some European countries, such as France, the Low Countries, Poland, Germany, and even England, explicit religious diversity existed, narrowly tolerated and often bitterly contested. These internal feuds dramatized the division of Christian truth in pointed fashion, and there can be no doubt but that as the division of Western Christendom continued and increased the Christian truth claims lessened. No wonder, Thomas More remarked in wise and "horrific" anticipation in 1533, that "some of us . . . live not in the day that we would gladly wish to be at league and composition with them to let them have their churches quietly to themselves, so that they would be content to let us have ours quietly to ourselves."[10]

The division of Christendom entailed a spectacular weakening of the power and authority of the Catholic Church, for the new Protestant churches grew on soil vacated by Catholicism. A glance at the map of Europe showing formal religious affiliations in 1600 might suggest that the Catholic losses were tolerable. Arguably, the desertion from Catholic ranks was less than some had hoped and what others had feared. Germany, for example, at one juncture seemingly on the way to complete acceptance of the new faith, eventually retained a Catholic majority, especially in the south and northwest. Poland, Hungary, and France, likewise at one time leaning toward Protestantism, eventually declared for the Catholic faith, while Italy, Spain, and Ireland escaped most of the religious turmoil altogether. It took the Catholic Church a long time to plot and implement its strategies for reasserting authority and

---

10. This reference is to William Roper's *Life of Thomas More* as cited in John M. Headley, "Thomas More's Horrific Vision," in *Confessionalization in Europe, 1555–1700* (ed. John M. Headley, Hans J. Hillerbrand, and Anthony J. Papalas; Aldershot: 2004), 340.

power, which did not come about until the opening sessions of the Council of Trent. But both self-confidence and self-assertion were quickly restored, so that the Roman Catholic Church entered the second half of the sixteenth and subsequently the seventeenth century with surprising vigor and assertion.

The significance of the division in Protestant ranks calls for further comment. Neither historically nor theologically was there ever a single Reformation movement; rather, there were several, prompting recent scholars to speak pointedly of plural "Reformations."[11] The Protestant Reformation was never a monolithic phenomenon, but almost from the beginning a house divided against itself. When Bishop Jacques Bossuet of France wrote his famous history of Protestantism, he gave it the telling title *Histoire des variations des églises protestantes* (1688). Although, in contrast to official twentieth-century Catholic language, Bossuet was quite willing to recognize the Protestant assemblies as "churches," he argued that the very divisions within Protestantism, the lack of unity in doctrine, were persuasive proof of its falsehood. Truth was one, not many, and since there were many Protestant "truths," Protestantism could not be truth.

The seemingly endless divisions among the Protestants, so grotesquely manifested during the Protectorate in seventeenth-century England, also called into question the fundamental Protestant notion that Scripture was clear and self-evident and that all individuals of goodwill would readily agree on its meaning. Luther, who had first made this assertion, was to learn its weakness in his controversy with Zwingli over the interpretation of Jesus's words of institution at the Lord's Supper. His dismay over such disagreements fueled his increasingly rigid intolerance of alternate scriptural interpretations—for example, that of the Anabaptists.

One must add that the Reformers themselves had great difficulty acknowledging spiritual and theological kinship with those who disagreed with them. At the Marburg Colloquy of 1529, Luther refused the fraternal handshake with Zwingli, Oecolampadius, and Bucer with the telling words, "you have a different spirit." Indeed, as I have argued, the seeming unanimity in the first few years of the controversy was more one of pious desires than theological reality, and after 1523 theological divisions came tangibly to the fore. It was the Catholic protagonists, for whom all varieties of Protestant reform were regurgitations of ancient heresies, who imposed the notion of a unified Reformation on the various strands of reform impulses.

A second controversial topic has been whether the Protestant Reformation constituted a radical break with the past. That the Reformation brought a break, namely the division of Christendom with all its implications, is clear enough. But was it radical? Was there discontinuity with the past?

Several realities come to mind. Perhaps foremost among them is the fundamental assertion of the Reformation: that salvation was divorced from any agency of the church and was based solely on the faith of the believing Christian. The individual

11. For example, James D. Tracy, *Europe's Reformations 1450–1650* (Lanham: 2006); Carter Lindberg, *The European Reformations* (Oxford: 1996); Alec Ryre, *Palgrave Advances in The European Reformations* (New York: 2006). This use of the plural is an outgrowth of trends in cultural studies, which discipline uses plurals throughout (i.e., Christianities, Augustinianisms, Catholicisms, Enlightenments, etc.) to denote the empirical diversity beneath certain collective or "mass") nouns.

stood alone, spiritually naked, *coram Dei* (in the face of God), and trusted in the divine promise of forgiveness and acceptance. This Protestant affirmation concomitantly meant the utter disparagement of all external markers of religion and religiosity, except for the two sacraments of baptism and the Lord's Supper. As Archbishop Cranmer wrote in his preface to the 1540 Bible, "ceremonies, pilgrimages, purgatory, saints, images, works and such like, as hath these three hundred or four hundred years been corruptly taught," were irrelevant for one's salvation.

The Copernican revolution brought about by the Reformation was the disavowal of those sensory aids, such as images, incense, and relics, that for centuries had accompanied the faithful on their life journeys. They all were replaced by the Word. The sensual culture of Catholic Christendom, in the seventeenth century so flamboyantly expressed in the baroque, was replaced by the austerity and simplicity of the Word. Although it is overlooked these days by much of contemporary Protestant theology, this entailed a lessening of the role of the sacraments by connecting baptism and the Lord's Supper to the primacy of the Word, making it understandable how, by the mid-seventeenth century, the celebration of the Lord's Supper had disappeared from the regular Protestant Sunday service. Indeed, in all Protestant churches the Lord's Supper was understood as but a tangible proclamation of the Word, making the "proclamation" of the "words of institution" crucial to the celebration of the sacrament.

The disavowal of the expressions of Catholicism's material culture led harmoniously to the rejection of monasticism, with its presupposition of a dual morality, one for those who desired a "perfect" spiritual life and another for everyone else, and the priority given to the spiritual over the mundane life. This Protestant rejection touched the heart of traditional Catholic piety and its ramifications in the cultural and societal realms; it also introduced a new understanding of Christian living that did not distinguish between levels of moral perfection, which had allowed the veneration of certain women and men canonized as saints. The secular realm and the entire sweep of occupations, from the most exalted to the lowliest, were given spiritual meaning and significance.

There were other breaks with Catholic tradition. One was the end of the heresy laws, promulgated and honored in the church from late antiquity onward. It occurred when in 1555 the imperial diet gave full legal recognition to Lutherans, whom the Catholic Church had declared to be heretics. That was, indeed, truly revolutionary.

THE NEW CHURCHES

Those who rallied to the cause of reform in the early years of the controversy had some clear notions about the practical consequences of the reform message. They demanded evangelical preaching based on the Word and the abolition of the "abomination" of the Mass. Whatever hopes they may have harbored about the Roman church seeing things their way quickly dissipated after Luther's excommunication, and by 1522 it had become evident that the movement of reform was turning into new, Protestant churches. The heavy burden of separate permanence settled upon them. The more time passed, the further out of the question reconciliation became, even as the frenetic eschatological sentiment of the early sixteenth century waned and no longer afforded grounds for considering matters of practical churchmanship moot. The new churches were forced to settle down to everyday life.

The emergence of these new churches was a slow and haphazard process, which, suggests that for a while the Reformers were overwhelmed by a task that they had neither anticipated nor wanted. The growing awareness that the break with the Catholic Church was unbridgeable (and probably permanent) triggered a determination to reforming church life that was increasingly comprehensive and led to new organizational structures. Before long the practical reordering of church life according to the principles of the Word became the Reformers' foremost assignment. At the end of that path stood the newly formed Protestant churches. Needless to say, some changes in worship were undertaken with relative dispatch, while others (especially changes in ethos) proved complicated. The process of Protestant confessionalization took the better part of the century.

The initial changes in church life were relatively moderate and lacked revolutionary fervor, underscoring that the weight of tradition hung heavily over all reforming efforts. Foremost was the demand for "evangelical" preaching. Despite an understandable heterogeneity of style and emphasis on the part of the large phalanx of preachers, this widely accepted demand showed a remarkable uniformity.[12] At its core was the Protestant insistence on the centrality of Scripture, the Word. This Word proclaimed that salvation was altogether God's doing, appropriated by the individual by faith, and by faith alone. God's promise of forgiveness and salvation came directly to the individual, who as "free lord of all" was called to serve the neighbor with faith active in love. This demand for evangelical preaching was a profoundly religious summons, though in itself it did not entail the radical rejection of existing church structures and patterns of worship. Nonetheless, the proclamation of the Word had to be made central.

At the same time, the dynamic of evangelical preaching triggered an awareness that the new evangelical message challenged the theological grounding of prevailing worship practices. All of a sudden the advocates of reform saw themselves faced with a host of practical issues that arose from their new theological perspectives. What should be done about the side altars in the churches, for example, since they served mainly to allow priests to celebrate private masses? What about the prayers to the saints during the service? What about the monasteries and convents, often wealthy and prosperous, located self-confidently in the midst of communities? Quite to the point, Andreas Carlstadt wrote a pamphlet *Von Abtuhung der Bylder* (Concerning the Removal of Images), because a great many of the questions begging for answers had to do with existing practices and patterns. Little by little, cautiously in some places, audaciously in others, practical changes began to be made in both churches and communities, and it soon became evident that these changes entailed consequences. The

---

12. We are largely in the dark as to firsthand evidence of actual preaching. However, a subgenre of the "pamphlet literature" of the time consists of printed sermon "summaries," which gives us a glimpse of what must have been preached. See Bernd Moeller, "Was wurde in der Frühzeit der Reformation in den deutschen Städten gepredigt?" *Archiv für Reformationsgeschichte* 75 (1984): 176–93. There is scholarly disagreement about the theological cohesiveness of this initial preaching: see Berndt Hamm, ed., *Reformationstheorien* (Göttingen: 1995).

dissolution of a community's monasteries and convents raised not only the issue of what the monks and nuns were to do, but also a multitude of legal problems that became more complicated as time went on. What should be done with the endowments that provided for the celebration of private masses, or with monastic property that no longer served a religious function? In England in the mid-1530s, Henry VIII found a simple solution. He used the sale of monastic property both to stabilize government finances and to create a core of supporters of his religious policies. In Germany, where the issue was first faced, the solutions were more complex. The legal bequests and endowments that churches, monasteries, and convents had received over many years were used to provide support for numerous good causes, such as the upkeep of convents or the support of priests. In some instances, a noble family had won the right to nominate an incumbent for a parish. These extensive and formidable legal relationships did not lend themselves to speedy modification.

It was the result of the evangelical preaching that led, quickly and consistently, to the question of what constituted proper biblical worship. The earliest public challenge of traditional worship came in Wittenberg in December 1521, when Luther's colleague Carlstadt conducted a worship service in a new mode: according to (admittedly hostile) observers he celebrated Communion in street clothes and shirtsleeves, using the German vernacular and distributing both bread and wine to the communicants.[13] Although the abolition of the Mass quickly became a hallmark of evangelical agitation, many congregations lacked pastors with the creative talent necessary for developing a new order of worship, and for the time being most congregations continued their worship with a foggy mix of the old and the new. Luther's great antagonist Thomas Müntzer quickly weighed in, publishing in 1523 a new "evangelical" order of worship, the *Deutsch-evangelisches Kirchenamt* (German Evangelical Church Order), which was characterized by the deletion of all references to a "Mass" and by the use of the German vernacular. In Nuremberg that same year Communion was celebrated with both bread and wine, and one year later a rudimentary service in German was attempted. In Erfurt Johann Lang also wrote an order of worship for local use.

These attempts at liturgical reform prompted Luther, who did not particularly relish conceding priority of place and theological insight to his challenger Müntzer, to publish his *Formula missae et communionis* (Formula of the Mass and Communion) in 1523 and his *Taufbüchlein* (Little Book on Baptism), which laid out biblical worship, both theologically and practically, as he understood it. Luther's stance was broadminded, allowing, even encouraging, local variations in worship. As long as the gospel was proclaimed, he argued, detailed and rigid patterns of worship were secondary issues. Uniformity of worship was neither necessary nor desirable.

An overriding principle characterized the early patterns of the reform of worship: the local congregation was envisioned as the center of Christian life and worship, which also became responsible for carrying Christian social obligations. Although these two aspects may carry overtones of redundancy today, in the early sixteenth cen-

---

13. James Preuss summarized the complex developments in Wittenberg in 1521/1522: *Carlstadt's Ordinaciones and Luther's Liberty: A Study of the Wittenberg Movement, 1521–22* (Cambridge: 1974), though he too makes too much of the alleged disruption of law and order.

tury they were nothing less than revolutionary, for the centrality of the local congregation meant the rejection of the existing complexity of parish life, where parish churches existed alongside churches of the various monastic orders and even cathedral churches. The mandate for Christian charity had been mainly the responsibility of the monastic orders. The dissolution of the monasteries and convents meant that the churches connected to them disappeared, so the parish churches had to assume responsibility for the works of Christian mercy. Reform meant simplification. Wherever the Reformation was adopted, monastic property as well as existing endowments for spiritual purposes no longer considered valid were converted into endowments for the livelihood of the clergy (most of whom were now married and had greater financial needs than single Catholic priests) and for the care of the poor.

This development paralleled the increasing role of the political authorities in ecclesiastical affairs, a role that had been gradually but significantly enhanced in the course of the late fifteenth century. By 1524 it became obvious not only that the cause of reform and renewal meshed with the determination of the political elites to increase their role in ecclesiastical affairs, but also that carrying out ecclesiastical reform depended on the support of the political authorities—city councils in the cities and rulers in the territories. The new church, organized along the political boundaries of cities and territories, came into being with the active support (and never against the opposition) of the rulers. Eventually two distinct patterns of Protestant church structure emerged out of the Reformation controversy: a congregational pattern that vested power in the local congregation, which characterized the Zwinglian-Calvinist-Reformed tradition; and an episcopal pattern that subjected local congregations to regional oversight, which characterized the Anglican, Scandinavian Lutheran, and German Lutheran churches, the first two with the office of the bishop. Although the areas in which these two patterns were concentrated had their particular histories and thus their own rationales, the situation in the empire, with its Lutheran and Zwinglian divergence, finds its explanation in the different environments of Zurich and Wittenberg, the one a significantly large territory, the other a city republic. Patterns of governance differed, and both Luther and Zwingli latched on to structures with which they were familiar.

In Zurich the role of the city council in ecclesiastical affairs was clear from the beginning, certainly after the January Disputation of 1523, when the decision of the council to support Zwingli's preaching dramatized the council's pivotal role in the city's ecclesiastical affairs. The defenders of the old church shook their heads in consternation: how could a city council usurp the authority to render theological judgments, which had been the province of the councils of the church since early Christianity? It was the Zurich city council that in April 1525 authorized a new order of worship, and somewhat later the *Ordnung der christlichen Kirche zu Zürich* (Order of the Christian Church in Zurich).[14] In electoral Saxony, on the other hand, the sentiment of the Wittenberg city fathers was irrelevant compared to the power and authority of the elector. In Sweden and England royal fiat determined that the traditional episcopal structure was to be maintained. Virtually all the ecclesiastical

14. *Zwinglis Werke*, 4:671ff.

legislation in England that severed ties with Rome was passed by Parliament and not by the convocations of York or Canterbury.

The challenge facing the early Reformers was how to organize the church. What could be retained, in light of biblical insights, of the traditional structures, and what had to be changed? Since the early days of Christianity, spiritual as well as administrative oversight of the churches had been vested in bishops, whose unbroken continuity from apostolic times was understood to vouchsafe—more than the sequence of popes and councils—the apostolic heritage of the Christian community. This historical legacy of the apostolic succession of bishops threw its long shadow over the reforming efforts of all Protestant churches. The hope that such continuity might be retained quickly turned out to be groundless, for no incumbent Catholic bishop in Germany converted to the new faith. This meant that, in terms of the traditional assumption, the new Protestant churches lacked the legitimation of historical episcopal continuity and succession. Even more important, Luther's theology (unlike that which took hold in England and Scandinavia), with its insistence on the unmitigated centrality of the Word, made the topic of apostolic succession of secondary consideration. Luther asserted that authentic apostolic succession meant fidelity to apostolic teaching, rather than an empirical succession of laying on of hands from bishop to bishop. He derived this notion from his understanding of the history of the church (the historical episcopate had not always retained apostolic teaching) and his judgment that the true evangelical faith had existed in centuries past quite apart from the formal apostolic succession.

Luther understood his suggestions for a new ordering of church life as emergency notions, to be revised or changed once the larger question of how the church was going to respond to the challenges of reform had been answered. He fully recognized the need for a regional administrative structure, though he had problems with the office of bishop as a separate order in the church. In line with this approach, he introduced the office of the "emergency bishop" (*Notbischof*) to temporarily supervise ecclesiastical affairs during the crucial period of transition from the old to the new faith. The office fell to the political authorities, so the affairs of the new churches were placed into the hands of the city councils (in the imperial free cities) and the territorial rulers—not only the major ones, such as electoral Saxony or Hesse, but the smaller ones as well. The rulers rarely hesitated to exercise their prerogative. This aspect of Protestantism connects the early Reformation in Germany with that in other European countries, such as England. King Henry VIII and his European counterparts all saw themselves (be it as the result of religious conviction or of lust for power) as "supreme heads" of their respective churches. The magistracy began to exercise final ecclesiastical authority and assume broad responsibilities. The government supervised ecclesiastical affairs, the training of the clergy, and their remuneration, and through official "visitations" monitored the life and belief of the faithful. Luther had conceded the ruler's role in ecclesiastical affairs only with great reluctance, though the preface to his *Unterricht der Visitatoren* (Instructions for the Visitors for the Clergy) of 1527 indicated that he had given up the idea of effecting the building of a new church by way of a spontaneous evolution of forms, structures, and patterns on the local level.

This development had significant bearing on the subsequent relationship between church and state in Protestant countries. In England and Sweden, where Catholic bishops embraced the changes—and participated in the consecration of episcopal candidates—the traditional episcopacy and the historic episcopate were retained, though it was not until the end of the century that Anglican theologians formulated the theological justification for the special order of the episcopacy. In those countries, however, the ruler could hardly be involved in detailed church affairs. In Germany, on the other hand, the territorial rulers could indeed see themselves as "diocesan bishops" and thereby void the episcopal office of both authority and power. Only in Scandinavia and England was there a seamless transition from the "old" church to the "new," as bishops of the old church converted (for whatever reason) to the "new" and thereby, in their own eyes, allowed for the continuation of the historical episcopate.

Issues pertaining to the local congregation had surfaced first, for the new gospel had to find embodiment in the daily routine of church life and worship. The issues addressed ranged all the way from the use of Latin in the worship service to the celebration of the Mass to the support of the poor, the widows, and the sick in a community. Traditionally, these latter functions had been carried out by nuns and monks, but the repudiation of monasticism meant the monasteries and convents disappeared while the social needs they served remained.[15]

A variety of local solutions were proposed and put into practice in the early 1520s, for example, the *Ordnung der Stadt Wittenberg* of January 1522, or the *Leisniger Kastenordnung* of the following year. These orders reflected the spirit of liberating exuberance with which problems large and small, old and new, were addressed. In Germany reflections on the structure of congregational life were influenced by Luther's nonchalance and a concomitant concern not to undertake too many changes too quickly. Luther wrote several orders of worship, beginning with the *Formula Missae et Communionis* of 1523, the *Taufbüchlein verdeutscht*, and the *Deutsche Messe* (German Mass and Order of Service) of 1526. Here Luther asserted his fundamental principle: "In sum and substance this church order and all others are to be used so that, if there is abuse, they are promptly abolished and a new one put in its place. Forms and orders of worship should be for the promotion of faith and the service of love, and not to harm faith. When they have no more to do, they are dead and no longer of any worth. If good coin is counterfeit, it is done away with and destroyed for fear of misuse, or, when new shoes have become old and worn, we stop wearing them and throw them away and buy new ones. Order is an outward matter."[16]

In his *Formula* Luther also suggested that the "serious Christians" in a local congregation should meet separately for prayer and Bible study—a rather striking notion that has had a lengthy history, even though Luther subsequently abandoned his suggestion because it smacked of sectarianism. Nonetheless, a group of Zwingli's disciples, who subsequently broke with him over the issue of infant baptism, insisted that

---

15. For Zurich we have the study of Lee Palmer Wandel, *Always Among Us: Images of the Poor in Zwingli's Zurich* (Cambridge: 1990).
16. WA 9:113.

he implement such groups in Zurich. A century and a half later, Philip Jakob Spener, the father of German Pietism, reintroduced the same notion with his proposal to establish *collegia pietatis*, circles of serious Christians.

Also in 1523 Luther addressed a specific issue that had surfaced in the Thuringian town of Altenburg, where both city council and citizens had demanded the right to appoint an evangelical minister but had been thwarted by the neighboring Augustinian monastery, which had the legal right to make that appointment but refused to do so. Luther's *Dass eine christliche Versammlung oder Gemeinde Recht und Macht habe, alle Lehre zu urteilen und Lehrer zu berufen, ein-und abzusetzen* (That a Christian Assembly or Congregation Has the Authority and Power to Judge All Teaching, to Call, Install, and Dismiss Teachers) was a forceful argument for the centrality of the local congregation.[17] Here was a declaration of autonomy for the local congregation. However, Luther promptly discovered that things were not quite that simple. Many congregations were entangled in legal structures (for example, in some congregations endowments with trustees and legal rights paid for clergy) that could not easily be ignored. Confronted with this reality, Luther gradually abandoned his democratic notions of local church government. In a letter to the Bohemian Utraquist church Luther outlined how, in the absence of an ordaining bishop, the local congregation could install candidates to the ministry.[18] Luther's stance was one of considerable latitude and largesse, and the churches following his lead generally embraced his relaxed point of view. Beyond fidelity to the proclamation of the Word and the proper administration of the sacraments, patterns and styles of worship could develop along lines of local custom and precedent. When a fellow reformer proposed a council to bring about ecclesiastical uniformity among the adherents of the new faith, Luther retorted that uniformity was neither necessary nor advisable. Structures and forms would issue spontaneously and creatively from the local congregation. Indeed, in a few instances this actually happened.

Since Luther and the other Reformers acknowledged only two of the seven Catholic sacraments, the question quickly arose about the traditional sacrament of penance, so crucial for the faithful because it gave them the opportunity to confess their sins and receive absolution. In his *Formula Missae*, Luther advocated that only those should be admitted to Communion who had informed their pastor of their intention and, in so doing, had confessed their sins. More than that, Luther stipulated that they had to recite Jesus's words of institution from memory, a rather formidable requirement. Melanchthon's *Augsburg Confession* essentially reiterated this sentiment, and in the Saxon visitation of 1529 the stipulation is clear: "We forbid anyone to be given the holy Sacrament of the body and blood of Christ unless he can recite from memory the Ten Commandments, the Creed, and the Lord's Prayer and unless he laments his misdeeds beforehand to the pastor or the deacon."[19] Before long the last requirement triggered a discussion about whether pastors had to find a fellow pastor to whom to confess and from whom to obtain absolution before receiving the elements!

---

17. WA 11:408ff.
18. Luther, *De instituendis ministris ecclesiae*, WA 12:193ff.
19. As quoted in S. Karant-Nunn, *The Reformation of Ritual* (New York: 2002), 97.

By the early 1530s the liturgical and organizational changes in the new Protestant churches had in many places reached the point where an element of permanence began to characterize the scene. No matter what the professed commitments of the Reformers concerning the unity of the church, the realities of life spoke a language of their own. Evangelical sermons had to be preached, the sacraments administered, clergy educated, and congregations properly organized. In short, a new church had to be nurtured. This was the eminent internal task of Protestant church leaders in the 1530s and 1540s. We will return to this important aspect in our reflections on the emergence of a new church.

The laity's voice in church affairs was heard only indirectly; ordinary laypeople had no voice. In the territories a measure of congregational participation existed only in Hesse, where the organizational structure was less bureaucratic than elsewhere. The same held true for the imperial cities, influenced no doubt by the limited geographic confines and the representative character of the governing city councils. Protestants, of course, espoused the principle of the priesthood of all believers as a splendid ideal, but in actual practice severe restrictions prevailed with respect to the involvement of the laity, and so the actual situation in Protestant lands differed little from that in Catholic ones.

Nonetheless, the common people were not beyond making their will known and their sentiment heard. Recent researchers have suggested that lay folk were not altogether passive when it came to the introduction of new dogmas and new rituals; they accepted, resisted, and adapted. The clergy were another story.

In 1544 visitors made this report about a pastor: "There is not much knowledge or intellect in the little man. He preaches from memory, it is true, but he has a strange way and is very faulty in his pronunciation and, besides, he shouts. He swallows his last words and syllables, and has an odd way of overusing certain words; he repeats them again and again in his sermons. Consequently, he is unpleasant to listen to."[20] Luther, who observed that preaching simply was a great art, wrote a number of times on preaching, noting that a preacher also needs to know when to stop.[21]

At another occasion, Luther was asked, "Reverend Father, teach me in a brief way how to preach." Luther responded briefly, "First, you must learn to go up to the pulpit. Second, you must know that you should say there for a time. Third, you must learn to get down again. Anybody who keeps this order will be a good preacher. First, he must learn to go up to the pulpit, that is, he should have a regular and a divine call. Second, he must learn to stay there for a time, that is, he should have the pure and genuine doctrine. Third, he must also learn to get down again, that is, he should preach not more than an hour."[22]

Of course, there also were many dedicated and competent ministers who carried out their ministerial responsibilities with proficiency and conscientiousness. The field officers of the Reformation, they translated Protestant theory into practice. They proclaimed the new gospel, nurtured their congregations, and dealt with the political authorities. In sum, they added religious vitality to theological pronouncements.

20. W. Pauck, op. cit., 129.
21. WA TR 4:447.
22. WA TR 5171b.

Though Protestantism had espoused the notion of the priesthood of all believers, in practice it became a *Pastorenkirche*, a church guided by the clergy.

All Protestant churches insisted on an educated clergy. Moreover, because the Catholic ideal of celibacy had been rejected by the Reformers, the new Protestant pastor was not only more educated than the typical Catholic priest had been, he was also head of a family. The difference in education meant, over time, that pastors, especially in rural areas, seemed demonstrably of a higher class than the village folk. Their married status meant they had a greater need for adequate income. The visitation records from the late sixteenth century are full of whining pastors who complained about their insufficient earnings. Fees for pastoral services became important again—a terrible turn, for the denunciation of such fees in Catholic practice had been a major topic of Protestant polemic in the early years of the controversy. In all of this, Catholics promptly followed suit, understanding full well that the absence of a properly trained clergy was one of the main reasons for the striking success of the Reformation. The Council of Trent quickly issued detailed instructions for stringent clerical education.

The task of the Protestant pastors was to preach the Word and to administer the sacraments. Given the centrality of the Word in the Protestant affirmation, it should come as no surprise that the sermon quickly became the heart and hallmark of the Protestant service. With this emphasis went the explicit accusations of the Reformers, important and not so important, that the medieval church had disparaged preaching—an indictment widely echoed subsequently by historians of the Reformation. In fact, there had been a good deal of preaching before the Reformation, as Bernard of Clairveaux, Savonarola, or Johann Geiler von Kaisersberg attest, but the sermon had not occupied a central place. That was held by the Mass. The new Protestant emphasis upon preaching revolutionized worship, even though on the face of things the essential structures of the traditional Mass were retained. Preaching aroused the excitement and enthusiasm of the common people, and one indication of the widespread absence of meaningful preaching prior to the Reformation is that the defenders of the old church were hard put to counter Reform preaching with eloquent preaching of their own, even though, intriguingly, the initial wave of Reformers came out of the same milieu as did those in the church who did not waver in their loyalty to Rome.

In the Mass, the worshipers' attention had focused on what was happening at the altar, a ritual that was familiar and, in the interchange between officiating priest and God, made the worshipers into spectators. The sermon, on the other hand, engaged the worshiper directly, to exhort, proclaim, comfort—though there undoubtedly were sleepers and daydreamers during (lengthy) sermons as well. Over time, the significant consequence of the Protestant emphasis on preaching was the installation of pews in churches, when the physical demands of listening to lengthy (and surely at times utterly tedious) sermons became obvious.

The medieval church had commanded its faithful to receive the sacrament of the altar at least on Easter, a realistic minimum requirement that nonetheless was more often honored only in the breach. The Reformation brought little change in this regard, certainly as regards the conscientiousness of the people. Nonetheless, most Protestant worship continued to include the celebration of Communion, and it was not until the later part of the century that two types of Protestant services became firmly established: the regular service, with its focus on the sermon, and the special service, celebrated perhaps once a month, of Communion.

The new emphasis on preaching as the core of the service placed a heavy responsibility upon the clergy and was far more easily postulated than put into practice. Theological and biblical literacy was rather low among the pre-Reformation clergy, though this reality was not quite as disastrous as Protestant polemic made it out; after all, the central function of priests was not to preach, but to celebrate the Mass. The impact of the Reformation meant that a nonexistent (or, at any rate, rarely exercised) function became the heart of the ministerial responsibilities. It speaks for Luther's sense of practical churchmanship that during his stay at the Wartburg he wrote a book of sermons as examples of scriptural preaching. It proved enormously successful and has found numerous imitators all the way to the present. The so-called *Wartburg Postil* saw almost thirty editions. The sermons of the *Postil* were to be study guides, to be used by clergy in the preparation of their sermons. Of course, they could also be declared the clergyman's "own." The zeal for the gospel was more important than questions of authorship. Thus the words of the Reformer were heard from Protestant pulpits everywhere throughout Protestant lands. No doubt, scores of simple worshipers thus heard profound expositions of the gospel, to which they would not have been exposed had they depended solely on the exegetical and theological insights of their own pastors. Plagiarism thus enhanced the propagation of the Protestant (and subsequently Catholic) agenda.

CHURCH LIFE AND POPULAR RELIGION

On the eve of the Reformation the Catholic Church appeared resplendent in its magnificent power and ritual—a feast for the senses. From the sprinkled water in baptism to the awesome imposition of oil in extreme unction, the rituals of the church accompanied the earthly pilgrimage of the faithful. One suspects that much of the deep symbolism of water, oil, bread, even spittle was beyond the understanding of the rank and file, because a great deal of misunderstanding prevailed about their meanings; for example, the consecrated wafer might have been taken for a love potion. Nonetheless, ritual more than doctrine and theology exemplified what the church was and what the church stood for.

Most Protestants reacted to a greater or lesser degree against this ritualized Christian faith, and this reaction may have occurred on two levels: the theological affirmations that rendered such ritual moot and the persistence or modification of Catholic ritual despite its formal rejection.[23] At the same time, the Reformation also raised questions about the popular understanding of religion. A great deal has been written (not only in these pages) about the ideas and actions of the elites in church and society— about Luther's notions of worship or marriage, for example, or Cranmer's *Book of Common Prayer*. It is easy indeed to romanticize about these splendid ideas and appealing notions on the assumption that in the course of the story of the Reformation, theory

23. Susan Karant-Nunn, *The Reformation of Ritual* (New York: 2002).

routinely translated into practice. Recent research has called attention to the method-
ological (not to mention factual) flaws in this assumption. We have learned that popular religion is sui generis and deserves consideration on its own.

The effort to sketch how the Reformation's lofty ideas about church and society
affected the common people must begin with an elementary observation. The Reformation movement heralded the pivotal centrality of the Word as the ubiquitous center of the Christian faith. It therefore called for and required literacy—the ability to
read sacred Scripture and understand that its proclamation stood at the heart of worship. Given the era's extensive illiteracy, especially among the common people, that
requirement constituted a challenge. Of course, the medieval church had also confronted the challenge of how to communicate the Christian message to the common
people. It had employed the visual dimension of communication in a rich variety of
ways. It had offered the concept of "implicit faith" (*fides implicita*), which meant that
the theological ignorance of the faithful could be overcome with the affirmation that
they believed everything the church believes, even if they were ignorant of it. The
medieval church provided the rich ornamentation of Gothic churches: stained-glass
windows depicting salvation history from the garden of Eden to Armageddon, the
representation in stone of the Last Judgment. It also had the Mass at the center of its
worship, which meant the engagement of the senses: the sight of the priest's movements of hands and body at the altar, the sound of the bells, the aroma of incense.

The Reformation churches declared much of this to be unbiblical or unnecessary—a dramatic pronouncement, weighty both theologically and practically. The
new focus was on the Word, and this at a time when few men and women were able
to read, and the statues and paintings in the churches as well as the ritual of the Mass
served as their instruction manuals in the faith. The new, self-confident, and self-
conscious burghers joined the new biblical principle with a new practical reality.

There was an appallingly low level of religious literacy among the people. There may
have been a few who, with nothing at their disposal but a good portion of intelligence
and the Bible, confounded the academic theologians, but they were the exceptions. The
masses of the people were illiterate, a handicap even goodwill could rarely overcome.
After all, the ability to read is generally a prerequisite for theological competence.

With widespread religious illiteracy came also a good deal of superstition and belief
in magic and astrology, which was hardly congenial to an informed understanding of
religious controversies. The tolling of bells during thunderstorms, for example,
supposedly kept lightning from striking within hearing range of the bells. Religious
ignorance was universal, even more in the rural areas than in the cities. The church
visitation records offer ample evidence. Those for Lüneberg in 1568 indicated that
the people almost without exception were unwilling to come to the midweek cate-
chetical instruction. There were gross misunderstandings of the Decalogue, which in
one village version was rendered as, "The first shall have no other goal; the second
shall not use the name of God in vain; the third shall keep the Sabbath holy." In a village near Magdeburg only three people of fifty-two families knew the Lord's Prayer.

The task of the new churches was to indoctrinate the rank and file in the new theological tenets. That was a pedagogical challenge of major proportions, for the men and
women of the sixteenth century were hardly preoccupied with religion to the point that

they thought of nothing else. It is risky to generalize about Europe at large, about all religious factions, or about developments extending over several decades, but the evidence suggests that after an initial period of religious engagement and exuberance, preoccupation with religion declined in most countries. Only a few individuals were concerned about matters of the spirit. There are some indirect clues, such as persistent governmental pronouncements exhorting church attendance, religious illiteracy, and the Reformers' embarrassingly pathetic self-indictments. For example, the quasi-official homily *The Place and Time of Prayer,* issued in England in 1571, painted a rather unattractive picture of how people observed Sundays: "They rest in ungodliness and filthiness, prancing in their pride, prancing and pricking, pointing and painting themselves, to be gorgeous and gay; they rest in excess and superfluity, in gluttony and drunkenness, like rats and swine; they rest in brawling and railing in quarreling and fighting." Even in Protestant lands the kingdom of heaven had not been ushered in with the Reformation.

The hallmark of those unconcerned with religion was that they ignored the church and its activities. Dissent from the established form of religion was precarious, and those who expressed it, such as Sebastian Franck or the Anabaptists, suffered for their conviction, candor, and courage. Most people pursued their daily rounds, circumventing the church's moral teaching, and lived their lives unencumbered by ecclesiastical pronouncements. As long as governmental authority enforced ecclesiastical standards, overt violations of these standards were rare; but wherever a lenient atmosphere prevailed—for stretches of time in England, for example—much dissent came to the fore. At issue was outright opposition, which was rare indeed and came mainly from a few religious zealots, such as the Anabaptists or later the Puritans, and not from indifferent unbelievers. The anatomical posture where the head nodded and the heart remained uninvolved was surely not infrequent and undoubtedly increased as theologizing among Protestants became more sophisticated.

The religious ignorance of the common people was attributable to ubiquitous illiteracy rather than to any conspiratorial attempt on the part of the Catholic (or Protestant) Church to keep the common people in darkness. This situation presented problems for the new Protestant churches' educational efforts. Competent teachers were necessary—not just a few, but one for every parish. Educational manuals had to be written. Luther's Small Catechism, printed both in pamphlet form and abbreviated on cardboard to be hung on the walls of living rooms, was one of the earliest attempts to kill two birds with one stone: to supply materials for a literate public and to enhance religious competence. Some two hundred catechisms were published in the sixteenth century, all expressing a universal concern with increasing the level of religious and biblical literacy among the common people.[24] And this was not an exclusively Protestant hallmark. Catholics faced the same educational challenge and used the catechism as a pedagogical tool—witness Peter Canisius's popular effort, with so many biblical references in the margins as to suggest a Protestant approach.

As matters turned out, many people were neither willing to go through the rigid intellectual exercise nor able to devote the time required for an active involvement in

---

24. A useful reference tool in this regard is the multivolume *Verzeichnis der im deutschen Sprachraum im XVI. Jahrhundert erschienenen Schriften* (ed. Irmgard Bezzel; Stuttgart: 1983ff.).

church life. In the first few years of the Reformation religious matters had stirred much excitement among the people; but their exuberance faded rather quickly, as evidenced in the visitation records. The Lord's Prayer, the Apostles' Creed, and the Decalogue became fundamentals of the instruction of both youth and adults, yet these few items were hardly sufficient to express the fullness of the Protestant or, for that matter, the Catholic faith. The numerous visitation records indicate that the Decalogue was as much a mystery as the Trinity and that the simple recitation of the Apostles' Creed seemed unsurpassably difficult. The clergy, at least according to the visitations, despaired. The common people know nothing of Christianity, observed one clergyman, and a visitation record tells about one individual who, when asked to explain who Jesus is, was only able to respond, "he's up there, above us."

The clergy themselves were not much better. The oft-quoted visitation of the clergy of Gloucester by Bishop John Hooper in 1551 revealed appalling clerical ignorance.[25] Most men of the cloth hardly knew the basic affirmations of the faith, not to mention the specific Protestant affirmations. Obviously, a causal relationship existed between clerical incompetence and popular ignorance. Only as ministerial standards rose in the second half of the sixteenth century did the situation improve. More and more Protestant pastors had a university education and the competence to function as teachers. At the same time, many pastors, especially in villages and rural areas, continued in difficult economic circumstances that offered few, if any, financial attractions. Such had been the case even before the Reformation, when it had led to all sorts of clerical involvement in fiscal matters that raised eyebrows. The presence of married clergy only intensified the problem.

Both Catholics and Protestants emerged from the Reformation era with two gigantic educational tasks: to dispel religious ignorance and to advance spirituality. The former task enjoyed the advantage of the increasing emphasis on education and extensive literacy, but also labored under the handicap of the religious apathy that followed the intense preoccupation with religion during the Reformation.

The dynamics of Protestant worship called for changes in the configuration of sacred space. An obvious offense for the Reformers was the numerous side altars in the churches, manifestations of the proliferation of private masses in the late medieval period. In Protestant churches these altars ceased to have religious significance and were no longer needed. In the Zwinglian/Reformed tradition the altar became the simple Communion table, although in the Anglican and Lutheran setting the altar remained. However, in Lutheran and Calvinist churches the altar was moved away from the rear wall of the chancel so that the minister, standing behind the altar, faced the congregation. Luther, for one, was quite insistent that whatever the place of the minister in the sanctuary, the congregation had to be able to hear his words clearly. At the same time, pulpits became essential. The most obvious (and easiest) solution was to place the pulpit somewhere in the nave, hugging one of its pillars. As long as there were no pews, the location of the pulpit was no problem, for the worshipers could easily face the pulpit no matter where they stood. But the centrality of the sermon in the Protestant service made pews a necessity, because unlike the Mass, with

25. "Bishop Hooper's Visitation of Gloucester," *English Historical Review* 19 (1904): 101f.

its ever-changing choreography in which the action of the priest was divorced from the participation of the worshipers, the sermon meant interaction between preacher and congregation. To stand during the homiletical expositions, generally fairly lengthy, of Protestant pastors called for more persistence of body and mind than could be expected of the faithful. Pews provided the solution.

In Calvinist settings, the solution was often to place the pulpit in the center of the chancel, generally somewhat elevated, with the Communion table in front of the pulpit. In Lutheran architecture, the altar retained its centrality, and various other places in the sanctuary were selected for the pulpit. Where new churches were built, a common solution was to retain the altar in the center but place the pulpit, also in a central position, high in the wall behind the altar.

Music

Luther's famous "A Mighty Fortress Is Our God," the "Marseillaise of the Reformation," expressed symbolically that the Reformation movement proclaimed the Word in both sermon and vernacular hymn. The Reformation was a singing movement, and Lutheran hymns, Clément Marot's French paraphrases of the Psalms in Calvinist France, and the simple words and tunes of the Anabaptist hymnal *Ausbund* conveyed that singing congregations were at the very heart of the Reformation impulse.

Of course, the Christian church had not only employed music in the divine service through the centuries but had also been a singing church ever since the days of the apostles. Some of the hymns that became Protestant favorites derived both words and tunes from the medieval church. The Reformation stood in this tradition, and certainly the Lutheran churches retained the traditional melodies of the liturgy. The incisive difference, however, was that the hymn became part of the proclamation of the Word, proclaimed by the entire congregation. It was thus no mere peripheral matter, but a central part of the service. Quite consistently, the hymns were in the vernacular, not in Latin.

There was historical precedent for vernacular hymns, but they had been viewed with considerable suspicion; they jarred with the normative Latin language of the Mass, and many communities, such as Basel and Cologne, prohibited vernacular singing during Mass outright. The change brought by the Reformation had to confront the fact of low levels of literacy, especially in rural areas, which created a wedge between theory and practice. The congregations had to learn the new hymns mostly by rote. In the cities, with their higher literacy rates, the active participation of the congregation in the service through singing came more easily.[26]

Luther had early on complained about the lack of vernacular hymns—perhaps not surprisingly, given his love of music—and had publicly expressed his hope for hymns in German, to be sung by the people during Mass. He deplored the dearth of writers who might write new hymns, though he had conceded that they might well exist but were unknown. Responding to Luther's challenge, Nikolaus Decius wrote two hymns

---

26. P. Wackernagel's bibliography of German hymns remains unsurpassed. *Bibliographie zur Geschichte des deutschen Kirchenlieds im XVI. Jahrhundert* (Hildesheim: 1961).

in the Low German dialect for Easter 1523, and a bit later Luther himself composed two German hymns to memorialize the first two evangelical martyrs burned at the stake in Brussels, including "Aus tiefer Not schrei ich zu Dir" ("Out of deep distress I cry to thee"). The following year, the vernacular hymnal was published, with hymns written by a number of Reformers. It comprised eight hymns, a small but impressive number because not only the texts, but also the musical settings were newly composed. It took the name of *Achtliederbuch* (The Eight Hymns Book), and it included eight metrical chorales. Luther himself composed four of the hymns. Other efforts followed, especially the use of rhymed translations of psalms intended to be sung as hymns. The music for these hymnals was a mixture of medieval melodies, Latin hymns, popular religious songs, and secular tunes recast in a religious tone. In 1524 Luther arranged for the publication of a German hymnal, the Wittenberg *Gesangbuch*, and contributed twenty-four of its thirty-two hymns.

Other Reformers also wrote and composed hymns, at times using popular tunes of the day, at times translating ancient Latin hymns, at times rendering psalms into vernacular rhymes. The latter were considered particularly attractive because they demonstrated the Reformation's biblical orientation. Calvin insisted that only biblical words be used in the divine service, and the first French Protestant hymnal, published in 1539, consisted of vernacular paraphrases of the psalms from the pens of Calvin and Clément Marot. Subsequent hymnals in the Calvinist tradition made the same literal use of the psalms, using both contemporary and Gregorian chant–based melodies. Marot's psalm translations exercised a powerful influence wherever the French language was spoken. Just as Luther's hymns helped advance the Protestant cause in Germany, so did Marot's translation, set to music in the Genevan Psalter, play a crucial role in advancing the Calvinist cause in France—far more, some have argued, than the French translations of the Bible. Not surprisingly, the psalm translations got Marot into trouble with the Sorbonne, and he fled to that safe haven of French Protestants, Geneva. But Calvin's city also proved inhospitable; Marot was said to lack proper spiritual devotion. Ironically, the man who through his translations did so much to advance and buttress the Calvinist cause was forced to leave Geneva for Turin, where he died in 1544.

The publication of hymnals was paralleled by the publication of hymns in poster form, to allow the congregation the use of the new hymns. In 1531 an extensive hymnal was published by Michael Weisse, an Augustinian friar turned Bohemian Brother. His *Ein hübsch christlich gesang buchlen* (A Splendid Christian Song Book) included no fewer than 157 hymns, an indication (as uniformly noted by twentieth- and twenty-first-century hymnologists) of the superabundance of available material.

In short, the Reformation found splendid expression in the realm of music. Wherever the teachings of the Reformers found entrance, a singing church resulted. To be sure, Christians had been singing ever since the apostolic church, but what was now happening made the hymn a central part of worship. This is not surprising, for it was in worship that the liturgical life of the church allowed the new principle of the centrality of the local congregation to be directly applied. Vernacular hymns became the mainstay of worship, with important psychological consequences that can hardly be overestimated: the corporate singing of hymns was the most visible (and audible) manifestation of a new understanding of Christian community, for the laity was released from its passive role in the Mass and occupied a pivotal place in the liturgy of the service.

There were exceptions. Carlstadt compared singing in the service to "shrieking geese" and was adamantly hostile to it, while in Zurich music in worship was thought to be an abomination, and worship without congregational singing prevailed there until the end of the sixteenth century. On the whole, however, the Reformation was a singing movement. The Protestant hymn was the expression of the entire congregation, its integration with the service a manifestation of the concept of the priesthood of all believers. And because its lyrics were in the vernacular, all the people could understand what they were singing.

On the Catholic side, the notion of congregational singing was accepted with surprising speed. The difficulty lay elsewhere. The rich and ornate Italian musical tradition had gained not only increasing importance but also polyphonic sophistication in the course of the sixteenth century. It was precisely polyphony that caused controversy and disagreement in the Catholic Church, for it seemed to threaten the clarity of the sung text deemed so essential for the Mass. Not surprisingly, the Council of Trent discussed the matter at great length. The intervention of none other than composer Giovanni Pierluigi da Palestrina brought a favorable decision: the example of his textually clear settings convinced the Council that the problem lay not with polyphony as such but with muddy texts. This was more an issue of principle than of practicality. Polyphonic motets and Masses could not be sung by a congregation; the 3-, 4-, 5-, 6-, etc.-part harmony was too difficult and required not only verbal but also musical literacy. Sixteenth-century Masses and motets would *never* have been sung congregationally. Sacred polyphony was sung by trained choirs attached to a chapel or cathedral. Polyphony was used for the Ordinary of the Mass; the Proper was still monophonic. The only place congregational singing took place in the Catholic liturgy was in antiphonal responses, which were in the monophonic Proper. The reason congregations could sing the Protestant hymns was that they were monophonic, not polyphonic. The harmonizations with which we today are familiar, such as Bach's, came well after Luther.

CHURCH AND SOCIETY

In some sense, all Western society in the late medieval period was "Christian," the religious and the civic community, church and society, fused into a single *corpus christianum*, where (to cite one example) many legal issues in society were decided by canon law, the law of the church. Any effort at religious reform or renewal would therefore inevitably affect society, and that is exactly what happened in the sixteenth century. Christianity was not only characterized by dramatic theological and ecclesiastical developments; it also reached beyond the realm of ecclesiastical affairs and, in a variety of ways, affected society at large. This is not to suggest that the Reformation was the alpha and omega of the sixteenth century, or that nothing of significance beyond religion happened in that eventful century, or even that every religious happening, such as the theological controversies in German Lutheranism after Luther's death, was profoundly important. Many of that century's momentous events were related neither to the Reformation movement nor to Christianity at large. The European geographic discoveries, for example, took place altogether independently from any religious happenings, and in due time and season they exerted a forceful impact on Europeans quite apart from ecclesiastical affairs.

Moreover, the assertion that the effects of the Reformation reached into society does not mean that the relationship between the two was a one-way street—though some scholars, especially in the nineteenth century, have been disposed to see things that way, attributing to the Reformation all the blessings (or curses) of subsequent European history, from capitalism to indoor plumbing, or insisting that the Reformation as a religious phenomenon was the result of societal change. This has been argued by Marxist scholars, who have insissted on describing the Reformation as the "early bourgeois" revolution.

The interaction between religion and society was mutual. At the outset of the Reformation controversy a matrix of diverse social, political, and religious concerns merged into an overarching notion of reform in which religion was increasingly paramount, while other, secular concerns, though real, were subordinate. In turn, the notion of religious reform proved catalytic for all sorts of societal reform proposals and measures. Although the Reformation exerted a variety of forceful stimuli on society, causing change, realignment, and innovation, society exerted its own influence on religion, and the Reformation's religious turbulences in a way reflected society's. It seems inappropriate, therefore, to posit a causal priority for one or the other. Rather, both were present, somehow related, and somewhat influenced by one another.

Furthermore, beginning in the late fifteenth century European society had become increasingly restrictive, as all dissenters and those on the margins of society, be they beggars, lepers, heretics, or Jews, came to learn. Feeling threatened, civic and religious authorities undertook to subject their communities to increasingly restrictive canons of social discipline.[27] Illustrations abound. Earlier in the fifteenth century, prostitutes had been able to receive their place, however limited, in society, even in church. Late in that century, this began to change: formerly prostitutes could be buried in the church cemetery, but now this was no longer possible.[28] Even the European witch craze, which dominated so much of the sixteenth and early seventeenth centuries, must be seen in this context.

Moreover, it was one thing for the Protestant Reformers to pontificate on the social or economic issues of their day; it was quite another to effect actual change. In most places the Reformers were far removed from the centers of power. What they thought, felt, or wrote did not automatically have a societal impact. Any exploration of the Reformation's impact upon society must do more than list the Reformers' programmatic pronouncements.

In the early sixteenth century society was undergoing rapid social and economic change, with steep inflation and increased poverty. Although none of these problems

---

27. Such threat could easily be merely imagined but could also relate to the experience of the plague, the Hussite movement, as well as other developments seen as disturbing.

28. See, for example, *Randgruppen der spätmittelalterlichen Gesellschaft* (ed. Bernd-Ulrich Hergemöller; Warendorf: 2001).

was drastic enough to create a sense of societal crisis, as we have seen, certain issues (for example, the updating of ancient governance structures) did call for amelioration. Such was the case in the town of Mühlhausen, in central Germany, for example, where tension and turbulence were eventually resolved by the adoption of a "recess" that provided for the establishment of a new government.

From the very beginning of the Indulgences Controversy, the cause of religion intertwined with societal affairs. Even Luther's Ninety-five Theses touched, if only peripherally, on the financial implications of the sale of indulgences, and social issues became very much part of the agenda. Luther's *Open Letter to the Christian Nobility* of 1520 reiterated the traditional German grievances about the state of religion and society: the import of costly spices, the restriction of luxury, and the problem of university reform. Luther also wrote tracts on usury, *Vom Kaufhandel und Wucher* (Concerning Trading and Usury) and on the establishment of schools. Other writers likewise combined religious and societal concerns. Heinrich von Kettenbach's *Klage an den Adel des Reiches* emulated Luther's *Open Letter*. Ulrich von Hutten blamed German social problems on all things Roman and foreign. Johann Eberlin von Günzburg combined enthusiasm for Luther's religious message with a concern for German society's economic conditions. He wrote about high prices and juridical procedures, and in his *Bundtgenossen* pamphlets even sketched a picture of a model society he called "Wolfaria," where "things fare well" (*wohlfahren*).

The juxtaposition of religious and societal problems found graphic expression in the *Twelve Articles* of the south German peasants, of 1525. The *Articles* were hardly unique or new. Many of the Lutheran pamphlets of the preceding years had, like the Articles, advocated a renewal of both religion and society, insisting that both went hand in hand, the former indeed providing the momentum for the latter. The *Twelve Articles* summarized concrete economic and social concerns that had been already variously expressed, for example, the peasants' use of the "flowing waters" (rivers, brooks for fishing), the restriction of service to the lords, or the reduction of the "Todfall," an estate tax. At the same time, however, the *Articles* explicitly related these societal issues to the teachings of Scripture. The catastrophe of the Peasants' War, together with Luther's emotional denunciation of the peasants, gloomily disparaged the advocacy of reform in society. Indeed, after 1525 the Lutheran Reformers tended to be pointedly cautious in this regard. Luther's categorical pronouncement that the "gospel" and "politics" (in the Aristotelian sense) did not mix proved to be a leitmotif for the Lutheran tradition. The impact of the Lutheran ethos upon society was indirect at best, for it declared the public square to have its own autonomy, albeit "under God." In other words, there was no "Christian" politics or economics. Society was not "baptized" with Christian principles, for things Christian related only to the strictly religious issue of salvation brought by the Son of God. Luther and the Lutheran tradition sought to make clear, nonetheless, that society was under a divine mandate, one that was universally applicable to all people in all societies at all times.

This turn of events in Germany did not, however, deprive the Reformation movement of a direct societal thrust elsewhere in Europe. Other Reformers, notably Zwingli in Zurich, Bucer in Strassburg, and later Calvin in Geneva, propounded a notion of religious reform that explicitly encompassed societal concerns as well, and from an explicitly Christian orientation.

Among the many social pronouncements of the Protestant Reformers, two topics appeared more frequently than any other: the alleviation of the plight of the poor and the improvement of education. One writer put the two problems under one umbrella by noting that the "suppressinge of Abbeyes, Cloysters, Colleges, and Chauntries" would bring about a "better releve of the pore, the maintenaunce of learning, and setinge forth of goddes worde."

The first generation of Reformers consisted of visionaries who had caught a glimpse of what they took to be the true gospel and set out to translate that glimpse into practice. They were unperturbed by burdensome past experiences, unbothered by the complexity of practical problems, and undeterred by the sloth and nonchalance of human beings. They were convinced that once the true gospel was proclaimed, people would joyfully and determinedly cling to it. Once poverty had been recognized as a Christian problem, measures toward its alleviation would follow as a matter of course.

Traditionally, the care of the poor had been carried out by the monastic orders, but concerned civic authorities increasingly sought solutions of their own. The official orders for the poor promulgated in such cities as Nuremberg, Regensburg, or Ypres in the early 1520s, at a time when municipal self-consciousness was on the rise and the incipient Reformation movement was still of slight consequence, illustrate that concern for the alleviation of this social issue existed independently of the religious controversy. The poor were, after all, the city's poor. The foremost theoretician of poor relief in the early sixteenth century, the Spanish humanist Luis Vives, was anything but a Protestant reformer.

The Reformers' statements on the issue of poverty were numerous, but there was a kind of monotony to what they wrote. The Reformers sought to outdo one another with practical and theological pronouncements. They stood against poverty, hardly a revolutionary or startling position. Intriguingly, Luther's comment, in his *Sermon vom Wucher* (Sermon on Usury), that there should be no begging in Christendom was included among the condemned propositions in the papal censure of 1520. Other Reformers echoed the sentiment, precipitating a kind of literary-theological war on poverty. Importantly, the legal introduction of the Reformation in a community was ubiquitously accompanied by formal expression of concern for the problem. The newness of the Reformation orders for the poor lay in the dismissal of begging as a practice unworthy of a Christian community, in contrast to the traditional Catholic understanding, which saw begging, so extensively practiced by the mendicant orders, as a good work because it alleviated the plight of the poor.

As early as 1522, Carlstadt and Luther had a hand in drawing up an "order of the common chest" for the town of Wittenberg, the first of many such Protestant orders. The order sought to offer a comprehensive scheme for dealing with poverty. Begging students were to be expelled from town, and needy burghers were to be given loans from the "common chest." The term "chest" was to be taken quite literally: an actual chest with two separate locks and two separate keepers of keys contained the coins necessary for the support of the poor. The funds were to be derived from church property that had been confiscated.

These orders for the poor may be seen as vigorous expression of the Reformers' social concerns and the communal component of the Reformation. All the same, the Reformers' engagement was also simply part of a widespread societal concern. Communities became aware of the growing number of poor and destitute folk in their midst, and community leaders became convinced that amelioration was the task of the entire community and not merely that of the church. The Reformers shared both the concern and the solution, and in so doing they revived ancient Christian practices.

Protestant charities emphasized the role of the laity. Traditionally the Catholic Church had handled the problem on its own terms: it had the moral precepts and the resources. By the early sixteenth century it was obvious, however, that the church had failed to provide a satisfactory solution, for the poor continued to be very much with the communities and cities. The new self-consciousness of the increasingly important cities and towns merged with the conviction that the church had failed and the body politic needed to step in. A new sense of communal responsibility became evident. New solutions were needed—and were possible. The wealth of the church appeared to be the appropriate source for addressing various societal ills, because some of this wealth had been acquired through donations earmarked for a variety of good purposes now no longer considered spiritually legitimate (such as the endowment of private masses), while other purposes, such as endowments for the poor, were associated with stipulations (to pray for the souls of the donors) that the Reformers considered inappropriate. Although in the end the greedy hand of the powerful caused a good many theoretical schemes to be as words spoken in the wind, the Reformation "baptized" the various lay efforts by acknowledging that the civic community had a function to perform in this regard. The emphasis on lay activity with regard to relief for the poor was both the outgrowth of trends discernible in the late fifteenth century and a consequence of the repudiation of existing ecclesiastical structures. With the rejection of the Catholic ecclesiastical structure, only the laity were able to formulate the necessary policies and undertake changes. The Reformation's emphasis on the laity—what Luther called the "priesthood of all believers"—meshed with the need to find practical solutions to communal ills.

The Reformers' pronouncements fit with trends then in the air, notably the increased involvement of secular authorities in ecclesiastical affairs. In other words, Nuremberg might have issued an order for the poor in the 1520s even if the world had never heard of Luther. The influence of the Reformation was felt less in new practical proposals than in a new ethos: the notion of a proper disposition, a joyful, spontaneous service to one's neighbor.

With respect to the economic and social dimensions of society, the Protestant Reformation was indirectly revolutionary and directly conservative. Luther's concept of "vocation," which held that all professions and endeavors were spiritually blessed, was of immense significance. It made all work, no matter how lowly and mundane, if performed in the proper spirit, pleasing to God, and thereby undoubtedly released creative and stimulating forces. The significance of this idea lies in the fact that this secularization of vocation redirected much of the talent that previously had wound up in the ministerial profession and the church. In the early eighteenth century the first of the English physico-theologians, William Derham, was to calculate how much labor had been lost to European society through the monasteries.[29] His point was naive but well taken. Instead of disappearing behind the walls of the monasteries, men in Protestant lands strove to live their religious faith in the classroom or the court chamber. To use a modern term, they secularized the gospel. The impact, though beyond verification, must have been substantial.

On the level of economic and social considerations, however, the Reformers were conservative. Though they differed over the mandates of the gospel for economic and social realms, they hoped to explicate these mandates and, moreover, to express their distrust of the marketplace. Rather like their scholastic predecessors, the Reformers pondered endlessly such problems as just prices, the legitimacy of charging interest on loans, and poverty. They propounded new notions (Calvin, for example, rejected the economic dogma of the Middle Ages that money was sterile), but they sought to influence society by insisting on the rigorous ethical concepts of the gospel rather than by offering innovations in economic theory. If Luther had had his way, economic life would have continued as before.

The plain fact was that commerce and trade were no more receptive to Protestant ethical counsel than they had been to Catholic. Indeed, new empirical developments, such as generous supplies of silver from the New World and precious spices from Asia, the rise of chartered trading companies, and European expansion to the west and south of the Atlantic, not to mention dramatic population increases, also influenced the economic development of the sixteenth century. Real economic development and innovation of a capitalist sort did not come until the seventeenth century, by which time the Calvinist version of Protestantism had come to play an important role in economic affairs.

Undoubtedly, as Max Weber suggested a century ago, religious ethos has a way of influencing the economic endeavors and behavior of some individuals, even groups of individuals, and the idea that certain religious virtues, such as thrift, self-denial, or self-discipline, have tremendous economic relevance should not drive us to cynicism. To be sure, some individuals have pursued their economic endeavors with technical competence rather than religious faith, and the development of capitalism in Western Europe was influenced by a configuration of forces, of which religious ethos was only one. The Augustinian theologian Peter of Aragon provided an apt commentary on the whole matter toward the end of the sixteenth century when he confessed that "the marketplace has its own laws."[30]

The Reformers inveighed against sundry social abuses, such as prostitution, drinking, and luxury in dress, as Catholic authorities had done all along, though initially the Reformers showed little of the accommodating spirit in which the medieval church had often juxtaposed theological condemnation and practical tolerance—for example, as regards prostitution, which was condemned as a sin while brothels were tolerated. The intensity of the Reformers' strictures raises the suspicion that they recognized the colos-

---

29. William Derham, *Physico-theology: or, A demonstration of the being and attributes of God, from his works of creation. Being the substance of sixteen sermons preached in St. Mary-le-Bow-Church, London; at the Honourable Mr. Boyle's lectures, in the years 1711, and 1712. With large notes, and many curious observations* (London: 1727).

30. As quoted in W. Köhler, *Dogmengeschichte* (Zurich: 1951), 16.

sus against which they were struggling. Luther (witness his *Open Letter to the Christian Nobility*) had strong opinions concerning these matters but argued that the secular authorities (the "Christian" nobility) should formulate and execute the proper policies, with the church providing the ethos that inspired the authorities' actions. Accordingly, there were few formal pronouncements from Lutheran bodies, only proposals offered by individuals or governmental edicts, although the number of those was legion. It is hard to say, however, whether they were always issued (or received) with the religious ethos Luther desired; certainly they were not always successful.

Among the Calvinists the story was different, for there the moral mandates of the gospel were seen to apply directly in society. In Geneva, for example (though never in Wittenberg or Canterbury), certain activities, such as dancing or playing cards, were prohibited, and in place of the time-honored institution of the tavern Calvin substituted (unsuccessfully, as it turned out) a new one in which the beverages were weak and the theology strong. Calvinists elsewhere sought to do the same. They relied on governmental mandates, and wherever those were issued, the transparent religious impulse was clear.

Education likewise was heavily influenced by the religious controversy. In the late Middle Ages education was in the hands mainly of monastic orders that provided schooling for future church functionaries. It was not characterized by any effort to educate as many youth as possible; rather, it focused on a talented few. At the beginning of the controversy the Reformers had appeared to be hostile to education. Luther's attack on scholastic learning seemed to be a blunt repudiation of traditional learning. Had not the Reformers charged that the universities were teaching abominable errors, and that the study of Aristotle was despicable? Luther had asserted that the learned theologians and academicians were in error and that it was given to simple and unlearned men and women to understand the gospel. This was not an attack on education as such, however, but on a certain kind of education, sterile scholastic learning against which the humanists had inveighed.

Importantly, the Reformers argued that the education of the young was a matter of utmost importance to a community and therefore a civic, not an ecclesiastical, responsibility. Luther argued the case in his 1524 tract *An die Ratsherren aller Städte deutschen Landes* (To the Councillors of All German Cities That They Establish and Maintain Christian Schools), and this was the way it worked out in Protestant areas. The secular authorities, both in the cities and in the territories, embraced the notion of their responsibility in this regard, and the property of the Catholic Church, mainly that of the monastic orders, was routinely used to pay for the new educational efforts.

The Reformers zealously advocated the establishment of grammar or grade schools, for both boys and girls. Before too long the Catholic Church followed suit. The intention of both parties was not so much the advocacy of the liberal arts or what we might nowadays call "general education." It was education for a purpose: on the Protestant side, to enable people to read the Bible as sole source of religious authority; on the Catholic side, to enable people to understand the teachings of the church. Education was called upon to be the handmaiden of religion. The contribution of the Reformation to education was thus twofold. There was the insistence, put forward repeatedly, first, that schools be established, and second, the responsibility for educating the young be moved from the church to the state. This did not mean that the church abdicated its educational involvement. The ties between church and school remained strong, and the Peace of Westphalia of 1648, which ended the Thirty Years' War, explicitly stated that schools were *annexum religionis*, a part of religion.

Many of the Reformers were humanists, and they echoed humanist goals for the content of education. They stressed the study of languages (Latin for clarity of thought, Greek and Hebrew for understanding Scripture) and advocated textual criticism and literary analysis. At the same time they emphasized the value of historical studies. The motivation for these ancillary areas of study was that they provided the basis for theological education and understanding (along lines congenial to Protestant thought). The training of teachers, lawyers, and doctors was a corollary concern.

Protestant educational efforts enjoyed the advantage of freedom from the weight of tradition. The Reformers were able to explore new venues. In particular, although the purpose of education was defined rather narrowly, the practical initiatives undertaken in its behalf were much broader. The Nuremberg reformer Andreas Osiander contributed a preface to Nikolaus Copernicus's famous work, *The Revolutions of the Heavenly Bodies*, in which he defended the scientist's right to offer hypotheses. In part this attitude found its explanation in Protestant self-confidence, the conviction that all pursuit of truth would confirm rather than deny religious truth. Of course, medieval scholastics, such as Thomas Aquinas, would have agreed with this assertion, but sixteenth-century Catholicism showed itself utterly closed, as for example the promulgation of the *Index of Prohibited Books* makes clear.

More important may have been a kind of pragmatic self-limitation on the part of those Protestants who were in positions to exercise power. Protestantism, after all, was a divided house and nowhere possessed Catholicism's universal stature. The condemnation of Galileo by a Saxon consistory would have looked rather foolish (and would have been ineffectual besides) next to the weighty verdict of the Roman curia. The divisions of Protestantism made it relatively congenial to scientific endeavor.

In the arts, Calvinist austerity cast a shadow over whatever creative exuberance the new faith generated. In the centuries of Christian experience, religious artistic endeavor was always related to the liturgical life of the church—intended to embellish, glorify, suggest, and even teach. The complexity of the late Gothic style took this momentum to its extreme. Calvinist churches, following Zwingli's notions, became exemplars of the idea that art was unnecessary. Whitewashed and plain, devoid of ornamentation and decorations, they were the consequence above all of a literal application of the Old Testament proscription of graven images. Wherever this temperament made its appearance—in Zurich, Geneva, or England—treasured works of art were destroyed, but no new creative forces were released. The twenty-first-century visitor to English cathedrals still encounters the painful destruction wrought by the Henrician and Edwardian Reformations, from the shrine of St. Thomas à Becket at Canterbury to the decapitated statues of saints at Ely Cathedral. The same had happened on the Continent—in Wittenberg, Münster, and Zurich, for example—and each time the men who attacked the churches with paintbrush and hammer saw not precious works of art, but idolatry; not spirituality embodied in stone or canvas, but blasphemy to be obliterated.

The Calvinist tradition seems to have had a greater propensity for such confrontations. Both Lutheran and Anglican traditions (except, as noted, the Puritan offspring of Anglicanism) content to accept the "images" in and around churches as either neutral ornamentation or as acceptable devotional aids. But the issue of images raised a much more profound problem. The Reformation argued the centrality of the written Word. It therefore called for and required literacy: the ability to take the Scriptures and read. What had been so characteristic of medieval houses of worship—the rich ornamentation of Gothic churches, their ubiquitous symbolism, their stained-glass windows depicting salvation history from the garden of Eden to Armageddon, their stone portrayals of the Last Judgment—so needful when few men and even fewer women were able to read, became unnecessary. A demographic and societal revolution was under way. The statues and paintings and stained-glass windows, aimed at the illiterate as graphic instructions in faith, were no longer needed. A new, self-confident, and self-conscious class was emerging, and it was literate, able to concentrate on the text. A new theological principle meshed harmoniously with a new practical reality.

That the Reformation had cultural consequences needs little verification. The difficult question pertains to their extent and significance. The Reformation instilled a new ethos into society: the notion of direct, personal responsibility; the concept of personal (and corporate) election; the postulate of personal discipline; and the claim of the autonomy of secular authorities. However, this is neither to suggest that such notions were absent before the Reformation nor to argue that the simple fact of their propagation proves their practical influence.

The question of the cultural consequences of the Reformation, in the final analysis, raises the question of the role of ideas in human affairs. Religious ideas were present in the sixteenth century, forceful, daring, revolutionary ideas, though not all that had the label was really religious; nor did authentic religious ideas always appear in pristine form. But they made their impact within Protestant churches and within society, and thereby helped transform Western civilization.

The various societal initiatives triggered by the Reformation remained tradition bound in one crucial and sad respect: the European witch hunts. This sordid and complicated phenomenon had long-standing antecedents but acquired a new dynamic in the late fifteenth century with the publication in 1486 of the *Malleus maleficarum* (Witch Hammer). Meant as a comprehensive reference manual on magic, good and evil, the book described the world of witches in graphic language. The broader theological context of the witch hunts, however, was offered in a bull of Pope Innocent VIII that summarized the church's case against witches. Although the *Malleus maleficarum* had been a private expression of two theologians, the papal bull was the official pronouncement:

> Many persons of both sexes, unmindful of their own salvation and straying from the Catholic faith, have abandoned themselves to devils, incubi and succubi, and by their incantations, spells, conjurations, and other accursed charms and crafts, enormities and horrid offenses, have slain infants yet in the mother's womb, as also the offspring of cattle, have blasted the produce of the earth, the grapes of the vine, the fruits of the trees, nay, men and women, beasts of burden, herd beasts, as well as animals of other kinds, vineyards, orchards, meadows, pastureland, corn, wheat, and all other cereals; these wretches furthermore afflict

and torment men and women, beasts of burden, herd beasts, as well as animals of other kinds, with terrible and piteous pains and sore diseases, both internal and external; they hinder men from performing the sexual act and women from conceiving, whence husbands cannot know their wives nor wives receive their husbands; over and above this, they blasphemously renounce the faith.

These sentences demonstrate that more was at issue than deviation from the true faith; they clearly express notions of a society gone awry and profoundly threatened. All possible means of defense had to be mustered. The bull underscored the church's position that the renunciation of the faith went hand in hand with personal and societal evil, and because it did not restrict itself to description but also offered policy guidelines on how to deal with this threat, it suggests once more that a society becomes a persecuting society whenever it feels itself under attack. Even later, when the Protestant Reformers were called upon to render opinion and judgment about the reality of a witches' world, they faithfully echoed what society had come to affirm and believe.

Thus began the European witch hunts in the late fifteenth century. By the time they ended, an interminably long two centuries later, they had claimed a horrifying number of victims—young and old, rich and poor, beautiful and ugly, loathed and respected by their neighbors. Although a few were male, the overwhelming majority were female, indicating that, no matter how serious was the notion of a threatened society turning to persecution, long-standing misogynist sentiment also played a significant role.

THE REFORMATION AND WOMEN

Women's place in the historical course of events has had a way of being ignored, and women's voices have often been forgotten. Recent historiographical developments have sought to redress these omissions, and in this regard the Reformation is in a way a superb laboratory, for the period allows a keen insight into the presence and absence of women in the course of its events.

The traditional Christian view of woman, embraced as normative by medieval society, was ambiguous. It spoke appreciatively as well as skeptically of women, glowingly as well as negatively, an ambivalence strikingly expressed by an early-seventeenth-century writer who remarked that "woman is a stinking rose, a pleasing wound, a sweete poyson, a bitter sweete, a delightful disease, a pleasant punishment, a flattering death." In the late fifteenth century, the *Malleus maleficarum* had been more categorically one-sided, describing women as "without faith" and as the natural embodiment of witches. The European witch craze victimized women for over a century with a determination worthy of a nobler cause.

On another level, however, the European witch craze accentuated a long-standing and deep-seated ambivalence about women. The Christian tradition, in a precarious paradox, affirmed two exemplars of womanhood, Eve and Mary. The biblical story of Eve afforded ever new possibilities for establishing woman's loathsome character: she had been formed from the side of man; she had been created last; above all, she had yielded to the serpent. According to biblical tradition, the apostle Paul had insisted that women were to be subject to their husbands and commanded them to be silent in church. But then there was the paradigm of Mary, chosen to bear the Son of God, honored as Mother of God. The purity of her soul and the strength of her faith, both so superbly expressed in the Magnificat, made her increasingly a figure of salvation history. No wonder that in many churches her iconographic presence overshadowed that of her son. The theological issue was the notion of original sin, which forced theologians to account for the transmission of sin from one generation to the next, with the sexual act the obvious means. That act seemed particularly to indict women, who were viewed as more promiscuous than men, as could be gleaned from the story of Adam and Eve.

Accordingly, the church espoused the ideal of virginity and permanent chastity, which meant that the sexual and reproductive role of women was deemed inferior. The church's attitude also reflected a particular understanding of the meaning of femininity. Theologians distinguished the physical, sexual side of people on the one hand from the spiritual, intellectual side on the other, denouncing the former with stereotyped vehemence while commending the latter. Women religious, who wished to live a perfect spiritual life, committed themselves to poverty, obedience, and chastity— three vows indicating a pointed rejection of the physical. Nuns hid their hair (described by the apostle Paul as the "glory" of women), even had it shorn, and their monastic habits were devoid of all feminine trappings. The powerful sway of the Song of Songs, whose inclusion in the Bible provoked periodic expressions of unease, found expression in Christian interpretation in the notion of a spiritual union of the believer with the bridegroom, Christ. As the writings of female medieval mystics suggest, this understanding was bound to be attractive for women. The disparagement of the body and thereby of sexuality had profound and far-reaching ramifications.

A deep gulf existed between the natural and the spiritual life. The men and women who sought to live the perfect spiritual life were instructed that it consisted of a daily round of unceasing meditation, worship, and prayer. Attention paid by women to beauty and appearance, to motherhood or to being a homemaker, was seen as unbecoming to their spiritual destiny. The ideal of virginity, though applicable to men and women alike, came to be more significantly identified with women, probably because of the biblical story of Adam and Eve, because the theologians were male, and because lapses from the ideal of chastity were more easily established for women.

It is appropriate to begin an account of the impact on women of the sixteenth-century Protestant Reformation with reflections on the role of women in late medieval religion and society because whatever new insights the Reformation formulated have to be seen in continuity with traditional notions and understandings. The new emerged from the old. At the same time, the discovery of gender as a valid and important category of historical examination does not negate the continued importance of traditional categories, such as social standing or education.

In the early stages of the Reformation controversy a host of issues, notions, and judgments about women surfaced, and a plethora of scholarly publications has recently sought to throw light on the place women occupied in sixteenth-century thought and action. This abundance of scholarly writings suggests that women—generally relegated to the status of silent partners in the course of events—played an important public role in the Reformation. Women became involved in the public debate about the new faith because they, like men, had to make a decision either for or against the new gospel. Some women became ardent and even public partisans of the new faith. Some did so through personal activism, exhibiting qualities not frequently found in women in that male-oriented age. Other women, such as Katherina Zell, Argula von Grumbach, or Ursula von Münsterberg, were literary advocates for the reform and impressed all with their biblical literacy. An uncommonly high number of the sixteenth-century martyrs burned at the stake or drowned were women, Anne Askew in England and the Anabaptist martyr Elisabeth, for example, as the Anabaptist *Martyrs' Mirror* makes quite evident. In the sixteenth- and seventeenth-century martyrologies, such as those of Rabus, Crespin, and van Braght, the percentage of female martyrs is as high as 30 percent; and although that number may not seem striking, one must take into account once more that women in those days were generally condemned to silence. John Foxe, in the later editions of his *Acts and Monuments*, steadily increased the accounts of women martyrs.

For the proponents of the old faith, this public role truly was the abomination of abominations. As far as the early Catholic protagonists of the controversy were concerned, the perversity of the Reformers' message was manifested in the fact that women felt called to proclaim the new gospel. When Anne Askew was interrogated in a first examination, she was chided for "uttering the Scriptures," and it was pointed out to her that "S. Paul (he said) forbade women to speak or to talk of the word of God. I answered him, that I knew Paul's meanyng so well as he, which is, i. Corinthiorum 11:22 that a woman ought not to speak in the congregation by the way of teaching."[31] The opposition to Anne's public testimonies to the new evangelical faith suggests that Catholics were quite aware of the important place of women in the Reformation movement.

As was the case with the central messages of the Christian faith, the affirmations of the sixteenth-century Protestant Reformers were in themselves gender neutral. The notions of justification by faith alone and of the sole authority of Scripture had no gender-specific aspect. Even so, women had to make a decision about staying with the old church or converting to the new one. To be sure, in many cases that decision was formally made for them by husbands or fathers, but their spiritual comfort (or lack thereof) in the new evangelical service was theirs and theirs alone.

Why, then, did the message of the Reformation appeal to women? One answer is simple: women embraced the Reformation message for the same reasons as men did. Yet, strikingly, the limited evidence we have from those notoriously unreliable sixteenth-century statistics suggests that women in particular seem to have been attracted to the Reformation message. For example, a disproportionately large number of women lived in Anabaptist Münster, both among the Münster burghers who stayed in the city after the Anabaptists had gained control and also among the refugees who flocked there from places in northwest Germany upon hearing that the "new Jerusalem" had been established in the city.

At the same time, however, two major Reformation affirmations, held across the board by all Reformers, called into question in principle the role and place of women

31. *The Examination of Anne Askew* (ed. Elaine V. Bailin; New York: 1996), 35ff.

in church and society. One was Luther's dictum of the priesthood of all believers, enunciated in 1520, which repudiated the traditional dichotomy between priests and laity. His insistence that all Christians were priests included in principle women no less than men: "All Christian men are priests, even as all Christian women are priestesses."[32] Luther underscored the universality of his notion when he talked about the ministerial office. The foremost criterion for such office was the "call" by the congregation— and that, in principle, following Luther's reasoning, extended to a woman no less than a man. Accordingly, Luther interpreted the apostle Paul's dictum about women keeping silent in the churches not in terms of a commandment, but rather in terms of women's physical inability to perform the responsibilities of the ministerial office.[33] Women were said not to have the vigorous voice needed for proper preaching, as their physiology revealed. It goes without saying that deeply rooted patriarchical notions sustained Luther's curtailment of women's role in the congregation and the pulpit, but assuredly the categorical rejection of women for the ministerial office had been abrogated. Luther was much concerned about the education of the young, but he clearly did not envision education as a means to allow women to obtain the qualifications needed to stand in the pulpit. Indeed, despite biblical precedent, he had little use for female rulers.[34] At issue was his concern for a structured society, in which everyone had an assigned place. For women, that was the place of wife and mother.

This new theme found expression in the church orders promulgated wherever the Reformation understanding of the Christian faith became official. Johannes Bugenhagen's several church orders, such as that of Lübeck in 1531, explicitly acknowledged the role and place of women in the church. Midwives, for example, were authorized to baptize, if only in emergencies, and women teachers were allowed to expound Scripture.

A second relevant affirmation was the Reformation insistence on the sacredness of human endeavors. Luther had voiced this notion rather early in the controversy. Even the most menial of human undertakings (in his tract *Married Life*, of 1522, Luther used the illustration of changing a baby's dirty diaper) became a God-pleasing work, filled with spiritual meaning. The theological presupposition was that God had instituted societal "orders" or "structures" so as to allow all humans to live in peace and harmony. Thus rulers were necessary in society, as were teachers, and peasants, and butchers, and bakers, and candlestick makers. All their work had divine approval— as long as it was carried out in the conviction that it served the common good. For women, deprived of any public role (as were, of course, most men) and confined to kitchen and hearth, this liberating word meant that their mundane chores of housekeeping and childrearing were spiritually meaningful. This insistence on the spiritual worth of ordinary work was reinforced by the Reformers' affirmation that human sexuality was a divine gift and that for most men and women chastity was neither possible nor, in fact, desirable. Pregnancy, far from another "fall," was part of the divine order of things that wanted men and women to multiply and populate the earth.

---

32. WA 6:370. A penetrating discussion of Luther's concept is found in Harald Goertz, *Allgemeines Priestertum und Ordiniertes Amt bei Luther* (Marburg: 1997), especially 185ff.

33. WA 8:497, "weyl eynem man viel mehr zu reden eygent" ("because a man is more capable of speaking").

34. WA 50:633, "weyber kein regiment können" ("women cannot rule").

The Protestant Reformers' first reaction to the traditional view of women and marriage was their vehement indictment of clerical celibacy. Luther's treatise *Married Life* expounded, in classical fashion, the Reformation position: marriage is ordained by God, and thus a good. The disparagement of women and marriage—for Luther the two went hand in hand—was a pagan principle that should be rejected: "There are many pagan books which treat of nothing but the depravity of womankind and the unhappiness of the estate of marriage, such that some have thought that even if Wisdom itself were a woman one should not marry." The polemic was specifically directed against the traditional notion of clerical celibacy; in order to counter it, the Reformers had to paint a broad picture of the values of marriage and womanhood. The implications went beyond the narrow issue of the marriage of clerics. Tyndale put it rather pointedly: "Why hath God geven us these membres? Why these pryckes and provocations? Why hath he added the power of begettynge, if bachelorshyp be taken for a praise?"

The affirmation of marriage entailed the acknowledgment of the physical side of men and women. Sex was seen as a divine gift, no more, though also no less, under the curse of humanity's fall than the rest of creation. Thus the "physical" and the "natural" received a striking affirmation. Yet sex was seen as a theological rather than a physiological problem: although writers reflected on its significance at the time of creation or the implications of the Fall, when it came to the present their voices became remarkably muted.

The Reformers' affirmation of the "natural," "physical" dimension of existence was reinforced by their insistence that all human endeavors have a positive good. Indeed, these two facets were but the two sides of the same fundamental purview. Although the affirmation of sexuality pertained to men and women alike, the Protestant notion of vocation had a special applicability to women in that women's daily round of chores received uncommon appreciation. Luther summed it up by saying, "If the wife is honorable, virtuous, and pious, she shares in all the cares, endeavors, duties, and functions of her husband. With this end in view, she was created in the beginning; and for this reason she is called woman, or a 'she-man'." Expounding the creation narrative of the book of Genesis, Luther observed that "in the household the wife is a partner in the management and has a common interest in the children and the property." Luther emphatically affirmed the sanctity of the body and the spirituality of the ordinary life.

The English reformer Miles Coverdale, in a tract entitled *The Christian State of Matrimony*, echoed these themes. The superiority of man was for him beyond question. The proof text was the account in Genesis of Eve's creation: "Yet was she not made of the head; for the husband is the head and Maister of the wyfe . . . but even out of thy side, as one that is set next unto man, to be his helpe and companion." Husband and wife were to respect each other mutually: "The one ought to be an eye, eare, mouth, hand, and foote to the other. In trouble the one must be the comfort of the other." In practice, however, man's superiority entailed a division of functions. Woman was subordinate to man, though she occupied her own sphere of responsibility: "Whatsoever is to be done without the home, that belongeth to the man, and the woman to study for things within to be done."

Of course, few people in the sixteenth century enjoyed what we call "vertical mobility"; most men were as much tied to their station without any ability to move, as were women. There was little freedom for men, very little for women. Not much changed with the Reformation. What changed, and changed dramatically, was that chores that had theretofore been afforded only carefully circumscribed spiritual meaning, as for example in St. Benedict's Rule, were now exalted as spiritually on the same level as good works. This liberation from the traditional Catholic value system came at a price. It was not immediately obvious, for the Reformation message of the sacred vocation of all individuals seemed to overshadow everything else.

Although women's everyday work was thus given spiritual meaning, the Reformation repudiation of monasticism closed an avenue of practical and spiritual importance that had been open to women. The monastic ideal and practice had offered this opportunity to women both before and after the sixteenth century, making the history of Catholic thought and reflection unthinkable without such figures as Julian of Norwich, Hildegard of Bingen, or Teresa of Ávila, not to mention all the women religious who as teachers, nurses, and counselors helped make the Catholic Church and about whom we know far more than about the simple Catholic women in the pews. The Catholic Church astutely acknowledged this importance when it named Teresa a doctor of the church and canonized her at the same time as Ignatius of Loyola.

It should not come as a surprise that the religious life had faithful and loyal adherents, especially among nuns, despite the Reformers' assaults and attacks. Even though nuns had to battle the misconceptions that theirs were lives of leisure and that their religious houses were brothels, the resistance put up when the houses were to be shut down is most remarkable. Perhaps gender roles offer here at least a partial explanation. The Reformation denunciation of the monastic life meant for monks that they could leave the monastery, get married, and somewhere find a position as pastor. Nuns had no alternatives other than to marry. Moreover, the Reformation had raised some fundamental issues: Was God better served in a family or in the religious life? Should the family community or the monastic community, physical or spiritual motherhood, have priority? Thus Katharina Ebner, twenty years of age, told her mother, who had come to take her from the Nuremberg convent of St. Clare, "You are my mother according to the flesh, but not according to my spirit, for you did not give me my soul, and therefore I am not obligated to be obedient to you in matters pertaining to my soul."[35]

In Nuremberg and Braunschweig, as well as other places, some nuns insisted that they wished to be true to their vows; they were quiet witnesses to a piety with a thousand-year history. In Geneva fistfights and near-riots occurred between nuns and protagonists of the Reformation. Caritas Pirckheimer, abbess of the convent of St. Clare in Nuremberg, valiantly opposed the efforts of both the city council and the reformer Andreas Osiander, despite the pleas of the nuns to be left alone to live their vows, to shut down her convent.

There was to be no such parallel on the Protestant side, certainly not after the initial wave of sturm und drang had passed. The Protestant churches were run by men, except that early on in Anabaptist conventicles some women played leadership roles.[36]

35. Josef Pfanner, *Die Denkwürdigkeiten der Caritas Pirckheimer* (Landshut: 1962), 80.
36. Marion Kobelt-Groch, *Aufsässige Töchter Gottes. Fraven im Bauernkrieg und in den Täuferbewegungen* (Frankfurt: 1993).

Later, in the seventeenth century, there were sporadic instances of active female leadership roles in religious affairs, among the followers of George Fox, for example, and then, later in the eighteenth century, on the Continent in the Pietist *collegia* or in Britain among the followers of John Wesley. But these were exceptions to the rule that could be found at times of nascent religious movements.

The Reformers were far from proclaiming notions of equality between men and women, except, as we saw, in the spiritual realm; women were declared to be the equals of men only there and in the domestic sphere, where—again in the pronouncements of the Reformers—they exercised their own particular authority.

In recent years some scholars have argued that the coming of the Reformation hardly constituted a great divide, while others have argued that what was new should hardly be viewed in a positive light.[37] Moreover, how (and whether) the ideals of the Reformers were translated into practice is quite another question. Their words about the virtuous woman or woman's positive role in the domestic sphere did not necessarily translate into action. What happened in the home, the marketplace—the bedroom—was a different matter. We are thus left with the question of the effectiveness of the new ideals, that is, how much practical change did occur in the self-understanding and role of women as the result of the Reformation. The evidence for actual change is hard to come by. We have correspondence between spouses, and between parents and children, that bespeaks both tenderness and an awareness of the underlying Christian assumptions of marriage and family.[38]

Even where change can be observed, the sources remain in doubt. Indeed, there were other forces and developments in the early sixteenth century that antedated the changes in religion and may well have been the more fundamental causes of change. The artistic evidence is a case in point. Beginning in the late fifteenth century artists rediscovered woman in full bodily form, much like the ancients. To speak more precisely, artists discovered the female figure, for woman, needless to say, had been known to artists all along. But heretofore she had been ethereal and spiritual, an otherworldly beauty evoking few emotions. The Virgin Mary epitomized the spiritual qualities of womanhood.

Nude female (and male) figures were not absent from art before the sixteenth century, but they lacked all naturalism. There is an air of innocence about Botticelli's *Birth of Venus* or *Primavera*, an evident hesitancy to depict the female body in physical detail. Marsilio Ficino, Botticelli's patron, found that Venus's "eyes [are] Dignity and Magnanimity, her hands Liberality and Magnificence, her feet Comeliness and Modesty. The whole, then, is Temperance and Honesty, Charm and Splendor." Such words clad an aesthetic notion of woman, a philosophical idea of beauty that harmonized with the theologians' understanding. Even Albrecht Dürer's 1504 etching *Adam and Eve* conveys this ethereal air, especially when compared, for example, with Jan van Mabuse's *Adam and Eve* or Lucas Cranach's *Venus and Amor*.

---

37. For example, Judith Bennett, "Medieval Women, Modern Women: Across the Great Divide," in *Culture and History 1350–1600: Essays in English Communities, Identities, and Writing* (ed. David Aers; London: 1992), 147–75.

38. For example, Steven E. Ozment, *Flesh and Spirit: Private Life in Early Modern Germany* (New York: 1999).

The artistic perception of women and also men changed. Even a novice in the finer points of sixteenth-century art will note that the paintings of such artists as Cesare de Sesto, Giorgione, or Titian convey noticeable differences from the asceticism of the medieval period: the subject matter was frequently not only no longer religious, but secular and even pagan; the women were depicted nude.

Thus Cesare de Sesto's *Leda*, while still a figure from classical mythology, is a woman of flesh and blood. Geometric harmony disappeared and voluptuousness took its place. Titian's nudes, notably his *Danae* and *Venus and the Organ Player*, expressed the same. Even Lucas Cranach's *Judgment of Paris* conveyed a new touch. These painters and many others depicted a new kind of woman in whom ethereal or spiritual beauty gave way to earthiness and even sensuousness.

The evidence is similar in the realm of literature in that the very quantity of publications of the time intimates the lure of the subject. Beyond doubt, the proper understanding and appreciation of woman must have been prominent in many minds, as is signified by such names as Vives (*A Very Fruitful and Pleasant Booke Called the Instruction of Christian Woman*) or John Aylmer (*An Harborough for Faithful Subjects*), or such titles as *Of the Beauty of Women*, *The Prayse of All Women*, *A Woman's Worth*, and *A Lyttel Treatyse of the Beaute of Women*. Of course, these books stand in continuity with the medieval courtly-love literature, but at the same time they indicate the interest of the sixteenth century in the topic of women.[39]

The ferment in the sixteenth century was at once theological, artistic, and literary. A new concept of womanhood was formulated not merely by Protestant theologians; it occurred in society at large as well. Whether these conceptual changes translated into new roles actually played by women in home and society is difficult to say. Probably not, apart from the social changes that sooner or later were to affect women as well, such as literacy. If women were happier or more frustrated, less frequently beaten by their husbands or more, more aware of their femininity or humanity or less, given more say in domestic finances and logistics or less, cannot be ascertained from this distance. One suspects that the actual roles of women hardly changed—wife beating may have been more than an occasional exercise of male prerogatives, childbirth continued to be thought to make women "unclean," and the widespread witch craze in early modern Europe exemplified a ruthlessly cruel anti-woman sentiment. None of these situations could have continued or developed without the concomitant continuation of the traditional notions concerning woman.

That the divine order ordained the subordination of woman, just as it ordained the subordination of some men to others; that woman was particularly susceptible to the temptations of the flesh; that her virtues were few and her faults many; that her destiny lay in the domestic sphere—all this can be widely read in sixteenth-century literature, both religious and secular. The Protestant Reformation, while not fundamentally challenging this worldview, sought to modify it, subtly, one suspects, in order to demonstrate here too the new insights of the movement of reform.

---

39. Axel Erdmann, *My Gracious Silence: Women in the Mirror of Sixteenth Century Printing in Western Europe* (Luzern: 1999).

The Reformers asserted that the claimed inferiority of women meant a difference in function: the man outside the home, the woman within. Alongside such difference in function stood a different definition of the meaning of womanhood. Woman was pulled down to earth, so to speak. She was told that she should be proud of her vocation, her calling, in *Kirche, Küche, und Kinder* (church, kitchen, and children). Subsequent decades and centuries would show that even this marginally positive view was not without its serious problems, especially once social and economic mobility began increasingly to affect men.

POLITICS

There can be no doubt: without the intervention of the political authorities, the Reformation movement would not have been formally established. This reality must not be taken to reflect negatively on the power of the ideas in the Reformation. Ideas have their own persuasiveness; once generated and propounded, external forces can do little to affect their course. Indeed, history is a rich laboratory of ideas, generated, endorsed, rejected, suppressed, imposed.

Nor do ideas need a formal organizational or institutional support for their effectiveness; the European Enlightenment is splendid proof that they do not. Yet though the ideas propounded by the Protestant Reformers went their own unfettered way in the sixteenth century, gaining approval as well as disapproval, the organizational consolidation of the Reformation movement was something else. Here the support of the governmental authorities was crucial. Because the theological disputes had quickly fastened onto issues of practical churchmanship, the secular authorities, whether territorial rulers or city councils, had to go on record as either rejecting or endorsing the formal changes called for by the new Reformation ideas. Behind this function of secular government (which caused intermittent uneasiness on the part of the Catholic hierarchy) lay the medieval notion of a Christian society, in which government played an important, albeit not always crisply defined role in ecclesiastical affairs and where church and state were but two sides of the same coin. Change in the one sphere, therefore, had to be supported, or rejected, by the other.

In the sixteenth century a favorable governmental decision formalized the organizational success of the movement of reform, whereas a negative one meant failure. However, we must be careful not to attribute such decisions to crude power politics or idiosyncratic whim. Genuine religious commitment undoubtedly determined many decisions for or against the new faith. Additional forces were always at work as well, such as popular support for religious change, fiscal exigency, or lust for power. These factors converged to provide the context for decisions favoring or opposing formal ecclesiastical change.

Emperor Charles V is a splendid illustration of this convergence. Deeply influenced by the notions of Erasmus, Charles was a loyal Catholic, determined to resolve the religious conflict in a way that would safeguard the honor and integrity of the Catholic Church and deal with heresy the way good Catholics did. By background, conviction, and temperament Charles was destined to be a forceful guardian of

Catholic truth. By the same token, more than most other key figures Charles aided the spread of the Reformation in Germany, and thereby in the rest of Europe as well. Charles was also consumed by universal dynastic interests that intermittently assumed priority over matters of religion in Germany. During the thirty-five years of his rule as emperor, Charles spent less than half a decade in Germany; during the first two decades, he was in Germany less than three years. To be sure, at the time Charles had good and cogent reasons for his absences. In 1521, and then again in 1530, the religious controversy seemed to have been brought under control, while conditions in his hereditary lands were anything but tranquil and called for his attention. Moreover, though Charles's direct power in the empire was limited, his voice counted. More than anybody else, he personified efforts to resolve the controversy along lines congenial to the Catholic faith. Even if his presence in Germany, in the end, would not have altered events, his absence assured that they followed the course they did.

Elector Frederick the Wise of Saxony also comes to mind, for without his involvement Luther would have suffered the routine fate of a convicted heretic. Had it not been for Frederick's hand, Luther would not have survived the first years of controversy, and one may wonder whether a Reformation movement would even have come about. Frederick protected Luther by insisting, in 1518, that he be examined in Germany rather than in Rome; by not recognizing, in 1520, the authority of the bull *Exsurge Domine*; by demanding, in 1521, that Luther be given a hearing before the German diet; and by hiding Luther at the Wartburg. Surely, this is an impressive string of actions. To this day scholars disagree about Frederick's motivation, for there is no evidence to suggest that he was a partisan of Luther's religious cause. One suspects that Frederick, as noted earlier, had two intertwining considerations: to make sure that the emperor understood the importance of the power and authority of the territorial rulers, making the Luther affair an issue of governance in the empire, and to make sure that fundamental fairness governed the church's query of Luther's orthodoxy.

Charles and Frederick also personified the complex administrative structure of the empire, with its deep tensions between imperial and territorial interests—over which Charles stumbled fatefully when, after his victory in the war against the League of Schmalkald, he sought to redress these tensions in favor of imperial power. This complexity proved to be the decisive factor in the ultimate success of the Reformation movement. The ineffectiveness of the *Reichsregiment*, which was to function as the central authority during the emperor's absence from Germany, is a good illustration. Between 1522 and 1524 its members discussed at length how to suppress the Lutheran heresy, but they got lost in the quagmire of cross-purposes, which—compounded with their lack of real power—allowed no determined and unified action, indeed no action of any kind other than policy pronouncements.

The Ottoman Empire was a factor of enormous political importance, another indication of the complex interweaving of religious and political forces that impinged on the course of events. From the second decade of the century onward, the specter of a Turkish attack upon central Europe was real, and the powerful in Europe, led by pope and emperor, sought for ways to prepare for such a possible onslaught. Pamphlets on the Turkish threat were published galore during this time, and they expressed the anxiety prevalent in Europe. No agreement prevailed, however, on whether the threat was real or, if so, on how to deal with it. The obvious answer was to strengthen the armed defenses, but precisely that scenario created a problem: it required financial support. Because a possible Turkish attack threatened all of Europe, support for raising an army seemed to call for the common effort of all of Christendom. But only Austrian and German lands were within immediate reach of a Turkish attack, and countries farther from the sound of the hoofs of the Ottoman forces saw little urgency in the threat. In Germany the emperor depended on the territorial rulers to contribute financially to the cause, but he ran directly into long-standing disputes over his and their respective powers and authority. After 1520 the unresolved controversy in Christendom aggravated these tensions.

Not surprisingly, the estates with Lutheran sympathies quickly discovered that the Ottoman threat offered a splendid opportunity for religious blackmail. At the diet at Speyer, in 1529, these estates announced that they would provide no financial assistance against the Turks unless the religious controversy was satisfactorily solved. What they meant, of course, was solved to their particular satisfaction. The Catholic estates balked. On that particular occasion the Lutheran strategy of "no aid without religious concessions" was ignored, for in the end the Lutheran estates agreed to provide support despite the lack of a favorable religious settlement. But the basic strategy, having now been articulated, proved to be the decisive element in the years that followed. As matters turned out, the Protestants scored their greatest legal achievements in the context of acute Turkish threats: in 1532, in the late 1530s, and finally the early 1550s. In each instance they were able to consolidate their ecclesiastical achievements because they shrewdly took advantage of the emperor's political predicament.

Of course, the Protestants had not manufactured the Turkish threat (it was preexistent), but they certainly exploited it. The Catholic estates, which monotonously insisted that the Turkish and the religious problems were unconnected, inadvertently contributed to the precarious situation by refusing to supply sufficient financial and military aid against the Turks to render Protestant assistance superfluous. Had they been willing to reach deeper into their pockets, the Protestant strategy would not have worked. Their parsimoniousness made money as much of an issue as religion, however; so the Protestant contribution was all the more necessary.

Religion and politics converged in the Reformation in yet another way, once more accruing decisive benefit to the Protestants. After the German Peasants' War, the cause of the Reformation in Germany was tied to an alliance established to assure that the Catholics would not use military means to solve a religious problem. Landgrave Philip of Hesse first suggested that the new faith, that is, the new forms of worship and belief, would need to be safeguarded by military strength. He proposed an alliance that (thanks to his persistence) eventually led to the formation of the League of Schmalkald. There can be little doubt that the league grew out of the awareness that force might be the means by which Catholics would subdue the Reformation movement; its survival, therefore, likewise had to be secured by military might.

The role of the alliance for safeguarding the Protestant faith strikingly paralleled that played in the drama (however inadvertently) by the Ottoman Empire. Religious concessions were to be effected on political grounds. The difficulties attending the formation of the league revealed that some Protestants saw the relationship of religion and politics quite differently. Saxon officials openly expressed the suspicion that those who urged the formation of an alliance had rather more mundane considerations on their mind: they were interested in political advantages rather than religious commitment. Such doubts were justified in the case of Landgrave Philip of Hesse. As he saw it, a Protestant alliance would bound to be anti-Habsburg (because of the staunch Catholic attitude of the Habsburgs), and because his own political troubles related to the Habsburgs, he was staunchly in support of a Protestant alliance.[40] His involvement in the Pack Affair in 1528 showed that he was not beyond using religion as a ploy to get out of political hot water. The League of Schmalkald was not only a defensive alliance against the Catholic estates; it was also directed against the emperor, on the grounds both of religion and of the emperor's encroachment upon territorial prerogatives.

In short, the rulers made the religious decisions. It is difficult to fathom fully why individual decisions were made, though different reasons undoubtedly prevailed at different times and in different places. The heart of the matter, such aspects as personal commitment and religious conviction, is beyond the historian's reach. Moreover, the decision in favor of the Reformation made in Germany in the late 1530s had a different context from a similar decision made ten years earlier and was thus likely made for different reasons. In the 1520s the larger ecclesiastical situation was still very much in a state of flux, as was the political setting within which the change occurred. From 1531 onward, the League of Schmalkald cast a protective mantle (despite the uncertain legal situation) over the Protestant territories and cities.

In the early years of the controversy the political advantages of supporting the new faith were not immediately obvious. The political authorities were very reluctant to support the movement of reform during the early phase of the controversy. If it had been clear that the prize of subjecting the church to secular control could have been had for the asking, they would scarcely have hesitated.

At some places the reform movement was forcefully opposed—in England, for example—and yet the momentum of reform remained strong despite a somewhat fickle king. External forces could hardly suppress the Reformation as a movement of ideas. An unspoken alliance between religion and regime existed, the latter supporting, by way of either active policies or latent neutrality, the former frequently sustaining the cause of ecclesiastical reform. The Reformers in turn by declared government have been ordained by God to support true religion. They seemed never bothered by the fact that the victory of their ideas was made possible by governmental action.

There were other situations as well—government authorities that were outrightly hostile or, at best, reluctant to endorse precarious schemes of ecclesiastical change. When that happened, for example, in Alstedt with Müntzer in 1523, in Geneva with Calvin in 1538, or in Scotland with Knox in 1554, the Reformers rose like the prophets of the Old Testament with fiery words of condemnation, threats of divine wrath, and solemn moods of defiance. Müntzer told the count of Mansfeld in the heat of the Peasants' War: "The living and eternal God has ordered us to remove you from

---

40. The case for Philip the politician rather than martyr of the faith is argued by Wilhelm Ernst Winterhager, "Zwischen Glaubenseifer und Machtpolitik: Zum Problem der 'Fürstenreformation' am Beispiel Philipps von Hessen," in *Glaube und Macht: Theologie, Politik und Kunst im Jahrhundert der Reformation* (ed. Enno Bünz, Stefan Rhein, and Günther Wartenberg; Leipzig: 2005), 49–68.

your place by force, for you are of no benefit to Christendom, you are nothing but a miserable dust broom of the friends of God."[41] Initially Müntzer's distinction between the "elect" and the "godless" had entailed no political significance; in his famous sermon to the Saxon rulers in August 1524, he simply challenged the rulers to join the elect and carry out the divine will. By the time the peasants' uprising had coalesced in the fall of 1524, the tone had changed. Because the rulers had shown themselves unwilling to carry out God's will, they were *gotlose regenten* (godless rulers), whose godlessness deprived them of their divinely ordained authority. The banner of carrying out the divine will had thus fallen to the peasants. Müntzer's challenge of established authority, if it failed to side with the cause of the true gospel, was taken up by other Reformers whenever they had to confront hostile political powers: somewhat gingerly by Calvin, more confidently by Knox, whose *Godly Letter of Warning and Admonition to the Faithful* (1554) included the telling phrase, "for all those that would draw us from God (be they kings or queens), being of the devil's nature, are enemies unto God, and therefore will that we declare ourselves enemies unto them."

The developing notion of a right of resistance and, by implication, of revolution, was a consistent extension of these premises. Governmental support for ecclesiastical change was necessary in the sixteenth century, and the Protestant divines spared no efforts at eloquence and persuasion to make the case for such support. Wherever the political authorities decided to throw their weight behind the Roman Church, when hoped-for support turned into grim hostility, the Reformers rose up in protest—and threatened with arms. Calvinists in France, Scotland, and the Low Countries, such as John Ponnet (*A Short Treatise of Politique Power*, 1556), Christopher Goodman (*How Superior Powers oght to Be Obeyed of Their Subjects*, 1558), or even John Knox (*Appellation*, 1558), developed a full-fledged theory of resistance, precipitated by the hostile circumstances they faced. The French monarchomachists Languet, Hotman, and Duplessis-Mornay argued the case with an interesting juxtaposition of biblical and secular argumentation: the "tyrant" who violated the laws of God and of the land had to be resisted. This argument received formal theological respectability in the Scots Confession of 1560, which included "the repudiation of tyranny" among the good works of the faithful.

The German Lutherans, who were not particularly in the forefront of such reflections and were only hesitatingly supportive of the League of Schmalkald, had their defining moment after the War of Schmalkald, when the city of Magdeburg defied the emperor's imposition of the Interim and valiantly withstood the siege of the city. The avalanche of pamphlets published in Magdeburg during the siege defended the city's defiance of the emperor, prompting Lutheran theologians to develop a full-fledged theological theory of resistance.[42] Unlike the Calvinist tradition, which widely (in Scotland, France, and the Low Countries) faced the reality of hostile governmental authority, Lutherans faced it only in Magdeburg; and in the centuries that followed the alliance between throne and altar was so harmonious that the Magdeburg episode

41. Thomas Müntzer, *Schriften und Briefe*, 468.
42. Thomas Kaufmann, *Das Ende der Reformation: Magdeburgs "Herrgotts Kanzlei" (1548–1551/2)* (Tübingen: 2003).

in Lutheran history was soon forgotten. It was rediscovered after World War II, when Lutheran theologians and laity asked searching questions about the all-too-easy compliance of the Lutheran churches in Germany with Nazi totalitarianism.

During the reign of Queen Elizabeth, William Cardinal Allen spearheaded the attempts of émigré English Catholics on the Continent to develop a theory of resistance and rebellion against a heretical queen. Thus all sixteenth-century religious parties, including even at times the Anabaptists, were altogether prepared, if suppressed by a hostile governmental dictum, to invoke a theory of resistance. Religious outsiders, regardless of ecclesiastical label, propounded theories of resistance when political circumstances warranted it.

This almost universal sixteenth-century phenomenon is all the more intriguing because when the question first arose some voices expressed concerns and misgivings. Luther, for one, was reluctant to concede anything other than passive suffering by the faithful in the face of governmental adversity. He argued that resistance against governmental authority was justified only in worldly matters in which the rulers had violated their legal, constitutional responsibilities. Subjects were not to rebel because of religious grievances; after all, in the Sermon on the Mount Jesus exhorted the believer to be long-suffering. By 1531 Luther had modified his sentiment and showed himself prepared to support resistance against the emperor, but again purely on political grounds, the argument being that the emperor, by suppressing the Protestants, had violated his election agreement and therefore had to be resisted. Because the emperor was both a political and a religious foe, however, Luther's notion was not as clear in practice as it was in theory.

Politically, the main significance of the Reformation was the repudiation of ecclesiastical control over government. The perennial struggle in the Middle Ages between political and ecclesiastical authority, graphically evidenced by Pope Boniface VIII's bull *Unam Sanctam*, was resolved in favor of the former. One might see this as the culmination of a trend appearing in the later Middle Ages. Indeed, some political theorists, such as Stephen Gardiner in England, insisted that the authority of the ruler embraced ecclesiastical matters as well. The most dramatic reversal of the relationship between church and state occurred in England under Henry VIII, where the king's new title, "Supreme Head of the Church," was a spectacular symbol of the change. Later in the century Thomas Lüber (Erastus) wrote his *Explicatio gravissimae quaestionis* (Examination of That Most Grave Question) to argue for the complete submission of ecclesiastical affairs to political authority. Even Catholic countries espoused this notion. Little difference existed between Catholic and Protestant countries in this respect.

The acquisition of ecclesiastical authority on the part of governmental authorities was only one of several developments that grew out of the religious turbulence of the sixteenth century. The state declared itself autonomous, no longer under the jurisdiction of the church; it began consistently to exercise educational and charitable functions that previously had been under the aegis of the church. The state thereby assumed a moral stature it had previously lacked. The Reformation's theoretical justification may have been an ex post facto *pièce justificative* or a revolutionary innovation. Nonetheless, the reality proved to be of immense significance. A new kind of state began to make its appearance. No longer did it wrestle with the church, for it had acquired the power and prerogatives it desired. Although the state was still far from secular—religion continued to be of the utmost importance—the English propagandist for Henry VIII, Richard Morison, wrote in his tract *A Remedy for Sedition* that "religion is that which keeps subjects in obedience," three hundred years before Karl Marx—surely an intriguing sentence! All countries had an "established" church whose main function was to support the state's efforts at social discipline and thus ensure peace and tranquility. However, religion was only one facet of many in the body politic, akin to trade and commerce. Just as the proper care of ecclesiastical affairs was the responsibility of the ruler, so loyalty and obedience on the part of the subjects were affirmed as the proper expression of the pious Christian life. Religion was considered the cohesive factor in society, its moral handmaiden (with a very modest cost to the state).

The changes in the political realm were few. The public expression of religious dissent continued to be unthinkable and was suppressed with varying degrees of sternness, oppression, persecution—and death. Neither tolerance nor religious freedom was part of the vocabulary of the sixteenth century, though generally the harshest punishments—death by drowning (for rebaptism) or fire (for heresy)—were reserved for the Anabaptists, who suffered the additional liability of being branded revolutionaries and rebels. Confiscation of property, compulsory emigration, and imprisonment were all normal legal measures against religious dissent. All countries, Catholic and Protestant alike, clung to the notion that religious uniformity was indispensable for the tranquility of the body politic, and the notion of the "Christian commonwealth" continued.

THE CALL FOR TOLERATION

At the beginning of the sixteenth century, few people in Europe had the faintest inkling of the words "toleration" or "tolerance," not to mention their meaning, as could painfully have been attested by women accused as witches, theological dissenters, heretics, and—once the Reformation controversy had erupted—Anabaptists and other reformers.[43] Those who knew Latin were aware, of course, that the root of the word was "to accept, to suffer, to bear," but the word was meaningless for sixteenth-century Europeans, for the fact was that the church taught the timeless message that there was one truth and dissent from that truth was dissent from the eternal order of things. Tolerance of dissent was abominable blasphemy if not outright rebellion against the divine order, and neither church nor state would have any of it. Intriguingly, the lack of toleration so profoundly characteristic of the medieval world encompassed not only the realm of ideas, but also their practical enforcement. The former was the domain of the church, the latter the responsibility of the secular government. The church pronounced the verdict; the state carried it out.

43. The standard work on the topic continues to be Joseph Lecler, *Toleration and the Reformation*, 2 vols. (New York: 1960). See also Henry Arthur Francis Kamen, *The Rise of Toleration* (London: 1967). Two broader works are Perez Zagorin, *How the Idea of Religious Toleration Came to the West* (Princeton: 2003), and John Christian Laursen et al., eds., *Beyond the Persecuting Society: Religious Toleration before the Enlightenment* (Philadelphia: 1998).

The concept of toleration, on the other hand, acknowledges and accepts the "other." The diverse arguments advanced in support of toleration either offered a different interpretation of the Christian religion or proposed a hierarchy of points of belief in which only the most fundamental, such as the denial of God's existence, should be penalized.

If anything characterized rulers, theologians, and churchmen in the early sixteenth century it was that—with a few exceptions—they were incapable of entertaining the notion of a religiously diverse society. Not only did the universally held concept of truth mandate that only one truth could be possible and therefore the claimed possession of this truth rendered impossible any divergent validation, but the Constantinian revolution in the fourth century had also bestowed on government the responsibility for guarding and protecting this Christian truth (and the church which was the guardian of this truth). Thus, theological dissent was both a religious matter and a political offense. The heretic faced not only the censure of the church, which judged that deviation from the teachings of the church consigned the heretic eternally to the fires of hell; the heretic also faced a secular court of law, which condemned him to the fires of the stake.

Two forces converged to create the phenomenon of heresy: the conceptual impossibility of diverse truth claims and the determination of the political authorities to suppress with fire and sword any manifestation of dissent. Even before Christianity became the officially enjoined religion of Europe, theologians had inveighed with humorless determination against heretics, categorically disallowing them the label Christian and a place in the Christian firmament. Most of the heretics of early Christianity enjoyed the luxury of merely being expelled and sent into exile for their beliefs. Before long, however, the normative punishment was the loss of freedom and even of life, as Jan Hus, for example, was to experience in 1416 despite the promise of a safe conduct in Constance.

The Reformation intensified the issue of dissent, for it made starkly evident that the unity of the church was a thing of the past. The course of events in sixteenth-century Europe saw a wholesale desertion from the ranks of the Catholic Church, which meant that the category of heresy found a formidable quantitative extension. Moreover, because some city governments and rulers formally supported the reform movement, it came to be characterized by a new twist in the relationship between theological dissent and governmental authority. No longer was what was called heresy propounded by isolated individuals or fringe movements; it encompassed whole towns, regions, and countries. And because the reform movement quickly became a house divided, different groups of Reformers had to decide what steps to take against those who abhorred the Roman church as much as they themselves, yet but who propounded a different understanding of the authentic gospel.

The ranks of those who did not know the words tolerance and toleration were large and widespread. At issue was the proper acceptance of the Christian religion, in both ideology and practice—both the insistence that religious dissent was tantamount to blasphemy and the use of the public judiciary to hunt down all those who dissented from the established religion of the realm. The differences between Catholic and Protestant attitude in this regard were minor, more a matter of degree than of kind, as the Anabaptists were to learn.

This overwhelming consensus notwithstanding, a few solitary individuals cautiously yet pointedly propounded novel notions about religious disagreement and diversity, compelled to do so because it was theirs that was the "different" understanding of the Christian religion. Later, during the seventeenth and eighteenth centuries, those who rejected the notion of uniformity in religious thought and practice not only became more and more numerous; they also began to advance nonreligious arguments, notably economic considerations, in support of their contention for universal toleration.

Early in the Reformation controversy, Luther recorded his feeling that the burning of heretics was not in keeping with the Christian gospel. Indeed, one of the forty-one sentences culled from his writings in the papal bull of condemnation rebuked him for that very view. Luther reiterated this sentiment—no doubt because his theological dissent had put his life on the line—in subsequent years. In his 1523 treatise *Concerning Secular Government*, Luther argued that secular government had no role in religion and could therefore neither coerce nor punish anyone for religious reasons. Conscience (which Luther had invoked in his famous response at the diet of Worms) was free; its only confinement was Scripture. Of course, Luther did not mean to embrace toleration as we have come to understand it today. Rather, his pronouncement sought to remove governmental authority from the arena of religion.

Beginning in the late 1520s, however, a different tone began to enter Luther's writings, and it seemed that he had forgotten his own argument in his tract on governmental authority. A cynic might observe that by that time Luther knew himself to be beyond the reach of pope and emperor, while a more benign (and, by all odds, more authentic) explanation is that the legacy of over a millennium of tradition began to weigh heavily on him—all the more because the Peasants' War and the Anabaptists had demonstrated that political insurgency could be tied to religious reform. The consequence was that Luther increasingly conceded an important role for government in ecclesiastical affairs.

The juxtaposition of charges of political disloyalty and theological aberration became normative in early modern Europe. Accordingly, the Anabaptists were uniformly considered potential insurrectionists, persecuted not only for their theological dissent but also their political threat. Luther had no problem, therefore, supporting the death penalty for Anabaptists.

The Reformers displayed intolerance with a zeal worthy of a nobler cause, though the number of those executed by fire or sword in Protestant jurisdictions was far more modest than the number of those suffering the same fate at the hands of Catholics, especially once the Inquisition had swung into action. The total number of executions in the towns of Bruges, Ghent, Antwerp, and Brussels between 1530 and 1580 came to slightly over 800, of whom some 427 were Anabaptists and 289 were Calvinists.[44] The Anabaptist Felix Mantz was drowned in the Limmat River by order of the Zurich city council in 1527 for rejecting infant baptism; Protestant Basel's city council

---

44. These figures are compiled by Gerhard Güldner, *Das Toleranz-Problem in den Niederlanden im Ausgang des 16. Jahrhunderts* (Hamburg: 1968), 175. The modest number of Lutheran martyrs finds its explanation, of course, in the disappearance of Lutheran influence in the second half of the century.

ordered the death by burning of an Anabaptist named Konrad in 1530.[45] In England, Henry VIII executed both Catholic traditionalists and Protestant gospelers. The most notorious instance of the Protestant pursuit of "heretics" came on October 27, 1553, when the Spanish antitrinitarian Michael Servetus was burned in the market square of the Genevan suburb of Champel for having denied the Trinity and the baptism of infants. It was in the aftermath of this event that the first wave of clamors for toleration could be heard in Europe.

The first voices to express disagreement with the treatment of dissenters came from individuals who had found the quarrels between the adherents of the old and the new faith to be over trivia. Erasmus of Rotterdam never tired of positing the centrality of the *philosophia Christi,* the imitation of Christ in one's daily life, and of arguing against Sophistic theological speculation. The fundamental affirmations of the Christian faith were few, and only those deserved universal acceptance. Sebastian Franck, who made the transition from Catholic priest to disciple of Luther, then to Anabaptist and eventually to spiritualist, disavowed all the quarrelling religious factions. He followed in Erasmus's steps with his insistence that the controversies of the age were not over issues that pertained to eternal salvation. In his folio-sized *Chronica, Zeitbuch und Geschychtbibell* (1531), which serves as a masterful illustration that some non-expert authors have an uncanny ability to identify just the right kind of secondary sources to create a new brilliant whole, Franck included a "chronicle of heretics," in which he wrote: "Dear reader, you must not conclude that I consider as heretics all those I have described on these pages and have included in this roster of heretics. I offer not my judgment but that of the pope, of his followers and the councils which are the judges. If it were my own judgment, I would turn the tables and canonize many of those who are here decried as heretics and would, in fact, include them in the company of the saints."[46]

Franck's was a frontal attack on the traditional understanding of the relationship between the ecclesiastical and civic communities and a challenge to the traditional understanding of truth. Franck argued the same kind of reductionist understanding of the Christian gospel as had Erasmus: the fundamentals of the Christian religion were few, and most of the theological controversies and disagreements had to do with matters of secondary importance.

Franck's notions were taken up by another spiritualist, whom we also have already encountered: Sebastian Castellio, translator, teacher, Bible student, and linguist. Castellio was principal of a seminary–preparatory school in Geneva, and even though he had attained this position on John Calvin's recommendation, the two men soon got into an argument. Calvin insisted it was because of Castellio's shameless ambitions and pride, while Castellio argued that the cause was Calvin's tyrannical demeanor in Geneva. Castellio moved to Basel to become professor of the Greek language, and by all odds he would have ended his life quietly as a distinguished linguistic scholar unknown to the world at large had it not been for Servetus's execution in Geneva. Castellio took pen in hand and in 1554 published a special kind of volume entitled

45. Nikolaus Paulus, *Protestantismus und Toleranz im 16. Jahrhundert* (Freiburg: 1911), offers an exhaustive inventory of Protestant intolerance in the sixteenth century.
46. Sebastian Franck, *Chronica, Zeitbuch und Geschychtbibell* (Ulm, 1536; new ed. Darmstadt, 1969), 81.

De haereticis: an sint persequendi (Should Heretics be Persecuted?). The book was in fact an anthology, a compilation of statements by theologians from Augustine and Chrysostom to Luther and Calvin. Although Servetus was not mentioned in the book, the author was an unknown "Martinus Bellius," and the place of publication was Magdeburg, far to the north, it did not take long for Calvin's supporters to grasp that the publication had to do with Servetus's execution, to identify the real author, and to launch a spirited literary counterattack. Those who embraced traditional notions of the collaboration of church and state in sustaining pure religion were vigorous and aggressive in their defense. Calvin himself reacted with ill-concealed fury to the criticism of Servetus's execution and his role in it. Toward the end of January 1554 appeared his intransigent *Defensio orthodoxae fidei de Sacra Trinitate contra prodigiosas errores Michaelis Serveti Hispani* (Defense of the Orthodox Faith Concerning the Holy Trinity against the Abominable Errors of Michael Servet from Spain), with the subtitle *ubi ostenditur haereticos jure gladii coercendos esse* (where will be demonstrated that heretics must be compelled with the law of the sword). Calvin's associate and eventual successor, Theodore Beza, similarly pronounced on the topic with his *De haereticis a civili magistratu puniendis libellus* (Should Heretics Be Punished by the Civil Magistracy?), in which he inveighed against "shameless academics" who failed to understand the true nature of heresy (namely, anything that disturbed the peace of the church) and the right of secular authorities to suppress it.[47] It was malicious, and not love, Beza argued, to expose the faithful to theological predators; those who felt sorrow for Servetus were destroyers of the church. Moreover, wrote Beza, it was the sacred responsibility of the magistracy to carry out the punishment of heretics, because heresy threatened to destroy the community.

Sebastian Castellio, however, based his argument not only on the impressive array of eminent theologians who through the centuries had rejected the use of force in religion; he also invoked Jesus's principle of forgiveness, which he contrasted with the severity and cruelty with which heretics were punished. "People hardly hear this word 'heretic' and they disdain an individual only for this reason. They have deaf ears when it comes to that person's defense and they angrily and furiously persecute not only him but also all those who dare to open their mouths in his defense."[48] Castellio went on to argue the two grave dangers of this traditional state of affairs: first, some individuals are taken to be heretics when in fact they are not, and second, those who are heretics are punished more severely than the principles of the Christian faith warrant. This last point is especially noteworthy, for it suggested an understanding of toleration that went beyond the pragmatic considerations of his argument. His simple argument was that the Christian religion did not allow the cruel treatment customarily imposed on heretics.

Castellio's pragmatic disposition, far more controversial in the sixteenth century than one might expect, found striking expression in a French publication of 1561. Published anonymously on the eve of the first of the French Wars of Religion, the *Exhortation aux Princes et Seigneurs du Conseil privé du Roy, pour obvier aux seditions*

47. Théodore de Bèze, *De haereticis a ciuili magistratu puniendis libellus, aduersus Martini Bellii farraginem, & nouorum academicorum sectam* (Geneva: Oliva Roberti Stephani, 1554; reprint Frankfurt: 1973).

48. Roland H. Bainton, ed., *Concerning Heretics, Whether They Are to Be Persecuted?* (New York: 1935).

qui semblent nous menacer pour le faict de la Religion (Exhortation to the Princes and Lords of the Priory, Council of the King) combined arguments both old and new.[49]

Castellio propounded the Erasmian notion that secondary theological points were not worth such ferocious disagreements and cruel punishments. But the book also argued a new view. Religious peace—and thus toleration—was indispensable for the harmonious unity of the realm. Persecution of dissent was divisive. At the same time, Michel de L'Hôpital urged his fellow citizens to make a distinction between *séditeux* (seditionists) and *hérétique* (heretics), between those who sought to destroy the commonwealth and those who merely held dissenting religious opinions. Although these voices minimized the political forces in the conflict, they were prophetic pleas for France to be spared the turmoil of what became almost half a century of civil strife. L'Hôpital reiterated the notion that conscience cannot be coerced.[50] He called for toleration, saying the unity of France was at stake. Later in the century, the Dutchman Dirk Volkertszon Coornheert (1522–1590), artist and lay theologian, developed a deep personal commitment to propagate Castellio's ideas and publications in the Netherlands.[51] And he added some pointed publications of his own.[52]

Beyond these few isolated figures not much was said in the sixteenth century on behalf of religious toleration. To be sure, where religion touched on political issues—such as in Switzerland after the War of Kappel, in Germany after the Peace of Augsburg, and in France after the Edict of Amboise of March 1560—the sheer inability of one religion to impose its will categorically on any other led to a kind of formal, juridical toleration of the several branches of Christianity. However, nowhere did this mean that the traditional understanding of a single truth that all had to be coerced to accept and acknowledge was forfeit. These legal pronouncements simply reflected the real world, where no party was able to subdue any other(s) by rational argument or brute force. What began as expedience settled as habit, so that by the eighteenth century religious uniformity was no longer pursued by governmental action.

Finally, the sixteenth century showed itself intolerant not only of those whose religious beliefs were out of joint with the prevailing religion of a commonwealth. Intolerance also characterized the treatment of Jews and those, mainly women, who were labeled witches. I noted in an earlier chapter that societies turn into persecuting societies when they feel threatened and see the social and political order at risk. The determination to persecute antedates the coming of the Reformation—the *Malleus Maleficarum*, for example, was published in 1486—but the strife and controversies of the Reformation accentuated a pervasive sense of uncertainty and threat. What is deeply ironic, however, is that those who themselves had challenged the existing order of religion and society, such as Luther and Calvin, who in their later years never tired of labeling the pope the Antichrist, found any challenge to their own new order tantamount to blasphemy.

---

49. An excellent survey with abundant references to secondary and primary literature is Malcolm C. Smith, "Early French Advocates of Religious Freedom," *Sixteenth Century Journal* 25 (1994): 44.

50. Michel de L'Hôpital, *Ouevres completes*, ed. P. J. S. Duféy (Paris: 1824), 1:421.

51. There is a rich literature, most recently Gerrit Voogt, *Constraint on Trial: Dirck Volckertsz Coornhert and Religious Freedom* (Kirksville, MO: 2000).

52. For example, his *A l'aurore des libertés modernes: synode sur la liberté de conscience* (1582).

THE END OR THE BEGINNING:
CONFESSIONALIZATION IN EUROPE

The end of the Reformation, which may be defined as the time when the political decision for or against the new faith was definitively made (in Germany in 1555, in Scotland in 1560, in England in 1559, and in France in 1598), is increasingly seen in recent scholarship also as the beginning of a new epoch, and indeed the claim is made that this new epoch surpassed the Reformation in significance as the harbinger of modernity, especially as regards the emergence of the modern state. This thesis has become known as "confessionalization," and it is seen as a process ubiquitous throughout Europe, in both Catholic and Protestant lands, where the normative belief or confession led to far-reaching changes in all aspects of society.[53] According to Heinz Schilling, the German historian who introduced the concept, confessionalization meant fundamental ecclesiastical and theological as well as cultural, political, and social change in European societies.[54] It meant a comprehensive transformation of both public and private life and had a bearing on the evolution of the modern state and of the modern society of disciplined subjects. Confessionalization, in other words, was the driving force that transformed the status-governed world into the democratic world of modernity.

The process of confessionalization embraced all aspects of society and therefore should be seen as a comprehensive development that encompassed art, literature, music, education, and law in addition to piety. Confessionalization took place at a time when the several new forms of Christianity that had tentatively come into being in the course of the Reformation emerged as self-conscious entities. The confessions became aware of the need to delineate their particular truth claims and, in so doing, to differentiate themselves from each other. For example, in the Lutheran tradition changes in worship began to be made so as to make it conform to the Lutheran "confession." Although early on in the Reformation many features of Catholic worship had been retained, now Lutheran worship began to be pronouncedly "Lutheran."

The point of departure was that by the second half of the sixteenth century an awareness had developed that the division of Western Christendom was, at least for the time being, irreversible. No fewer than half a dozen Christian traditions stood alongside one another in sharp competition, hostility, and disagreement. Yet each of these churches claimed to represent the true faith, denouncing all the others for various forms of biblical or theological aberration. It is not surprising, therefore, that it was during the second half of the sixteenth century that the new Protestant churches drafted and accepted confessions of faith: in 1560 the Scottish, in 1561 the Belgic, in 1566 the Second Helvetic, in 1577 the Lutheran Formula of Concord, and in 1605

---

53. The best appraisal of the "confessionalization thesis" or "paradigm," with extensive references to the literature, is by Thomas Kaufmann, "Die Konfessionalisierung von Kirche und Gesellschaft," *Theologische Literaturzeitung* 121 (1996): 1112–21.

54. Heinz Schilling, "Die Konfessionalisierung von Kirche, Staat und Gesellschaft—Profil, Leistung, Defizite und Perspektiven eines geschichtswissenschaftlichen Paradigmas," in *Die Katholische Konfessionalisierung* (ed. W. Reinhardt and H. Schilling; Gütersloh: 1995), 11–49.

the Racovian Catechism. This has been long understood as "confession formation," the attainment of a confessional and, of course, theological identity in the face of competing theological truth claims.

The notion of confessionalization, as it is currently affirmed in historical scholarship, holds that the intimate relationship between church and society in early modern Europe meant that when religion changed, society was bound to change as well. The process of forming the confession went hand in hand with the process of forming the state. Confessionalization not only brought the confessional homogenization of the people in a given realm; it also aided the formation of the modern state in its initial, absolutist form (the aggrandizement of state power began, after all, with state control over the church). Confessionalization entailed a number of mechanisms that facilitated the process. Pure doctrine was declared, its enforcement aided by both censure and propaganda as well as by social discipline in the form of visitations.

Confessionalization is what we have come to call "meta-history," "big" history, in contrast to the approaches of social history, with its postulate of the primacy of socioeconomic factors in the historical process. The confessionalization paradigm seeks to ask (and answer) the fundamental question about the role of religion in the dynamics of the emergence in Europe of modern society and states. The paradigm affirms categorically the importance, if not the centrality, of religion in the course of events, for it sees the confession of a territory or state as its driving force. At the same time, however, the argument that around the 1580s European societies began to undergo the radical change labeled "confessionalization" means that the Reformation, deemed by Protestant historians the pinnacle of the transformation of the medieval into the modern world and the decisive revolution in both religion and society, gets short shrift.

In the confessionaliation paradigm the Reformation becomes a preparatory phase, a notable beginning, of the changes that were to follow. The paradigm thus raises two quite different questions: whether its description of developments in European society, both Protestant and Catholic, in the second half of the sixteenth century is accurate; and whether these developments were more crucial than those traditionally associated with the Reformation. While the answer to the first question surely must be positive, to the second requires a resounding no.

As one would expect from a concept so comprehensive, so persuasive in its broad context, one finds problems as soon as one reflects on specifics and details—in which, according to the proverb, resides the devil. Thus as early as the 1520s one can observe social changes as outgrowths of the Reformation movement in Germany. In fact, everywhere the Reformation was formally introduced in a community or territory, efforts at social and economic reform were undertaken at the same time. Calvin's Geneva serves as a case in point. One must be careful not to yield to the mistaken notion that it was not until the end of the century that the Protestant territories and cities awakened to the idea that their particular theologies had ramifications for the public square. Moreover, those who framed the Lutheran *Book of Concord* in 1577 or offered Lutheran theologizing about doctrine or worship toward the end of the century always explicitly declared themselves to be heirs of Luther, thereby invoking continuity, rather than distance, from the Reformation proper.

Finally, a word of caution seems also appropriate with respect to the use of the word "confession" in all of its derivations, such as "confessional age" or even "confessionalization." The word "confession" (German *Konfession*) is of nineteenth-century coinage. To be sure, it was used in the sixteenth century, but it received its current meaning in the nineteenth century, when "confessions" began to be understood as legally equal variants of the Christian religion. In the sixteenth century, the term saw Lutheran, Reformed, Anglican, and Catholic Christianity as different expressions— old and new, true and false, papal and "protesting"—of the one Christian religion. Needless to say, this is a different understanding from ours, and we do well, therefore, to restrict the notion of a "confessional age" to the modern era.

THE WIDER WORLD

In August 1523, barely three decades after Christopher Columbus's landfall in what came to be known by Europeans as the Americas, two Franciscan friars from Flanders established the first Christian congregation in the new world. To be sure, there had been priests on just about every European vessel that had ventured across the seas, but that ecclesiastical presence was meant to provide spiritual guidance (often ignored) for the conquistadores so as to assure that their demeanor corresponded to the principles of the religion they claimed as theirs. What began in 1523, however, was the concerted missionary effort to convert the native peoples of the Americas to Christianity. Because these lands new to the Europeans were vast and the native peoples many, those in Rome and elsewhere who directed this missionary effort established zones of influence, so that Franciscan missionaries, for example, would not compete with Jesuits. One may well argue that that August 1523 a new chapter in the history of Christianity began, a long and tedious one of which only the early years of the twenty-first century offer the penultimate conclusion: the slow turn of the Christian faith from a European to a global religion, in which Europe and North America increasingly play only a modest role.

In the sixteenth century the story of Christianity was arguably what it had been for centuries—a European story. More precisely, and more narrowly, it was a central and Western European story that perforce says little, if anything, about developments and events in the Orthodox churches of Eastern Europe. One may find justification for such Western parochialism in the fact that until the twentieth century, the stories of Eastern and Western Christianity have had few points of contact. For example, the Lutheran Augsburg Confession was translated into Greek to make it accessible to Orthodox Christians. But both theologically and institutionally there have been two stories, two narratives.

The focus shifts if we turn to lands west and south of the Atlantic Ocean, for in those regions European expansionism sowed the seed for a chain of events, dramatically intensified in the nineteenth century, that made non-European and non–North American Christianity in the late twentieth century more widespread and, according to many observers, more vibrant. The foundations are to be found in the sixteenth century, when European merchants, con men, and conquistadores sailed forth for adventure and gold and silver. By all odds, these men, as a group, were no worse (or better) than other groups of men, before or after their time, who set out on similar missions. But before long the element of exploitation and confrontation began to carry the day, and the story of the European discoveries turned into a sordid one.

In all of this, the Christian cross was never far behind, for the adventurers and conquistadores were everywhere accompanied by men of the cloth who saw as their assignment the conversion of the natives to the Christian religion. They too may have been enraptured by exotic tales and promises of riches, or they may have been but puppets in the hands of men of power and determination. But evangelize they did, and before too long the church had added a new region to its vastly stretched empire. New dioceses were established, bishops and even archbishops appointed, so that by the end of the sixteenth century a new administrative network existed in what the Europeans called New Spain and later the new world.

The European expansion revived, for the first time in many centuries, the missionary impulse of European Christianity. The new lands and new peoples beckoned Christian missionaries, and they came, hundreds and hundreds of them, Franciscans, Dominicans, Augustinians, Jesuits. What was beginning was intriguingly anticipated in Zurich in 1525, when the first Anabaptists, confronted with suppression and persecution, pondered migration to the newly discovered Americas. The missionary activities were made possible by the engaged support of the Spanish crown, which paid for the travel of the priests across the Atlantic and built chapels and churches throughout Central and South America.

The first diocese in the New World was established by Pope Clement VII in Mexico in 1530. By the end of the century, there were no fewer than eleven, and the diocese of Mexico had become an archdiocese in 1546. Much the same took place in South America, except that there missionary impulse was characterized by a triumphalist hegemonic propensity absent from the north. As matters turned out, the external success of the missionary effort did not hide the reality that the native peoples converted to Christianity retained essential elements of their old religions. How many were converted is hard to say. The Catholic missionaries themselves spoke of "millions," but one suspects that a more modest number is likely to be more accurate, especially because these missionary impulses occurred in the context of a dramatic decline in the native population.

The most spectacular missionary impulse came from the members of the Society of Jesus in the second half of the century. Francis Xavier set the tone, indefatigably traveling southward to Africa, rounding the Cape of Good Hope, then forging on to India, while other Jesuit missionaries even reached Japan, where they suffered martyrdom. Xavier's reports back to Europe were as spectacular as was the number of claimed converts. A sample account conveys, rather dramatically and perhaps all too exuberantly, Xavier's strategy and approach: "He went up and down the streets and squares with a bell in his hand, crying to the children and others to come to the instructions. The novelty of the proceeding, never before seen in Goa, brought a large crowd around him which he then led to the church. He began by singing the lessons which he had rhymed and then made the children sing them so that they might become better fixed in their memories. Afterwards he explained each point in the simplest way. . . . By this method, which has since been adopted everywhere in the Indies, he so deeply engrained the truths and precepts of the faith in the hearts of the people that men and women, children and old folk, took to singing the Ten Commandments while they walked the streets." Xavier also could be quite credulous. About the Indonesian islands he wrote: "There are islands whose folk eat the bodies of enemies killed in their tribal wars. When one of them dies from sickness his hands and heels are eaten, and considered a great delicacy. Such barbarians are they on some islands that a man, wishing to hold a great feast, will ask his neighbour for the loan of his father, if he is very old, to serve him up as a dish, at the same time promising to give his own father when ripe for the purpose and the neighbour is desirous of having a banquet."[55] The account shows an intriguing strategy: Xavier challenged his hearers to embrace the basic tenets of the Christian religion but did not insist on any change in prevailing cultural patterns.

By the early seventeenth century, the ancient Christian missionary impulse had been revived, almost exclusively by a resurgent Catholicism. It had spread the Christian gospel under the protection of the Spanish and Portuguese crowns and had been, in both South and Central America, strikingly successful. The African continent, which did not seem to harbor the treasures of gold and silver that Europeans sought, was more or less ignored and bypassed as the British and Dutch vessels plowed the seas to the Indies. The Protestant impulses were far more restrained, even when in the early seventeenth century Protestant dissenters from England began to settle the east coast of North America. The obvious explanation for such Protestant missionary restraint is geopolitical: Spain and Portugal were strategically located on the Atlantic coast, and in the sixteenth century, no less than in the nineteenth, missionaries tended to operate under the banner of the body politic. In all instances the new emerging Christian communities were appendages of European Christianity.

Nonetheless, the encounter of Europeans with peoples and cultures different and theretofore unknown had other and far-reaching consequences. These peoples, new to European awareness, were in fact not all new. They were known in theology as "heathen" or "pagan" because they did not know the true God of the Bible. Consequently, they were deemed inferior, not only in religion but also in their morality. The first encounters between European explorers and native peoples seemed to vindicate such traditional judgments—the native peoples were all but naked. But as European observers came to a better understanding of the native cultures (this did not happen until the late seventeenth century), many of them concluded that the stereotypes were far from the mark and that the native peoples possessed values, norms, and morals just as Europeans did. Over time, it became obvious that the topic of religion was far more complex than had ever been assumed. The European mind-set began to change.

Furthermore, the European encounters challenged, before long, not only the traditional understanding of religion but also the traditional system of values. The matter was quite simple. A gulf separated the European traders and native peoples, apparent, for example, when Europeans were able to barter precious furs for a few glass beads that possessed no real value in Europe. Medieval scholastics had talked of the "just price" of an item, and now it was beginning to be obvious that there was no such thing—it all depended, as economists were to say centuries later, on supply and demand.

---

55. Both quotations from the *Monumenta Xaveriana* in Hans J. Hillerbrand, *The Reformation* (New York: 1965), 455–56.

Anno Domini 1600 the face of European Christianity, and what it meant to be a Christian, had changed dramatically from what it had been a hundred years earlier. It had been a century of turbulence. The Christian religion had experienced more turmoil in three generations than in the previous millennium and a half of Christian history.

Yet turbulence and turmoil notwithstanding, by the end of the century ancient beliefs had been reaffirmed, and new beliefs, claimed to be ancient, had been affirmed. New churches had come into being, and the old church had reasserted itself in no uncertain terms. A process of consolidation and reinvigoration was well on its way, affording the Christian religion, represented in churches old and new, a fresh dynamic and new self-confidence. There was still, as there seems always to be, a discrepancy between the lofty ideals propounded by the several churches and the reality of popular belief and loyalty in town and village, that the church and its affirmations were at the very core of the lives of individuals and society can hardly be questioned. Soon, however, these churches, and those who adhered to them, were to face the challenge even more radical than that which had begun in the fall of 1517 in the reflections of an unknown professor of theology in Wittenberg, Germany: the rise of modernity. Once more church and believers were changed beyond recognition. Old Christendom was divided. A new Christianity made its appearance.

Anno Domini 1600 Christians little realized that the decades and centuries yet to come were to bring, alas, even greater conflagration.

Epilogue

HISTORIOGRAPHY

For a long time historians—not surprisingly, since they were mostly Protestant in their orientation—declared the "Reformation" of the sixteenth century to have been one of the most incisive epochs of European history. Leopold von Ranke, the founder of modern historical scholarship in the nineteenth century, saw Luther and the Reformation movement he triggered as the beginnings of modernity. Ranke spoke of the "Age of the Reformation," roughly marked by the years 1517 and 1555, to denote that this one man and this one movement defined an entire epoch.[1] Ranke's conceptualization became the standard interpretive scheme of historians from the middle of the nineteenth century onward. In England Thomas Carlyle opined that Luther's Ninety-five Theses had been more influential for the course of European history than the Battle of Waterloo.

Historians and theologians of Catholic propensity begged to differ. Not only did they see Luther as a convicted heretic, but they also took the theology of the Reformation as replete with ignorance and heresy.

Of late, there has been some skepticism about these two traditional perspectives. It was nurtured by the realization that the break between the late Middle Ages and what happened beginning in 1517 with Luther's Ninety-five Theses may not have been as dramatic as Ranke and other historians had argued. Numerous lines of continuity between the late Middle Ages and the sixteenth century began to be recognized, in theology as well as in intellectuality. The radical newness of Luther's and the other Reformers was questioned, and above all the state of affairs in church and society before 1517 was seen in a far mellower light than had been the case previously. The notion of a corrupt, worldly, perverted church was replaced by the picture of a church full of vitality and spirituality, despite obvious (and extensive) deviations from the professed ideal.

The absence of a sharp break with the past, triggered by Luther and others early in the sixteenth century, has led some historians to conceptualize a much longer time period, extending from the thirteenth to the seventeenth century, as an "Age of Reforms," suggesting that from the fourteenth to the seventeenth century numerous "reforms" increasingly altered both church and society, of which those associated with Luther and "the" Reformation hardly deserve special recognition.[2]

---

1. The title of his work was *Deutsche Geschichte im Zeitalter der Reformation* (German History in the Time of the Reformation). Ranke wrote it after having completed his history of the popes, feeling that he should also let Protestant voices be heard.

2. See here the proceedings of a meeting of the German Verein für Reformationsgeschichte under the title *Die frühe Reformation in Deutschland als Umbruch: Wissenschaftliches Symposium des Vereins für Reformationsgeschichte* (ed. Stephen E. Buckwalter and Bernd Moeller; Gütersloh: 1998).

In short, recent historiography has posed the question of the significance of the changes brought about by the Reformation. Were those changes simply the continuation of developments that had their beginning in the late Middle Ages, or were they something new, a real break with the past? The former notion points to the long-term qualitative changes in all areas of society and church in the decades and centuries prior to 1517. It suggests, supported by a myriad of detailed studies and monographs, that what historians of earlier generations self-confidently stated to be the "theological discoveries" of the Reformation (for example, the emphasis on divine grace rather than human merit; the repudiation of the papacy, of pilgrimages, of canon law; the centrality of Scripture, the use of the vernacular) can be confidently found well before 1500. If seen this way, the traditional understanding of the Reformation evaporates: there will be nothing exciting to record because the truly exciting, indeed, revolutionary changes occurred well before Luther started his university career.

There is, of course, the alternate notion that argues for revolutionary change. The traditional Catholic notion of sainthood serves as a good illustration. This notion sees sainthood as an extraordinary gift from God, bestowed upon some humans for their meritorious efforts. Saints are bearers of an extraordinary spiritual depth, which not only places them close to God but also compels others to approach them, solicit their aid, and venerate their relics. The Reformation fundamentally repudiated the underlying notion of merit, satisfaction, purgatory, indulgences, virginity, celibacy, the monastic profession—and thereby offered something strikingly new.

Our current uncertainty about the significance of the Reformation may be related to the fact that historians of different interests (cultural historians, social historians, theological historians, etc.) have drawn on the areas of their particular expertise to reflect on the larger issues in the period from 1400 to 1600, and they have understandably come up with divergent results. It should come as no surprise that social historians will view the sweep of events between 1400 and 1600 differently than a religious historian. Accordingly, the divergent perspectives on the Reformation, when seen in this broader context, become rather obvious.

A further consideration has little to do with the important question as to what were the theological, social, cultural, and political innovations in the late Middle Ages. Rather, it focuses on the public consciousness of whatever innovations or changes were taking place. After all, Norse seafarers, such as Eric, may well have reached what we now call North America centuries before Columbus, but only Columbus's voyage created a new consciousness and mind-set in Europe, forever changing European affairs and history. So the fundamental question is if, say in the latter fifteenth century, the faithful understood the call for Scripture or a vernacular Bible as truly revolutionary and perceived that they were living in a time of revolutionary innovation and change, a perception quite different from Ulrich von Hutten's exuberant "O tempora, O mores! What a delight it is to be living in this time."

The answer takes us to the events triggered by Luther's Ninety-five Theses, commonly called the Reformation, to Thomas More's resignation from the chancellorship in England when Parliament acceded to the king's will or to Duke George's exclamation "das walt die Sucht" upon hearing Luther's declaration about the errors of church councils at the Leipzig debate in 1519. These men, and countless others, expressed their perception of the radicalism of the changes happening around them. For Wycliffe to talk of the pope as the antichrist was one thing; Luther's reiteration of such sentiment, echoed by a host of contemporaries, raised the consciousness of an entire society and indeed coalesced such sentiment into a movement. Luther's antichrist notion derived its significance from the far-reaching echo it received, not necessarily from its possible newness.

In short, if the category of public consciousness is seen as being at the heart of how historians are to understand the past—namely, as men and women in the past understood themselves and their own present—the significance of the Reformation appears in a quite different light. The evidence, as I seek to unfold it, suggests that people in the sixteenth century perceived the happenings around them as novel, striking, indeed as revolutionary.

There is another consideration. The notion of a distinctive epoch called the "Reformation" presupposes that the entire period was characterized by a particular consciousness and self-understanding. This is expressed in the current vogue of speaking of "early modern Europe" as a more or less cohesive historical period with varying chronological parameters within the broader time frame of 1400 to 1789. This broad chronological expanse raises troubling questions of periodization.[3]

Yet the term "early modern" would seem to be problematic. Its use means that a periodization category (not unproblematic) from political, perhaps also intellectual, history is applied to an entire epoch.[4] This includes, prominently, the use of the term for church history.[5]

Nonetheless, the use of "early modern" as a comprehensive historical epoch is not without serious problems. Two come to mind in particular: to what extent was the sixteenth century incisively characterized by its "modern" aspects; and, second, is it possible to subsume the entire era under this heading? The latter point takes us, inter alia, to the question if in the history of Christianity the first half of the century allows for no better label than the rather evasive "early modern."

The same conceptual issue surrounds the use of the term "Renaissance" as a historical epoch, and that quite apart from the propriety of its applicability for the history of Christianity during that time. The term "modern" is used without an appropriate and persuasive definition of what that term means. It is, of course, a highly malleable term, meaning that each generation, whether in the thirteenth century or the twenty-first, has seen itself as "modern" or, as in our own time, "postmodern," that is, distinctive. It appears to say much about our time that only the term "postmodern" has suggested

3. The *Handbook of European History, 1400–1600: Late Middle Ages, Renaissance, and Reformation* (ed. Thomas A. Brady Jr., Heiko A. Oberman, and James D. Tracy; Leiden: 1994), would appear to wish to have its cake and eat it as well, since it identifies "the Late Middle Ages, Renaissance, and Reformation" as evidently discrete and distinct periods within that two-hundred-year sweep.

4. In German scholarship, aided by that fascinating ability of the German language to coin new words, the term *Frühneuzeit* has appeared as a noun.

5. John O'Malley's presidential address to the American Catholic Historical Association preferred the term "early modern Catholicism" over the possible two alternatives "Counter-Reformation" or "Catholic Reform." The reason for such preference would seem rather obvious; it is to disconnect the history of sixteenth-century Catholicism from the Protestant Reformation.

itself, a rather strange designation, which causes some to shudder if the next historical label will be "post-postmodern."

Aspects of the sixteenth century did indeed intimate new ideas. The incipient ideas about religious freedom come to mind, as one case in point. By the same token, however, those "modern" ideas are few and far between in the sixteenth century, and traditional notions, norms, and values continued to dominate. Since we are here concerned primarily with religious history, we might point to such factors as the retention of the medieval worldview, the absence of critical scholarship of the Bible, and the continued dominance of Aristotelianism in the universities.

To argue that the Protestant Reformation was an essentially medieval phenomenon does not preclude the acknowledgment that certain ideas were new. Ernst Troeltsch, in his famous book *Protestantism and Progress,* argued the point rather cogently.[6] The Protestant Reformers offered new answers to traditional medieval problems, but in a myriad of ways, the sixteenth century (most assuredly the early sixteenth century) remained deeply embedded in the medieval value system. It retained the notion of the *corpus christianum,* the society that was at once identical to the church. The epistemology was Aristotelian, even as the understanding of divine providence was traditional, that is, deeply anthropomorphic. Luther may never have thrown the inkpot against the devil at the Wartburg, as pious tradition has it, but the story receives its credence in that he well might have. Luther was able to note in utter seriousness that in a neighboring town a woman had given birth to a mouse, or that the devil was responsible for bad beer.[7]

One should not read these statements as facetious frivolities but as profoundly indicative of the medieval zeitgeist. The European witch craze or the persecutions of dissenters are further illustrations for the persistence of the medieval value system. Sixteenth-century people could not envision a religiously divided community. Accordingly, the Anabaptists and Jews, ubiquitously oppressed or persecuted, would have been shockingly surprised to be told that they were enjoying a premodern age.

In short, as Ernst Troeltsch was at pains to note, there is little "modern" in the Protestant Reformation (and in the Council of Trent), and there is not much more in the sixteenth century in general. Much of the world was still subsumed under the heading of magic. But this reality (surely not revelatory truth to students of the sixteenth century) poses the question why the term "early modern" has almost universally come to encompass the early part of the sixteenth century and the Protestant Reformation. The explanation lies in that historians have become uneasy and unwilling to attribute to the Reformation as a religious phenomenon an epoch-forming significance. Historians do not find sufficient dynamic in the religious turbulence of the first half of the sixteenth century to see it as a discrete historical period. The term "early modern," by way of contrast, is becomingly septic.

The consequence has been that the problematic term "early modern" has come to be employed to denote a historical epoch, albeit with unspecified chronological para-

---

6. Ernst Troeltsch, *Protestantism and Progress: A Historical Study of the Relation of Protestantism to the Modern World* (trans. W. Montgomery; London: 1912).
7. WA 43:692.

meters. The Protestant Reformation is subsumed under this period, with the proponents of confessionalization arguing the essential priority of importance for the end of the sixteenth century. But, whatever legitimacy one might conjure up for the use of the term, its dynamic does not capture the dynamic of the Reformation, however understood. The preoccupation with the alleged centrality of "early modern Europe" distorts the meaning and significance of the Reformation.

This book has focused on roughly the first half of the sixteenth century and has simply sought to tell the story of how Luther stumbled into a conflagration and how a movement coalesced from this conflagration—and how this movement rightly marks a historical period. This book thus treads familiar ground, though it does not stake out claims of a "world-historical significance" of the Reformation even as it has told the story quite differently from the way it was told in the past. In the past, historians generally were of one mind as to how to explain this story.

Historians agreed that the cue to what happened after 1517 must be sought in the years before. They pointed out how in a variety of ways church and society in the early sixteenth century were characterized by weaknesses, which, in various ways, facilitated the progression of an individual's protest to a movement. Indeed, some historians talk about a systemic crisis of society at the time, while others pointed to a variety of stark abuses and perversions in the church.

The reason is obvious. If society and church in the late fifteenth and early sixteenth centuries revealed signs of fateful weaknesses or tensions, if there were telltale symptoms of a deepening crisis, if the handwriting was on the wall, the task of explaining the phenomenon "Reformation" becomes one of relating this systemic crisis of church or society to the religious and even societal upheaval. This smacks of some form of historical determinism, and, indeed, traditionally historians of the Reformation, especially Protestant historians, have so paid homage: politics, the state of the church, German nationalism, or social class became the catalyst for events. According to this perspective, an analysis of late-fifteenth-century church and society can identify a variety of forces that constituted an irresistible, inevitable dynamic for an upheaval of any sort. There would have been a Reformation, in other words, even if Luther or Zwingli had died in the cradle.

The purest form of such historical determinism was propounded by Marxist historians in former Communist East Germany in the 1970s and 1980s.[8] These historians argued a "crisis" in early-sixteenth-century German society, characterized, as suggested by traditional Marxist theory, by the emergence of new modes of economic production and new holders of economic power, who wished to exercise political power as well. Thus it was a society in crisis. Thus the Reformation at its heart was the ideological (religious) expression of a new economic order that sought to overcome the decaying political and economic feudal system.

This perspective entails the argument that the causalities between pre-Reformation society and the Reformation were plain and direct. This means, for example, that the immorality of the clergy or the new vision of humanism created a situation that was

8. See Adolf Laube, et al., eds., *Illustrierte Geschichte der deutschen frühbürgerlichen Revolution* (Berlin: 1974).

as precarious as it was overt. It also means that the intellectuals had deserted the societal consensus in the late fifteenth century; that people were alienated, hostile, and dissatisfied from church and society; and that the critical voices in theology, in literature, and in society, far from benign solitary naysayers, were deeply symptomatic.

Another approach sees the causes of the upheaval not so much in overt matters as in certain fundamental characteristics of society at the time: the "crisis" of the early sixteenth century was structural, existing even though society and church on the surface may have been peaceful and tranquil; the other characteristics always cited, such as the worldly cleric, were an exception, and ecclesiastical greed was not widespread. Externals notwithstanding, the balance of forces that formed a cohesive mantle over society disappeared. Changing political, economic, and social conditions began to challenge the place of the church, which became increasingly meaningless and redundant. This turn took place, as often as not, underneath the surface and found few dramatic expressions. The influx of people into towns, for example, meant that a sizable number lived "uprooted," as it were, in a new social setting. Unrelated to the traditional guilds, they were particularly open to new ideas, and seemingly predestined to accept the Reformation changes.

The argument of these pages has suggested a different understanding of the dynamics of the course of events. Most accounts of the Reformation subtly convey the notion that the state of affairs in the early sixteenth century was akin to an avalanche poised to begin its path down the mountain. History, however, rarely if ever moves in so deterministic a fashion. At each particular point in time, in the course of events, there are likely to be several options for the future, an openness that eschews determinism. A whole range of forces, all the way from the weather to personal temperament, acts upon the historical situation at a given time, and it is difficult to predict the outcome of events. The historian, who ought not to engage in writing history in the subjunctive, should never forget that numerous "ifs" are strewn, as it were, across the historical landscape, and that any of them might well have found realization and categorically influenced the course of events.

In addition to such general presuppositions having to do with the nature of the historical process, other considerations must be mentioned: the matter of geographic delimitation, for example. Geographically, should the purview be restricted to Germany, where, after all, the controversy had its beginning; or should the scope be extended to all of Europe? The answer is not at all self-evident. It is both difficult and precarious to categorize Europe as a whole, for in so doing one blithely overlooks the differences, for instance, between Scotland and Italy, or between Spain and Sweden. Each of these countries, not to mention others, had its own particular propensity and dynamic, and all generalizations about European developments and patterns must be modified by numerous exceptions. Especially if one uses such bold slogans as "the impact of the Renaissance," the "rise of cities," the "decline of feudalism," or the "rise of nationalism," to mention but a few, the complexity provided by different places and countries cannot be adequately evaluated.

The narrative focus here has been on Germany, and there is justification for so centering the discussion. The turbulence began there; indeed, it had its most dramatic phase there as well, so that one may make the point that German events constituted the beachhead, which made the advances elsewhere in Europe possible. Broadly speaking, the fate of the European Reformation was decided in Germany. If Luther had suffered the fate appointed for a heretic and outlaw in 1521, the story of the sixteenth century would need to be written differently.

Bibliography

A work of this sort might easily generate a bibliography as extensive as the text itself—Reformation scholarship has been lively and dynamic for the better part of two centuries. I have decided that it is best to concentrate on a few seminal works that either have stood the test of time or, if of recent vintage, have influenced and directed scholarship. One might call the bibliography that follows the "bibliography of my indebtedness." Given the readership of this book, it draws heavily on English-language publications.

General Aids to the Sixteenth Century

The Reformation of the sixteenth century has been one of the major areas of scholarly interest, both for historians and theologians, within the broader spectrum of the history of Christianity. Accordingly, a rich panoply of both scholarly and bibliographical helps is available. The best access to the field is found in *The Oxford Encyclopedia of the Reformation*, ed. Hans J. Hillerbrand, 4 vols. (New York: Oxford University Press, 1996), and the handbook of Thomas A. Brady Jr., Heiko A. Oberman, and James D. Tracy, eds., *Handbook of European History, 1400–1600*, 2 vols. (New York: Brill, 1994). More specifically, other useful recent introductions should be noted: Alec Ryrie, *Palgrave Advances in the European Reformation* (New York: Palgrave Macmillan, 2006); R. Po-chia Hsia, ed., *A Companion to the Reformation World* (Malden, MA: Blackwell, 2004); and Andrew Pettegree, ed., *The Reformation World* (London: Routledge, 2000).

A useful historiographical survey of Reformation historiography is A. G. Dickens, *The Reformation in Historical Thought* (Cambridge, MA: Harvard University Press, 1985).

General Histories

Given the plethora of general introductions and surveys, it is difficult to select the most useful. A whole phalanx of British historians have in recent years presented general histories of the Reformation: Euan Cameron, *The European Reformation* (Oxford: Clarendon, 1991), is a most useful text, encyclopedic in approach. Diarmaid MacCulloch, *Reformation: Europe's House Divided, 1490–1700* (London: Allen Lane, 2003), is well written, focuses heavily on the British Isles, and is useful on Eastern Europe. Owen Chadwick, *The Early Reformation on the Continent* (Oxford, 2001) is helpful, as is Patrick Collinson, *The Reformation: A History* (New York, 2004), both books from the pens of specialists in British history. Insightful is the collection of essays edited by Andrew W. Pettegree, ed., *The Reformation World* (New York: Routledge, 2000). Ulinka Rublack, *Reformation Europe* (Cambridge, 2005), focuses on general European history. Broad in its sweep is John Bossy, *Christianity in the West, 1400–1700* (Oxford: Oxford University Press, 1987). Felipe Fernández-Armesto and Derek Wilson, *Reformations: A Radical Interpretation of Christianity and the World, 1500–2000* (New York: Scribner, 1997), argues a provocative thesis. A useful introduction is Mark Greengrass, *The Longman Companion to the European Reformation, c. 1500–1618* (New York: Longman, 1998). Another recent general study is Peter George Wallace, *The Long European Reformation: Religion, Political Conflict, and the Search for Conformity, 1350–1750* (New York: Palgrave Macmillan, 2004).

The *Theologische Realenzyklopädie* (TRE), published in Germany in no fewer than thirty-six volumes, covers more than the sixteenth century, but its coverage of major sixteenth-century events and personages is superb. A parallel reference work, offering both a Catholic perspective and details of Catholic phenomena, is the *Lexikon für Theologie und Kirche* in eleven volumes. Another exceedingly helpful resource—an impressive encyclopedia of Christian biographies—is T. Bautz et al., eds., *Biographisch-Bibliographisches Kirchenlexikon* (Hamm, 1990ff.). It is accessible on the Internet.

Martin Luther and Germany

Understandably, Martin Luther has enjoyed immense attention from both secular and religious historians. A good introduction is Donald K. McKim, ed., *The Cambridge Companion to Martin Luther* (New York: Cambridge University Press, 2003). The most thorough biography of Luther in English is the three-volume series by Martin Brecht, *Martin Luther* (Philadelphia: Fortress, 1985). Other biographies are by Heiko A. Oberman, *Luther: Man between God and Devil* (New Haven, CT: Yale University Press, 1989), and Richard Marius, *Martin Luther: The Christian between God and Death* (Cambridge, MA: Belknap, 1999), both somewhat unorthodox. Specific aspects of Luther and the German Reformation are treated in Mark Edwards, *Luther's Last Battles: Politics and Polemics, 1531–46* (Ithaca, NY: Cornell University, 1983), and his *Printing, Propaganda, and Martin Luther* (Berkeley, 1994). See also Gerald Strauss, *Luther's House of Learning: Indoctrination of the Young in the German Reformation* (Baltimore: Johns Hopkins University Press, 1978). On the important figure of Philipp of Hesse, see Richard Andrew Cahill, *Philipp of Hesse and the Reformation* (Mainz: von Zabern, 2001).

An excellent introduction to the German Reformation is C. Scott Dixon, *The Reformation in Germany* (Malden: Blackwell, 2002). The older volume by Rainer Wohlfeil, *Einführung in die Geschichte der deutschen Reformation* (Munich: Beck, 1982), contains brilliant insights.

Individual Reformers

Martin Greschat, *Martin Bucer: A Reformer and His Times* (Louisville, KY: Westminster John Knox, 2004); James Martin Estes, *Peace, Order and the Glory of God: Secular Authority and the Church in the Thought of Luther and Melanchthon, 1518–1559* (Leiden: Brill, 2005); Günter Frank und Ulrich Köpf, eds., *Melanchthon und die Neuzeit* (Stuttgart-Bad Cannstatt: Frommann-Holzboog, 2003); Hellmut Zschoch,

Reformatorische Existenz und konfessionelle Identität: Urbanus Rhegius als evangelischer Theologe in den Jahren 1520 bis 1530 (Tübingen: J. C. B. Mohr [Paul Siebeck], 1995). E. Gordon Rupp, *Patterns of Reformation* (Philadelphia: Fortress, 1969), is an older book but still eminently readable.

The Reform Movement Coalesces

Rebecca Oettinger, *Music as Propaganda in the German Reformation* (Burlington, VT: Ashgate, 2001); Paul Russell, *Lay Theology in the Reformation: Popular Pamphleteers in Southwest Germany, 1521–1525* (New York: Cambridge University Press, 1985). Two interesting studies are by Peter Matheson, *The Rhetoric of the Reformation* (Edinburgh: T. & T. Clark, 1998), and *The Imaginative World of the Reformation* (Edinburgh: T. & T. Clark, 2000). Robert Scribner, *For the Sake of Simple Folk: Popular Propaganda for the German Reformation* (New York: Clarendon, 1994), is one of the most influential monographs. Geoffery Dipple, *Antifraternalism and Anticlericalism in the German Reformation: Johann Eberlin Von Günzburg and the Campaign against the Friars* (Brookfield, VT: Scholar Press, 1996).

The Peasants' War in Germany has received much attention since Günther Franz published his epoch-making *Der deutsche Bauernkrieg* (most recent edition: Darmstadt: Wissenschaftliche Buchgesellschaft, 1977), with its thesis of the distinction between "ancient law" and "divine law." Peter Blickle, *The Revolution of 1525: The German Peasants' War from a New Perspective* (Baltimore: Johns Hopkins University Press, 1998), extended this argument to include the uprisings in the towns and cities as crucially important for understanding the events. Useful is *The German Peasants' War: A History in Documents*, ed., trans., and with an introduction by Tom Scott and Bob Scribner (Atlantic City, NJ: Humanities, 1991). See also Peter Blickle, *Der Bauernkrieg: die Revolution des Gemeinen Mannes*, 2nd ed. (Munich: C. H. Beck, 2002). A historiographical survey is offered by Peter Blickle, ed., *Der Deutsche Bauernkrieg von 1525* (Darmstadt: Wissenschaftliche Buchgesellschaft, 1985).

Cities

Bernd Moeller, *Imperial Cities and the Reformation: Three Essays* (Philadelphia: Fortress, 1972); Steven Ozment, *The Reformation in the Cities: The Appeal of Protestantism to Sixteenth-Century Germany and Switzerland* (New Haven, CT: Yale University Press, 1975). A crisp survey of the literature is Berndt Hamm, "The Urban Reformation in the Holy Roman Empire," in Thomas A. Brady, Heiko A. Oberman, and James D. Tracy, eds., *Handbook of European History, 1400–1600*, (Grand Rapids: Eerdmans, 1996), 2:193–227.

The Division of Reform Impulses

Zwingli and the Reformation in Switzerland

The older survey by Gottfried W. Locher is still indispensable: *Huldrych Zwingli in neuer Sicht* (Zürich: Zwingli Verlag, 1969). See also Ulrich Gäbler, *Huldrych Zwingli: His Life and Work* (Edinburgh: T. & T. Clark, 1987); Bruce Gordon, *The Swiss Reformation* (New York: Manchester University Press, 2002); Fritz Büsser, *Wurzeln der Reformation in Zürich: zum 500. Geburtstag des Reformators Huldrych Zwingli* (Leiden: Brill, 1985). A collection of translated sources is found in *Ulrich Zwingli: Early Writings*, ed. Samuel Jackson (Durham: Labyrinth, 1987).

The Dissidents: Radical Reformers

A good general introduction is Hans-Jürgen Goertz. *Religiöse Bewegungen in der frühen Neuzeit* (Munich: R. Oldenbourg, 1993).

Thomas Müntzer

Thomas Müntzer has received much attention, first from Lutheran theologians who found much fault with his theology, then from Marxist historians who saw in him the truly radical visionary of the Reformation. See Abraham Friesen, *Thomas Müntzer: A Destroyer of the Godless* (Berkeley: University of California Press, 1990). Also available is *The Collected Works of Thomas Müntzer*, edited by Peter Matheson (Edinburgh, 1988); Hans-Jürgen Goertz and Peter Matheson, eds., *Thomas Müntzer: Apocalyptic, Mystic, and Revolutionary* (Edinburgh: T. & T. Clark, 1993).

Anabaptists

Two works are basic to the sixteenth-century Anabaptist phenomenon: Harold S. Bender and Henry Smith, eds., *The Mennonite Encyclopedia: A Comprehensive Work on the Anabaptist-Mennonite Movement* (Hillsboro, KS: Mennonite Brethren Publishing House, 1955), and George H. Williams, *The Radical Reformation* (Kirksville, MO: Sixteenth Century Publishers, 1992). The *Encyclopedia* expresses the notion of a theologically cohesive Anabaptist mainstream, of which those Anabaptist groups and groupings with different theologies did not belong. A revisionist historiography has challenged this perspective. See Hans J. Goertz, *The Anabaptists* (New York: Routledge, 1996). Important source collections are *Menno Simons: Complete Writings*, trans. from the Dutch by Leonard Verduin and edited by John Christian Wenger (Scottdale, PA: Herald, 1956). The most recent biography by Sjouke Voolstra is brief but thorough: *Menno Simons: His Image and Message* (North Newton, KS: Bethel College, 1997). Also: Leland Harder, ed., *The Sources of Swiss Anabaptism: The Grebel Letters and Related Documents* (Scottdale, PA: Herald Press, 1985); Arnold Snyder, ed., *Sources of South German/Austrian Anabaptism* (Kitchener, Ont.: Pandora, 2001); Cornelius J. Dyck, ed., *Confessions of Faith in the Anabaptist Tradition, 1527–1660* (Kitchener, Ont.: Pandora Press, 2006).

The important series of source collections are the *Quellen zur Geschichte der* (*Wieder*) *Täufer*, published under the aegis of the German Verein für Reformationsgeschichte since 1930, of which some sixteen volumes have appeared. There are English translations of important Anabaptist writings (from Michael Sattler to Peter Riedemann) in the series *Classics of the Radical Reformation*, of which eleven volumes have been published. A good illustration for the latter is *The Anabaptist Writings of*

David Joris, 1535–1543, trans. and ed. Gary K. Waite (Scottdale, PA: Herald, 1994). Other helpful studies on Anabaptism include two theological assessments: Arnold Snyder, *Anabaptist History and Theology* (Kitchener, Ont.: Pandora, 1997), and Walter Klaassen, *Anabaptism: Neither Catholic nor Protestant* (Kitchener, Ont.: Pandora, 2001); Stephen Boyd, *Pilgram Marpeck: His Life and Social Theology* (Durham, NC: Duke University Press, 1992); and Klaus Deppermann, *Melchior Hofmann: Social Unrest and Apocalyptic Visions in the Age of the Reformation* (Edinburgh: T. & T. Clark, 1987).

Broader topics are analyzed in Brad Gregory, *Salvation at Stake: Christian Martyrdom in Early Modern Europe* (Cambridge, MA: Harvard University Press, 1999), and Hans Guggisberg, *Sebastian Castellio, 1515–1563: Humanist and Defender of Religious Toleration in a Confessional Age* (Burlington, VT: Ashgate, 2002).

Münster Anabaptism

Sigrun Haude, *In the Shadow of "Savage Wolves": Anabaptist Münster and the German Reformation during the 1530s* (Boston: Humanities, 2000); Ralf Klötzer, *Die Täuferherrschaft von Münster: Stadtreformation und Welterneuerung* (Münster: Aschendorff, 1992); Karl-Heinz Kirchhoff, *Die Täufer in Münster 1534/35: Untersuchungen zum Umfang und zur Sozialstruktur der Bewegung* (Münster: Aschendorff, 1973).

Hutterite Anabaptists

Peter Riedemann's Hutterite Confession of Faith (translation of the 1565 German edition of *Confession of Our Religion, Teaching, and Faith, by the Brothers Who Are Known as the Hutterites*), trans. and ed. John J. Friesen (Scottdale, PA: Herald Press, 1999); Leonard Gross, *The Golden Years of the Hutterites: The Witness and Thought of the Communal Moravian Anabaptists during the Walpot Era, 1565–1578* (Scottdale, PA: Herald, 1968); and Werner Packull, *Hutterite Beginnings: Communitarian Experiments during the Reformation* (Baltimore: Johns Hopkins University Press, 1995).

Reform in Europe

Bob Scribner et al. eds., *The Reformation in National Context* (Cambridge: Cambridge University Press, 1994).

Events in Sweden

Still basic is Michael Roberts, *The Early Vasas: A History of Sweden 1523–1611* (Cambridge: Cambridge University Press, 1968); Matthias Asche, ed., *Dänemark, Norwegen und Schweden im Zeitalter der Reformation und Konfessionalisierung: nordische Königreiche und Konfession 1500 bis 1660* (Münster: Aschendorff, 2003).

The Reformation in Poland

Stanislaw Lubieniecki, *History of the Polish Reformation, and Nine Related Documents*, trans. George Huntston Williams (Minneapolis: Fortress, 1995); Christoph Schmidt,

Auf Felsen gesät: die Reformation in Polen und Livland (Göttingen: Vandenhoeck & Ruprecht, 2000); Gottfried Schramm, *Der polnische Adel und die Reformation. 1548–1607* (Wiesbaden: F. Steiner, 1965).

The Reformation in France

Mack P. Holt, *The French Wars of Religion, 1562–1629* (Cambridge, UK; New York: Cambridge University Press, 2005); Glenn S. Sunshine, *Reforming French Protestantism: The Development of Huguenot Ecclesiastical Institutions, 1557–1572* (Kirksville, MO: Truman State University, 2003); *Les Deux Réformes Chrétiennes: Propagation et Diffusion*, ed. Ilana Zinguer and Myriam Yardeni (Leiden: Brill, 2004).

The Reformation in England

Walter H. Frere and William M. Kennedy, eds., *Visitation Articles and Injunctions of the Period of the Reformation 1536–1558*, 3 vols. (London: Longmans, Green, 1910).

Scholarship on the English Reformation has undergone drastic changes in perspectives from the time A. G. Dickens published his *The English Reformation* in 1964 (new ed.: University Park: Pennsylvania State University, 1991), with the argument that religious change in England took place from the ground up, supported by the people. He found support in a number of publications, such as the superb biography of G. R. Elton, *Reform and Reformation: England, 1509–1558* (Cambridge, MA: Harvard University Press, 1977). Recent studies have contested Dickens's thesis, calling attention to England's flourishing religious life and the essential conservatism of the English people; see, in particular, Christopher Haigh, ed., *The English Reformation Revisited* (New York: Cambridge University Press, 1987), and Christopher Haigh, *English Reformations: Religion, Politics, and Society under the Tudors* (New York: Clarendon, 1993). Specifically dealing with the local changes is Robert Whiting, *Local Responses to the English Reformation* (New York, 1998). See also Eamon Duffy, *The Stripping of the Altars: The Tradition Religion in England, c. 1400—c. 1580* (New Haven, CT: Yale University Press, 2005); Peter Marshall, *Religious Identities in Henry VIII's England* (Aldershot, 2006); Peter Marshall and Alex Ryrie, eds., *The Beginnings of English Protestantism* (Cambridge, UK: Cambridge University Press, 2002).

Superb specific studies are G. R. Elton, *Politics and Police: The Enforcement of the Reformation in the Age of Thomas Cromwell* (Cambridge: Cambridge University Press, 1985); Kenneth Carleton, *Bishops and Reform in the English Church, 1520–1559* (Rochester, NY: Boydell, 2001); and J. J. Scarisbrick, *The English Reformation and the English People* (Oxford: Blackwell, 1994). See also Eamon Duffy, *The Voices of Morebath: Reformation and Rebellion in an English Village* (New Haven, CT: Yale University, 2001); and Rory McEntegart, *Henry VIII, the League of Schmalkalden, and the English Reformation* (Rochester, NY: Boydell, 2002).

A good collection of sources is found in John King, ed., *Voices of the English Reformation: A Sourcebook* (Philadelphia: University of Pennsylvania, 2004); Norman Jones, *The English Reformation: Religion and Cultural Adaptation* (Malden, MA: Blackwell, 2001).

Important biographies are Arthur Ogle, *The Tragedy of the Lollards' Tower* (Oxford: Pen-in-Hand, 1949); Richard Marius, *Thomas More: A Biography* (New York: Knopf, 1984); Diarmaid MacCulloch, *Thomas Cranmer: A Life* (New Haven, CT: Yale University Press, 1996); Retha M. Warnicke, *The Rise and Fall of Anne Boleyn* (Cambridge, 1989); E. W. Ives, *The Life and Death of Anne Boleyn* (Malden, MA: Blackwell, 2004); Thomas Mayer, *Cardinal Pole in European Context: A Via Media in the Reformation* (Burlington, VT: Ashgate, 2000); Christopher Highley and John King, eds., *John Foxe and His World* (Burlington, VT: Ashgate, 2002); and Brian Moynahan, *God's Bestseller: William Tyndale, Thomas More, and the Writing of the English Bible: A Story of Martyrdom and Betrayal* (New York: St. Martin's, 2003).

On Henry VIII see J. J. Scarisbrick, *Henry VIII* (Berkeley: University of California Press, 1969); G. W. Bernard, *The King's Reformation: Henry VIII and the Remaking of the English Church* (New Haven, CT: Yale University Press, 2005); Patrick Coby, *Henry VIII and the Reformation Parliament* (New York: Pearson Longman, 2006).

Catholicism in the Sixteenth Century

Scholars of sixteenth-century Catholicism have either tended to ignore the Protestant happenings or they have reacted defensively to the dominance of Protestant themes and events during that time. Nomenclature has played an important role, with "Catholic Reformation," "Counter Reformation," "Catholic Reformation and Counter Reformation" the most frequently used terms. See Jean Delumeau, *Catholicism between Luther and Voltaire: A New View of the Counter-Reformation* (Philadelphia: Westminster, 1977); Louis Chatellier, *The Europe of the Devout: The Catholic Reformation and the Formation of New Society* (New York: Cambridge University Press, 1989); R. Pochia Hsia, *The World of Catholic Renewal, 1540–1770* (New York: Cambridge University Press, 2005); John W. O'Malley, *Trent and All That: Renaming Catholicism in the Early Modern Era* (Cambridge, MA: Harvard University Press, 2000); A. D. Wright, *The Counter-Reformation: Catholic Europe and the Non-Christian World* (Burlington, VT: Ashgate, 2005); Robert Bireley, *The Refashioning of Catholicism, 1450–1700: A Reassessment of the Counter Reformation* (Washington, DC: Catholic University, 1999); and Martin D. W. Jones, *The Counter-Reformation: Religion and Society in Early Modern Europe* (Cambridge: Cambridge University Press, 1995).

Important monographs are Peter Godman, *The Saint as Censor: Robert Bellarmine between Inquisition and Index* (Boston: Brill, 2000); Peter Burke, "How to Become a Counter-Reformation Saint," in *The Counter-Reformation: The Essential Readings*, ed. David M. Luebke (Oxford: Blackwell, 1999), 130–42; Allyson Poska, *Regulating the People: The Catholic Reformation in Seventeenth-Century Spain* (Boston: Brill, 1998); Lucy E. C. Wooding, *Rethinking Catholicism in Reformation England* (New York: Clarendon, 2000); and A. D. Wright, *The Counter-Reformation: Catholic Europe and the Non-Christian World* (Burlington, VT: Ashgate, 2005).

The Popes of the Sixteenth Century

Götz-Rüdiger Tewes, *Die römische Kurie und die europäischen Länder am Vorabend der Reformation* (Tübingen: Niemeyer, 2001); Eamon Duffy, *Saints & Sinners: A History of the Popes* (New Haven, CT: Yale University Press, 2002); Ludwig Pastor, *Geschichte der Päpste seit dem Ausgang des Mittelalters* (Freiburg im Breisgau: Herder, 1923ff. [English trans.: *The History of the Popes, from the Close of the Middle Ages* London: Kegan, 1899–1953]); Johann Posner, *Der deutsche Papst Adrian VI* (Recklinghausen: Paulus Verlag, 1962); Roberto Zapperi, *Die vier Frauen des Papstes: das Leben Pauls III.zwischen Legende und Zensur* (Munich: Beck, 1997); Kenneth Gouwens and Sheryl Reiss, eds., *The Pontificate of Clement VII: History, Politics, Culture* (Burlington, VT: Ashgate, 2005).

New Religious Orders

John P. Donnelly, "The New Religious Orders, 1517–1648," in *Handbook of European History 1400–1600*, 2 vols., ed. Thomas A. Brady, Heiko A. Oberman, and James D. Tracy (New York: Brill, 1996), 2:283–315; Jodi Bilinkhoff, *The Avila of Saint Teresa: Religious Reform in a Sixteenth-Century City* (Ithaca, NY: Cornell University Press, 1989).

John O'Malley, *The First Jesuits* (Cambridge, MA: Harvard, 1993); Jonathan Wright, *The Jesuits: Missions, Myths, and Histories* (London: HarperCollins, 2004); John C. Olin, *Catholic Reform: From Cardinal Ximenes to the Council of Trent, 1495–1563* (Fordham University Press, 1990); Georg Schurhammer, *Francis Xavier: His Life, His Times*, trans. M. Joseph Costelloe (Rome: Jesuit Historical Institute, 1973–1982); John Patrick Donnelly, *Ignatius of Loyola: Founder of the Jesuits* (New York: Longman, 2004); Joseph F. Conwell, *Impelling Spirit: Revisiting a Founding Experience, 1539, Ignatius of Loyola and His Companions: An Exploration into the Spirit and Aims of the Society of Jesus as Revealed in the Founders' Proposed Papal Letter Approving the Society* (Chicago: Loyola, 1997); John M. Headley et al., eds., *San Carlo Borromeo: Catholic Reform and Ecclesiastical Politics in the Second Half of the Sixteenth Century* (London: Associated University, 1988).

Council of Trent

Sources in Decrees and Canons of the Council of Trent, ed. H. J. Schroeder (St. Louis: Herder, 1955). The basic study on the council continues to be Hubert Jedin, *A History of the Council of Trent* (London: Nelson, 1963). See also Paolo Prodi, *Das Konzil von Trient und die Moderne* (Berlin: Duncker & Humblot, 2001); Leo Scheffczyk, *Das Konzil von Trient und die Reformation: zum Versuch eines Brückenschlags* (Munich: Verlag der Bayerischen Akademie der Wissenschaften, 1992); Bernhard Steinhauf, *Giovanni Ludovico Madruzzo (1532–1600): katholische Reformation zwischen Kaiser und Papst; das Konzept zur praktischen Gestaltung der Kirche der Neuzeit im Anschluß an das Konzil von Trient* (Münster: Aschendorff, 1993).

League of Schmalkald

Ekkehart Fabian, *Die Entstehung des Schmalkaldischen Bundes und seiner Verfassung 1524/29–1531/35: Brück, Philipp von Hessen und Jakob Sturm; Darstellung und Quellen mit einer Brück-Bibliographie* (Tübingen: Osiandersche Buchhandlung,

1962); Armin Kohnle, *Reichstag und Reformation: Kaiserliche und Ständische Religionspolitik von den Anfängen der Causa Lutheri bis zum Nürnberger Religionsfrieden* (Gütersloh: Gütersloher Verlagshaus, 2001); Gabriele Haug-Moritz, *Der Schmalkaldische Bund 1530–1541/42: eine Studie zu den genossenschaftlichen Strukturelementen der politischen Ordnung des Heiligen Römischen Reiches Deutscher Nation* (Leinfelden-Echterdingen: DRW-Verlag, 2002); Luise Schorn-Schütte, ed., *Das Interim 1548/50: Herrschaftskrise und Glaubenskonflikt* (Gütersloh: Gütersloher Verlagshaus, 2005).

Religion and Society

P. R. Baehr and Gordon Wells, *The Protestant Ethic and the "Spirit" of Capitalism and Other Writings* (Penguin: New York, 2002); William Swatos and Lutz Kaelber, eds., *The Protestant Ethic Turns 100: Essays on the Centenary of the Weber Thesis* (Boulder, CO: Paradigm Publishers, 2005). Other important studies are S. Michael Wilcox, *Fire in the Bones: William Tyndale, Martyr, Father of the English Bible* (Salt Lake City: Desert Book Company, 2004); John M. Headley, Hans J. Hillerbrand, and Anthony J. Paplas, eds., *Confessionalization in Europe, 1555–1700: Essays in Honor and Memory of Bodo Nischan* (Burlington, VT: Ashgate, 2004); John Tedeschi, James Lattis, and Massimo Firpo, eds., *The Italian Reformation of the Sixteenth Century and the Diffusion of Renaissance Culture: A Bibliography of the Secondary Literature, ca. 1750–1997* (Modena: ISR, 2000). See also Peter Blickle, *Communal Reformation: The Quest for Salvation in Sixteenth-Century Germany* (Atlantic Highlands: Humanities, 1992), and John Bohnstedt, *The Infidel Scourge of God: The Turkish Menace as Seen by Protestant Pamphleteers of the Reformation Era* (Philadelphia: American Philosophical Society, 1968).

Puritanism

For developments after Henry VIII, see Patrick Collinson, *English Puritanism* (London: Historical Association, 1983); Diarmaid MacCulloch, *Tudor Church Militant: Edward VI and the Protestant Reformation* (London: Allen Lane, 1999); Diarmaid MacCulloch, *The Later Reformation in England, 1547–1603* (New York: Palgrave, 2001); Dan G. Danner, *Pilgrimage to Puritanism: History and Theology of the Marian Exiles at Geneva, 1555 to 1560* (New York: P. Lang, 1999); Henry Birt, *The Elizabethan Religious Settlement: A Study of Contemporary Documents* (London: G. Bell, 1907); Everett H. Emerson, *English Puritanism from John Hooper to John Milton* (Durham, NC: Duke University Press, 1968); Gary Jenkins, *John Jewel and the English National Church: The Dilemmas of an Erastian Reformer* (Burlington, VT: Ashgate, 2006). For the later developments, see also Patrick Collinson, *The Religion of Protestants: The Church in English Society, 1559–1625* (New York: Clarendon, 1982); Norman Jones, *Faith by Statute: Parliament and the Settlement of Religion, 1559* (London: Humanities, 1982).

Antitrinitarianism

George Huntston Williams, *The Polish Brethren: Documentation of the History and Thought of Unitarianism in the Polish-Lithuanian Commonwealth and the Diaspora,*

1601–1685 (Missoula, MT: Scholars, 1980); Williams's *The Radical Reformation* (Kirksville, MO: Sixteenth Century Publishers, 1992) offers a detailed account. Paul Wrzecionko, *Reformation und Frühaufklärung in Polen: Studien über den Sozinianismus und seinen Einfluß auf das westeuropäische Denken im 17. Jahrhundert* (Göttingen: Vandenhoeck und Ruprecht, 1977). The works of two eminent antitrinitarian theologians have been published: *Opere: Lelio Sozzini*, ed. Antonio Rotondò (Firenze: Olschki, 1986), and *Opere: Camillo Renato* (Firenze: G. C. Sansoni, 1968).

The Lutheran Theological Controversies

The sources for the eventual resolution of the controversies are available in a new English edition: *The Book of Concord*, ed. Robert Kolb, Timothy Wengert et al. (Minneapolis: 2000). See also Matthias Richter, *Gesetz und Heil: eine Untersuchung zur Vorgeschichte und zum Verlauf des sogenannten zweiten antinomistischen Streits* (Göttingen: Vandenhoeck & Ruprecht, 1996); Robert Kolb, *Luther's Heirs Define His Legacy: Studies on Lutheran Confessionalization* (Aldershot: Variorum, 1996).

John Calvin and the Tradition That Came to Bear His Name

For Calvin, see William Bouwsma, *John Calvin: A Sixteenth-Century Portrait* (New York: Oxford University Press, 1988); Bernard Cottret, *Calvin: A Biography* (Grand Rapids: Eerdmans, 2000); Paul Helm, *John Calvin's Ideas* (Oxford: Oxford University Press, 2004); Randall Zachman, *John Calvin as Teacher, Pastor, and Theologian: The Shape of His Writings and Thought* (Grand Rapids: Baker Academic, 2006).

A good introduction to Calvin and Calvinism is Donald K. McKim, ed., *The Cambridge Companion to John Calvin* (New York: Cambridge University Press, 2004). Insightful for France is also Barbara Diefendorf, *Beneath the Cross: Catholics and Huguenots in Sixteenth-Century Paris* (New York: Oxford University Press, 1991).

A number of helpful anthologies are available. See Menna Prestwich, ed., *International Calvinism, 1541–1715* (Oxford: Clarendon, 1985), and *Calvinism in Europe, 1540–1620*, ed. Andrew Pettegree, Alastair Duke, and Gillian Lewis (Cambridge: Cambridge University, 1994); a corollary volume has select texts: *Calvinism in Europe, 1540–1610: A Collection of Documents*, ed. Alastair Duke, Gillian Lewis, and Andrew Pettegree (New York: St. Martin's, 1992). A brilliant account is Philip Benedict, *Christ's Churches Purely Reformed: A Social History of Calvinism* (New Haven, CT: Yale University Press, 2002). The older book by John T. McNeill, *The History and Character of Calvinism* (New York: Oxford University Press, 1954), is still helpful. On specific issues see Robert M. Kingdon et al., eds., *Registers of the Consistory of Geneva in the Time of Calvin*, Vol. 1: *1542–1544* (Grand Rapids: Eerdmans, 2000); Robert M. Kingdon, *Adultery and Divorce in Calvin's Geneva* (Cambridge: Cambridge University Press, 1995).

Women

Basic (though also controversial) for the understanding of the Reformation consequences is Lyndal Roper, *Holy Household* (New York: Oxford, 1989). Susan C. Karant-

Nunn and Merry Wiesner-Hanks, *Luther on Women: A Sourcebook* (Cambridge: Cambridge University Press, 2003), collects important texts of the Reformer. See also Joel Harrington, *Reordering Marriage and Society in Reformation Germany* (New York: Cambridge, 1995); Susan Dinan and Debra Meyers, eds., *Women and Religion in Old and New Worlds* (New York: Routledge, 2001); Merry Wiesner-Hanks, *Christianity and Sexuality in the Early Modern World: Regulating Desire, Reforming Practice* (New York: Routledge, 2000); Hermina Joldersma and Louis Grijp, *"Elizabeth's Manly Courage": Testimonials and Songs of Martyred Anabaptist Women in the Low Countries* (Milwaukee: Marquette University, 2001); M. L. King and A. Rabil, eds., *Teaching Other Voices: Women and Religion in Early Modern Europe* (Chicago, 2006); Patricia Crawford, *Women and Religion in England, 1500–1720* (New York: Routledge, 1993); and Mark Chaves, *Ordaining Women: Culture and Conflict in Religious Organizations* (Cambridge, MA: Harvard University Press, 1997). Elsie McKee has a thorough two-volume study on an important early Reformation partisan: *Katharine Schütz Zell* (Leiden: Brill, 1999). See also Amy Leonard, *Nails in the Wall: Catholic Nuns in Reformation Germany* (Chicago: University of Chicago, 2005).

The Arts

Carl C. Christensen, *Art and the Reformation in Germany* (Athens: Ohio University, 1979); Joseph Leo Koerner, *The Reformation of the Image* (London: Reaktion Books, 2004); Ingrid Schulze, *Lucas Cranach d. J. und die protestantische Bildkunst in Sachsen und Thüringen: Frömmigkeit, Theologie, Fürstenreformation* (Bucha bei Jena: Quartus-Verlag, 2004); John Dillenberger, *Images and Relics: Theological Perceptions and Visual Images in Sixteenth-Century Europe* (New York: Oxford University, 1999); Jan Harasimowicz, *Kunst als Glaubensbekenntnis: Beiträge zur Kunst-und Kulturgeschichte der Reformationszeit* (Baden-Baden: Koerner, 1996); and Peter Blickle, ed., *Macht und Ohnmacht der Bilder: Reformatorischer Bildersturm im Kontext der Europäischen Geschichte* (Munich: Oldenbourg, 2002).

Worship

Emil Sehling, ed., *Die evangelischen Kirchenordnungen des XVI. Jahrhunderts*, 5 vols. (Tübingen: Mohr Siebeck, 1902ff.); Carlos Eire, *War against the Idols: The Reformation of Worship from Erasmus to Calvin* (Cambridge: Cambridge University, 1986); and Christopher Brown, *Singing the Gospel: Lutheran Hymns and the Success of the Reformation* (Cambridge, MA: Harvard University Press, 2005); Susan Karant-Nunn, *The Reformation of Ritual: An Interpretation of Early Modern Germany* (New York: Routledge, 1997); C. Scott Dixon and Luise Schorn-Schütte, eds., *The Protestant Clergy of Early Modern Europe* (New York: Palgrave Macmillan, 2003).

Poverty

Lee Wandel, *Always among Us: Images of the Poor in Zwingli's Zurich* (Cambridge: Cambridge University Press, 1990); Timothy G. Fehler, *Poor Relief and Protestantism: The Evolution of Social Welfare in Sixteenth-Century Emden* (Aldershot: Ashgate,

1999); Ole Peter Grell et al., *Health Care and Poor Relief in Counter-Reformation Europe* (London: Routledge, 1999); Sebastian Kreiker, *Armut, Schule, Obrigkeit: Armenversorgung und Schulwesen in den evangelischen Kirchenordnungen des 16. Jahrhunderts* (Bielefeld: Verlag für Regionalgeschichte, 1997); Bronislaw Geremek, *Geschichte der Armut: Elend und Barmherzigkeit in Europa* (Munich: Artemis-Verlag, 1988); Thomas Fischer, *Städtische Armut und Armenfürsorge im 15. und 16. Jahrhundert: sozialgeschichtliche Untersuchungen am Beispiel der Städte Basel, Freiburg i. Br. und Straßburg* (Göttingen: Schwartz, 1979); and Sebastian Schmidt, *Norm und Praxis der Armenfürsorge in Spätmittelalter und früher Neuzeit* (Stuttgart: Steiner, 2006).

Overseas

Markus Wriedt, "Kirche und Kolonien in der frühen Neuzeit: Der Aufbau des lateinamerikanischen Kirchenwesens im 16. Jahrhundert," *Saeculum: Jahrbuch für Universalgeschichte* 44 (1993): 220–42; Wolfgang Reinhard, *Missionare, Humanisten, Indianer im 16. Jahrhundert: ein gescheiterter Dialog zwischen Kulturen?* (Regensburg: Pustet, 1993); John Howgego, ed., *Encyclopedia of Exploration to 1800: A Comprehensive Reference Guide to the History and Literature of Exploration, Travel, and Colonization from Earliest Times to the Year 1800* (Sydney: Hordern House, 2004); Herbert Frey, *Die Entdeckung Amerikas und die Entstehung der Moderne* (Frankfurt am Main: Lang, 2000); and Ivo Kamps and Jyotsna G. Singh, eds., *Travel Knowledge: European "Discoveries" in the Early Modern Period* (New York: Palgrave, 2001).

Propaganda

An excellent collection of sources is Adolf Laube et al., eds., *Flugschriften der frühen Reformationsbewegung (1518–1524)*, 2 vols. (Berlin: Akademie-Verlag, 1983). See also Heinz Dannenbauer, *Luther als religiöser Volksschriftsteller 1517–1520: Ein Beitrag zur Frage nach den Ursachen der Reformation* (Tübingen: Mohr Siebeck, 1930), and Miriam U. Chrisman, *Conflicting Visions of Reform: German Lay Propaganda Pamphlets, 1519–1530* (Atlantic Highlands, NJ: Humanities, 1996).

Ilonka van Gülpen, *Der Deutsche Humanismus und die Frühe Reformations-Propaganda 1520–1526: Das Lutherporträt im Dienst der Bildpublizistik* (New York: Georg Olms, 2002), and Wolfram Wettges, *Reformation und Propaganda: Studien zur Kommunikation des Aufruhrs in süddeutschen Reichsstädten* (Stuttgart: Klett-Cotta, 1978). For Catholic propaganda efforts, see Philip M. Soergel, *Wondrous in His Saints: Counter-Reformation Propaganda in Bavaria* (Berkeley: University of California, 1993). See also Rebecca Wagner Oettinger, *Music as Propaganda in the German Reformation* (Aldershot; Burlington, VT: Ashgate, 2001), and Karel Hruza, ed., *Propaganda, Kommunikation und Öffentlichkeit (11.—16. Jahrhundert)* (Vienna: Verlag der Österreichischen Akademie der Wissenschaften, 2002).

Confessionalization

Heinz Schilling, "Confessional Europe," in Thomas A. Brady, Heiko A. Oberman, and James D. Tracy, eds., *Handbook of European History, 1400–1600*, 2 vols. (Grand

Rapids: Eerdmans, 1996), 2:641–81; Heinz Schilling, "Die Konfessionalisierung im Reich." *Historische Zeitschrift* 246 (1988): 1–45.

Conclusion

Berndt Hamm, "Wie innovativ war die Reformation?" *Zeitschrift für Historische Forschung* 27 (2000): 481–97.

Index